SALES PROMOTION
Concepts, Methods, and Strategies

ROBERT C. BLATTBERG
University of Chicago

SCOTT A. NESLIN
Dartmouth College

PRENTICE HALL, Englewood Cliffs, New Jersey 07632

Library of Congress Cataloging-in-Publication Data

Blattberg, Robert C. (date)
   Sales promotion—concepts, methods, and strategies / Robert C.
Blattberg, Scott A. Neslin.
      p.   cm.
   Includes bibliographical references.
   ISBN 0-13-788167-3
   1. Sales promotion.   I. Neslin, Scott A. (date).   II. Title.
HF5438.5.B57   1990
658.8′2—dc20   89-29223
                                                        CIP

To our parents

Editorial/production supervision and
   interior design: Barbara Grasso
Cover design: Wanda Lubelska
Manufacturing buyer: Peter Havens

 © 1990 by Prentice-Hall, Inc.
A Division of Simon & Schuster
Englewood Cliffs, New Jersey 07632

Printed in the United States of America

10   9   8   7   6   5   4   3   2   1

ISBN 0-13-788167-3

Prentice-Hall International (UK) Limited, *London*
Prentice-Hall of Australia Pty. Limited, *Sydney*
Prentice-Hall Canada Inc., *Toronto*
Prentice-Hall Hispanoamericana, S.A., *Mexico*
Prentice-Hall of India Private Limited, *New Delhi*
Prentice-Hall of Japan, Inc., *Tokyo*
Simon & Schuster Asia Pte. Ltd., *Singapore*
Editora Prentice-Hall do Brasil, Ltda., *Rio de Janeiro*

Contents

PART TWO
METHODS FOR ANALYZING SALES PROMOTIONS

PART FOUR
SALES PROMOTION PLANNING

Preface

In deciding to write a book on sales promotion, we recognized that practitioners and academics need a reference book to assist them in understanding how sales promotions work and what is known about sales promotions. Our book is intended to serve as a comprehensive guide to the sales promotion literature as well as to assist the reader in understanding the research and practical issues associated with the design and execution of sales promotions.

The emergence in the early 1980s of sales promotion as a significant marketing issue probably occurred first among practitioners. This was fueled by spiraling sales promotion costs. Academics then began to devote increased attention to the topic, the impetus being the availability of data and timely conceptual work in the fields of consumer behavior and economics. The net result has been an explosion in research activity and increased attention to planning, implementing, and evaluating sales promotion.

In our view, much of the increased level of activity involving sales promotion is taking place without the benefit of a unified synthesis of what is and is not known about the subject. Today promotions represent two-thirds of the marketing expenditures for many consumer products firms and advertising only one third. Ironically, there are many more books written and courses offered on advertising. Yet, most marketing managers of consumer product companies, service companies, and industrial firms need to understand sales promotion.

In the spring of 1985 we mapped out plans for a book that would address this need. We envisaged the project as a two-year endeavor. Clearly, we made the common mistake of thinking of sales promotion as a short-term investment.

The specific purpose of this book therefore is to provide a synthesis and exposition of contemporary research and practice that is of use to both academics and practitioners. We hope that this book will allow researchers to make further advances to the field, and help practitioners to better manage sales promotion. The book is organized as follows: Chapter 1 defines sales promotion; Chapters

2–5 present the conceptual underpinnings of the field; Chapters 6–9 discuss methodological approaches to measuring promotional effectiveness; Chapters 10–12 describe the three major types of promotions offered—coupons, trade deals, and retailer promotions—and compile substantive findings about these promotions; Chapters 13 and 14 discuss how manufacturers and retailers plan promotions; Chapter 15 discusses strategic issues associated with promotions. These chapters relate to the particular needs of our target audience in the following ways:

Academic Researchers. These users should draw most directly on the particular chapter relevant to the area in which they are generating a contribution.

Practitioners Evaluating Sales Promotion. These users should draw most directly on the methods chapters, and indirectly on the substantive findings chapters.

Practitioners Developing Sales Promotion Plans and Strategies. These users should draw most directly on the planning and strategic chapters, as well as on the substantive findings chapters.

MBA Students. MBA students in courses on brand management, marketing communications, or sales promotion, will find the descriptive and planning chapters (10–15) of most immediate use. We have used Chapters 10, 11, 12, and 15 in an MBA brand management course. MBA students in marketing research or marketing models courses will draw on the methodology chapters.

We recommend that all users examine the conceptual chapters. Chapter 2 provides the consumer behavior underpinnings of sales promotion, and Chapter 4 provides economic foundations. Chapters 3 and 5 apply these concepts. Chapter 3 discusses the deal prone consumer, while Chapter 5 integrates Chapters 2, 3, and 4 into an exposition of how promotions affect sales.

In an effort to be as complete as possible in writing this book, we have drawn on the expertise of a large set of academic and business colleagues. Among academics, Bob Shoemaker was particularly important in stimulating our ideas and in setting a high standard for research in the field. We have benefitted immensely from the comments and encouragement of colleagues at our respective schools, including Gert Assmus, John Deighton, Rohit Deshpande, Caroline Henderson, Bob Johnson, Victor McGee, Linda Schneider, Fred Webster, and the Spring, 1985 Sales Promotion Seminar at Tuck, and Greg Allenby, Chakravarthi Narasimhan, Robert Schindler, Mary Sullivan, and the Fall, 1986 Ph.D. Seminar on Marketing at University of Chicago. Dick Wittink and students of the Spring, 1988 Marketing Seminar at Cornell provided detailed and invaluable feedback on early versions of the book. Randy Bucklin, Dipanker Chakravarti, Gilbert Churchill, Charles Jacobson, Rajiv Lal, Gilles Laurent, John Little, and four reviewers for Prentice Hall also provided insightful comments and stimulating ideas that are incorporated in the book.

Several business colleagues have provided both ideas and examples for this book. These include Rick Goldberg (Gillette), William Hawkes (A. C. Nielsen),

Leonora Jungerwirth (Procter & Gamble), Mark Moody (SAMI-Burke), Donald Tassone (Procter & Gamble), Bob Wade (Hannaford Brothers), and Tony Yannantuono (General Foods). Ken Johnson (Hannaford Brothers) and Thomas Richardson (A. C. Nielsen) provided important insight on how retailers make forward buying and promotion decisions. Keith Jones (Colgate-Palmolive) gave us the idea for retailer-manufacturer cooperative push and the hostage index in Chapter 15. Data has been provided by A. C. Nielsen, General Foods, Hannaford Brothers, Information Resources, Inc., and Jewel Food Stores.

We also benefitted from generous financial support provided by our respective institutions. We are very grateful to the Marketing Center at the University of Chicago and the Tuck Associates Program for this support.

A project of this magnitude does not go forward without ample logistical support. Lori Cantin, Sabina Dougherty-Wiebkin, Karen Maurice, Fay Morris, Karen Pistey, and Carolyn Steller provided patient, diligent word processing. Patricia Peat organized and executed the arduous task of securing permissions for reproducing tables and figures. Santosh Nabar and Peter Cibulskis provided valuable research assistance. Dorothy Bower proved several times that she is the best computer programmer an analysis-happy professor could every find.

Finally, the backbone to this entire effort is our families—our parents, Abbey and Helen Blattberg and Stanley and Lenora Neslin, for instilling in us the sense of perseverance needed to bring this project to fruition, our wives, Rebecca and Betsey, for putting up with the early morning hours, late night hours, and weekends that come with this perseverance, and Scott and Betsey's daughters, Jenny and Louise, for reminding us of the bigger things in life.

Robert C. Blattberg   Scott A. Neslin
University of Chicago   Dartmouth College

1

Introduction

DEFINING SALES PROMOTION

Sales promotion has become a ubiquitous element of marketing, and therefore of the customer's purchase environment: A coupon in the Sunday newspaper clearly indicates a 40 cent savings on brand X coffee. The end-of-aisle display confronts the impulse buyer with a wall of snackfood. A family buys a camcorder and gets a free traveling case, or buys a car and gets a check for a $500 rebate. An appliance retailer is given a 10 percent manufacturer discount on January's orders if the retailer advertises the product in the local newspaper. We see that not only are sales promotions commonplace, but they are strikingly direct. Despite this directness, however, the term "sales promotion" is not particularly straightforward to define. This reflects the fact that despite its directness, sales promotion is a rather rich and complex marketing instrument, and one that is in the midst of conceptual change.

Table 1.1 quotes four alternative definitions of sales promotion as stated in various published sources. We believe these suggest five themes that should be retained in a good working definition. These are as follows:

1. Sales promotions are *action focused*: Perhaps the most distinguishing characteristic of sales promotions is their emphasis on getting the customer to take action. In fact, many promotions are participative in nature: Coupons require clipping, saving, and redemption; rebates require mailing; contests and sweepstakes require consumer effort; trade deals often involve retailer participation in cooperative advertising; and retailer feature advertising only works if consumers scan weekly store circulars. Another important element of sales promotion's action orientation is its common reliance on a limited duration time frame. The price cut for brand X coffee pertains to a given week; the appliance dealer is given a discount on all orders received during a particular month. Not all promotions are of limited duration, nor are they all actively participative. However, they all contain elements which impel the customer to take action.

TABLE 1.1 Alternative Definitions of Sales Promotion

- "Sales promotion consists of a diverse collection of incentive tools, mostly short-term, designed to stimulate quicker and/or greater purchase of a particular product by consumers or the trade" (Kotler, 1988, p. 645).

- "Sales promotion is the direct inducement or incentive to the sales force, the distributor, or the consumer, with the primary objective of creating an immediate sale" (Schultz and Robinson, 1982, p. 8).

- "Sales promotion, deals, and display can be defined under the general term of 'short-term inducements to customer buying action.'" (Webster, 1971, p. 556)

- "Sales promotion represents those marketing efforts that are supplementary in nature, are conducted for a limited period of time, and seek to induce buying." (Davis, 1981, p. 536)

---

2. Sales promotions are *marketing events*: Sales promotions span the spectrum from concrete price discounts to creative tie-ins and premiums. Perhaps most traditionally sales promotions have taken the form of price discounts. However, as they have spread in popularity to durable goods and services, and as packaged goods companies have become more sophisticated in designing promotions, nonfinancial incentives have grown in importance. Premiums and gifts have become important nonfinancial tools. Innovative promotions such as American Express extending the warranty on durables purchased with an American Express card are clearly broader than are a cents-off incentive. We use the word "marketing" because sales promotions involve a relationship between a manufacturer and its customers: end users, retailers, or distributors. The word "event" is used to connote the theme that promotions are often collections of distinct incentives—for example, the June consumer promotion for brand X coffee may consist of a coupon drop, a contest, a premium offer, and a trade deal. The sum of these constitute an "event." Some firms even use the word "campaign."

3. Sales promotions are designed to have a *direct impact on behavior*: This is a particularly salient characteristic of sales promotion. Many theories of consumer behavior posit that consumers go through some cognitive process and then take action. The cognitive process involves steps such as problem recognition, awareness, attitude, and purchase intentions (e.g., see Chapter 2, "The Consumer Decision Process"). Advertising is often thought to work on this cognitive process. Sales promotion, however, works directly on behavior. While the most common behavior to be influenced by promotion is the act of purchasing, other forms of behavior may be influenced as well. An automobile dealer may offer $10 to all those test driving a certain vehicle. A food manufacturer may offer a recipe book or cooking utensil because that spurs product usage.

    Another way to look at this issue is that sales promotions often offer a reason to buy the product that is extrinsic from the product itself. A common assumption is that advertising, word-of-mouth, or the salesperson has informed the consumer about the product. Now an additional inducement is needed to get the sale: "Buy this camcorder and get a free traveling case."

    Despite the "direct behavior" orientation, it is important to recognize that sales promotions can indeed have very strong effects on the cognitive state of the consumer. Buying on promotion may weaken brand attitude—a topic of much debate—or teach the consumer to anticipate future promotions. However, these effects occur after the purchase. Another example is the ability of special displays to increase primary demand. The display for snack food reminds the consumer of how good the snack tastes and that it has been a while since the consumer bought this snack. The consumer concludes he or she needs the snack (this is called "problem recognition") and proceeds to buy it. This example shows that response to promotion can certainly involve cognitive activity about the product itself. However, the action focus of the promotion moves the consumer quickly toward behavior.

4. Sales promotions are designed to influence *consumers or marketing intermediaries*: Consumers obviously are the ultimate targets of all promotions, but the immediate target depends on whose behavior the manufacturer wants to influence directly. For example, the firm may want a marketing intermediary such as a retailer to feature its product so that consumers will buy more of it, but must offer a promotion to retailers for retailers to do the featuring. Many times, a sales promotion event works on both the trade and consumers at once. The trade is offered an advertising allowance and price discount so they will promote the product to consumers, and 30 million coupons are distributed directly to consumers to coincide with the retailer promotions.

By the "trade," we mean marketing intermediaries such as retailers and distributors who are customers of the manufacturer but resell the product to consumers or to other trade entities. We do not include incentives to the firm's own sales force in our definition of sales promotion. Members of the sales force respond to a broader set of motivations and policies that are best described by the field of sales force management. We believe sales force incentives therefore are best studied within that context rather than within the context of sales promotion. However, we do include incentives that a manufacturer might offer to a retailer's sales personnel. These are called "spiffs."

To summarize this discussion, we have developed the following definition of sales promotion:

Sales promotion is an action-focused marketing event whose purpose is to have a direct impact on the behavior of the firm's customers.

One theme mentioned in Table 1.1 but not included in the foregoing definition is that of sales promotion "creating an immediate sale" or getting the customer to buy now. These phrases imply that promotions merely shift the timing of behavior that would have occurred anyway. There is some empirical evidence that promotions can do this, but certainly this is not always their effect. For example, coupons are the quintessential sales promotion, yet their focus is more on brand switching or repeat purchasing than on purchase acceleration.

A second element not in our definition is the descriptor "short term." Short term might imply that the effects of the promotion are temporary. Limited duration is often a critical ingredient of a promotion's action orientation, but this does not mean that the effects of the promotion are short term. The direction and magnitude of the long-term effects of sales promotion are a matter of intense theoretical and empirical debate. We therefore do not include it in our working definition.

TYPES OF SALES PROMOTIONS

There are three major types of sales promotion: consumer promotions, retailer promotions, and trade promotions. We will discuss these types in detail in Chapters 10, 11, and 12. In this section, we point out the principal distinctions among the types of promotion and provide illustrations.

Figure 1.1 depicts the major agents involved with sales promotion. The consumer, or end user, is the ultimate target of all sales promotion activities. The manufacturer can offer promotions directly to consumers. These are called "consumer promotions." The retailer can also offer promotions to consumers. These are called "retailer promotions." The manufacturer can offer promotions to retailers or other trade entities. These are called "trade promotions." Trade entities can promote to each other. For example, a distributor can offer a steep temporary price cut to retailers in order to sell its excess inventories. We call these trade promotions since the recipient of the promotion is a marketing intermediary.

Sometimes several manufacturers or several retailers combine in one promotion. These are called "cooperative promotions" (Varadarajan, 1986) or "promotion partnerships" (Farris and Quelch, 1983, Ch. 8). Partnership promotions often "tie in" a sample or other promotion for one product with the purchase of another. For example, a snack food company that offers coupons for a soda brand on its package is engaging in a tie-in consumer promotion.

Strategically, trade promotions and the resultant retailer promotions are elements of the "push" component of a manufacturer's marketing effort, while consumer promotions are part of the "pull" effort. It is important that the push and pull elements of sales promotion strategy work hand-in-hand with the push and pull elements of the rest of a firm's marketing strategy. For example, trade promotions often must be coordinated with sales activity, while consumer promotions often coordinate with advertising.

Table 1.2 provides a list of specific retailer, trade, and consumer promotions. This list is by no means exhaustive. The reader should refer to Chapters 10, 11, and 12 of this book, as well as Schultz and Robinson (1982) Ailloni-Charas (1984), and Totten and Block (1987) for more detailed descriptions of the many variations of sales promotions.

Figures 1.2A through 1.2J provide a compendium of examples of sales promotions to illustrate Table 1.2. Figure 1.2A shows feature advertising taken out by a pharmacy in a local market. This feature clearly displays regular (or suggested "reference") prices. The sale price, or price cut, is possibly the result of the pharmacy passing along a trade promotion. The upper left item is perhaps the ultimate promotion. The regular price is $3.19–$3.49, the sale price is $2.00, and there is a manufacturer rebate available for $2.00. As a result, the net price of

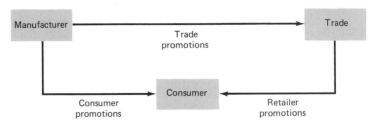

FIGURE 1.1 A Schematic Framework of the Major Types of Sales Promotion

TABLE 1.2 Specific Sales Promotion Tools

Retailer Promotions	Trade Promotions	Consumer Promotions
Price cuts	Case allowances	Couponing
Displays	Advertising allowances	Sampling
Feature advertising	Display allowances	Price packs
Free goods	Trade coupons	Value packs
Retailer coupons	"Spiffs"	Refunds
Contests/premiums	Financing incentives	Continuity programs
	Contests	Financing incentives
		Bonus packs
		Special events
		Sweepstakes
		Contests
		Premiums
		Tie-ins

the item is zero. Many feature advertisements do not advertise any price cut. They merely advertise products at their regular prices. This is especially common for everyday low-pricing supermarkets.

Figures 1.2B through 1.2E show durable goods and service promotions, including rebates, coupons, price cuts, and accessory premium tie-ins. Note that the brands using these promotions are well-known names. Note also the listing of potential rebates in Figure 1.2E.

Figure 1.2F shows the ubiquitous packaged goods coupon, in this case coupled with a premium offer. Note the advertising message of "quality." Some marketers doubt that any advertising message can get through the clutter of a coupon delivery, especially combined with a premium overlay. Others argue that such promotions draw attention to the message and prevent "counterarguing" of that message (see Chapter 10).

Figure 1.2G shows a coupon for a small restaurant. Restaurant coupons can be used to stimulate trial of particular items as well as increase profits (see Chapman, 1986). Figure 1.2H is a rather wry commentary on how coupons have become a part of everyday life. Indeed, present estimates are that approximately 80% of American households redeem coupons (see Chapter 10). Coupons, as well as other sales promotions, are truly woven into the fabric of modern society.

Perhaps the most important point suggested by Table 1.2 and Figures 1.2A through 1.2H is the variety of sales promotions tools. Unfortunately, much of the research on sales promotion has concentrated on only a few types, or considered promotion more generically. For example, couponing by far is the most researched form of consumer promotion, so that we can devote an entire chapter to it in this book. In one sense, this is appropriate since coupons are clearly the most important consumer promotion for packaged goods marketers (Donnelley Marketing, 1988, p. 19). However, contests and sweepstakes, continuity offers, price packs, and premiums are clearly underresearched. Rebates, which are the durable

FIGURE 1.2A Feature Advertising of Price Cuts and Rebates

Courtesy of CVS Pharmacy (Melville Corp.), Woonsocket, RI.

FIGURE 1.2B An Advertised Rebate

Courtesy of Armstrong World Industries, Lancaster, PA.

Think thrice before thy move.

Yes, three times. Your first option is to call a van line. Your second option is to make umpteen trips with family cars. Your third option is to move-it-yourself the safest, most dependable way in a Ryder truck — and still save a lot of money.

Even more savings, with this special offer to HOME BUYERS.

Ryder trucks are newer, tougher, stronger. Their components are specified more critically when they're ordered from the factory. And they're maintained in the strictest preventive-maintenance program in the industry.

They have the kind of options you'd expect in a car: automatic transmissions, air conditioning, power steering, radios.

Moving it yourself *can* be made more pleasant than ever. That's why:

IT'S RYDER. OR IT'S WRONG.

RYDER TRUCK RENTAL

While you're weighing your choices, clip this coupon and keep it handy.

$10 OFF ON A LOCAL MOVE

$30 OFF ON A ONE-WAY MOVE TO ANOTHER CITY.

Just present this coupon to your nearby Ryder location or Ryder authorized dealer. They'll discount the appropriate amount on your rental contract.

RYDER TRUCK RENTAL

Offer expires Feb. 28, 1987. Not valid during any other special promotion, though you will get the benefit of whichever is the better offer for you. Drive safely.

FIGURE 1.2C   A Coupon for a Service

Courtesy of Ryder Truck Rental, Miami, FL.

FIGURE 1.2D An Accessory Premium Tie-in Promotion

Courtesy of The Toro Company, Minneapolis, MN.

FIGURE 1.2E A Rebate Certificate

Courtesy of Leica USA, Northvale, NJ.

This certificate is valid toward the Leitz rebate program when the following conditions are met:

1. Item purchased must be warranteed by E. Leitz, Inc., Rockleigh, NJ (international warranty not acceptable) and be purchased through an authorized Leitz dealer.

2. This Rebate Certificate, your store receipt showing the date of purchase and the E. Leitz, Inc., U.S. Warranty Registration Card (filled in completely) must be sent to E. Leitz, Inc., 24 Link Drive, Rockleigh, NJ 07647. Attn: Registration Dept.

3. E. Leitz, Inc. will mail you a check in the amount of your rebate upon receipt of the items in paragraph 2 above. Allow 6–8 weeks for processing.

4. Only one certificate can be applied to each individual item purchased. Facsimilies will not be accepted.

5. This offer is good for purchases of specified new Leica equipment from February 1, 1985 through July 31, 1985. Certificates, store receipts and warranty cards must be mailed no later than August 31, 1985.

6. Rebate items, values and conditions may be modified or rescinded at any time. Employees of E. Leitz, Inc., Leitz dealers, agents of E. Leitz, Inc. as well as their employees and/or families are not eligible for this offer.

Leitz, Leica and Trinovid are trademarks of E. Leitz, Inc.

FIGURE 1.2E (Continued)

Rebates available on these products

Camera bodies	Cat.#	Rebate
R4 Black	10043	$200.00
R4 Silver	10041	200.00
R4S Black	10045	100.00
M4-P Black	10415	100.00
M4-P Silver	10416	100.00

Reflex Lenses	Cat.#	Rebate
24mm f/2.8 Elmarit R	11221	$ 50.00
28mm f/2.8 Elmarit R	11204	100.00
35mm f/2.8 Elmarit R	11231	100.00
50mm f/2.0 Summicron R	11216	100.00
60mm f/2.8 Elmarit R	11212	50.00
90mm f/2.8 Elmarit R	11211	50.00
135mm f/2.8 Elmarit R	11806	50.00
180mm f/2.8 Elmarit R	11923	150.00
500mm f/8.0 MR-Telyt R	11243	150.00
35–70mm f/3.5 Leitz	11244	200.00
2x Extender-R3/R4	11236	50.00
2x Extender-SU/SL2	11237	50.00

Rangefinder lenses	Cat.#	Rebate
35mm f/2.0 Summicron M	11310	$ 50.00
50mm f/2.0 Summicron M	11819	50.00
75mm f/1.4 Summilux M	11815	100.00
90mm f/2.8 Tele-Elmarit M	11800	50.00

Accessories	Cat.#	Rebate
Motor Winder-R4/R4S	14282	$100.00
Motor Drive-R4/R4S	14292	150.00

Trinovid® binoculars		Rebate
All full size (except 7×35)		$100.00
All compact B		25.00

Pradolux® projectors	Cat.#	Rebate
RT300/AV	200010—22	$ 50.00

To help us evaluate our marketing programs, would you take a moment to answer a few questions?

1. This purchase was a: ☐ Body ☐ Lens
   ☐ Accessory ☐ Other____

2. What is the main reason you purchase Leica equipment? (answer only one)
   ☐ To get the best picture quality possible.
   ☐ It is the most full-featured equipment available.
   ☐ It is the most precise and durable equipment available.
   ☐ Leica is the top-of-the-line product.
   ☐ Other____

3. If any, what **brand** of 35mm SLR camera(s) did you own prior to this purchase?
   ☐ No 35mm owned previously
   ☐ Owned a____

4. How did you first become aware of the Leitz rebate program? (Check one)
   Dealer's ☐ store ☐ mailing ☐ ad
   ☐ radio commercial
   Leica's ☐ ad (specify magazine)
   Other____

Items ordered by July 31, 1985, but delivered after that date are not eligible for refunds.

This refund offer may be rescinded or modified at any time.

11

FIGURE 1.2F A Packaged Goods Coupon with a Mail-in Premium

Courtesy of Clorox, Inc., Oakland, CA.

FIGURE 1.2G A Coupon for a Small Restaurant

Courtesy of Everything But Anchovies, Hanover, NH.

goods analog of couponing, have received very little attention. The use of premiums and financing incentives in a durable goods context is also vastly underresearched.

The most commonly researched sales promotions are coupons, trade allowances, and retailer promotions. Even among retailer promotions, only recently have researchers begun to distinguish among price cuts, displays, and features, and even now, those are often subsumed under one "promotion" or "deal-offer" variable.

SALES PROMOTIONS EXPENDITURES

An accurate dollar estimate for total sales promotions expenditures does not exist. However, the following evidence suggests that the financial commitment is large, in fact larger than the commitment to advertising.

- A 1984 study using the PIMS database found promotion, as a percentage of advertising and promotion, was 66 percent for 190 consumer durables businesses and 58 percent for 265 nondurables businesses (Quelch et al., 1984).
- A 1985 survey found 76 percent of major appliance purchasers reported having bought on deal (Wilkie and Dickson, 1985).
- Packaged goods manufacturers distributed 221.7 billion coupons in 1988 (Manufacturers Coupon Control Center, 1989b).
- Sales promotion agencies are doing a booming business. Many advertising agencies have either acquired sales promotion agencies or developed their own subsidiaries (Strazewski, 1986).
- Consumer and trade promotion accounted for 64.8 percent of the combined advertising/promotion budgets of 68 packaged goods manufacturers in 1987 (Donnelley Marketing, 1988).

FIGURE 1.2H Coupons for Father's Day

- Merchandise markdowns accounted for 19.3 percent of total sales in department stores and 15 percent of total sales in specialty stores in 1986 (National Retail Merchants Association, 1987).

Sales promotions are still probably most associated with packaged goods marketing. However, the preceding figures plus many of the examples shown earlier suggest that this is not the case (see Quelch et al., 1987, for a discussion of durable goods promotions and Lovelock and Quelch, 1983, for a discussion of promotions in the service sector). Nevertheless, much of the academic research to date has been in the packaged goods industry. This is probably due to packaged goods firms' long history of using sales promotion, coupled with the availability of panel and sales data.

TRENDS IN SALES PROMOTION EXPENDITURES

Although we cannot pinpoint the current size of sales promotion expenditures, we can be sure that the trend is up. The following facts are indicators of this:

- Combined consumer and trade promotion as a percentage of advertising/promotion budgets grew from 58 percent in 1976 to 65 percent in 1987 (Donnelley Marketing, 1988, p. 11).
- Manufacturers distributed 75 billion coupons in 1977, and 221.7 billion in 1988, an annual rate of increase of 10.4% percent (Nielsen Clearing House, 1985; Manufacturers Coupon Control Center, 1989b).
- Markdowns as a percentage of total sales has grown from 6.0 percent in 1963 to 19.3 percent in 1986 for department stores, and 10.2 percent to 15.0 percent for specialty stores during the same period (National Retail Merchants Association, 1972, 1987).
- While using a broader definition of sales promotion than we use, a recent study found advertising expenditures increased at a rate of 10 percent per year over the previous ten years, while sales promotion expenditures increased at a rate of 12 percent (Bowman, 1986).

There are many potential explanations for these trends, all of which provide fertile areas for research. We list several of them (many of them are suggested by Quelch et al., 1987). There are certainly counterarguments to many of these explanations, but the plausibility, number, and complexity of these explanations demonstrate the challenge in understanding sales promotion.

- *Advertising has become less effective.* The consumer is bombarded by too much advertising and, with the advent of the VCR, no longer has to watch television advertising.
- *Consumers are more price sensitive.* The rampant inflation of the 1970s raised consumers' general price-consciousness. Many "baby boomers" reached adulthood during this period and learned to be a purchasing consumer in this atmosphere. (Note that the direction of causality is open to debate here. Many could claim that promotions make consumers more price oriented.)

- *Many product categories are mature.* Population growth has slowed, and many households have what used to be considered luxuries. Companies find themselves fighting for market share using every tool they can find.
- *Retailers are more powerful.* Retailing has become more sophisticated and more competitive. Retailers often find themselves in a position to demand price breaks and play off one manufacturer against another (see Quelch, 1982).
- *Many product categories offer undifferentiated commodity products.* In many product categories, several brands within a given "price tier" are virtually indistinguishable. Manufacturers therefore do not compete based on product, and their advertising message cannot establish a point of difference. Sales promotion is the only marketing tool that can influence sales.
- *Managers increasingly have a short-term orientation.* Increased competitiveness as well as internal management incentives have made marketing managers more short term in their outlook. If managers sacrifice short-term sales to wean their brands of sales promotion, neither they nor their brands may be around in a few years.
- *Sales promotions are more acceptable to the consumer.* Packaged goods brands taught consumers that (1) there are ample rewards to "smart shopping" and (2) the brand on promotion is not necessarily of lower quality. As a result, the consumer readily transfers this knowledge to durable goods and services.
- *It is more difficult to forecast demand.* Due to the proliferation of new brands, retailers and manufacturers find it difficult to forecast sales and often find themselves with excess inventory. As a result, they must offer more inventory-clearing promotions (Pashigian, 1987).
- *Sales promotion is in a "prisoner's dilemma" spiral.* Similar to a price war or even a wage-price spiral, manufacturers are currently locked in a defensive, reactive escalation of sales promotion expenditures. If one manufacturer cuts sales promotion, it suffers a short-term loss that may or may not be reciprocated by the competition. If the manufacturer increases sales promotion, it achieves a short-term gain that is whittled away after the competitor reacts. This induces the manufacturer to promote even more.
- *Sales promotions are "optimal."* Many economic theories conclude that profits can be maximized by using promotions (see Chapter 4). Some of these theories are based on price discrimination arguments, essentially allowing the brand to compete in two or more market segments. Sales promotions may allow a premium brand to compete with a lower-tier brand among price sensitive consumers, or with a new brand among consumer innovators. The increased use of sales promotion may be optimal because of the increased size and more distinct definition of the price-conscious segment or because of the proliferation of new products.
- *Consumers expect prices to decrease.* A growing segment of consumers has learned that prices of durable goods, for example, will eventually decline. They therefore hold off purchasing. Sales promotions are needed to accelerate purchasing among this segment.
- *More and more businesses emphasize volume.* The popularity of experience curve and market share strategies pushes manufacturers to seek high sales volumes as a path toward long-term profits. Sales promotion is a proven volume generator.
- *In-store sales support has declined.* Either due to the general decline of service or to the manufacturer's lack of control of the retail floor, the manufacturer can no longer count on an effective sales/consumer relationship. The manufacturer must therefore "hardsell" with sales promotions.

- *Sales promotion specialists are becoming more effective.* Traditionally, sales promotion specialists were not highly paid for their low-prestige jobs. Due to the increased importance of sales promotion, these roles have attracted a more sophisticated manager. Increased experience with sales promotion has also increased expertise. As a result, the growth in sales promotion receives a further boost.
- *Trends in retailer ordering policies result in excess inventory.* Increased retailer emphasis on reporting and control has increased the cost per order of retailers. As a result, retailers make fewer orders and run the risk of accumulating unsold inventory. This inventory can most easily be sold by using a promotion.

It is difficult to gauge the validity or relative importance of these explanations for growth in sales promotion. Undoubtedly, they all contribute, in varying degrees, depending on the industry. The marketing manager must identify the particular explanation applicable to his or her industry and then develop appropriate promotion strategies. The researcher must distill whatever generalizations can be made while developing methods for diagnosing sales promotion expenditures on a market-by-market basis.

As we survey the foregoing list, however, it seems clear that the growth will not continue ad infinitum. The possible decrease in advertising effectiveness will bottom out. The effectiveness of sales promotion may start to decline. Consumer price sensitivity will top off. Mergers among manufacturers may counteract the new found power of retailers. Manufacturers, as well as gas stations, have demonstrated that they eventually can wrestle themselves out of prisoner's dilemmas. The challenge, if indeed the prisoner's dilemma is at work, is to do it sooner rather than later.

PURPOSE AND ORGANIZATION OF THE BOOK

This book is a compilation and synthesis of research on sales promotion. The result is an integrated summary and analysis of what we know and do not know about sales promotion. Our goal, however, is more active than providing an encyclopedia of knowledge on sales promotion. We hope that researchers will be better able to study sales promotion as a result of reading this book and that executives will be better able to manage and analyze sales promotions. Our specific purposes are therefore as follows:

- Provide a reference that summarizes the field.
- Organize and standardize the field so as to provide common ground for further advances.
- Identify the gaps in current knowledge of sales promotion.
- Provide significant guidance on how to analyze the effectiveness of promotion.
- Attempt to integrate and reconcile the disparate theories and findings regarding sales promotion.
- Present concepts of why promotions are used and how they influence sales.

Accordingly, we organize the book in four main sections: (1) conceptual underpinnings, (2) methods for analyzing sales promotions, (3) substantive knowledge on sales promotions, and (4) sales promotion planning. The conceptual chapters include consumer behavior and economic theories of sales promotion, as well as an identification of how sales promotion affects sales. The methods chapters contain expositions of the statistical techniques for analyzing sales promotions. The substantive findings chapters review what we know about three main types of sales promotions: couponing, retailer promotions, and trade promotions. The planning chapters describe the planning process for both manufacturers and retailers.

2

Theories and Concepts of Consumer Behavior Applied to Sales Promotion

INTRODUCTION

Sales promotions set in motion a complex interaction of management decisions and consumer behavior. If managers are ever to assume the "driver's seat" in this interaction, they must understand not only how but *why* consumers respond to promotions. The field of consumer behavior provides a rich collection of concepts and theories that shed light on this question. The purpose of this chapter is to describe these frameworks, examine how they apply to the field of sales promotion, and identify areas where further understanding is needed.

Table 2.1 presents the list of topics that will be covered in this chapter. We do not cover the entire field of consumer behavior, but have selected the topics that are most applicable to sales promotion. The theories described in this chapter can be grouped into three categories. Behavioral learning theories concentrate on the consumer's environment and behavior, but do not consider the inner cognitive processing the consumer might undertake. In contrast, attribution, price perception, perceived risk, and prospect and mental accounting theories are chiefly concerned with these cognitive processes, especially with how the consumer perceives the environment. Attitude and consumer decision-making models include consumer perceptions in their core, but also consider how perceptions translate into actual choices.

BEHAVIORAL LEARNING THEORIES

Classical Conditioning

Classical conditioning is best defined by the well-known example of Pavlov's experiments with dogs. Pavlov noticed that the presence of food would always cause a dog to salivate. He then repeatedly paired a previously neutral stimulus,

TABLE 2.1	Topics in Consumer Behavior Relevant to Sales Promotion

I. Behavioral learning theories
    Classical conditioning
    Operant conditioning
    Hullian model

II. Attribution and dissonance theories
    Person perception theory
    Object perception theory
    Self-perception theory
    Dissonance theory

III. Price perception theories
    Weber's law
    Adaptation-level theory
    Assimilation-contrast theory

IV. Perceived risk

V. Prospect theory and mental accounting

VI. Attitude models

VII. Consumer decision-making models
    Low involvement
    High involvement

the ringing of a bell, with the presentation of food. Eventually, the dog would salivate simply if the bell were rung, even if food did not accompany the bell. In conditioning terminology, the food serves as an *unconditioned stimulus*, and salivation is the *response*. The ringing of a bell is a *conditioned stimulus*. The dog will not naturally emit the response upon the ringing of the bell, but will after he or she has been conditioned to respond to the bell. Note that a stimulus that has been conditioned strongly enough can be thought of as an unconditioned stimulus and used in turn to "condition" another stimulus. For example, subsequent coupling of the bell with the verbal command "salivate" could result in that command becoming a conditioned stimulus.

Table 2.2 reviews the foregoing definition and presents applications to sales promotion. In the first application, a premium or prize serves as an unconditioned

TABLE 2.2 Examples of Classical Conditioning

	Unconditioned Stimulus	Conditioned Stimulus	Response
Pavlov	Food	Bell	Salivation
Promotions	Premium or prize	Brand	Excitement, affect
	Sale/price discount	Display	Purchase
	Sale/price discount	Feature advertising	Purchase

stimulus—it naturally elicits a response of excitement. By frequently coupling the premium or prize with a particular brand, the brand itself eventually becomes a conditioned stimulus. That is, the brand comes to elicit a sense of excitement, which, it is hoped, leads to favorable attitude and, finally, purchase. For example, fast-food establishments often offer toys and prizes and hold special events targeted at children. These promotions serve as unconditioned stimuli while the fast-food establishment can become a conditioned stimulus. Eventually, the simple mention of McDonald's or Burger King or Wendy's to a child elicits a sense of excitement that translates into a visit to the restaurant.[1] Potentially, this positive effect can remain even as the child progresses into adulthood.

The second and third promotion examples in Table 2.2 provide insight as to why special displays or feature advertising, *even if not accompanied by a price discount*, can elicit strong sales effects. Since these activities often *are* associated with price discounts, which do naturally elicit a strong response, they become conditioned stimuli. A display is like the ringing of Pavlov's bell: It automatically makes the consumer salivate in anticipation of a sale. A similar example along these lines would be in-store special announcements of sales that are often used in discount department stores. The announcement coming over a loudspeaker is a conditioned stimulus—the shopper has learned to associate this announcement with unusually attractive price cuts.

The idea of promotions serving as conditioned or unconditioned stimuli has a certain logical appeal. One has only to observe consumers in a local supermarket snatching up coffee from a special display to be struck by the apparently automatic nature of the response. Similarly, the keen excitement kids exhibit when parents mention a trip to the local fast-food restaurant seems disproportional to the actual event of eating lunch. Beyond these casual, although compelling observations, there is little empirical work that supports the applicability of classical conditioning in a promotions context. There is some mixed evidence from research that was not explicitly investigating classical conditioning, Shimp et al. (1976) found that children were more likely to want to purchase a cereal that included a premium, but this did not translate into positive feelings for the cereal itself. However, this study only included a single exposure to the premium. Blair and Landon (1981) found consumers inferred that advertised prices for durable goods were lower than regular prices, even if no regular price was stated in the advertisement. However, this study did not attempt to determine whether classical conditioning was the cause of this effect (see the upcoming discussion for a reference price explanation of the results).

There is some strong evidence on the applicability of classical conditioning to the effects of advertising, and it is from these studies that researchers should

---

[1] Note that the traditional response considered by classical conditioning has been emotional or psychosomatic (e.g., salivation). Indeed, its use in advertising has been to induce favorable emotional feelings (Nord and Peter, 1980). Even though classical conditioning is mostly concerned with affective response, there is ample theoretical support for the translation of affect into behavior (see the later discussion on attitude models in this chapter).

borrow in investigating sales promotion (Gorn, 1982; Stuart et al. 1987). For example, Stuart et al. found in a series of laboratory experiments that (1) consumers developed positive attitudes toward brands (conditioned stimuli) if those brands were repeatedly coupled with pleasing photographs (unconditioned stimuli), (2) the conditioning effect was lessened if the consumer was exposed to the brand several times before the pairing with photographs began, and (3) the conditioning effect was stronger when the consumer first saw the brand and then the photograph than if the photograph came first (that is, it was better to ring the bell and then present the food than to present the food and then ring the bell). Logically, premiums, coupons, or other promotions could also serve as unconditioned stimuli, but this awaits further research.

To summarize, the central theme of classical conditioning is that the consumer can be induced to form positive feelings toward a "conditioned stimulus" by associating that stimulus with an "unconditioned stimulus" that naturally generates positive feelings. Price cuts, premiums, and coupons can serve as unconditioned stimuli, while specific brands or nonfinancial promotions such as displays, feature advertisements, or in-store announcements can become conditioned stimuli. For additional discussion, the reader is referred to the marketing applications covered in Nord and Peter (1980) and Assael (1987, Ch. 3) as well as the theoretical development in Hilgard and Bower (1975).

Operant Conditioning

The Basic Theory. The basic tenant of operant conditioning is that a reinforced behavior is more likely to persist. The concept of operant conditioning emerged most directly from the work of B. F. Skinner (Skinner, 1938) and is best illustrated by the workings of a "Skinner box." In the Skinner box is a lever which a small animal such as a pigeon or rat can press. If the animal does press the lever, reinforcement is delivered in the form of food. As this response (pressing the lever)–reinforcement (food) sequence is repeated, the animal becomes more and more likely to press the leaver in any given period of time. Once the reinforcement is removed, the likelihood of pressing the lever decreases to some long-run value. This is known as "extinction." In a marketing context, purchasing the brand is the behavior we wish to teach consumers, and a promotion such as a coupon or premium is the reinforcement. The goal is to use promotions to build up purchase frequency, but do this in a way so as to mitigate the extinction effect.

A good example of operant conditioning would be in-pack coupons (see Rothschild and Gaidis, 1981). The coupon serves as a reward that the consumer finds at the bottom of the cereal box once all the cereal is consumed. The coupon specifically rewards the behavior of purchasing and consuming the product. Another example is the American Express "Buyer's Assurance Program," under which American Express automatically extends the warranty of any warrantied product bought with an American Express card. The behavior being learned by the consumer is to use the American Express card to purchase durable products.

The reward is the extended warranty. If the purchasing behavior has become successfully operant conditioned, it will persist even after the Buyer's Assurance promotion is terminated.

There are a number of rich concepts associated with operant conditioning that have application to sales promotion. We first point out some distinctions between operant and classical conditioning. The distinction between classical and operant conditioning can be understood most easily as a difference in sequence. In classical conditioning, a stimulus occurs first, and a response is *elicited*. Classical conditioning can thus be called a stimulus-response (SR) theory. In operant conditioning, the response is first *emitted* and then reinforced. Operant conditioning can thus be called a response-reinforcement (RR) theory. Referring back to our earlier examples, the premium had to be presented first before the child would become excited. The premium is therefore an unconditioned stimulus that comes before the excitement response. In the case of the in-pack coupon, the cereal is purchased and consumed, and *then* this behavior is rewarded by the coupon.

Primary Versus Secondary Reinforcement. Rather than just one reinforcer, several different reinforcements can reward a single behavior. An important distinction arises between primary and secondary reinforcers. Primary reinforcers are rewards that have "intrinsic utility" as opposed to secondary reinforcers which have no direct usefulness but must be "converted" to have value (Rothschild and Gaidis, 1981). A traditional example of a primary reinforcer would be food, while a secondary reinforcer might be money that can be used to buy food. In the promotion context, we would *like* to think that the consumer's consumption experience with the brand is the primary reinforcer while the promotion (e.g., coupon) is the secondary reinforcer. Eventually, we can withdraw the coupon and the behavior will still persist, rewarded continually by consumption of the brand.

Unfortunately, it may not be realistic to think of specific brands as primary reinforcers. There are usually many alternative brands that satisfy the same basic need and often there is little differentiation among those brands. In this situation, the promotion (especially one with monetary value) may be the primary reinforcer, or at least, more primary than the product itself. As a result, purchase behavior becomes extinct very quickly once the promotion is withdrawn. There are two strategies for avoiding this situation: (1) do not make the promotion too rewarding (e.g., too high in monetary value), and (2) be sure the promoted brand has enough intrinsic utility so as not to be overshadowed by the promotion.

Another interesting view of this situation is the concept of a "conditioned reinforcement" (Hilgard and Bower, 1975, p. 220). The concept is simply that "a stimulus that is not originally a reinforcing one . . . can become reinforcing through repeated association with one that is" (Keller and Schoenfeld, 1950, p. 232). For example, experiments with a Skinner box, by coupling food reinforcement with a light, have resulted in light having reinforcing properties by itself. In the case of promotion, if in fact a given brand is a weak reinforcer, we may be able to increase its reinforcing properties by associating it with a strong reinforcer, namely, a coupon.

Reinforcement Schedules. An integral part of operant conditioning is the frequency or timing in which reinforcement is applied. A variety of such schedules have been devised and tested in the context of animal behavior (Hilgard and Bower, 1975, pp. 214–219). The application to promotions is particularly clear: Reinforcement schedules address the issue of how often to promote. The bulk of experimental evidence would indicate that the answer to this question is, "intermittently." As noted by Ray (1973, p. 54), "In the learning laboratory, the basic finding is that partial reinforcement produces effects which are more resistant to extinction than does continuous reinforcement." There is a compelling logic to this finding: Under continuous reinforcement, the reward (i.e., the promotion) is more likely to become the only reason to perform the behavior. If the promotion is sometimes not available, the consumer is more apt to become aware of the rewards the product has to offer.

Although the intermittent reinforcement recommendation is very powerful, it has received little published research attention in a marketing context. One directly relevant study was undertaken by Deslauriers and Everett (1977). They conducted a field experiment in which bus ridership was the behavior and couponlike tokens were the reinforcement. The experiment was a time series design in which partial reinforcement was first applied, then continuous reinforcement, and then partial reinforcement. The authors concluded that the partial reinforcement schedule was as successful as the continuous reinforcement in increasing bus ridership. Unfortunately, the authors were not able to compare extinction effects for the partial versus continuous reinforcement schedules, and the time series nature of the design means that the schedules were not administered independently. However, this research is important as a rare example of testing operant conditioning in a promotions context. Future research needs to replicate and build on this work.

Shaping. While operant conditioning was originally applied to simple behaviors (e.g., pressing a lever), it was also used to induce very complex behaviors (e.g., pigeons playing Ping-Pong!). One way to develop these behaviors is to condition the organism to perform progressively more complex behaviors, leading up to the final desired activity. The application of this procedure to promotions is particularly relevant to durable goods, but also to packaged goods. Table 2.3 illustrates applications to durables and to packaged goods (borrowed from Rothschild and Gaidis, 1981). In the durables example, the ultimate desired behavior is for the consumer to purchase an automobile. Before that can be accomplished, however, the consumer must visit the automobile showroom and test drive the automobile. These intermediate behaviors are reinforced by refreshments and a small amount of cash. In the packaged goods example, the manufacturer wants the consumer to purchase the brand on a sustained basis. Before that occurs, however, the consumer is reinforced through the behaviors of using a product sample and then

TABLE 2.3 Shaping Procedures Applied to Promotion

Durables

Behavior	Visit automobile show-room	→	Test drive	→	Purchase automobile
Reinforcement	Coffee and donuts		$10 cash; product perfor-mance		

Packaged goods*

Behavior	Use sample of new deter-gent	→	First purchase of deter-gent	→	Repeat purchase
Reinforcement	Product performance; monetary savings from not using regular deter-gent; availability of coupon *inside* box for future savings		Product performance; savings from coupon		Product performance

* *Source:* This example is adapted from Michael L. Rothschild and William C. Gaidis, "Behavioral Learning Theory: Its Relevance to Marketing and Promotions," *Journal of Marketing*, 45 (Spring, 1981), p. 72.

purchasing the brand for the first time.[2] The lesson from these examples is that while promotion is most often seen as a method to bring about an immediate *sale*, there are a number of intermediate behaviors which are also potentially induced by promotions.

Stimulus Discrimination. A stimulus that occurs at the same time as reinforcement may become a signal to the consumer in future situations that reinforcement is about to occur. This is called a "discriminative stimulus." This could happen within the world of pigeons by rewarding pecking when a light is turned on, but not rewarding it when the light is turned out. The light eventually works analogously to a conditioned stimulus in classical conditioning: Pecking will occur only when the light is turned on (see Sahakian, 1976, p. 147). From a technical point of view, the light is not, strictly speaking, a conditioned stimulus, because it took on its conditioning properties under a different process from that which occurs in classical conditioning. However, in terms of the way the discriminative stimulus can be used to induce response, it is very similar to a conditioned stimulus.

The application of this concept to sales promotion is an important one. Merchandising activities such as displays, feature advertising, or point-of-purchase material can become discriminative stimuli if they are frequently coupled with a reward such as a price cut. These stimuli may elicit brand buying behavior even if the reward (a true savings) is not there.[3] However, analogously to the pigeon

---

[2] Peter and Nord (1982, pp. 104–105) criticize this example as not exactly following the concept of shaping. For example, they argue that the terminal behavior, repeat purchasing, is essentially the same as the first purchase. Their point is well taken: Shaping refers to reinforcing progressively more complex behaviors.

[3] The reader should compare this explanation for the role of displays and feature advertising with that given during the discussion of classical conditioning. While the difference should be clear conceptually, it would be difficult in practice to decide whether a display or feature was serving as a conditioned stimulus or a discriminitive stimulus.

not pecking when the light is turned off, the consumer will not buy the brand when discriminative stimuli are absent. Discriminative stimuli can therefore either help or hinder the manufacturer: That such stimuli may bring about sales increases even when no true savings are offered is attractive to the manufacturer, yet if the stimuli have truly become discriminative, sales will occur only when the stimuli are present, and it costs the manufacturer money to keep these stimuli present.

Note that the concept of discriminative stimulus is different from that of a conditioned reinforcement as discussed earlier. A conditioned reinforcement is something that acquires reinforcing properties by association with a reward. A discriminative stimulus acquires the properties of a conditioned stimulus by association with a reward. The difference is very important, because discriminative stimuli become necessary for a response to occur (that is, the pigeon will only peck if the light is turned on), whereas the conditioned reinforcement can be used to reinforce behavior as part of operant conditioning. The question of whether a stimulus paired with a reward becomes a conditioned reinforcement or a discriminative stimulus is a crucial one. The question might be resolved depending upon the reinforcement schedule. If a stimulus is always associated with the reward, it becomes a discriminative stimulus, whereas if the stimulus is associated intermittently with the reward, it becomes a conditioned reinforcement.

An interesting extension of the discriminative stimulus concept is that of stimulus sampling. Estes (1950) posited that all stimuli present when a behavior is rewarded can potentially become discriminative stimuli. Over time, the sample of stimuli present when a behavior is rewarded changes, so the conditioning strength of some discriminative stimuli becomes greater than for others. Once the reward is removed, the likelihood of the behavior taking place depends on the total conditioning power of the sample of discriminative stimuli present at the occasion. As a result, behavior becomes probabilistic. As discussed in Chapter 8, stochastic models of consumer behavior have found important application in the study of sales promotion.

Summary.   Operant conditioning as well as classical conditioning provide a rich conceptual basis for understanding promotions. The ideas of reinforcement schedules, primary versus secondary reinforcement, and shaping especially have concrete application to the design of promotion programs.

These theories also have more strategic implications. For example, perhaps manufacturers are conditioning consumers, as intended, but the behavior that gets reinforced is deal usage, not brand usage (see Rothschild, 1987). The consumer is learning that by spending a relative modicum of effort to shop carefully and buy on deal (the behavior), he or she can realize huge financial savings (the reward). A secondary reward in this learning process is that the promoted products are just as good as the nonpromoted ones, and thus product satisfaction is not adversely affected. Along this theme, Henderson (1984) presents the conjecture that deal proneness is a learned skill, and in operant terms, is a shaped behavior. Under this conjecture, the final behavior is the deal seeking use of all types of deals. Initial behaviors leading up to this are purchasing items on display (this is easiest to do), followed by more complex behaviors such as coupon clipping and store switching. For manufacturers, the way out of this cycle is either to provide fewer promotions (adjust the reinforcement schedule) or make sure that the reward delivered by their particular brand is stronger than the reward of the promotion (primary rather than secondary reinforcer).

A major frustration with the operant and classical conditioning viewpoint is its explicit exclusion of attitude and mental processes. Managerially, this apparently erases the usefulness of concepts such as product positioning and brand image. Intellectually, this seemingly relegates consumer decision making to the same level as pigeons pecking levers to obtain their food. Indeed, the behaviorist tradition is probably less in favor today as opposed to 30 years ago. However, there are compelling arguments for the behaviorist viewpoint. First, many of the general ideas emerging from these theories make good intuitive sense. Second, there is a certain consistency between the role of promotions in *directly* influencing behavior and the orientation of the behaviorist view of stimulus-response-reward. Third, the marketing world has long been frustrated in attempts to link "mental states" such as personality and attitude to brand choice. Linkages have been found, but the percentage of behavior explained is not high. Fourth, one might conjecture that many consumers are not highly "involved" in their purchase decisions. Under low-involvement decision making (see the upcoming section on the consumer decision process), one would expect little cognitive activity on the part of the consumer, making him or her susceptible to behavioral conditioning.

A second problem with operant and classical conditioning is the confusion that can arise between them. Both these theories grew out of a laboratory experiment paradigm in which the theoretical constructs of stimulus, response, and reinforcement could be easily manipulated. In applying these concepts, it is often unclear exactly what the role is for promotion. For example, is a display a conditioned stimulus, a discriminative stimulus, or a conditioned reinforcer? The answer to this depends on how we assume the display acquired its reinforcing properties and the extent to which we believe the display has become a necessary condition for purchase. The important general lesson is that we may not be able to apply behavioral learning theories too literally.

A final problem with operant and classical conditioning theories is the lack of empirical research in the area. Experimental research is especially needed in the areas of reinforcement schedules, primary versus secondary reinforcement, and shaping.

The Hullian Model

The Hullian model is similar to classical and operant conditioning in that it includes the notions of stimulus and reinforcement, but differs importantly in that it incorporates the concepts of "drive" and "habit." The theory was developed by Clark Hull (1943) using postulates and mathematical formulations (see Sahakian,

1976, Ch. 6; Hilgard and Bower, 1975, pp. 152–205; and Howard, 1981, for good discussions of the theory). Over the years Hullian theory has undergone various transformations. We can summarize, however, the major components of the theory. Let

V = stimulus-intensity dynamism, essentially the strength of a stimulus

K = incentive motivation, that is, the reward(s) associated with performing the particular behavior.

D = drive, which (although behaviorists would object to the word) is basically the state of *need*

H = habit strength, which is the extent to which performing the behavior has been rewarded in the past

E = reaction potential, or the inclination to perform the behavior, resulting from the foregoing four factors

These concepts are most often combined in a multiplicative way:

$$E = V*K*H*D \tag{2.1}$$

For example, consider a frequent-flyer program for an airline and the traveler's choice of an airline on which to fly. D might represent the traveler's need to get to his or her destination by a certain time. V might be the attractiveness of the frequent-flyer program for the particular airline. This attractiveness would depend on the number of bonus miles awarded per miles traveled, among other things. K might be the intrinsic reward of flying with this airline, essentially, how good the airline was on service, reliability, and so on. H might be the extent to which the traveler had reaped the rewards of service, reliability, and so on provided by this airline by previously traveling on it. Finally, E would be the consumer's intention to use the airline for the upcoming trip.

One component of the theory of particular interest is that it was originally proposed as a *stochastic* theory of behavior (Hilgard and Bower, 1975, pp. 160, 168). Reaction potential was not stable, but "oscillated" from "instant to instant." The momentary reaction potential had to exceed a "reaction threshold" for the behavior to occur. In fact the probability of this happening "is a normal (Ogival) function of the extent to which the effective reaction potential exceeds the reaction potential" (Hull, 1943, p. 344). This is similar conceptually to a probit model, or if a Weibul rather than a normal distribution is used, a binomial logit model. The logit model of Guadagni and Little (1983) can be viewed in Hullian terms. Their model includes brand loyalty (a type of H), presence of promotion (stimulus intensity, V), and intrinsic brand utility (reward, K). Their model does not include drive in that they do not model the consumer's need to make a purchase (e.g., through modeling interpurchase time or household inventory). Hull's theory therefore allows us to interpret more richly the consumer choice models that are increasingly being applied to sales promotion (see Chapter 8). It has not, however, been directly applied to studying the effects of sales promotion, and further research is needed to exploit the theory's potential.

ATTRIBUTION THEORY

Conceptual Underpinnings

Attribution theory describes how consumers explain the causes of events. These explanations are called "attributions." Attributions result directly in attitude change rather than behavioral change, and attribution theory does not formally address the behavioral consequences of a consumer's attributions. However, to the extent that attitudes are the antecedents of behavior (see the later discussions on attitude models and the consumer decision process), the theory is very relevant. (See Mizerski et al. 1979; Sternthal and Craig, 1982, Ch. 6; and Zaltman and Wallendorf, 1983, Ch. 16, for excellent discussions of attribution theory.)

There are many promotional events that potentially beg explanation in the minds of the consumer. For example,

> Why did I use a coupon to buy brand X?
>
> Why is Brand X being promoted?
>
> Why did the salesperson talk more about brand Y, when it was brand X that was advertised as being on sale?

How the consumer answers these questions has critical implications for subsequent purchase behavior. Here are some possible attributions based on the foregoing questions:

> I used this coupon because I happened to have it available, and why shouldn't I get a price discount once in a while on brands that I like.
>
> Manufacturers distribute coupons so that consumers will keep buying their brand. I'm simply taking advantage of these efforts and saving substantially at the same time.
>
> I used this coupon to get a price break.
>
> The coupon induced me to purchase this brand. I would not have bought it otherwise.
>
> Brand X is being promoted because they can't sell it at its regular price. It's probably a low-quality product.
>
> Brand X is being promoted because the store manager knows brand X is so popular that this will bring in more customers into the store. Brand X is serving as a loss leader.
>
> The store probably does not make much money on brand X when it's on sale. That is why the salesperson is trying to get me to buy brand Y.
>
> The salesman is talking up brand Y because he believes it best fits my needs.

As these examples illustrate, a number of possible attributions are possible based on the same question. This means that predictions from attribution theory can often be equivocal.

Three types of attribution theories can be distinguished: self-perception, object perception, and person perception (see Mizerski et al., 1979). These differ in terms of the object about which the attribution is being made. Attributions about one's own motives are the subject of self-perception (the "why-did-I-buy" question). Attributions directly about products are the domain of object perception (the "why-is-brand-X-on-promotion" question). If an attribution is being made about another person, the relevant theory is person perception (the salesperson example).

Self-perception theory is ascribed to the work of Bem (1972). According to the theory, "individuals form *their* attitudes by observing their past behavior and inferring dispositions or attitudes consistent with those actions" (Scott, 1981, p. 296). The key question individuals ask is whether the action they take is due to external causes (e.g., a promotion) or internal causes (e.g., favorable brand attitude). For example, if strong external causes are present, the individual invokes the "discounting principle," whereby internal causes are disregarded. As a result, brand attitude can remain unchanged or could even diminish (Scott, 1981, p. 297). Diminishing of attitude could occur either because of direct attribution (e.g., "I bought this brand on promotion so, since it took a big incentive to get me to buy the brand, I must not really like it") or simply because the consumer forgets characteristics of the brand after being so caught up with the promotion.

Self-perception theory is most readily applicable to repeat purchasing after a promotion. According to the theory, if the promotion is sufficiently strong, the consumer will attribute the purchase to an external cause, internal causes such as favorable brand attitude will be discounted, and repeat purchase probabilities will remain the same or perhaps diminish, compared to what they would be if the consumer had purchased the brand on his or her own.

Another application of self-perception theory to promotions is the case of the "foot-in-the-door" technique. This technique of selling is to induce the consumer to comply with an intermediate behavior (e.g., use a sample) in the hope that the consumer will then be more likely to engage in more complex behavior (e.g., purchase the brand at full price). (The reader will notice the similarity between this and the "shaping" concept of operant conditioning). The self-perception explanation as to why this strategy works is that the consumer is more likely to ascribe an internal cause to compliance with a small request ("I tried the sample because I was curious") than with a large request ("I bought this product because the salesperson sold me on it and offered a rebate gimmick").

Object-perception theory (Kelley, 1967; Mizerski et al., 1979) considers three factors that affect the attribution made concerning an object: (1) the distinctiveness of the event involving the object, (2) the consistency of that event over time or situation, and (3) the observations of others. Consider the case of judging the quality of a brand based on the event that it is being promoted. If only this brand or a small subset of brands promote, this event is relatively distinct. If, in addition the promotion occurs often, and at all stores, it is consistent over time and situation. It thus becomes easier for the consumer to draw an attribution about the brand ("this brand must be low quality—they're trying to give it away"). If a neighbor notices the same events and begins to form the same opinion, the attribution becomes even more solid.

An implication of object-perception theory to the current retailing environment for packaged goods is that promotion will not degrade any one brand's image, because all brands promote often (promotion of a particular brand is therefore not distinctive). However, the risks of brand image deterioration are clear to the durable goods manufacturer who may be the first in the industry to use promotion.

Jones and Davis (1965) developed three rules people use in making inferences about other individuals (Mizerski et al., 1979):

1. Choice		Other individuals are assumed to have choice as to which action they take.
2. Commonality		Only actions specific to the behavior in question are used to make attributions. These actions are called "noncommon effects."
3. Desirability		It is easier to make an attribution if the individual's behavior is seemingly not desirable.

In the salesperson example mentioned earlier, the consumer might assume that the salesperson *chose* to talk up brand Y at this *specific* store visit. Since the store advertising indicated that store management wanted to sell brand X (not the advertised brand Y), this is an *undesirable* action. However, an explanation of why the salesperson chose to take this seemingly inconsistent action at this time is that he or she must make more commission for brand Y.

It is important to note that dissonance theory (Festinger, 1957) underlies many of the attribution theories. The theory is based on the notion that behaviors frequently give rise to inconsistent facts for the consumer, and the consumer needs to resolve this dissonance. One way to resolve the dissonance is to change one belief that may be dissonant with others. For example, if a consumer buys a brand on promotion and finds the brand to be unsatisfactory, this contradiction ("why did I buy this no-good brand?") can be resolved by ascribing the purchase to the promotion. In the language of self-perception theory, an external cause is available to explain the contradiction. As another example, dissonance is created for the consumer when a brand thought to be high quality offers a promotion. This dissonance may be resolved by the consumer changing his or her belief that the brand is high quality, unless all brands are promoting and the consumer explains the high quality brand's promoting as something all brands have to do.

Empirical Studies

A number of attempts have been made to study attribution theory in a promotions context. Most of these focus on self-perception theory and the conditions under which the consumer will attribute behavior to an external cause (a promotional incentive).

Scott (1976) used self-perception theory to test two hypotheses: first, that participants contacted for an initial small request will be more likely to agree to a subsequent large request (this is the "foot-in-the-door approach"), and second, among those asked to comply with an initial request, compliance with the subsequent request will be larger for those whose initial request was not accompanied by an incentive. Further, Scott varied the degree of incentive without hypothesizing the effects. However, it would appear that stronger incentives give more plausible bases for external causes of the behavior, and hence the consumer is more likely to discount internal causes.

The hypotheses were tested using a field experiment in which the initial request was to receive a new newspaper on a trial basis. Coincident with this request was no incentive (regular price), a 50 percent discount, free trial, or free trial plus a premium. A randomly selected control group did not receive any initial request. Later, all subjects were asked to subscribe to the newspaper at its regular price. The results of this experiment were as follows:

Condition		Percentage Complying to Full Request (Subscribing)	N
With initial request	No incentive	13.2%	121
	50% discount	18.1%[a,b]	116
	Free trial	3.9%	51
	Free trial plus premium incentive	16.7%[b]	42
	No initial request	9.0%	100

[a] Significantly greater than no initial request group, $p < .05$.
[b] Significantly greater than free trial group, $p < .05$.

The results provide directional support for hypothesis 1. Three of the four initial-request groups have higher subscription rates than does the no-initial-request group. The second hypothesis was that subsequent subscription rates would be lowest for those given an incentive to accept the trial request. The results were directionally contrary to this hypothesis. The group receiving the 50 percent discount had the highest subscription rate—the only rate that was significantly higher than the no initial request group. Free trial plus a premium also did relatively well in generating subscriptions, while free trial alone was the only one of the three trial incentive treatments to yield lower subscription rates than the no incentive trial condition.[4]

Scott invokes some interesting potential explanations for these results. For example, the 50 percent discount might have worked so well because this incentive "may have been small enough to serve as a positive reinforcer rather than a discounting cue" (Scott, 1976, p. 267). The free trial plus premium might have generated "a sufficiently high degree of positive affect toward the newspaper to obviate any discounting that may have taken place" (Scott, 1976, p. 267). These comments illustrate the rich conceptual interplay that can transpire between at-

---

[4] One might argue that the subscription rates of real interest are those among *acceptors* of the initial trial request, for this corresponds to repeat rates among new triers. Scott cautions against this because of potential self-selection biases in comparing acceptors among the experimental groups. However, she reports that the 50 percent discount treatment yielded a directionally higher initial acceptance rate than did the regular price treatment (29.3 percent versus 28.1 percent) yet also a higher subscription rate among acceptors (44.1 percent versus 32.4 percent). The free trial and free trial plus premium treatments yielded much higher acceptance rates (70.6 percent and 76.2 percent, respectively) but also lower subscription rates among acceptors (2.8 percent and 18.8 percent, respectively).

tribution theory and behavioral learning theory. One explanation for the poor performance of the free trial condition would be that the free trial was a strong incentive and so evoked discounting and at the same time did not benefit from the affect generated by the premium.

In summary, this important experimental study provided "only equivocal support for self-perception theory" (Scott, 1976, p. 267). However, as indicated by Scott, there was a clear need for further research. For example, what is the effect of promotions for ongoing brands, where the promotion is not part of an introductory strategy. Second, what is the internal validity of attribution theory experiments? Do subjects actually make attributions, or is there some other explanation for the results? A third avenue of research was to investigate the conditions under which discounting would occur. The results of the 1976 paper indicated that the simple provision of an incentive was not enough by itself to stimulate discounting of internal reasons for purchasing or trying a brand.

This third line of inquiry was pursued with three studies (Scott and Yalch, 1980; Scott and Tybout, 1979; Tybout and Scott, 1983). Scott and Yalch (1980) offered subjects the choice of whether to taste a new soft drink under a $2 \times 2 \times 3$ crossed experimental design: The three-level factor was the quality of the "objective" taste of the soft drink as prejudged by the experimenters. The two two-level factors were the availability of a coupon and the opportunity to examine the product visually prior to tasting. The examination manipulation was the key treatment in the experiment. Scott and Yalch hypothesized that this examination would encourage the subjects to think about the reasons for their choice of a soft drink to taste. As a result, subjects given a coupon and encouraged to think about the reasons for their choice would attribute the causes to external factors and therefore would not be as receptive to the taste of the new soft drink, compared to those not given a coupon. Alternatively, when subjects were not encouraged to think about the reasons for their choices, Scott and Yalch conjectured that the coupon might serve as a positive reinforcement.

The results were in the hypothesized direction. In the examination condition, provision of an incentive resulted in generally lower taste evaluations than if no incentive were provided. When subjects were in the no-examination condition, provision of an incentive resulted in generally higher taste evaluations than if no incentive were provided. A very important additional finding related to the second question raised, namely, did subjects actually make the attributions that are hypothesized to cause the results? Using a survey of their subjects, Scott and Yalch found that "rewarded subjects who examined the product before tasting it would report the most external attributions" (Scott and Yalch, 1980, p. 37). This provides evidence on internal validity that indeed subjects made attributions as to why they undertook certain behaviors.[5]

---

[5] Scott (1977) conducted another experiment in which an attempt was made, through surveying, to determine whether subjects actually made attributions. She obtained directionally similar results, although not as strong in terms of statistical significance.

Scott and Tybout (1979) ran a 2×2 taste test experiment in which the two factors were provision of incentive (coupon or no coupon) and time at which the subjects were encouraged to think about the reasons for their behavior (cognitive work immediately versus cognitive work delayed). The hypothesis was that there should be an interaction between provision of incentive and timing of cognitive work: The cognitive work immediately condition was assumed to initiate the self-perception process, whereby the presence of an incentive would serve as a discounting cue. However, if subjects were not encouraged immediately to think about their behavior, the incentive would "be interpreted as a reinforcing rather than discounting cue" (Scott and Yalch, 1980, p. 51) and positive taste evaluations would result. Results were consistent with this hypothesis.

Tybout and Scott (1983) used very similar experiments as Scott and Tybout (1979) but proposed a different theoretical argument. They hypothesized that subjects with well-formed internal knowledge about a brand would attribute their choice of that brand to internal causes. In that case, a financial incentive would serve as a reinforcement and enhance brand attitude. However, subjects without well-formed internal knowledge would attribute their choice of the brand to external causes (see Hastorf et al., 1970, pp. 88–89). In that case, the incentive would serve as a plausible external cause of the choice and would undermine attitudes toward the brand. Tybout and Scott manipulated the order in which subjects either tasted the brand or received information on other people's taste evaluations of the brand, under the assumption that those tasting the brand first would develop more well-formed internal knowledge about the brand. Results were consistent with their hypothesis: Subjects tasting the brand first formed more favorable attitudes toward the brand when an incentive was present than when an incentive was not present, while subjects receiving others' taste evaluations first formed less favorable attitudes toward the brand when an incentive was present than when an incentive was not present.

The results of the Scott et al. experiments are that promotions such as coupons can have either negative or positive effects on evaluations of brands. Negative effects occur when the choice context or internal state of the consumer encourages the consumer to attribute choice to a promotion. Positive effects are observed when consumers are not encouraged to attribute their choosing the brand to a promotion. The important question is whether the natural consumer environment or state of the consumer encourages attribution to promotion or discourages it. The papers reviewed here suggest that encouraging consumers to think about their choices before using the product, having consumers explicitly compare the product to its competition, or offering promotions to consumers who have poorly formed internal knowledge about the brand induce negative attributions and undermine evaluation of the product. The salience of these conditions in consumers' information environments needs to be investigated.

A related study to the Scott et al. experiments was conducted by Doob et al. (1969). This study was cast in a dissonance theory framework, in particular, "the more effort in any form a person exerts to attain a goal, the more dissonance is aroused if the goal is less valuable than expected. The individual reduces this dissonance by increasing his liking for the goal, and therefore the greater the effort, the more he should like the goal" (Doob et al., 1969, p. 345). Doob et al. thus predict that a brand introduced at a low price will eventually enjoy fewer sales than will the same brand if introduced at a higher (and thus more likely to induce dissonance) price. The authors tested this hypothesis in five replicated field experiments, each time matching two sets of stores. In each experiment, a new "house" brand or brand size was introduced either at a lower than usual price or the "normal" price. In either case, prices were not advertised or reinforced with point-of-purchase material. After a brief time (one to three weeks), price in the low-price stores was increased to normal. Results for these five experiments were very similar, indicating that while the low introductory price condition induced much higher sales initially, eventually the sales rate in the normal introductory price stores exceeded that in the low-price stores. The results for one product category, aluminum foil, are displayed in Figure 2.1.

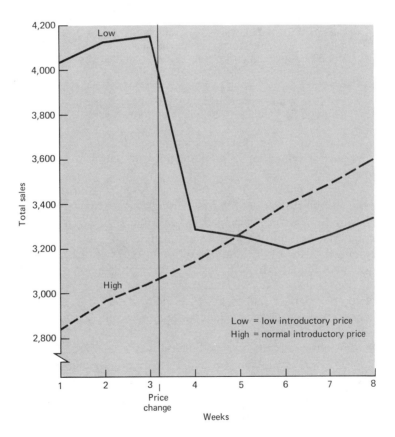

FIGURE 2.1   Results of the Doob et al. Experiment for Aluminum Foil

Source: Anthony N. Doob, J. Merrill Carlsmith, Jonathan L. Freedman, Thomas K. Landauer, and Tom Soleng, Jr., "Effect of Initial Selling Price on Subsequent Sales," *Journal of Personality and Social Psychology,* Vol. 11, no. 4 (1969), p. 347.

These results are intriguing. As with most field research, however, while the external validity of the experiment is clear, the internal validity is not. As the authors note, there are several interpretations of the results.

1. *Dissonance theory.* Indeed, consumers who initially bought at the normal price resolved dissonance by developing more favorable attitudes.
2. *Object perception.* Consumers in the low-price condition may have inferred that the brand was lower quality because of the low price. This could have attracted price conscious consumers rather than quality conscious consumers as the initial brand franchise. These consumers are more likely to be brand switchers and hence have lower repeat rates.
3. *Adaptation-level theory.* Consumers were more likely to resist the price increase because of the initial low price. They needed time to adapt to the new price or may never have adapted (see "Theories of Price Perception").
4. *Purchase acceleration.* The low introductory price might have induced consumers to stock up on the brand (buy multiple items) or purchase earlier than they needed to. The authors state that this is not a good explanation because the number of weeks studied was greater than the interpurchase time (except for light bulbs). In addition, the mouthwash data were also examined 20 weeks out, and the same sales discrepancy was evident. However, interpurchase times for toothpaste and aluminum foil could be longer than the time frame examined. For example, the Blattberg et al. (1981) data indicate the interpurchase time for aluminum foil is on the order of 10 weeks.
5. *Self-perception theory.* The low introductory price provided a plausible external cause of the purchase. This inhibited formation of favorable brand attitude.

It is unfortunate that the experiment did not allow distinguishing among these alternative explanations, for the managerial implications of each theory are different.

Influenced strongly by Scott et al.'s work, Dodson et al. (1978) studied the extent to which deal purchases were associated with switching and repeat purchasing for existing packaged goods brands. Shoemaker and Shoaf (1977) had noted that deal purchasing was associated with lower repeat rates. Dodson et al. extended this work by studying different types of deals and by using self-perception theory to form hypotheses. The three deals examined were media-distributed coupons, cents-off marked packages, and on/in-package coupons. Since the media coupons generally had higher face value, Dodson et al. reasoned that, from an economic perspective, media coupons should induce more switching than cents-off packages and package coupons and all deals should induce more switching than would be obtained when no deal was available or used.

Dodson et al. then applied self-perception theory to predict repeat rates associated with dealing. They considered two factors: consumer effort to utilize the promotion and the promotion's economic value. They looked at three deals and categorized them in terms of these factors as follows[6]:

---

[6] The classifications were made based on the authors' judgment.

Promotion Type	Effort Required	Economic Value
Cents-off price marked	Low	Low
Media-distributed coupon	Moderate	Substantial
Package coupon	High	Low

Dodson et al. then hypothesized that since media coupons had substantial economic value and required moderate effort to redeem, consumers would attribute their purchasing the brand to the media coupon. They would reason: "Why did I go to the effort to redeem this coupon? Because of its economic value" (Dodson et al., 1978, p. 74). Since cents-off deals required minimal effort for low reward, they were less likely to be attributed as an external influence than would be media coupons but more likely than package coupons. Package coupons also had low economic value but required relatively more effort. The consumer would thus reason that he or she must have really liked the brand (attribution of internal cause) to buy it using this coupon. The resulting hypothesis is that use of media-distributed coupons and cents-off packages will undermine repeat purchase probabilities when they are retracted, with the effect for media-distributed coupons being greater. However, use of package coupons should enhance repeat purchase probabilities once they are retracted.

Table 2.4 summarizes the results of their study. Note, first, that there are two repeat purchasing situations—one where the consumer had just switched brands, the other where the consumer had just purchased the same brand twice in a row. The results appear to be largely well in accord with Dodson et al.'s hypotheses. They therefore conclude that "media-distributed coupons induced substantial switching, cents-off deals somewhat less switching, and package coupons either decreased or did not affect brand switching. Second, the retraction of a deal had a significant effect on the incidence of brand repeat purchasing . . . media-distributed coupons undermined repeat purchasing to a greater extent than either cents-off deals or package coupons, whereas cents-off labels undermined repeat purchasing to a greater extent than package coupons" (Dodson et al., 1978, p. 79).

Dodson et al. make a valuable contribution to the conceptual issue of how to apply self-perception theory to the analysis of deal repeat purchase effects. However, it is not clear whether the data are causal enough to warrant conclusions such as "induced" or "undermined." An alternative explanation of Table 2.4 is as follows: Because of differences in economic value and effort required, media-distributed coupons attracted more switchers than did cents-off price deals, which in turn attracted more switchers than did package coupons. Switchers are those who would have a low probability of buying the brand if the promotion had not been available. *By definition*, then, switchers have lower repeat rates. We therefore expect a negative association between the amount of switching generated by a promotion and repeat rates observed after the promotion purchase, and this is what is displayed in Table 2.4. The key data analysis problem is that switching behavior is by definition inversely related to repeat purchasing. Neslin and Shoe-

TABLE 2.4 Switching and Repeat Purchase Probabilities

	Hypothesized		cents-off purchase		package coupon		no deal
Switching[a]	media coupon	>	cents-off purchase	=	package coupon	>	no deal
Margarine	65%		44%		41%		40%
Flour	82%		48%		32%		43%
Switching transaction[c] Hypothesized[e]	media coupon	<	cents-off purchase	<	package coupon	>	no deal
Margarine	13%		13%		—		28%
Flour	16%		34%		—		36%
Repeat purchase[b] **Loyalty transaction**[d] Hypothesized[e]	media	<	cents-off purchase	<	package coupon	>	no deal
Margarine	51%		62%		83%		77%
Flour	44%		62%		72%		74%

[a] Table entries are percentage of purchase occasions in which a brand switch took place, given that the particular deal (or no deal) was used in the purchase occasion.

[b] Table entries are the percentage of purchase occasions in which the brand bought was repurchased, given that the particular deal (or no deal) was used.

[c] Switching transactions were instances when the consumer used a promotion in switching brands, and then Dodson et al. observed the probability of repeat purchasing the switched-to brand on the next occasion.

[d] Loyalty transactions were instances when the consumer bought the same brand two times in a row, the second purchase being on promotion. Dodson et al. then observed the probability of repeat purchasing that same brand on the next occasion.

[e] The hypothesized relationship among media coupon, cents-off purchase, and no deal is media coupon < cents-off purchase < no deal.

Source: Joe A. Dodson, Alice M. Tybout, and Brian Sternthal, "Impact of Deals and Deal Retraction on Brand Switching," *Journal of Marketing Research,* Vol. 15 (February 1978), adapted from pp. 76–79. Adapted from the *Journal of Marketing Research,* published by the American Marketing Association.

maker (1989) expand upon this problem. They note that even if promotions have no effect upon individual purchase probabilities, aggregate level analyses can reveal an apparent negative relationship, especially to the extent that the promotion draws a large number of switchers (consumers with low nonpromotion purchase probabilities) to the brand (see Chapter 5 and Chapter 8).

In summary, the Dodson et al. study is intriguing and stimulating. However, as the authors note, "it was not possible to rule out competing explanations for the observed effects . . . research is needed which minimizes threats to both internal and external validity" (Dodson et al., 1978, p. 80).

Two recent laboratory experiments have further investigated the role of promotions in determining repeat purchase probabilities. Cole and Chakraborty (1987) ran an experiment in which they manipulated the economic value of a coupon and the effort required to redeem the coupon. They studied the effects of these factors on redemption rates and repeat purchases for a new product. They found generally that effort was more important than economic value. Effort had a negative effect upon redemption and a positive effect upon repeat purchases. Cole and Chakraborty report that their sample sizes were low so that some of their observed effects are marginal. However, their work is indicative of the research that is needed in this area.

Kahn and Louie (1988) used a laboratory experiment to examine the effects of three contingencies on repeat purchasing in a promotion environment: the variety-seeking versus brand-loyal orientation of subjects, the pervasiveness of promotions in the product category, and the time pattern of promotions. They found, for example, that promotions undermined the repeat purchase probabilities of loyal subjects when only the promoted brand used promotions, but this effect vanished if all brands in the category were promoting. They also found that a regular pattern of promotions resulted in higher repeat purchases for variety-seeking subjects. The overall finding is that the effects of promotions upon repeat purchasing depend on consumer characteristics and the promotion environment.

Summary

In summary, attribution theory provides a framework for studying how the use of sales promotions affects the consumer's attitude toward the brand. These attitudes are influenced as the consumer seeks to explain his or her own actions (self-perception theory), the actions of others (person-perception theory), or the reasons behind the promotion of particular brands (object-perception theory). In this section, we also discussed dissonance theory, a related framework that applies to situations where the consumer observes discrepancies in behavior or actions that must be resolved. Self-perception theory has received the most attention of these theories, and the empirical research in this area suggests that promotions can have either positive or negative effects on brand attitudes, depending on the promotion itself, the purchase environment, or the internal state of the consumer prior to using the promotion.

Presently, the task for researchers is to replicate and extend previous work on attribution theory. The ample work in the area of self-perception theory needs to be replicated and consolidated. For example, additional laboratory experiments are needed to manipulate the context variables (economic value, consumer experience, provision of information, consumer effort required, etc.) that have been shown to mediate the attribution effects of promotions. An important context variable that has received little direct attention is whether the promoted product is a new or existing brand. One would expect that negative attributions would be more prevalent in the case of a new product, where brand attitudes are not firmly entrenched (e.g., see Tybout and Scott, 1983). It is hoped that these contingency studies will lead to results that can be generalized to the real world.

Methodologically, both field experiments and nonexperimental data analysis are needed, but previous efforts have been subject to problems of internal validity. One way to overcome these problems is to include survey instruments along with observation of behavior. (Scott has done this, with mixed results. See Mazursky et al., 1984, for another example of integrating survey and behavior data.) Another approach, suggested by Neslin and Shoemaker (1989), is to conduct data analysis at the individual consumer level.

The implication for managers of this line of research is to consider the possible long-term effects of promotions. Viewing promotions as switching devices without any long-term implications is probably a mistake. Sawyer and Dickson (1984) recommend that prior to implementing a promotion, managers should go beyond strict financial planning (profit, revenues, costs) and ask conceptual questions such as "What will the consumer learn from the promotion? What behavior will be reinforced?" and "How will the consumer perceive the promotion?" The discussion and results concerning attribution theory suggest this is sound advice.

THEORIES OF PRICE PERCEPTION

Many sales promotions involve price reductions, and hence the process by which consumers perceive prices becomes critical for determining the appropriate size and presentation of price decreases. Three theories have particular relevance: Weber's law, adaptation-level theory, and assimilation-contrast theory.

Weber's Law

Weber's law is concerned with the question of how much of a stimulus change is necessary in order for it to be noticed. The law postulates that this "just noticeable difference" is proportional to the absolute magnitude of the original stimulus. That is, let

ΔS = size of stimulus change that will be noticed

S = original magnitude of the stimulus

k = constant of proportionality

Weber's law is then

$$\frac{\Delta S}{S} = k \tag{2.2}$$

In pricing terms, if a \$1 price decrease in a \$10 item is the minimum price decrease that will be noticed, then $k = .1$, and a \$2 price change in a \$20 item is required to have any effect.

Weber's law has received mixed confirmation in a pricing context (Monroe, 1973). A concern in applying the theory to the promotions context is that promotions are of short duration and they are usually announced to the consumer. Weber's law is perhaps more applicable in the pricing context than in the case of price *promotions*. However, Weber's law suggests two critical concepts: first, that price cuts within a given small range may be completely ineffective and, second, that a base or original price is important for determining the effectiveness of a price reduction. These concepts are elaborated upon in adaptation-level and assimilation-contrast theories.

Adaptation-Level Theory: The Concept of a Reference Price

Adaptation-level theory (Helson, 1964) proposes that perceptions of new stimuli are formed relative to a standard or "adaptation level." The adaptation level is determined by previous and current stimuli to which a person has been exposed. It thus changes over time as a person is exposed to new stimuli. The adaptation level for judging the price of a particular item is called the "reference price." A consumer's reference price might be based on previous prices paid for the item or similar items, previous prices observed, prices for comparable items available at the time of purchase, the context within which the purchase occasion is taking place, a reservation price (Chapter 4), or some subjective judgment of what the item is worth. Whatever the basis for the consumer's reference price, the key implication of adaptation-level theory is that the price of an item will be judged relative to that reference price.

Researchers have thought of the reference price as an "expected price" (e.g., Winer, 1986; Kalwani et al., 1988), a "fair price" (e.g., Kamen and Toman, 1970; Nagle, 1987), or a "target price" (Monroe, 1973, p. 77). Research is needed to determine which if any of these conceptualizations most closely describes the reference prices consumers use. One could easily imagine circumstances under which these prices would differ. For example, one might expect that a box of chocolate chip cookies will cost \$2.59, the target price (i.e., the price one is looking for) might be \$2.29, yet the perceived fair price might be \$2.00. Each of these could serve as the reference price relative to which the actual price of the cookies will be judged.

Manufacturers and retailers generally would like consumers' reference prices to be high. That way, any price decrease appears even more attractive to consumers, and regular prices do not seem so unattractive. Therefore, the important questions are: (1) "Do consumers utilize reference prices?" if so (2) "How are they formed?" and (3) "How do various promotions affect reference prices?" An understanding of how various promotions affect reference prices would allow manufacturers and retailers to utilize an appropriate mix and schedule of promotions so as to sustain high reference prices.

One indication of whether consumers have reference prices in mind is consumer awareness of item prices. The literature on price awareness is somewhat inconclusive in this regard (see summaries in Monroe, 1973, and Dickson and Sawyer, 1986). Much of this research has concentrated on price recall accuracy, with the results being that accuracy varies greatly across brands and product classes. For example, in the often cited study by Gabor and Granger (1961), accuracy ranged from 34.8 percent for breakfast cereal to 79.3 percent for tea. In addition, Dickson and Sawyer concluded after reviewing several studies that recall accuracy has not increased over the years, despite the belief that consumer demand sensitivity to price is increasing. In fact, Dickson and Sawyer interviewed consumers literally seconds after they had placed an item in their shopping carts and found that only 47 percent could state the exact price of the item and 56 percent were able to quote the price to within five percentage points (see the upcoming discussion on evidence of point-of-purchase perceptions for more detail on the results of this study with respect to price reductions).

One might argue that it is not price recall accuracy but rather consumers' opinions of whether they know prices that is important. The evidence on this is also mixed. Gabor and Granger (1961) report that 82 percent of respondents were willing to at least answer the question about the price of a specific item, while for Dickson and Sawyer, the percentage is 79 percent. However, both studies did not probe for respondents' confidence in their answers.

Monroe (1973, p. 77) cites studies other than price recall tests that suggest consumers' judgments of prices are influenced by an internal adaptation price level. For example, Kamen and Toman (1970) find evidence that consumers were more likely to switch brands of gasoline, for a given price differential, if the general price level were higher. (This contradicts Weber's law discussed earlier.) The explanation is that consumers have views on what products should cost, and as actual prices deviate from that fair price, they switch brands. If this is actually the mechanism that explains Kamen and Toman's findings, it suggests that perceived fair price serves as the reference price.

Della Bitta and Monroe (1974) conducted a laboratory experiment to identify the existence of reference prices. They presented subjects with either ascending or descending series of prices for various items and solicited judgments for each price on a seven-point "high-low" measurement scale. The hypothesis was that the descending series of prices would generally be judged to be lower than the ascending series on the seven-point scale. The reason for this hypothesis is that the first prices presented in a series enable the subject to form a reference price for the item. For the ascending series, the reference price will be low compared to that formed from the descending series, so that prices in general for the ascending series will be perceived as high, while those for the descending series will be perceived as low. This hypothesis was strongly confirmed, and the concept of reference prices provides a compelling explanation for the results. The research suggests that reference prices can be created in the laboratory. Winer (1986) has formulated a model to test whether reference prices play a role in actual consumer purchasing.

Winer (1986) formulated a brand choice model based on the expected price notion of a reference price. He developed a two-stage model, in which the first stage described the formation of the reference price, and the second incorporated the reference price in a choice model. Winer tested two reference price formation models. The first model was that consumers simply extrapolate the last price they observed and a trend to form the reference price. That is,

$$P^r_{ijt} = \delta_o + \delta_1 P^o_{ijt-1} + \delta_2 \text{TREND} + \epsilon_{ijt} \tag{2.3}$$

where

P^r_{ijt} = reference price for consumer i for brand j at purchase occasion t

P^o_{ijt-1} = consumer i's observed price of brand j at purchase occasion $t - 1$

TREND = trend term

ϵ_{ijt} = error term

Equation (2.3) implicitly assumes a high level of awareness for prices, even for brands the consumer did not purchase on the previous purchase occasion. This is reflected by the P^o_{ijt-1} term. An alternative would be to use the price last paid for the item.

The second model Winer used for reference price formation was a rational expectations model:

$$P^r_{ijt} = \theta_o + \theta_1 P_{jt-1} + \theta_2 MS_{jt-1} + \theta_3 \text{TREND} + v_{ijt} \tag{2.4}$$

where

P_{jt-1} = retail price for brand j at purchase occasion $t - 1$

MS_{jt-1} = market share for brand j at purchase occasion $t - 1$

v_{ijt} = error term

The key assumptions here are that equation (2.4) describes the process by which manufacturers adjust their price and the consumer learns this decision rule and therefore comes to expect the appropriate price.

Actual measures of reference price, the dependent variable in equations (2.3) and (2.4), were not available. Winer assumed, however, that consumer's expectations were unbiased, so that actual price could be inserted as the dependent variable in these equations for the purposes of estimation. Winer did not display estimated coefficients for either equation (2.3) or equation (2.4). However, he did observe that the predictive accuracy of the choice model did not depend on the reference price model.

The choice model used by Winer was as follows:

$$\text{PROB}_{ijt} = \alpha_0 + \alpha_1 \text{PURCH}_{ijt-1} + \alpha_2 \text{ADV}_{ijt}$$
$$+ \alpha_3(RP^r_{ijt} - RP^o_{ijt}) + \alpha_4 RP^o_{ijt} + \epsilon_{ijt} \tag{2.5}$$

where

PROB_{ijt} = the probability consumer i buys brand j at purchase occasion t

PURCH_{ijt-1} = a zero-one indicator of whether brand j was bought on the previous purchase occasion

ADV_{ijt} = relative advertising exposure of brand j to household i prior to purchase occasion t

RP^o_{ijt}, RP^r_{ijt} = relative observed and reference prices, respectively.

ϵ_{ijt} = error term

Note that both observed and reference prices included in the model were computed *relative* to the average across all brands. Given our discussion of adaptation-level theory, this can be interpreted as including two potential reference prices: expected price computed using either equation (2.3) or (2.4) and prices of comparable items. Winer refers to $RP^r_{ijt} - RP^o_{ijt}$ as a "sticker shock" variable. If the variable is highly negative, this means the actual price is above expectations. In the event that the actual price is below the reference price, the variable can be interpreted as perceived savings. Winer's results indicated that the reference price coefficient (α_3 in equation 2.5) was positive as expected and statistically significant for two out of three brands. For those brands, including the reference price variable in the model significantly improved choice prediction.

Winer's model is important because it rigorously incorporates the concept of reference price in an individual choice model. It contains the formation of reference price and how that price influences brand choice. Two caveats, however, are in order. First, as Winer notes (1986, p. 255), "Since many of the constructs utilized in this study were estimates of nonmeasured quantities, the reported results must be treated as indications of the underlying consumer behavior at best." Second, the reference price effect needs to be disentangled from other possible "promotional price cut" effects. For example, since the reference price will be highly correlated with previous price, the $RP^r_{ijt} - RP^o_{ijt}$ variable will be close to zero when the retailer is charging regular price and positive when the retailer is cutting price. The variable could then be interpreted as a price cut variable, and price cuts are often communicated at the point of purchase (Chapter 12). Guadagni and Little (1983) find evidence of both a regular price and promotional price cut effect. Another possibility along these lines is that the reference price effect measured in this research is confounded with an interaction between advertising and price. (See Chapter 6 for experimental evidence of this interaction.)

In summary, there is some evidence that reference prices do exist and play a role in product choice. However, there is clearly the need to research this important area further, in two potential directions. One would be to investigate further the role of reference prices in determining consumer choice (see Büyük-kurt, 1986; Kalwani et al., 1988). The second direction would be to directly measure the concept and study the various determinants of reference price. This line of research will be especially challenging but potentially very rewarding. New techniques are needed to measure the standard (if any) to which consumers compare prices when they shop.

Assimilation-Contrast Theory

Assimilation-contrast theory (Sherif and Hovland, 1953; Sherif, 1963) provides one conceptualization of how reference prices might change. The key notion here is that the degree of change in an individual's initial belief depends on the discrepancy between the initial belief and the position advocated by a newly observed communication (Fishbein and Ajzen, 1975, p. 458). Less discrepant new information is easily assimilated by the individual, while highly discrepant information provides a stark contrast to initial beliefs. In either situation, the effect on belief change will be small. Larger belief changes occur for moderately discrepant information, which is neither completely assimilated nor contrasted with initial beliefs (see also Engel and Blackwell, 1982, pp. 467–469).

In the case of reference prices, the consumer's current perceived reference price can be considered the initial belief, while the newly observed or advertised price is new information. The discrepancy between reference price and observed price might be very small, moderate, or very large (these regions can be labeled the ''latitude of acceptance,'' ''latitude of noncommitment,'' and ''latitude of rejection,'' respectively). Only if the discrepancy is moderate will the consumer's reference price change. If the discrepancy is small, it may be seen as a slight aberration. If the discrepancy is large, the consumer might see the observed price as an ''exception.'' In either case the consumer's current perceived reference price will barely change.

Managing the assimilation-contrast process is a strategic challenge. A small price cut will probably not change reference prices (it is assimilated) but also probably will not be large enough to provide a strong economic incentive. A moderate price cut might be large enough to provide a meaningful economic incentive, but may also decrease reference price. A large price cut will be contrasted and will not change reference price, but will provide too large an incentive and cost the firm too much in lost revenues.

One strategy for dealing with the assimilation-contrast process is to try to increase the consumer's perceived reference price, or at least prevent the current reference price from changing, at the same time as offering a price cut. This is commonly done by providing a ''suggested'' reference price in the advertised or in-store communication of the price cut. This is a delicate task. For example, the suggested reference price might be much higher than the consumer's current reference price, and is therefore rejected (contrasted). The price cut might therefore appear to be in the moderate range and be used to revise downward the perceived reference price. Retailers try to avoid downward revision of the consumer's reference price by using the word "sale" or "special" to accompany the reduced price. This essentially tells the consumer that the reduced price is temporary and should not be used to decrease the consumer's reference price. The best way the suggested reference price strategy could work is if the suggested reference price is only moderately higher than the consumer's current reference price, so it increases it slightly. Then the price cut seems very large, so large that it communicates a strong economic incentive but does not decrease the consumer's perceived reference price. A few interesting studies have looked at these issues and are summarized next.

Blair and Landon (1981) and Nystrom et al. (1975) both found that presentation of a reference price increases perceptions of the amount of savings involved in a price cut. The results of the Blair and Landon study are displayed in Table 2.5. In this research, consumers were asked what the "normal" store price of various durable goods items were, after they were exposed to a store advertisement for the items. All advertisements contained a currently available price. Some also included a suggested reference price (treatment B) while others did not (treatment A). The store used in the treatment advertisements was fictitious, and both the advertised and reference prices were on the high end of the market. Table 2.5 shows that the average consumer-stated normal price was greater when a suggested reference price was provided. Blair and Landon also found that the consumer's perception of the lowest price available for the product was also increased by provision of the reference price, although the results were not as strong (see also Ahmed and Gulas, 1982).

TABLE 2.5 Results of the Blair and Landon Study on Reference Prices

Item	Mean Subject-Estimated "Normal Price" for Store		Statistical Significance of Difference	Available Price Presented in Treatments A and B	Reference Price Provided Treatment B
	Without Reference Price (Treatment A)	With Reference Price (Treatment B)			
Sony television	517.20	522.24	NS	459.00	544.00
Store-brand television	368.02	393.42	.07	324.00	419.00
G.E. food processor	66.98	74.79	.01	59.95	79.95
Store-brand food processor	50.98	61.49	.01	44.55	69.95

NS – Not significant.

Source: Edward A. Blair and E. Laird Landon, Jr., "The Effects of Reference Prices in Retail Advertisement," *Journal of Marketing*, Vol. 45, no. 2 (Spring 1981), adapted from pp. 63, 66. Adapted from the *Journal of Marketing*, published by the American Marketing Association.

Nystrom et al. (1975) compared two formats for presenting a price reduction of a shirt in a Swedish department store. Again, one format provided a suggested reference price (49:00 Crowns crossed out to indicate that the price had been cut), while the other did not. The results are in Table 2.6 and show that the actual price was judged more favorably when the reference price was provided.

Liefeld and Heslop (1985) found different results than the two studies just reviewed. In a study of Canadian consumers, these researchers found that using suggested reference prices had no bearing on perceptions of "normal prices." This could have been caused by the suggested reference prices being much larger than consumers' own reference prices. Liefeld and Heslop attribute the finding more probably to a lack of source credibility (1985, p. 874). In addition, Liefeld and Heslop found that use of the term "sale" resulted in a lower perception of normal price and, hence, lower perceived savings. This shows that use of additional terms such as "sale" or "special" can backfire. Perhaps in this case, consumers executed an object-perception attribution, concluding that the brand was on sale because the brand was low quality, and therefore probably had a fairly low price.

Evidence of Point-of-Purchase Perceptions

Dickson and Sawyer (1986) conducted a broad price-perception study at the point of purchase. More than 800 supermarket shoppers were questioned within seconds of selecting an item and placing it in their shopping baskets. Dickson and Sawyer's study is unique in that not only did it explore issues of general price awareness, but it uncovered some interesting findings regarding perceptions of price promotions. We summarize and comment on three of these findings.

1. Among consumers who purchased an item on price promotion, 49.1 percent were aware that it was on promotion, 27.2 percent thought it was at its usual price, and 23.7 percent were not sure. Therefore, fewer than half of those buying on promotion knew they had bought on promotion! One's immediate reaction is that this is a small number. It raises the challenge that only a minority of consumers go through the process of forming reference prices and assimilating/contrasting a new price. However, these theories are really only models and cannot be expected to apply to every

TABLE 2.6 Results of the Nystrom et al. Study on Reference Prices

Presentation	Men's shirt wash and wear (65% terital, 35% linen)	Men's shirt wash and wear (65% terital, 35% linen)
	~~49:75 Crowns~~	
	37:00 Crowns	37:00 Crowns
Mean judgment of price	6.08	5.73

Note: Higher number means more favorable judgment; difference in means is statistically significant, $p < .01$.

Source: Harry Nystrom, Hans Tamsons, and Tober Thams, "An Experiment in Price Generalizations and Discrimination," *Journal of Marketing Research*, Vol. 12 (May 1975), adapted from pp. 178, 180. Adapted from the *Journal of Marketing Research*, published by the American Marketing Association.

consumer. If only 50 percent of those aware they had bought on promotion had in fact been *influenced to buy* because of the promotion, this would still mean a 33% increase in sales due to the promotion.

2. Among those aware that they had bought on promotion, 56.2 percent could not/ would not guess the amount of the price *reduction*, 28.9 percent guessed wrong, and only 12.9 percent could actually state the amount of the reduction. However, 50 percent were able to state correctly (without looking in their baskets) the exact amount they paid for the item. The conclusion therefore is that relatively speaking, consumers were aware of the final price and aware they had bought on promotion, but did not know the amount of reduction. This appears to challenge the notion that consumers go through the reference price–assimilation-contrast process.

3. There was a tendency for consumers to understate the amount of the price reduction (when they were willing to voice an estimate) yet also understate the price they paid. Taken together, this implies that if consumers had internal reference prices, they were lower than the true regular prices. That is the only way consumers could understate the amount of the reduction yet still understate the actual price paid. Perhaps frequent promotions had lowered the average reference price.

The Dickson and Sawyer study provides fascinating insight but also shows the potential for further work in this area. It is noteworthy, for example, that the shelf labels used to communicate price promotions stated "Cost Cutter Bonus Buy" and showed the price, but did not say "sale" or show a reference price. This might explain consumers' lack of *belief* that they had bought on promotion. In addition, a very useful extension would be to couple the price awareness information with evidence of past purchase behavior. In this way, price perception could be linked to brand switching. Past purchase behavior could be recorded in a self-report survey at the point of purchase or possibly using scanner panelists.

Summary

In summary, Weber's law, adaptation-level theory, and assimilation-contrast theory provide a rich framework for establishing the perceptual consequences of price promotions. Key to that framework is that a price promotion is compared to a *perceived* benchmark—a reference price—and that comparison yields consumer perception of savings. Previous and current prices of a particular brand and its competition undoubtedly play an important role in determining a consumer's reference price. However, other factors such as advertised reference prices, advertised sale prices, use of the word "sale," use of unit pricing (Anderson, 1974), the inflationary environment (Sawyer and Dickson, 1984), and the use situation in which the purchase takes place (Monroe et al., 1977) all might affect the consumer's reference price. In addition, the level of consumer involvement in the product category can have important effects on what constitues small, medium, or large discrepancies in an assimilation-contrast context (e.g., see Fishbein and Ajzen, 1975. p. 458). The effects of these various mediating factors must be sorted out before we have a clear understanding of the role of price perception in sales promotion.

PERCEIVED RISK

Risk taking is an inherent element of purchasing new brands (Bauer, 1960; also see Beem and Schaeffer, 1981). As identified by Cunningham (1966), there are two components of risk the consumer faces in purchasing an untried product: uncertainty about how the brand will perform and the consequences of poor performance. Accordingly, consumers can reduce risk either by reducing uncertainty or reducing the consequences of an incorrect choice. It is to this latter case that sales promotions can be applied, in particular, to reducing the risk for consumers who are unfamiliar with the brand. The concept of perceived risk is thus especially relevant for new products.

Roselius (1971) surveyed consumers regarding their opinions on the best ways to reduce risk. Free samples were the only promotion tested, and they did score high on ability to reduce financial loss as well as the risk of "feeling foolish." However, buying major well-known brands as well as buying the same brand one has been satisfied with scored much higher. This study uses self-report, and it may be difficult for consumers to articulate the methods they use to reduce risk. In addition, the study took place before the explosion in use of promotions. However, the results underscore the importance of brand and even manufacturer image in reducing perceived risk.

Shoemaker and Shoaf (1975) found evidence that consumers buy a smaller size when trying a brand than when they repurchase the brand. This is consistent with the idea that buying a smaller size is a risk reduction mechanism. Interestingly though, Shoemaker and Shoaf found that free samples distributed prior to purchase did not decrease the tendency for the first *purchase* to be of a smaller size than subsequent purchases. This is inconsistent with the hypothesis that samples serve as a risk-reduction mechanism. It appears to be too drastic for the consumer to move from trying a small free sample to spending money on a regular size. This would be consistent with the concept of behavioral shaping. Alternatively, the sample may be too small to allow the consumer to assess completely the brand's attributes, and so the first actual purchase of a brand will still be of a smaller size. Also, as noted by Shoemaker and Shoaf, the samples might have encouraged more trial purchases, and the additional new triers might have been relatively risk averse. In addition, the free sample used in their study may have attracted a different type of new tryer, perhaps more likely to be a light user. In summary, then, Shoemaker and Shoaf's results suggest that consumers purchase smaller sizes as a risk reduction mechanism, but the results are equivocal as to whether using samples is another risk reduction mechanism.

One explanation for how promotions address risk is the utility-theoretic notion of a risk premium. For example, assume that brand A provides benefits y for sure and brand B might provide either benefits x or z, where $x > y > z$. The risk premium in this case would be for example the price reduction for brand B needed to induce the consumer to risk obtaining benefits z. In utility lottery terms,

	Choice	*Probability*	*Benefit*
Lottery 1	Brand A	1	y
Lottery 2	Brand B	p_1	z
		$1 - p_1$	x

The term p_1 is the probability that brand B will deliver benefits z. Assuming the consumer is risk averse,[7] a price reduction can be seen as a risk premium necessary for leaving the consumer indifferent between obtaining benefits y for sure and entering the lottery that is represented by purchasing brand B.

While we motivate the utility-theoretic explanation in terms of a price reduction, nonfinancial sales promotions such as gifts, sweepstakes, and contests could also serve as risk premiums. They provide an extra benefit that compensates the consumer for assuming the risk of trying the product. Managers often think of sales promotions as a compensation to the consumer for incurring risk. Unfortunately, the role of sales promotions as a risk premium has not been addressed empirically.

PROSPECT THEORY AND MENTAL ACCOUNTING

Much of price perception theory is centered on the concept of a reference price. The general notion is that consumer judgments are made relative to some base case. This notion is the foundation of prospect theory (Kahneman and Tversky, 1979). Prospect theory proposes that consumer decisions are based on how they value the potential gains or losses from making that decision. The theory has three principal tenets which are encompassed in the consumer's "value function" (see Figure 2.2):

1. The value function $V(\cdot)$ is defined in terms of gains and losses from some natural reference point.
2. The value function is concave for gains and convex for losses.
3. The value function is steeper for losses than it is for gains. That is, losses of an amount x seem greater than gains of an amount x.

Thaler (1985) was concerned with the mental process by which consumers code multiple gains and losses. He applied prospect theory to derive some interesting principles that are relevant for promotions. First is his "segregate gains" principle. This says that it is better to have consumers code several gains separately (segregate) than think of the several gains as one net gain (integrate). Mathematically, this follows from the concavity of $V(X)$ for $X > 0$: that is, if $X > 0$ and $Y > 0$, $V(X) + V(Y) > V(X + Y)$. To apply the segregate gains principle, consider

---

[7] Technically, the utility function for product benefits must be concave for the consumer to be risk averse. If utility for the product is linear in benefits, as is implicitly assumed by a linear attitude model, then the consumer is risk neutral and no risk premium is necessary (see Hauser and Urban, 1979).

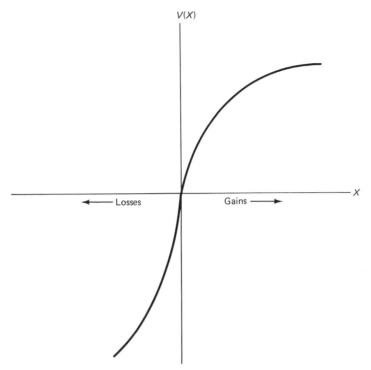

FIGURE 2.2 The Value Function for Prospect Theory

Source: Richard Thaler, "Mental Accounting and Consumer Choice," *Marketing Science,*
4, 3 (Summer, 1985), adapted from p. 203.

the retailer who is lowering the price of a $275 item to $250, and then helping to distribute a manufacturer rebate worth an additional $50. It would be better to communicate and make clear to the consumer he or she was getting two reductions, one of $25 and one of $50, from the regular $275 price than to say simply that an item regularly priced at $275 would be available at a $75 reduction. According to the segregate gains principle, $V(25) + V(50) > V(75)$.

A second idea developed by Thaler is the "silver lining" principle. This says that it is better to segregate a large loss and a small gain (and better to integrate when the gains and losses are roughly equal or the gain is bigger than the loss). Consider $X > 0$, $Y > 0$, and $Y >> X$. Because of the steepness of the value function for losses, $V(X) + V(-Y) > V(X - Y)$. X represents the silver lining to a rather large loss Y. Thaler applies the silver lining principle to the use of rebates for automobiles; the loss of, say, $10,000 for the price of the automobile is more effectively compensated by a rebate of $500 than is a statement of price at $9,500.

A third area explored by Thaler is the nature by which consumers evaluate a transaction. He proposes that the total value of a transaction to a consumer is the sum of acquisition utility and transaction utility. Acquisition utility is the result of comparing the price paid for an item to its "value." The value of an item is defined as the amount of money that would leave one indifferent between receiving that money and receiving the item. Transaction utility is the result of comparing the price paid to a reference price, where in Thaler's view, reference price is most closely determined by fairness. The immediate effect of a price cut is to increase both acquisition and transaction utility, since price paid is part of both types of utility. However, frequent promotions can erode the perceived value of an item (perhaps through a self-perception process, see the attribution theory discussion) and erode the reference price (see the section on adaptation-level theory). In the longer term, both acquisition and transaction utility will decrease, for a given price. There are two strategies for counteracting this problem. One is to enhance the perceived value of an item, through advertising or through the quality of the product. The other is to influence the reference price through a suggested reference price or other purchase context cues as discussed in the earlier section on assimilation-contrast theory. From a theoretical standpoint, the concepts of acquisition and transaction utility suggest that choice models should include a price term (representing acquisition utility) and a reference price term (representing transaction utility). This is the path followed by Winer (1986).

The foregoing discussion demonstrates the richness of integration, segregation, acquisition utility, and transaction utility concepts. Unfortunately, the application of both prospect theory and Thaler's principles to sales promotion has not been empirically investigated. One interesting issue is how the principles could be applied to the situation when the consumer incurs a loss in utility by switching brands, while gaining in the form of a price decrease. A final issue is to determine the circumstances under which a consumer will integrate or segregate, as a function of the type of promotion(s) offered and the purchase situation.

ATTITUDE MODELS

Theory

Attitude models specify the linkage between consumer beliefs and behavior. These models have enjoyed ample attention in the marketing literature (e.g., see Wilkie and Pessemier, 1973; Ryan and Bonfield, 1975; Shocker and Srinivasan, 1979; as well as Fishbein and Ajzen, 1975, for an in-depth treatment). The model has been applied most often as the basis for product or advertising decisions, because these actions have a direct impact on beliefs. Application of attitude models to the promotions context is still in its infancy.

The theory has gone through many gestations over its many applications, but the general model can be represented in Figure 2.3 (based most closely on Fishbein and Ajzen, 1975, e.g., Ch. 1).

Figure 2.3 shows that attitude models depict the consumer's decision to perform a specific behavior as the logical consequence of a progression of sub-

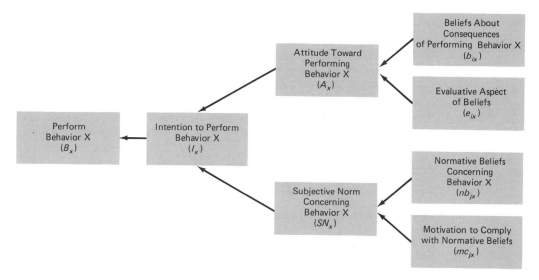

FIGURE 2.3 The Fishbein-Ajzen Attitude Model

Source: Martin Fishbein and Icek Ajzen, *Belief, Attitude, Intention, and Behavior: An Introduction to Theory and Research,* © 1975, Addison-Wesley Publishing Co., Inc., Reading, Massachusetts, adapted with permission from pp. 16, 301–302.

jective beliefs, attitudes, and intentions with regard to that behavior. In fact, a more modern label for attitude models is the "theory of reasoned action" (see, e.g., Shimp and Kavas, 1984). The model makes an important distinction between personally held beliefs and attitudes and the beliefs and attitudes of others with regard to the specific behavior. This aspect is very relevant for sales promotion, since social pressures and consequences of buying on deal might be expected to have an important impact on consumers' decisions to take advantage of promotion.

To describe the theory more completely, we need to define the terms in Figure 2.3 more specifically. Included in each definition that follows is an example based on a consumer's decision to use a rebate for a kitchen appliance.

B_x = performing behavior X (using the rebate)

I_x = the consumer's intention to perform behavior X (intention to use the rebate)

A_x = the consumer's overall attitude toward performing behavior X (the consumer's overall feeling of whether using the rebate would be worthwhile); (also labeled A_{act} in the literature)

SN_x = subjective norm—the consumer's belief of whether relevant others taken as a group would look favorably upon the consumer performing the behavior. (the consumer's belief that friends, spouses, children, etc., would look favorably toward the consumer using the rebate)

b_{ix} = the consumer's belief that performing behavior X will have certain consequences, $i = 1, \ldots, I$, labeling these consequences (e.g., the belief that the process of using the rebate—filling out the rebate form, mailing in the rebate, etc.—will take a lot of time)

e_{ix} = the consumer's evaluative feelings about consequence i; that is, is the consequence a good or a bad one (e.g., how much the consumer cares if the process of using the rebate takes a lot of time)

nb_{jx} = normative belief—the consumer's beliefs that reference group or individual j thinks the consumer should perform behavior X, $j = 1, \ldots, J$ labels these individuals (e.g., the consumer's belief that his or her spouse thinks he or she should use the rebate)

mc_{jx} = motivation to comply, or the importance the consumer places on normative belief j (e.g., the extent to which the consumer cares whether his or her spouse thinks he or she should use the rebate)

The following two terms then complete the definitions necessary to specify the model:

w_1 = importance the consumer places on his or her own attitude in determining intention to perform the behavior (the extent to which the consumer's own attitude toward using the rebate will influence his or her intentions to use it)

w_2 = importance the consumer places on social influences in determining his or her intention to perform the behavior (the extent to which the consumer's beliefs regarding the views of others influences the consumer's intention to use the rebate)

The model is then as follows:

$$A_x = \sum_i e_{ix} b_{ix} \tag{2.6}$$

$$SN_x = \sum_j mc_{jx} nb_{jx} \tag{2.7}$$

$$I_x = w_1 A_x + w_2 SN_x \tag{2.8}$$

$$B_x \sim I_x \tag{2.9}$$

Equation (2.6) says that overall attitude toward performing a behavior is a weighted sum of the consumer's beliefs about the consequences of performing that behavior, the weights being the valences or evaluative aspects of these consequences. Equation (2.7) says that the consumer's overall belief of whether relevant others would look favorably upon his or her performing the behavior can be expressed as a weighted sum of beliefs regarding specific relevant others' feelings toward the consumer performing the behavior, the weights being the importances of these feelings in the eyes of the consumer. Equation (2.8) says that the consumer's intention to perform the behavior is a weighted sum of the consumer's own attitude toward the behavior and consumer's overall belief regarding how others would look upon he or she performing the behavior, the weights reflecting the relative impact of personal feelings versus external pressures.

As Equation (2.9) indicates, the actual act of performing the behavior is seen as some not-well-defined function of intentions. Attitude models typically do not explicitly model the translation between intentions and behavior, although several researchers have devoted attention to this issue (e.g., Morrison, 1979, and Kalwani and Silk, 1982, from a management science viewpoint, and Fishbein and Azjen, 1975, pp. 368–381, Warshaw, 1980, Bagozzi, 1982, and Shimp and Kavas, 1984, from a behavioral perspective).

Application 1: Why a Price Reduction Results in Increased Sales

When the behavior in question is purchasing a brand, one of the relevant belief items (b_{ix}) is whether the brand is expensive. Depending on how price conscious the consumer is (this would be reflected in large e_{ix}'s), these beliefs can exert a strong influence on whether the brand is purchased. A price reduction alters these beliefs in a favorable direction, and thus purchase behavior is more likely to result.

Two issues are worth noting. First, the process by which an objectively determined stimulus changes beliefs is not explicitly incorporated in the typical attitude model (see Holbrook, 1981, or Neslin, 1981, 1983, for illustrations of how this influence process can formally be included in the model. See the earlier section on theories of price perception for a discussion of price perception formation). Second, the usual composition rule by which beliefs influence attitude is referred to as "additive compensatory." That is, a low price as effected by a promotion can compensate for low perceived quality, especially if quality is not quite as important as price (it has lower e_{ix}). There are a number of other possible composition rules. For example, there may be a level of perceived quality for which no price or economic incentive could compensate. As another example, the relationship between beliefs and attitude may be compensatory, but nonlinear (see Einhorn, 1970, for a discussion of alternative composition rules).

This example brings out the rationality of consumer decision making assumed by attitude models. In fact, though arising from a very different theoretical base, attitude models are often indistinguishable from economic utility models (Lancaster, 1971; Ratchford, 1979). One distinctive characteristic of attitude models, however, is the explicit attention to views of relevant others. This is a factor generally unrelated to the intrinsic utility of the product. A second philosophical difference between attitude models and economic utility models is that in the former, price is considered to be another attribute, no different from "quality," "reliability," or "effectiveness," whereas with economic models, price is given an explicit role in a budget constraint and seen as a critical yardstick for determining how much of certain attributes will be purchased by the consumer. In fact, some researchers in the economic tradition scale attributes relative to price, so that attributes are thought of as "quality per dollar" and so on (see Hauser and Shugan, 1983). While the differences between attitude models and economic models can have important implications for how researchers tackle a consumer choice problem, many of the philosophical differences can be ironed out. For example, attitude models can implicitly include a budget constraint by having a large importance (e_{ix}) attached to price. Similarly, economic models can include the normative beliefs regarding relevant others by thinking of this factor as a product attribute.

Application 2: Coupon Usage

Shimp and Kavas (1984) applied the attitude model framework to understanding the consumer's decision to use coupons. They measured all the constructs of the attitude model as defined earlier. The following are the belief items (b_{ix}) that were measured, and their correlation with the consumer's overall attitude toward using coupons[8] (abstracted from Shimp and Kavas, 1984, p. 802).

Belief Item (b_{ix})	Correlation With Overall Attitude Toward Using Coupons (A_x)
Inconveniences	
Time/effort clipping coupons	−.39
Time/effort redeeming coupons	−.28
Encumberances	
Subscribing to extra media	−.10
Purchasing nonpreferred brands	−.11
Shopping at nonfavorite stores	.01
Rewards	
Saving on grocery bills	.56
Feeling of being a thrifty and smart shopper	.58

It is dangerous to interpret relative effects based on pairwise correlations; however, it is striking that beliefs in the rewards of couponing correlate highly with attitude, inconveniences in actually using coupons correlate less so, and more broadly defined inconveniences ("encumbrances") correlate weakly. Figure 2.4 presents standardized path coefficient estimates relating the components of the attitude model (from Shimp and Kavas, 1984, p. 801). These correspond to Equations (2.6) through (2.9).

Both the social influence and subjective attitude components of coupon usage appear to be very important. The impact of social influence is especially interesting. It implies that coupon usage will increase as it becomes more socially acceptable. The linkage between the sum of subjective beliefs (b_{ix}) times evaluative aspects (e_{ix}) and attitude is statistically significant, although noticeably smaller than would be expected given the correlations noted earlier. This could be the result of measurement error in the evaluative components e_{ix}. Finally,

---

[8] Overall attitude was measured as the sum of semantic differential scales where the anchors were foolish/wise, good/bad, valuable/worthless, waste of time/wise use of time, and useful/useless.

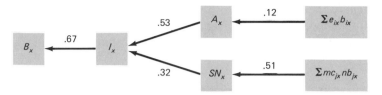

Standardized coefficients (all were statistically significant at the .01 level)

FIGURE 2.4 Results of Applying the Fishbein-Ajzen Model to Coupon
Usage

Source: Terence A. Shimp and Alican Kavas, "The Theory of Reasoned Action Applied
to Coupon Usage," *Journal of Consumer Research*, Vol. 11 (December 1984), adapted
from pp. 797, 801 (Model 1).

there is a clear link between consumer's intentions to use coupons and their self-
reported behavior in actually doing so.[9]

Summary

Attitude models provide a potentially valuable basis for understanding the various
factors that influence the consumer's decision to use promotions. The model contrasts markedly with behavioral learning theory, which ignores all internal "rational" processes. The resolution of this difference is probably that consumer
behavior contains elements of both highly rational belief-attitude-intention structures and mindless behavioral conditioning. Attitude models offer much potential
for improving managerial decisions. For example, if as suggested by the Shimp
and Kavas correlations, increasing the rewards in using coupons has higher
valence than decreasing the inconvenience, managers should use higher face values rather than rely on more convenient (and hence more expensive) distribution
vehicles. Attitude models provide the structure by which this type of guidance
can be obtained.

The results of the Shimp and Kavas research are encouraging and represent
a rigorous effort to apply attitude models to the context of sales promotion. There
are several avenues for future research in this area. One issue is to investigate
different models for relating the various components of the attitude model. For
example, Shimp and Kavas explored "cross-over" effects between overall attitude and subjective norm. Another important topic for research would be to estimate the feedback from behavior to beliefs. This could provide evidence of
attribution effects. As presently structured, this model would not be identified
econometrically (all the variables in Figure 2.5 would be endogenous). Adding
some objectively defined exogenous variables, such as face value, could help to

---

[9] Note that one should be careful in ascribing causality to these results. It is possible, for
example, that in the study, consumers "backward" reasoned their attitudes after first knowing their
intentions. This is in general a difficult problem in studying attitude models.

identify the model. A final potential avenue for research would be to apply an attitude model toward the behavior of using a specific coupon to buy a particular brand. This would involve considering two behaviors: buying the brand and using the coupon.

THE CONSUMER DECISION PROCESS

A number of comprehensive consumer behavior models have been developed that attempt to integrate all aspects of how and why consumers arrive at a particular decision. These include the Howard-Sheth model (1969), the Nicosia model (1966), and the Engel-Kollat-Blackwell (EKB) model (1982). Perhaps because of the comprehensiveness of these models, they have not been fully tested (although see Farley and Ring, 1970), and no single model is fully accepted among academicians. However, they do provide an important conceptual integration of many aspects of consumer decision making and lend important insight to the effectiveness of promotions (see Sternthal and Craig, 1982, p. 46).

The discussion in this section will be based on the EKB model. The core of the EKB model is that the consumer must recognize the need to purchase the product category (this is called "problem recognition"), then goes through a process to arrive at a choice, and after the choice, uses and evaluates the particular product that was purchased. Along this path, the consumer may draw upon memory to activate problem recognition and aid in the choice decision. Memory may contain a detailed structure of beliefs, attitudes, and intentions with regard to purchasing various brands. Information from the marketing environment filters into memory through a process of exposure, attention, comprehension, and retention.

An important feature of the EKB model is that it consists of high-involvement and low-involvement versions. The concept of involvement is a significant theme underlying much research in the consumer behavior area (Kassarjian, 1978). There are many dimensions to the concept, and measuring involvement or identifying low- versus high-involvement situations is a challenging task (Cohen, 1983; Zaichkowsky, 1985). However, there are several distinctions that can be made between low- and high-involvement decision making (we draw from Assael, 1987, p. 96, in the following discussion). High-involvement consumers are active information seekers and processors, whereas low-involvement consumers rarely seek information, and when information is provided, they process it "passively." High-involvement consumers attempt to maximize satisfaction with their purchases, while low-involvement consumers seek an "acceptable" level of satisfaction. Products are closely tied to the high-involvement consumer's identity and belief system, whereas no such link exists for the low-involvement consumer. High-involvement consumers evaluate brands in detail before purchasing and then assess their satisfaction with the product after it is used. Low-involvement consumers buy first and then may or may not evaluate the product after use. If post-usage evaluation is undertaken, it is undoubtedly less rigorous and demanding for the low-involvement consumer.

Promotions can influence both high- and low-involvement decision making. Some examples are as follows:

PROBLEM RECOGNITION. A promotion such as a special display can trigger problem recognition. The display reminds the consumer that he or she wants the promoted product or perhaps stimulates latent demand for the product category. This may explain why displays for items such as soft drinks or cookies can be particularly effective. Problem recognition can be triggered in both high- and low-involvement situations; however, the sales effect for low-involvement will be much more immediate. In the high-involvement case, problem recognition triggered by an attractive rebate for a durable good would more likely result in search for information rather than an immediate purchase.

INTENTION-CHOICE TRANSLATION. A promotion such as an end-of-aisle display can make it more convenient for a consumer to follow through on intentions formed as a result of high involvement. Alternatively, a promotion can act as an unanticipated circumstance and cause a different brand to be purchased than intended ("I intended to buy Brand X but Brand Y was on sale so I bought Brand Y").

PROBLEM RECOGNITION–CHOICE TRANSLATION. The low-involvement consumer may go to the store with the knowledge that he or she needs to purchase from the product category, but an in-store promotion will then determine which of several acceptable brands is bought. Deshpande et al. (1982) conjecture that in an effort to minimize the amount of cognitive effort, low-involvement consumers will attempt to use simple choice rules in making purchase decisions. The prevalence of promotions makes the adoption of rules such as "buy cheapest brand" or "buy coupon-advertised brand" more likely. For example, the low-involvement consumer might refer to his or her collection of coupons to determine which brand will be purchased. This simple function of a promotion, to give a reason for the uninvolved consumer to choose one of several equivalent brands, is particularly relevant in today's competitive environment. Because of the power of this phenomenon, one might conjecture that in-store promotions and various price breaks are more effective for low-involvement than high-involvement consumers (Assael, 1987, pp. 92–93).

EFFECTS ON BRAND LOYALTY. Consistent repurchasing of the same brand can occur for both low- and high-involvement consumers. In the low-involvement case, this "brand loyalty" can develop because the consumer has found a brand that works and does not want to expend the effort to find anything better. As just discussed, a promotion can disrupt this routinized repurchase behavior, and the consumer can resort to the simple choice heuristic of buying whatever brand is on promotion. The result will be less frequent repurchasing of the same brand.

The high-involvement consumer can arrive at the same end although by a different process. In the high-involvement case, brand loyalty is the result of a well-thought-out evaluation of brands. However, by offering an economic incentive, a promotion can interrupt the consumer's intention to repurchase a brand. Since the consumer is highly involved, he or she carefully evaluates the outcome of this decision. In a market where real differences among brands are nonexistent, the consumer begins to learn that several brands are the same, and the decision process becomes one of low-involvement choice of whatever brand is on promotion.

There are counter-arguments to both these scenarios. In the low-involvement case, the consumer may not wish to take the time searching for price deals, and may find that repurchasing the same brand is easier than finding a brand on discount. The high-involvement consumer may use promotions to try new brands, but by evaluating those brands in detail, will discover the fine differences that do exist between brands, and stick with the brand most compatible with his or her tastes.

These examples point out the benefits of considering a comprehensive model of consumer decision making. It is not necessary to validate the entire EKB model. The model serves to generate hypotheses as listed, which need to be tested empirically.

SUMMARY

Table 2.7 highlights the areas to which each of the theories reviewed in this chapter can be applied (see Chapter 5). The table indicates there is no paucity of theories, and all types of promotions and all types of sales effects can be covered by these theories. Many of the theories can yield different predictions depending upon various contingencies. For example, operant conditioning would predict that promotions can enhance brand loyalty, *if* the appropriate reinforcement schedule is applied. Similarly, self-perception theory may or may not predict a decrease in brand attitude, depending on whether the consumer is encouraged to invoke the discounting principle. In applying various theories to sales promotion, researchers must therefore be careful to consider all possible contingencies.

Perhaps two areas where more consumer theory is needed are the topics of purchase acceleration and primary demand. Purchase acceleration, the tendency of promotions to increase purchase quantity and move purchase timing forward, is most commonly explained by economic models focusing on household inventory and resource variables. The consumer decision-making framework explains purchase acceleration as resulting from the timely stimulation of problem recognition. However, there may be a deeper psychological explanation of why consumers are willing to accelerate their purchases. Similarly, the underlying reasons why sales promotion can increase total product category sales need to be elaborated. For example, through what mechanism can promotions influence the consumption rate of a product?

In terms of specific promotions, the effects of rebates need to be explained

TABLE 2.7 Most Immediate Areas of Applicability for Consumer Behavior Theories

Theory	Type of Promotion	Type of Sales Effect
Classical conditioning	Premiums, feature advertising, displays	Brand switching, repeat purchases
Operant conditioning	Price cuts, coupons, premiums, rebates	Repeat purchases, purchase acceleration timing
Hullian model	All promotions	Brand switching, repeat purchases
Object perception	Premiums, price cuts, coupons, rebates	Brand switching
Self-perception	Premiums, price cuts, coupons, rebates	Repeat purchasing
Perceived risk	Samples, premiums, price cuts, coupons, rebates	Brand switching
Price perception	Price cuts, coupons	Brand switching, repeat purchasing
Attitude models	Price cuts, coupons	Brand switching
Consumer decision-making process	All promotions	Brand switching, repeat switching, purchase acceleration, primary demand
Prospect theory and mental accounting	Price cuts, premiums	Brand switching

more fully. Operant conditioning would view rebates as less effective than coupons, because the reward from the rebate is delayed. A theory for understanding the interplay between information search, perceived product quality, and a rebate would be useful. It would be important to understand which part of the decision process is influenced by a rebate.

While there are some opportunities for theory development, the more immediate research need is in the area of theory testing. The areas of behavioral theory, attribution, attitude models, and price perception especially need a more complete empirical base. The research reviewed in this chapter indicates that both laboratory and field study experiments can successfully contribute to this base.

Table 2.7 points out clearly that more than one theory can typically be applied in a given situation. When several theories suggest the same hypothesis, this yields problems of internal validity in interpreting experiments. Managerially at least, we can be content that a number of theories all point to the same conclusion. From a research perspective, however, this presents a particular challenge, for the researcher is interested in establishing a particular theory so that

TABLE 2.8 Application of Consumer Behavior Theories to Commonly Made Statements About Promotion

Statement	Example of One Appropriate Theory
1. "Coupons are a way for us to reward our loyal users."	Operant conditioning
2. "Promotions destroy the brand franchise."	Self-perception theory
3. "We're afraid to use promotions because they cheapen the brand image."	Object-perception theory
4. "All we're accomplishing with our promotional strategy is training consumers to use coupons."	Operant conditioning
5. "The consumer has a range of acceptable brands and really doesn't care which among these he or she buys. We just use promotions to get our brand to be top of mind."	Consumer decision-making process (especially low involvement)
6. "Only our current users take advantage of our promotions."	Hullian
7. "We use coupons and price-off promotions to appeal to the price-sensitive segments."	Attitude models
8. "Promotions merely get consumers to buy brands earlier that they eventually would have bought anyway."	Consumer decision-making process (low and high involvement)
9. "Promotions should tie in with brand attributes."	Self-perception theory, operant conditioning
10. "Promotions should offer the consumer something besides reduced price."	Self-perception theory, operant conditioning
11. "Promotions provide consumers with a safe way to try a new brand."	Perceived risk
12. "We've taught consumers that if they time their purchases right and buy large quantities, they can always buy at a reduced price."	Operant conditioning
13. "We don't like to engage in price promotions because then consumers won't get used to buying at the regular price."	Adaptation-level theory
14. "We find that even a small token gift accompanying the purchase of our expensive product induces the consumer to buy."	Prospect theory and mental accounting (silver lining principle)

it can be used to make predictions in new situations. Researchers must then design their studies so that the theory they are investigating implies a unique prediction in the specific situation and that this prediction would not be implied by other theories. In addition, they should attempt to take "process" measures that verify that the particular mechanism implied by the theory was at work. This is a common dilemma in behavioral research. However, it seems particularly salient in the case of sales promotion.

As an additional summary, Table 2.8 juxtaposes common statements made about promotions with at least one appropriate consumer behavior theory. The table demonstrates the applicability of these theories to more strategic aspects of sales promotion and thus underscores the need for definitive empirical testing of these theories.

Most of the examples in Table 2.8 are self-explanatory. However, a few of the examples warrant some comment.

EXAMPLE 5.   The notion of there being many acceptable brands, with promotions serving to cast the final vote on which is chosen, could be consistent with several theories. In the language of attitude models or high-involvement decision making, consumers may have well-established cognitions regarding the brands, but the brands are basically the same physical items. Therefore, purchase intent strength is equal for all the brands, and promotions elevate these equal intentions to actual choice. However, the low-involvement model is probably most relevant to this situation. Under this interpretation, the consumer does not want to make a great deal of effort in making a brand choice. Low-involvement consumers like to move directly from problem recognition to brand choice. Under these circumstances, the brand that is most top of mind for the consumer will be chosen, and continual promotion of the brand might help ensure a high level of brand awareness.

EXAMPLE 6.   The statement here is meant in a negative way: Only current users purchase on promotion, and hence few promotion sales are incremental. The Hullian model applies best here because of its explicit reference to the role of reinforced habit. Loyal consumers are more likely to have found their promotional purchases of the brand in question reinforced by satisfactory product experience at a bargain price.

EXAMPLE 7.   The possibility of a price-sensitive segment follows directly from attitude models. Price-sensitive consumers care more about price and value and thus will have higher attribute importance weights for these factors. A given price break will thus have more significant impact in changing attitudes and intentions among these consumers.

EXAMPLE 8.   This statement is similar to that in example 12, except that statement 8 refers to just one purchase, whereas example 12 makes a conjecture about consumer learning. As far as the immediate purchase is concerned, purchase timing can be affected through the initiation of problem recognition or of information search.

EXAMPLES 9 AND 10.   These statements go together and are concerned with preventing the promotion reward from becoming the sole reason for purchase. In self-perception terms, this mitigates the potentially damaging interpretation of promotions as an *external* motivator. In operant terms, this prevents the promotion from being the primary reinforcer. If the promotion is a secondary reinforcer, it is more likely that the desired behavior (brand choice) will persist even after the promotion is withdrawn.

3

The Deal-Prone Consumer

INTRODUCTION

Managers and researchers alike have spent considerable effort trying to identify and understand the "deal-prone" consumer. Two streams of research bear most directly on this issue. The first attempts to characterize the deal-prone consumer in terms of demographic, psychographic, behavioral, and personality traits. The second stream integrates the concept of deal proneness into market segmentation schemes based on consumer choice strategies. These two streams have developed in an intermingling way, but we will separate them, examining the "characterization" stream first and then the "segmentation" stream.

CHARACTERIZING THE "DEAL-PRONE" CONSUMER

Motivation

The motivation to characterize the deal-prone consumer stems from both managerial and theoretical considerations. On the managerial side, an understanding of which types of consumers are deal prone would lead to better targeting of promotions. Managers designing new promotions could anticipate what types of consumers would respond in which ways to various promotion alternatives. Understanding the deal-prone consumer would be especially beneficial for managers using direct-mail promotions such as coupons, samples, and other offers. The growing ability of direct-mail marketers to pinpoint consumers satisfying various demographic, psychographic, and behavioral criteria (e.g., see Alsop, 1985; Stern, 1985) offers an attractive opportunity to apply the results of deal proneness studies.

On the theoretical side, the ability to identify the deal-prone consumer provides a better understanding of the conceptual underpinnings of why promotions work. For example, if personality traits such as the desire to control one's environment correlate well with coupon proneness, this would provide support for the "smart shopper" phenomenon (see Chapter 10, "The Redemption Decision"). In turn, managers would understand that they should design promotions that appeal to consumers' needs to believe they are smart shoppers. As another example, if deal-prone consumers turn out to be more price sensitive, this would support the economic theory of price discrimination as it applies to promotions (see Chapter 4).

The potential payoff in being able to characterize the deal-prone consumer is therefore very high. In the next section, we elaborate some of the conceptual issues in studying deal proneness and then summarize what is currently known about the deal-prone consumer.

Conceptual Issues

Defining Deal Proneness.   The first issue in studying deal proneness is to define it. Most authors have not explicitly defined deal proneness, but instead move quickly to their operationalization of the concept. Drawing from this previous work, however, and considering the managerial viewpoint of deal proneness, we propose the following definition:

> Deal proneness is the degree to which the consumer is influenced by sales promotion, in terms of behaviors such as purchase timing, brand choice, purchase quantity, category consumption, store choice, or search behavior.

The key word in this definition is "influenced." It is easy to try to define deal proneness as the degree to which the consumer simply uses sales promotions, without worrying about whether the promotions are influencing behavior. This definition would lack managerial relevance, however, and also lead to some illogical conclusions. For example, under this definition, the consumer who is highly loyal to a brand that happens to promote 80 percent of the time would by definition be more deal prone than would the consumer who searches for coupons for a more expensive, preferred brand, finding them 40 percent of the time.

Another important aspect of our definition is that the influence of sales promotion can be exerted in several ways. The consumer can be influenced to change purchase timing or purchase quantity (we call this "purchase acceleration," see Chapter 5), switch brands, try a new brand, increase consumption of the product category, switch stores, or search for promotions. However, not all consumers need be influenced in the same ways. For example, some consumers might be influenced to switch brands but not change purchase timing, while others might be influenced to change timing but not brands. Still others might be influenced in both ways. Deal proneness is therefore a multidimensional consumer trait.

We also note that consumers might be deal prone with respect to one promotion but not another. For example, the smart shopper might search for coupons but not pay attention to in-store displays. Most researchers simplify this situation by investigating the influence of one type of promotion, for example, couponing, on one type of behavior, for example, new product trial (Teel et al., 1980). Henderson (1984) and Schneider and Currim (1989) are exceptions, studying and explicitly differentiating among several types of promotions.

Figure 3.1 summarizes the foregoing discussion. The top half of the table shows that deal proneness is concerned with the degree to which promotions influence a complex and interrelated set of behaviors. The problem of characterizing the deal-prone consumer is to relate demographic, psychographic, behavioral, and personality variables to these influences.

Measures of Deal Proneness   Given our definition of deal proneness, one would measure the construct by estimating the influence that one or several promotions have on one or several types of behaviors. Because of the multidimensional nature of this task, and because of the need to detect influence, it is not easy to accomplish this measurement. Studies of deal proneness have used one of four types of measures: percentage-of-purchases, demand elasticities, self-report, and choice model–derived measures. These measures tend to tap varying types of influence.

In their simplest form, percentage of purchases measures involve calculating the percentage of category purchases made on promotion. They may also involve absolute quantities such as the number of coupons used or the quantity purchased on deal. However, in this simple form, these measures do not explicitly measure any aspect of influence—one consumer might appear to be more deal prone than another because the first happens to prefer a brand that promotes often. We see

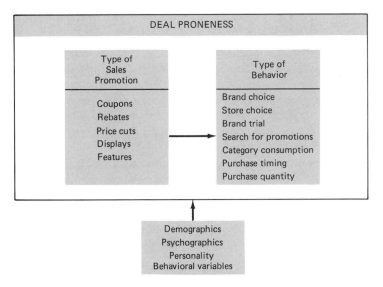

FIGURE 3.1   Characterizing the Deal-Prone Consumer

that at a minimum, there is a need to control for both the availability of promotions and the consumer's brand preference.

Webster (1965) conducted one of the first deal proneness studies, using a relatively sophisticated formula for calculating deal proneness. The formula adjusted for how often each of the brands the consumer bought was on promotion and the share of requirements each brand satisfied for the consumer. It therefore attempted to take into account the availability of promotions as well as consumer preferences. The formula was defined as follows (see Webster, 1965, p. 187):

Let

c_{ij} = the percentage of household i's purchases of brand j made on promotion

e_j = the percentage of all sales for brand j made on promotion

r_{ij} = the percentage of all category purchases for household i made of brand j

L_i = the deal proneness measure for household i

$$L_i = \sum_j (c_{ij} - e_j) * r_{ij} \tag{3.1}$$

This measure will be large if a consumer's purchases of a brand are more likely to be on promotion than the average consumer's purchases of that brand, and if that brand is purchased often by the consumer. The measure therefore is attempting to detect the degree to which the consumer is seeking out promotions for brands that he or she prefers. Thus, consider the following example:

Brand X has 60 percent of sales on deal.
Brand Y has 20 percent of sales on deal.
Consumer A buys brand X 70 percent of the time, 60 percent of the time on deal, and Y 30 percent of the time, 20 percent of the time on deal.
Consumer B buys brand X 20 percent of the time, 60 percent of the time on deal, and Y 80 percent of the time, 30 percent of the time on deal.

Consumer A would have a deal proneness measure of $(.60 - .60) * .70 + (.20 - .20) * .30 = 0$, and consumer B would have a deal proneness measure of $(.60 - .60) * .20 + (.30 - .20) * .80 = .08$. Consumer B would be considered more deal prone than consumer A, although consumer B has 36 percent of his or her total purchases on deal, whereas consumer A has 48 percent. Consumer B seems to be seeking out promotions for brand Y, which appears to be that consumer's preferred brand.

Webster's measure appears to provide a viable index of the degree to which a consumer is influenced to search for promotions for his or her preferred brand. Note, however, that it is not a measure of switching or acceleration behavior. For example, we cannot tell from this measure whether consumer B was induced by promotions to switch between brands X and Y because the index does not take into account the sequence of purchases nor consider whether promotions were available for both brands at particular purchase occasions. There is also some ambiguity with respect to r_{ij}, the measure of preference. This measure, being the percentage of times that the consumer buys a particular brand, may not reflect preference. The consumer may use the decision rule of purchasing whatever brand can be found on promotion, and so the consumer appears to prefer the brand for which he or she has been able to find the most promotions. Related to this, a consumer may decide to become a "loyal" purchaser of a particular brand because in fact that brand is heavily promoted. Even though that consumer may then purchase that brand on promotion no more than the average, the consumer is in at least one sense highly deal prone.

Although Webster's measure of deal proneness is not perfect, it does attempt to adjust for availability and preference in a reasonable way. One must be careful in interpreting the results of studies that utilize a percentage-of-purchases measure but do not attempt to make these adjustments.

Promotional elasticity measures of deal proneness are typically calculated using an econometric model. McCann (1974) and Massy and Frank (1965) estimated econometric models in which deal availability was an independent variable and sales or market share served as the dependent variable. The models were estimated within various segments to determine whether certain segments had higher deal elasticities than others. It is difficult to determine which aspect(s) of behavior influence was being measured by these studies. Sales could be affected by either brand switching or increased category consumption, and neither the McCann nor the Massy and Frank model attempt to distinguish between the two. However, the elasticity measure of deal proneness does appear to represent some type of influence on brand sales, whereas Webster's measure seems more focused on the issue of consumer search for promotions.

Self-report measures of deal proneness are based on consumers' responses to survey questions regarding how they are influenced by their use of promotions.[1] These measures allow the researcher to define explicitly the type of deal proneness that is being measured, because the type of behavior and type of promotion under consideration can be easily stated. Teel et al. (1980) simply asked consumers to report the frequency with which the decision to purchase a new brand was influenced by a coupon. Neslin and Clarke (1987) used self-report data to measure the extent to which coupons induced consumers to switch brands. Jolson et al. (1987) used self-reported measures of the extent to which rebates "trigger" purchases. The obvious problem with self-report measures is that the consumer may not be able to report accurately in what way, if any, a particular promotion has influenced him or her. However, these measures have clear face validity.

Choice model–derived measures have been used by Fader and McAlister (1985) to quantify deal proneness (see Chapter 8 for a discussion of choice models). They estimate an individual-level choice coefficient (gamma), which they interpret as the percentage-of-purchase occasions in which a consumer restricts choice to

---

[1] Note that percentage-of-purchase measures can be calculated based on consumer diary data, where the consumer *self-reports* whether each purchase was made on promotion. We still consider this a percentage of purchase measure rather than a self-report measure. The self-report measures are characterized by consumers reporting the *influence* that promotions have on their behavior, not merely whether they use promotions.

only promoted brands. The measure is therefore an index of a type of brand switching.

More recently, Schneider and Currim (1989) quantify consumer purchase strategies and derive measures of different types of deal proneness from these models. These measures represent the degree to which different promotions are associated with particular strategies used by the consumer.[2] Both the Fader and McAlister and Schneider and Currim studies estimate household-level statistical models and infer individual deal proneness measures from these models. They provide a statistically revealed counterpoint to self-report measures.

In summary, deal proneness has been measured in four ways: percentage of purchases on deal, promotion elasticities, self-report, and choice model–derived measures. All four can provide useful measures of deal proneness, but each has its own problems: Percentage-of-purchases measures must be adjusted for promotion availability and brand preference; econometric models are subject to misspecification error; self-reports can be of questionable validity; and choice models at the individual level utilize only a few observations. In addition, the various methods can measure different types of deal proneness. Percentage-of-purchases measures probably detect search behavior, elasticity measures detect some kind of sales influence, self-reports can theoretically measure any kind of behavior influence, and choice model–derived measures quantify influence of the particular choice being modeled, which could be brand, store, quantity, timing, or some combination of these.

What Is a Deal?   As suggested by our definition of deal proneness, it is important to specify the type of promotion under investigation. In the early days of deal proneness research, this was not explicitly done. Since diary panel data were employed, a deal was defined as when the consumer reported in his or her diary that the purchase had been made "on deal." In practice, this often meant a special price. Currently, when promotions are increasing in diversity, the need to distinguish among types of deals is more immediate. Perhaps because of their popularity, coupons have often been singled out for study. However, a consumer may be coupon prone because he or she is a smart shopper, or display prone because he or she is an impulse buyer, or premium prone because he or she has kids, or price cut prone because he or she is price sensitive. Henderson (1984) and Schneider and Currim (1988) are noteworthy in that they consider various types of promotions in the same study. Future deal proneness research will clearly have to follow these examples.

Theory.   Deal proneness studies have often not proceeded from a theoretical base. They can be viewed more as the empirical building blocks of theory then as theory

---

[2] Schneider and Currim's deal proneness measures are based on the "concept learning system" algorithm first used by Currim, Meyer, and Le (1988). Their deal proneness measure is not a coefficient from an equation, but is inferred from the ability of a promotion variable to discriminate between chosen and not chosen purchase alternatives.

testing. One exception to this is the work of Blattberg et al. (1978). These authors visualize the household as an inventory management unit. The household seeks to satisfy its own demand for products at a minimum total cost. Included as costs are transaction costs of time required to purchase as well as transportation, inventory costs reflected in tying up the household's capital as well as its storage space, stockout costs reflecting the disutility of not having a product on hand if it is needed, and purchase cost as reflected by price. These costs are included in a probabilistic dynamic programming model (demand as well as prices are assumed to be probabilistic). Although the model was not explicitly operationalized, it was used to generate hypotheses about the correlates of deal proneness. These hypotheses were as follows:

   a. Homeowners should be more deal prone. They face lower storage costs and hence can store as inventory product that they do not immediately need.
   b. Car owners should be more deal prone. They face lower transaction costs in the form of transportation. They can seek out the best deals more cheaply.
   c. Households with no children under the age of 6 should be more deal prone. Adults who are parents of children over 6, or have no children, face fewer demands upon their time. Hence, the transaction costs of time are lower for such households.
   d. Households without working wives should be more deal-prone. The traditional housewife has lower transaction costs of time. She can afford to spend the time looking for deals.

   Although not explicitly hypothesized, Blattberg et al. conjectured that family income should be negatively related to deal proneness, because higher-income families generally have higher opportunity costs of time. However, since income is often confounded with home and car ownership, Blattberg et al. recognized the need to control for these variables when examining the relationship between income and deal proneness. The results of their study are as follows: Hypotheses a, b, and d were clearly supported, while hypothesis c was not. The conjecture concerning income was only partially supported. Eliminating the effects of home and car ownership did erase an otherwise positive correlation between income and deal proneness, but the resultant relationship was not consistently negative.

   Other than the Blattberg et al. work, there are other studies that have suggested or tested theories of deal proneness. Henderson (1984) proposes a learning hypothesis, that is, that consumers learn to become more deal prone and to take advantage of a greater variety of deals. This is consistent with shaping procedures in operant conditioning. However, Henderson does not explicitly test this theory. Narasimhan (1984b) bases many of his hypotheses on the Blattberg et al. model and on his own model of price discrimination in couponing (Narasimhan, 1984a). Bawa and Shoemaker (1987a) derive a model of coupon usage based on handling and brand substitution costs balanced against financial benefits. They use this model to investigate the consistency of coupon usage across product classes. Schneider and Currim (1989) propose a distinction between "active" and "passive" deal proneness, the former referring to promotions such as coupons that require effort or search, the latter referring to promotions such as displays that require no special effort. Schneider and Currim test hypotheses based on these concepts.

The potential to test theories of consumer behavior is ample and should be the basis of much of the future work on deal proneness. As an example, the smart-shopper phenomenon would suggest that coupon proneness be correlated with psychological traits such as the need to control one's environment. Perceived risk theory would suggest that deal proneness be positively correlated with risk-taking ability and venturesomeness and inversely related to income. Self-perception theory would predict that deal proneness could be negatively correlated with brand loyalty. Operant conditioning would predict a curvilinear relationship between deal proneness and brand loyalty. The partial reinforcement and primary reinforcer concepts would imply that brand loyalty would be highest for medium levels of deal proneness (partial reinforcement is most effective and medium levels of deal proneness indicate a deal is not the primary reinforcer), but lowest for very low or very high levels of deal proneness (in the former case, no reinforcement has occurred, while in the latter case, the reinforcement is continuous and probably serving as a primary reinforcer).

Explanatory Variables Considered.   Four types of variables have been considered in the deal-proneness literature: demographics, psychographics, behavioral, and personality. Demographics include the usual well-defined household descriptors. Psychographics include the consumer's general activities, interests, and opinions (Assael, 1987, Ch. 10). Behavioral characteristics include variables pertaining to consumer purchasing behavior such as brand loyalty and category usage.[3] Personality includes basic psychological traits such as gregariousness, Machiavellianism, and the like. Among the four types of variables, demographics, behavioral, and psychographic characteristics have received the most attention, followed by personality. Demographic, behavioral, and psychographic variables can yield a well-defined profile of deal-prone consumers that can easily be translated into targeting goals. Personality measures provide less directly operational recommendations, and perhaps are more useful for theory testing. However, the emphasis on these variables should increase as creative design of promotions becomes more important.

Methods Used.   The general approach in the deal proneness literature is to first define a measure of proneness. This can then serve as the dependent variable in either a regression or a discriminant analysis, or simply be cross-tabulated against the various demographic, psychographic, behavioral, and personality descriptors.

---

[3] Note that brand loyalty can be thought of in attitudinal terms as well as in terms of repeat purchasing patterns (e.g., Assael, 1987, pp. 73–77). We use the label "behavioral" for convenience.

Findings

Table 3.1 summarizes the methods and results of 18 deal proneness studies. In general, Table 3.1 indicates that demographics and behavioral characteristics yield a much less clear portrait of the deal prone consumer than do other variables. In terms of demographics, various studies have found, for example, that older, younger, or middle-aged consumers are more deal prone. Variables found significant in one study, for example, education (Narasimhan, 1984a, 1984b; Bawa and Shoemaker, 1987a) do not surface in other studies (Webster, 1965; Teel et al., 1980).

Psychographically, however, we find a somewhat more consistent picture of the deal-prone consumer as price conscious (Teel et al., 1980; Rosen, 1985; McCann, 1974; Jolson et al., 1987), involved with media (Teel et al., 1980; Montgomery, 1971; Rosen, 1985; McCann, 1974), and involved with shopping (Teel et al., 1980; Rosen, 1985). In summary, the deal-prone consumer is more likely to be an expert, sophisticated shopper.

There are various reasons for the inconsistency of demographic and behavioral results across studies: The studies use different measures, methods, and study different types of promotions. However, the relative success of psychographic variables suggests that the real reasons for deal proneness lie more deeply than the cold statistics of demographics or buying patterns. One perhaps cynical view of the success of psychographic variables in portraying the deal-prone consumer is that the variables that consistently emerge are the obvious ones (e.g., price consciousness). As a counter to this, the demographic variable income would appear to be obviously negatively associated with deal proneness; however, the income effect has been obscured by confounded demographics (such as home ownership) and psychographics (e.g., involvement in media). In closing this summary, we conclude with a few observations of results (or nonresults) that are particularly important both managerially and theoretically:

1. *Brand loyalty.* A few studies have found a negative correlation between deal proneness and brand loyalty (Webster, 1965; Teel et al., 1980; Montgomery, 1971; Bawa and Shoemaker, 1987a), while a few others have found no relationship (Rosen, 1985; McCann, 1974; Massy and Frank, 1965). Even if a relationship can be found, the critical question here is causality. That is, does deal proneness cause one to become a brand switcher, or are brand switchers naturally deal prone? The issue is obviously confounded by the type of deal proneness with which we are concerned. If the concern is with proneness to use promotions to switch brands, then the relationship with brand loyalty is tautologically negative. However, if the type of deal proneness of interest is propensity to use promotions to accelerate purchases, the hypothesized relationship is less obvious. One might expect that brand-loyal consumers would be more apt to accelerate, because they incur no disutility cost in stocking up on one brand. Brand-loyal consumers might also be more apt to search for promotions, because they do not want to use most of the promotions they would come across on a random basis. Another interesting issue concerning the relationship between brand loyalty and deal proneness is that operant conditioning would predict a nonlinear relationship between the two. Too frequent usage of deals might undermine

TABLE 3.1 Summary of Deal Proneness Studies

Study	Measure of Deal Proneness	Promotions Examined	Product Category	Method	Variables Considered	Findings
Massy and Frank (1965)	Deal elasticity	Consumer-recognized deal	Frequently purchased product	Used regression to estimate market-response model for various segments	Behavioral variables	No difference in sensitivity based on loyalty. Chain store purchases are much more sensitive to deals than are independent store purchases.
Webster (1965)	Percent of purchases on deal, adjusted for promotion frequency and share of requirements	Consumer-recognized deal	Food product	Regression	More than 200 demographic, psychographic, and behavioral variables	Older consumers are more deal-prone. Switchers and light users are more deal-prone.
Montgomery (1971)	Percent of purchases on deal	Consumer-recognized deal	Toothpaste (before and after Crest endorsement by ADA)	Regression	Behavioral variables, psychographics, and personality	In general, brand switching is positively related to deal proneness. Before ADA endorsement, venturesomeness and media exposure were positively related to deal proneness. After endorsement only brand switching was still related.
McCann (1974)	Deal elasticity	Consumer-recognized deal	Low-priced frequently purchased product	Used regression to estimate market response model for various segments	Demographic, psychographic, and behavioral variables	Smaller households, heavy deal users, and households that buy multiple brands on a purchase occasion are more deal sensitive. No difference in deal sensitivity in terms of brand switching, loyalty, or income.
McCann (1974)	Percent of purchases on deal	Consumer-recognized deal	Low-priced frequently purchased product	Divide sample in half based on deal proneness. Estimate market response models for each half.	Price and media sensitivity	Deal prone are much more sensitive to price.
Teel et al. (1980)	Self-report	Coupons	New products in general	Cross-tabulation	Demographic, psychographic, and behavioral variables	Younger, higher-income, larger families are more deal sensitive. Deal sensitive are price-conscious bargain hunters who use advertising, buy on impulse, are less brand loyal, enjoy shopping, and perceive high benefits and low costs to using coupons.

Study	Measure	Promotion type	Category	Method	Variables	Findings
Blattberg et al. (1978)	Classification as national brand switcher or loyal, deal, or deal oriented	Consumer-recognized deal	Five nonfood packaged goods	Cross-tabulation	Demographics	Deal prone own cars and homes, female not working. Income and children not clearly related to deal proneness.
Nielsen (1985)	Usage-rate of coupons	Coupons	General	One-way breakdowns	Demographics	Coupon usage peaks at middle income, middle age; increases with family size.
Manufacturers Coupon Control Center (1989b)	Usage rate of coupons	Coupons	General	One-way breakdowns	Family size	Strong positive relationship with family size.
Rosen (1985)	Frequency of coupon use	Coupons	General	Discriminant analysis	Several demographics and psychographics	Psychographics much better discriminators than demographics. Sex is only clear demographic discriminator: households size also has some discriminatory power. Deal prone are price conscious, venturesome, highly involved with shopping, plan shopping, read and are involved with advertising, compulsive, clip magazine recipes, opinion leaders about products, smaller households, and female. Brand loyalty was not a good discriminator. Different discriminators for males versus females.
Narasimhan (1984b)	Quantity bought using promotion	Coupon	Twelve grocery categories	Tobit analysis	Demographics	Middle-income group is most deal prone. Education is positively related to deal proneness. Presence of children somewhat negatively related.
Narasimhan (1984a)	Quantity bought using promotion	Coupon	Nineteen grocery categories	Regression	Demographics	Middle-income is most deal prone. Education is positively related to deal proneness. Presence of children negatively relate to deal proneness.
Henderson (1984)	Multivariate, percent of purchases	Deal packs, manufacturer and retailer local advertising, price cuts, coupons	Toilet tissue, coffee	Clustering followed by discriminant analysis	Demographic, psychographic, and behavioral variables	Stable clusters of deal-prone consumers exist, homogeneous in terms of the types of promotions used. Clusters fairly consistent across categories, but membership was not. Many significant differences among clusters in terms of demographic, psychographic, and behavioral variables.

TABLE 3.1 *(continued)*

Study	Measure of Deal Proneness	Promotions Examined	Product Category	Method	Variables Considered	Findings
Fader and McAlister (1985)	Choice model parameter and frequency of promotion use	Coupons, in-store promotions	Coffee	Regression	Demographic and behavioral variables	Store patronage is highly significant and only good discriminator.
Bawa and Shoemaker (1987a)	Percentage of purchase measure across product classes	Coupons	Seven packaged goods	Regression	Demographic, psychographic, and behavioral variables	Huband's education and urban counties are positively related. Store and brand loyalty are negatively related. Income significantly positive in univariate analysis but insignificant in regression. Coupon proneness or lack of proneness is somewhat consistent across product categories.
Jolson et al. (1987)	Self-reported number of purchases "triggered" by rebates	Rebates	Small home appliances	Discriminant analysis, comparisons of means	Demographic, psychographic, and behavioral variables	Light users have higher income than do frequent users who have higher income than nonusers. Frequent users less likely to perceive rebates as requiring effort, more aware of prices, more likely to accelerate purchases.
Schneider and Currim (1989)	Statistics from consumer choice model	Coupons, features, displays	Coffee	Regression	Behavioral variables	Coupon proneness is associated with greater purchase quantities and accelerated purchase timing when buying on deal. Display proneness is associated with smaller quantities. Feature proneness is associated with accelerated timing, larger purchase quantities, and larger choice set size.
Moody (1987a)	Redemptions per week ("frequency"); redemptions per $100 shopping bill ("propensity")	Coupons	Grocery products	Automatic Interaction Detection (AID)	Demographic variables	The profile of high frequency households is: larger households, subscribe to Sunday newspaper, female head of household not full time employed. The profile of high propensity households is: annual income < $30,000, subscribe to Sunday newspaper, single family dwelling.

loyalty because the promotion becomes the reward. Too infrequent usage of deals might not be enough of a reward to habituate the behavior of buying one brand. The inconsistency of results across studies may reflect these nonlinearities. Clearly, this is an issue that needs much more attention.

2. *Income.* As mentioned earlier, researchers have not found a consistent negative relationship between income and deal proneness, even after controlling for other variables. It may indeed be the case that income is too intimately confounded with other variables such as education, or there may be a need to better conceptualize the role of income in household purchasing behavior.

3. *Price sensitivity.* The evidence as just cited points toward price sensitivity to be strongly related to deal proneness. This bodes well for the confirmation of price discrimination theory and its managerial implications. The general conclusion is that manufacturers should price their products high and use promotions that require effort on the part of the consumer. Only the price sensitive will find this effort worthwhile. These results strongly support the use of coupons, which allow the price sensitive consumers to self select to use the promotion.

In conclusion, the deal proneness literature has yielded some important definitive results, but they are far from completely understood. The work of Bawa and Shoemaker (1987a) as well as Blattberg et al. (1976) provides encouraging support to the view that a consumer deal proneness trait does exist across product categories. The challenge is for researchers to identify *better* those consumers who possess that trait.

DEAL PRONENESS AND CONSUMER CHOICE SEGMENTS

Blattberg and Sen (1975, 1976) developed a taxonomy of consumer purchasing strategies that can yield significant managerial as well as theoretical insight. Their initial taxonomy had three variables, as follows:

> Brand loyalty
> > Single brand
> > Last purchase loyal
> > Many brands
>
> Type of brand preferred
> > National
> > National and private label
> > Private label
>
> Deal proneness
> > Not deal prone
> > Deal prone

From this taxonomy, Blattberg and Sen identified 16 potential choice segments. (There are 18 combinations of the foregoing variables, but the 2 segments involving single-brand-loyal and national and private label are logical impossibilities). The brand loyalty variable needs some explanation. In particular, single brand and many brands represent the extremes of brand loyalty. The last purchase

PURCHASE HISTORIES OF INDIVIDUAL CONSUMERS, FACIAL TISSUE

	Consumer 1731				Consumer 1611				Consumer 1439			
	High National Brand Loyal				National Brand Loyal				National Brand Switcher			
Purchase number	Brand	Store	Size (# tissues)	Price (¢)	Brand	Store	Size (# tissues)	Price (¢)	Brand	Store	Size (# tissues)	Price (¢)
1	1	10	24	5	7	8	400	2/31*	8	3	400	19
2	1	2	400	27*	2	3	400	29	8	3	400	19
3	8	3	400	19	2	7	400	29	8	3	400	19
4	1	3	400	29	1	7	200	15	1	7	400	29
5	1	3	400	25*	1	3	400	25*	1	7	400	23*
6	1	3	400	29	2	7	400	25*	2	7	400	29
7	1	3	400	29	1	3	400	2/49*	14	9	402	29
8	1	3	400	29	7	8	300	9*	2	7	400	29
9	1	3	400	2/49*	13	5	400	31	1	9	400	25*
10	1	2	400	29	2	3	400	29	2	7	400	29
11	1	2	400	29	2	3	400	29	1	9	400	31
12	1	2	400	25*	2	7	400	29	16	9	400	27 N
13	1	2	400	29	2	3	400	29	2	7	400	29
14	1	3	400	29	8	3	400	19	2	7	400	29
15	8	3	400	2/39	2	3	400	29	2	7	400	29
16	1	3	400	25*	2	3	400	29	2	7	400	29
17	1	3	400	25*	2	3	400	29	1	7	400	29
18	1	2	400	29	2	3	400	29	2	7	400	29
19	1	3	400	29	2	3	400	29	2	10	400	29 N
20	1	3	200	15	2	3	400	29	2	7	400	29
21	1	2	400	29	8	3	400	22	1	7	400	2/49*
22	1	2	400	2/49*	2	3	400	25*	1	7	400	29
23	1	2	400	29	2	3	400	29	1	7	400	29
24	1	2	400	29	2	3	400	29	3	3	400	2/39
25	1	2	200	29	2	3	400	29	1	7	400	29
26	8	3	400	17*	2	3	400	29	2	3	400	29
27	1	6	400	29	2	3	400	25*	2	7	400	29
28		6	400	29	2	3	400	25*	1	7	400	29
29	1	6	400	29	1	3	400	29	2	7	400	29
30	1	6	200	2/39	2	3	400	29	1	7	400	3/98
31	1	6	400	29	2	3	400	23*	1	7	400	29
32	1	6	400	29	2	3	400	29	1	7	400	2/49*
33					2	3	400	23*				
34					2	3	400	23*				
35					2	7	400	29				
36					2	7	400	29				

*Deal price.
N: Not known whether or not this is a deal price.

	Consumer 1217				Consumer 947				Consumer 569			
	National/Private Switcher				Last Purchase Loyal				Private Label Loyal			
Purchase number	Brand	Store	Size (# tissues)	Price (¢)	Brand	Store	Size (# tissues)	Price (¢)	Brand	Store	Size (# tissues)	Price (¢)
1	8	3	400	19	4	1	400	2/35*	8	3	400	19
2	8	3	400	19	4	1	400	2/35*	3	3	400	19
3	8	3	400	19	4	1	400	2/35*	3	3	400	19
4	1	2	400	29	4	1	400	2/35*	3	3	200	19 N
5	2	2	400	29	4	1	400	21	3	3	400	19
6	2	1	400	29	4	1	400	21	3	3	400	19
7	8	3	400	19	4	1	400	21	3	3	400	19
8	2	3	400	19*	4	1	400	21	3	3	400	19
9	11	7	400	2/45*	4	1	400	21	3	3	400	19
10	13	5	400	29	4	1	400	21	3	3	400	18*
11	1	1	400	29	4	1	400	21	3	3	400	18*
12	1	2	400	29	4	1	400	21	8	3	400	19
13	1	7	400	29	4	1	400	21	3	3	400	19
14	1	1	400	29	4	1	400	2/35*	3	3	400	2/35*
15	1	7	400	29	4	1	400	2/35*	3	3	400	19
16	3	1	400	2/35 N	4	1	400	2/35*	3	3	400	19
17	8	3	400	19	14	10	402	21	5	6	400	20
18	2	5	400	29	4	1	400	2/35*	3	3	400	19
19	11	5	400	6/125	14	10	402	21	5	2	200	20 N
20	4	1	400	2/39	14	10	402	28	3	3	400	20
21	1	1	400	29	14	10	402	19	3	3	200	19 N
22	5	2	400	2/39	14	10	402	2/39	3	3	400	20
23	8	3	400	19	14	10	402	2/39	3	3	400	2/37*
24	5	5	400	2/43	14	10	402	2/39	3	3	400	18*
25	8	3	400	19	14	10	402	2/39	3	3	400	2/39
26	1	1	400	29	14	10	402	2/39	3	3	400	2/39
27	8	3	400	19	14	10	402	2/39	3	3	400	17*
28	8	3	400	19	14	10	402	2/39	3	3	400	2/39
29	2	2	400	2/49*	15	10	400	18*	3	3	400	20
30	1	9	24	5	14	10	402	2/39	3	3	400	2/39
31	1	1	400	29	14	10	402	2/39	3	3	400	16*
32	8	3	400	2/39	14	10	402	2/39	3	3	400	2/35*
33	1	1	400	29	15	10	400	3/50*	3	3	400	2/39
34	14	5	402	9/190*	15	10	400	3/50*	3	3	400	2/39
35	4	1	400	2/35*	14	10	402	2/39	3	3	400	2/39

*Deal price.
N: Not known whether or not this is a deal price.

FIGURE 3.2 Consumer Choice Segments Derived by Blattberg and Sen

loyal descriptor means that the consumer tends to be loyal to one brand, but occasionally switch, and after doing so, remain loyal to that brand.

Blattberg and Sen investigated slightly different segmentation schemes (e.g., also considering store loyalty, or four gradations of loyalty), developed a method for classifying consumers in various segments, and examined the consistency of consumer classifications across product categories (Blattberg and Sen, 1975, 1976; Blattberg et al., 1976). However, the conceptual richness of their approach is best illustrated by examples in Figure 3.2, reprinted from Blattberg and Sen (1976). Note, for example, the clear decrease in loyalty as we move from consumer 1,732 to consumer 1,611 to consumer 1,439. Like consumer 1,439, consumer 589 is also a national brand switcher, but is clearly more deal oriented. As a further extreme, the deal-oriented consumer (1,440) shops at many stores, obviously for the lowest-

PURCHASE HISTORIES OF INDIVIDUAL CONSUMERS, FACIAL TISSUE

Purchase number	Consumer 1135				Consumer 589				Consumer 1440			
	Private Label Switcher				Nat'l Brand Switcher (Deal)				Deal-Oriented			
	Brand	Store	Size (# tissues)	Price (¢)	Brand	Store	Size (# tissues)	Price (¢)	Brand	Store	Size (# tissues)	Price (¢)
1	1	6	400	31	2	7	400	24*	4	1	400	2/35*
2	2	6	400	25	1	7	400	19*	7	8	400	17*
3	11	6	400	25	2	7	400	23*	7	8	400	17*
4	8	3	400	19	1	7	200	19	4	1	400	2/45
5	4	1	400	21	1	7	400	29	11	5	400	2/49
6	4	1	400	19*	2	7	400	19*	7	8	400	17*
7	3	3	400	19	2	7	400	19*	11	5	400	2/49
8	4	1	400	20	1	7	400	19*	4	1	400	2/35*
9	16	3	400	19 N	2	7	400	29	4	1	400	2/35*
10	3	3	400	19	1	7	200	19	1	5	400	20*
11	8	3	400	19	1	7	200	19	4	1	400	2/35*
12	3	3	400	20	1	7	200	12*	4	1	400	2/35*
13	3	3	400	20	2	7	400	19*	7	8	400	17*
14	1	6	400	25*	1	7	400	19*	1	5	400	20*
15	5	2	400	20	1	7	400	29	11	6	400	2/49
16	3	3	400	18*	1	7	200	19	7	8	400	17*
17	5	6	400	20	1	7	200	12*	7	8	400	17*
18	4	7	400	20	1	7	400	29	1	5	400	20*
19	3	3	400	20	1	7	200	19	1	5	400	20*
20	5	2	400	20	2	7	400	19*	1	5	400	20*
21	16	6	400	20 N	1	7	400	19*	7	8	400	2/31*
22	3	3	400	20	1	7	200	19	4	1	400	2/45
23	4	7	400	20	1	7	200	19	1	8	400	2/37*
24	3	3	400	20	12	7	400	19*	7	8	400	17*
25	2	6	400	29	12	7	400	19*	1	10	400	2/25*
26	1	6	200	2/29	2	7	400	19*	7	8	400	2/29*
27	4	7	400	20	2	7	400	19*	7	8	400	2/31*
28	5	7	400	18*	2	7	400	19*	3	3	400	2/39
29	12	6	400	20	2	7	400	19*	1	6	400	23*
30	3	3	400	20	2	7	400	19*	7	8	400	17*
31	3	3	400	20	1	7	400	29	3	3	400	5/88*
32	3	3	400	20	2	7	400	19*	9	4	400	2/45
33	3	3	400	20	2	7	400	19*	15	10	400	3/47*
34					2	7	400	23*	3	3	400	2/39

*Deal price.
N: Not known whether or not this is a deal price.

FIGURE 3.2 (Continued)   Consumer Choice Segments Derived by Blattberg and Sen

Source: Robert C. Blattberg and Subrata Sen, "Market Segments and Stochastic Brand Choice Models," *Journal of Marketing Research*, Vol. 13 (February 1976), pp. 36–38. Reprinted from the *Journal of Marketing Research*, published by the American Marketing Association.

price brand available. Almost all purchases are on a deal basis. The last purchase-loyal consumer is also of interest. If many consumers fall into this category, and if a promotion can help induce a switch, the repeat purchases generated by the promotion can greatly increase the profitability of the promotion.

Using panel data, Blattberg and Sen classified consumers in three product categories, with the results displayed in Table 3.2. Due to statistical considerations, only "heavy users" were classified (Blattberg and Sen, 1976, p. 40). As can be seen, there is a great deal of brand loyalty in all three product categories. Whether this finding holds across all consumers, different product categories, and in today's promotion environment is an open and important question. The hypothesis based on self-perception theory would be that many more consumers are now deal oriented or national brand switchers (deal). The testing of this hypothesis is obviously an important area for future research.

McAlister (1986) has made important extensions of the Blattberg and Sen segments, adapting them to today's more promotion-intensive environment. For example, she adds a stockpiler variable to differentiate between those who do and do not accelerate their product purchases due to promotion. Her segments are as follows:

Loyal, not deal prone
Loyal, deal prone—stockpiler
Loyal, deal prone—will switch due to promotion
Loyal, deal prone—will switch and stockpile due to promotion
Switchers, not deal prone
Switchers, deal prone—restrict choice to brands on deal
Switchers, deal prone—restrict choice to brands on deal, will stockpile

TABLE 3.2 The Percentage of "Heavy Buyer" Households in Various Choice Segments

	Facial Tissue	Waxed Paper	Aluminum Foil
Highly national-brand loyal	12.7%	34.9%	24.5%
National-brand loyal	14.7	25.6	20.4
Private-label loyal	22.0	7.0	4.1
Last-purchase loyal	11.3	7.0	10.2
National-brand switcher	5.3	11.6	16.3
National/private switcher	10.0	7.0	6.1
Private-label switcher	14.0	0.0	4.1
National-brand switcher (deal)	1.3	2.3	6.1
Deal oriented	8.7	4.7	8.2

Source: Robert C. Blattberg and Subrata Sen, "Market Segments and Stochastic Brand Choice Models," *Journal of Marketing Research*, Vol. 13 (February 1976), adapted from p. 42. Adapted from the *Journal of Marketing Research*, published by the American Marketing Association.

McAlister then models the profitability of each segment, using a different underlying choice model for each segment. This approach is immediately applicable to the management of promotions. Note also that clear distinctions are drawn regarding the type of influence that promotions are having on the consumer with respect to switching and stockpiling.

Currim and Schneider (1988) utilize a similar taxonomy as McAlister. They consider brand loyalty, sensitivity to promotion, and stockpiling behavior. They then provide empirical results showing how often consumers utilize the choice strategies implied by the taxonomy.[4] They find the following choice strategies and percentages of times the strategies are used:

- Household purchases regular brand and quantity—not influenced by promotions (22 percent).
- Promotions influence household to switch brands but not stockpile (25 percent).
- Promotions influence household to switch brands and stockpile (18 percent).
- Promotions influence household to stockpile brand to which the household is loyal (16 percent).
- Household switches brands but not related to the presence of promotions (19 percent).

These results say, for example, that on 19 percent of purchase occasions, consumers switch brands for reasons unrelated to the presence of promotions; on 18 percent of purchase occasions, promotions are associated with a brand switch and stockpiling; and so on. The Currim and Schneider results correspond well with the classification scheme proposed by McAlister. For example, Currim and Schneider's first purchase strategy corresponds to McAlister's "Loyal, not deal prone" segment.

The brand choice segment approach has much promise as both a managerial technique and a tool for testing the effects of promotion on brand loyalty. The recent extensions by McAlister and Currim and Schneider lead us toward that promise, but more empirical results are needed. One difficulty in operationalizing the approach is the classification of consumers. Blattberg and Sen (1975) developed a statistical procedure for classifying consumers, while Currim and Schneider used cluster analysis. However, both procedures rely on a meaningful specification of cut-off points. For example, if a consumer buys 50 percent of the time on deal, is the consumer deal prone? If one brand accounts for 60 percent of the consumer's purchases, is the consumer brand loyal? Blattberg and Sen need cut-off points to classify consumers, while Currim and Schneider need cut-off points to interpret their clusters. Of course, cut-offs can be defined in terms of medians, but to compare segments across categories, a more meaningful standard is needed.

---

[4] Note that Currim and Schneider quantify the percentage of times that consumers use various purchase strategies rather than the percentage of consumers who use a given strategy. This is in contrast to Blattberg and Sen, who classify consumers into various strategies (see Table 3.2).

DIRECTIONS FOR FUTURE RESEARCH

In this chapter, we have taken an in-depth look at the concept of deal proneness and the research that has been undertaken to understand the phenomenon better. This research has been insightful but the area is still very fertile for further research. The following topics appear to be especially important:

1. *Better measurement.* Future researchers need to be more specific in terms of which type of deal proneness they are measuring and develop measures that accurately reflect that type of deal proneness. For example, little has been done to improve upon the percentage-of-purchases measure developed by Webster that we interpreted to measure promotion search behavior. The validity of self-report measures of all types of deal proneness has not been investigated. A convergent-discriminant validity study of the four major measures of deal proneness identified in this chapter—percentage-of-purchases, promotion elasticity, self-report, and choice model–derived measures—would be a welcome addition to the literature.

2. *Theories of deal proneness.* Deal proneness is very rich in behavioral connotations, but there is a strong need for a consumer behavior–based theory of the phenomenon. This theory should explain and integrate the various dimensions of deal proneness elaborated in Figure 3.1. One specific area that probably needs better conceptualization is the relationship between income and deal proneness.

3. *More empirical results.* The relationship between deal proneness and brand loyalty is a very important managerial issue that warrants further investigation. The general role of personality in explaining deal proneness needs to be investigated further. The Blattberg and Sen typology and its embellishments need to be quantified in today's promotion environment. Finally, broad studies that consider the several types of deal proneness with respect to several types of promotions are needed.

In summary, there is ample room for methodological, theoretical, and empirical work in the area of deal proneness.

4

Economic Theories of Promotions

An important way in which firms vary price is through the use of promotions. An important question is: "Why are promotions used rather than simply changing prices?" There are many explanations ranging from product obsolescence or perishability to price discrimination between informed and uninformed consumers. The purpose of this chapter is to offer "economic" explanations of promotions. These explanations will give the reader insights into when and why promotions work.

The chapter is organized as follows: First, we show that the optimal pricing policy when demand is uncertain is to promote; then we show that promotions result when inventory carrying costs and transaction costs differ across retailers and consumers; then we analyze differential information as a cause; next we study how promotions allow firms to price discriminate between different market segments; then we analyze switchers versus loyals; then we study competitive reasons for using promotions; and finally we give implications for marketing managers.

DEMAND UNCERTAINTY

Department stores, fashion catalogs, or any firm that sells products for which it is difficult to predict demand, have priced the product "high" at the beginning of the season and then reduced the price near the end of the season. Most marketers intuitively understand this form of pricing. However, no one in marketing has ever shown why it is "optimal" to price using "end of season" promotions. Lazear (1986) has developed a clever model using item demand uncertainty as an explanation of promotions. Pashigian (1987) acknowledges Lazear's explanation but adds a second reason, shifting economic conditions and increased fashion orientation which causes buyers to overestimate total demand, resulting in item markdowns. Only Lazear's model will be discussed here.

Lazear's Model

Suppose there is only one buyer in the market and that buyer is willing to pay V for the good. The seller does not know V but has a prior distribution for V. The problem is to set the price R to maximize expected profits. To make matters simple suppose the cost is zero.

The firm's problem is to maximize expected profit (Π):

$$\Pi = \max_R R[1 - F(R)] \qquad (4.1)$$

where R is the price the firm sets, $F(R)$ is the probability that R does not exceed V, $[F(R) = Pr(V \leq R)]$, and hence $1 - F(R)$ is the probability V exceeds R and the consumer buys the brand.

If the prior distribution of V is uniform, then Lazear shows that the optimal price is one-half and the expected profit is one-fourth.[1]

In the two-period model, the firm has two chances to sell the product. If the good does not sell during the first period, the seller faces *another* buyer during the second period who is identical to the customer in the first period. If the product sells in period 1, the price is R_1; if it sells in period 2, the price is R_2. The problem is to set the price for the two periods R_1 and R_2 to maximize profits,

$$\max_{R_1,R_2} R_1[1 - F(R_1)] + R_2[1 - F_2(R_2)][F(R_1)] \qquad (4.2)$$

where $F_2(R_2)$ is the probability that the price in period 2 exceeds the second customer's reservation price, V, given the first customer did not buy in period 1. $F(R_1)$ is the same as in the one-period problem.

Lazear shows that the solution is a dynamic programming problem. The firm's problem in period 2 is

$$\max_{R_2} R_2[1 - F_2(R_2)] \qquad (4.3)$$

where

$$F_2(R_2) = \frac{F(R_2)}{F(R_1)}, \qquad R_2 < R_1$$

Maximizing (4.3) with respect to R_2 gives

$$R_2 = \frac{F(R_1) - F(R_2)}{f(R_2)}$$

In the case where V is uniform, $F(R_1) = R_1$, $F(R_2) = R_2$, and $f(R_2) = 1$, then

$$R_2 = \frac{R_1}{2}$$

---

[1] To see this result, begin by noting that $F(R) = R$ for the uniform distribution. Then $d\pi/dR = 1 - 2R = 0$ or $R = \frac{1}{2}$.

Next substitute R_2 into (4.2) and solve for R_1. Noting that $R_2 = R_1/2$, $F(R_1) = R_1$, and $F_2(R_2) = R_2/R_1 = \frac{1}{2}$, the problem becomes

$$\max\{R_1[1 - R_1] + R_{\frac{1}{2}}[1 - \tfrac{1}{2}]R_1\} = R_1 - \tfrac{3}{4}R_1^2 \tag{4.4}$$

Taking derivatives and setting them equal to 0, gives $R_1 = \frac{2}{3}$. Substituting $R_1 = \frac{2}{3}$ into $R_1 - \frac{3}{4}R_1^2$ shows that profits are $\frac{1}{3}$ for the two-period problem.

Thus, Lazear shows, assuming a uniform distribution, that the optimal price for period 1 is $\frac{2}{3}$ and for period 2 is $\frac{1}{3}$. More important, the profits are higher by being able to set the price in two separate periods. For the one-period pricing model, the profit is $\frac{1}{4}$, and for the two-period pricing model, the profit is $\frac{1}{3}$.

The intuition underlying Lazear's results can be understood by the fact that firms should try a high price in case the customer has a high reservation price. If the customer does have a high reservation price, then the firm receives a higher profit. By setting the price at $\frac{2}{3}$, there is a $\frac{1}{3}$ chance the customer will buy. If the customer does buy, then the profit is higher. If the customer does not buy, then the firm has learned that V is less than $\frac{2}{3}$ and can reprice the product lower and still make a profit. (This assumes that customers do not expect lower future prices.)

Lazear's results show that when the demand curve for a product is unknown, it is optimal (under certain conditions) to price the product high in the first period and then run a promotion in the second period. This is obviously the practice used by many retailers.

Further Results from Lazear's Model

Lazear analyzes several other cases. The first relates to the number of customers in the market. In his initial model, the firm was selling one product and there was one customer per period. Suppose there are N customers, P are just "shoppers" and $1 - P$ are "buyers" who are willing to pay V. A shopper is someone who comes into the store but does not buy. Lazear examines the condition that there are very few "buyers" in the market and asks the question: "What is the optimal pricing strategy?" When there are very few buyers (versus shoppers) in the market, then a lower initial price is superior and less discounting is optimal because the firm may miss selling to a key customer. Once the customer has left the store, it is no longer possible to attract them back to the store.

An example would be a retailer selling a "one of a kind" expensive designer dress. In this situation the retailer would be better off charging a lower initial price and offering a lower markdown when it goes on sale than simply charging a high initial price and then offering a very high markdown. This is the opposite strategy followed by many retailers pricing unique expensive designer clothes.

Another issue Lazear analyzes is: "How should goods be priced that become obsolete?" Suppose children's toys must be sold by Christmas. After Christmas, they have a much lower value. Should the firm charge a higher initial price and then discount the item more after Christmas or should it charge a lower initial price and discount less?

By letting the item have a value V/K in period 2 where $K > 1$ in the model given in Equation (4.2), the problem becomes

$$\max_{R_1, R_2} R_1[1 - F(R_1)] + R_2[1 - F_2(KR_2)]F(R_1) \tag{4.5}$$

Lazear shows (p. 25) that

$$R_2 = \frac{R_1}{2K} \quad \text{and} \quad R_1 = \frac{2K}{(4K - 1)}$$

Suppose $K = 2$; then $R_1 = \frac{4}{7}$ and $R_2 = \frac{1}{7}$. Comparing this to the case where there is no obsolescence, $K = 1$ ($R_1 = \frac{2}{3}$ and $R_2 = \frac{1}{3}$), one sees the period 1 price is lower and the period 2 price drops much more than in the case of no obsolescence. Thus, a lower initial price (markup) should be offered to attract customers and avoid a large "write-off" in period 2. Also note that the percentage discount is greater in the "obsolescence" case.

Summary of Lazear's Results

Based on his analysis of pricing when the firm does not know the customer's reservation price, Lazear concludes that

1. Being able to offer a promotion in the second period rather than simply having a fixed one-period price increases firm profitability.
2. Pricing products with few buyers (e.g., high-fashion items) should result in a lower price in the first period ceteris paribus than products with many buyers.
3. Pricing products which become obsolete should again result in a lower price in the first period ceteris paribus than products with no obsolescence and the markdown should be higher in the second period.

These results offer managers general guidelines for pricing, though obviously Lazear's model is restrictive. However, his results are intuitively reasonable and therefore offer an explanation why promotions are optimal when demand is uncertain. It would be interesting to extend Lazear's results using other statistical distributions and allowing multiple purchases of the item.

INVENTORY COST SHIFTING

Inventory "stockpiling" is prevalent in nondurables. It can work one of two ways: Consumers buy larger quantities when the product is sold on deal or the consumer can shift purchase timing to buy before the expected time of the next purchase. In some cases, consumers increase their "stock" of durable goods before they might normally purchase. When General Motors offers a special financing package (e.g., 2.9 percent interest), potential buyers may accelerate their purchase timing. The result is consumers are increasing their stock ("newness") of car ownership (see Chapter 5).

Because consumers stockpile products much the same way retailers do, one explanation of the cause of dealing is shifting inventory costs from retailers to consumers. This explanation is controversial but does not assume certain market "imperfections" are required to cause promotions to occur such as informed versus uninformed consumers which will be discussed in the next section. It also does not assume promotions are driven by competitive behavior in which retailers or manufacturers are "cutting each others throats."

Blattberg, Eppen, and Lieberman

Blattberg et al. (1981) developed a model which analyzed how consumers and retailers purchase in a category. The consumer is assumed to minimize holding costs, and the retailer is assumed to maximize profits which depend upon the consumer's behavior.

The consumer's objective is to minimize holding costs given he or she will consume c units per period. The total cost to the consumer is

$$TC(q) = \int_0^{q/c} h(q - ct)dt - Dq \tag{4.6}$$

where

h = holding costs

c = consumption rate per period

D = deal discount

t = time

q/c = time to consume q units bought at time 0

Consumers are divided into two types:

1. High-holding-cost consumers
2. Low-holding-cost consumers

The retailers would offer a promotion if the low-holding-cost consumer "forward buys" (stockpiles) and holds inventory rather than the retailer. The retailer would hold inventory for the high-holding-cost consumers. If there is a consumer segment in the market that has holding costs low enough so that it pays to allow them to hold inventory rather than retailers, then a promotion is offered; otherwise, it is not economically advantageous for the retailer to promote. In the latter case retailers would prefer to charge consumers a high price and not pass the savings on to the consumer because the retailer is more efficient in holding inventories.

The model makes certain predictions regarding dealing actively:

1. As consumption (c) increases, deal discounts decrease but the frequency of deals increases.
2. As holding costs increase, deal discounts increase and frequency increases.

3. As the percentage of low-holding-cost consumers increase, deal discounts decrease but deal frequency increases.

Although it is difficult, these implications can be tested. The problem is that it is difficult to measure the percentage of consumers who have low holding costs in a given category. Consumption rate is also difficult to define since the unit of measurement is different across categories and may not be constant.

Blattberg et al., using diary panel data, did attempt to test the model and compared its implications to an alternative model which assumed that promotions were used to induce trial for a brand. The empirical results showed that consumers stockpile products. Analyzing four product categories (aluminum foil, facial tissue, liquid detergent, and waxed paper), consumers stockpile in one of two ways: (1) purchase a greater quantity on deal and (2) purchase before they normally would if no deal is offered. Two tables are presented showing this effect. Table 4.1 shows that for the 25-ft aluminum foil, facial tissue, and the 100-ft and 125-ft

---

TABLE 4.1A Consumers' Response to Deals Through Stockpiling

Product Category	Package Size	Mean Number of Units Bought per Deal Transaction	Number of Deal Transactions[f]	Mean Number of Units Bought per Nondeal Transaction	Number of Nondeal Transactions	Difference	P-value[g]
Aluminum foil[a]	25.0 ft	1.21 (0.035)[e]	160	1.04 (0.01)	441	+0.17	Less than .001
	37.5 ft	1.01 (0.005)	102	1.03 (0.03)	97	−0.02	.07
	75.0 ft	1.03 (0.015)	60	1.00 (0.00)	230	+0.03	.05
Facial tissue[b]	400 ts	1.99 (0.03)	733	1.24 (0.01)	2,510	+0.75	Less than .0001
Liquid detergent[c]	12 oz	1.03 (0.006)	250	1.02 (0.005)	1,061	+0.01	.20
	22 oz	1.03 (0.005)	602	1.01 (0.003)	891	+0.02	.001
	32 oz	1.08 (0.0296)	165	1.02 (0.009)	572	+0.06	.05
Waxed paper[d]	100 ft	1.68 (0.043)	69	1.25 (0.016)	789	+0.43	Less than .0001
	125 ft	1.29 (0.024)	106	1.02 (0.004)	1,409	+0.27	Less than .0001

[a] Reynolds and Alcoa in Jewel.

[b] Kleenex and Scotties in A & P, National, Jewel, Kroger, and Walgreens.

[c] Ivory, Joy, and Lux (and 22-oz Gentle Fels) in A & P, National, and Jewel.

[d] Rapinwax, Freshrap (100 ft) and Cut Rite (125 ft) in A & P, National, and Jewel.

[e] Number in parentheses is standard error.

[f] Some transactions were eliminated when it was uncertain whether they were deal or nondeal purchases.

[g] P-value is the significance level for which the null hypothesis is rejected.

Source: Robert C. Blattberg, Gary D. Eppen, and Joshua Lieberman, "A Theoretical and Empirical Evaluation of Price Deals for Consumer Nondurables," *Journal of Marketing,* Vol. 45, no. 1 (Winter 1981), pp. 116–129. Reprinted from the *Journal of Marketing,* published by the American Marketing Association.

TABLE 4.1B The Effect of Deals on Postdeal Purchase Timing

Product Category	Mean Time Interval (in days) Between Deal and Nondeal Purchases	Number of Intervals	Mean Time Interval (in days) Between Deal and Nondeal Purchases	Number of Intervals	Difference (in days)	P-value[b]
Aluminum foil	95.65 (5.55)[a]	374	71.65 (0.575)	1,198	24.00	Less than .0001
Facial tissue	63.61 (2.4)	935	47.6 (1.2)	3,543	15.98	Less than .0001
Liquid detergent	66.18 (3.39)	745	53.72 (1.58)	2,524	12.36	.0005
Waxed paper	135.88 (8.88)	255	100.25 (3.625)	1,005	35.63	.0002

[a] ( ) indicates standard error.

[b] P-value is the significance level for which the null hypothesis is rejected.

Source: Robert C. Blattberg, Gary D. Eppen, and Joshua Lieberman, "A Theoretical and Empirical Evaluation of Price Deals for Consumer Nondurables," *Journal of Marketing*, Vol. 45, no. 1 (Winter 1981), pp. 116–129. Reprinted from the *Journal of Marketing*, published by the American Marketing Association.

waxed paper, consumers buy larger quantities on deal than when no deal is offered. Second, for all four categories, the purchase interval is longer between the deal to nondeal purchase than nondeal to nondeal purchases. The evidence shows that consumers stockpile. (See Chapter 5 for further evidence of stockpiling.)

The other test of the theory was deal magnitude and deal frequency. The theory implies that brands with higher sales will be offered on deal more frequently and with lower deal discounts. Table 4.2 shows that approximately 60 percent of the cases fit this prediction.

In summary, consumers appear to stockpile products through purchasing a larger than normal number of units and change their purchase timing. Predictions made regarding the frequency and magnitude offer some evidence that brands with higher volumes receive more promotions and have lower deal magnitudes. However, the evidence supporting this part of the theory is weaker.

The unique feature of Blattberg et al.'s model is that it is one of the few models tested empirically. While the model cannot explain some causes of promotion and omits trade deals as a cause of promotions by retailers, their empirical results are consistent with the model.

If trade dealing is added to the model, then retailers' costs are reduced in the periods in which the trade deal is offered. However, the question still becomes: "Why do manufacturers offer retailers trade deals?" The answer should be related to the willingness of the retailer to pass the trade deal through to the consumer. If the retailer does not pass through the trade deal, then the manufacturer has no

TABLE 4.2A Summary of Predictions for Aluminum Foil

Dealing Parameters	Deal Magnitude[a]	Dealing Frequency
Number of predictions	5	7
Number of correct predictions	5[b]	5[c]
Percentage of correct predictions	100.0	71.4

[a] Fewer deal magnitude predictions exist because no deals occurred for Kaiser at Jewel. Thus, the deal magnitude is unknown.

[b] 25.00 ft (Reynolds, Kaiser) and (Reynolds, Alcoa) in National and Jewel and (Reynolds, Alcoa) in Jewel; 37.50 ft (Reynolds, Alcoa) in Jewel.

[c] 25.00 ft (Reynolds, Alcoa) in National and Jewel (Reynolds, Alcoa) and (Alcoa, Kaiser) in Jewel; 37.50 ft (Reynolds, Alcoa) in Jewel.

incentive to trade deal. If the retailer has lower holding costs than consumers, why not hold the extra inventory and not pass through the trade deal? Thus, trade dealing does not change the theory put forth by Blattberg et al.

Retail promotions may increase category consumption but Blattberg et al. do not consider this case. They assume consumption rate, c, is fixed. For certain types of categories, facial tissue, aluminum foil, and so on, it is not clear how much increased consumption results from occasional lower prices. For other categories, tuna, snacks, and so on, reduced prices may increase consumption. When this does occur, promotions may be used to "price discriminate." This theory will be covered in the section on price discrimination.

In summary, inventory transfer may explain some elements of why promotions are used. Clearly firms with excess inventories frequently discount to sell off inventories. Whether this is because some consumers have lower holding costs or it increases consumption of the good needs to be the focus of future empirical research.

TABLE 4.2B Summary of Predictions for Brand Dealing Parameters: All Product Categories

Dealing Parameters	Deal Magnitude	Dealing Frequency
Number of predictions	46	49
Number of correct predictions	29	31
Percentage of correct predictions	59.2	63.3

Source: Robert C. Blattberg, Gary D. Eppen, and Joshua Lieberman, "A Theoretical and Empirical Evaluation of Price Deals for Consumer Nondurables," *Journal of Marketing*, Vol. 45, no. 1 (Winter 1981), pp. 116–129. Reprinted from the *Journal of Marketing*, published by the American Marketing Association.

Other Inventory Cost Models

Several economists have shown that a two-price equilibrium results when consumer inventory costs, transaction costs, and search behavior is considered. The significance of a "two-price" equilibrium is that there is a high and low price in the market which is similar to some firms promoting and other firms not promoting. Salop and Stiglitz (1982) use the following model to demonstrate that a low and high price are the equilibrium[2] price distribution. The equilibrium prices are based on the following assumptions (Salop and Stiglitz, 1982, p. 1123):

1. *Profit maximization.* Each small firm chooses a price, p, to maximize profits given the prices of the other firm.
2. *Equal profits.* Each firm earns identical ("normal") profits.
3. *Search equilibrium.* Each consumer searches optimally given the distribution of prices, $f(p)$.
4. *Entry equilibrium.* Each consumer enters the market if and only if expected consumer's surplus is nonnegative.

In addition, the consumer is modeled as follows:

1. Every consumer "lives" two periods; that is, the consumer is in the market for two periods.
2. In each period a consumer demands one unit of the commodity at any price no greater than some reservation price, u.
3. The consumer may enter and purchase in *each* period or purchase two units in period 1 and store the one unit for period 2. The consumer saves the transaction cost c but incurs the storage cost δ.

Let $\hat{p}$ denote the "reservation price" which leaves the consumer indifferent between purchasing for storage and purchasing for consumption with the intention of entering the market in the next period. The consumer *must* buy at the price observed in period 2. Noting that the consumer will pay the average price $\bar{p}$ next period, and must also pay transaction cost c, $\hat{p}$ is given by

$$\hat{p} + \delta = \bar{p} + c \tag{4.7}$$

Using these assumptions, Salop and Stiglitz show that $1 - \lambda$ and λ firms charge P_l and P_h, respectively, where P_l is the low price and P_h is the high price. Further $P_l = \hat{p}$ and $P_h = u$. They then show that

$$P_l = \frac{u + (\delta - c)}{2}$$

$$P_h = u \tag{4.8}$$

Thus, holding costs and transaction costs drive the two-price equilibrium. They further show that if holding costs are too high, there will be a single-price equilibrium.

---

[2] Equilibrium means that no firm can vary price and increase profits. Because they assume a competitive market, all firms have a profit of zero in equilibrium.

The *key* assumption in the Salop and Stiglitz model is search behavior. They assume that sales are unadvertised. They state (p. 1121): "Those customers who (unluckily) arrive at a high-price firm purchase only for their immediate needs and re-enter the market later. Those who (luckily) arrive at a low-price store economize by purchasing more than is required for immediate consumption, storing the excess for future consumption."

Thus, the cause of the two-price equilibrium is a combination of search and the trade-off between storage costs and transaction costs. Consumers can search again in the next period but may not find a promotion. Therefore, they can buy for inventory and do not have to buy next period when their expected price is $\bar{p}$.

"Sales" or promotions occur because some retailers are charging a lower price to obtain extra business from the low-holding-cost consumers. "Promotions" result because of consumers' search and transaction costs. It is optimal for some retailers to reduce the consumers' transaction costs. In equilibrium, at random, some retailers will reduce prices to save some consumers future transaction costs.

The Salop and Stiglitz explanation for promotions requires consumers to search randomly. This is unlikely. Stores, in fact, differentiate themselves on price image and spend large advertising budgets[3] on "informing" the consumer about promotions and price image. Without the consumer's "random" behavior, everyone would arrive at the low-priced store, even if the consumers' transaction cost is high. Therefore, the average price in the market would not be $\bar{p}$ but rather p_l.

Based on the foregoing discussion, the lack of differential information is critical to Salop and Stiglitz's explanation for promotion. However, it is not for the Blattberg et al. explanation. Theirs requires the consumer to have lower holding cost than the retailer.

DIFFERENTIAL INFORMATION

Economists, since Stigler's path-breaking article, have shown that customers may not find the lowest price in the market because the search cost is too high. This has caused price dispersion in a market. Marketers and retailers obviously have understood this phenomenon but did not develop theories explaining why this behavior exists. Several articles in the economic literature have developed models of consumers and then showed that the optimal pricing pattern is to have two pricing levels in a market. In a separate article from the one just discussed, Salop and Stiglitz (1977) derive a "two-price equilibrium" in the market in which some retailers price low and others price high.[4] Varian (1980) argues that this equilibrium is not viable in the long run and develops an alternative explanation

---

[3] A typical department store spends 3 percent of its sales on advertising. Food retailers advertise once to twice a week in the local newspapers.

[4] In equilibrium means no firm can increase its profits by changing price.

which shows that occasional promotions (randomized prices) are optimal for the retailer in attracting "informed" customers. This section will discuss both explanations.

Differential Information Causing a Two-Price Equilibrium

Because consumers have different costs of search and different abilities to process information, it is possible to have a two- (or multiple-) price equilibrium. Thus, it is optimal for different stores to segment themselves into high- and low-priced stores. While this does not lead to a promotional strategy, Varian, in the next section, argues that a "two-price equilibrium" can only be implemented through promotions. It is important to understand Salop and Stiglitz before discussing Varian's article.

The basic concept developed by Salop and Stiglitz begins with two sets of customers: (1) customers who are informed because they have a low cost of search for information and (2) customers who have a high cost of information and therefore are less (uninformed) informed. Let

α = proportion of informed

$1 - \alpha$ = proportion who are uninformed

β = proportion of low-priced stores

N = total number of stores

L = total number of buyers

It is assumed that uninformed consumers shop at random and the expected number of uninformed consumers shopping at each store is $(1 - \alpha) L/N = q_u$, where q_u is the average number of uninformed customers per store. Informed customers will only shop at low-priced stores. The expected number of informed customers, q_I, shopping at low-priced stores is

$$q_I = \frac{\alpha L}{\beta N}$$

Then, the total number of customers shopping at low-priced stores is

$$q_I + q_u = (1 - \alpha) \frac{L}{N} + \frac{\alpha L}{\beta N}$$

The equilibrium price is determined by assuming that price per unit is equal to the average cost per unit.[5] If each customer makes one purchase, then

$$P_L = A(q_I + q_u) \tag{4.9a}$$

$$P_H = A(q_u) \tag{4.9b}$$

where $A(q)$ is the average cost of q units sold.

---

[5] In equilibrium, zero profits are earned. Therefore, price per unit equals average cost.

To reach this equilibrium, several key assumptions are required. The first is that the average cost curve is declining in the number of customers. This is a reasonable assumption since most retailers have high fixed costs of space, equipment, and so on. The second assumption is that uninformed customers shop at random. This is a very difficult assumption to accept. If a customer shops at random on the first trip and finds a low-priced store, it is likely he or she will continue to shop at the low-priced store. Therefore, there must be some mechanism that requires uninformed consumers to continue to be uninformed and not learn from searching.

For marketers the important concept is that stores that cater to more informed consumers have lower prices. Becoming "informed" results from reading newspaper advertisements indicating which items are offered at special prices. Thus, stores use promotions to differentiate between "informed" and "uninformed" consumers.

A problem arises in the cost analysis. To advertise price promotions, stores incur a cost. Thus, catering to the informed consumers has a fixed cost which must be absorbed by higher volume received from the informed consumers. Only if there are enough shoppers willing to switch to low-priced stores will it pay to advertise. Thus, when the cost of obtaining the information is low and the savings high, a two-price equilibrium can result.

For retailers determining optimal pricing strategies, it is essential to understand how large each segment is likely to be. When the cost of disseminating information is low *and* two segments are likely to exist (informed and uninformed consumers), then the retailer must decide whether to advertise and use periodic promotions. An example is low-priced versus high-priced optical centers where purchases are infrequent. In markets where it pays consumers to shop (auto dealers), it is unlikely that one will see a two-price equilibrium. An empirical evaluation of the types of retailing in which one sees "high"- and "low"-priced retailers compared to the cases in which a one-price equilibrium would offer evidence regarding the variables explaining when information is costly relative to the return from shopping. Unfortunately, in its current state, the Salop and Stiglitz explanation does not offer marketers actionable strategies.

Randomization to Discriminate Against Uninformed Consumers

Varian (1980) argues that Salop and Stiglitz's justification for price dispersion cannot hold because low-priced stores would dominate the market. Uninformed consumers would eventually find the low-priced stores, and the high-priced stores would be forced out of the market. Empirically, prices vary overtime and are not just "static" low or high prices. Varian, therefore, developed an alternative model and theory.

Let

R = the reservation price above which no consumer will buy

P = the price offered by the store

I = the number of informed consumers

M = the number of uninformed consumers

n = number of stores

Then, if it is assumed uninformed consumers randomly shop, the number of uninformed consumers per store is simply $U = M/n$. If the price of an outlet is lower than the competition, its sales are $I + U$.

For the market to have two prices, the retailers will randomize between the two prices. P_h will be the reservation price, and P_l will be determined by the number of informed consumers and several other factors. Retailers will occasionally charge a low price to attract informed consumers. By *randomizing* prices uninformed consumers who accidentally found a low-priced store cannot use this past knowledge of low-priced stores to shop efficiently.[6] They must learn what is low priced "today." Therefore, they must continue to be informed consumers or they will pay higher prices.

Using his randomization argument, Varian derives the optimal high- and low-price retailers should charge. The high price is r, the reservation price of the uninformed consumers. The low price, $p = C(I + U)/(I + U)$, where $C(I + U)$, is the cost of the $I + U$ units. $C(I + U)$ is assumed to be a strictly decreasing function. As the number of informed consumers increase in the market, p will decline. The result is a lower average cost.

Varian's model may at first appear to result in an unrealistic solution. Retailers probably do not think they "randomize." However, the key concept is that the consumer cannot anticipate when an item will be promoted. Food retailers offer advertised, weekly promotions. These can be interpreted as offering varying prices for the basket of groceries a customer buys. Mass merchandisers such as Ward, Sears, and Penney also offer advertised weekly price discounts. Informed consumers are likely to respond. Therefore, Varian's argument may offer a partial explanation of why dealing is used by retailers.

PRICE DISCRIMINATION

The three explanations just given have focused on either uncertainty about demand or costs (inventory carrying costs or search costs). This section is going to use price discrimination as the explanation for promotions.[7]

Price discrimination allows the firm to charge customers different prices depending upon their demand curves. Two variables to discriminate between consumer segments are (1) time and (2) inventory carrying costs. The explanations

---

[6] Uninformed consumers means they do not search for information. If they accidentally obtain it, they are still not "informed."

[7] Search costs or inventory carrying costs can be used as a basis to price discriminate. In fact, Varian and Salop and Stiglitz are discriminating between informed and uninformed consumers.

used in this section could also be included under cost explanations, since time (lost wages) and inventory carrying costs are also related to different consumer costs. However, in this section promotions are being used to charge customers different prices in order to price discriminate.

The basic concept used in this section is simple. Two segments of consumers exist, one with low elasticities (high transaction or holding costs), the other high elasticities (low transaction or holding costs). By offering different prices to these two segments, the firm can increase its profits because the low-cost consumers have a higher elasticity of demand. Retailer promotions or coupons are the vehicle used to offer different prices to these segments.

Coupons as a Form of Price Discrimination

Narasimhan (1984a) developed a model to explain how coupons are used to price discriminate. Several other articles also assume coupons are a price discrimination device. White (1983) argues that coupons are a mechanism which allows manufacturers to discriminate between consumers who comparison shop (coupon users) and consumers who do not (noncoupon users). Levedahl (1983) also finds evidence that coupons serve as a marketing tool to price discriminate between consumers. Narasimhan's article will be used as the basis of this section because it has been widely quoted and offers both theoretical and empirical evidence. (See Chapter 10 for further discussion.)

The theory begins by assuming that the consumer is required to devote time to using coupons. The higher the consumer's wage rate, the greater the value of the time used to redeem coupons. However, some consumers may be more efficient in using coupons because of education. While they may have higher wage rates, they also may require less time. Narasimhan uses these concepts and develops a model of the consumer.

His model begins by assuming there are two goods X and L. X is the good being studied, and L represents leisure time. The consumer's goal is to maximize utility for X and L. The consumer faces three constraints: (1) an income constraint, total income must equal total expenditures; (2) a time constraint, time devoted to work plus leisure plus time to consume good X plus the time to use coupons for good X must be less than or equal to the total time available; and (3) the quantity of X purchased must exceed the quantity of X bought with coupons.

Given this series of constraints the consumer maximizes utility of the goods purchased subject to the three constraints stated. Mathematically,

$$\max U(X, L)$$

subject to:

$$\alpha w(H) + A = P_1 X - S X_1 + P_2 L \qquad \textbf{(4.10a)}$$

$$T = t_1 X + t_2 X_1 + L + H \qquad \textbf{(4.10b)}$$

$$X \geq X_1 \qquad \textbf{(4.10c)}$$

$$X \geq 0 \qquad \textbf{(4.10d)}$$

where

P_1 = price of one unit of X

P_2 = price of one unit of L

X_1 = quantity of X bought with a coupon

S = savings per unit bought with a coupon

H = hours the consumer spends in the labor market

t_1 = time input into the consumption of X_1

t_2 = time input for using one coupon

A = wage income

$w(H)$ = effective number of hours

α = wage rate

T = total number of hours available

L = leisure time

Based on this model, Narasimhan derives several implications:

1. As the wage rate and opportunity cost of time decreases, coupon usage increases.
2. More intensive users of coupons are more price elastic.
3. Higher-priced brands will offer larger coupon savings.
4. Savings per unit of the product will be inversely related to the size.
5. Certain demographic groups will be heavier users of coupons, for example,
   a. Better educated consumers
   b. Nonworking women
   c. Lower-income groups

Note in the analysis of demographics it is assumed other demographic variables are held constant. (For example, better educated, lower-income consumers are heavier users of coupons than are better educated, higher-income consumers.) To evaluate his model, Narasimhan developed two alternative tests. The first concentrated on evaluating whether consumers who use coupons are more price sensitive. The second evaluated different hypotheses about coupon sensitivity for specific demographic groups.

To test the first hypothesis, differences in demand elasticities between users and nonusers of coupons, the following model was used.

$$\ln[QTY(i)] = \alpha_1 \ln[PRICE(i)] + \alpha_2[INCOME(i)]$$
$$+ \alpha_3 \ln[FAMSIZ(i)] + \alpha_4 \ln[EDUFEM(i)] \qquad (4.11)$$
$$+ \alpha_5 \ln[FEMEMP(i)] + \alpha_6 \ln[AGEFEM(i)] + \epsilon(i)$$

where

$QTY(i)$ = annual quantity purchased by the ith household

$PRICE(i)$ = average price paid by the ith household

INCOME(i) = annual income of the ith household

FAMSIZ(i) = number of members in the ith household

EDUFEM(i) = educational level of the female head of the ith household

AGEFEM(i) = age of the female head of the ith household

FEMEMP(i) = employment status of the female head of the ith household

A dummy variable was created to test whether coupon users had different demand elasticities. DRP(i) = α_7[d(i) ln PRICE(i)]. d(i) takes on a value of 1 if the ith household is a coupon user and 0 otherwise. Thus, DRP(i) is used to test the hypothesis that coupon users are more price elastic than are nonusers.

Table 4.3 gives the results. It shows that coupon users are more price elastic. Sixteen of the 20 cases have the correct sign, and almost all the t-ratios are significant. Thus, Narasimhan's work has shown that there is a difference in price responsiveness between coupon users and noncoupon users.

The next hypothesis Narasimhan evaluated was demographic differences between coupon users. Again a model is used to test for significant effects. The

TABLE 4.3 Results of Regression to Test Differences in Demand Elasticities Between Users and Nonusers of Coupons

Product	N	R2	Price		DPR[a]		Income	
Toilet tissues	979	0.21	−0.596	(−5.35)[b]	−0.060	(−4.66)	0.009	(0.27)
Paper towels	932	0.09	−0.518	(−3.18)	0.062	(−0.22)	0.163	(1.96)
Stuffing/dressing	434	0.15	−0.711	(−5.50)	−0.245	(−5.42)	0.077	(1.18)
Hair coloring	205	0.09	−0.455	(−2.70)	0.032	(0.80)	0.166	(1.65)
Hair spray	450	0.13	−0.065	(−7.13)	−0.202	(−2.74)	−0.003	(−0.04)
Shampoo	834	0.37	−0.838	(−16.02)	−0.200	(−5.60)	0.256	(4.96)
Cooking/salad oil	946	0.21	−1.221	(−9.85)	−0.099	(−5.29)	0.129	(−2.64)
Ready to eat cereal	952	0.29	−1.577	(−5.96)	0.856	(2.28)	0.22	(−2.91)
Dog food[c]	432	0.42	−1.498	(−9.69)	0.63	(2.64)	0.202	(2.45)
Dry mix dinners	647	0.24	−0.876	(−9.42)	−0.210	(−6.23)	−0.217	(−3.04)
Bars and squares	247	0.14	0.546	(2.16)	−0.348	(−5.35)	−0.123	(−1.06)
Cake mix	886	0.18	−0.210	(−1.35)	−0.219	(−10.71)	−0.153	(−2.82)
Cat food[c]	329	0.21	−0.485	(−2.13)	−0.642	(−3.96)	0.235	(2.07)
Frozen entrees	715	0.16	−0.601	(−5.30)	−0.346	(−8.46)	−0.044	(−0.59)
Gelatin	773	0.23	−0.971	(−11.05)	−0.278	(−8.57)	−0.067	(−1.09)
Spaghetti sauces	619	0.48	−1.653	(−20.94)	−0.161	(−4.88)	0.045	(0.60)
Creme rinse/ conditioners	493	0.34	−0.824	(−12.44)	−0.295	(−4.60)	0.202	(2.62)
Soups	959	0.30	−1.052	(−15.27)	−0.165	(−8.73)	−0.027	(−8.73)
Other mixes	596	0.22	−0.958	(−9.68)	−0.244	(−9.13)	−0.159	(−2.60)
Hot dogs	884	0.20	−0.585	(−4.08)	−0.182	(−6.20)	−0.162	(−2.94)

[a] *DPR* is 0 for nonusers and equals price for users.
[b] Figures in parentheses are *t*-values.
[c] For dog food and cat food, family size was replaced by number of dogs and number of cats, respectively.

Source: Chakravarthi Narasimhan, "A Price Discrimination Theory of Coupons," *Marketing Science*, Vol. 3 (Spring 1984), pp. 128–146.

model is

$$
\begin{aligned}
\text{Cupont}(i) = {} & \alpha_0 + \alpha_1 \text{ INCOME}(i) + \alpha_2 \text{ INCOME}^2(i) \\
& + \alpha_3 \text{ EDUFEM}(i) + \alpha_4 \text{ FEMEMP}(i) + \alpha_5 \text{ QTY}(i) \\
& + \alpha_6 \text{ QTY}^2(i) + \alpha_7 \text{ DUMCHD}(i) + \alpha_8 \text{ OCC1}(c) \\
& + \alpha_9 \text{ OCC2}(i) + \epsilon(i)
\end{aligned}
\tag{4.12}
$$

where

$\text{Cupont}(i) = $ quantity bought using coupons

$\text{DUMCHD}(i) = $ 1 if household i has children under 18 and 0 otherwise

$\text{QTY}(i) = $ quantity purchased by household i

$\text{OCC1}(i) = $ dummy variable for one set of occupations

$\text{OCC2}(i) = $ dummy variable for another set of occupations

$\text{INCOME}(i)$, $\text{EDUFEM}(i)$, and $\text{FEMEMP}(i)$ were defined in equation (4.11).

Table 4.4 shows the empirical results. The income effect is nonlinear and the effect is an inverted U. Thus, low-income and high-income households behave similarly. The highest-coupon-prone consumer is the middle-income households. Two of the demographic variables have the correct sign. Education of the female head is a positive coefficient in 25 out of 31 cases. Similarly, presence of children has the correct sign in 20 out of 27 cases. Thus, these two variables imply that higher-educated women with children were heavier coupon users.

The variable with the wrong sign is female employment. Narasimhan hypothesized that due to time constraints working women would be less likely to redeem coupons. The explanation may be that it is more lucrative to redeem coupons than work. Suppose it takes one hour to clip $10 worth of coupons. If the average face value of a coupon is $.50, then it is possible that 20 coupons could be clipped within an hour. The $10 is higher than the alternative wage rate, particularly after taxes. If coupons are redeemed every week, this amounts to $500 per year. Thus, working women may find it more advantageous to clip coupons for an hour rather than work for the extra hour. Unfortunately, Narasimhan did not try to determine the alternative return from these various activities. Only women earning significantly higher incomes than they could receive from clipping coupons would choose to substitute an hour of work.[8]

In evaluating Narasimhan's model, can manufacturers justify price discrimination given the cost of couponing? Because it is so difficult to identify heavy coupon users demographically, it is not possible to price discriminate directly. Rather, it is only possible to use self-selection mechanisms (consumers choose to use coupons because they are more price sensitive). On average, 4 percent of coupons are redeemed and there is a large fixed cost of distributing the coupons.

---

[8] Narasimhan actually used opportunity cost of time. Wage rate may only be a proxy. A high value of leisure time results in a high opportunity cost, but opportunity cost is difficult to measure.

TABLE 4.4 Test of Intensity of Coupon Usage

Product	N	R^2	Income	Income²	EDUFEM I[a]	EDUFEM II	EDUFEM III	DUMCHD I	DUMCHD II	DUMCHD III	FEMEMP I	FEMEMP II	FEMEMP III
Toilet tissues	979	0.32	8.2×10^{-3} (2.54)	-2.58×10^{-7} (−2.18)	8.43 (2.80)[b]	—[c]	—	9.24 (1.48)	—	—	−0.38 (−1.40)	—	—
Paper towels	933	0.43	0.0001 (0.57)	-3.89×10^{-3} (−0.52)	0.67 (3.30)	—	—	0.31 (0.21)	−0.44 (−0.81)	0.90 (1.50)	−0.03 (−1.71)	—	—
Stuffing/dressing	434	0.20	0.0002 (0.55)	-4.55×10^{-9} (−0.45)	0.51 (1.49)	—	—	0.90 (1.33)	—	—	—	—	—
Hair coloring	205	0.12	-8.67×10^{-7} (−1.88)	1.86×10^{-11} (1.58)	0.0007 (1.83)	0.0007 (1.83)	−0.0006 (−1.23)	0.00002 (0.03)	—	—	6.8×10^{-5} (1.09)	—	-3.6×10^{-4} (−1.06)
Shampoo	845	0.18	-4.9×10^{-9} (−0.97)	1.43×10^{-8} (0.70)	0.98 (2.27)	—	—	0.16 (0.18)	—	—	0.04 (1.07)	—	—
Cooking/salad oil	946	0.27	0.001 (0.65)	-6.36×10^{-8} (−1.05)	3.25 (2.04)	—	—	1.87 (0.58)	—	—	−0.028 (−0.21)	—	—
Ready to eat cereal	952	0.55	0.0665 (0.76)	-2.91×10^{-7} (−1.12)	23.3 (1.18)	5.01 (0.83)	18.29 (2.60)	17.26 (1.76)	—	—	−0.76 (−1.65)	—	—
Dog food	492	0.34	0.039 (1.03)	-1.5×10^{-5} (−1.27)	100.67 (2.83)	—	—	87.73 (1.30)	—	—	1.09 (0.37)	—	—
Dry mix dinners	648	0.23	1.6×10^{4} (0.15)	2.68×10^{-9} (0.09)	−0.62 (−0.22)	0.39 (0.44)	1.68 (1.69)	3.06 (2.31)	—	—	−0.12 (−1.93)	—	—
Bars and squares	247	0.33	2.2×10^{4} (0.24)	-4.82×10^{-9} (−0.16)	−0.07 (−0.05)	—	—	−1.93 (−0.79)	—	—	0.026 (0.28)	—	—
Cake mix	886	0.50	0.008 (1.88)	-1.61×10^{-7} (−1.18)	9.50 (0.89)	4.11 (1.25)	8.39 (2.29)	−10.47 (−0.60)	14.46 (2.04)	10.60 (1.44)	−0.31 (−1.27)	—	—
Cat food	328	0.43	0.008 (0.49)	-7.90×10^{-7} (−1.40)	8.07 (0.42)	—	—	−31.27 (−0.16)	70.28 (−1.30)	70.50 (1.39)	−3.49 (−2.21)	—	—
Frozen entrees	715	0.18	0.005 (2.31)	-7.90×10^{-8} (−0.91)	1.35 (0.77)	—	—	−1.76 (−0.48)	—	—	−0.89 (−2.78)	—	0.005 (0.06)
Gelatin	774	0.28	4.5×10^{-5} (0.06)	-4.07×10^{-9} (−0.17)	0.65 (1.41)	—	—	−0.83 (0.22)	−0.64 (−0.49)	2.21 (1.58)	−0.03 (−0.68)	—	—
Spaghetti sauces	620	0.22	−0.0003 (−0.14)	1.67×10^{-8} (0.25)	5.25 (1.25)	0.50 (0.32)	4.1 (2.74)	4.21 (1.59)	—	—	−0.13 (−1.03)	—	—
Creme rinse conditioners	499	0.21	0.0002 (0.50)	-6.80×10^{-9} (−0.38)	1.39 (3.46)	—	—	.13 (.17)	—	—	−0.05 (−1.55)	—	—
Soups	959	0.17	0.0016 (1.27)	-4.72×10^{-8} (−0.92)	−1.49 (1.14)	—	—	5.39 (1.99)	—	—	−0.013 (−0.12)	—	—
Other mixes	596	0.33	0.003 (1.65)	-5.55×10^{-8} (−1.12)	−1.05 (−0.34)	0.32 (0.40)	3.34 (2.66)	4.63 (2.08)	—	—	−0.13 (−1.27)	—	—
Hot dogs	885	0.20	0.00037 (2.34)	-9.47×10^{-8} (−2.07)	−0.91 (−0.33)	0.24 (0.20)	2.33 (1.69)	2.05 (1.09)	—	—	−0.53 (−2.94)	—	−0.20 (−1.95)

[a] I, II, and III refer to the following groups, respectively: household with no male head, household with female not employed, household where both are employed.

[b] Figures in parentheses are t-values.

[c] A "—" means that the hypothesis of homogeneity of response across groups could not be rejected and consequently the estimates are the same for all groups for that variable. The critical value of t (for large degrees of freedom) for a one-tailed test is 1.29 at 0.10 level of significance and 1.65 at 0.05 level.

Source: Chakravarthi Narasimhan, "A Price Discrimination Theory of Coupons," *Marketing Science*, Vol. 3 (Spring 1984), pp. 128–146.

While conceptually the self-select argument is correct, the cost of distributing coupons to nonusers may be too great. Thus, self-selection may not pay out.

Retailer Promotions as a Price Discrimination Tool

Narasimhan developed his model to show that couponing was used to price discriminate. In subsequent research, Jeuland and Narasimhan (1985) developed a model based on the idea that consumers have different holding costs and retailers can price discriminate between consumers by using price promotions. This differs from Blattberg et al. Jeuland and Narasimhan are assuming that the goal of promotions is price discrimination, not differential holding costs between the retailer and consumers. The reason is that high-holding-cost consumers will buy when there is no promotion and will hold very little inventory even if there is a promotion.

The following assumptions were used in the Jeuland and Narasimhan model:

1. Buyers are heterogeneous in their demand.
2. Customers differ in their cost to inventory a product.
3. Customers incur no transaction or shopping costs.
4. There is a positive correlation between consumption and holding cost.
5. The seller is more efficient in stocking the product than buyers.

Given these assumptions, Jeuland and Narasimhan derived several implications.

1. Dealing increases demand by attracting consumers with lower reservation prices.
2. No trough will be observed after a promotion.
3. Occasional buyers stockpile whereas "regular" buyers do not.
4. Bulkier items will not necessarily be dealt more frequently.
5. Some selling establishments are more likely to promote than others.

Implication 1 follows from heterogeneous demand. Implication 2 results from their assumption that the retailer is more efficient in stocking the product than the consumer and that only occasional buyers stockpile. Implication 3 is based on the assumption that low-holding-cost consumers have lower consumption rates. Implication 4 comes from the assumption that promotions are demand driven not cost driven. Implication 5 comes from the assumption that different retail establishments cater to different demand segments.

The problem is that it is very difficult to test the implications of this model. How can one evaluate whether higher-holding-cost consumers consume more? Causal empiricism would refute this claim. Does an individual over 70 years old who lives in a small apartment in the city have a lower holding cost than a family of four living in the suburbs? Unlikely. Yet the family of four has much greater consumption for most grocery products. Troughs after deals are also difficult to measure because of the high frequency of dealing in many categories. Consumers do not need to stockpile because next week a deal is offered on a comparable item.

While one can raise many issues about the testability of the model presented, it does offer a plausible explanation for promotions. No doubt some promotions are run to price discriminate. Further research is needed to understand better when promotions can be used to price discriminate.

LOYALS VERSUS SWITCHERS

The section on differential information described Varian's theory that promotions are used to discriminate between informed and uninformed consumers. Narasimhan (1988), Rao (1987), and subsequently Raju et al. (1988) use a model similar to Varian's to explain promotions, but rather than informed and uninformed consumers, they use switchers and nonswitchers. Lattin (1988) and Lal (1988) add the retailer and the manufacturer to the switchers and loyals model to explain trade dealing. This section begins with a discussion of loyals and switchers and then describes Narasimhan's model.

Loyals, Switchers, and the Deal-Prone Consumers

Blattberg and Sen (1974) analyzed consumer panel data and found that one could divide consumers into several segments based on (1) loyalty to a single brand, (2) loyalty to type of brand bought (national versus private label), and (3) deal proneness (deal versus nondeal buyer). Segments of buyers were created based on these three criteria. (See Chapter 3.)

Obviously different product categories will have a higher or lower percentage of deal-oriented buyers as well as potential switchers. When a brand's sales are primarily made up of loyal customers, it becomes costly to promote because the firm is simply reducing price to its regular customers. A brand whose main source of business is from switchers requires frequent promotions to maintain its sales levels. Therefore, the issue becomes what strategies should each firm follow depending on its market position.

Promotional Strategies for Markets with Switchers and Loyals

Narasimhan's (1988) model begins with the following assumptions:

1. Each consumer buys one unit as long as the price is less than or equal to r.
2. There are two firms in the market, each offering a branded product.
3. Consumers can be divided into the following three segments.
   a. Loyal to firm 1 (α_1)
   b. Loyal to firm 2 (α_2)
   c. Switchers (β)
4. There are no intertemporal effects either in terms of quantity bought or changing loyalties.
5. Marginal cost is 0 (for simplicity).

The profit function for the two brands is then

$$\pi_1 = \alpha_1 P_1 + \delta_{12}\beta P_1 \tag{4.13a}$$

$$\pi_2 = \alpha_2 P_2 + \delta_{21}\beta P_2 \tag{4.13b}$$

where

$$\delta_{12} = \begin{cases} 1 \text{ if } P_1 < P_2 \\ \tfrac{1}{2} \text{ if } P_1 = P_2 \\ 0 \text{ if } P_2 < P_1 \end{cases}$$

$$\delta_{21} = \begin{cases} 1 \text{ if } P_2 < P_1 \\ \tfrac{1}{2} \text{ if } P_2 = P_1 \\ 0 \text{ if } P_1 < P_2 \end{cases}$$

Narasimhan shows that no pair of prices results in an equilibrium, because if one firm fixes price, a competitor can increase (short-run) profits by reducing price. This means the two firms have an incentive to randomize prices so that the competitor can not anticipate the firm's price. Therefore, the optimal strategy for each firm will be to vary its price randomly.

Based on the foregoing assumptions, Narasimhan shows that

1. The average price for firm 1 (the one with more loyal consumers) will be higher than for firm 2 (the firm with fewer loyal customers).
2. The more loyalty brand 1 has (α_1) relative to brand 2, the fewer promotions they will run.

The concept of "random" prices does not fit what a manager does. However, analyzing the optimal policy when two firms are "stealing" switchers is relevant. Very little research has addressed this issue. It shows that brands with a strong consumer franchise (high loyalty) are vulnerable to brands that constantly cut price.

There are many potential extensions of the basic model, one of which Narasimhan considers. Suppose the weaker brand (fewer loyals) also has a lower reservation price (valued less by consumers). The same results hold as with the case of equal reservation prices, but the weaker brand operates at lower prices. If $r_1 > r_2$ and $\delta > 0$, the pricing range for the "stronger" brand is (P_1^*, r_1) where P^* is the lowest discount offered. For the weaker brand, the range will be $(P^* - \delta, r_2)$, where δ adjusts price downward.

Another important extension of the model is differences in cost structure. If the brand with significant brand loyalty is also spending a fixed cost on advertising and may have a higher variable cost, then what is the optimal promotional strategy? The weaker brand may want to discount frequently, and the "stronger" brand will not retaliate according to Narasimhan. However, if there are economies of scale in the market, the constant promotion by the weaker brand may result in retaliation by the strong brand, and with high fixed costs and lower variable costs, volume is a key determinant of profit. The strong brand may increase its promotions even though it reduces its profits from loyal customers. Narasimhan does not consider the cost structure of the firms, but this is an obvious extension.

The other issue not considered is the actual mechanism through which brands adjust price. Manufacturers reduce price to the retailer (channel of distribution) who then determines which promotions to pass through. The retailer has a different motivation from that of the manufacturer. The retailer wants to attract traffic to the store or to gain incremental sales for the category. Strong brands are more desirable to promote because more consumers purchase the product and are more likely to change stores to shop for a strong brand. Thus, while the manufacturer of weak brands may promote more frequently, some percentage of these promotions do not reach consumers. On the other hand, the strong brands may promote less often, but when they promote the retailer passes it through.

Rao (1987) used a similar model to Narasimhan, though his goal was to explain private versus national brand promotions. He assumes that the buyer has a higher reservation price for the national brand. The national brand promotes to attract private-label customers. However, there are conditions under which the national brand will not promote. If the number of switchers is small, the national brand will not promote because it is too costly to attract private-label customers. Thus, his explanation for promotions is driven by the national brand "randomizing" price to avoid the private label from being able to price slightly below the differences in reservation prices. By randomizing the national brand captures the optimal mixture of loyal and nonloyal sales.

The private label will not promote because it has only nonloyal customers. It attracts a segment of nonloyal customers except when the national brand promotes. It has no incentive to promote because it increases the frequency of promotions by the national brand, thus eroding its share.

While the empirical evidence would show that private labels are promoted, generic brands are rarely promoted. Thus, promotions and their frequency may be a function of the price tier the brand is in. (See Blattberg and Wisniewski, 1988, for a discussion of price tiers.)

Rao's paper, like Narasimhan's, omits the retailer. However, Lattin (1988) and Lal (1988) use arguments similar to Rao's and explain promotions are driven by competition between brands from different price tiers. This is discussed in the next section.

Raju et al. (1988) use a similar approach to Narasimhan. The difference is in the way loyal and switchers are defined. The implications also are different. For example, Raju et al. find that stronger brands offer deeper discounts than weaker brands but stronger brands promote less frequently. Narasimhan shows that the stronger brand has smaller discounts than the weaker brands. In evaluating these differences, it is disconcerting to see that similar models lead to different implications. Obviously, the models' implications are very sensitive to the assumptions.

The tests of these models are also difficult to do because the data required are for manufacturer's actions. Unfortunately, the manufacturer's promotional activities are translated into retailer activities. Most of the empirical work uses frequency and depth of the retailer's promotions. Unfortunately, these data do not test these models.

Trade Deals and the Retailer

An important extension to the ideas discussed in Rao, Narasimhan, and Raju et al. is the inclusion of the retailers into the market structure. Lattin (1988) uses an argument similar to Rao's and shows that the manufacturer should offer occasional trade deals to lower the manufacturer's price to induce the retailer to promote. The remainder of the argument is similar to Rao's. The retailer, however, is maximizing profits and hence will promote if a lower price is offered (trade deal) for the national brand and there is a large enough switcher segment.

Lattin argues that the national brand has no incentive to promote if there is no private label or if the size of this segment is small. Because his model does not include other manufacturers fighting for switchers, there will be no incentive to offer a trade deal to capture the national brand switcher segment.

Lal (1988) also uses the concept of brands in different price tiers "causing" trade deals. Rather than a mixed strategy, he argues that trade deals are the result of "implicit collusion" among national brands. In his model there are two national brands and one private label (or lower-price tier brand). To compete in the price-sensitive market segment, the national brands alternate trade deals, and the retailer passes the trade deal on to the consumer. By alternating price, the higher-priced national brands capture a significant share of the price-sensitive consumers. Implicit collusion occurs because both national-brand manufacturers recognize it is not in their interest to cut one another's throat. They, therefore, alternate promotions.

Lal presents empirical evidence from Coke and Pepsi alternating promotions (26 weeks each) as evidence of this behavior. There are many retail categories in which one national brand is promoted every week. Whether this is evidence of a mixed strategy, implicit collusion, or another theory is difficult to evaluate. Lal would not predict that private labels would be promoted, and yet they are.

Both Lattin and Lal make important extension to the literature on the causes of promotions. Both miss an important issue: forward buying. Forward buying decreases the profitability of the trade deal and may make it far too costly to try to price discriminate. Only if the manufacturer can reduce forward buying will it then be possible to properly discriminate between higher- and lower-price tier buyers.

COMPETITIVE EXPLANATIONS

One of the most commonly used explanations for why promotions are used is the "prisoner's dilemma." The concept is that if firm A cuts price, firm B must match the price or else lose profits. While it is optimal for each firm to price at a higher level, the problem is that it is profitable for each firm to cut price if the other does not match. Thus, the firms end up at a lower price than if they colluded. This section explains the theory of the prisoner's dilemma and discusses its implications for promotional strategies. (Also see Chapter 15 for a discussion of the prisoner's dilemma.)

Theory of the Prisoner's Dilemma

The prisoner's dilemma is a two-person *noncooperative* game. The name is developed from the original example of this problem. Its structure is simple. There are two guilty persons who have been captured, put into prison, and then interrogated. If prisoner A confesses that they both did it and prisoner B does not confess, prisoner A is set free and prisoner B receives a 10-year prison sentence. Similarly, if prisoner B confesses, and prisoner A does not confess, B is set free and A receives a 10-year sentence. If both confess, each receives a 5-year sentence. If neither confesses, each receives a 2-year sentence.

The problem can be structured using a payoff matrix.

		Prisoner B	
		Does Not Confess	*Confesses*
Prisoner A	Does Not Confess	(2, 2)	(10, 0)
	Confesses	(0, 10)	(5, 5)

The matrix is read as follows: The first element is the sentence for prisoner A; the second element is the sentence for prisoner B. Thus, for row 1, column 1, in which A and B do not confess, the entry is (2, 2). This indicates that prisoner A receives a sentence of 2 years and prisoner B receives a sentence of 2 years. The other cells of the matrix are read in similar manner.

In designing a strategy, prisoner A has two options: confess or not confess. The payoff matrix for prisoner A is

		Prisoner B	
		Does Not Confess	*Confesses*
Prisoner A	Does Not Confess	2	10
	Confesses	0	5

If prisoner B does not confess, the best strategy for prisoner A is to confess (0- versus 2-year sentence). If prisoner B does confess, the best strategy for prisoner A is to confess (5- versus 10-year sentence). Thus, no matter what prisoner B does, prisoner A should confess.

A similar analysis for prisoner B shows it is optimal to confess. Thus, both prisoners will confess. Yet, it is optimal for both prisoners not to confess; 2-year sentences for each rather than 5 years for each if they both confess. Hence the name, "the prisoner's dilemma." The result is that it would be optimal for both prisoners to collude and agree not to confess. The problem is that they are not allowed to meet.

The Prisoner's Dilemma Applied to Promotions

It is easy to apply the prisoner's dilemma to promotions, particularly to retailer promotions and manufacturer's trade deals. If there are two firm's competing, then the payoff matrix looks like the example given in the previous section, except that the decisions are changed.

		Firm B	
		No Promotion	*Promotion*
Firm A	No Promotion	(High, High)	(Lowest, Highest)
	Promotion	(Highest, Lowest)	(Low, Low)

The pattern is the same as in the preceding section. If one firm promotes and the other does not, then the firm promoting has the highest profits and the firm not promoting has the lowest profits.

In many circumstances both firms are better off not promoting. However, if one firm promotes and the other does not, then the firm that promotes captures an increased market share at the expense of the firm that does not promote. The result is each firm promotes just as each prisoner confesses.

The real issue then becomes: "How can firms signal each other not to promote?" The answer is not easy. However, some research has been conducted on prisoner dilemma games in which the players (firms) have multiple plays. Axelrod (1980a, b) has written several articles analyzing strategies for playing these types of games. His research shows that a "tit-for-tat" strategy results in the highest profits. "Tit-for-tat" means you always *follow* the moves your opponent is making. If they promote, you promote. If they stop promoting, you stop promoting.

The best example is a gas station who starts a price war. When gas station 1 drops price, all stations on the same corner (same vicinity) drop price. The result is identical prices for all stations but now at a lower price. Quickly, they realize they have not gained an advantage relative to one another and when one raises price they all follow, recognizing there is no advantage to pricing lower.

For trade deals and retailer promotions, "tit-for-tat" is more difficult to execute. For retailer promotions there are long lead times between internal decisions and when the competitor finds out the action taken. Many retailer promotions require 4 to 6 weeks to produce the ads in which the price reductions appear. Second, the decisions are less reversible in the short run. Even if a retailer announces the elimination of all promotions, it would take 6 weeks before it reaches the market and then another 6 weeks before its competitor could change its promotional policy.

For trade deals, competitors do not always know their competition's trade deals. Therefore, it is easy for each side to "cheat." Both firms have a strong incentive to cheat, and therefore because of the difficulty of monitoring the other's activity, it becomes difficult to know what their competitor's actions are.

"Tit-for-tat" is actually part of a more general concept called signaling. In effect, by making well-defined moves (always matching a competition), the firm is signaling to its competitor what actions it will take. There are other types of signals such as general announcements in the press. The president of General Foods could announce that his firm will match its competitors' trade deals dollar for dollar, *but* he thinks trade dealing is hurting the industry. This "signal" is trying to tell General Foods' competitors that trade dealing is not in anyone's interest, *but* if the competitors trade deal, General Foods will match their offers. This is a "tit-for-tat" strategy in which General Foods is indicating it is willing to stop heavy trade dealing. There are many other types of signals that can be used. Porter (1980) describes many of these and gives examples.

In summary, the prisoner's dilemma is a commonly used explanation of why promotions continue even though they might not be profitable. The major question is: "How can firms stop promoting if it is unprofitable?" Several approaches such as "tit-for-tat" and signaling may offer a solution in some situations. However, to date, the answers to this question are not very satisfactory. (See Chapter 15 for a further discussion of the prisoner's dilemma and signaling.)

IMPLICATIONS FOR MARKETING MANAGERS

While the theory of why promotions are used is of academic interest, it is also important to marketing managers because the types of strategies and tactics they use will depend upon the underlying reasons why promotions increase a firm's sales. This section describes the implications for marketing managers of the different economic theories given in the preceding sections.

The easiest explanation for managers to understand is the use of promotions to reduce excess inventories or sell obsolete goods. Therefore, little more needs to be said about this explanation.

One of the most interesting explanations of promotions was given by Lazear. He indicated that it is optimal to promote when demand is uncertain and the retailer has only one shot at the customer. In this situation it is better to price high and then drop price overtime because one cannot estimate what the customer will pay for the good. Intuitively most retailers, real estate brokers, and others selling goods where it is difficult to estimate the customer's willingness to pay for the good understand this pricing policy. However, Lazear also showed that for products in which there are very few potential customers, a firm must be very careful about charging too high a price on the first pass because they may lose the few customers willing to buy the product. Thus, very expensive high-fashion clothing or an expensive home should receive lower percentage discounts overtime than should products with a large number of prospective buyers. This type of strategy is not understood by most retailers.

There is one other implication of Lazear's model that offers some insight for management. It is clear that learning the shape of the demand curve is highly valuable to a firm selling an item. Research techniques should be developed to try to estimate demand early in the "selling season" and then modify price based on these estimates. Lazear assumes that only one unit is being sold. However, if multiple units are sold then the retailer may be able to adjust price on the basis of early returns. Developing a database of information about early sales of each item then allows the retailer or firm to modify its price depending on the information received. While modifying price early is not a promotion, it is optimal when demand is uncertain.

Two articles showed that promotions were caused by retailers discriminating between informed and uninformed consumers. Obviously, if this is true, then retailers should analyze those items for which informed customers devote considerable time learning prices. Clearly for expensive items consumers spend more time trying to find low prices. These types of items may not be very good items to promote because all retailers will try to price them competitively. It may be that items that represent less significant expenditures but are heavily shopped by informed consumers may be the best items to promote if the theory is correct.

For researchers it would be interesting to try to determine whether informational differences is the basis for promotions. To do this would require analyzing those items that are heavily promoted and determining the degree to which consumers know the promoted prices. Dickson and Sawyer (1986) indicated 50 percent of consumers know promoted prices. If the theory is correct, consumers who know the prices in the market will shop at stores that have the lowest prices. This should be testable. One could ask informed consumers if they shop more stores.

The model of loyals versus switchers developed by Narasimhan if modified to incorporate the retailer has strong implications for brand managers. Lattin (1988) and Lal (1988) have attempted to do this. First, if a brand has a large number of switchers making up its sales, then it should be heavily promoted because the brand with a large number of loyal customers cannot cost effectively promote as frequently. Thus, weaker brands (in term of loyalty) should use promotions as an offensive weapon.

If one looks at brands market by market (e.g., Standard Metropolitan Statistical Area), it is possible to develop a different strategy for every market depending on the degree of loyalty the brand exhibits. With scanner diary panel becoming available on a local level, it will become possible for the brand manager to analyze the degree of loyalty exhibited by his or her brand and then design a special promotional strategy for each market.

There are several implications for both retailers and manufacturers based on the theory of shifting inventory costs. For the manufacturers, those items which have high storage costs for the retailer may be very good items to promote because the retailer will not stockpile them. The retailer will pass the promotion on to the consumer. Examples are items such as paper products and liquid bleach. Those items which can be stockpiled by the retailer at a low cost such as canned tuna may not be as good an item to trade deal because the retailer has a low holding cost and therefore is willing to "forward buy" a large number of weeks supplies of the item. (Also see Chapter 11 and 14 for a discussion of this issue.)

For the retailer, inventory behavior by the consumer determines the types of items that should be promoted. First, if an item can be more cost effectively stored by the consumer, then the retailer will want to promote it. Examples may be soft drinks which are direct store delivered and which cannot be easily stockpiled by the store unless they can be put in a special warehouse. The low-holding-cost consumers simply store soft drinks in their garages or basements. Other items which fit this classification are paper products or any product whose price per cubic inch is low. More analysis of relative holding costs of retailers and consumers should be able to determine promotion-sensitive items.

The use of coupons as a means to price discriminate has potential application to most packaged goods companies. Currently new databases are being generated in which information will be available for (1) consumers' willingness to redeem coupons and (2) the regular brands the consumer buys. Once these data are available it will be possible to offer coupons to consumers willing to redeem who regularly buy the competitor's brand. For example, if a consumer regularly buys Folgers coffee and is a user of coupons, then General Foods can offer a $1 coupon to that consumer to buy Maxwell House Coffee. If, on the other hand, a consumer regularly buys Maxwell House Coffee, then General Foods does not send that consumer a coupon. Thus, coupons can become a highly effective tool for price discriminating between different types of consumers. (See Chapter 10.)

Finally the most important explanation to most marketing managers is the prisoner's dilemma. Most manufacturers and retailers believe they are in a prisoner's dilemma. The issue becomes: How they can overcome the dilemma? The methods described (such as tit-for-tat or signaling) may not work. As data become available from scanners, manufacturers may notice that it is not in their interest to promote even if their competitor can gain a short-term advantage because the category is not promotion sensitive. Even though a firm increases its volume through offering a trade promotion, the retailer's forward buying may be too costly such that the increase in share will not compensate for the lower average price received. However, if this is not the case, then signaling may be the only solution. (See Chapter 15.)

In summary, the theories described in this chapter were not intended for managers when they were originally developed. However, a retailer or brand manager will need to understand the reason that promotions increase sales to maximize the effectiveness of the promotions offered.

The explanations given can be summarized as follows:

1. Reduce excess or obsolete inventories.
2. Price high and then reduce price overtime when there is significant uncertainty about the demand for a product. For this strategy to hold, the customer will return to buy only if the price is reduced.

3. Variation in the price is a way for retailers and other types of firms to discriminate between informed and uninformed customers.

4. Promotions allow firms to battle each other for the brand switchers. Weaker firms (with fewer loyal customers) can compete effectively against stronger firms through the use of promotions.

5. Retailers use promotions to induce low-holding-cost customers to inventory items for which they can more cost effectively stockpile than the retailer.

6. Coupons can be used as a mechanism for price discriminating between regular and occasional users of a product.

7. Promotional wars are caused by each firm in the market being afraid that if it does not promote it will lose significant market share and profits if its competitors promote. This is called the prisoner's dilemma. Signaling and tit-for-tat may be ways to reduce promotional activity.

5

How Promotions Affect Sales

In this chapter we examine four basic mechanisms by which promotions affect sales: brand switching, repeat purchasing, purchase acceleration, and category expansion. These mechanisms are defined as follows:

Brand switching	The consumer is induced to purchase a different brand from that which would have been purchased had the promotion not been available.
Repeat purchasing	The consumer's probability of buying the brand again in the future is influenced by purchasing the brand on promotion.
Purchase acceleration	The consumer's purchase timing or purchase quantity is changed by the promotion.
Category expansion	The consumer's total consumption of the product category is increased by the promotion.

In this chapter, we study these effects in depth. For each mechanism, we elaborate upon the foregoing definition and then examine relevant theory and empirical evidence pertaining to the mechanism. The theories we draw upon are those described in Chapters 2 and 4. We conclude with a discussion of the combined impact of these mechanisms.

BRAND SWITCHING

Conceptual Issues

A useful distinction can be made between "aggressive" and "defensive" brand switching effects due to promotion. An aggressive switching effect occurs when the promotion induces the consumer to buy a different brand on the current purchase occasion than the brand he or she bought on the previous occasion. A defensive switching effect occurs when a promotion for brand A on the current purchase occasion induces the consumer who previously bought brand A to purchase brand A on the current purchase occasion, rather than purchase a different brand. Empirical analyses do not usually distinguish between aggressive and defensive brand switching. For example, econometric models with cross-elasticity terms calculate the net amount of aggressive and defensive brand switching. However, it is important for a manager to know whether promotions are serving to keep current customers or attract new ones.

While the manufacturer is concerned with purchase of one brand versus another, for the retailer, the "brand" in question might refer to a particular store. A consumer may respond to a retailer promotion by switching stores, that is, shopping at a different store than the store he or she would have had the retailer promotion not been offered. From the retailer's point of view, store switching can be much more important than brand switching. It is also interesting to consider the relationship between store switching and brand switching. For example, a consumer promotion might induce a consumer to switch brands, but the consumer might then decide to switch stores because he or she knows that the switched-to brand is more likely to be available at a different store. Similarly, a decision to switch stores might also cause the consumer to switch brands, because the new store represents a different purchase environment. In conclusion, store switching and brand switching can be related to each other simultaneously.

Theory

A simple theoretical explanation of why promotions induce brand switching is based on the linear attitude model. By offering a price discount, promotions increase the consumer's overall attitude toward buying the brand. The degree to which this occurs depends on the size of the discount (this influences the consumer's belief that the brand is low priced) and the importance the consumer attaches to low price. If overall attitude for the brand would have been much lower than some competing brand had the promotion not been offered, then the promotion is likely to cause a switch to the promoted brand.

The utility-theoretic view of a price cut would provide a similar view of brand switching. In this case, the price cut changes the nature of the budget constraint faced by the consumer. It may allow the consumer to fit into his or her budget an expensive brand that otherwise could not have been "afforded" or may induce the consumer to buy a brand that previously could be afforded, but whose purchase now at an even lower price will allow the consumer to buy other items in different product categories from the promoted brand.

The utility and attitude arguments do not explain why nonprice promotions such as features and displays induce brand switching, why certain forms of offering the same discount may be more effective than others, or why promotions may help to induce a switch to a new product. Classical conditioning, the consumer decision process, price perception theories, and perceived risk are helpful here (see Chapter 2 for full discussions of these theories).

From a classical conditioning viewpoint, features and displays may induce switching because such promotions serve as conditioned stimuli associated with price reductions. That is, the consumer has been "trained" to associate features and displays with price reductions, so responds to the feature and display even if a price reduction is not also present.

Consumer decision-making models, both low and high involvement, also provide important explanations for why nonprice promotions may induce brand switching. In the low-involvement situation, consumers may simply buy the brand most readily available, which would be the displayed brand. A simple newspaper advertisement may remind the consumer that he or she needs coffee, and since the brand name is attached to the ad, the consumer goes to the store thinking, "I need brand X coffee." In high-involvement situations, promotions can structure information search toward a particular brand (e.g., test driving a particular automobile) or interrupt a well-reasoned intention to buy a particular brand (e.g., the consumer was going to buy Brand X, but Brand Y was conveniently on display).

Price perception theories would suggest that alternative forms of expressing a price promotion can have different effects on brand switching. The critical issues here include provision of a suggested reference price and using a "sale" sign or other signal. The key to an effective price discount is the extent to which the consumer is convinced that the price discount is substantial. Provision of a suggested reference price or other point-of-purchase materials are tools for doing this. For example, one explanation for why coupons are effective is the certainty of the reference price. Consider the case that the consumer bought brand C last time, but has only a slight preference for that brand. Brands A and B are equally preferred. The consumer has a 40¢ coupon for brand B, and the following information is available to the consumer at the point of purchase:

Brand A	Brand B	Brand C
SALE!	$1.99	$1.99
Reg. $1.99		
Now $1.59		

Since the consumer has only a slight preference for brand C, he or she will be willing to switch away from that brand if the competition offers a price reduction. Since the consumer has a coupon for brand B, he or she has no doubt that 40 cents will be saved in buying brand B. However, belief in the discount available from buying brand A depends on the consumer's perceived reference price for brand A, and how readily he or she accepts the suggested reference price and "SALE" sign. We learned in Chapter 2 that consumers do not fully accept suggested reference prices and that a "SALE" sign can sometimes be viewed suspiciously. This would suggest that for an equal discount level, coupons would be more effective switch inducers than in-store price reductions.

Another potential reason why alternative forms of price reduction induce different degrees of switching is the smart-shopper phenomenon (see Chapter 10).

The smart-shopper phenomenon suggests that consumers will buy a brand with a coupon simply because of the pride the consumer takes in proactively obtaining a lower price. Therefore, if the consumer is faced with a choice between two equally acceptable brands, one displayed as on sale and the other not on sale but one for which the consumer has a coupon, the sense of control and pride associated with using a coupon will shift the purchase probability in the direction of the couponed brand.

Trial of a new product is a special type of brand-switching situation, because of the risk to the consumer in switching to a new brand with uncertain performance characteristics. The theory of perceived risk suggests that a price reduction for the new product serves as a risk premium to compensate the consumer for risking trial of the new product.

An important question involving price promotion–induced brand switching is what causes asymmetry in price cross-elasticities. That is, why might brand A draw from brand B but brand B not draw from brand A? Blattberg and Wisniewski (1986) have developed a theoretical explanation for this based on the distribution of quality/price preferences in the population. For example, consider the case that the bulk of the population prefers low price at the expense of high quality. Also assume that there are two brands, high and low quality, with the former priced higher than the latter. If the high-quality brand now cuts its price, many sales will be drawn from the low-quality brand, because the high-quality brand is now positioning itself closer to what the bulk of the population wants— low price. If instead the low-quality brand cuts its price even further below that of the high-quality brand, there are not many sales to be gained, because the bulk of price-conscious consumers are already purchasing that brand. As a result, price cuts for the high-quality brand draw sales from the low-quality brand, but price cuts for the low-quality brand do not draw from the high-quality brand. Blattberg and Wisniewski evolve from this idea a theory of price tiers, whereby brands in different tiers would be expected to compete asymmetrically with respect to price cuts.

In summary, then, there are many theories that explain why promotions induce brand switching, and why some promotions might be more effective than others. We now turn to the empirical evidence of promotion-induced brand switching.

Empirical Evidence

Despite the apparent simplicity of the concept of brand switching, it is not easy to find a simple example of brand switching at work. One cannot simply look at an increase in sales associated with a promotion and conclude that switching has occurred. The increase in sales may be due to category expansion or to purchase acceleration. Figure 5.1, however, presents a relatively clear-cut example.

Figure 5.1 presents sales of two competing brands in one chain of supermarkets located in the same geographic area. Brand A was heavily discounted in

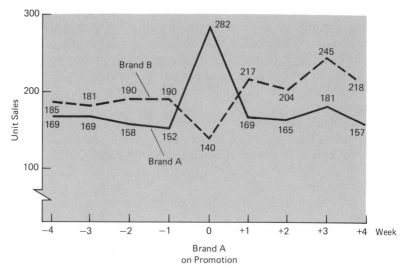

FIGURE 5.1 An Example of Brand Switching (Brand A on Promotion in Week 0)

Data courtesy of Hannaford Bros. Co., Scarborough, Maine

week 0 and experienced a clear increase in sales. If we average the prior four weeks, the increase up to 282 packages represents an increase of 120 packages. It appears that at least some of these sales represent switches from brand B. Averaging brand B's prior four weeks, brand B experienced a drop of 46 packages in the week brand A was promoted. Note that we have not explained brand A's total sales increase. Acceleration and category expansion effects may also be at work, as well as switching from other brands or from other stores. We will return later in this chapter to the question of how the different sales effect mechanisms can interact. At this point, Figure 5.1 does serve the important purpose of documenting brand switching.

Table 5.1 presents calculations for the regular caffeinated and instant caffeinated coffee product categories that provide insights on the comparative switching effects of coupons versus in-store promotions. The table displays the likelihood that purchases using various promotions are of a different brand than that purchased on the previous occasion. Note that the displayed numbers represent associations and not necessarily causality and that we are measuring aggressive and not defensive brand switches as discussed earlier.

Given these caveats, however, the results in Table 5.1 offer some interesting insights. They show that coupons, either manufacturer or retailer distributed, are very strongly associated with brand switching. Various combinations of retailer promotions can have a stronger association with brand-switching than do coupons. However, as a single promotional tool, coupons generally have the strongest associations with brand switching. These results are consistent with Johnson's (1984, Fig. 3). In an analysis of 14 brands, Johnson found that coupons were more

TABLE 5.1   Associations Between Deal Purchases and Purchasing Different Brand on Successive Purchase Occasions

Promotion(s) Used in Purchase	Percentage of Current Purchases That Was of a Different Brand from the Previous Purchase			
	Regular Caffeinated Coffee		Instant Caffeinated Coffee	
	No. of Occasions	% Brand Switching	No. of Occasions	% Brand Switching
No promotion	8,071	32.1%	4,438	32.2%
Manufacturer coupon only	874	56.1	1,200	47.1
Store coupon only	316	47.2	177	45.2
Feature only	725	41.5	163	35.6
Display only	576	31.9	65	47.7
Price cut only	919	33.4	337	38.6
Feature/store coupon	1,484	46.0	276	41.3
Feature/display	909	53.9	111	54.1
Store coupon/feature/display	1,023	66.0	221	45.7
Display/price cut	263	55.9	41	46.3
Feature/price cut	942	48.3	137	46.0
Feature/price cut/display	1,875	66.6	238	45.0
Other combinations	811	53.4	586	52.0
Total	18,788	43.4	7,990	38.3

Source: Data courtesy of Information Resources, Inc., Chicago, Illinois.

strongly associated with brand switching than was consumers' self-reported purchasing on "store specials."

Table 5.1 is not conclusive because of issues of causality and interpretation as noted. However, it challenges us to uncover an explanation for the apparent brand-switching power of coupons. A few possible explanations are:

1. Coupons are indeed more effective switch inducers. This is because of the clear, believable communication of a price discount and the smart-shopper phenomenon.
2. Coupons are used by switchers. Either natural switchers seek out coupons or coupons are targeted toward those who are known to be switchers.
3. The type of switching induced by in-store promotions is more likely to be defensive (i.e., the store promotion keeps the consumer in the franchise) than aggressive (i.e., the store promotion attracts other brands' loyal customers).
4. The previous purchase for coupon users is more likely also to involve a coupon, and coupons break down brand loyalty. The effect in Table 5.1 is therefore more an illustration of the deleterious repeat purchase effects of couponing than their switching abilities.

While the data as displayed in Table 5.1 do not allow one to choose among the preceding explanations, the data illustrate the complexity of the switching phenomenon and the need to understand it more fully.

More statistically rigorous evidence of switching due to promotions comes from econometric models. The measure of brand switching calculated using these models is cross-elasticity. Kumar and Leone (1988) examined a market dominated by three brands. Brand A was lowest price and moderate quality, while brands B and C were of comparable levels of price and quality, both being higher than brand A. Kumar and Leone found that brand B and brand C attracted sales from each other when they reduced price. Brand A's price reductions, however, did not draw from either brand B or brand C. Brand C's price reductions did draw from brand A.

The first important finding is that the cross-elasticities are asymmetric. Second, brand C, a higher-tier brand, draws from brand A, a lower-tier brand, although brand A does not draw from either of the higher-tier brands. The view that emerges is that a brand's promotions draw from other brands within its own price tier or from brands in lower tiers. This is exactly what Blattberg and Wisniewski (1986) find, using a similar econometric model but in four different product categories. For example, they estimate that the sales of 14 out of 15 premium brands were affected by price cuts of other premium brands, but only 2 out of 15 premium brands were affected by the price cuts of middle-tier brands, and only 1 out of 10 premium brands were affected by generic brands. Similarly, the sales of middle-tier brands were affected by price cuts by high- and other middle-tier brands, but not by price cuts by generics. Generics were moderately affected by price cuts from premium and middle-tier brands.

Both Kumar and Leone's and Blattberg and Wisniewski's results provide substantial evidence that promotion-induced brand switching is asymmetric between brands. The results also show that a significant portion of the variation in these asymmetries can be explained by price tiers, and this provides evidence of the importance of Blattberg and Wisniewski's theory. Future research is needed to explain these asymmetries still further.

Evidence on store switching is less plentiful than is evidence on brand switching. Kumar and Leone (1988) found statistically significant price cross-elasticities between stores for sales of diapers. That is, when one store decreased its price, a competing store would have lower sales. Walters and MacKenzie (1988), however, found little association between store traffic and the particular product category promoted as a loss leader, or the use of double couponing (see also Walters and Rinne, 1986). Clearly, there is a need to expand upon this pioneering research.

REPEAT PURCHASING

Conceptual Issues

There are two types of repeat purchase effects connected with sales promotion. The first occurs simply because any purchase of a brand has implications beyond the immediate purchase occasion: The consumer forms a habit toward purchasing the brand, sustains that habit, or learns about the performance of the brand.

Because sales promotions can induce purchases that would not otherwise occur (e.g., by causing a brand switch or category expansion), this effect becomes very relevant in the study of sales promotion. We call it the "purchase effect." The second effect involves a change in purchase probability due to purchasing the brand *on promotion*. For example, purchasing a brand on promotion may weaken the consumer's attitude toward the brand, and therefore decrease his or her probability of subsequently buying the brand. We call this the "promotion usage" effect. The promotion usage effect occurs distinctly because a purchase has been made on promotion.

The purchase and promotion usage effects on repeat purchasing can occur simultaneously. For example, a consumer might purchase brand A as a result of a promotion and, due to habit formation, be more likely to buy it next time than if he or she had not bought the brand at all. However, the consumer's repurchase probability might be lower than it would have been had the purchase taken place "naturally" because use of the promotion denigrates brand A in the eyes of the consumer. Again, the difference between the purchase and promotion usage effects is that the purchase effect takes place simply because the brand is purchased, while the promotion usage effect takes place because the brand is purchased *on promotion*.

Repeat purchase effects due to promotion take on a broader meaning with respect to durable goods. In this case, repeat purchasing may mean more than simply repurchasing the same brand again. The effect may be on repeat purchasing the same product line or continued use of the manufacturer's service facilities. For example, the satisfied user of a particular manufacturer's refrigerator may be more likely subsequently to buy that manufacturer's dishwasher or microwave oven. The tendency of common branding for durables is consistent with this repeat purchase effect. In the case of automobiles, purchase of a dealer's automobile may encourage subsequent use of the dealer's service facilities. Dhebar et al. (1987) illustrate how important this type of repeat purchasing can be. While not the same as the classic buy-brand-A-again repeat purchase effect, these examples are still repeat purchase effects in that they represent sales benefits that occur after a purchase on promotion.

Theory

The two prevalent (and often conflicting) theories addressing the promotion usage repeat purchase effect are operant conditioning and attribution theory. Operant conditioning views promotions as rewards that enable the consumer to learn to continue buying the product. As discussed in Chapter 2, the nature of this reward has important implications for future purchasing behavior. The key is to design the reward so that it is strong enough to provide the encouragement and reinforcement the consumer needs to sustain the behavior, yet not so strong that the consumer learns only to seek out promotions in the future.

Attribution theory considers the causal judgments consumers make when they purchase a brand. The concern is that when the purchase involves use of a promotion, these judgments may be negative. For example, the thought that "I must have bought this brand because it was on promotion" weakens the consumer's intrinsic interest in or preference for the brand. Once the promotion is no longer available, there is no firm cognitive reason for the consumer to continue buying. This is an example of self-perception theory.

Another example of negative attribution is when the brand is directly perceived as lower quality as a result of the promotion. The consumer asks: "Why is this brand on promotion?" and answers: "Because it's low quality and the store manager wants to get rid of it." As a result, the consumer may buy once because the price is so low, but has made a negative inference about the quality of the brand that will lower the probability of a subsequent purchase of the brand.

In fact, the results of this "object perception" might color the product consumption experience by setting up a bias on the part of the consumer to confirm poor quality. In particular, the poor quality judgment the consumer forms at the point of purchase causes him or her to look for the signs of poor quality once the product is consumed (e.g., "I didn't expect this paper towel to be absorbent. That's why they had to give it away," or, after taking a test drive: "Just as I thought, this confirms why they're offering a rebate on this car: It simply rides terribly.") Deighton (1984) documented this type of effect in the case of advertising, and the point is well taken: Attributions made at the point of purchase can disadvantage the brand before it is even consumed.

The purchase effect on repeat purchasing is supported by theories of habit formation and learning (see Assael, 1987, Ch. 3, for a thorough discussion and further references). For example, in the Hullian model (Chapter 2) habit is one of four major forces contributing to sustained behavior. By causing the consumer to purchase brand A, a promotion is taking the consumer along the first step toward establishing a habit. By keeping another consumer from wandering away from an already established behavior, the promotion is helping to sustain a habit. Habit also plays an important role in the low-involvement decision-making model. The low-involvement consumer does not want to spend a great deal of time thinking about decision-making. Forming a habit is a convenient way to simplify the question of what brand to buy.

Consumer learning is presumed to occur when the consumer examines actual brand performance. Learning in this sense is an important element of the high-involvement decision model. Even low-involvement consumers often examine their product's performance, if only to decide whether to make purchasing it a habit. The concept of learning about the brand is embedded in choice models such as the linear learning model and the bargain value model reviewed in Chapter 8.

In summary, there is ample theory to support both a purchase effect and a promotion usage effect on repeat purchasing. The purchase effect, if it exists, is expected to be positive, but there is theoretical debate as to whether the promotion usage effect should be positive or negative. If the effect is negative, the question becomes: Which effect is greater, the positive purchase effect or the negative promotion usage effect? We will investigate this issue shortly. It is noteworthy, however, that neither effect may be at work. First, the purchase effect may not exist in a very-high-involvement brand category, where each purchase is carefully considered and consumers know a great deal about the alternative brands available (many durables categories might fit this description). Second, consumers may be objective about evaluating the consumption experience, and are not influenced by the fact that the brand was bought about promotion. They may put less thought in the evaluation process than the attribution theorists assume, and more thought than the operant conditioning theorists assume.

Empirical Evidence

Aaker's New Trier Model: The Purchase Effect on Repeat Purchasing.   Aaker (1971) developed a model that explicitly considered the purchase effect on repeat purchases. He proposed that a "new trier" of a particular brand would initially have a high probability of repeat purchasing the brand, but that probability would decrease to some long-run probability after a few purchase occasions. Consistent with our earlier discussion of the purchase effect, Aaker assumed that the timing and magnitude of the decrease would depend on the consumer learning about the product while at the same time forming a habit toward buying it. The brand was considered to be on "trial" for the first few purchase occasions after it is purchased; that is, the brand must be experienced for a few periods for the consumer to learn about the brand's attributes. During this period, probability of purchase is assumed to be high. Once the consumer fully learns about the brand, purchase probability then begins to decline to its long-term value. The brand is also vulnerable to outright rejection because habit strength is not yet firmly established. For example, promotion of some competing brand could cause rejection of the brand.

Aaker's findings were that the trial period is probably only one purchase occasion in duration. This might be explained by the fact that the product class examined was a familiar one to consumers, and consumers could tell fairly quickly whether they liked the product. Their attitudes toward buying the brand thus became established soon, but the habit of buying the product was not firmly established, and it was this factor that resulted in the purchase probability beginning to decline fairly soon. Aaker's graphical results indicated that an equilibrium purchase probability was reached after two to six purchase occasions.

Aaker's model was an important contribution to understanding the roles of habit formation and learning in the development of purchase probabilities. While Aaker's model was developed for new products, it seems that the factors he describes hold for any situation where a promotion induces a brand purchase that would not otherwise have occurred (see Aaker 1973; Neslin and Shoemaker, 1983a). However, Aaker did not explicitly examine the effects of promotion-induced purchases on repeat rates, so he did not examine the promotion usage effect.

Empirical Studies of the Promotion Usage Effect on Repeat Purchases.   There are two streams of research that have investigated the promotion usage effect on repeat purchases: laboratory experiments and panel data analyses. In Chapter 2, we described laboratory experiment research. One conclusion of this research is that a promotion incentive can either have negative or positive effects on repeat purchasing. The attribution theory explanation of these results is that negative effects occur if the consumer is encouraged to attribute the cause of his or her purchasing the brand to the promotion. Positive effects occur if the consumer is not encouraged to attribute the cause to the promotion.

The panel data analyses of the promotion usage effect consist of two approaches: analysis of purchase sequences (Shoemaker and Shoaf, 1977; Dodson et al., 1978; Bawa and Shoemaker, 1987b) and logit choice models (Jones and Zufryden, 1981; Guadagni and Little, 1983). All these studies except Bawa and Shoemaker's find a negative association between promotion and repurchase rate—the probability of repurchasing a brand is lower if the purchase is made using a promotion than if a promotion is not used. We will review the Shoemaker and Shoaf results here because they are representative of these findings. We then discuss a methodological note by Neslin and Shoemaker (1989) and the paper by Bawa and Shoemaker (1987b).

Shoemaker and Shoaf (1977) were among the first researchers to investigate the promotion usage effect on repeat purchases. They conducted an analysis of repeat rates following deal purchases by examining the first two purchases in a sequence and then observing the probability of buying the brand in question on the next purchase occasion. In particular, let

   1 = purchase of the brand in question without a deal

   $1'$ = purchase of the brand in question with a deal

   0 = purchase of another brand, not on deal

   $0'$ = purchase of another brand, on deal

Therefore, $P(01'0)$ = the probability that the brand in question is purchased on the third occasion not on deal, given that the prior purchase was of that brand on deal, and the second prior purchase was of another brand not on deal. Shoemaker and Shoaf formulated hypotheses for the relative sizes of these probabilities. They used the utility-theoretic argument that nondeal purchases suggested the consumer had high nonprice utility for the brand, yet deal purchases were ambiguous: The brand might have been purchased for price reasons alone. Table 5.2 reports their basic findings. The results show that the average probability of purchasing a brand is lower if a previous purchase of it involved a promotion.

One possible interpretation of the Shoemaker and Shoaf results is that deal purchases cause a decrease in the consumer's probability of repurchasing the brand. However, Neslin and Shoemaker (1989) propose an alternative explanation of the results. The explanation is that individual purchase probabilities do not change. Rather, the promotion temporarily attracts a large number of consumers

TABLE 5.2 Weighted Average Purchase
Probabilities for 30 Brands

Past Purchase Sequence	Probability of Purchasing Subject Brand on Next Purchase
11	.806
1'1	.708
11'	.691
1'1'	.635
0'1	.427
01	.412
0'1'	.296
01'	.271
10'	.338
10	.277
1'0'	.270
1'0	.243
0'0'	.042
00'	.043
0'0	.042
00	.029

1 = purchase of subject brand, not on promotion.

1' = purchase of subject brand, on promotion.

0 = purchase of competitor brand, not on promotion.

0' = purchase of competitor brand, on promotion.

Source: Robert W. Shoemaker and F. Robert Shoaf, "Repeat Rates of Deal Purchases," *Journal of Advertising Research*, Vol. 17, no. 2 (April 1977), p. 43, Table 6. Reprinted from the *Journal of Advertising Research*, © Copyright (1977), by the Advertising Research Foundation.

with low nonpromotion purchase probabilities for the brand. The aggregate repeat rates following promotion purchases are then lowered by these low purchase-probability households who repurchase at their usual low probability. Neslin and Shoemaker investigate the potential for this effect and find that a key component of their explanation is that the promotion draws a disproportionately large number of low-probability consumers. This assumption seems plausible because the high-probability consumers will buy the brand without the promotion, so the potential for increased sales is among the low-probability consumers. It is also consistent with economic arguments for promotion that are based on the existence of a large segment of switchers who have low nonpromotion probabilities of buying the brand, but are attracted by promotions (see Blattberg and Sen, 1976; Narasimhan, 1988; Rao, 1987; Raju et al., 1988; Ch. 4). In addition, Neslin and Shoemaker conduct an exploratory empirical analysis that suggests the difference in repeat rates for promotion versus nonpromotion purchases corresponds closely to differences in the prepromotion purchase probabilities for promotion versus non-promotion purchasers.

One methodological implication of the Neslin and Shoemaker research is that repeat rates should be investigated on an individual household basis. Bawa and Shoemaker (1987b) perform an analysis that is consistent with this approach. They examine household panel data from a coupon field experiment. For each household that redeemed the coupon, Bawa and Shoemaker observed purchase behavior for six occasions before and after the redemption. Brand A's market share was 11.2 percent before redemption and 11.9 percent after redemption. This slight increase did not appear to be significant. However, Bawa and Shoemaker divided redeemers into "users" versus "nonusers" of brand A. They found that market share among users decreased slightly after redemption, and the decrease was not statistically significant. However, share among nonusers almost doubled, from 5.4 percent to 9.1 percent, and the increase was statistically significant. Bawa and Shoemaker's results do not distinguish between a purchase effect and a promotion usage effect: The nonusers might have learned more about brand A, developed a more sustained habit toward buying brand A, or developed a positive attitude toward the brand because of the coupon. However, their analysis is consistent with the cautions raised by Neslin and Shoemaker.

To summarize, the existence and direction of a promotion usage effect on repeat purchasing has not been resolved. There is research that supports a negative effect, no effect, or a positive effect. The research does seem to tell us that the effect depends on the types of attributions encouraged for the consumer using the promotion, the type of consumer being exposed to the promotion, and the promotion environment. Future research needs to examine these contingencies. (See Chapter 2 for additional discussion.)

Choice Models and Repeat Purchases: Examining Both the Purchase and Promotion Usage Effects.   Research on choice models has taken the work just described one step further, to examine jointly both the purchase and promotion usage effects on repeat purchasing. Efforts in this area include logit models formulated by Jones and Zufryden (1981) and Guadagni and Little (1983) (see Chapter 8 for a more detailed discussion of logit models). These models predict the probability that a consumer will purchase a particular brand on the current purchase occasion, as a function of the current promotion environment and the consumer's previous purchase history. In this section, we will use a simple logit model to illustrate how to investigate how the purchase and promotion usage effects might balance out. This expands upon an analysis originally undertaken by Guadagni and Little (1983, pp. 222–223). We first describe this logit model, and then use it for the illustrative calculations.

Using similar definitions as Jones and Zufryden and Guadagni and Little, we first define the variables that we will use to represent the current promotion environment and a consumer's purchase history. The current promotion environment can be captured by a dummy variable defined as follows:

$$
P_t = \begin{cases}
1 \text{ if a particular brand (the ``subject brand'') is on} \\
\text{promotion on the current purchase occasion.} \\
\\
0 \text{ if the subject brand is not on promotion on the} \\
\text{current purchase occasion.}
\end{cases}
$$

The consumer's purchase history can be represented by two variables defined as follows:

$$
LP_{t-1} = \begin{cases}
1 \text{ if the consumer purchased the subject brand on} \\
\text{his or her previous purchase occasion, either on or} \\
\text{off promotion.} \\
\\
0 \text{ if the consumer did not purchase the subject} \\
\text{brand on his or her previous purchase occasion.}
\end{cases}
$$

$$
LPP_{t-1} = \begin{cases}
1 \text{ if the consumer purchased the subject brand on} \\
\text{promotion on his or her previous purchase occasion.} \\
\\
0 \text{ if the consumer did not purchase the subject} \\
\text{brand on promotion on his or her previous purchase} \\
\text{occasion.}
\end{cases}
$$

Given these definitions, there are three possible combinations for LP_{t-1} and LPP_{t-1}: $LP_{t-1} = 0$ and $LPP_{t-1} = 0$ means that the consumer did not buy the subject brand on his or her previous purchase occasion, $LP_{t-1} = 1$ and $LPP_{t-1} = 0$ means that the consumer bought the subject brand on his or her previous purchase occasion, but not on promotion, and $LP_{t-1} = 1$ and $LPP_{t-1} = 1$ means that the consumer bought the subject brand on his or her previous purchase occasion, and the brand was on promotion when this purchase took place. ($LP_{t-1} = 0$ and $LPP_{t-1} = 1$ is not a possibility because LP_{t-1} must equal 1 if any purchase took place, whether it be a promotion purchase or nonpromotion purchase.)

The variables P_t, LP_{t-1}, and LPP_{t-1} could be incorporated in a "binomial" logit model as follows[1]:

PROB$_t$ = the probability the consumer chooses the subject brand on the current purchase occasion.

$$
V_t = \beta_0 + \beta_1 * P_t + \beta_2 * LP_{t-1} + \beta_3 * LPP_{t-1}
$$

$$
\text{PROB}_t = 1/[1 + e^{-V_t}]
$$

---

[1] The binomial logit model calculates the probability of purchasing a particular subject brand. One minus that probability is the probability of purchasing a competing brand. Multinomial logit models calculate the probability of purchasing each of several competing brands separately (see Chapter 8). The binomial logit model is used by Jones and Zufryden (1981), while Guadagni and Little use a multinomial logit model (1983). We use a binomial logit model for simplicity, but the principles illustrated in this section would be equally applicable to the multinomial model.

Under these definitions, PROB$_t$ ranges between 0 and 1 and is an increasing function of V_t. V_t in turn is a function of the promotion environment and purchase history variables. We therefore would expect the promotion coefficient β_1 to be positive. The coefficient for last purchase (β_2) reflects the purchase effect, and we would therefore expect it to be positive. The coefficient for last purchase on promotion (β_3) reflects the promotion usage effect and will be negative if there is a negative promotion usage effect.

For the purpose of our illustration, we will assume $\beta_0 = -2.2$, $\beta_1 = 2.2$, $\beta_2 = 2.6$, and $\beta_3 = -.5$. Using these coefficient values and substituting in our equation for PROB$_t$, we calculate the following probabilities:

P_t	LP_{t-1}	LPP_{t-1}	PROB$_t$
0	0	0	.10
1	0	0	.50
0	1	0	.60
0	1	1	.48
1	1	1	.89
1	1	0	.93

These probabilities reflect a strong current promotion effect (e.g., purchase probability increases from .10 to .50 if a consumer who did not previously purchase the brand is exposed to a promotion on the current purchase occasion), a positive purchase effect (e.g., purchase probability increases from .10 to .60 for a consumer who purchased the brand on the previous occasion *not on promotion* and there is also no promotion on the current purchase occasion), and a negative promotion usage effect (e.g., purchase probability is .48 rather than .60 for the consumer who purchased the brand last time *on promotion* and there is no promotion on the current purchase occasion).

We will now illustrate how to calculate the net effect of promotion on the number of purchases occurring after the promotion, netting out the purchase and promotion usage effects. The calculation utilizes the probabilities calculated above and is shown in Figure 5.2.

Figure 5.2 shows the progression of purchase probabilities over purchase occasions t and $t + 1$ for a consumer who had not purchased the brand on purchase occasion $t - 1$. This progression is calculated under two conditions—presence or absence of a promotion on purchase occasion t. The figure shows that the expected number of purchases on purchase occasion $t + 1$ is larger for the promotion case than for the no-promotion case (.29 versus .15), although there is a negative promotion usage effect. The key point is that although it is less likely that the consumer will repurchase the brand if it is bought on promotion on occasion t than if it is bought not on promotion (.48 versus .60), he or she is still more likely to repurchase the brand than if the brand were not purchased at all on purchase occasion t (.48 versus .10). The expected number of purchases in period $t + 1$ is then larger under the promotion condition because the promotion makes it less likely that the consumer will be subject to the .10 purchase probability

Case 1: Promotion Occurs on Purchase Occasion t
Promotion Does Not Occur on Purchase Occasion $t + 1$

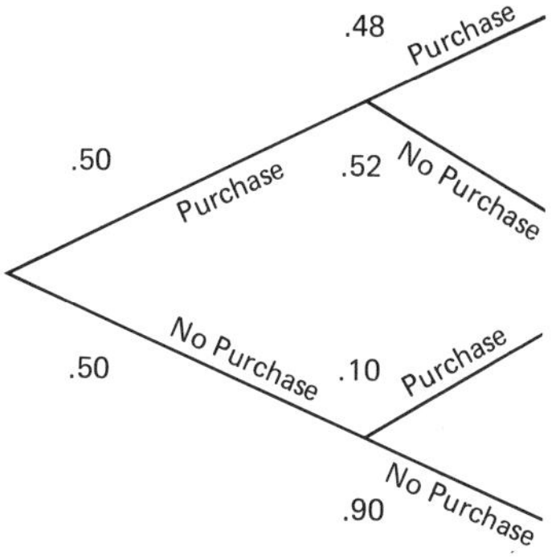

	Branch Probability	Number of Purchases	Expected Number of Purchases
.48 Purchase	.24	2	.48
.50 Purchase .52 No Purchase	.26	1	.26
.50 No Purchase .10 Purchase	.05	1	.05
.90 No Purchase	.45	0	0
			.79

Purchase Occasion t $t + 1$

Expected number of purchases on occasion $t + 1$ = .79 − .50* = .29

Case 2: No Promotion Occurs on Purchase Occasion t
No Promotion Occurs on Purchase Occasion $t + 1$

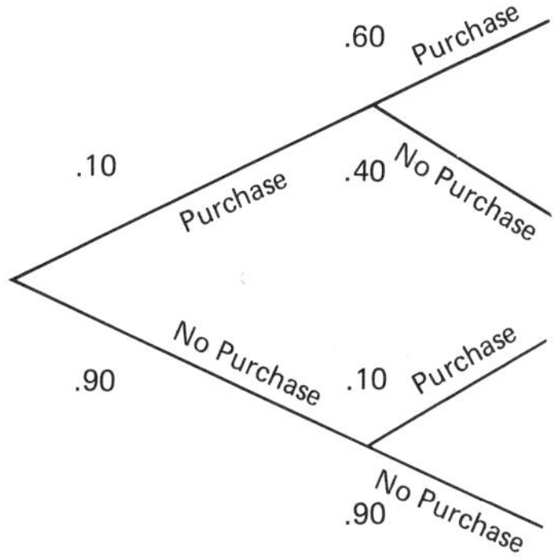

	Branch Probability	Number of Purchases	Expected Number of Purchases
.60 Purchase	.06	2	.12
.10 Purchase .40 No Purchase	.04	1	.04
.90 No Purchase .10 Purchase	.09	1	.09
.90 No Purchase	.81	0	0
			.25

Purchase Occasion t $t + 1$

Expected number of purchases on occasion $t + 1$ = .25 − .10** = .15

* .50 = Case 1 expected number of purchases on occasion t, = .5(1) + .5(0)
** .10 = Case 2 expected number of purchases on occasion t, = .1(1) + .9(0)

Note: Calculations assume brand was not purchased on purchase occasion $t − 1$. The binomial logit model described in the text was used to make these calculations.

FIGURE 5.2 Predicted Purchase Probabilities for Purchase Occasions t and $t + 1$ Under Promotion Versus No Promotion Conditions in Period t

which occurs if the consumer has not bought the brand last time. The promotion makes it more likely that the consumer will be subject to a .48 repurchase probability, which is not as large as the .60 repurchase probability that occurs if the consumer purchases the brand in period t not on promotion, but the consumer is unlikely to be subject to this probability in the no-promotion condition.

The foregoing simulation is meant only to be an illustration of how a logit model could be used to investigate the repeat purchase effects of promotion, and we do not wish to draw any empirical conclusions. However, the following points emerge:

- Even with a negative promotion usage effect, it is possible that the presence of promotion can increase the number of purchases after the promotion. This occurs if the promotion usage effect does not obliterate the purchase effect. The promotion then makes it more likely that the consumer will be subject to a high repurchase probability on the next purchase occasion.
- The above analysis only looked one period ahead after the promotion. If the promotion usage effect lasts only one period, as is assumed by the above model, the purchase probability tree in Figure 5.2 will look the same for promotion and no-promotion conditions in periods $t + 2$, $t + 3$, etc., and so the net gain due to promotion will hold up over time. However, if a negative promotion usage effect is permanent, or persists for several periods, it is possible that the net effect of promotion will be negative.
- The above analysis assumed that the logit model was causal and could be applied to an individual consumer. As Neslin and Shoemaker (1989) caution, and as discussed earlier, this may not be appropriate if the model has been estimated across consumers.

The above analysis needs to be conducted more extensively, for all consumers purchasing in a given category, under a variety of promotion scenarios, and using more sophisticated choice models. The key dimensions in which the model could be improved would be (1) a more detailed definition of promotion, e.g., amount of price discount, presence of feature advertising, etc., (2) a more refined definition of last purchase variables (see Guadagni and Little (1983)), and (3) a more precise modeling of the promotion usage effect, e.g., of how long the promotion usage effect persists (Guadagni and Little find that it persists for two periods, but do not show how it changes after that, and implicitly assume that the effect vanishes after two periods).

PURCHASE ACCELERATION

Conceptual Issues

Purchase acceleration refers to consumers buying different quantitites or purchasing at different times than they would have had a promotion not been available. This often takes the form of larger purchase quantities and purchase occasions moved forward ("accelerated") in time. Purchase acceleration is a very real phenomenon for retailer sales as well as consumer sales. Purchase acceleration for retailers is known as "forward buying" (see Chapter 12). A fascinating process is the cascading purchase acceleration that occurs as manufacturers accelerate retailers using trade deals, and retailers in turn accelerate consumers using retailer promotions.

The most direct consequence of purchase acceleration is that it merely shifts purchases forward that would have occurred anyway. Other important effects can take place, however. For example, by taking the consumer out of the market, a manufacturer can preempt the marketing plans of a competitor. Therefore, purchase acceleration can prevent switching away from the manufacturer's brand. As a second example, purchase acceleration might increase the consumer's consumption rate, because the consumer has been "loaded up" with inventory.

While we usually think of purchase acceleration in the sense of increased quantities and decreased purchase timing moved forward, quantities may also be smaller, and purchase occasions can actually be moved backward in time due to promotions. Smaller quantities might result because the promotion is inducing the consumer to switch brands, and the consumer buys a smaller quantity of that brand because of the risk involved in trying something new. "Decelerated" purchase timing can occur because the consumer learns in advance or anticipates that a promotion will occur and waits for the event.

Purchase acceleration can be applied to durable goods through the concept of "stock." For example, the stock of automobiles held by consumers is the number of automobiles owned times the average quality per vehicle. Quality is related to vehicle age, performance, reliability, level of luxury, and so on. For any period t, we can write

$$\text{stock}_t = \text{stock}_{t-1} - \text{retired stock}_t - \text{depreciation}_t + \text{new stock}_t \qquad (5.1)$$

Retired stock corresponds to vehicles that are no longer used for transportation (they are sold for scrap). Depreciation represents a deterioration in quality among nonretired stock, due to wear and tear. New stock represents new vehicles purchased by consumers. In any given time period, stock can either increase or decrease. It will increase to the extent that consumers purchase many new high-quality vehicles, do not retire many old vehicles, and do not wear their vehicles as much as usual (there will then be less depreciation).

A sales promotion accelerates the process of replenishing lost and depreciated stock. It can induce consumers to purchase new automobiles sooner than they ordinarily would, and as a result retire more old vehicles. A promotion might encourage consumers to buy higher-quality automobiles. The promotions might actually be for the higher-end "loaded" models, or consumers might apply an incentive such as a rebate toward purchasing additional options. As a result of the accelerated acquisition of new stock, there will be fewer retirements and generally higher stock levels in the future. This in turn will lower the demand for new stock. The net result is the same mortgaging of future sales that occurs with frequently purchased products.

Theory

One compelling explanation for how price promotions cause purchase acceleration is based on the economic theory developed by Blattberg et al. (1981) (see Chapter 4 for a complete discussion). In this theory, the retailer wishes to maximize profits. By lowering price, the retailer may reduce revenues but will also reduce inventory costs. The consumer wants to minimize the cost of satisfying his or her household's demand for the product. By buying on deal at a lower price, the consumer can decrease household purchase costs but may incur a cost of carrying more inventory of the product than is needed to satisfy immediate consumption. Some households, perhaps those with minimal storage space, have high holding costs and will not respond to price deals. Other households have relatively low inventory holding costs and will potentially respond to deals. Thus retailers will find it profitable to offer temporary price cuts, to be taken advantage of by low-holding-cost consumers. Purchase acceleration therefore is the result of retailers shifting inventory to consumers. This shift can be mutually beneficial if among at least one segment of consumers, household inventory costs are significantly lower than retailer inventory costs.

Blattberg et al.'s theory is an elegant one. It suggests a reason for the existence of promotions based simply on the benefits of accelerated consumer purchasing. The theory contains certain critical assumptions that make the model less than complete. These include (Blattberg et al., p. 118): There is a single retailer in the market, only one brand is promoted, the regular (nonpromoted) price is fixed, and manufacturers do not offer trade deals to the retailers. Expanding the theory to take into account these factors would undoubtedly increase the realism of the theory. However, the central theme of the theory is a compelling economic argument: Consumers will accelerate purchases because the economic benefits (lower price) of acceleration outweigh the inconvenience and added costs of buying larger quantities and buying earlier.

The consumer behavior theories covered in Chapter 2 do not directly address the issue of purchase acceleration. However, operant conditioning and low-involvement decision making are somewhat relevant. The operant conditioning argument is that frequent promotions teach the consumer to buy on deal rather than to buy any particular brand (see Chapter 2). Consumers learn that economic benefits of buying on deal outweigh the inventory costs as well as substitution costs of not necessarily buying their favorite brand. The low-involvement decision paradigm suggests that purchase acceleration of timing can result because the promotion stimulates problem recognition. The feature or display reminds the consumer that his or her inventory of the product is low, and a purchase is made. In this sense, features and displays are functioning as surrogate shopping lists.

Empirical Evidence

Several researchers, including Wilson et al. (1979), Shoemaker (1979), and Grover and Rao (1985), as well as Blattberg et al., have provided empirical evidence that promotions are associated with increased purchase quantities and decreased in-

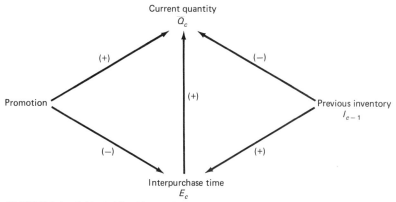

FIGURE 5.3   A Model for Measuring Purchase Acceleration

Source: Scott A. Neslin, Caroline Henderson, and John Quelch, "Consumer Promotions and the Acceleration of Product Purchases," *Marketing Science* (Spring 1985), p. 150, Fig. 1.

terpurchase times. This was usually accomplished simply by comparing average quantities and average interpurchase times associated with promotion versus non-promotion purchases.

Neslin et al. (1985) expanded this empirical line of inquiry by developing a model of purchase acceleration. Let

Q_c = quantity of the product class bought at the current purchase occasion

E_c = the elapsed time (or "interpurchase time") between the current and previous purchases of the product class

I_{c-1} = the household inventory of the product class that existed directly after the previous purchase

The model is best described by Figure 5.3. As the figure shows, promotion is hypothesized to have a positive effect on quantity Q_c and a negative impact on interpurchase time E_c. However, to measure the effect correctly, one must take into account the household's inventory I_{c-1} and the relationship between inter-purchase time and quantity. In particular, if the previous household inventory was large, the household will (1) wait longer until purchasing again and (2) for a given interpurchase time, tend to purchase less of the product class at the next occasion. In addition, interpurchase time on its own is positively related to pur-chase quantity. If the household has waited longer than usual between purchases, it will probably purchase a larger than usual quantity.

Neslin et al. estimated their model for two product classes: bathroom tissue and coffee. The model was also estimated in various consumer segments and several promotion vehicles were considered. Their important conclusions were as follows:

1. Purchase quantity is accelerated by both price and nonprice promotions. Coupons, temporary price cuts, and featured price cuts are all associated with higher purchase quantities, and so is feature advertising by itself. The range of quantity increases is from 8 percent to 35 percent.

2. Interpurchase time is less likely to be accelerated by promotions. Coupons, feature advertising, and temporary price cuts are not associated with decreased interpurchase times. However, featured price cuts can accelerate timing, being associated with an average 10 percent reduction in interpurchase time.

3. Consumers "make up" for the added inventory they take on by both waiting longer until the next purchase and by buying less on the next purchase. However, the waiting longer strategy appears to be more common. This supports the notion that an accelerated sale takes the consumer out of the market for a longer time.

4. Purchases of brands to which the consumer is loyal are not the only purchases that are associated with acceleration. In one product category, loyal purchases were more accelerated than nonloyal purchases, however, in the other category, both loyal and nonloyal purchases were equally accelerated. This suggests that accelerators may not only be those stocking up on their favorite brand.

5. Purchase acceleration is stronger among heavy users of the category, but there is no difference in acceleration tendencies between high- and low-income groups.

Litvack et al. (1985) conducted an interesting experiment related to the issue of purchase acceleration. They examined the effects of a price cut on sales of "stock-up" versus "non-stock-up" items. Stock-up items were defined as "any nonperishable good in a unit size that is consumed frequently by a purchaser's household" (p. 10). Their experiment divided 72 products into stock-up versus non-stock-up groups, and sales of these items were observed before, during, and after a price cut. The authors found that sales of stock-up items were significantly more price sensitive than were those of non-stock-up items. Interestingly, the authors did not observe the postpromotion dip in sales among the stock-up items that would be expected if the sales of the stock-up items had been accelerated. This may be due to the relatively short postpromotion period (two weeks) or to a variety of other factors (see the Combined Impact of Separate Sales Effects of this chapter, Independent Variables of Chapter 7, and Stockpiling of Chapter 12 for further discussion).

Purchase acceleration has rarely been studied in durables markets, and it is here that the economic argument would appear to be very relevant. The amount of consumer dollar savings could be significant and retailer inventory costs would be relatively large. There is, however, some emerging research in this area. Doyle and Saunders (1985) found a deceleration effect in studying a furniture promotion. Sales in the weeks before the promotion were lower than normal. Doyle and Saunders trace this phenomenon to the higher commission rates offered to sales people during the promotion. It is possible that as a result of these higher commission rates, sales people lessened their sales efforts or simply informed consumers of the upcoming sale. Thompson and Noordewier (1989) found a strong acceleration effect for national automobile promotions conducted in 1985, 1986, and 1987. Sales were significantly lower than normal during the periods following these promotions. Bayus (1988) used consumer survey data to study the mean replacement times for television sets. He found that lower price paid and higher advertising expenditures were associated with shorter replacement times. An interesting follow-up to this study would be to investigate the replacement times *after* a promotion purchase. In this way, one could determine whether consumers make up for the accelerated purchase by waiting longer until they buy again. One could then distinguish between a pure acceleration effect and an increase in category demand (see the next section).

In summary, there is a good deal of theoretical and empirical support for the acceleration effects of sales promotions. It should be emphasized, however, that the specific empirical findings are tied to the range of data and categories examined. Most of the empirical results are for frequently promoted packaged goods categories. If in fact many consumers in these categories have been conditioned to purchase mainly on deal, the acceleration effects will be underestimated. For example, a consumer who purchases every two weeks on deal will not appear to be accelerating, yet the timing of purchases may really be dictated by the presence of a deal for an acceptable brand. A related area that warrants increased research attention is how consumers form expectations of the timing of sales promotion, and in turn, how these expectations affect the timing of their purchases.

CATEGORY EXPANSION

Conceptual Issues

It appears that promotions could stimulate primary demand in at least three ways:

- By creating a new purchase occasion.
- By increasing consumption rate.
- By causing the consumer to accelerate purchase timing yet not to make up for the earlier purchase by purchasing later or purchasing less next time.

A good example of a promotion creating a new purchase occasion is the display that reminds the consumer that potato chips are a good snack to bring along on a picnic. It is plausible that consumer durables demand could also be created by promotions. This might include discretionary products such as portable hair dryers, portable vacuum cleaners, and car stereos.

Increasing usage rate is a common goal for many packaged goods manufacturers. For example, it might be relatively easy to get consumers to stockpile tuna fish or soup or a cake mix, but getting the consumer actually to use these products is a different problem. Promotions such as free recipe book or tie-ins with perishable products (e.g., buy the tuna and get a free loaf of bread) can help to stimulate usage.

As suggested by the results of Neslin et al., consumers can make up for stockpiling by repurchasing the category later or by purchasing less of the category on the next occasion. In some categories, however, it might be possible to counteract these purchase strategies. For example, a family may normally purchase an automobile every four years. A promotion may accelerate that interpurchase time by six months (see the preceding discussion of Bayus, 1988). The key question is whether the family will wait four and a half years before purchasing again, four years, or three and one-half years. In the first case, the purchase was only accelerated; in the second case, the old interpurchase time is retained; and in the third case, the new interpurchase time is retained. In the latter two cases, there has been an increase in category demand. While the issue is clear and very important, it has not been studied in depth in a durables context.

Theory

Low-involvement decision making can explain the ability of promotions to increase primary demand by creating a purchase occasion. In particular, promotions can stimulate problem recognition (e.g., a display reminds the consumer that potato chips are a good snack to bring along on picnics). Promotions could also stimulate primary demand in a high-involvement situation. For example, a promotion could remind the consumer of the appropriateness of a particular product as a gift. Also, a personal computer promotion consisting of a free instruction course could help translate purchase intentions into actual behavior. An economic explanation for price promotions creating a purchase occasion would be based on the concept of reservation price. Reservation prices play an important role in many economic models (see Chapter 4). The reservation price explanation is simply that there are prices above which consumers will forgo consumption. A price promotion lowers the price of the product category below the reservation price, and so a purchase occasion is created.

There is a lack of theoretical explanation for how promotions can increase consumption rate or establish a new interpurchase time. The Neslin et al. framework and the stock model proposed in the preceding section provide an empirical basis for studying the relationship between timing acceleration and increases in primary demand. However, they do not provide theoretical explanations of when, for example, consumers would be expected to make up for increased inventory or stock by waiting longer until the next purchase versus consuming the product faster or repurchasing at their normal times.

Perhaps operant conditioning could be applied to training consumers to purchase durable goods more frequently. It seems plausible that frequent promotions in the automobile industry could induce the habit of buying every three rather than four years. At first the theory would appear not to apply, for *individual* consumers would still not purchase an automobile often enough for the repetitive aspects of operant conditioning to become entrenched. Perhaps, however, the relevant learning is with respect to durables in general. That is, all durables promotions are teaching individual consumers to buy durables more frequently. Consumers then apply that habit to particular categories.

Empirical Evidence

There is a lack of empirical demonstration of category expansion effects. Ward and Davis (1978a) conducted an econometric time series study of the orange juice market and concluded that use of coupons was associated with increased category sales of orange juice. The increase could have come from newly created purchase occasions or a faster use rate stimulated by having stockpiled orange juice.

Moore and Winer (1978) conducted a field experiment to determine whether getting consumers to stockpile a product could increase usage rate. The particular method of stockpiling investigated was the purchase of larger package sizes, and the categories studied were colas and spaghetti. Thirty-five consumers were divided into four groups in which the package sizes made available to them on a weekly basis were either large or small. The hypothesis was that those who were exposed to and bought the larger package size would have higher consumption rates. After ten weeks, weekly consumption rates were analyzed and no package size effect was found. The experiment thus was unable to confirm the possibility of using consumer stockpiling to stimulate consumption rate. The experience is similar to the problem that makers of soup, desserts, and so on have when promotions merely cause stockpiling but no usage.

Clearly there is a great need for further study, both theoretical and empirical, in this area. For many products, for example, those with very high market share, category expansion is the only way to increase sales. A theory is needed that includes the determinants of consumption rate, purchase occasion, and interpurchase time. Empirical testing, using both field experiments and time series analyses, is then needed to test this theory.

THE COMBINED IMPACT OF SEPARATE SALES EFFECTS

In the real-world marketplace, it is likely that brand switching, repeat purchasing, acceleration, and category expansion occur at the same time. Neslin and Shoemaker (1983a) constructed a simulation model that included brand switching, repeat purchasing, and acceleration effects. While we will not derive the model here, we will state and interpret it, and examine the ideal behavior implied by the model. Let

$SPRO_t$ = sales made on promotion in period t. (This corresponds to either $LREDEEM_t$ for coupons or $PROPUR_t$ for in-store promotions in the Neslin and Shoemaker model.)

ACC = percentage of promotional sales that represent sales accelerated from future periods.

MSU = percentage of unaccelerated promotional sales that would have been sales of the brand even if the promotion had not been offered.

MSA = percentage of accelerated promotional sales that would have been eventual sales of the brand even if the promotion had not been offered.

$S(X)$ = the fraction of accelerated sales drawn from X periods ahead.

$NEWREP(X)$ = the fraction of promotional sales that result in incremental sales X periods after the promotional sales.

ΔSALES$_t$ = The total increment or decrement in sales that occurs in time t due to current and previous promotions. (This corresponds to either COUPGAIN$_t$ or RETPROGAIN$_t$ in the Neslin and Shoemaker model.)

SPRO$_t$ is simply a count of the number of promotional purchases made at time t. Neslin and Shoemaker distinguish between coupons and in-store promotions, but that is not necessary for our discussion. ACC represents the acceleration phenomenon, and MSU and MSA represent switching. The larger these quantities are, the less switching that occurs. Neslin and Shoemaker assumed that different percentages of switching are found among accelerators versus nonaccelerators. In particular, they assumed that MSU < MSA, because they considered it more difficult to induce a consumer to both accelerate and switch. S(X) represents the time periods from which accelerated sales are drawn. Neslin and Shoemaker assumed that more accelerated sales would be drawn from periods closer to when the promotion took place: S(X) > S($X + 1$). NEWREP(X) represents *additional* repeat purchases that occur from promotional sales. Note that Neslin and Shoemaker think of the net repeat purchase rate as being positive, as in Figure 5.2 discussed earlier. However, a negative repeat purchase effect could be considered simply by having NEWREP(X) be negative. Neslin and Shoemaker derive the following model:

$$\Delta\text{SALES}_t = \text{SPRO}_t * [\text{ACC} + (1 - \text{ACC}) * (1 - \text{MSU})]$$
$$+ \sum_x \text{SPRO}_{t-x} * [\text{NEWREP}(X) - \text{ACC} * \text{MSA} * \text{S}(X)]$$

The first term in this equation represents the immediate sources of incremental sales: ACC% of those promotion sales are accelerated and thus represent incremental sales in the current period. Among the $(1 - \text{ACC})$ nonaccelerated sales, $(1 - \text{MSU})$ represent switchers and hence incremental sales. The second term in the equation represents the effects of previous promotional sales on current sales. NEWREP(X)% of the promotional sales made X periods ago (SPRO$_{t-x}$) result in incremental sales in the current period. A total of ACC$*$ MSA $*$ S(X)% of sales made X periods ago represent accelerators who would have bought the brand anyway but were accelerated X periods in advance.

Figure 5.4 illustrates the simulated behavior of the model. The model produces a quintessential promotion effect: an immediate increase in sales followed by a postpromotion dip and then a slight increase over the brand's baseline. The immediate increase comes from the combined effects of switching and accelerating. The postpromotion dip is due to accelerated sales being drawn from periods immediately after the promotion. The subsequent small increase comes from new repeat purchases.

The net incremental sales impact of a promotion is of course the sum of the "overages" and "underages" compared to baseline sales. This nets out the combined effects of switching, repeat purchasing, and acceleration. Interestingly, Neslin and Shoemaker found that although the repeat purchase impact in this calculation might be small, the margin from these sales is much larger than is the

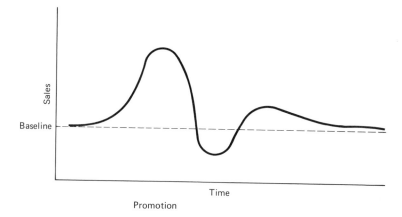

FIGURE 5.4   The Combined Effect of Switching and Accelerated and Repeat
Purchasing upon Brand Sales, Simulated Using the Neslin and
Shoemaker Model

Source: Scott A. Neslin and Robert W. Shoemaker, "A Model for Evaluating the Profitability of
Coupon Promotion," *Marketing Science*, Vol. 2, no. 4 (Fall 1983), adapted from p. 375, Figure
4.

margin from immediately incremental sales. Thus a positive repeat purchase effect
can be an important source of profit for a promotion.

While the Neslin and Shoemaker model provides insights on how the various
promotional effects combine to produce a total effect, the quintessential sales
curve shown in Figure 5.4 is rarely seen in practice. Figure 5.5, taken from Little
(1979), shows more common sales curves (see also Chapter 11 and Chapter 12).

Actual sales graphs can deviate from the ideal simulated curve for several
reasons:

- The $S(X)$ function could draw uniformly from subsequent periods, making it difficult
to see postpromotion troughs. This could occur if acceleration is due to a combination
of timing and quantity effects. Figure 5.5 assumes only a timing effect of acceleration,
with accelerators drawn from the closest periods. If acceleration is also of quantity,
then purchases will also be drawn from time periods occurring roughly one interpurchase period after the promotion. As a result, the promotion draws more or less
uniformly from subsequent periods (see the "Independent Variables" section of
Chapter 7).
- The $NEWREP(X)$ function could be negative or zero. That is, promotions could
cause a net decrease in repeat purchases, or could have no effect on repeat purchases
(see the concluding section of this chapter).
- Frequent successive promotions could swamp the relatively subtle effects of repeat
purchasing and a more uniform acceleration effect.
- Acceleration and repeat purchasing could cancel each other out. For example, a
slight increase in new repeat purchases coming an average of one purchase cycle
after the promotion would be canceled by a slight dip coming one purchase cycle
after a promotion due to accelerated quantity.
- A large number of consumers may have their purchase timing determined by promotions and hence permanently depress a brand's baseline.

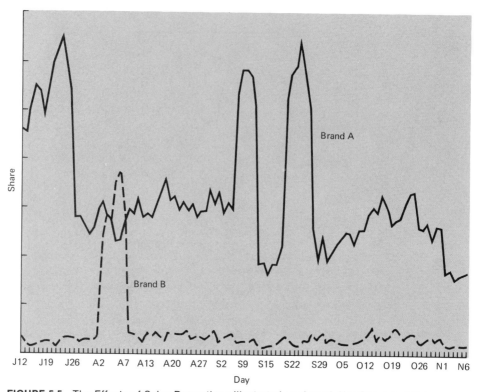

FIGURE 5.5 The Effects of Sales Promotions Illustrated on Actual, Not Simulated Data

Source: John D. C. Little, "Decision Support Systems for Marketing Managers," *Journal of Marketing*, Vol. 43 (Summer 1979), p. 16. Reprinted from the *Journal of Marketing*, published by the American Marketing Association.

This discussion suggests several reasons why actual sales response curves to promotion look the way they do. Undoubtedly, a combination of all the foregoing reasons are at work. It is very important to note that evidence of repeat purchase and acceleration effects come largely from panel data or experimental analyses. Rarely have such effects been observed using sales data (Doyle and Saunders, 1985; Leone, 1987; and Thompson and Noordeweir, 1989, are exceptions). This raises a challenging research topic—to determine why we rarely observe postpromotion effects in sales data (see Chapter 12, Stockpiling for further discussion).

Gupta (1988) proposed a multi-equation model to capture brand switching and purchase acceleration effects (both of quantity and timing) in the same analysis. There are two major assumptions to Gupta's model. First, consumers make choices in a particular sequence: They first decide when to buy, and then decide how much and what brand. Second, Gupta assumes that the brand choice and quantity decisions are independent. One might indeed quarrel with these assumptions, and even Gupta suggests that a simultaneous model among quantity, timing, and choice might be appropriate. However, Gupta makes some logical conditional probability arguments for his structure, and his assumptions are very clear, so future researchers can easily build upon his work.

Gupta estimated his model for nine brand sizes in the regular coffee market. He then decomposed the sales elasticity of each brand with respect to promotion into switching, acceleration of timing, and acceleration of quantity subelasticities. For all brands, the switching effect dominated, with timing far behind and second in influence, and quantity acceleration had very little impact. One reason for the small estimated impact of quantity acceleration is that the 16-ounce size dominated the market and two 16-ounce packages or a 32-ounce package (the next higher available size) may have been more than the consumer wished to purchase. However, Gupta's research represents a welcome empirical analysis decomposing the effects of promotions into the mechanisms described in this chapter (see also Moriarty, 1985, and Krishnamurthi and Raj, 1988).

DISCUSSION AND SUMMARY

In summary, we have described and provided both theoretical and empirical evidence for how promotions affect sales. In particular, we have reviewed switching, repeat purchase, acceleration, and category expansion effects. The switching phenomenon probably has the strongest theoretical base and has been the most clearly measured. Important research issues for this topic include the relative switching power of various types of promotions and the causes for asymmetries between brands. Purchase acceleration has been explained most clearly as the result of shifting inventory carrying costs, either from the manufacturer to the retailer or from the retailer to the consumer. However, a theory is also needed to help determine the role of consumer expectations. Purchase acceleration has been established to exist empirically, but there are questions as to whether its magnitude has been underestimated. The category expansion effect of sales promotion is potentially very relevant to the durable goods industry, but there are very few theories or empirical studies bearing on this issue.

There are several rich theories regarding the repeat purchase effects of promotions, but these theories are often in conflict: Operant conditioning predicts a positive effect, while attribution theory is most often applied to predict a negative effect of using a promotion to purchase a brand. The empirical evidence has also been ambiguous—positive, negative, and no effects have been found. The issue is also clouded by the fact that there are two types of repeat purchase effects, one due to the phenomenon that any purchase of a brand reinforces further purchase (the purchase effect), and the second, the promotion usage effect, distinctly due to the use of a promotion to purchase a brand. Operant conditioning and attribution theory refer to this promotion usage effect. We saw, however, that even if the promotion usage effect is negative, the purchase effect on repeat purchases may overshadow this effect, so that the net impact of promotions on repeat purchases may be positive. The definitive sorting out of these issues is a very important area for future research.

Another major area for future research is the joint consideration of switching, repeat purchase, acceleration, and category expansion effects. For example, Gupta's work discussed earlier could be expanded to incorporate repeat purchase and category expansion effects. The key issue here is how to model the interrelationships among these phenomena. Should brand choice be considered to be independent of the quantity decision? Do timing, quantity, and brand decisions occur sequentially or simultaneously? These theoretical issues need to be resolved before definitive empirical results can be generated on this topic.

A final important area for future research is the long-term effects of promotion—where "long-term" is measured in years rather than the next few purchase occasions. This would sort out the long-term effects of repeat purchasing, acceleration, and category expansion. The effects of promotion, advertising, and regular price could also be contrasted in such research.

6

Sales Promotion Experiments

OVERVIEW

The salient characteristic of experiments is that an experimental treatment, in this case the occurrence of a promotion, is manipulated in such a way that we can observe its effects. It is this deliberate, planned control of sales promotion that distinguishes experimental data from traditional historical data. An important issue in studying experiments is the design of the experimental manipulation and data collection procedure. These data can then be analyzed using regression, time series analysis, choice models, or simple descriptive statistics. In this chapter, we examine both the design and analysis of experiments as they apply to the study of sales promotion. The reader may also want to consult Chapters 7, 8, and 9 for a more in-depth treatment of analysis techniques.

TIME SERIES QUASI-EXPERIMENTS

Design

A very common type of promotion experiment utilizes the "time series quasi-experiment" design (Campbell and Stanley, 1963, p. 40). In this design, sales are observed for some period of time, a promotion is then instituted, and sales are observed both during and after the promotion. Sales may be observed in one or more stores or one or more cities, or among a panel of consumers. Specifically, let O_t denote the observation of sales in time period (usually week) t, and X_t denote the placement of a promotion in time t. The time series quasi-experimental design can be diagrammed as follows:

$$O_1 \; O_2 \; O_3 \; O_4 \; X_5 \; O_5 \; O_6 \; O_7 \; O_8 \; O_9$$

In this case, we observe four weeks of prepromotion sales and then insert a promotion of one week duration. We then observe sales during the promotion week and for four subsequent weeks.

Analysis

A common method for analyzing time series experiments is first to compute average weekly sales across the prepromotion period as a forecast of what sales in the promotion period were expected to be without the promotion. This "baseline" is then subtracted from average weekly actual sales during the promotion period to derive an estimate of the promotion effect. (Baseline sales can also be subtracted from sales in weeks after the promotion to estimate long-term effects.) If we let O_p equal average weekly sales during the promotion period, and O_{pre} equal average weekly sales during the prepromotion period, the estimated weekly promotion effect is $O_p - O_{pre}$.

One problem that can bias $O_p - O_{pre}$ as an estimate of the promotion effect is if the marketing environment or experimental units during the promotion period are systematically different from their counterparts during the prepromotion period. For example, there could be an upward trend in the data due to increasing loyalty among the households (experimental units) in the experiment. For example, consider the following sales data,

$$10 \quad 20 \quad 30 \quad 40 \quad 50 \quad 90$$

where the first five periods are prepromotion and a promotion is implemented in the sixth period. In this case, $O_p - O_{pre} = 90 - 30 = 60$. This is obviously an overstatement of the promotion effect. The trend in the data suggests that sales in period 6 would have equaled 60 had the promotion not been implemented, so the estimate of the promotion effect should be $90 - 60 = 30$. A regression, time series, or logit analysis could be performed on the prepromotion data to estimate the trend and provide an adjusted baseline for the promotion period.

Another important reason to use regression or similar analyses is to produce a narrower confidence interval estimate for the promotion effect. Figure 6.1 illustrates this point. In panel (a), the mean of the prepromotion data is 150, and the standard deviation is 25. Without incorporating any information on the marketing environment present in a particular week, our forecasted sales for that week in the absence of promotion will be 150, with a 95% confidence interval of plus-or-minus 2 times 25, or 50. This is because, without any further information, we must view each week's sales as a random pick from a distribution with mean 150 and standard deviation 25. Regression analysis, however, takes account of the marketing environment present in the particular week for which it is forecasting sales. The result is a narrower confidence interval, as illustrated in panel (b) of Figure 6.1. Since with regression analysis, we have a narrower confidence interval for what sales would be without the promotion, we have a more precise estimate of the promotion effect (see the forthcoming section, "Increasing Precision Through Multivariate Regression," for a full numerial example).

This example suggests that regression analysis should automatically be used to evaluate time series experiments. However, there can be substantial cost in data collection and computing to use regression. If the current marketing environment is not very competitive, sales data would be relatively stable and the effect of a promotion could be clearly measured without regression analysis. Sales data would look like this:

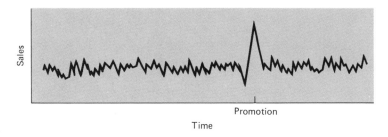

rather than this:

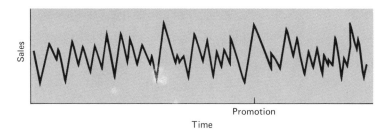

A simple $O_p - O_{pre}$ calculation might provide a narrow confidence interval for the promotion effect in the first case, but a regression model might be needed in the second case to derive a narrow confidence interval.

Problems

The biggest statistical problem with time series promotion experiments is the presence of an unusual marketing event at the same time of the experimental promotion that plausibly could explain the change in sales observed. This is referred to as the effect of "history" by Campbell and Stanley (1963). For example, consider a time series experiment for candy with a 20-week prepromotion period, where the promotion week exactly coincides with Halloween. The simple $O_p - O_{pre}$ estimate will be biased because the estimated promotion effect also includes the effect of Halloween. If we quantify Halloween using a dummy variable and attempt to include it in a regression, the Halloween variable will be exactly collinear with the promotion variable, and the regression will be unable to separate the Halloween effect from the promotion effect. (This is manifested in the regression by the estimated effects being displayed as incomputable or of infinite variance, depending upon the computer program.) If the historical event is not very

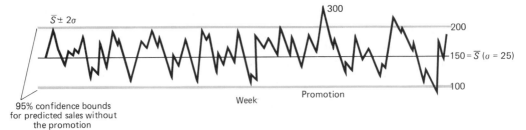

(a) Analysis based on average prepromotion sales

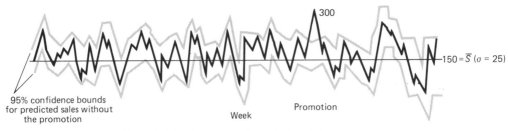

(b) Analysis based upon regression or logit model

$\overline{S}$ = average weekly sales in prepromotion period

σ = standard deviation of weekly prepromotion sales

Heavy jagged lines are weekly sales

FIGURE 6.1   Use of Regression Analysis to Measure More Precisely the Promotion Effect in a Time Series Quasi-Experiment

unusual, for example, a competitor also ran a promotion during the promotion period, a variable capturing competition can be included in the regression model without it being perfectly collinear with the promotion effect. The prepromotion data must have at least some occurrences of competitive promotion for this to work.

Another commonly acknowledged problem with the time series experiment is called "interactive testing" (Campbell and Stanley, 1963, p. 8, 18). Interactive testing occurs when previous measurements cause the experimental units to react in a particular way to the experimental treatment. For example, we might ask consumers participating in an experiment to keep a diary or answer a marketing survey. This may pique their interest in marketing events and cause them to react differently to the promotion than they naturally would. The estimated promotion effect will therefore not apply to any real-world market.

The obvious way to address the interactive testing problem is not to take any premeasurements. However, this will deprive us of deriving a baseline against which to judge the promotion effect. Another solution is to make measurements less obtrusive. For example, scanner panels, where consumers merely present a card when checking out, are less obtrusive than traditional handwritten diaries. A final solution is to move to a more elaborate design. A common remedy for the interactive testing effect is a four-group design, where two of the groups receive no premeasurements and one of those groups receives the experimental treatment. By subtracting the no-premeasurement promotion group from the premeasurement promotion group, we can isolate the interactive testing effect (see Cambell and Stanley, 1963, pp. 8, 24–25; Churchill, 1987, pp. 125–126).

A final subtle but nevertheless important problem can arise with using the $O_p - O_{pre}$ estimate of the promotion effect. If the prepromotion period includes a number of brand promotions, O_{pre} will provide an inflated baseline, and the result will be an underestimate of the effect of the experimental promotion. In this case, a regression model that quantifies the brand's own promotions should be used to provide a forecast of baseline sales during the promotion period (see Chapter 7, Omitted Variables Bias).

Implementation

Time series quasi-experiments are perhaps the easiest experiments to implement. The most basic implementation decision is what should be the unit of data collection. Consumer panels are amenable to direct-mail coupon or sampling experiments, and these yield consumer-level data. In-store experiments are best for examining retailer promotions, so often the unit of analysis will be the store-week.

Another consideration is the desired length of prepromotion and promotion periods. For prepromotion, enough time is needed so that one can ascertain whether there is a trend in brand sales and gauge the "normal" week-to-week variation in sales for the product. If regression is being used to analyze the data, there must be enough time periods to estimate a statistically sound model. Examples of prepromotion periods in the literature have ranged anywhere from 4 weeks (*Nielsen Researcher*, 1982; Cotton and Babb, 1978) to 40 weeks (Hee, 1981).

The promotion period should be long enough to capture any long-term effects of the promotion. A minimum postpromotion period would be one purchase cycle for the product class. While these guidelines are easy to state, they are not always easy to realize. For example, one might run into another promotion for the brand. If a long enough promotion period is available, we can assume that at some point the promotion effect is no longer present. In this case, we can use these periods to help infer a baseline, combining them with O_{pre} or with a more sophisticated regression or time series model (see discussion of "PROMOTER" in Chapter 9).

Another important factor in implementing time series experiments is the requirement to monitor marketing events before, during, and after the promotion, so as to determine whether an unusual historical event has unfortunately occurred at the same time as the experimental promotion. Since promotion treatments are short-lived, this is not a particularly critical problem. However, similar to the Halloween problem just discussed, if during the week of an in-store signing experiment for a given brand, the store happens to run an unusual sale, it will be virtually impossible to disentangle the effect of the signs from that of the sale. In practice, not only should the marketing environment be monitored, but *controlled*. For example, a manufacturer can ask retailers not to do anything unusual during the promotion treatment period. Failing that, the manufacturer can ask the retailer for a calendar of activities so periods of unusual activity can be avoided.

A final consideration is the selection of experimental units for inclusion in the experiment. Ideally, the selection should be made randomly from the population to which one wishes to project the results. For example, if stores are randomly selected from one geographic region, the results are projectable only to that region and not to the rest of the country.

Example

This example illustrates the evaluation of a free-standing insert coupon (*Nielsen Researcher*, 1982). The following sales indices for Listerine mouthwash were observed (the first week of the prepromotion period was indexed at 100):

Average Weekly Sales over Four-Week Prepromotion Period	Week of Coupon Drop	Week After Coupon Drop
119	200	168

The immediate interpretation is that the coupon almost doubled sales in the week it was dropped ($O_p - O_{pre} = 200 - 119 = 81$) and also increased sales in the succeeding week ($O_p - O_{pre} = 168 - 119 = 49$). This "long-term" effect makes sense because not all coupons are redeemed in the first week. However, Figure 6.2 presents a more complete picture of what actually occurred. As the figure indicates, in-store retailer support (i.e., retailer promotions) had been increasing during the four weeks prior to the coupon drop, with a coincident increase in sales. Likewise, sales in the drop week as well as subsequent weeks also reflect retailer support.

Does this mean that the coupon had no effect on sales? Not necessarily. Figure 6.2 is aggregated across all stores. The following statistics show what occurred in stores where there was retailer support versus those where there was no retailer support:

	No Retailer Support	Retailer Support
Week of coupon drop	100	338
Week after coupon drop	123	232

The data now show that a coupon by itself induces a delayed increase in sales, but that the coupon together with retailer support produces an immediate and larger increase.

The example points out (1) the need to examine several time periods before and during an experimental promotion treatment, (2) the need to measure other

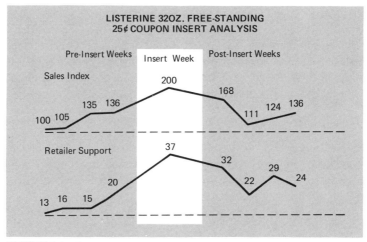

FIGURE 6.2 Examining a Coupon Experiment

Source: Nielsen Researcher, 1982, "Analyzing Promotions: The Free-Standing Insert Coupon," No. 4 (Chicago: A. C. Nielsen Company, 1982), p. 17.

marketing activities besides the promotion treatment, and (3) the importance of examining disaggregate data, for example, on the store level, rather than across stores. (Note that if we had weekly sales data for all weeks in stores with and without retailer support, we could use regression to analyze the experiment.)

A final word of warning is in order for the analysis of sales promotion time series quasi-experiments. Often the data available in such instances are not experimental in that the insertion of the promotion was not controlled by the researcher. There is nothing necessarily that eliminates the usefulness of such data. However, the lack of experimental control raises the likelihood that an historical event could be confounding the results. Again, experimental control is the key difference between experimental and nonexperimental data. In any case, one should collect complete brand and competitive marketing data for the period covering a promotion "experiment" to evaluate it accurately.

TWO-GROUP PRE-POST EXPERIMENTS

Design

While the time series experiment suffers from the potentially confounding effects of unusual historical events, the two-group experiment potentially eliminates that problem. The two group pre-post experiment can be diagrammed as follows:

Promotion Group: O_1 O_2 O_3 O_4 X_5 O_5 O_6 O_7 O_8 O_9
Control Group: O_1' O_2' O_3' O_4' $\quad$ O_5' O_6' O_7' O_8' O_9'

The groups might consist of "experimental units" such as stores. Experimental units should be *randomly assigned* to groups. In this case, the experimental units will be equivalent on average. It is also important that the groups be exposed to the same marketing environment. An unusual "Halloween" event will then be common to both groups. The direct effect of the unusual event can therefore be "subtracted out" in estimating the impact of the promotion.

Analysis

The differences $O_1 - O_1'$, $O_2 - O_2'$, and so on, represent prepromotion differences between the groups, which if units were randomly assigned from the same competitive environment, should average out to equal zero. If the average is not zero, it should be subtracted out from the $O_5 - O_5'$, $O_6 - O_6'$ differences to provide estimates of the promotion effect. For example, consider the following data:

	Prepromotion				Promotion	Postpromotion			
Promotion Group:	100	105	110	105	170	140	120	110	100
Control Group:	90	95	100	95	120	130	110	100	90

Then, the average prepromotion difference between the groups is 10. It would be unfair to attribute a $170 - 120 = 50$ unit gain to the promotion since we know that on average sales are 10 units higher in the promotion group. We therefore subtract out the built-in difference between the promotion and control groups (10) from $O_5 - O_5'$ and get 40 as our estimated incremental impact on sales.

In most general terms, our estimate of the promotion effect for the two group design is $(O_p - O_p') - (O_{pre} - O_{pre}')$, where O_p is sales during a particular week during the promotion period or the average weekly sales during the promotion period, O_p' is the level of sales in the control group corresponding to O_p, O_{pre} represents average weekly sales in the promotion group during the prepromotion period, while O_{pre}' represents average weekly sales in the control group during the prepromotion period.

One might ask how $O_{pre} - O_{pre}'$ could be anything but zero if units were randomly assigned to the same marketing environment. First, it is difficult to find identical marketing environments. For example, stores even located in the same town might face different marketing environments depending on their exact location. The store assigned to the promotion group might be from the east side of town, while the store randomly assigned to the control group might be from the west side and faces a different set of competitors. Second, the assignment may not have been random. For example, the store from the east side of town might have been willing to run an experimental promotion, but the west side store was not. There may be systematic differences between stores willing and not willing to cooperate that show up in differences in prepromotion period sales. Finally, even if experimental units have been assigned randomly to the same marketing environment, random fluctuations within the groups will cause $O_{pre} - O_{pre}'$ to be nonzero.

Multivariate analysis such as regression, logit, or analysis of covariance can be used to analyze two-group experiments. As with the one-group time series experiment, the multivariate analysis can increase the precision or, more specifically, decrease the width of the confidence interval we place around our estimate of the promotion effect. This is especially important in the event that the groups are not drawn from the same marketing environment, because then, week-to-week differences between the groups might be explainable in terms of differences in the environment.

Problems

The two-group design does not control for the interactive testing effect described earlier in this chapter. If the promotion group has been unduly sensitized to anticipate or react to a promotion, the gain in sales in that group versus the control group will not be projectable to the actual marketplace. Notice this occurs even if both the promotion and control groups are sensitized. The control group does not see an experimental promotion so does not get the chance to react to it. The promotion group does, and their reaction is not representative of what would be obtained in a real-world situation.

Another more subtle problem with two-group experiments stems from their basic strategy of subtracting out the effects of marketing events common to both groups. For example, assume that a competitor launches a competitive promotion coincident with the experimental brand's promotion. The competitive promotion is subtracted out in the term $(O_p - O'_p)$ only if both groups react the same to the competitor promotion. However, if there are systematic differences between the two groups, caused by either lack of random assignment or differences in the marketing environment, they may not react the same. The promotion group may be more loyal to the experimental brand and hence not be as severely influenced by the competition promotion. As another example, the store that cooperated in running the promotion might create an in-store environment that is more conducive to promotion purchasing. Let

P = promotion effect for the experimental brand

C = effect of competitive promotion in the promotion group

C' = effect of competitive promotion in the control group

We then have $(O_p - O'_p) = P + C - C'$. If $C \neq C'$, we have not subtracted out the effect of the competitive promotion.

As long as we randomly assign experimental units to treatment groups and the marketing environments for the two groups are identical, we should obtain $C = C'$ *on average*. However, this is of little comfort to the researcher who can run an experiment just once. In addition, sometimes we may be setting up experimental groups for repeated testing. In that case, we would not want a built-in bias caused by one group having a different loyalty profile from another.

"Matching" the promotion and control groups can potentially address this issue. This is done, for example, by making sure an equal number of "everyday-low-pricing" supermarkets are assigned to each group, or by making sure each group has an equal number of high-income consumers. Ideally, we would want to match the two groups perfectly on all variables that could potentially cause differences in reactions to environmental factors. This is never practical, so usually only a few matching characteristics are used.

Implementation

The two-group design is beautifully simple and potentially can address the problem of history that plagues the time series quasi-experiment. However, in practice, it is rare that the design is implemented in its ideal form. In particular, the experimental units are often from different competitive environments. For example, a promotion might have been run in one city but not the other. Alternatively, an experiment may be run in one year and sales in the previous year used as a "control." Once we stray from the "random assignment/same competitive environment" desiderata of the two-group design, our experiment is open to the problem of unusual historical events discussed earlier. A precaution is to measure all marketing events and environmental factors as they occur in each group. If there are strong differences in these variables, the best way to analyze the data is with a regression analysis.

Even if we obtain experimental units from the same marketing environment, but do not randomly assign them to groups, we run the risk of obtaining a biased estimate of the promotion effect. For example, consider a two-group experiment where the promotion group consists of loyal users of the brand, and the control group consists of nonusers. A researcher might do this if further cooperation were needed from the promotion group, and loyal users were more likely to cooperate. The estimated promotion effect might then apply only to loyal users. There is no way of telling whether nonusers would have reacted the same to the promotion.

Example

A good example of a two-group pre-post experiment used for promotion is the Couponlab series of experiments (Klein, 1981). Between 60 and 70 experiments were run in this series, each testing the effectiveness of a coupon in inducing incremental sales. The experimental units used in the test were over 2,000 households located in Kansas City, Missouri. The households were randomly divided into three groups. The groups were matched on the basis of store loyalty, income, and family size. For example, if there were 300 four-person families loyal to store A and with high annual income in the panel, 100 of these families would be randomly assigned to each of the three experimental groups. Purchases of all families were monitored in UPC scanner–equipped stores.

Notice that the three panels were not balanced on the basis of loyalty to any specific brand. The reason for this is that Couponlab experiments involved several brand coupons being tested at once, matching on the basis of loyalty to

TABLE 6.1 Experimental Design for a Typical Metric Coupon Laboratory Experiment

Panel A	Panel B	Panel C
10c Brand S snack	10c Brand T snack	Control
Control	35c Brand A cleaner	35c Brand B cleaner
45c Coffee	Control	45c Coffee with sample
25c Detergent	25c Detergent	Control
Control	35c Dog food	35c Dog food
10c Toothpaste	Control	10c Toothpaste

Source: Robert L. Klein, "Using Supermarket Scanner Panels to Measure the Effectiveness of Coupon Promotions," in *Marketing: Measurement and Analysis, 1981, Proceedings of the Third ORSA/TIMS Special Interest Conference on Market Measurement and Analysis*, ed. John W. Keon, p. 119 (Providence, RI: The Institute of Management Sciences, 1981).

one brand would not ensure balance with respect to loyalty in several product categories. Potential balancing problems could have been avoided if the panels were re-formed for each coupon mailing, but then only one coupon could be mailed each mailing. This would have been expensive and also less realistic—solo direct-mail coupons are rare. Table 6.1 shows the design of a typical coupon mailing for the coupon laboratory.

Figure 6.3 shows week-by-week test minus control minus prepromotion difference, $(O_p - O_p') - (O_{pre} - O_{pre}')$, in share points for one brand. Notice first

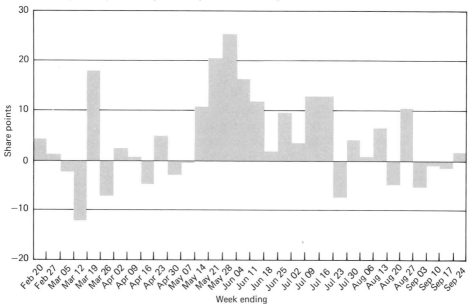

FIGURE 6.3 Results from a Typical Couponlab Experiment (Test Minus Control Minus Average Difference in Prepromotion Weeks)

Source: Robert L. Klein, "Using Supermarket Scanner Panels to Measure the Effectiveness of Coupon Promotions," in *Marketing: Measurement and Analysis, 1981, Proceedings of the Third ORSA/TIMS Special Interest Conference on Market Measurement and Analysis*, ed. John W. Keon, p. 121 (Providence, RI: The Institute of Management Sciences, 1981).

that there is a fair amount of variation in the data before the coupon drop, although the variation appears random and sums approximately to zero. It may be surprising that the noise level is as high as it is, but calculation of the approximate standard errors involved show how this occurs. Klein states that for the example shown in Figure 6.3, an average of 60 panelists purchased in the category each week. Therefore, the "n" on which weekly market share is calculated in each week is only 60. If we assume the brand in question has roughly a 20 percent market share in each panel, then the standard error of differences in market share (test $-$ control) would be $\sqrt{(.20)(.80)/60 + (.20)(.80)/60} = .073$; two standard errors would be .146. Indeed, 11 of the 12 differences shown in the test period (92 percent) are within 0.146 of zero.

DETAILED DISCUSSION OF THE PRECISION OF THE TIME SERIES QUASI-EXPERIMENT AND THE TWO-GROUP PRE-POST EXPERIMENT

Even if one is willing to assume that the estimated promotion effect obtained from these experiments is unbiased—that is, on average will equal the true promotion effect—the particular estimate obtained in one run of the experiment will not equal the true promotion effect. If one were to rerun the experiment several times, a different estimate would be obtained each time. The average estimate will equal the true effect; however, the variance around this average represents how close any particular estimate tends to be to the true effect. By precision of the experiment, therefore, we mean the variance of the estimated promotion effect.

In this section, we first discuss how to calculate the variance of the promotion effect estimate for both the time series quasi-experiment and the two-group pre-post experiment. We discuss conditions under which one experiment might be more precise than the other, illustrate these points with a numerical example, and discuss strategies including blocking, matching, and regression analysis, for improving the precision of these experiments.

Analysis Using Descriptive Statistics

Following the notation introduced earlier, let O_p equal sales in the treatment group during a promotion, let O_{pre} equal average sales in the treatment group before the promotion, and let O'_p and O'_{pre} be the corresponding quantities for the control group (present only in the two-group experiment). Our estimates for the promotion effect are

$$\text{Time series quasi-experiment:} \quad O_p - O_{pre} \tag{6.1}$$

$$\text{Two-group pre-post experiment:} \quad (O_p - O'_p) - (O_{pre} - O'_{pre}) \tag{6.2a}$$

$$= (O_p - O_{pre}) - (O'_p - O'_{pre}) \tag{6.2b}$$

We see then that the two-group estimate equals the time series experiment estimate adjusted for changes in sales occurring in the control group during the time of the promotion.

Another way to think of the comparison between the time series experiment and the two-group experiment is in terms of their estimates of "baseline" sales—sales that would have occurred in the treatment group during the promotion period had the promotion not been implemented. The time series experiment estimate of this baseline is O_{pre}. The two-group baseline estimate is $O_{pre} + (O'_p - O'_{pre})$. The second term in this expression uses the deviation from average sales in the control group during the promotion week to infer what would have occurred in the promotion week for the treatment group, had there been no promotion.

To derive the variance of the estimates, we take the variance of equations (6.1) and (6.2a), obtaining:

Variance of the
quasi-experiment estimate $= \text{var}(O_p) + \text{var}(O_{pre}) - 2[\text{var}(O_p)\text{var}(O_{pre})]^{(1/2)}\rho_{opre}$ **(6.3)**

Variance of the
two-group estimate $= \text{var}(O_p - O'_p) + \text{var}(O_{pre} - O'_{pre})$

$$- 2[\text{var}(O_p - O'_p)\text{var}(O_{pre} - O'_{pre})]^{(1/2)}\rho_{odifpre} \qquad \textbf{(6.4)}$$

where ρ_{opre} is the correlation between O_p and O_{pre} and $\rho_{odifpre}$ is the correlation between $O_p - O'_p$ and $O_{pre} - O'_{pre}$. We will assume for the moment that the correlations between promotion period and prepromotion period sales are zero, although in the next section we will discuss what happens if we deviate from this assumption of no serial correlation. Our focus is then on the four variance terms in equations (6.3) and (6.4).

Assume that the sales data will be obtained on a weekly basis and that the promotion takes place over a one-week period.[1] Consider then the $\text{var}(O_p)$ term in equation (6.3). Conceptually, this is the variance in sales during the promotion week one would observe if the experiment were to be repeated an infinite number of times. The promotion effect is included in the promotion week's sales, but this effect is a constant so does not contribute to variance. The variance we are looking for should therefore be manifested in the normal week-to-week variation in sales. This can be estimated from the prepromotion period data. If we have n prepromotion data points, we can simply calculate the variance of the data points (call this S^2) and use that as an estimate of $\text{var}(O_p)$. The task would be similar in calculating $\text{var}(O_p - O'_p)$. In this case, we are interested in the variance in the difference between the promotion and control groups. This could be obtained by calculating the differences for each week in the prepromotion period, calculating the variance of these numbers (call this S'^2), and using that as an estimate of $\text{var}(O_p - O'_p)$.

---

[1] We make this assumption to simplify the exposition. We discuss at the end of this section how to change the analysis if the promotion period lasts more than time period—in this case, more than one week.

Note that an important assumption implicit in the foregoing discussion is that the variance in sales is the same during the promotion period as it is during the prepromotion period. This was justified on the basis that the promotion effect during that period is like a constant added to sales that would not vary in reruns of the experiment. If in fact the variance of sales is different in the promotion period than in the prepromotion period, this is called heteroscedasticity and will be discussed shortly.

Now consider the $\text{var}(O_{pre})$ term in equation (6.3). This is the variance of an average, the average of the n prepromotion weeks. We could therefore use S^2/n as the estimated variance of the average. Again implicit in this suggestion are two assumptions: (1) that the weekly sales data are not autocorrelated and (2) that each weekly sales number has the same variance, estimated by S^2. Similarly we could estimate the $\text{var}(O_{pre} - O'_{pre})$ term in equation (6.4) by S'^2/n. Putting these arguments together, we have as the estimates of variance for each of the promotion effect estimates:

$$\begin{array}{ll}\text{Estimated variance of} \\ \text{quasi-experiment estimate} \end{array} = S^2 + \frac{S^2}{n} \qquad (6.5)$$

$$\begin{array}{ll}\text{Estimated variance of} \\ \text{two-group estimate} \end{array} = S'^2 + \frac{S'^2}{n} \qquad (6.6)$$

Note that in deriving equations (6.5) and (6.6), we assumed that the data are collected weekly and that the sales promotion lasted one week. If the promotion lasted n^+ weeks where $n^+ > 1$, for the time series experiment we could calculate O_p as *average* weekly sales during the promotion period, and then the first term in equation (6.5) would be S^2/n^+. Similarly, for the two-group experiment, we would calculate $O_p - O'_p$ as the *average* weekly difference in sales between the promotion and control groups during the promotion period, and then the first term in equation (6.6) would be S'^2/n^+.

We see from equations (6.5) and (6.6) that the relative precision of the time series versus the two-group experiment will depend on the relative magnitudes of S^2 and S'^2. To investigate the relationship between these terms, let S^{*2} be the variance in sales in the control group, and let r be the correlation of weekly sales between the promotion and control groups. We can then write[2].

$$S'^2 = S^2 + S^{*2} - (2 \cdot S \cdot S^* \cdot r) \qquad (6.7)$$

We see from equation (6.7) that the variance of the difference in sales between the two groups equals the variance of sales in the promotion group plus the variance of sales in the control group minus a term that will be largely positive if sales are highly correlated between the groups.

---

[2] This follows because the variance of a difference between two random variables is the sum of the variances of these variables minus two times the first standard deviation times the second standard deviation times the correlation between the random variables (e.g., see Olson and Picconi, 1983, p. 234).

Equations (6.5)–(6.7) imply that to the extent that the variance in sales in the control group is small or the correlation between sales in the promotion and control groups is large, the variance of the two-group estimate can be smaller than the variance of the time series experiment. However, this may not be the case. The variance of the control group can be very large and sales between the groups may not at all be correlated. The situation of low correlation would occur if the control and promotion groups were subject to completely different geographic and marketing environments. If the two groups were subject to the same marketing environment, sales for those groups would likely be correlated, because a marketing event that increases (decreases) sales in one group should also increase (decrease) sales in the other group. In this case, the variance of the two-group estimate would tend to be smaller than that of the time series estimate.

Equation (6.7) therefore suggests a rationale for how the two-group experiment can be more precise than the time series experiment. Adding a control group adds noise to the error, because the control group itself will experience variation in sales over time. However, if the control group can be selected from the same geographic and marketing environment, we would expect that sales in that group will be correlated with those in the promotion group. This lowers the variance of the difference in sales between the two groups, and hence lowers the variance of the estimated promotion effect.

Analysis Using Univariate Regression

Another way to analyze the time series and two-group experiments is to cast the problem in terms of a regression equation. This yields exactly the same estimates and variances as the methods described in the previous section. However, the use of regression allows us to discuss the assumptions of no heteroscedasticity and no autocorrelation we used in deriving equations (6.5) and (6.6). Also, given the widespread availability of regression packages, some analysts find it easier to use the regression approach.

In particular, define the variable D_t as a zero-one dummy variable equaling one in the promotion week and zero in the prepromotion weeks, let ϵ_{qt} and ϵ_{gt} equal the error terms in the quasi-experiment and two-group experiment regression, respectively, for week t, and let Y_{pt} and Y_{ct} be defined as sales in the promotion and control groups, respectively, in week t. Then we could estimate the following regression models:

quasi-experiment
regression:
$$Y_{pt} = \alpha_q + \beta_q D_t + \epsilon_{qt} \tag{6.8}$$

two-group experiment
regression:
$$Y_{dif} = Y_{pt} - Y_{ct} = \alpha_g + \beta_g D_t + \epsilon_{gt} \tag{6.9}$$

If these equations are estimated using ordinary least squares regression, their estimated parameters will correspond to those in equations (6.1) and (6.2a). This is because the constant terms in equations (6.8) and (6.9) represent sales or differences in sales in the absence of promotion, and the regression coefficient for D_t represents the estimated effect of the promotion. Specifically, the constant term α_q will correspond to O_{pre} in equation (6.1), and β_q will correspond to $O_p - O'_{pre}$ in equation (6.1). The constant term α_g will correspond to $O_{pre} - O'_{pre}$ in equation (6.2a), and the term β_g will correspond to $(O_p - O'_p) - (O_{pre} - O'_{pre})$ in equation (6.2a).

As mentioned, regression analysis provides a framework for diagnosing and if necessary adjusting for the presence of heteroscedasticity and serial correlation. The consequence of both heteroscedasticity and serial correlation is biased estimates of the variances of the promotion effect estimates. That is, variances estimated using equations (6.5) and (6.6) or ordinary least squares estimation of equations (6.8) and (6.9) will be biased estimates of the true variances of the estimated promotion effect. Confidence intervals for the promotion effect using these estimates will be incorrect. There are econometric methods which potentially not only correct the bias but produce estimates of the promotion effect that have lower variance than the estimates derived from equations (6.5) and (6.6) or (6.8) and (6.9) (see Pindyck and Rubinfeld, 1981, Ch. 6, esp. pp. 145–146 on correcting for heteroscedasticity and pp. 154–58 on correcting for serial correlation).

In summary, ordinary least squares estimation of equations (6.8) and (6.9) provides the same results as equations (6.5) and (6.6). In addition, the regression framework allows one to test for the presence of heteroscedasticity and serial correlation. If these problems are present, advanced regression techniques can be used to produce lower variance estimates of the promotion effect.

An Example Using Simulated Data

In this section we will use Monte Carlo simulation to generate sales data using a known model and then use both the descriptive statistics and regression approaches to analyze the data. We will demonstrate the equivalence of the two methods and also illustrate the circumstances under which the two-group experiment can yield higher or lower variance estimates of the promotion effect than does the time series experiment.

We generate data using the following model:

$$S_{it} = \alpha + \beta P_{it} + \delta R_t + \epsilon_{it} \tag{6.10}$$

where

S_{it} = sales for group i during week t

P_{it} = dummy variable for presence of sales promotion in group i during week t

R_t = marketing environment (same for both groups) during week t

ϵ_{it} = other causes of sales in group i during week t

i = 1 or 2 corresponding to the promotion group or the control group, respectively

t = 1, 2, . . . , 50 corresponding to 50 weeks

The promotion dummy always equals zero for the control group, and for the promotion group, equals zero in all weeks except week 50, when it equals 1 to signify a promotion in that week. For this illustration, the marketing environment is assumed to be the same for both groups. Implicitly, then, we are assuming that the two experimental groups are from exactly the same geographic area. The Couponlab experiments are an example of this case. The actual marketing environment data (R_t) were generated as independent draws from a uniform distribution between zero and one. These data can be viewed as the sum total of marketing variables affecting sales in any given week. Included in this total would be the brand's own promotions and advertising, as well as its competitors'.

The ϵ_{it} terms include other causes of sales that are not the same for both groups (note the i subscript in ϵ_{it}). These causes might include factors intrinsic to the experimental units themselves. For example, if the experimental units are households, the level of household inventory, brand loyalty, purchase history, interpurchase time, and so on will all vary over time. Since the two groups consist of two different sets of consumers, these factors will not be common between the groups. A mathematical way of stating this is that the correlation between ϵ_{1t} and ϵ_{2t} is zero.

Using these assumptions, we simulate two cases of equation (6.10). These cases are presented in Table 6.2. There are two differences between case 1 and case 2: (1) The marketing environment is a more important determinant of sales in case 1 than in case 2, and (2) the variance in the ϵ_{it} term is greater in case 2 than in case 1. These differences were specified to create case 2 as an example where there would be less correlation between sales of the two groups over time, and the variance of the control group would be relatively large, compared to the situation in case 1. As discussed earlier, under these circumstances, we would expect that the two-group estimate will have lower variance than the time series estimate for case 1, but higher variance than the time series estimate for case 2.

We first consider case 1. Using equation (6.1) and the data in Table 6.1, the time series estimate of the promotion effect is

$$O_p - O_{pre} = 3{,}303.07 - 1{,}374.54 = 1{,}928.53$$

Using equation (6.5), the variance of that estimate is

$$S^2 + \frac{S^2}{n} = (216.77)^2 + \frac{(216.77)^2}{49} = 47{,}948.20$$

The square root of this variance, 218.97, is the standard error of the estimate and can be used to form a 95 percent confidence interval for the promotion effect. That confidence interval would be $1{,}928.53 \pm (2 \cdot 218.97)$, or $1{,}928 \pm 437.94$. We see that this interval does contain the true promotion effect, which was 2000 (see Table 6.2). Using ordinary least squares estimation of equation (6.8), we obtained the following result (standard errors are in parentheses):

$$Y_{pt} = 1{,}374.54 + 1{,}928.53D_t$$
$$\quad\;\; (30.97) \quad\;\; (218.97)$$

TABLE 6.2 Simulated Data for a Two-Group Promotion Experiment

General Assumptions

$$S_{it} = \alpha + \beta P_{it} + \delta R_t + \epsilon_{it}$$

where
- $t = 1, \ldots, 50$ labeling weeks
- $i = 1, 2$ labeling groups (1 = promotion group, 2 = control group)
- S_{it} = sales in group i during week t
- P_{it} = presence or absence of promotion for group i at week t. ($P_{it} = 0$ for $i = 1, 2$ and $t = 1, \ldots, 49$; $P_{1,50} = 1$, $P_{2,50} = 0$) (a promotion takes place in week 50 for group 1)
- R_t = marketing environment factors common to both groups in week t (R_t is drawn each week from a uniform distribution between 0 and 1, each draw is independent)
- ϵ_{it} = other factors affecting sales in group i during week t (ϵ_{it} are drawn from a normal distribution with mean 0 and standard deviation σ which varied between cases. All draws were independent, both over time and between groups)

Simulation Results

Case I

$$S_{it} = 1,000 + 2,000P_{it} + 700R_t + \epsilon_{it}$$

$$\sigma^2 = 10,208$$

	Prepromotion Period		Promotion Period
	Mean Sales	Standard Deviation (using 48 as divisor)	Sales
Test group	1,374.54	216.77	3,303.07
Control group	1,346.61	245.67	1,210.97
Difference	27.93	147.50	2,092.10

Correlation between sales of test and control = .804

Case II

$$S_{it} = 1,000 + 2,000P_{it} + 550R_t + \epsilon_{it}$$

$$\sigma^2 = 163,333$$

	Prepromotion Period		Promotion Period
	Mean Sales	Standard Deviation (using 48 as divisor)	Sales
Test group	1,231.58	370.08	3,595.24
Control group	1,387.23	439.30	2,238.17
Difference	155.66	524.91	1,357.07

Correlation between sales of test and control = .167

This yields identical estimates of the promotion effect and its variance as does the descriptive statistics approach shown.

Analyzing the data in Table 6.2 as a two-group experiment, we use equation (6.2a) to obtain the following estimate of the promotion effect:

$$(O_p - O_p') - (O_{pre} - O_{pre}') = 2,092.10 - 27.93 = 2,064.17$$

Using equation (6.6) and the data in Table 6.2, we obtain the following for the variance of the promotion effect estimate:

$$S'^2 + \frac{S'^2}{n} = (147.50)^2 + \frac{(147.50)^2}{49} = 22,200.26$$

The square root of this is 149.00, so the confidence interval for the true promotion effect is $2,064.17 \pm (2 \cdot 149)$, or $2,064 \pm 298$. Note that this interval is narrower than the interval derived using the time series estimate, and also contains the true promotion effect of 2,000. As hypothesized, then, in case 1, the two-group estimate yielded a more precise estimate—lower variance—than did the time series estimate. Note the correlation of prepromotion period sales between the promotion and control groups is .804. Referring back to equation (6.7), this results in a lower variance for the two-group estimate.

For case 2, we just provide the ordinary least squares estimates of equations (6.8) and (6.9), since they are equivalent to the estimates based on equations (6.1), (6.2a), (6.5), and (6.6):

Time series estimate: $Y_{pt} = 1,231.58 + 2,363.66 D_t$
                                          (52.87)   (373.84)

Two-group estimate: $Y_{dif} = -155.65 + 1,512.72 D_t$
                                          (74.99)   (530.24)

Note first that both estimates are within one standard error of the true promotion effect, but that the standard errors are much larger than for case 1. This is because the error variance was much larger (see Table 6.2). Second, as hypothesized, the two-group estimate is less precise than the time series estimate. This is due to the large variance of the control group in this case compared to case 1, and the lower importance of marketing environment, which was common to both groups, in determining sales. As a result, Table 6.2 shows that the correlation of sales between promotion and control groups in the prepromotion periods is only .167. Referring back to equation (6.7), this results in a higher variance for the two-group estimate, compared to the time series estimate.

Increasing Precision of the Two-Group Design Through Blocking or Matching

Blocking and matching are methods for assigning experimental units to treatment groups. These procedures work by finding experimental units that are equivalent on one or more variables and then equally and randomly dividing these units between the promotion group and the control group. Matching and blocking differ in that matching is usually thought of as pertaining to pairs of units, while blocking involves several units (Reichardt, 1979, pp. 175–178). For example, we might pair up or match stores whose sales were practically equal and then randomly assign the pair members to either the promotion or control group. With blocking, we could create three categories—large, medium, and small stores—and find ten stores in each block. We then assign five from each block to the promotion and control groups.

Blocking or matching can increase the precision of our experiment in two ways. First, these techniques can help to assure that sales for the experimental groups are correlated over time. Second, we can include the blocking or matching factors in the analysis, thereby explaining or controlling for the variance they cause in the data.[3] We discuss this second benefit in more depth shortly. The first benefit will be discussed here.

From equation (6.7) we know that our two-group estimate will have lower variance to the extent that sales are highly correlated between the two groups. Earlier, we illustrated that the correlation between sales for the two groups will be higher to the extent that the groups are equivalent over time on variables that are important determinants of sales. Blocking or matching provides a means of assuring that the two groups will be equivalent throughout the experiment on these determinants. For example, when one draws experimental units from the same geographic area, the units will be equivalent on marketing variables, seasonality, and the weather. Several stores might be selected from the same sales region. These stores will be offered the same trade promotions, and television advertising will be the same. As a result, important marketing determinants of sales will be correlated over time between the stores; this will result in high correlation in sales between the stores and will lower the variance of the estimated promotion effect.

Another way to block or match experimental groups is on internal characteristics of the experimental units. For example, one could make sure that households in a two-group experiment begin the experiment with the same distribution of brand loyalty toward the test brand. If the groups are also well matched on marketing environment, one might then expect that loyalty will evolve similarly over time for the two groups, resulting in a higher correlation between sales. It is often difficult to measure characteristics such as loyalty before an experiment begins. Demographic characteristics might be used as a surrogate for this factor.

Increasing Precision Through Multivariate Regression

Another method for increasing the precision of either the time series or two-group experiment is to estimate a multivariate regression model and use it to measure the promotion effect. For example, one could quantify some of the marketing

---

[3] Note that another motivation for using blocking or matching is to control bias in the experiment, which might arise if experimental units were not randomly assigned to groups (see the preceding discussion; Reichardt, 1979, pp. 175–182; and Campbell and Stanley, 1963, p. 15).

variables that were a part of equation (6.10) but were ignored in using equations (6.8) and (6.9) to measure the promotion effect. Intuitively, by quantifying other variables besides the experimental promotion and estimating their effect upon sales, we can derive a more precise estimate (narrower confidence interval) of what sales would have been during the promotion period. This is because we know the other variables present during that period and we have an estimate of how they affect sales. If we leave out those variables, our confidence interval for baseline sales during the promotion period will be wider.

The Chapman experiment described later uses a multivariate econometric model to help provide more precise estimates of a promotion effect. Hee (1981) describes the use of logit to decrease uncertainty in the estimate of the promotion effect. The logit model has the advantage of taking into account both environmental variables (e.g., in-store promotions) and internal characteristics of the experimental units (e.g., household purchase history), so it attempts to control for a broader variety of variables. The logit model uses panel data to quantify internal characteristics.

To illustrate the potential of multivariate regression, we incorporated the actual values of R_t from cases 1 and 2 in Table 6.2 into a regression model that expanded upon equation (6.8). The following estimates were obtained:

Case 1: $Y_{pt} = 1,011.87 + 2,029.19D_t + 661.65R_t$
$$\phantom{Case 1: Y_{pt} = }(31.58)(103.77)(51.06)$$

Case 2: $Y_{pt} = 920.36 + 2,168.15D_t + 519.73R_t$
$$\phantom{Case 2: Y_{pt} = }(124.21)(358.15)(190.16)$$

Referring back to "An Example Using Simulated Data," we see that the standard error for the promotion effect estimate in case 1 decreased from 218.97 to 103.77. For case 2, the decrease was less impressive, from 373.84 to 358.15. This is because R_t is a more important determinant of sales in case 1, both in terms of absolute impact and relative to the impact of other causes of sales.

EXPERIMENTS THAT INCORPORATE MORE THAN ONE VARIABLE

Design

The need to incorporate more than one variable occurs often in sales promotion research. For example, one might want to study how coupons affect sales, how displays affect sales, and how the two together affect sales. A critical question is whether the joint sales effect of a simultaneous in-store display and manufacturer coupon is greater than the sum of the sales effects that would occur if each promotion were implemented in separate time periods. If the joint effect is larger, we have a positive "interaction," or "synergy," between the promotions. The existence of such synergy is a major assumption justifying "big-bang" multi-event promotions.

One might also incorporate more than one variable in an experiment as a means of controlling experimental noise. For example, we may be interested only in investigating the effect of in-store price cuts on sales and want to run an experiment in a geographic area with, for example, 24 stores. Response to the price cut will vary from store to store because of differences in store size. If we do not explicitly consider this in designing and then analyzing our experiment, differences in stores may swamp the effect of the price cut.

Another very important reason for incorporating several variables in an experiment is to avoid confounding the promotion effect with some other factor. For example, if we randomly assign the price cut to 12 of the 24 stores, we might inadvertently assign the price cut disproportionately to the large stores. If *only* large stores receive a price cut, its effect will be completely confounded with the store size factor. This is similar to the Halloween example discussed earlier. By systematically making sure that both large and small stores receive a price cut, we ensure that the effects of store size and price cut can be separated in the analysis. Often we are not able to separate perfectly the effects of different factors in our experimental design. This will manifest itself as multicollinearity in the data. We will review an example of this shortly, when we discuss Chapman's (1986) coupon experiment.

We will briefly discuss four types of experiments that incorporate more than one variable: randomized blocks, Latin squares, full factorials, and fractional factorials. The first two designs are often used to control experimental noise, while the last two are often used to examine more than one promotion instrument. There is a significant body of literature pertaining to the design of these experiments. Winer (1971) provides excellent and readable detail of how to design and analyze such experiments. Doyle and Gidengil (1977) also provide good examples and perspective on sales promotion experiments in particular.

Randomized Blocks. Following our example of investigating the effect of a price cut, assume that we could divide the 24 stores available into three equal groups on the basis of store volume: small, medium, and large. Suppose then that for each group of 8 stores, we randomly have 4 institute a price cut and 4 serve as a control by not instituting a price cut. The design would be as follows:

	Price Cut	
Store Size	*No*	*Yes*
Small	4 stores	4 stores
Medium	4 stores	4 stores
Large	4 stores	4 stores

Notice the design is balanced in that the price cut is instituted equally often in small, medium, and large stores. This will allow us to measure the effect of the price cut separately from the store size factor. If we had used the following design,

| | Price Cut | |
Store Size	No	Yes
Small	0	8
Medium	4	4
Large	8	0

we would not be able to dissociate the effect of the price cut from store size, since any apparent effect (or lack of it) of the price cut might be due to the small stores in which it was instituted.

Returning to our balanced *randomized block* design, it is easy to see how consideration of the store-size factor will allow us to get a more precise estimate of the price cut effect. For example, assume the data (in number of sales during the price cut period) were as follows:

No Price Cut	Price Cut
30, 135, 190, 20, 140, 120, 35, 200, 230	40, 120, 250, 25, 160, 170, 30, 190, 250

The data appear to be very noisy; there are several stores in the price cut condition that achieved lower sales than in the no price cut condition. However, if we arrange the data by the blocking factor store size, we have the following:

| | Price Cut | |
Store Size	No	Yes
Small	30, 20, 35	40, 25, 30
Medium	135, 140, 120	120, 160, 170
Large	190, 200, 230	250, 190, 250

We now can see much more clearly that indeed the price cut did have an effect. In the formal analysis of a randomized block experiment, the blocking factor is included as an additional variable influencing sales. By helping to explain a good portion of the noise in the data, it allows the promotion effect to be estimated more clearly against the unexplained noise (see Winer, 1971, pp. 240–244; Lapin, 1987, pp. 411–419).

Latin Squares.   Another type of blocking design is the Latin square. Following on the preceding example, assume that we wanted to test three levels of price cut—none, 10 percent, and 20 percent—and also suspected that store pricing strategy—little, moderate, or heavy use of price promotions—was an important blocking variable along with store size. We could formulate the following design (with one store in each cell):

| Pricing Strategy: Reliance on Price Promotions | Store Size | | |
	Small	Medium	Large
Little	No price cut	10% price cut	20% price cut
Moderate	10% price cut	20% price cut	No price cut
Heavy	20% price cut	No price cut	10% price cut

The design is balanced in that each store size is exposed to each level of price cut, and each pricing strategy is exposed to each level of price cut. The design is also parsimonious: we need only 9 stores. If we were to use a full randomized block design with two blocking factors, we would have needed $3 \times 3 \times 3 = 27$ stores. The Latin square saves on the number of stores needed because not every strategy-size *combination* appears with every price cut level.

The Latin square is easy to use and provides a parsimonious balanced design. However, it has a few drawbacks: (1) It requires an equal number of levels for each factor. This can be artificial. (2) The small sample sizes encouraged by the Latin square may be too small to detect significant effects. (3) It is impossible to dissociate the effects of the main treatment variable from interactions between the two blocking variables. For example, stores relying heavily on promotions may generally have larger sales than stores relying moderately on promotions, and larger stores may have more sales than medium stores. This reflects the "main effects" of store size and pricing strategy. However, these two factors may interact, so that large stores relying heavily on promotions have much larger sales than medium-sized stores relying moderately on promotions, in fact, much more than would be predicted based on the main effects alone. If we look at our design, however, this will distort the effect we estimate of the 10 percent reduction, because this is the only reduction paired with the "large-heavy" store combination. The 10 percent reduction might appear to be very effective only because it was the only reduction paired with the store combination with exceptionally high sales. The problem would be rectified if we paired every level of price reduction with every store combination, but then we would be back to a 27-cell experiment.

Likewise, we can deduce that any interactions between the price reduction and one of the blocking factors, say, pricing strategy, will be confounded with the main effect of the other blocking variable, for example, store size. For example, a 20 percent price cut might be especially effective in stores relying heavily on price promotion, but that effect would be masked by the fact that the 20 percent reduction in a heavy-reliance store was only used when the store was small, and small stores generally achieve smaller sales.

Full and Fractional Factorials. As mentioned, the most complete experimental design is the "full factorial," where each factor level appears with each combination of the foregoing factors. A full factorial allows the researcher to explore all potential interactions among the factors. For example, in a three-factor experiment involving couponing, price reduction, and display, a full factorial would allow for a clear conclusion as to whether the three promotions in combination performed better than the separate contributions of each promotion. The problem with full factorial designs is that they require a large sample. For example, consider the design of a four-factor experiment with couponing (none, 15 cent face value, 30 cent face value), price reduction (none, 10 percent, 20 percent), display (none or end-of-aisle), and retailer advertising (none, small ad, large ad). The full factorial would require $3 \times 3 \times 2 \times 3 = 54$ cells, or 54 stores for its implementation.

An alternative to the full factorial is a fractional factorial. For example, the 54 cells could be reduced to 27. The reduction from the full factorial means that some interactions will be confounded with some main effects, so that, for example, we may not be able to dissociate the independent main effect of couponing from the interaction between retailer advertising and display. The reason for this is exactly the same as for the confounding that occurs in the Latin square design. However, with judicious selection of experimental cells, one can plan on confounding main effects with interactions that can be assumed to equal zero. We can then interpret the main effect result as the only effect measured. For example, we might assume that the interaction between retailer advertising and display would be small. Displays rely on impulse buying and will be equally effective whether or not the brand was advertised that week. In that case, we can design our experiment so that the main effect of couponing would be confounded with the interaction between display and retailer advertising. Since we are willing to assume that interaction is zero, the main effect for couponing we calculate will be interpreted as purely the effect of couponing.

Fractional factorials are a very practical tool for incorporating several variables in an experiment. They do require a great deal of planning, for example, in deciding which interactions are likely to be negligible and in actually selecting the cells for factor combinations, to be included in the experiment. The reader is referred to Winer (1971) for some of the detail on how to construct fractional designs as well as to Green (1974), Addleman (1962), and Cochran and Cox (1957).

Analysis

Randomized block, Latin square, full factorial, and fractional factorial experiments are analyzed using analysis of variance, analysis of covariance, or regression. Analysis of variance is designed for the situation where all factors to be considered in the analysis have been considered explicitly in the design of the experiment. Analysis of covariance is designed for the situation where another factor has not been controlled for in the design of the experiment but may exert some influence on sales. For example, in the Latin square experiment described earlier, competitive promotion activity was not explicitly considered in formulating the experiment, but may influence sales. Competitive promotion activity would then serve as a "covariate" in an analysis of covariance. Regression analysis can be used in the extreme case that none of the factors is explicitly controlled, or the control has been minimal. We will provide a detailed example of using regression to analyze a promotion experiment in the next section.

The reader should note that both analysis of variance and analysis of covariance can be formulated in terms of a regression model, and the same results will be obtained. The analyst simply codes the experimental treatment factors as dummy variables, thinks of any covariates as additional independent variables, and runs a regression. The use of a particular technique then depends on the preferences of the analyst. Analysis of variance and analysis of covariance are described in Winer (1971) and many statistical packages include these techniques.

One advantage of using analysis of variance or covariance is that the software is deliberately designed to allow the analyst to easily examine interaction effects and other particular hypotheses. However, an equivalently formulated regression model will yield the same results.

Examples

Our first example will be a Latin square experiment devised by Woodside and Waddle (1975). The experiment investigated the effect of price reduction and retailer point-of-sale advertising promotions on sales of instant coffee. Store and time period were used as the blocking factors, each at four levels. The design is displayed in Table 6.3. Notice that Woodside and Waddle really investigated two promotion variables—price reduction and advertising promotion—each at two levels, but combined them into one four-level promotion variable. The time period blocking variable consisted of one week at each level. This raises the possibility of carry-over effects from one week to the next. For example, the heavy promotion in week 1 for store D might result in lower sales in week 2, thereby making the low promotion condition in the next week look especially bad. Woodside and Waddle investigated this possibility by adding a fifth week of their experiment which replicated their fourth week. By examining this week, they concluded that there were no carry-over effects.

Graphical results from the Woodside and Waddle experiment are shown in Figure 6.4. Both point-of-sale advertising and price reduction seem to produce higher sales, but these two types of promotion interact—an advertised price reduction is especially effective.

TABLE 6.3   Design of the Woodside and Waddle Signing Experiment

Time Period	Retail Store	Design and Results of Extra-Period Latin Square Design Experiment in Product Unit Sales							
		A		B		C		D	
I		T_3	30	T_1	14	T_2	22	T_4	51
II		T_4	70	T_2	27	T_3	34	T_1	11
III		T_2	23	T_4	84	T_1	19	T_3	32
IV		T_1	19	T_3	31	T_4	85	T_2	23
V		T_1	25	T_3	36	T_4	45[a]	T_2	23

Overall total unit sales (0) = 704
Overall mean unit sales (0) = 35.20

T_1 = no price reduction, no promotion; T_2 = price reduction, no promotion; T_3 = no price reduction, promotion; T_4 = price reduction, promotion.

[a] A stockout of the item occurred in store C during the fifth week.

Source: Arch G. Woodside and Gerald L. Waddle, "Sales Effects of In-Store Advertising," *Journal of Advertising Research,* Vol. 15, no. 3 (June 1975), p. 31. Reprinted from the *Journal of Advertising Research,* © Copyright (1975), by the Advertising Research Foundation.

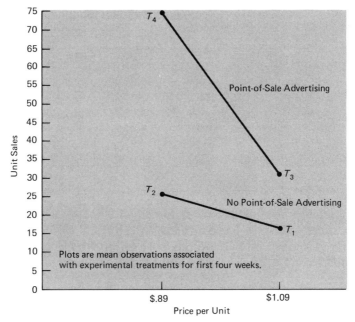

FIGURE 6.4 Results from the Woodside and Waddle Experiment

Source: Arch G. Woodside and Gerald L. Waddle, "Sales Effects of In-Store Advertising," *Journal of Advertising Research*, Vol. 15, no. 3 (June 1975), p. 33. Reprinted from the *Journal of Advertising Research*, © Copyright (1975) by the Advertising Research Foundation.

McKinnon, Kelly, and Robison (1981) utilized a slightly more complicated design to study the effects of in-store signing and price reduction on sales. Their design is summarized in Table 6.4. The promotion variable is a combination of price reduction and signing combined into a six-level promotion treatment, and is incorporated in a Latin square using time period and product as blocking variables. A different Latin square was used for each of three stores.

The McKinnon study concluded that an in-store sign that communicated some product benefits in addition to price information induced more sales than signs which just communicated price, although the effect interacted with the actual price. The benefits sign was especially effective when the price was reduced.

Wilkinson, Mason, and Paksoy (1982) used a full factorial experiment to investigate the sales effects of price reduction, display, and advertising. There were three price levels, three display levels, and two advertising levels, resulting in $3 \times 3 \times 2 = 18$ treatment cells. The experiment was run in one store over several weeks, so the experimental unit of analysis was the store week. The experiment was repeated twice (each repetition is called a "replication"). The experiment was run for four products and treated as four separate experiments.

TABLE 6.4 The Basic Latin Square Used for the McKinnon et al. Signing Experiment[a]

Time Period	Product					
	1	*2*	*3*	*4*	*5*	*6*
1	1A	2A	3A	1B	2B	3B
2	2B	3A	1A	2A	3B	1B
3	3B	1B	2A	3A	1A	2B
4	1B	2B	3B	1A	2A	3A
5	2A	3B	1B	2B	3A	1A
6	3A	1A	2B	3B	1B	2A

Key:
1A: Regular price, no sign
2A: Regular price, price sign
3A: Regular price, benefit sign
1B: Sale price, no sign
2B: Sale price, price sign
3B: Sale price, benefit sign

[a] The design was rotated for each store.

Source: Gary F. McKinnon, J. Patrick Kelly, and E. Doyle Robison, "Sales Effects of Point-of-Purchase In-Store Signing," *Journal of Retailing*, Vol. 57, no. 2 (Summer 1981), p. 56.

At least one week was required between treatments, first for reasons of easier implementation but also to guard against carry-over effects. As a result, 36 weeks were needed for each replication, for a total of 72 weeks. Taking into account holidays, the experiment lasted 80 weeks. In running an experiment over such a long time period, one runs the risk of having seasonal distortions. Seasonality was therefore used as a covariate in the analysis.

This experimental design is relatively straightforward. The use of only one store perhaps limits the generalizability of the results across all types of stores and resulted in the experiment being very long. If 18 stores had been available, a Latin square could have been used with stores and 18 weeks used as blocking factors. More advanced designs involving randomized blocking and fractional factorials could have been used. For example, with three stores, we could assign 6 of the 18 treatments to each store so that the store effect would have been confounded with only a limited number of interactions (Winer, 1971, pp. 661–676).

Wilkinson, Mason, and Paksoy examined four products and found many interesting results. For example, for "Piggly Wiggly" pie shells, they found the main effects for price and display were statistically significant, but advertising was not. That is, advertising by itself did not increase sales. Price and display interacted, in that a price reduction was especially effective when the product was on special display. Unlike the Woodside and Waddle experiment, there was no interaction between advertising and price. This could be because advertising in the Wilkinson et al. experiment was store circular feature advertising, whereas in the Woodside and Waddle experiment it was in-store signing.

As a final example, Chapman (1986) analyzed the effect of a direct-mail coupon on sales in a pizza restaurant. There were three levels of couponing—no coupon (C), coupon with menu and brochure (EG1), and coupon with menu (EG2). The design is shown in Table 6.5.

Table 6.5 shows that there were 12 census tracts. Notice that 3 tracts served as control, 4 served as EG1, and 5 as EG2. The reason for the unbalanced allocation is that the restaurant owner had high expectations for the coupon and

TABLE 6.5 Experimental Design for the Pizza Restaurant Couponing Experiment

| | Experimental Treatment Assignments and Measurement Plan[a] | | | Tract Characteristics | | | |
| | | | | Number of Households[b] | | | |
Tract	Group[c]	Starting Week	Experimental Treatment Weeks	Ending Week	Apart.	Homes	Total	Location[d]
1	EG2	2	5–7	10	850	1,520	2,370	3
2	C	1		9	995	900	1,875	2
3	EG1	1	4–6	9	325	1,415	1,740	2
4	EG2	4	7–9	12	460	1,560	2,030	2
5	C	1		9	1,410	650	2,060	2
6	C	1		9	305	1,475	1,780	1
7	EG1	3	6–8	11	1,530	725	2,255	1
8	EG1	1	4–6	9	2,255	1,215	3,470	0
9	EG2	4	7–9	12	2,175	725	2,900	1
10	EG1	3	6–8	11	1,830	1,900	3,730	2
11	EG2	4	7–9	12	0	500	500	3
12	EG2	2	5–7	10	2,080	1,075	3,155	3

[a] For each of these census tracts, measurement of sales began in the week indicated under Starting Week and terminated in the week indicated under Ending Week. Coupons were actually delivered starting at the beginning of the first week indicated under Experimental Treatment Weeks; their expiration date was the end of the third week after the beginning of delivery.

[b] Under Number of Households, Apart. refers to number of apartment units and Homes refers to number of single family dwellings.

[c] The Group column refers to the allocation of this census tract to control and experimental treatment groups. The coding is as follows:

C = control group
EG1 = experimental group 1
EG2 = experimental group 2

[d] The codes under Location refer to the distance of the census tract to the retail outlet, in terms of the number of census tract boundaries that have to be crossed.

Source: Randall G. Chapman, "Assessing the Profitability of Retailer Couponing with a Low-Cost Field Experiment," *Journal of Retailing*, Vol. 62, no. 1 (Spring 1986), p. 27.

did not want to sacrifice sales by having too many control groups. This unbalance will make the analysis much easier using a regression framework.

Note also in Table 6.5 that there were several other factors that could influence sales: time period, apartment-home mix, and location. These factors were not explicitly controlled in the design and would be used as covariates in the analysis. The experiment was analyzed by a series of regressions. The early analysis revealed that the two coupon distribution techniques had the same effect, so this was combined into one variable. However, the effect of the coupon varied week by week and so different variables were used for each week of the coupon promotion. In particular, define the following variables:

MIX = proportion of dwellings that are in apartments

DISTANCE = distance of census tract from the restaurant (on the 0–3 scale labeled Location in Table 6.5)

TIME = time index for the 12 weeks of the experiment

W_i = 1 if the observation was from a tract that received a coupon $i - 1$ periods ago, i = 1 to 6; 0 otherwise

The final regression model estimated was:

$$\text{sales per household} = .0671 - .0108 \text{ MIX} - .00117 \text{ DISTANCE}$$
$$- .0013 \text{ TIME} + .0831 \ W_1 + .0663 \ W_2$$
$$+ .0570 \ W_3 + .0237 \ W_4 + .0342 \ W_5$$
$$+ .0396 \ W_6$$
$$R^2 = .509 \qquad \text{SEE} = .030 \qquad n = 108$$

The coefficients for MIX and TIME were not significant. The others were significant at the 5 percent level. Most important, the coupon exhibits a significant effect on sales, approximately doubling sales in the first three weeks after being distributed, and having significant contribution for the next three weeks after that.

The Chapman experiment represents a pragmatic design in the face of several potentially influential variables and management wanting to inject managerial rather than statistical considerations into the design. The cost of this unbalanced design is that the coupon variables are somewhat correlated with the covariates, for example, DISTANCE, and this makes the measurement of coupon effects less precise than it might have been. Formally, this shows up as multicollinearity among the independent variables in the model. Chapman reports that indeed there was some multicollinearity in the model. However, the 95 percent confidence interval for the first week effect of a coupon drop is .0831 ± .0220, which appears to be acceptably precise. Certainly the effect is different from zero. Therefore, despite the problems of multicollinearity, Chapman was able to measure the effects of couponing with good precision.

SUMMARY

We have presented an overview of the design, analysis, and application of experiments involving sales promotion. We have seen examples of highly controlled single-factor experiments (e.g., Couponlab) and loosely controlled multifactor experiments (e.g., Chapman, 1986). Both these experiments appeared to have worked well, so it is difficult to recommend any generally best design. The design of any promotion experiment will therefore be influenced by the number of promotion factors being investigated, the presence and potential measurement of blocking factors and covariates, and the managerial as well as financial resources available.

Experiments are often evaluated in terms of their internal and external validity. Internal validity refers to the certainty with which the manipulated treatment variable caused the observed sales effect. Generally, the more control exerted, the more we can be sure of internal validity. For example, Chapman ran the risk that the coupon effect would be confounded with the DISTANCE effect. In fact, there was some confounding, manifested in multicollinearity, but the problem was mild enough so as not to seriously weaken the results. Balanced designs such as Latin squares or factorials can guard against confounding a priori, but even these methods are less than perfect. For the Latin square, there are still confoundings involving main and interaction effects. Even the seemingly foolproof design of the Couponlab experiments—randomly dividing the population in half and giving one-half a coupon—can run into internal validity problems if one half happens to be more loyal to the couponed brand than the other half and therefore reacts differently to the coupon than the other half would have. In summary, internal validity is always a problem with experimental research, and is particularly relevant in the rich world of promotion research.

External validity refers to the extent to which the experiment is generalizable to some universe. Many of the experiments cited here lack generalizability because they are run in only one locality. This is especially relevant for brand managers needing to formulate national marketing plans. Sales promotion experiments can also lack external validity in more subtle ways. For example, a signing experiment might be unrealistic because it did not allow the natural support sales personnel give to a sale item, or used an unrepresentative set of stores. A coupon lab experiment may be unrealistic because it does not allow for higher levels of retailer support that often accompany a coupon drop.

7

Regression Analysis Applied to Sales Promotion

OVERVIEW

Multivariate regression is applicable to estimating the separate contributions of several variables acting jointly upon a single dependent variable. By its basic nature, the analysis of promotions tends to fit this situation well: A given brand uses several different types of promotion, each of which would be expected to have a different effect.

Table 7.1 outlines the specific issues involved with estimating regression models for analyzing sales promotion. We will discuss these issues in more detail on the ensuing pages. Throughout, we assume the reader is at least somewhat familiar with regression analysis. For those who are not, there are several excellent textbooks, including (in order of ascending complexity) Mansfield (1983), Wonnacott and Wonnacott (1979), Pindyck and Rubinfeld (1981), Johnston (1972), and Theil (1971).

DATA

Experimental Versus Nonexperimental Data

As discussed in Chapter 6, regression can be used to analyze both experimental and nonexperimental data. The only practical difference is that multicollinearity is less likely to be a problem with experimental data. This is because experimenters usually manipulate the treatments in an experiment to avoid confounding their effects (see Chapter 6). For example, if both feature and display were studied in an experiment, the experimenter would make sure there were an equal number of instances in which the brand was featured and not displayed, not displayed

TABLE 7.1 Issues in Using Regression to Analyze Promotion's Effect on Sales

Data	Experimental versus nonexperimental
	Panel versus store
	Consumer sales versus warehouse withdrawals versus factory shipments
Omitted variables bias	
Level of aggregation	Temporal
	Across stores
	Across brand size/style/flavor
	Across consumer
Dependent variables	Category sales
	Brand sales
	Market share
Independent variables	Promotion (features, deals, price, displays, etc.)
	Advertising
	Distribution
	Price
	Lags
	Interactions
	Competition
	Other variables (e.g., weather, seasonality)
Functional form	Linear
	Multiplicative
	Attraction
	Semilog
Estimation procedures	Ordinary least squares
	Generalized least squares
	Seemingly unrelated regression
	Nonlinear regression
	Constrained estimation
	Stein rule and shrinkage estimates
Multicollinearity	

and featured, featured and displayed, and not featured and not displayed. Once the feature and display treatments are converted to dummy variables for use in a regression analysis, these variables would be uncorrelated, and hence there would be no problems with multicollinearity.

Panel Data Versus Aggregate Sales

A second data issue is whether the data are for a panel of consumers or for aggregate sales in a geographic area or store. Panel data provide information on individual household purchases. Store data contain all sales in a given store or collection of stores over a period of time. "Scanner data" come in two varieties, store data and panel data. (See Totten and Block, 1987, pp. 28–29.) The data are collected by a computer attached to each checkout counter's scanning equipment.

As each item is scanned, the count is updated for the particular UPC code on the purchased package. In this way, all sales are counted. For panel data, a set of consumers, the panel, is given special laminated credit-type cards, which they present upon checking out. The computer then stores not only purchases, but the consumer's identification number as indicated on his or her card. As a result, the computer keeps on file a history of each consumer's purchases. Store data therefore contain aggregate sales from all consumers shopping in the store(s), whereas panel data contain household-level sales for a subset of these consumers.

Panel data contain more information than store data and are potentially more useful. For example, if we wanted to study the effect of promotion or consumer brand loyalty, we would need panel data in order to calculate measures of brand loyalty (see Jacoby and Chestnut (1978) for a review of brand-loyalty measures). One way to investigate this issue would be with a consumer choice model (Chapter 8). However, one might also want to model changes in aggregate brand loyalty over time using a regression framework.

The price of the additional information contained in panel data is that these data will be inherently more "noisy" than the corresponding store data collected from the stores where the panel members shop. The source of the additional noise in panel data is that sales are generated from a smaller sample size of consumers, and smaller sample sizes result in more week-to-week variation.[1] The lower noise level for aggregate store data is one factor in favor of using that data source for many types of regression modeling (see Chapter 12).

An additional factor influencing both panel and store data is noncoverage. That is, the stores, or the panelists, used to generate the data may not represent the entire retail universe. For example, we may have collected data in one chain of supermarket stores that is representative of all other supermarkets, but a significant volume in the category may be accumulated in discount stores or convenience stores. We can still infer the effect of in-store promotions on sales in supermarkets, but we will not be able to gauge the effect of a coupon or, more important, the *net* effect of in-store promotions on sales. For example, perhaps a supermarket promotion for the brand in question takes away from sales in convenience stores or discount stores. In general, researchers must be careful in interpreting the results of regression analyses when noncoverage is an issue.

In summary, aggregate store sales data are less noisy than panel data and therefore can yield more precise regression models. Panel data, however, allow the researcher to calculate and consider variables such as brand loyalty which

---

[1] Assume that $p * 100\%$ of a panel of size N would purchase a particular brand if all panel members purchased the category at the same time. In any given week, only n members of the panel actually purchase the category, where n is on average equal to N divided by average interpurchase time. We can therefore think of market share in any week as the outcome of a binomial sampling process, with parameters p and n. The brand's average market share will equal p, but the variance around that share will be $p(1 - p)/n$, which increases as n gets smaller. n gets smaller when the panel size N is smaller, so we see how small panel sizes add noise to the data. In fact, the situation is more complicated than this, because n itself is a random variable. However, the basic binomial argument still holds once n has been determined.

cannot be obtained from aggregate data. The best data to use will therefore depend on the particular application.

Retail Sales Versus Warehouse Withdrawals Versus Factory Shipments

Retail sales represent sales directly to the consumer; factory shipments represent "sales" from the manufacturer usually to the retailer. These shipments often go to the retailer warehouse, where they are withdrawn by the retailer as needed. The advantages of factory shipment data are that they are usually easily available to the manufacturer and can be matched up quite well with trade promotion periods. Factory sales data generally correlate highly with trade promotion variables. The danger with factory data is that they do not depict what the end consumer is actually purchasing and therefore can mask true promotion effects, especially when retailers purchase "deal to deal" (see Lodish and Reibstein, 1986; Abraham and Lodish, 1987; and Chapter 11).

In studying trade deals, therefore, factory shipment data can yield misleading results because retailer inventory and consumer sales are not included. Using just retail sales data to evaluate trade deals will not be much more successful, however, because the trade deal will lag retail sales depending on the various stores' promotion policies, and it will thus become difficult to match the trade deal and the consumer sales *caused* by the trade deal. It is for this reason that Blattberg and Levin (1987) propose a multi-equation model (factory sales, retailer inventory, and retail sales) for evaluating the effect of a trade deal (see Chapter 11).

In studying retailer or consumer promotions, retail sales alone should suffice. Retail sales are best measured by point-of-purchase data, such as provided by scanners. Diary panels may also be useful, especially for durable goods. Warehouse withdrawals are often close to packaged goods consumer sales, perhaps lagging them by a few weeks.

OMITTED VARIABLES BIAS

The Problem

As just discussed, a primary motivation for using multivariate regression is to measure the effect upon sales of several independent variables. The question often arises, however, as to what penalties are incurred by not taking into account all the variables that theoretically should influence sales. For example, one might believe that couponing and retailer promotions are important determinants of sales, but data might not be available for couponing, or simply due to the interests of parsimony, the analyst might omit couponing from the regression equation.

The potential consequence of omitting relevant variables from a model is biased estimates of the coefficients for variables included in the model. The degree of bias depends on how highly correlated the omitted variable(s) is (are) with the included variable(s). For example, couponing and retailer promotion efforts often are deliberately planned by the manufacturer to take place at about the same time (see Neslin and Shoemaker, 1983a). As a result, couponing and retailer promotion data will be correlated over time. In addition, both couponing and retailer promotions are known to have a significant impact on sales (see Chapters 10 and 12). As a result, if we estimate a regression model with retailer promotions included and coupon promotions excluded, the retailer promotion variable picks up some of the "credit" for increases in sales that are due to the coupons.

Consider the case that retailer promotions add on average 1,000 units to sales, coupons add on average 1,000 units to sales, but these promotions are implemented at exactly the same times. Running a regression with retailer promotions included but coupons omitted will result in an estimated coefficient for retailer promotions of 2,000. The regression only sees that when retailer promotions are run, sales tend to go up by 2,000, so assigns it a coefficient of 2,000. In practice, retailer promotions and coupons will not be perfectly correlated as in the foregoing example, however, to the extent that these promotions are highly correlated, the coefficient for the promotion included in the regression model will pick up part of the effect of the other promotion. (See Johnston, 1972, pp. 168–169, and Pindyck and Rubinfeld, 1981, pp. 128–130, for exact derivations and further discussion.)

Omitted variables bias is dangerous if the regression model is to be used for managerial diagnostics. In the foregoing example, the manager would gain a distorted overestimate of the sales influence of retailer promotions. As a result, he or she might allocate too much money toward the trade deals that stimulate these promotions. Couponing is one variable often omitted from promotion regression models. Other potential omitted variables are advertising, competitive activities, seasonalities, and product changes.

There are not many good solutions for omitted variables bias other than to include the omitted variables. There are three problems with doing this. First, data may not be availabile for the omitted variables. Second, including all the theoretically relevant variables can result in too many parameters to be estimated with too few observations. Third, including all theoretically relevant variables can result in multicollinearity. The consequence of these last two problems is higher standard errors, although no bias, for the estimated coefficients. The solution then of including as many variables as possible in the model comes down to a trade-off betweeen lower standard errors and degree of bias. The concept of "mean square error" quantifies that trade-off.

Mean square error (MSE) is defined as the expected square distance of an estimator from the true value of the quantity it estimates. In the case of regression, let β be the true value of a coefficient and b its estimator. The following relationship can be derived (Johnston, 1972, p. 403):

$$E[(b - \beta)^2] = E\{[b - E(b)]^2\} + [E(b) - \beta]^2 \tag{7.1}$$

or

$$\text{MSE} = \text{variance} + \text{bias}^2$$

Equation (7.1) says that the average squared difference between the estimated regression coefficient and the true coefficient value equals the variance of that estimated coefficient around its average value plus the square of the difference between the average value and the true value. If a regression estimator is unbiased, then $E(b) = \beta$ and MSE equals the variance of the estimator. However, if the estimator is biased, MSE equals the variance plus the square of the bias. In the case of biased estimation, MSE is an appropriate measure of the "total error" of the estimator.

The problem with implementing equation (7.1) is that MSE cannot be explicitly measured because the true value of the coefficient is unknown. However, conceptually, the equation points out that at some point it is better to allow some bias in the estimated coefficients if it means lower variance, because this may minimize mean square error. In qualitative terms, it may better for an estimator to be off a little on average but most of the time hover close to that average, than to be correct on average but most of the time be far away from that average.

An Example

To illustrate the problem of omitted variables bias in a promotion setting, we simulate an example of estimating a baseline level of sales to serve as a benchmark for evaluating promotions in some future period (see Table 7.6 for another example of omitted variables bias). We will show the types of biases that can arise if the period during which the baseline level is being estimated also includes promotions, but these promotions are not quantified and are omitted from the regression model.

Our approach will be to generate simulated data using an assumed model and then apply regression analysis to analyze that data. Assume then that the true model underlying sales is

$$\text{SALES}_t = 1{,}000 + 50_t + 3{,}000\text{DEC} + 1{,}000\text{PROMO}_t + \epsilon_t \tag{7.2}$$

where

$$t = 1, 2, \ldots, 48 \text{ months}$$

$$\text{SALES}_t = \text{sales in month } t$$

$$\text{DEC} = 1 \text{ if the month is December, 0 otherwise}$$

$$\text{PROMO}_t = 1 \text{ if the brand is on promotion in time } t, 0 \text{ otherwise}$$

$$\epsilon_t = \text{other factors influencing sales in time } t$$

We will model the ϵ_t's as being independent, with each ϵ_t following a normal distribution with mean 0 and standard deviation 400. Equation (7.2) says that normal sales are 1,000 units per month, except December, where business regularly increases by 3,000 units. This is obviously a product with a heavy Christmas season—children's toys, for example. Sales are trending up at 50 units per month, and a promotional event, for example, a premium, will increase sales by 1,000 in the month it occurs.

The first step in this illustration was to generate 48 ϵ_t's using Monte Carlo simulation. We then generated sales figures using equation (7.2) under three scenarios: infrequent promotions uncorrelated with the December season, infrequent promotions correlated with the December season, and frequent promotions uncorrelated with the December season. (See Table 7.2.) In scenario 1, there are four promotions, one of which does happen to occur in December (month 12). In scenario 2, there are also four promotions, but three of them take place in December (months 12, 36, and 48). In scenario 3, the brand is on promotion 42 percent of the time, randomly distributed throughout the year.

We then estimate the following model,

$$\text{SALES}_t = \alpha + \beta t + \gamma \text{DEC} \tag{7.3}$$

where α represents non-December normal sales of 1,000 units, β represents the 50-per-month positive trend, and γ equals the 3,000-unit increase typically found in December. Equation (7.3) is misspecified because PROMO_t is an omitted variable. We hypothesize that in scenario 2, the December seasonality estimate should be biased upward, since promotions are correlated with the month of December and are omitted from the model. In scenario 3, the December seasonality estimate should be correct, but the normal sales estimate should be grossly inflated. This is because promotions will significantly elevate the apparent floor of the data.[2] Scenario 1 does not have the problems of scenarios 2 and 3. However, our estimate of normal sales should still be biased upward, albeit slightly, because of the omission of promotions from the estimated model.

Table 7.3 displays regression results for equation (7.3), as well as the results of estimating the correctly specified model using regression. The table shows that in scenario 1, the normal sales, trend, and seasonality estimates are all within two standard errors of the true values. Notice, however, that the normal sales estimate is a little high. Also, the estimate of the December seasonal is a bit high. This is because in this example, the correlation between December and promotion was low (.182) but not zero. In scenario 2, the December seasonality estimate, 3,996.5, is four standard errors away from its true value of 3,000. In fact, the estimate completely includes the 3,000 plus the 1,000 unit promotion effect. Because promotion is so closely tied with December, (the correlation between them equals .727), the statistical analysis sees an average gain of close to 4,000 for December, even though 1,000 of that gain is due to promotion. In scenario 3, trend and seasonality are correctly estimated, but the normal sales estimate is grossly inflated. This is because promotion is so ubiquitous in this case that its

---

[2] This is a somewhat different situation from the normal omitted variable problem, where the omitted variable is correlated with the included variable. In this case, the included variable is a constant, so the omitted variable is not correlated with it. The bias in the estimated constant term of the model occurs because of the standard assumption of regression that the mean of the error term in the model is zero (Johnston, 1972, p. 122; Pindyck and Rubinfeld 1981, p. 47). In equation (7.2), the error term has a mean of zero, but in equation (7.3), the promotion variable becomes part of the error term, and the mean effect of the promotion variable upon sales is much greater than zero. This effect becomes absorbed in the estimated constant term.

TABLE 7.2 Simulated Sales Data for Omitted Variables Example

	Scenario 1: Infrequent Promotion Uncorrelated with December			Scenario 2: Infrequent Promotion Correlated with December			Scenario 3: Frequent Promotion Uncorrelated with December	
Month	Sales	Promo	Month	Sales	Promo	Month	Sales	Promo
1	691.45	0	1	691.45	0	1	691.45	0
2	1,871.97	0	2	1,871.97	0	2	2,871.97	1
3	853.50	0	3	853.50	0	3	853.50	0
4	1,692.09	0	4	1,692.09	0	4	1,692.09	0
5	842.82	0	5	842.82	0	5	842.82	0
6	1,380.74	0	6	1,380.74	0	6	2,380.74	1
7	1,589.18	0	7	1,589.18	0	7	1,589.18	0
8	1,205.94	0	8	1,205.94	0	8	2,205.94	1
9	1,552.98	0	9	1,552.98	0	9	1,552.98	0
10	1,532.96	0	10	1,532.96	0	10	2,532.96	1
11	1,438.63	0	11	1,438.63	0	11	1,438.63	0
12	6,380.23	1	12	6,380.23	1	12	6,380.23	1
13	2,408.57	0	13	2,408.57	0	13	3,408.57	1
14	1,239.70	0	14	1,239.70	0	14	1,239.70	0
15	1,773.86	0	15	1,773.86	0	15	1,773.86	0
16	2,156.33	0	16	2,156.33	0	16	3,156.33	1
17	1,909.86	0	17	1,909.86	0	17	1,909.86	0
18	1,805.32	0	18	1,805.32	0	18	1,805.32	0
19	2,150.30	0	19	2,150.30	0	19	3,150.30	1
20	2,989.58	0	20	2,989.58	0	20	2,989.58	0
21	2,252.46	0	21	2,252.46	0	21	3,252.46	1
22	2,768.73	1	22	2,768.73	1	22	2,768.73	1
23	2,104.66	0	23	2,104.66	0	23	2,104.66	0
24	4,869.63	0	24	4,869.63	0	24	4,869.63	0
25	2,751.99	0	25	2,751.99	0	25	3,751.99	1
26	2,178.17	0	26	2,178.17	0	26	2,178.17	0
27	2,019.46	0	27	2,019.46	0	27	3,019.46	1
28	1,667.00	0	28	1,667.00	0	28	1,667.00	0
29	2,493.26	0	29	2,493.26	0	29	3,493.26	1
30	2,688.73	0	30	2,688.73	0	30	2,688.73	0
31	3,131.51	0	31	3,131.51	0	31	4,131.51	1
32	2,010.40	0	32	2,010.40	0	32	2,010.40	0
33	2,486.53	0	33	2,486.53	0	33	2,486.53	0
34	3,136.59	0	34	3,136.59	0	34	4,136.59	1
35	2,074.37	0	35	2,074.37	0	35	2,074.37	0
36	5,863.19	0	36	6,863.19	1	36	5,863.19	0
37	3,506.75	0	37	3,506.75	0	37	4,506.75	1
38	3,110.65	0	38	3,110.65	0	38	3,110.65	0
39	4,179.34	1	39	3,179.34	0	39	4,179.34	1
40	2,741.25	0	40	2,741.25	0	40	2,741.25	0
41	2,645.88	0	41	2,645.88	0	41	2,645.88	0
42	2,841.60	0	42	2,841.60	0	42	3,841.60	1
43	2,917.86	0	43	2,917.86	0	43	2,917.86	0
44	2,940.95	0	44	2,940.95	0	44	3,940.95	1
45	4,176.00	1	45	3,176.00	0	45	4,176.00	1
46	3,243.06	0	46	3,243.06	0	46	3,243.06	0
47	3,359.17	0	47	3,359.17	0	47	3,359.17	0
48	6,929.17	0	48	7,929.17	1	48	6,929.17	0

TABLE 7.3 Regression Estimates for the Data in Table 7.2 (numbers in parentheses are standard errors)

	Scenario	$\hat{\alpha}$	$\hat{\beta}$	$\hat{\gamma}$	$\hat{\delta}$	R^2
Estimated model[a]						
Sales = α + βt + γDEC	1	1,152.3 (148.3)	47.2 (5.3)	3,443.2 (265.8)	—	.86
	2	1,138.5 (134.8)	45.8 (4.8)	3,996.5 (241.5)	—	.90
	3	1,568.8 (223.0)	45.0 (8.0)	3,092.7 (399.7)	—	.70
Estimated model[a]						
Sales = α + βt + γDEC + δPROMO	1	1,123.7 (118.9)	45.2 (4.3)	3,254.0 (216.0)	1,104.8 (215.7)	.91
	2	1,124.5 (118.8)	45.3 (4.2)	3,162.0 (308.3)	1,151.7 (307.9)	.92
	3	988.4 (119.7)	45.5 (3.9)	3,327.8 (197.1)	1,311.8 (109.7)	.93

[a] In both cases, the true model is sales = 1,000 + 50t + 3,000 DEC + 1,000 PROMO.

effects appear to be embedded in the normal environment unless they are explicitly taken into account.

Using the misspecified model equation (7.3) for scenarios 2 and 3 would have grossly misleading implications. For example, a promotion in some future December, say, month 60, would produce, on average, additional sales of 1,000 units, for a total of 1,000 + 50(60) + 3,000 + 1,000 = 8,000 units. However, in scenario 2, the model would infer a baseline of 1,139 + 46(60) + 3,997 = 7,896 without the promotion, and we would infer only a slight increase of 104 units in sales. Note, however, that the model could be used to measure promotion effects for non-December months, since the non-December inferred baseline estimate of 1,139.5 + 45.8*t* is close to the true value of 1,000 + 50*t*. Using equation (7.3) under scenario 3 will grossly underestimate the effects of promotion in all periods. For example, if we promote in month 50 (a non-December month), we will on average obtain sales of 1,000 + 50(50) + 1,000 = 4,500 units. The model's baseline estimate, however, will be 1,569 + 45(50) = 3,819, so its estimate of incremental sales will be 681 rather than the true increase of 1,000.

After seeing these problems, one might question why one would ever omit a potentially relevant variable from a promotion analysis. There are several answers. First, if the omitted variable is not very important or is uncorrelated with variables included in the model, there is little harm done by omitting it, and one does not have to bear the data collection cost of including it. Second, as discussed earlier, including all relevant variables can increase variance in the estimated coefficients and therefore increase mean square error. Another way of looking at this is that if candy is almost always promoted on Halloween, leaving out promotion will result in a biased coefficient for an included Halloween variable, but including both the Halloween and promotion variables will result in high multicollinearity between these variables, which will manifest itself in high coefficient variances and large mean square error. Third, in practical terms, omitted variables always have the potential to bias our results, and all analyses of promotion effects require judgment as to the severity of the problem.

In summary, this section establishes the importance of thinking through the correct specification of a regression model, even if all the potentially relevant variables cannot be measured and included in the estimated model. One can at least understand the potential biases of omitting those variables and raise the appropriate caveats in applying the model.

LEVEL OF AGGREGATION

Aggregating over Time

The appropriate time interval (weekly, monthly, etc.) for which to analyze marketing variables has become a controversial topic in advertising research, where data interval can influence the estimated long-term impact of advertising (see

Clarke, 1976; Vanhonacker, 1983; Bass and Leone, 1983; Blattberg and Jeuland, 1981). The research suggests that using highly aggregate time periods (e.g., yearly) can produce misleadingly large post-advertising effects. The research on advertising has been within the context of a Koyck or partial adjustment model, and promotion's long-term effects may not follow such a pattern. However, the lessons learned from the study of advertising would point toward the use of small data intervals.

The very nature of promotions suggests that a short data interval would be appropriate. Promotions often taken place over a period of days or weeks, so it is intuitive that daily or weekly data will provide the most precise estimate of promotion's effect on sales. There are two more concrete reasons for using a short data interval to study promotion.

First, sample size is dramatically reduced when one aggregates, for example, from weekly to monthly data. Promotion regressions will often involve several promotion independent variables, and since promotions are often executed at the same time, a fair amount of multicollinearity may exist. A large sample size is needed (1) to counteract the tendency of multicollinearity to enlarge the standard errors of coefficients (Belsley et al., 1980) and (2) to provide an appropriate ratio of parameters to observations.

Second, aggregation is a smoothing process, and it is possible that aggregation can smooth out the promotion variable to the point where it does not have enough variation to manifest its leverage upon sales. For example, if a brand is promoted once a week every month, aggregation to a monthly basis will completely smooth out the promotion variable. Indeed, lack of variation in price has often been cited as a problem in price-elasticity studies (see Neslin and Shoemaker, 1983b).

These arguments would suggest a data interval of perhaps one week. One might also argue for smaller intervals, for example, daily data. This is practical with store scanner data, and would have at least two advantages: First, one could estimate day-of-the-week effects and their interaction with various promotion variables. Second, one could avoid the overlap problem that occurs when weeks are defined as Monday to Sunday yet promotions are run Thursday to Wednesday. Currently, there are no published reports of promotions regressions estimated on daily data. The availability of such data would allow researchers to study new issues and probably increase the precision of estimated promotion effects. To complete the discussion, however, we point out that since often the only data available are on a monthly or quarterly basis, an important research task would be to investigate potential temporal aggregation biases for promotion regression models.

Aggregating and Pooling Data Across Stores

There are times when the researcher has available time series data of sales and promotion only at the market level. The data have been aggregated across stores. The researcher will estimate a regression model of aggregate store sales as a function of aggregate promotion. At other times, the researcher has these data available for each store. We will refer to instances where aggregate data are employed as the "aggregation case" and instances where the disaggregate data are employed as the "pooling case." The aggregate data can be created by summing the disaggregate data.

It is very likely that in a competitive retail environment, stores will differ in the increase in sales resulting from using a particular promotion. This occurs because of differences in patron demographics and brand loyalties, and because of different in-store retailing environments. Heterogeneity in store response to promotion has important consequences for the estimation of regression models, in both the aggregation and pooling cases.

In the case of aggregation, the estimated aggregate promotion response coefficient will be biased in that it will not represent, on average, the sum of response coefficients across stores.[3] As shown by Theil (1971, pp. 556–567), the expected value of the estimated aggregate promotion coefficient will be a weighted average of each true store coefficient, *plus* a weighted average of true coefficients for other variables in the model. Therefore, for example, an aggregate coefficient for feature will include, on average, some of the impact for display (see also Parsons and Schultz, 1976, pp. 88–91).

In the aggregation case, there is little the researcher can do about the bias. One should simply recognize that the bias in the aggregated coefficient will be less to the extent that the individual store coefficients are equal. However, the bias vanishes if the promotion schedules in each store are exactly the same (see Theil, 1971, pp. 558–567, esp. p. 565). This suggests that a researcher may be able to avoid aggregation bias by collecting data at the store chain level, because promotion schedules for stores within a chain are likely to be similar.

A final issue regarding aggregation is the method for calculating the aggregate data. Theil's results for aggregation bias assume simple summing of the disaggregate data, but it would be possible and perhaps desirable to calculate weighted sums. The weights could be store size (in retail square footage), yearly category sales in the store, or yearly brand sales in the store. None of these schemes is perfect, but the potential problem with not weighting (besides the bias noted) is that a promotion is counted the same whether it takes place in a store with one-quarter the sales of the average store, or four times the average. The result is wide variation in promotion response for the same level of promotion.

Weighting by store size may be too gross a measure—even a large store may be frequented by customers who are light users of the brand under study. Weighting by category sales may not reflect differences in customer demographics which result in different consumer loyalty or potential loyalty to the brand in question. Weighting by brand market share becomes tautological and may introduce simultaneity into the model—brand sales are explicitly included in both the independent and dependent variable. With a fairly large sample size, this built-

---

[3] This assumes that the aggregate is the simple sum or average of the data across stores. We shortly discuss alternative weighting schemes for calculating aggregate data.

in correlation can be reduced, however, and it is therefore probably better to weight by long-term brand share. The resulting promotion variable reflects the strength of promotion in stores that are important to the brand. However, no one method is clearly best, and the effects on aggregation bias in promotion models have not been studied (see Wittink et al., 1987, for some discussion). Until these effects are better understood, it is important to recognize that the weighting scheme used to collect the aggregate data may influence the degree of bias in the model.

In the case of pooling, the researcher might be faced with 100 time periods of data from each of 20 stores. One approach to these data would be to estimate 20 separate regressions, each with 100 observations. However, another possibility would be to pool the data (literally, stack the 20 time series on top of each other) and estimate one model based on 2,000 observations. The potential gains from this are (1) only one model has to be estimated, saving analysis effort, and (2) the large number of observations for the pooled model will result in low estimated standard errors.

The problem with the pooling approach is again that of heterogeneity in promotion effects across stores. The results of Wallace (1972, p. 690), for example, imply that if there is heterogeneity, the estimated pooled promotion response coefficient (the single coefficient assumed to apply to each store) will be biased. The expected value of the single coefficient will equal a weighted combination of the individual store coefficients, the weights being determined by the variance-covariance matrix of the data in each store (this can be deduced from Wallace, 1972, p. 690).

In contrast to the aggregation case, there are several things the researcher can do to avoid the pooling bias. These options are available because the researcher has the data to make inferences regarding individual stores. First, statistical tests can be employed to test whether the individual store coefficients are equal (e.g., see Bass and Wittink, 1975, 1978; and Pindyck and Rubinfeld, 1981, pp. 254–255). Second, if the test is rejected, the researcher can estimate separate models for each store. Third, if the test is rejected, one can construct a varying parameters model, where the data are pooled but promotion coefficients are modeled as functions of store characteristics or other factors that cause the promotion coefficient to vary across stores (see Fomby et al., 1984, pp. 314–315, and Gatignon, 1984, for a marketing example).

Wallace takes the view that even if a statistical test indicates that the individual stores coefficients are not all equal, one might be better off proceeding to estimate a pooled model. He argues that the mean square error, the sum of bias plus variance, can be quite small in certain instances (see equation 7.1 of this chapter). That is, the estimated coefficient may be biased, but because of the large sample size with the pooled data, its standard error will be small, so on average, it may in fact be closer to the true regression coefficients for individual stores than if we estimate separate models for each store.

To summarize, both aggregation and pooling cases give rise to potential biases in estimated promotion response effects. There is little one can do in the aggregation case except try to obtain more disaggregate data or collect data at a level of aggregation where the promotion schedule is the same for all stores. In the pooling case, one can employ testing procedures to diagnose the problem and then estimate separate models if necessary or construct a varying parameters model. There is little research on the severity of aggregation and pooling problems in a promotions context. The area is a fertile one for research. Meanwhile, researchers should exhibit caution in aggregating and pooling data and attempt to address potential problems in the ways described above.

Aggregating and Pooling Across Brand Size/Style/Flavor

The issues here are much the same as for aggregating and pooling across stores. Aggregation over brand sizes, styles, or flavors yields a more manageable modeling task, but as with the case with aggregating over stores, the estimated aggregate promotion coefficient will be biased if the various versions of the brand respond differently to deals.

Similar conceptual issues arise with aggregating across brand versions as when aggregating across stores. For example, it is not clear how an aggregate measure of brand promotion should be calculated. Various weighting schemes can be used to compute aggregate promotion variables for brands. One idea would be to weight by brand version market share over the entire period of the data. This, however, would introduce some, albeit probably not very much, simultaneity in the model because current period sales would be on both sides of the regression equation. An alternative would be to weight by recent market share.

Note that the problem of calculating an aggregate promotion measure will be less relevant for certain types of promotions than for others. For example, coupons often apply to all versions of a brand, and hence it is easy to think of one coupon availability variable applying for all brand versions. However, many retailer coupons are specifically geared toward certain brand versions.

Current research provides little guidance on how to create aggregate variables for promotion analysis. In fact, Theil's findings on aggregation bias (discussed earlier in this chapter) are derived under the assumption that the aggregate data are calculated as unweighted averages of the raw disaggregate data. It would be interesting and important to investigate the effect of various aggregation weighting schemes on aggregation bias. It is conceivable that schemes could be devised that diminish the degree of bias.

Pooling over brand versions would also encounter the same problems and potential solutions as with the case of pooling over stores. In addition to worrying about heterogeneity in the promotion coefficients for different brand versions, the intercept term would obviously be heterogeneous, since there will be clear differences in baseline sales among the different versions of a brand. When considering the pooling of data across brand versions, researchers should use the tests and procedures outlined in "Aggregating and Pooling Data Across Stores."

Aggregating and Pooling Across Consumers

The same arguments apply here as for aggregating across stores and across brand variations. The most common practice is to pool across consumers, although there are some good examples of segment-specific regression modeling that has produced useful managerial diagnostics. For example, McCann (1974) found important differences in promotion response across various demographic segments. Fraser (1985) actually ran brand-specific, individual consumer-specific regressions in a study of heterogeneous response to promotion.

DEPENDENT VARIABLES

Potential dependent variables for examining the sales effects of promotions are category sales (CAT), brand sales (SALES), and market share (MS). We may then want to estimate models of the form

$$CAT = f(PROMOTION) \tag{7.4a}$$

$$MS = f(PROMOTION) \tag{7.4b}$$

$$SALES = f(PROMOTION) \tag{7.4c}$$

The justification for considering category sales as a dependent variable is the ample empirical as well as theoretical evidence that promotion often works to displace category sales or even increase primary demand (Shoemaker, 1979; Blattberg et al., 1981; Ward and Davis, 1978a; Neslin et al., 1985). The category equation can capture the effect of promotion displacing sales either by accelerating purchase timing or by inducing larger purchase quantities, and include the effect of stimulating primary demand.

The question of whether to model sales or market share depends on the purpose for which the analysis is being conducted. Market share is often of strategic interest, and raw coefficient estimates need not be converted to elasticities to compare results across product categories. Since profitability calculations depend on the actual number of units sold, sales models are preferred if the purpose of the analysis is to calculate profits. Both market share and sales models, however, can be misleading if category sales are also reacting to promotion. For example, a doubling of market share is a quadrupling of sales if category sales also double. Similarly, a doubling in sales can mean a much less than doubling of market share if the increase in sales is due to expansion of the category.

As the foregoing suggests, regardless of whether market share or sales is modeled, it is useful to also model category sales. The category model provides information on purchase acceleration and category expansion, whereas the sales or market share model can provide information on brand switching and acceleration. As an example, consider the following data:

Period	Category Sales	Brand Sales
1	1,000	300
2	1,000	300
3	1,000	300
4 (promotion)	1,200	600
5	850	200
6	1,000	300
7	1,000	300
8	1,000	300

If we estimate a brand sales model from these data, we will find that the promotion increased the brand's sales by 300 units in the current period, although 100 units of that were accelerated from its own future sales, so the net gain was 200 units. A category sales model would identify more specifically the source of those 200 units. The category model would find that category demand increased by 200 units during the promotion, 150 of which were accelerated from the next period. The promotion therefore increased primary demand by 50 units. Referring to brand sales, we can then conclude that of the 300 additional units generated during the promotion period, 100 were accelerated from its own future sales, 50 were drawn from future sales of competitors (since total category acceleration was 150), 50 came from an increase in primary demand, and 100 came from competitors in the current period.

This discussion illustrates the rich insight generated by modeling category sales in addition to either brand or market share. Another reason for modeling category and brand effects is potential gains in estimation efficiency. If the category sales and brand sales are generated by the same omitted variable (for example, the weather), the error terms in the category and brand equations will be correlated. In this case, seemingly unrelated regression will provide more precise estimates of the models' parameters (Pindyck and Rubinfeld, 1981, Ch. 11). Neslin and Shoemaker (1983b) investigated the use of seemingly unrelated regression in estimating a three-equation price/advertising model involving category sales and market share, and found little improvement. However, the potential for increased estimating efficiency in a sales promotion context has not been investigated.

Since category sales equal the sum of each brand's sales in the category, modeling a separate equation for each brand will generate the same and, in fact, more insights than are obtained by considering one brand plus category sales. In practice, however, it may be very difficult to specify such models completely. For example, to capture the effect of each brand's promotion capturing sales from competing brands in the current period, several current period cross-elasticity variables would be needed in each brand model. To capture the effect that a brand's promotion may gain future sales from other brands, we would need several *lagged* cross-elasticity variables in each brand model. Very quickly, such a model can exhaust the data available for estimation. The potential insights from these models is very attractive, however, and their specification and estimation in a promotion environment is a fertile area for research (see Allenby and Blattberg, 1988, and the next section of this chapter for further discussion). Until that research is completed, a two-equation model—category sales and either sales or market share—is a useful intermediate step.

INDEPENDENT VARIABLES

Table 7.1 suggests a plethora of potential independent variables to include in promotion regression models. This is similar to the predicament faced in most market response model situations. Two variables that are particularly relevant to promotion models are interactions and lagged terms (also see Chapter 12, Statistical Modeling of Store-Level Scanner Data).

Interaction Terms

Interactions among various promotion instruments have been found experimentally (e.g., Woodside and Waddle, 1975; also see Chapter 6) as well as in regression models (Moriarty, 1983), and many marketing plans are based on an assumed interaction. One statistical explanation for the particular importance of interactions in sales promotion models can be derived from the proposition that sales promotions exert a direct effect on both an individual's probability of purchasing a particular brand and on his or her likelihood of making a category purchase. These two quantities multiply together to produce the probability of a consumer buying a particular brand. If promotion is present in two quantities that multiply together, the promotion terms are essentially multiplying together, producing an interaction.

It is interesting to note that if interactions are left out of the model, omitted variables bias can become related to heteroscedasticity. Heteroscedasticity is a well-known problem in regression analysis. The consequence of heteroscedasticity is increased standard errors for the estimated coefficients, combined with biased estimates of those standard errors (Pindyck and Rubinfeld, 1981, Ch. 7). The coefficient estimates remain unbiased, and weighted least squares can be used to provide more efficient estimates. However, omitting interaction terms from a promotion model can appear as heteroscedasticity. As a result, the coefficient estimates will be biased even if weighted least squares is used.

The argument is as follows:

Let F = feature, D = display, and ϵ = an error term uncorrelated with both F and D. Assume that the true model should include $\beta_1 F$ and $\beta_2 FD$, but the $\beta_2 FD$ term is omitted. The error term implied by this misspecified model is $\beta_2 FD + \epsilon$. The variance of that error term for a fixed value of F will be $\beta_2^2 F^2 \text{var}(D) + \text{var}(\epsilon)$, which is increasing in F. As a result, the error variance will be larger during feature weeks than during nonfeature weeks. Estimating these different error variances and then using weighted least squares will correct the heteroscedasticity but not the bias in the estimated feature effect caused by omitting the feature/display interaction.

In summary, then, omitted interactions can cause heteroscedasticity in the model such that the variance during promotion periods will be greater than variance in nonpromotion periods. If the researcher discovers heteroscedasticity of this type, she or he should check the possibility of adding interactions to the model.

Interaction terms add parameters and absorb degrees of freedom available for estimation. For example, a model with four promotion variables (feature, display, price cut, and store coupon) would generate six two-way interactions, four three-way interactions, and one four-way interaction. The interaction terms will undoubtedly be correlated with the main effect terms and with each other, especially if the data are not collected experimentally. There is no simple method to specifying a promotion sales model with interactions. We might, however, outline a few approaches:

1. *Disregard all interactions*. This is the expedient strategy, but can result in poor fit and biased coefficients if significant interactions are left out of the model that are correlated with the included variables.

2. *Rely on theory*. Perhaps certain promotions have been designed to interact. For example, the feature advertising may use the same spokesperson and slogan used in the display. Alternatively, the promotions might be designed to not interact, for example, if they are targeted to two different groups.

3. *Use an F-test to determine whether interactions as a group add anything to the model*. One could run the model without the interactions and with the interactions, and use an F-test to decide whether the additional variables significantly improve fit (Pindyck and Rubinfeld, 1981, pp. 116–120).

4. *Use stepwise regression*. This will provide a relatively high R^2 and a parsimonious model. However, gross misspecifications can result. For example, an interaction might be included without the separate main effects. This could occur if the interaction was strong and highly correlated with the direct main effect variables. The resulting managerial implication would be *only* to run the promotions simultaneously.

5. *Include all interactions*. This strategy may result in multicollinearity and therefore imprecise coefficient estimates. One could then drop interactions clearly not significant and not highly correlated with other variables.

6. *Use a multiplicative model*. Multiplicative models implicitly include interactions because the effect on sales of one variable will depend on the level of all other variables. However, multiplicative models do not have the same flexibility in capturing interactions as do additive models, because the additive model adds an extra parameter.

Undoubtedly all six of these solutions are used in practice, and each has its own merits. The actual solution adopted should depend on the purpose of the model. If the purpose of the model is forecasting, overloading the model with too many variables can actually reduce the standard error of the estimate which determines the forecast error (see Plane and Opperman, 1981, p. 380). In this case, the analyst might use F-tests to determine the desirability of adding interactions or use a more parsimonious representation of interactions such as afforded by a multiplicative model. If the model is to be used for diagnostics, then the analyst will be forced to trade off possible bias by omitting interactions versus loss of efficiency (higher standard errors) by including them. In this case, theory must play a strong role in the specification of the model, coupled with F-tests to test the model.

Interactions can also occur between promotion and nonpromotion variables. For example, the effect of a featured price discount might be larger in off-season than in prime season. In off-season, there may be latent demand for the product that could be stimulated by a promotion. In prime season, the promotion may cannibalize more sales that would have occurred anyway. Another way of looking at the situation, in terms of equations (7.4a), (7.4b), and (7.4c), is that promotions may stimulate category sales during off-season and help the brand fight for market share during prime season. Promotion could also interact with other marketing instruments such as distribution and advertising.

Lagged Variables

A second major consideration in building promotion regression models is the use of lagged variables. As mentioned earlier, there is considerable empirical evidence that promotion accelerates sales, and this implies the need for lagged terms. The evidence on repeat purchasing is less definite (see Chapters 2 and 5), but there is a firm theoretical reason for including repeat purchase effects (see Chapter 2). Table 7.4 outlines some particular lag effects and the type of lagged variables required to estimate those effects.

As the table indicates, there are a number of complex lag phenomena that can be modeled. Most of them require lag structures that extend over at least one interpurchase period, and this implies several lag parameters to be estimated. With only a slight decrease in flexibility, polynomial distributed lags (Pindyck and Rubinfeld, 1981, pp. 238–244) can be used to lessen the number of parameters required. For example, if a third-degree polynomial can be used to measure a lagged effect taking place over ten periods, then four rather than ten parameters need to be estimated. While there are no published examples of using polynomial lags to measure the lag effects of promotion, the technique appears to be promising. There are also nonlinear lag functions (see the Decay in Effectiveness row in Table 7.4), although these might require nonlinear estimation.

Referring back to the ''Aggregating over Time'' section, the researcher should be cautioned of temporal aggregation biases in estimating lag structures. The problem is well studied for geometrically decaying Koyck-type lags, but not well investigated for the types of lags displayed in Table 7.4.

There are very few published findings of promotion's lagged effects. Massy and Frank (1965) found only marginally significant lagged effects for ''dealing'' using MRCA diary panel data. The estimated effects were in the positive direction. It is difficult, however, to see how a promotion in week 1 could increase sales in week 2, unless feature advertising associated with the deal had a delayed effect. Montgomery and Silk (1972) found significantly positive lags lasting up to five periods (months) for pharmaceutical products sold to physicians. The positive

TABLE 7.4 Potential Lag Phenomena and Lag Structures for Promotion Progression Models

Description	Graph	Required Lags
Acceleration of timing		Lag terms X_{t-1}, X_{t-2}, going back to X_{t-c}, where c is average interpurchase time, or polynomial distributed lag of order 1 or 2 over c periods.
Inducing extra quantity		Lag terms $X_{t-c+k}, \ldots, X_{t-c}, \ldots, X_{t-c-k}$.
Acceleration of timing and quantity		Lag terms back to X_{t-c-k}, or polynomial distributed lag of order 3 over $c + k$ periods.
Repeat purchasing effect		Polynomial distributed lag of order 3 over $c + k$ periods, or $2k + 1$ lag terms $X_{t-c-k}, \ldots, X_{t-c}, \ldots, X_{t-c+k}$.
Delayed effect for coupons, samples, etc.		Koyck lag, or several (e.g., $c + k$) lag terms X_{t-1}, X_{t-2}, etc.
Decay in effectiveness if promotion runs more than one time period		Nonlinear term: $\gamma e^{-\lambda(t-t_0)} X_t$.

t_0 = starting time of most recent promotion
c = mean interpurchase time
X_t = level of promotion in period t
k = the number of weeks centered around the mean interpurchase time after the promotion during which we might expect to notice repeat purchase or quantity acceleration effects. For example, if c equals 5, k might equal 2 or 3.

lags found relate to the types of promotions studied: journal advertising, direct-mail literature, and samples. In both studies, either separate lag terms or Koyck models were used to estimate the lag effect. Moriarty (1985) investigated the lagged effects of price cuts using weekly data and found them not to be very common or important. Time series models, built using ARIMA methods, also yield mixed findings, sometimes uncovering lagged effects and sometimes not (see Chapter 9, "Transfer Function Analysis" and "Intervention Analysis").

One formidable problem bearing upon the estimation of promotion lag structures is that the several rich phenomena depicted in Table 7.4 may cancel each
other out, resulting in a flat post-promotion period. For example, assume that for
a particular brand, there are no repeat purchase effects but that promotions accelerate both timing and quantity (as found by Neslin et al., 1985). Timing acceleration will probably draw sales from the immediate weeks after the promotion.
These sales are from people who buy earlier but buy their normal quantity. Quantity acceleration, however, represents people who buy at their normal time but
stock up. (Of course, a given consumer could accelerate both timing and quantity,
but for simplicity, we keep the effects separate here.) Quantity acceleration will
draw sales from one interpurchase period after the promotion. For example, rather
than buy 10 units at time 1 and 10 at time 6, the quantity accelerator (with interpurchase time of 5 weeks) might buy 15 at time 1 and 5 at time 6.

The accompanying table presents a hypothetical example that combines the
effects of timing and quantity acceleration. We assume an average interpurchase
time of five weeks, with some variation around it, and baseline sales at 2000.

Period	Timing Displacement	Quantity Displacement	Total Sales
1	0	0	2,000
2	0	0	2,000
3	0	0	2,000
4 (promotion)	1000	1000	4,000
5	− 300	0	1,700
6	− 275	0	1,725
7	− 200	− 100	1,700
8	− 125	− 150	1,725
9	− 50	− 220	1,730
10	− 30	− 200	1,770
11	− 20	− 150	1,830
12	0	− 125	1,875
13	0	− 55	1,945
14	0	0	2,000
15	0	0	2,000

Once the promotion takes place, sales do not return to their normal baseline level
until nine weeks after the promotion. If another promotion is offered at around
period 13, the cycle repeats itself and the baseline is maintained below its normal
sales level. What's more, the sales pattern between weeks 5 and 10 is relatively
flat, compared to the dramatic increase seen in week 5, and amid the additional
noise that will accompany these data, no lag effect will be discerned. If one considers the additional possibilities brought about by either positive or negative
repeat purchase effects, it is apparent that the post-promotion period can appear
misleadingly flat, and in the presence of frequent promotions, never recover to
its natural level.

FUNCTIONAL FORMS

The principal functional forms used in market response regression models are linear, multiplicative, and attraction. Versions of these are written as follows,

$$\text{Linear:} \quad MS_{jt} = \alpha_j + \sum_k \beta_{jk} X_{jkt} + \epsilon_{jt} \tag{7.5}$$

$$\text{Multiplicative:} \quad MS_{jt} = \alpha_j (\prod_k X_{jkt}^{\beta_{jk}}) \epsilon_{jt} \tag{7.6}$$

$$\text{Attraction:} \quad MS_{jt} = \frac{\alpha_j (\prod_k X_{jkt}^{\beta_{jk}}) \, \epsilon_{jt}}{\sum_h \alpha_h (\prod_k X_{hkt}^{\beta_{hk}})} \tag{7.7}$$

where

MS_{jt} = market share for brand j in time t

X_{jkt} = value for explanatory variable k for brand j in time t

ϵ_{jt} = other causes of market share for brand j in time t

α_j = intercept term for brand j

β_{jk} = regression response coefficient for brand j, variable k

The linear model is the simplest with which to work and can include nonlinear and interaction effects by using X^2 and $X_1 * X_2$ terms. The multiplicative model automatically includes a general interaction among all the independent variables and allows for a decreasing-returns-to-scale response to the independent variables. The attraction model has the advantage of logical consistency—an increase in the promotional variable will add share to the promoted brand and take away market share from other brands according to their natural share position as well as their current marketing efforts.

The disadvantage of the linear model is that it cannot parsimoniously include nonlinear and interaction effects. The multiplicative model includes simple forms of these effects more parsimoniously but is awkward when independent variables can equal zero (because after taking logs to linearize the model, the log of zero is negative infinity). Both linear and multiplicative models are not logically consistent, meaning the predictions of market share obtained from these models do not sum to one across brands. While logically consistent, the attraction model requires more effort in preprocessing of the data before it can be estimated (see Nakanishi and Cooper, 1974, 1982).

There is ample literature comparing these functional forms in terms of their ability to forecast market share (Naert and Weverbergh, 1981, 1985; Brodie and DeKluyver, 1984; Ghosh et al., 1984; Leeflang and Reuyl, 1984). A meta-analysis conducted by Naert and Weverbergh (1985) of the three 1984 studies concluded that no one functional form results in better predictive accuracy. Naert and Weverbergh's 1981 study concluded however that the attraction model obtained the best predictive accuracy. These studies included advertising and price but did not assess weekly forecasting ability in a promotion environment.

Additional functional forms are possible besides the linear, multiplicative, and attraction models. For example, the log-linear form is as follows:

$$MS_{jt} = \alpha_j e_k^{\sum \beta_{jk} X_{jkt} + \epsilon_{jt}} \tag{7.8}$$

This model can be made linear in the explanatory variables by taking the log of both sides, yielding

$$\ln MS_{jt} = \ln \alpha_j + \sum_k \beta_{jk} X_{jkt} + \epsilon_{jt} \tag{7.8a}$$

The log-linear model is multiplicative (e.g., $e^{\beta_1 X_1 + \beta_2 X_2} = e^{\beta_1 X} e^{\beta_2 X_2}$) but also can incorporate $0 - 1$ dummies, since only the log of the dependent variable need be computed. It thus combines some of the advantages of the linear and the multiplicative models. (See Chapter 12, "Blattberg and Wisniewski Model.")

In summary, there is a multitude of potential functional forms confronting researchers who wish to use regression to study promotion. Although there is some evidence that simple linear models estimated using ordinary least squares do very well for forecasting purposes, more sophisticated functional forms might be called for if there is a need to represent nonlinearities, interactions parsimoniously or achieve logical consistency.

ESTIMATION PROCEDURES

The models discussed in this chapter can be estimated using ordinary least squares. Ordinary least squares does not explicitly attempt to address potential problems such as heteroscedasticity, serial correlation, or multicollinearity, but the method has been shown to perform well in a variety of situations and is readily available.

Heteroscedasticity might arise in a promotion regression model because sales during promotion periods are at a much higher level than during nonpromotion periods, and because the effect of a promotion itself may not be a constant but may vary each time the same promotion is implemented. The consequences of heteroscedasticity are a loss of efficiency—the true standard errors of the coefficients are not minimum among all linear estimators—coupled with biased estimates of those standard errors.[4] There are specialized methods for detecting and correcting for heteroscedasticity (see Pindyck and Rubinfeld, 1981, pp. 143–152; Fomby et al., 1984, Ch. 9). Theoretically, these procedures provide unbiased estimates of coefficient standard errors, and small true standard errors. However, they have not been tested in a promotion situation.

Another issue that might call for advanced estimation procedures is serial

---

[4] Note that the estimates of the coefficients themselves are still unbiased. It is the estimates of the standard errors of these coefficients that are biased.

correlation. Serial correlation is when the error terms in the regression model are correlated over time. In a promotion context, this might occur if advertising is left out of the model. If advertising schedules consist of "flights," that is, periods of sustained advertising followed by periods of very low advertising, the level of advertising in one period will be correlated with that in the next period. As a result, the error term of which advertising is a part will be correlated over time. The consequences of serial correlation are the same for heteroscedasticity—there is a loss of efficiency and estimates of the standard errors are biased. There are specialized procedures for overcoming these problems (Pindyck and Rubinfeld, 1981, pp. 152–164; Fomby et al., 1984, Ch. 10).

If both heteroscedasticity and serial correlation are present in a particular situation, generalized least squares (GLS) can be used to simultaneously address both these problems. GLS has not been used in a promotions context but has been employed in estimating market share models including advertising and price (e.g., see Ghosh et al., 1984; Brodie and DeKluyver, 1984; Leeflang and Reuyl, 1984; Naert and Weverbergh, 1985).

In practical applications, the emphasis is on obtaining low standard errors for the promotion coefficients in a regression model. The need for greater efficiency is there even if heteroscedasticity and serial correlation are not issues. Procedures for increasing efficiency are the use of linear constraints and Stein-Rule or other shrinkage estimators. These procedures incorporate information, not contained in the data but known to the researcher, to obtain lower standard errors for regression coefficients. Linear constraints specify, for example, that the sum of several parameters might equal a constant. For example, in a market share model, the coefficient for a brand's own promotion should equal the sum of the coefficients for that brand's promotion's effects on other brands. Neslin (1989) used this idea in a study of couponing. (See Theil, 1971, Ch. 7 and 10, for detailed development of this topic.)

Stein-Rule and other shrinkage estimators allow the researcher to specify a hypothesis regarding the parameters. The estimate yielded by these procedures will be close to the hypothesis (shrink toward it) if the data support it, but further away if the data do not. For example, Allenby and Blattberg (1988) use the hypothesis that the effects of a certain competitor's promotion on a given brand are equal. If the data support that hypothesis, the estimated competitor effects will be about equal. Shrinkage estimators are thus similar to using linear constraints, except the constraints do not have to be exactly satisfied. (See Fomby et al., 1984; Jennrich and Oman, 1986; and Oman, 1982, for further discussion).

MULTICOLLINEARITY

Multicollinearity appears in sales promotion models for two reasons. First, pairs of promotion variables such as feature and display are likely to be correlated. Second, there are so many variables potentially to include in a promotion model, it is very easy for one of them to be a linear combination of several of the others. For example, if a retailer usually promotes one brand within a category per week, then the sum of promotion dummy variables across brands will sum to one in most weeks. As a result, one brand's promotion can be predicted as a linear combination of the others. If the retailer's promotion schedule is consistent—that is, exactly one brand is promoted every week—then the multicollinearity will be exact and estimation will not be possible. If, however, the retailer is only fairly consistent, the multicollinearity will be strong but not perfect, and this will be manifested in large standard errors for the promotion variables.

Multicollinearity has received a great deal of attention in the econometrics literature. Belsley et al. (1980), for example, describe sophisticated procedures for detecting whether multicollinearity is a problem and how it affects the regression estimates. These procedures have been implemented in full on certain regression software packages (e.g., SAS Institute, Inc., 1985).

There are also a number of advanced techniques for estimating regression models in the presence of multicollinearity. The common theme of these procedures is that since multicollinearity leaves estimates unbiased but inflates their standard errors, the procedures inject a little bias into the estimation but gain in smaller standard errors. As a result, mean square error (essentially bias plus standard error) is minimized (see equation 7.1).

The advanced procedures for estimation in the presence of multicollinearity include ridge estimators and principal components regression (see Fomby et al., 1984, Ch. 13) and equity estimators (Krishnamurthi and Rangaswamy, 1987). In addition, constrained estimation, Stein-Rule, and other shrinkage estimators described earlier can also be used to combat multicollinearity. These methods hold promise but have not been systematically studied and compared in a promotions context.

A common sense way to address multicollinearity is to combine variables that might be included in the model yet are highly interrelated. This can be done either intuitively or on the basis of a factor analysis. For example, all competitive promotion variables might be combined into one competitive promotion variable. The cost of doing this is the implicit assumption that each competitor has the same effect on the subject brand. If this assumption is wrong, the resulting estimated coefficient is biased, in the same way that the coefficients are biased if we mistakenly pool observations. However, the benefits of including competition with a single biased coefficient may be better than not including competition at all, and the assumption of equal effects can be tested statistically (e.g., Theil, 1971, pp. 137–145; Pindyck and Rubinfeld, 1981, pp. 117–123).

In summary, multicollinearity is endemic to promotion regression models, and there is no established method for consistently eliminating the problem. Researchers need to be aware of the problem and be careful in diagnosing and, if possible, addressing multicollinearity. We would caution the researcher against omitting several variables correlated with the few included in the model as a way of avoiding multicollinearity. If the omitted variables belong in the model, omitting them biases the estimates for the included variables (see the earlier section, Omitted Variables Bias).

AN EXAMPLE OF MODEL BUILDING

We will examine a detailed example of using regression analysis to investigate the sales effects of promotion. The data are 108 weeks of scanner panel data for the instant coffee category, provided by Information Resources, Inc. (IRI), as part of its Academic Data Base program. Data are from two small cities and include measures of display, feature activity, price, and coupon redemptions. Analysis will be at the brand level, aggregating across stores and brand sizes. Promotion variables were created by first aggregating for a given brand size across stores, weighted by the stores' shares for that brand size. Next, the variables were aggregated across brand sizes, weighting by the share of brand sales attributed to each size. Table 7.5 provides descriptive statistics for the eight brands.

Table 7.5 shows a variety of brand share positions, ranging from 4.6 percent to 20.7 percent. Brands 3 and 7 are the most promoted brands, although brand 4 has the highest average market share. Brand 6 is a small-share brand with very little promotion. Brands 1, 2, 5, and 8 are in the middle. The 2,000 panelists generate an average of 217 category sales per week.

TABLE 7.5 Descriptive Statistics, Instant Coffee Regression Example

Average Brand	Market Share		Feature Activity		Display Activity		Price Cut Activity	
	μ	σ	μ	σ	μ	σ	μ	σ
1	.129	.041	.0144	.031	.0044	.018	− .0024	.005
2	.110	.053	.0177	.039	.0098	.029	− .0025	.007
3	.162	.067	.0500	.062	.0343	.056	− .0054	.010
4	.207	.068	.0295	.055	.0181	.039	− .0060	.010
5	.084	.034	.0212	.041	.0099	.027	− .0051	.010
6	.046	.021	.0044	.024	.0026	.019	− .0006	.002
7	.206	.064	.0647	.070	.0339	.057	− .0058	.009
8	.056	.023	.0161	.053	.0041	.022	− .0009	.003

Note: Market share is share of units. μ = mean, σ = standard deviation over 108 weeks.

Feature activity is a weighted average of the number of the brand's sizes being featured and the number of stores featuring the various brand sizes. A value of "1" in a given week would mean that all stores were featuring all brand sizes of the brand. The weights used were total store share of each brand size and brand size share of total brand sales.

Display activity is constructed the same way as feature activity, except the promotion of concern is display.

Price cut activity is constructed the same way as feature activity, except the variable of concern is the change in price during a price cut.

Data courtesy of Information Resources, Inc., Chicago, Illinois.

We will first analyze market share, and then category sales. For market share, we will investigate omitted variable bias, interactions between the promotion variables, and competitive effects. These analyses are summarized in Tables 7.6 through 7.9. For category sales, we investigate lagged promotional variables. These analyses are summarized in Tables 7.10 and 7.11. For category sales, we investigate lagged promotional variables. Throughout, we rely on statistical tests for deciding whether adding a new phenomenon (e.g., interactions) improves the fit of the model. Underlying our consideration of the various phenomena is either strong theoretical reasons or previous research that suggests their inclusion.

Table 7.6 displays two sets of regression runs. One includes feature and price cut; the other includes feature, display, and price cut. Scanning the first set, we see that R^2's range from .058 to .612, and all have significant F-statistics except brand 6. It is not very surprising that promotion does little to explain variation in market share for this relatively less promoted brand. The Durbin-Watson statistics are generally in the satisfactory range, although there is some propensity toward serial correlation. Time trend variables had been added to four of the brands based on low initial Durbin-Watson statistics. The trends are obviously serving as surrogates for some other marketing factor, possibly advertising.

Again scanning the first set of regressions, there is ample variation in the effectiveness of both feature and price cut activity. Price cuts are especially effective for brands 1, 2, and 8, which are middle-share brands, while feature activity is especially effective for the high-share brands, 3, 4, and 7.

The second set of regressions adds the display variable. Uniformly, this has the effect of lowering the magnitudes of the other two promotion effects. Apparently, when display is left out of the model, the included feature and price cut effects are inflated, because the display variable is positively correlated with feature and price cut. Leaving display out of the model is a classic example of omitted variables bias. Fortunately, there does not appear to be an undue degree of multicollinearity problems in the regressions. Most of the standard errors do not increase appreciably when display is included. The correlations among the estimates of the promotion effects were not intolerably high—the highest was a .62 correlation between the feature and display coefficients for brand 1. We have demonstrated omitted variables bias when a promotion variable is omitted from the model and shown that including it will not necessarily induce too much multicollinearity.

Table 7.7 shows the impact of adding three second-order interaction terms to the feature–display–price cut model. The table shows an F-test for testing whether these terms add explanatory power to the model (Pindyck and Rubinfeld, 1981, pp. 117–119). In the case of brand 1, the incremental R^2 is significant at the .01 level, although in all other cases, the increase in R^2 is not ever significant at the .15 level. It seems that promotions interact for brand 1, but not for the other brands. The reason for lack of significance for these brands could be (1) the interaction effects are just not there, (2) there is not enough variation in the

TABLE 7.6 Two Sets of Regression Runs Including Direct Effects of Promotions, With and Without Display (standard errors in parentheses)

	Brand							
	1	2[a]	3	4[b]	5[b]	6[a]	7	8[a]
Without Display								
Intercept	.119 (.004)	.027 (.01)	.126 (.01)	.226 (.01)	.094 (.01)	.047 (.01)	.164 (.01)	.070 (.01)
Feature	.441 (.12)	.286 (.09)	.713 (.08)	.801 (.09)	.312 (.07)	.075 (.09)	.607 (.07)	.106 (.05)
Price cut	-1.25 (.83)	-3.76 (.62)	-.174 (.63)	-.052 (.52)	.000 (.30)	.385 (.91)	-.369 (.57)	-2.08 (.72)
R^2	.153	.612	.440	.523	.200	.058	.478	.278
F	9.47	40.65	41.16	37.95	8.67	1.60	48.13	9.19
DW	1.76	1.83	1.45	1.74	2.11	2.14	1.61	2.16
SEE	.038	.034	.051	.048	.031	.020	.047	.020
With Display								
Intercept	.120 (.004)	.023 (.01)	.125 (.01)	.225 (.01)	.087 (.01)	.047 (.01)	.166 (.01)	.071 (.01)
Feature	.395 (.16)	.142 (.10)	.515 (.09)	.517 (.11)	.294 (.07)	.075 (.09)	.476 (.08)	.044 (.05)
Display	.126 (.29)	.544 (.15)	.462 (.11)	.614 (.16)	.383 (.10)	.101 (.11)	.311 (.11)	.249 (.12)
Price cut	-1.17 (.85)	-2.83 (.55)	.84 (.54)	.59 (.51)	-.03 (.28)	.33 (.92)	.264 (.59)	-1.76 (.73)
R^2	.154	.659	.523	.585	.290	.067	.516	.306
F	6.33	39.45	37.97	36.33	10.52	1.46	36.92	8.99
DW	1.77	1.89	1.60	1.62	2.13	2.13	1.63	2.16
SEE	.038	.032	.047	.045	.029	.020	.045	.020

[a] t and t^2 were included as additional variables after inspection of the data.
[b] t was included as an additional variable after inspection of the data.
Data courtesy of Information Resources, Inc., Chicago, Illinois.

TABLE 7.7 Adding Interactions to the Regression Model

| | R^2 | | |
Brand	Model with Interactions[a]	Model without Interactions[b]	F[c]
1	.278	.154	5.78[d]
2	.671	.659	1.20[e]
3	.536	.523	.94[e]
4	.590	.585	.41[e]
5	.310	.290	.97[e]
6	.082	.067	1.65[e]
7	.527	.516	.78[e]
8	.333	.306	1.34[e]

FEAT = feature activity
DISP = display activity
PC   = price cut activity

[a] $MS = \alpha + \beta_1 FEAT + \beta_2 DISP + \beta_3 PC$
$+ \beta_4 FEAT \times DISP + \beta_5 FEAT \times PC$
$+ \beta_6 DISP \times PC + \frac{\text{trend variables}}{\text{as appropriate}} + \epsilon$

[b] $MS = \alpha + \beta_1 FEAT + \beta_2 DISP + \beta_3 PC + \frac{\text{trend variables}}{\text{as appropriate}} + \epsilon$

[c] $F = \dfrac{(R_a^2 - R_b^2)/3}{(1 - R_a^2)/(108 - k)}$

where

$R_a^2 = R^2$ for interactions model
$R_b^2 = R^2$ for noninteractions model

[d] Significant $p < .01$

[e] Not significant at .10 level.

k = number of independent variables (including the constant) in interactions model. k ranges from 7 to 9, depending on th brand.

Data courtesy of Information Resources, Inc., Chicago, Illinois.

interaction variables, or (3) the interaction variables are so highly correlated with the main promotion variables that the effect cannot be detected. In the event that the third reason has occurred, the model builder is left with a dilemma: Should one use the model with all main effects or should one drop the main effects and just use the interactions? Chances are that the interactions alone model will be just as good as the main effects model. In this situation, the goal of simplicity would make one lean toward the main effects only model. In addition, experimental results have rarely shown a nonsignificant main promotion effect and significant interactions. Prior research plus simplicity thus points toward using the main effects only model when the F-test shows that the interactions do not add anything to the model.

The interactions model for brand 1 is as follows:

Variable	Coefficient	t-Statistic
Constant	.118	27.9
FEATURE	.143	.8
DISPLAY	1.908	1.4
PRICECUT	−1.716	1.7
$F \times D$	−9.495	.7
$F \times P$	−82.380	2.2
$D \times P$	166.300	3.8

Some of the *t*-statistics are low, but there is multicollinearity in the model to explain this. For example, the correlation between the DISPLAY and $F \times D$ coefficients is −.969. Interestingly, the sign of the $F \times P$ coefficient is negative, indicating that features and price cuts synergize for this brand, that is, deliver extra sales than would be obtained if the two promotions were run in separate weeks. However, the $D \times P$ coefficient is positive, indicating that running a display and a price cut (P is then negative) results in fewer sales than if the promotions had been run in separate weeks.

Although the interactions model is best for brand 1, one would have to be careful in using the model. For example, it would be dangerous to forecast sales for using a display alone, since the main display effect is confounded with the

TABLE 7.8 Adding Competition to the Model

	R^2			F^a	
Brand	Model A Three Competitive Variables[b]	Model B One Competitive Variable[b]	Model C Without Competition	A over C	B over C
1	.381	.347	.278	5.4[c]	10.6[c]
2	.699	.685	.659	4.5[c]	8.3[c]
3	.588	.560	.523	5.3[c]	8.7[c]
4	.703	.628	.585	13.2[c]	11.8[c]
5	.393	.361	.290	5.7[c]	11.3[c]
6	.091	.075	.067	.9[e]	.9[e]
7	.598	.577	.516	6.9[c]	14.9[c]
8	.368	.358	.306	3.2[d]	8.2[c]

[a] $F = \dfrac{(R_A^2 - R_C^2)/3}{(1 - R_A^2)/(108 - k)}$ or $F = \dfrac{(R_B^2 - R_C^2)/1}{(1 - R_B^2)/(108 - k)}$

k = number of independent variables (including the constant) in model A or B. k ranges from 5 to 10, depending on the model and brand.

[b] Brand 1 model contains promotion interactions. Brand 2–8 models contain only main promotion effects.

[c] Significant at p < .01 level.

[d] Significant at p < .05 level.

[e] Not significant at p < .10 level.

Data courtesy of Information Resources, Inc., Chicago, Illinois.

interaction with featuring. This is manifested in the large standard error for the display coefficient—the 95 percent confidence interval for this coefficient is 1.91 ± 2.80. The model will do much better when predicting the effect of a simultaneous feature display promotion.

Table 7.8 shows the effects of adding competition to the models. This was done in two ways. First, three aggregate measures of competitive feature, display, and price cut activity were separately used (model A). The aggregate measures were created by simply summing the competitive promotion activity in each time period. Second, the three measures were standardized and added together to create one overall competitive promotion measure. As Table 7.8 shows, competition significantly improves model fit, and in most cases, the single aggregate measure appears to be sufficient.

Table 7.9 displays the competitive effect coefficients for all eight brands. Note the rough correspondence between these coefficients and the average market share of the brands (the correlation between them is .38). For example, brands 3, 4, and 7 lose the most market share to competition, but these are the brands with the most share to lose. We include the three separate competitive promotion coefficients for brand 4, since the F-statistic was higher when these effects were included separately (Table 7.8). Note that the sign for competitive price cut is "incorrect" and the t-statistics for display and price cut are weak. Although the bivariate correlations among all the coefficients were not large (the largest involving competitive price cuts was .33), it is likely that either multicollinearity is at work or the incorrect sign is simply a random finding (the coefficient is not significantly different from zero at a high level).

TABLE 7.9 Competitive Promotion Effects on Each Brand's Market Share

Brand	Competition Coefficient	t-Statistic	Average Market Share
1	−.0054	3.3	.129
2	−.0046	2.9	.110
3	−.0073	3.0	.162
4	−.0074	3.4	.207
5	−.0046	3.4	.084
6	−.0009	.9	.046
7	−.0088	3.9	.206
8	−.0028	2.9	.056
4 (Feature)	−.150	4.8	
(Display)	−.062	1.3	
(Price cut)	−.341	1.8	

Note: The competition variable in the first eight rows is aggregated across all competitive brands and all types of promotion. The last three rows display the separate effects of competitive features, displays, and price cuts on market share for brand 4.

Data courtesy of Information Resources, Inc., Chicago, Illinois.

The results of these regressions show clearly how competitive promotions take away market share from each brand. However, the models have not gone into the detail of assessing which brands steal share from which brands. This would require 7 rather than 1 competitive variable, or 21 rather than 3 promotion-specific competitive variables. Including several such variables could invite multicollinearity. Allenby (1988) uses shrinkage estimators (see the earlier discussion) to estimate models including such detail. As an alternative, Allenby (1988) has developed a theory for reducing the number of distinct coefficients to be estimated.

We now turn our attention to the effect of promotions on unit category sales. Table 7.10 presents an initial series of regressions for investigating this possibility. The promotion variables were created by summing promotional activity across brands in each week. In this illustration, the regressions tell us two things: First, features and displays significantly increase category sales while price cuts do not. Second, there are no interactions among the promotions. The first result makes good sense. A price cut *by itself*, without an attention-getting display or feature, will probably only be noticed by someone who is already interested in purchasing the category and therefore examining the instant coffee shelves. As a result, a price cut by itself can influence market share but is less apt to affect category sales. Models II and IV, however, investigate the possibility of interactions among

TABLE 7.10 Current Period Effects of Promotion Upon Category Sales

| | Model | | | |
Variable	I	II	III	IV
Constant	192.1[a]	193.3[a]	193.8[a]	191.2[a]
FEAT	54.7[a]	40.9[c]	53.8[a]	42.5[c]
DISP	94.0[a]	124.3[c]	102.9[a]	130.8[c]
PCUT	−91.0[c]	113.5[c]		
FEAT × PCUT		−1339.8[c]		−1157.4[b]
FEAT × DISPLAY		−65.0[c]		−59.5[c]
DISP × PCUT		619.6[c]		916.8[c]
R^2	.216	.237	.213	.236
F	9.6[a]	5.2[a]	14.20[a]	6.3[a]
DW	1.72	1.71	1.72	1.69
Improvement F over preceding model		.93[c]		1.02[c]

[a] Significant $p < .05$.

[b] Significant $p < .10$.

[c] Not significant at .10 level.

FEAT = category feature activity
DISP = category display activity
PCUT = category price cut activity
$n = 108$

Data courtesy of Information Resources, Inc., Chicago, Illinois.

TABLE 7.11 Lagged Effects of Promotion upon Category Sales

Variable	Model I	Model II	Model III	Model IV
	I	II	III	IV
Constraint	193.8[a]	200.7[a]	207.2[a]	199.9[a]
FEATURE	53.1[a]	49.0[a]	52.2[a]	49.6[a]
DISPLAY	101.7[a]	102.1[a]	99.4[a]	100.1[a]
LF1	—	−27.9[c]	−32.0[b]	−30.2[c]
LF2	—	—	−27.1[c]	—
LD1	—	—	—	11.9[c]
R^2	.209	.229	.247	.230
F	13.6	10.1	7.9	7.5
Durbin-Watson Statistic	1.72	1.75	1.75	1.75
Improvement F over model 1		2.65[c]	2.55[b]	1.38[c]

[a] Significant $p < .05$.

[b] Significant $p < .10$.

[c] Not significant at .10 level.

  LF1 = FEATURE lagged one period

  LF2 = FEATURE lagged two periods

  LD1 = DISPLAY lagged one period

    n = 106 for all models for comparison purposes

Data courtesy of Information Resources, Inc., Chicago, Illinois.

the promotion variables. While the inclusion increases R^2 as it must, the improvement is not statistically significant.

Table 7.11 explores the lagged effect of promotion upon category sales. Model IV shows that adding one-period lags for both feature and display does not improve R^2 by a significant amount. However, including only feature lagged one period improves R^2 by the same amount, and the result is somewhat significant ($p < .14$). If we include two lagged terms for feature, the overall improvement is significant at the .10 level. These exploratory results suggest the possibility that features have a long as well as short term effect on category sales, whereas the effect of display is only immediate.

In summary, our investigation of the effects of promotions on category sales shows that features influence both the current and future level of category sales. Display was determined to have only an immediate effect on category sales, and price cuts had no effect. The category model could undoubtedly be developed further. For example, the polynomial lag model could be investigated.

8

Choice and Purchase Timing Models

Most of the techniques reviewed in this book examine the effect of promotion on sales by dealing directly with sales or market share generated by a group of consumers. Choice models are distinctive in focusing on the individual consumer and modeling his or her choice behavior. Total sales are viewed as the sum of the choice outcomes over several consumers.

There is an extensive marketing literature written on the development and estimation of choice and purchase timing models. This chapter will focus on specific applications relevant to promotions. The data required for these models are panel data, which are now available through sources such as IRI, Nielsen, and SAMI/Burke.

The use of choice models differs from models applied to store- or market-level sales data because it is possible to analyze buyer behavior. This leads to an understanding of how consumer behavior changes when promotions are offered. For brand managers and marketing researchers this translates into insights into how promotions work.

Specific issues that brand choice and purchase timing models can analyze are

- Carry-over effects.
- Heterogeneity in deal response.
- Sources of promotional volume.
- Stockpiling.

Choice models are used to understand carry-over effects and heterogeneity; purchase timing models are used to analyze stockpiling behavior; both purchase timing and choice models are used to understand sources of volume.

The chapter is organized as follows: The first section covers choice models, including stochastic brand choice models, the linear learning model, and the bargain value model; the second discusses incorporating marketing mix variables into stochastic brand choice models; the third describes purchase timing models including the NBD model; and the fourth and last discusses how these models can be used to answer key promotional issues.

CHOICE MODELS

Stochastic Brand Choice Models

Since the 1950s marketers have been studying brand choice models. The purpose of these models is to predict behavior recognizing that consumers randomly (hence the word stochastic) switch from brand to brand. The early work is summarized in Massy et al. (1970).

Before describing some of the models used to analyze promotional behavior, it is important to study some basic properties of stochastic brand choice (SBC) models and introduce simple models (Bernoulli and Markov) commonly used by researchers. Three properties of SBC models which will be used throughout the discussion are (1) order of the process, (2) heterogeneity, and (3) stationarity. Each is described in the paragraphs that follow.

Order of the Process.   Order of the process refers to the influence of past purchases on the current purchase. If past purchases do not influence the current purchase, then the order is zero. Mathematically, a zero-order process has

$$Pr(X_t = 0 \mid X_{t-1}, \ldots, X_1) = Pr(X_t = 0) \tag{8.1}$$

where

$$X_t = \text{buy, no buy in period } t$$

with

$$X_t = \begin{cases} 0 = \text{no buy} \\ 1 = \text{buy} \end{cases}$$

In contrast, nonzero-order processes (e.g., Markov or linear learning models) assume that prior purchases influence the current purchase. If the order is one, then only the last purchase affects the current purchase; if the order is greater than one, then more than the last purchase affects the current purchase. Markov models have order equal to one; linear learning models have order greater than one.

What are the primary implications of the order of the process? Specifically, it is used to determine whether a carryover effect exists. If the last purchase influences the current purchase (nonzero order), then inducing a customer to switch through the use of a promotion increases (or decreases) his or her probability of repeat purchasing. If the past purchase does not affect the consumer (zero order), then the promotional effect is limited to one period.

To understand this discussion better, suppose the probability of choosing

TABLE 8.1 Zero-Order versus First-Order Models

		A. Zero-Order Process				B. First-Order Process	
		Current Purchase				Current Purchase	
	Brand	1	2		Brand	1	2
Last	1	.5	.5	Last	1	.8	.2
Purchase	2	.5	.5	Purchase	2	.2	.8

brand 1 or brand 2 is given in Tables 8.1A, and 8.1B. In Table 8.1A the probability does not depend upon the prior brand purchase. The probability to buy is .5 whether brand 1 or 2 was bought in the last period. However, in Table 8.1B it does depend upon whether brand 1 or brand 2 was bought on the prior purchase.

Suppose that there are 1,000 households in the market and that under normal conditions 500 bought brand 1 last period and 500 bought brand 2. In the next period 500 households will buy brand 1 and 500 will buy brand 2 *under* either set of repeat purchase probabilities. Now suppose that a promotion was offered in the last period and 800 households bought brand 1 and 200 bought brand 2. The repeat buying rate will be very different under the two sets of purchase probabilities. For the probabilities given in Table 8.1A, the number buying brand 1 in the next period is 800(.5) × 200(.5) = 500. For the probabilities given in Table 8.1B, the number buying brand 1 is 800(.8) + 200(.2) = 680. Thus, for the probabilities given in Table 8.1A, the number buying brand 1 in the next period is the same whether a promotion was offered or not. However, this is not true for the first-order process given in Table 8.1B. An incremental 180 customers bought in the next period ($t + 1$). In fact, in the period after ($t + 2$), there is also an additional effect. There are 608 buyers. Ultimately, the number of buyers of brand 1 will reach 500, but it will take a number of periods before this happens.

Based on the foregoing example, it is clear that the order of the process is important in evaluating promotions. Bass et al. (1984) analyzed a series of studies plus some diary panel data and concluded: "For many product categories a substantial majority of customers whose behavior may be characterized as stationary have purchase sequences for brands which are either a zero-order process or something close to it" (Bass et al., 1984, p. 284). If Bass et al. are correct, then promotional effects only have a one-period effect.

Heterogeneity. As is obvious not all consumers have the same probability of buying a brand or have the same degree of deal proneness. Early SBC models assumed that everyone had the same probability of buying, which led to some measurement problems as well as confounding the order of the process with consumer heterogeneity (Frank, 1962). Mathematically, the assumption of homogeneity is

$$Pr(X_{it} = 1 \mid X_{it-1}, \ldots) = p_{it} = p_t \qquad \text{for all } i \tag{8.2}$$

where p_{it} is the probability that the ith consumer buys the brand at time t. If i varies across consumers, then there is heterogeneity.

Uniformly, SBC models (and purchase incidence models) assume heterogeneity in the population. It is well documented that consumers do not all have the same purchase probabilities. Consumer loyalty and purchase rate vary. Therefore, most models include an assumption that consumers' preferences or purchase frequencies follow a specific distribution (e.g., beta distribution). Massy et al. (1970) discuss this issue in detail.

Stationarity.   Most SBC models assume that the process is stationary, which means that the probability of purchasing a given brand is constant over time. In equation (8.2) if $p_{it} = p_i$ for all t, then the process is "stationary." This assumption is rarely met in practice. Promotions vary from week to week, and so the assumption of stationarity is violated. Only by incorporating marketing variables into SBC models can the lack of stationarity be overcome. Logit models (discussed later) have been used extensively in marketing because they allow for the incorporation of marketing mix variables into a stochastic choice process. Jones and Zufryden (1980) and Guadagni and Little (1983) show how to include marketing mix variables into SBC models.

Bernoulli Models.   The most fundamental SBC model is a Bernoulli model. In its simplest form, it leads to a binomial distribution of purchases. The key assumptions are

1. The probability of buying the brand is p no matter what brand was bought on a prior purchase (independence over time).
2. p is constant over time (stationarity).
3. p is the same for all households (homogeneity).

If there are N households in the market, the market share for the brand is Np, where p is the probability of buying and does not vary over time.

Because most marketers believe there is heterogeneity in the market, it is possible to relax the assumption of homogeneity. This is done by assuming that p follows a beta distribution across the population. Then, by integrating over p, the probability distribution of p for the population is a beta binomial. (See Massy et al., 1970.)[1]

A binomial model (or beta binomial) can be used as a baseline model. Assume the probability of buying the brand of interest for a fixed purchase occasion is .3. Assume that there are 1,000 households purchasing. Then the *expected* number buying is 300. A promotion is run and 500 households buy the brand. Then, the incremental number of households purchasing is 200.

In theory, using a Bernoulli model (or another SBC model) to estimate a baseline is appealing. The problem is there are very few nonpromoted periods to estimate baseline probabilities. Therefore, it is necessary to incorporate marketing

---

[1] For the K brand case, a Diriclet multinomial is used.

TABLE 8.2 Transition Matrix

		Brand	Period t		
			1	2	3
Period $t-1$		1	.6	.2	.2
		2	.3	.5	.2
		3	.1	.1	.8

mix variables into SBC models (see the section entitled "Incorporating Marketing Mix Variables into Choice Models").

There are several problems with Bernoulli models. First, there is no mechanism to measure carry-over effects because of the assumption of independence over time. Second, promotions do not affect the purchase probability because of the assumption of constant probability over time (stationarity). Logit models have been used to overcome these restrictive assumptions.

Markov Models. To relax the assumption of independence over time, Markov models were introduced. They make the purchase in period t a function of the purchase in period $t-1$. A transition matrix is introduced that shows how the purchase in period $t-1$ influences the purchase in period t. Table 8.2 gives a transition matrix for a three-brand market. Notice that the probability of buying brand 1 is significantly higher if brand 1 was bought last period than if brand 2 or 3 was bought. The matrix is constructed so that brand 2 and brand 3 also have higher probabilities of not switching brands than of switching brands. This results in a positive carry-over effect because the last purchase positively influences the next purchase.

Heterogeneity is difficult to incorporate into a Markov model because no simple probability distribution across the population exists to characterize heterogeneity such as the beta distribution. Massy et al. (1970) discuss ways to incorporate heterogeneity into simple Markov models. Blattberg and Sen (1976) also discuss a procedure for incorporating heterogeneity into Markov models.

Markov models do offer an interesting way to analyze promotional carry-over effects. Table 8.3 defines the probability of purchase depending upon whether

TABLE 8.3 Markov Transition Matrix Incorporating Dialing

		Period t	
		Buy	No Buy
	Buy, no deal	.8	.2
	Buy, deal	.5	.5
Period $t-1$			
	No buy, no deal	.1	.9
	No buy, deal	.3	.7

a purchase was made or was not made. A negative carry-over effect was included by making the probability of repeat buying brand 1 lower if it was bought on promotion than if it was not bought on promotion. Displaying diary panel purchase data using a transition matrix is a useful way to see how a household's buying varies when a deal purchase is made versus no deal purchase.

To see how the model works, suppose that there are 1,000 households in the market. Exactly 500 bought the brand on deal in the last period; exactly 500 bought the brand at regular price. Then, the number repeat buying if no deal was present is 500(.7) = 350. The number buying if a deal was present is 500(.5) = 250. The result is a significant drop-off of deal buyers. The reason may be that deal buyers have a negative attribution to the product. (See Chapter 2.)

One can use this matrix to begin to analyze carry-over effects of promotions. In using this matrix, though, it is important to address aggregation across households, which can cause negative carry-over effects to appear artificially. (See Chapter 5.)

In summary, Markov models are more complex than a Bernoulli model. They can be used to study carry-over effects and offer a simple procedure to display data using transition matrices. However, it assumes that only the last purchase affects the next purchase. The linear learning model extends this concept to allow for higher-order effects.

The Linear Learning Model

The Basic Model. The linear learning model was first suggested by Bush and Mosteller (1955) and applied to consumer behavior by Kuehn (1962). The linear learning model attempts to model the reinforcing effect of previous purchases on current purchases. In operant terms, reinforcement can occur because consumption of the product serves as positive reinforcement and hence helps the consumer to learn the behavior of purchasing the brand. In Hullian terms, purchasing the brand increases the habit strength of performing that behavior, and hence the behavior is likely to be repeated. (See Chapter 2, "Behavioral Learning Theories.")

The linear learning model is formulated as follows (following the notation of Lilien and Kotler, 1983):

$$P_{t+1} = \alpha + \beta X_t + \lambda P_t \qquad t = 0, 1, \ldots \tag{8.3}$$

where

P_t = the probability a consumer will purchase the brand at purchase occasion t

$X_t = \begin{cases} 1 \text{ if the brand is purchased at purchase occasion } t \\ 0 \text{ otherwise} \end{cases}$

α, β, and λ are parameters.

Equation (8.3) calculates choice probability for the next purchase occasion as a smoothing process, depending on the proability of purchasing the brand at the current occasion, and whether or not the brand was purchased. For example, consider $\alpha = .1$, $\beta = .1$, $\lambda = .7$, and $P_t = .4$. If the consumer *purchases the brand* on the current occasion, the probability of purchasing it on the next occasion is

$$P_{t+1} = .1 + .1(1) + .7(.4) = .48 \tag{8.4a}$$

If the consumer *does not purchase the brand* on the current occasion, the probability of purchasing it is 0 on the next occasion:

$$P_{t+t} = .1 + .1(0) + .7(.4) = .38 \tag{8.4b}$$

Thus, if the brand is purchased, the purchase probability is boosted by $\beta = .1$ over what it would be if the brand were not purchased.

Figure 8.1 shows additional numerical examples to help interpret the parameters. The role of α is generally to keep purchase probability close to a central value. The relative values of β versus λ govern the extent to which the consumer will rely on the most recent purchase versus the history of previous purchases in reaching the decision on whether to purchase the brand. By investigating the long-run impact of continually purchasing or never purchasing the brand, the following

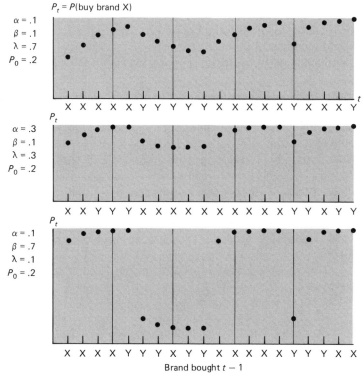

FIGURE 8.1 Illustrative Progression of Choice Probabilities for Period t, Using the Linear Learning Model, Assuming Purchases Made in Period $t - 1$

expressions can be derived for the upper and lower limits of P_t:

$$UL = \frac{\alpha + \beta}{1 - \lambda} \tag{8.5a}$$

$$LL = \frac{\alpha}{1 - \lambda} \tag{8.5b}$$

By taking the expected value of equation (8.3) and iterating recursively, it can be shown that the long-term expected value of P_t (see Lilien, 1974a) is

$$E(P) = \frac{\alpha}{[1 - (\beta + \lambda)]} \tag{8.6}$$

where the P is the long-run probability of buying the brand.

In summary, then, a consumer with parameters α, β, and λ and starting with some purchase probability P_0, will purchase the brand with probability between UL and LL over time, and eventually reach an equilibrium average probability of $E(P)$.

The parameters for the linear learning model theoretically vary from individual to individual. However, there may not be data for enough purchase occasions for each individual to provide reliable estimates of individual-specific coefficients. Lilien (1974a, 1974b) proposes considering that certain parameters follow some distributions (e.g., beta) across the population and then uses maximum likelihood to estimate the parameters of this distribution.

Kuehn and Rohloff's Application of the Linear Learning Model. The linear learning model does not explicitly include the potential effects of promotions, or for that matter, any other marketing instrument. However, Kuehn and Rohloff (1967) used the linear learning model to provide a baseline or "prepurchase" probability indicating how likely each consumer would be to purchase the brand had a promotion not been offered. (Ehrenberg, 1972, uses a similar strategy for purchase timing models. This is discussed in the section on purchase incidence models.) The average prepurchase probability across consumers buying the brand when a given promotion was in effect therefore is interpreted as the market share the brand would have achieved among deal purchasers had the promotion not been offered.

The specific formulation Kuehn and Rohloff used for the linear learning model was

$$P_{t+1} = \phi S + (\lambda' - \phi)X_t + (1 - \lambda)P_t \tag{8.7}$$

In terms of our original formulation, we have the following:

$$\phi S = \alpha \tag{8.8a}$$

$$\lambda' - \phi = \beta \tag{8.8b}$$

$$1 - \lambda' = \lambda \tag{8.8c}$$

Combining these equations, we obtain

$$E(P) = \frac{\alpha}{[1 - (\beta + \lambda)]} = S \qquad (8.9)$$

(from equation 8.4). Therefore, S is interpreted as the long-run equilibrium share for the brand. In addition, Kuehn and Rohloff let S vary by brand (so it is labeled S_i in their paper) but posited that λ and ϕ would be constant across brands.

Kuehn and Rohloff used their model to estimate both the average prepurchase probability among deal buyers for the purchase occasion of the deal and the degree to which postdeal purchase probabilities were increased among those buying on deal. The first quantity they call "trial" while the second is called "conversion." These correspond to the short-term and long-term effects of the promotion.

Kuehn and Rohloff's work is pioneering research on the application of stochastic models for evaluating promotions. The idea of using the linear learning model to provide baseline choice probabilities is very powerful, although it has not often been emulated by others (exceptions include Ehrenberg, 1972; Neslin, 1985). More recent research approaches have incorporated promotions directly in the model.

Lilien's Modified Linear Learning Model. Lilien (1974a, b) extended the linear learning model to include price. Strictly speaking, he included the price differential between two brands, whether or not the variation in this differential was large enough and of short enough duration to be considered a price promotion. He also did not consider the purchase timing and quantity effects that accompany promotions. However, since price promotions result in large price differentials, the modified linear learning model's independent variable (price differential) could be adapted quite readily to capturing the event of a price promotion. Lilien's modification to the linear learning model was simple yet captured the price difference factor quite well. In particular, his model was

$$P_{t+1} = (1 - C)(\alpha + \beta X_t + \lambda P_t) + C\phi(\delta_{t+1}) \qquad (8.10)$$

where

$$C = \text{price consciousness of the consumer}$$

$$\delta_{t+1} = \text{the price difference between the brands at purchase occasion } t + 1$$

$$\phi(\delta_{t+1}) = \text{the value of the price response function for a price differential of } \delta \text{ at time } t + 1$$

$$P_t = \text{the probability of buying the higher priced brand at time } t$$

Lilien oriented his analysis so that the brand in question was always higher priced (e.g., premium gasoline) and δ was the difference between the higher- and lower-priced brands. Therefore, $\phi(\delta)$ was a decreasing function of δ. The parameter C served as a weight to represent "roughly the fraction of his behavior determined by price." The modified linear learning model reduces to the basic linear learning model when $C = 0$.

In a sense, Lilien seems to include price sensitivity twice, once with C, which varies by consumers, and again by using $\phi(\delta)$, which does not vary by consumer. However, C can be viewed as the relative weight the consumer places on price, and $\phi(\delta)$ is the common response function consumers use when they consider price. Some function ϕ is needed in any case to rescale δ to be less than one.

Corresponding to equation (8.4), Lilien derives an expression for the long-term expected market share $E(\tilde{P})$, assuming a constant price difference δ:

$$E(\tilde{P}) = \frac{(1 - C) + C\phi(\delta)}{1 - (1 - C)(\beta + \lambda)} \tag{8.11}$$

As equation (8.11) shows, if the price differential (δ) is high and consumers are price sensitive (high C), then the denominator becomes larger and the numerator is weighted more toward $\phi(\delta)$, which will become smaller since $\phi(\delta)$ is decreasing in δ. As a result, the equilibrium share will be small.

Lilien estimated the modified linear learning model at the category level—premium versus standard gasoline. Lilien found that his model fit the data and predicted better than either the basic linear learning model or a zero-order Bernoulli model. His parameter estimates for the linear learning model were $\hat{\alpha} = .021$, $\hat{\beta} = .375$, and $\hat{\lambda} = .601$. The parameter C was allowed to vary according to a beta distribution across consumers. The estimated mean of this distribution was .316, and the distribution was unimodal. He also found fairly steep price response, since for example $\phi(2.79) = .189$, while $\phi(1.99) = .471$. Less than a 1-cent price difference would therefore have a pronounced effect on market share.

Lilien's modification of the linear learning model demonstrated that price promotion can be added to a simple choice model, and the result was a richer, better-fitting model. The linear learning model stream did not advance much further since Lilien's work. The current synthesis of these two models is the logit model. The linear learning model has been criticized, by Lilien himself, as cumbersome to extend to multibrand markets and to several marketing instruments (Lilien and Kotler, 1983, p. 245; Lilien, 1974b, p. 284).

However, a major criticism of the linear learning model is its association with the idea that purchase, including promotional induced purchase, serves as a reinforcement *enhancing* future choice probabilities. While this idea is based on the well-established theory of operant conditioning, the model builds in the reinforcement assumption rather than testing it. There is, however, no reason why the reinforcement parameter (β) could not be negative or zero, to reflect either variety seeking, product turn-off, or no influence of the consumption experience. The model could also be expanded to include both a promotion purchase effect versus a nonpromotion purchase effect. For example,

$$P_{t+1} = (1 - C)(\alpha + \beta X_t + \gamma X_t Z_t + \lambda P_t) + CZ_{t+1} \tag{8.12}$$

where $Z_t = 1$ if there was a promotion at purchase occasion t, 0 otherwise.

We would expect γ to be negative if using a promotion decreases the purchase probability relative to purchasing the brand not on promotion. The impact on the next purchase occasion choice probability would be β if the brand was not bought on promotion and $\beta + \gamma$ if the brand was bought on promotion. The parameter C in this case reflects the consumer's sensitivity to current period promotion. Because of its conceptual association with the operant conditioning reinforcement role of purchase and consumption, the linear learning model has been interpreted as mathematically ensuring confirmation of that theory, but that is not necessarily true. While equation (8.12) would be a logical extension of the modified linear learning model to test the reinforcing effects of promotion, the current logit models contain the same phenomena.

The Bargain Value Model

Keon (1980) introduced the bargain value model to the literature and positioned it as the antithesis of the linear learning model. The important implication of his model was that continual purchases of a "preferred" brand, including promotion induced purchases, result in successively higher probabilities of switching to a competitive brand. The role of promotions is therefore to build short-term share for the brand but not to build brand loyalty.

Keon postulated that brand choice was directly related to the "bargain values" of the brands in the consumer's evoked set. Bargain value was defined as the ratio of utility of the brand (expressed in monetary units) to price, so that the bargain value for brand X, BV_x, equals MV_x/P, where MV_x is the utility of brand X and P is price. The brand with the highest bargain value at the time of purchase is assumed to be chosen. However, the utility and hence bargain value of all brands *except the brand last purchased* is uncertain to the consumer. The utility of the current brand is certain because it was just used, while the consumer forgets the exact utility of nonpurchased brands. The key assumption incorporated into the bargain value model is that uncertainty for the nonpurchased brands increases over successive purchase occasions when those brands are not purchased, and hence the variance in the probability distribution of perceived utility of those brands increases.

To understand how the bargain value model works, assume there are two brands in the market, X and Y. Further assume that X was purchased last period but Y was not. Keon assumes that $BV_x = MV_x/P_x$ is known but $\tilde{BV}_y = \tilde{MV}_y/P_y$ is a random variable (˜ denotes a random variable). Keon uses a triangular distribution for $\tilde{MV}_y$, but we will use a normal distribution for $\tilde{MV}_y$ since it is easier to understand.

A consumer chooses brand X if $BV_x > BV_y$. Since $\tilde{BV}_y$ is a random variable, the probability the consumer chooses X is simply $Pr(\tilde{BV}_y < BV_x)$. Let $\tilde{MV}_y$ have mean μ_y and variance σ_y^2. Then,

$$Pr(\tilde{B}V_y < BV_x) = Pr\left[\frac{\tilde{B}V_y - \mu_y/P_y}{\sigma_y/P_y} < \frac{(MV_x/P_x) - (\mu_y/P_y)}{\sigma_y/P_y}\right]$$

$$= F\left[\frac{(MV_x/P_x) - \mu_y/P_y}{\sigma_y/P_y}\right] \tag{8.13}$$

where $F(\bullet)$ is the cumulative normal function.

As P_x decreases, the $Pr(\tilde{B}V_y < BV_x)$ increases. Thus, when X is promoted, the probability of buying X increases. Similarly, as P_y decreases or σ_y increases, the probability of choosing Y increases. Thus, when Y promotes, its probability increases.

Keon models σ_y as follows: $\sigma_y = k\sum_{i=1}^{t}\lambda^i$, where t is the number of periods since the consumer last bought. If $t = 0$, then $\sigma_y = 0$. λ is assumed to be between 0 and 1. As $t \to \infty$, $\sigma_y \to k/(1 - \lambda)$. The longer since a purchase of Y, the larger σ_y and the higher the probability of buying Y.

The key assumption made by Keon is that the variance increases over time, implying that the longer a brand has not been bought, the higher the probability of purchasing that brand. This is contrary to the generally used formulation of the linear learning model which assumes the probability of buying decreases the longer the brand has not been bought.

The bargain value model assumes the consumer is a risk preferrer (not risk adverse, which most random utility models assume) because as σ_y increases, the probability of buying y increases. This is a strange assumption. Most marketers would believe the variance of the consumer's evaluation of a nonpurchased brand increases over time. However, the mean might be reduced to the average of all brands in the category. Alternative formulations are required to consider how decreasing "knowledge" of the brand, which increases risk of buying the brand, should be incorporated into the choice process.

Keon has a complex formulation to consider the k brand case. However, the k brand case for the bargain value model can be formulated so that it becomes a probit model (see Amemiya, 1985). If there are k brands, then the consumer chooses brand 1 if $BV_1 > BV_2$, $BV_1 > BV_3$, . . . , $BV_1 > BV_k$. If all the BV's are random variables and are normally distributed, this becomes a probit model. Under another assumption about the error term (Weibull), the model becomes a logit model (see equation 8.15).

Because more standard models can be used (probit and logit), Keon's use of the triangular distribution adds little to the solution. However, Keon offers some interesting concepts required in formulating promotional choice models. Specifically, (1) the variance of the utility for the brand increases when the brand is not purchased, and (2) promotions should be combined with utility to create the bargain value (BV).

Keon's model is quite interesting because it can be generalized using a logit or probit model. Other researchers can try to modify the model to include other underlying assumptions.

INCORPORATING MARKETING MIX VARIABLES INTO CHOICE MODELS

The Logit Model

The Basic Model. The logit model has its roots in mathematical psychology (Luce, 1959) and transportation analysis (McFadden, 1973). Use of the logit model in marketing was pioneered by Green et al. (1977) and Jones and Zufryden (1980, 1981). Guadagni and Little (1983) were the first to use it to study promotions.

The model can be derived in a number of ways, but perhaps the simplest is the explanation given by Guadagni and Little (1983). In particular, for a given individual i, let

U_k = utility for brand k

V_k = deterministic component of utility for brand k

ϵ_k = random component of utility for brand k

S = choice set of brands considered {brands 1, 2, . . .}

Then, we assume for each $k \in S$

$$U_k = V_k + \epsilon_k \tag{8.14}$$

Equation (8.14) holds for a given individual at a specific choice occasion, although we avoid individual and choice occasion subscripts for ease of exposition. We may think of V_k, the deterministic component of utility, as representing utility that can be predicted by observed factors such as price and promotion. The random component, ϵ_k, can consist of unobserved factors that if we could quantify them, would be included in V_k, as well as truly random factors such as the weather, individual "mood," unquantifiable variety seeking, and so on.

We then assume that at a given choice occasion, individual i will choose the brand with highest utility U_k, but since ϵ_k and hence U_k is random, the brand with highest utility will vary from occasion to occasion. For a given occasion, we then have P_k, the probability of choosing brand k, which can be expressed as

$$P_k = P(U_k \geq U_j \text{ for every } j \in S) \tag{8.15}$$

Last, we make some explicit assumptions regarding the random component of utility, namely, that the ϵ_k's are independently distributed and follow a Weibull distribution. (The Weibull distribution is a unimodal distribution shaped similarly to the normal; see Guadagni and Little, 1983). This distribution is used for the mathematical convenience of the result that follows. If the normal distribution is used, the resulting somewhat less tractable model is called probit. (In practical applications, the probit and logit models do not differ substantially in their results.)

From equations (8.14) and (8.15), it can be shown (Theil, 1969; McFadden,

1973) that P_k can be expressed in terms of the V_k's as follows:

$$P_k = \frac{e^{V_k}}{\sum\limits_{m=1}^{K} e^{V_m}} \qquad k = 1, \ldots, k \tag{8.16}$$

Equation (8.16) is the logit model. It expresses the probability of choosing a brand as a function of quantifiable utility V_k. The approach of logit modelers is to express V_k as a function of measurable factors such as price and promotion. Therefore, if at a given choice occasion, we know these factors, we can calculate the V_k's and then the P_k's. Most commonly, the factors are assumed to be linearly related to V_k, so that

$$V_k = \sum_{j=1}^{J} \beta_{jk} X_{jk} \tag{8.17}$$

where X_{jk} equals deterministic factor j as it applies to brand k (e.g., the price of brand k). Although equation (8.17) is linear, equation (8.16) is nonlinear, and in fact the probability of purchase will be an S-shaped function of V_k. Since V_k is a linear function of the deterministic factors, purchase probability will be an S-shaped function of those factors, as shown in Figure 8.2.

Note also that the calculated purchase probability will be between 0 and 1 and will sum to one across brands. This is because of the "us divided by the market" form of equation (8.17). Therefore, if brand k is promoted and V_k enjoys a corresponding increase in size, the logit model will automatically reallocate market shares for all the brands.

For example, assume a three-brand market with

$$e^{V_1} = 1.0$$
$$e^{V_2} = .2$$
$$e^{V_3} = .8$$

so that .5, .1, and .4 correspond to the initial choice probabilities of the brands. Now assume that brand 3 is promoted so that $e^{V_3} = 1.2$, the new choice probability will be

Brand	Initial Share	New Share	Percentage Change
1	.50	.416	− 16%
2	.10	.083	− 16
3	.40	.500	+ 25

Notice that both brands 1 and 2 lose the same *proportional* amount of choice probability. Stated differently, brands lose sales in proportion to their original market shares. (We use market share and choice probability interchangeably, since market share is the result of aggregating across consumers.)

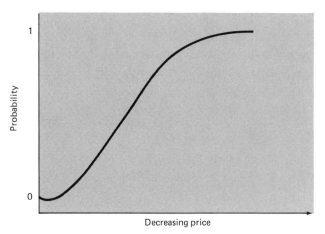

FIGURE 8.2 Purchase Probability as a Function of Price for the Logit Model

Estimating the logit model requires observations of the deterministic factors (*X*'s) and choice outcomes for either one consumer over several purchase occasions, several consumers over one purchase occasion, or several consumers over several purchase occasions. Most uses of logit models are estimated across consumers to generate enough observations. In this case, the β's in equation (8.14) are assumed to be equal across consumers. This opens up the aggregation bias problem.

Ortmeyer et al. (1987) modeled the way in which promotion response β's might vary across consumers and therefore explicitly included individual differences in promotion response. Jones and Landwehr (1988) discuss how choice probabilities can be biased if consumer heterogeneity in response to promotions is not incorporated into the logit model. They use demographic variables to account for these differences. Unfortunately demographic variables may not be the key explanatory factor describing deal proneness (see Chapter 3). Fader and McAlister (1985) use a different approach to modeling heterogeneity in response to promotions and show better results than a standard logit model. This is discussed later in this chapter.

Logit models can be estimated using either weighted least squares (see Jones and Zufryden, 1980, for a lucid discussion) or maximum likelihood (Guadagni and Little, 1983). The weighted least squares approach is available on SPSS; the maximum likelihood program is available from Ben-Akiva (1973). The weighted least squares approach requires forming groups of observations (consumer choice outcomes) so that all observations within a given group have the same values for the deterministic factors (independent variables). This limits its use to cases where there are relatively few discretely defined independent variables and there are several observations.

Using the Logit Model to Study Promotions. The richness of the choice models is reflected in the types of deterministic factors (X_{ij}'s, see equation 8.17) that are used in logit models. These variables have fallen into five main areas:

1. Brand dummies
2. Promotion occurrences
3. Last purchase on loyalty variables
4. Last purchase on promotion variables
5. Demographic characteristics

Jones and Zufryden (1981) use demographic characteristics and combined versions of loyalty and last purchase on promotion variables. The variables included in the Guadagni and Little model include loyalty, effects of past purchase, promotional effects, price elasticities, brand, and size effects. The basis model was a logit model which computes the probability of buying brand k for a specific consumer at a fixed point in time.

The model used is

$$P_k = \frac{e^{V_k}}{\sum_{j=1}^{J} e^{V_j}} \tag{8.18}$$

where

P_k = the probability of buying brand k

V_k = the utility of brand k

Then,

$$V_k = \sum_{j=1}^{J} \beta_{jk} X(j, k) \tag{8.19}$$

where

$X(1, k)$ = brand-size constant

= 0, not brand size k

= 1, brand size k

$X(2, k)$ = promotion indicator

= 0, not on promotion

= 1, on promotion

$X(3, k)$ = regular price in dollars per ounce

$X(4, k)$ = prior promotional purchase

= 0 if the previous purchase was not brand size k on promotion

= 1 if the previous purchase was brand size k on promotion

$X(5, k)$ = second prior promotional purchase

= 0 if the second previous purchase was not brand size k on promotion

= 1 if the second previous purchase was brand size k on promotion

$X(6, k, t) = \alpha X(6, k, t - 1) + (1 - \alpha)\delta_1(t)$

$\delta_1(t)$ = 0 if brand k was not bought on purchase $t - 1$

= 1 if brand k was bought on purchase $t - 1$

$X(7, k, t) = \gamma X(7, k, t - 1) + (1 - \gamma)\delta_2(t)$

$\delta_2(t)$ = 0 if size k was not bought on purchase $t - 1$

= 1 if size k was bought on purchase $t - 1$

The following is a discussion of the variables used in the model.

Loyalty.   For variable $X(6, k, t)$, Guadagni and Little estimated $\alpha = .875$, meaning that loyalty does not decrease too drastically if a consumer goes one purchase occasion without purchasing brand j. Note the striking correspondence between Guadagni and Little's operationalization of loyalty and the linear learning model: $\delta(t)$ is equivalent to X_t in that model, and $X(6, k, t - 1)$ is equivalent to P_{it}. In this sense, the Guadagni and Little loyalty variable reflects learning or habit formation.

Both Guadagni and Little and Jones and Zufryden capture habit formation. However, in models where consumer innate preference or utility is not explicitly included, the loyalty variables will undoubtedly pick up some of the utility effect. For example, assume Y_{ij} equals consumer i's utility (exclusive of promotion or habit effects) for brand j, measured on a constant sum scale. Since Y_{ij} will be correlated with $X(6, k, t - 1)$, the Guadagni and Little loyalty variable confounds habit formation and preference. Since both the Jones and Zufryden and Guadagni and Little models find very strong "loyalty" effects, this confounding is important to understand. For example, a consumer could be zero order (previous purchases do not affect present ones), yet the logit model could have significant loyalty variables. The potential misspecification is crucial for promotion evaluation, since a promotion can induce purchase and hence change "loyalty" and have a positive long-term effect. In this light, it is not surprising that Guadagni and Little obtain a large α in equation (8.19), implying that one deviant purchase does not change loyalty appreciably. This is what we would expect if the loyalty variable included a large component of innate preference. Further research is needed that combines survey measures of utility (Y_{ij}) with observed purchases for calculating a habit formation measure unconfounded with innate preference. The loyalty variables introduced by Jones and Zufryden and Guadagni and Little offer an important chance to study the long-term effects of promotion. However, one must be careful in interpreting the highly significant results typically found for this variable.

Promotional Variable.   The occurrence of promotion is a logical choice for an independent variable in a promotion model. Guadagni and Little (1983) demonstrate the power of such variables. In models such as theirs, which are estimated across individuals, there is typically one weight used for the promotion variable. However, if brand loyalty is included in the model, the promotion effect will implicitly differ across individuals and across brands. For example, assume we have estimated the following model in a two-brand market:

$$V_{ij} = .5 + .3B_j + 2.5P_j + 1.5L_{ij}$$

where

B_j = brand-specific constant indicator variable, equaling 1 if $j = 1$, 0 if $j = 2$

P_j = 1 if brand j is on promotion and 0 otherwise

L_{ij} = consumer i's loyalty for brand j

i = consumer i

Table 8.4 illustrates the calculation of purchase probabilities for two consumers, assuming that brand 1 and then brand 2 is on promotion. As the table shows, promotional response is greater for brand 2, which is the brand with the lower brand-specific constant. In addition, consumers 1 and 2 differ in their response to promotions. For example, a promotion for brand 1 makes purchase of it a virtual certainty for consumer 1, and makes it a very likely occurrence for

TABLE 8.4 The Effect of Brand Loyalty on Promotional Response

Consumer 1: $L_{11} = .8$, $L_{12} = .2$

Brand	On or Off Promotion		V_{ij}		P_{ij}	Difference On Promotion Versus Off
	Brand 1	Brand 2	Brand 1	Brand 2		
1	0	0	2.0	.8	.7685	
						.2074
1	1	0	4.5	.8	.9759	
2	0	0	2.0	.8	.2315	
						.5543
2	0	1	2.0	3.3	.7858	

Consumer 2: $L_{11} = .5$, $L_{12} = .5$

Brand	On or Off Promotion		V_{ij}		P_{ij}	Difference On Promotion Versus Off
	Brand 1	Brand 2	Brand 1	Brand 2		
1	0	0	1.55	1.25	.5744	
						.3683
1	1	0	4.05	1.25	.9427	
2	0	0	1.55	1.25	.4256	
						.4746
2	0	1	1.55	3.75	.9002	

consumer 2. Consumer 1, however, starts from a fairly high level of purchase probability, so the net effect is not as great. These differences in promotional response, across brands and across consumers, are due to the S-shaped sum-constrained character of the logit model and not to any theory. Ortmeyer et al. (1987) have embedded theory into a logit model to explain why promotional response might differ across individuals. Their model includes interaction terms involving loyalty and promotion.

Last Purchase Variables. The last purchase on promotion variables ostensibly provide a means for testing whether a promotion decreases the probability of a subsequent purchase relative to not buying on promotion. The *association* between promotional purchase and subsequent lower probabilities of purchase was originally noted by Shoemaker and Shoaf (1977), and as expected, both Jones and Zufryden and Guadagni and Little find a significant negative coefficient for the last purchase on promotion and the second to last purchase on promotion variable. To their credit, neither Jones and Zufryden nor Guadagni and Little ascribe causality to their findings. However, the temptation to do so is strong. To illustrate the potential problems in ascribing causality to this well-known result, consider the example depicted in Tables 8.5 and 8.6.

Table 8.5 describes a two-brand market where there are four types of *zero-order* consumers: (1) loyals, who have a high probability of buying brand A when

TABLE 8.5 Example of How A Heterogeneous Mix of Zero-Order Consumers Can Give Rise to Significant Last-Purchase Variables in the Aggregate

Consumer Population

| | Probability of Purchasing Brand A | | |
Group	Off Promotion	On Promotion	% of Population
I. Loyals	.70	.90	20
II. Nonloyals	.10	.60	30
III. Nonloyals: nondeal oriented	.10	.10	30
IV. Loyals: nondeal oriented	.80	.80	20

Resulting Purchase Probabilities

| | | Last Purchase | | |
		Bought Brand A Not on Deal	Bought Brand A on Deal	Bought Other Brand
Current Purchase	Brand A on deal	.8055	.7291	.4100
	Brand A not on deal	.6444	.5000	.1978

TABLE 8.6 A Logit Model Calibrated Using the Data in Table 8.5

Estimated Model

$$P_A = \frac{1}{1 + e^{-V_A}}$$

where	V_A	=	$-1.350 + .9668P_t + .1892L_{t-1} + 1.3652P_{t-1}$
	P_A	=	probability of choosing brand A
0–1	D_t	=	promotion available on current occasion
dummies	L_{t-1}	=	bought brand A last time, not on promotion
FIT	P_{t-1}	=	bought brand A last, on promotion

		Last Purchase					
		Bought brand A not on Deal		Bought brand A on Deal		Bought Other Brand	
		Actual	Predicted	Actual	Predicted	Actual	Predicted
Current Purchase	Brand A on deal	.8055	.8184	.7291	.7269	.4100	.4046
	Brand A not on deal	.6444	.6323	.5000	.5030	.1978	.2054

it is unpromoted and an even higher probability when it is promoted; (2) nonloyals, who have a low probability of buying the brand when it is not promoted and a fairly high probability of buying the brand when it is promoted; (3) nondeal-prone nonloyals who have a low probability of buying brand A whether or not it is promoted; and (4) nondeal-prone loyals, who have a high probability of buying the brand whether or not it is promoted. These groups are modeled after Blattberg and Sen's segmentation study (1976). Note that for all consumers, *the purchase of brand A on one occasion has no effect on purchasing it on the next occasion.*

The bottom of Table 8.5 shows the resultant aggregate purchase probabilities broken down by previous purchase and current promotional activity for brand A. For example, among consumers who bought brand A on promotion (on "deal") on their last purchase occasion, 50.0 percent of them would buy brand A at the current occasion if it were not on promotion. This is compared to a 64.4 percent purchase probability among those who purchased brand A last time but not on deal. If we interpret the results causally, we would infer that promotional purchase causes lower subsequent probabilities. However, we know this is not true, because the purchase probabilities arose from the zero-order world depicted in the top of Table 8.5.

What is happening is that a promotion selects a different mix of loyals versus nonloyals as purchasers, and hence subsequent purchase probabilities differ. In particular, a promotion skews the mix of purchasers more toward nonloyals. As a result, the probability of deal purchasers purchasing at the next occasion is lower than for nondeal purchasers. Table 8.6 shows the results of estimating a logit model on the data in Table 8.5, using the Jones and Zufryden approach. In particular, let

$$P_t = \begin{cases} 1 \text{ if brand A on promotion} \\ 0 \text{ otherwise} \end{cases}$$

$$L_{t-1} = \begin{cases} 1 \text{ if brand A bought last time, not on promotion} \\ 0 \text{ otherwise} \end{cases}$$

$$P_{t-1} = \begin{cases} 1 \text{ if brand A bought last time, on promotion} \\ 0 \text{ otherwise} \end{cases}$$

$$P_A = \text{probability of buying brand A at the current purchase occasion}$$

The model is

$$P_A = \frac{1}{1 + e^{-V_A}}$$

where

$$V_A = \beta_0 + \beta_1 P_t + \beta_2 L_{t-1} + \beta_3 P_{t-1}$$

From Table 8.5, we expect $\beta_1 > \beta_0$ and $\beta_2 > \beta_3 > 0$. The last inequality reflects the fact that purchasing the brand last time makes it more likely to purchase again, compared to if the brand were not purchased last time, but purchasing it on deal last time indicates not as high probability of repurchase compared to if it were purchased not on deal. Table 8.6 shows that this hypothesis is confirmed. The result mirrors Jones and Zufryden's. Guadagni and Little (1983) use a more sophisticated definition of variables, but their results are similar (Guadagni and Little, 1983, pp. 222–223).

The example shown in Table 8.6 depicts a type of aggregation-selection bias. (See Chapter 5 and Neslin and Shoemaker 1989, for a full elaboration of these results.) If the results are interpreted associatively, there is no problem. However, if causality is inferred, one runs the risk of this bias. The bias could be influencing the results of not only Jones and Zufryden and Guadagni and Little, but also of Shoemaker and Shoaf (1977) as well as Dodson et al. (1978). The issue is a critical one: Do promotions influence subsequent purchase probabilities? The issue has been a central theme for linear learning models, the bargain value model, and now logit models. (See also Chapters 2 and 5.) The methodological discussion here suggests that the issue may not yet be resolved. The answer could potentially lie in individual-level models, but this is an area for future research.

The foregoing discussion has demonstrated the rich insight that is generated by logit choice models. The Jones and Zufryden and Guadagni and Little papers have given impetus to a fertile research paradigm. The central issues discussed here—the construct validity of loyalty variables and the proper interpretation of last purchase on promotion variables—have not yet been resolved. However, current research has addressed other issues. These include formulation of price promotion variables based on price perception consumer theories (Winer, 1986), effect of promotion frequency on promotion response, and effect of noninde-pendence of error terms across purchase occasions.

Competitive Effects in the Logit Model

One of the key issues in promotional modeling is the incorporation of competitive effects. The logit model, as we stated earlier, does it indirectly through the use of proportional draw. Thus, when a promotion for brand *i* is run, sales for all other brands decline proportionally to their market share. This was shown earlier. Does this assumption make sense?

Suppose that the logit model is applied to the margarine category. There are two forms, stick and tub, and within each form there are five brands. The issue becomes: Do the brand types all compete with the same "intensity"? Should a promotion on Land 'O Lakes stick margarine affect Parkay tub margarine the same as Parkay stick margarine? The answer is likely to be no. Yet, stick and tub margarine do compete.

The answer to this problem may be the use of nested logit models introduced by McFadden (1981). Allenby (1988) uses this idea to develop a model of com-petition which can include different promotional responses within a submarket.

The idea underlying the nested logit model is that if an item in another submarket promotes, it affects all items in the other submarket less than items in the same submarket. Therefore, the assumption of proportional draw can be modified using a nested logit model.

Because nested logit models are complex, the reader is referred to McFadden (1978, 1981), Allenby (1988), or Maddala (1983) for further discussion of this model.

Markov Models

One of the earliest applications incorporating marketing mix variables into choice models was Telser (1963). He used least squares to incorporate marketing mix variables into Markov transition matrices. Specifically, he made the transition probabilities a function of advertising and promotion. Unfortunately, the models used aggregate-level data, not individual-level data, to estimate the parameters.

Zufryden (1986) proposed a method to incorporate marketing mix variables into the transition matrix of a Markov matrix. His procedure is similar to a logit model except that the probabilities to be fitted come from a Markov transition matrix rather than a multinominal distribution. This poses issues of logical con-sistency but has a distinct advantage: carry-over effects are directly modeled using the transition probabilities. To date, no one has applied Zufryden's methods for the analysis of promotions, but it offers a procedure to analyze carry-over effects using a stochastic model which has order higher than zero. (This addresses the problem discussed earlier about carry-over effects.)

Fader and McAlister's Noncompensatory Model

While choice models evaluating promotions have become a very active area of present research, and in fact this paradigm is not nearly exhausted, it is worthwhile reviewing a recent model due to Fader and McAlister (1989). The model is of interest in light of the progression we have charted from linear learning models through logit models. It is estimated at the individual level and is zero order in that prior purchases do not affect future purchases. It is also based on the assumption of a noncompensatory decision scheme, whereby with certain probability, γ, a consumer may restrict choice to only the brands on promotion. Because of these characteristics, the Fader and McAlister choice restriction model is an innovative departure from previous choice models used to analyze promotions. In particular, let

$$R(i, j, t) = \gamma_i \delta(i, t) \frac{V(i, j)\, P(j, t)}{\sum_k V(i, k)\, P(i, k, t)} + [1 - \gamma_i \delta(i, t)] \frac{V(i, j)}{\sum V(i, k)} \qquad \textbf{(8.20)}$$

where

$$\gamma_i = \text{promotional responsiveness of the } i\text{th consumer}$$

$$P(j, t) = \begin{cases} 0 \text{ when no promotion is run in period } t \text{ for the } j\text{th brand} \\ 1 \text{ when a promotion is run in period } t \text{ for the } j\text{th brand} \end{cases}$$

$$V(i, j) = \text{the utility for the } i\text{th consumer for the } j\text{th brand}$$

$$R(i, j, t) = \text{the probability of buying brand } j \text{ by the } i\text{th consumer at time } t$$

$$\delta(i, t) = \begin{cases} 0 \text{ if no acceptable brand is promoted for the} \\ \quad i\text{th consumer at time } t \\ 1 \text{ if an acceptable brand is promoted for the} \\ \quad i\text{th consumer at time } t \end{cases}$$

Fader and McAlister's model assumes that if no acceptable brands are on promotion, the consumer just considers the ratio of brand j's utility to all other brands' utilities. In this case, $\delta = 0$, so that the $1 - \gamma\delta$ term becomes 1. Then,

$$R(i, j, t) = \frac{V(i, j)}{\sum_k V(i, j)} \qquad \textbf{(8.21)}$$

which is simply a standard logit formulation. However, if acceptable brands are on promotion ($\delta = 1$), the consumer concentrates *only* on those brands with probability γ (the first term in equation 8.20) or considers all brands with probability $1 - \gamma$ (the second term in equation 8.20). The net probability of purchasing a particular brand is the weighted sum of the two terms in equation (8.20) (the weights being γ and $1 - \gamma$).

Fader and McAlister estimate their model for individual consumers and find that the median γ is .691, indicating high promotion sensitivity. They then compare their model to a compensatory model with the same number of parameters, also estimated at the individual level, and find that these two models fit the data and predict choice equally well.

There are some significant questions concerning the choice restriction model. First, it is not clear why a given consumer would sometimes restrict choice to only promoted brands and other times ignore all promotions, especially irrespective of the consumer's utilities for the brands involved. Second, the functional form of the model is essentially compensatory. A low-utility brand will have a higher probability of being purchased if it is on promotion. The parameter γ might simply be measuring the compensatory value of promotion and not the probability of restricting choice.

The Fader-McAlister model is still an interesting and innovative approach to modeling the effects of promotions. Perhaps their result of broadest significance is that both individual models they tested outperformed an aggregate (across consumers) logit model in hold-out data predictive ability, and both individual models assumed no postpurchase effects of promotion. In light of our review of other choice models applied to promotion, this is a very significant finding.

A final note of interest is the similarity between the γ coefficient and Lilien's C coefficient in this modified linear learning model. C measured the degree to which a consumer relied on price versus brand preference to make a choice. In Lilien's model, however, preference changed over time according to a linear learning process.

PURCHASE INCIDENCE MODELS

A promotion affects *when* the consumer purchases as well as *which* brand. Brand choice models focus on which brand whereas purchase incidence models focus on when. Purchase incidence models determine the probability of a given household purchasing a brand in a fixed period of time and therefore these models can be used as baseline models to evaluate promotions. Later in this section models that incorporate marketing mix variables into the purchase timing models will be discussed.

Poisson Purchase Incidence Model

Most marketing models of purchase incidence assume that the purchase probability follows a Poisson process. A Poisson process has a similar underlying assumption as the Bernoulli process; purchase behavior is independent over time. This assumption will be discussed later in this section.

The Poisson purchase incidence model can be derived from the following assumptions:

1. The decision to purchase in a time interval, Δt, is independent of when the last purchase is made.
2. During a short interval, Δt, the consumer either buys 0 or 1 unit.
3. The purchase rate, λ, is constant over time and across consumers.

Using these assumptions, the Poisson distribution gives the number of purchases, N, to be made in a fixed time period t (e.g., a week). The distribution is

$$Pr(\tilde{N} = i \mid \lambda, t) = \frac{(\lambda t)^i e^{-\lambda t}}{i!} \qquad i = 0, 1, \ldots \tag{8.22}$$

where λ is the purchase rate (e.g., once per month), t is the time interval, and i is the number of purchases ranging from 0 to infinity.

To see how this distribution can be used for promotional research, suppose all consumers have the same λ. Then, one could compute the probability of a household buying and multiply it by the total number of consumers who purchased. This is $[1 - Pr(\tilde{N} = 0 \mid \lambda, t = 1)] \cdot k$, where t and λ are expressed in weeks and k is the number of consumers in the market. If the actual number of consumers purchasing is significantly higher during the promotion, this increase is attributed to the promotion.

As an example suppose $\lambda = .25$ which means the average consumer buys once every four weeks and $t = 1$ which is a week. Then, $Pr(\tilde{N} = 0 \mid \lambda = .25, t = 1) = e^{-\lambda t} = e^{-.25} = .78$. $1 - .78 = .22$ or 22 percent of the households buy in a week. If there are 1,000 households ($k = 1,000$), then 220 would normally purchase in a week. Suppose a promotion is run and 400 customers purchase. In that case $400 - 220 = 180$ purchases were attributable to the promotion.

As was the case with brand choice models, consumers may not all have the same expected interval between purchases, λ. Therefore, it is necessary to allow λ to vary across the population. The commonly made assumption is that λ follows a gamma distribution whose shape is given in Figure 8.3. If λ follows a gamma distribution, then the number of consumers purchasing in a fixed time period follows a negative binomial distribution (NBD) (Ehrenberg, 1972). This distribution is

$$Pr(\tilde{N} = i \mid \alpha, \beta, t) = \left(\frac{\Gamma(\alpha + i)}{\Gamma(\alpha)\Gamma(i + 1)} \right) \left(\frac{t}{\beta + t} \right)^i \left(\frac{\beta}{\beta + t} \right)^\alpha \qquad i = 0, 1, \ldots$$

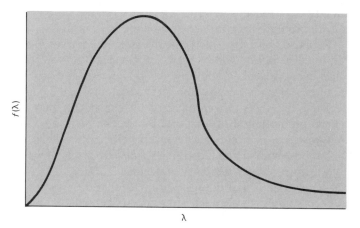

FIGURE 8.3 Gamma Distribution

The mean of the gamma distribution is $\alpha t/\beta$, which is $E(\tilde{\lambda})$. The mean of the NBD is $(\alpha/\beta)t$, where t is the interval being analyzed (e.g., one week). This is the same as the mean of the Poisson distribution except that instead of λ, the $E(\tilde{\lambda})$ is used. However, the variance of the NBD is larger than the Poisson distribution. The NBD can then be used to predict the baseline number of customers in the same way the Poisson distribution was used.

The Poisson and NBD models have several restrictive assumptions that are important to recognize:

1. Independence over time. The time of the last purchase does not affect the current purchase.
2. Stationarity. Constant purchase rate (λ).

Independence over time conceptually makes little sense if the interval (t) is short relative to λt. If a consumer buys last week and his or her average purchase rate is monthly, the probability of buying next period is significantly lower than if the consumer has not purchased in the last week. To solve this problem several authors have studied more complex distributions which allow the time between purchases to be a function of the time of the last purchase. An example of this type of distribution is the Erlang distribution (see Jeuland et al., 1976).

The other key assumption, stationarity, implies that promotions do not affect purchase timing. As was discussed in Chapter 5 and elsewhere in this book, this assumption is clearly violated. A model is required that incorporates marketing mix variables into the timing process. Thus, λ needs to become a function of marketing mix variables. By modeling λ or $E(\lambda)$ as a function of marketing mix variables, one can directly determine how promotions affect purchase timing. This is clearly an important direction for future research.

To make the preceding discussion more concrete, we shall show how promotional variables can affect the number of customers buying per period. Suppose $\lambda = \alpha(\beta^D)$, where $D = 0$ if no promotion occurs and 1 if a promotion occurs. λ is assumed the same for all consumers, α is the normal purchase rate, and β^D is the adjustment for a promotion. In weeks 1 and 2 no promotions are run, but in week 3 a promotion is run. Then, how do the purchase counts vary?

Suppose there are 1,000 customers in the market. To make matters simple a Poisson distribution will be used. t is in weeks, $\alpha = .25$ (normal purchase cycle of once every 4 weeks), and $\beta = 1.5$, which means that λ is increased (purchase rate increases) when a promotion is offered implying the purchase cycle is shorter.

Table 8.7 shows the probability of consumers shopping during the weeks when no promotion is offered and the week when the promotion is offered. It shows how customer counts increase significantly.

Suppose another parameter is added to the model of λ that indicates the purchase rate should decrease immediately after a deal. Let $\lambda(t) = \alpha(\beta^{D(t)})(\gamma^{D(t-1)})$, setting α and β to the prior level and $\gamma = .7$; λ will decrease after a deal occurs implying a trough after a deal. Table 8.8 shows the resulting weekly sales for weeks 1, . . . , 4. Customer counts show a trough. The Poisson/NBD

TABLE 8.7 Consumer Shopping Probabilities

	No Deal	Deal
Probability of shopping	.22	.33
Number shopping	220	310
Number of additional customers due to promotion	90	

α = .25; β = 1.5; 1,000 consumers; t = 1 week.

models can capture key promotional effects by making λ a function of promotional variables. Clearly, further research using panel data is required to study the best models to use to incorporate marketing mix variables into promotional models.

Quantity Decision

In making a purchase decision, a key decision is the quantity to purchase. Most of the modeling has focused on brand choice or purchase incidence, not quantity purchased. The assumption is the consumer will buy his or her average quantity when a promotion is run. However, in Chapter 5 stockpiling was discussed. There is ample evidence that consumers buy increased quantities when a promotion is run. Therefore, it is necessary to model not only the choice and timing decision, but also the quantity decision.

The modeling of quantity may require a more sophisticated approach than regression analysis. The reason is that the observations are truncated. For certain levels of the independent variables, only zero is observed. This limits the amount of information being offered. If one omits the zeros and models only purchase quantities not equal to zero, then the fact that no purchase was made when the independent variables had specific values is lost. If one includes the zeros, the regression line is biased because negative values or small positive values only appear as zero. Figure 8.4 shows an example of expenditure data for a hypothetical consumer versus prices for a given brand. Clearly, a high percentage of the points will be at zero. Because of the concentration of points at zero, the linearity assumption of least squares is violated (see Amemiya, 1985, p. 362). Therefore, an alternative procedure (tobit models) needs to be considered. This is discussed next.

TABLE 8.8 Consumer Timing Model

Week	1	2	3	4
Promotion	No	No	Yes	No
Number shopping	220	220	310	160
Difference from nonpromotional week	0	0	90	−60

α = .25; β = 1.5; γ = .7; 1,000 consumers.

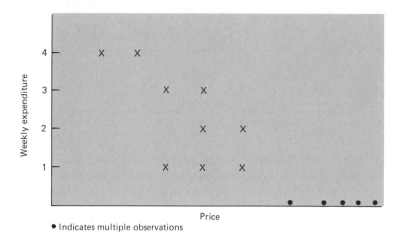

• Indicates multiple observations

FIGURE 8.4 Price Versus Weekly Expenditure

Tobit Model. Tobit models are part of a general class of models which analyze truncated data. In other words, one observes a zero if the quantity decision is equal to zero and Y_t if the quantity decision is greater than or equal to 0.

Mathematically,

$$y_t = \beta_0 + X_t\beta + u \quad t = 1, \ldots T \tag{8.23a}$$

$$y_t = y_t \quad \text{if } y_t \geq 1 \tag{8.23b}$$

$$ = 0 \quad \text{if } y_t < 1$$

X_t is the independent variable, y_t is the quantity purchased, and T is the time period ($y_t < 1$ means the consumer does not buy). To fit it into a standard tobit model, y_t is assumed continuous so one can use expenditure rather than quantity.

To understand why a tobit model is needed, it is useful to study the bias in a standard regression model when least squares estimation is used. Suppose that

$$y_t = \beta_0 + \tilde{X}_t\beta_1 + u_t$$

where $\tilde{X}_t$ is distributed normally with mean 0 and variance-covariance matrix Σ. u is also normally distributed and independent of $\tilde{X}_t$. Amemiya (1985) shows that plim $\tilde{\beta}_1 = F(\beta_0/\sigma_y)\beta_1$, where $\tilde{\beta}_1$ is the least squares estimate and plim is the probability limit. Since the mean of X_t is zero, the size of β_0 determines the likelihood of observing observations less than 0. As $\beta_0 \to \infty$ then $F(\beta_0/\sigma_y) \to 1$. As $\beta_0 \to -\infty$, $F(\beta_0/\beta\sigma_y) \to 0$. In other words, the frequency of observations at 0 is a critical determinant of the bias. In diary panel data, most observations are zero, indicating the bias is likely to be larger, hence the need to use a tobit model.

There are several alternative estimates of the tobit model. For example, Heckman has a two-step estimator. The tobit model can be rewritten as

$$y_i = X_t\beta + \sigma\lambda(X_t\alpha) + \epsilon_i \quad \text{for } i \text{ such that } y_i > 0 \tag{8.24}$$

where $\lambda(X_t\alpha) = f(X_t\alpha)/F(X_t\alpha)$ and $\alpha = \beta/\sigma$.

Heckman (1976) proposed the following estimator:

Step 1:   Estimate α by a probit MLE (maximum likelihood estimator) given in Amemiya (1985).

Step 2:   Regress y_i or X_i and $\lambda(X_t\alpha)$ by least squares using only positive observations of y_i.

$\lambda(X_t\alpha)$ is related to the probability of negative observations, $F(X_t\alpha)$, and the importance of the point $f(X_t\alpha)$.

In summary, tobit models can be used to estimate expenditures for promoted and nonpromoted variables. Then, it becomes possible to determine how the consumer stockpiles.

Application of the Tobit Model.   Pedrick (1987) gives an application of the tobit model for estimating quantity. The variables used in his model are

Q_{it}^k = quantity purchased by household k of brand i at purchase occasion t

DEAL_{it} = percent deal discount for ith brand at time t

$\text{SFAM}_{it}^k = \begin{cases} 1 \text{ if } k\text{th household owns own home} \\ 0 \text{ otherwise} \end{cases}$

$\text{FEMP}_{it}^k = \begin{cases} 1 \text{ if female head of } k\text{th household is employed} \\ 0 \text{ otherwise} \end{cases}$

VOLAVG^k = household k's average purchase quantity in preperiod

$\text{VOLAG}_t^k = Q_{it-1}^k - \text{VOLAVG}^k$

IPT_t^k = number of days since the last purchase in the category.

Pedrick included time since last purchase and VOLAG to attempt to see whether the household was buying above-average quantity on last purchase (VOLAG) or had longer than average time since last purchase (IPT). His results are given in Table 8.9.

The results show that households differ on volume used (VOLAVG). Deal has a larger effect on quantity purchased as evidenced by the size of the coefficient relative to its standard error. VOLAG is also highly significant indicating stockpiling is an important explanatory variable. Interpurchase time is less important in this category.

The conclusion is that tobit models fit the quantity data reasonably well. This type of research is important because stockpiling and changing interpurchase times have the same implications for purchase incidence models as carry-over effects do for brand choice models.

Brand Choice and Tobit Models.   There have been two recent applications of tobit models in combination with brand choice, Kristnamurthi and Raj (1988) and Pedrick (1987). In both models, it is assumed that brand choice and purchase quantity are correlated. This assumption is used in their choice of statistical techniques. Unfortunatey, this is an extremely difficult assumption to test, and neither paper studies the validity of this assumption. If brand choice and quantity decisions are independent, then a standard tobit model can be used.

TABLE 8.9   Estimates for Tobit Models

| Parameter | Brand | | | |
	Imperial	House	Blue Bonnet	Parkay
Intercept	−0.005	−0.029	0.011	−0.019
	(0.009) [a]	(0.035)	(0.031)	(0.029)
VOLAG	0.973	0.930	1.013	0.642
	(0.037)	(0.033)	(0.041)	(0.043)
DEAL	1.323	2.769	1.876	3.000
	(0.347)	(0.652)	(0.365)	(0.414)
IPT	0.001	0.002	0.002	0.001
	(0.001)	(0.001)	(0.001)	(0.001)
VOLAG	−0.210	−0.214	−0.155	−0.052
	(0.046)	(0.036)	(0.041)	(0.043)
	0.157	0.379	0.441	0.386
	(0.100)	(0.147)	(0.138)	(0.133)
SFAM	1.203	2.387	0.570	0.647
	(0.885)	(2.469)	(0.696)	(0.650)
FEMP	−0.539	−1.434	−0.689	−0.395
	(0.418)	(0.857)	(0.374)	(0.408)
R^2	0.458	0.362	0.398	0.326
RMSE	0.358	0.840	0.725	0.710

[a] Numbers in parentheses are standard errors.

Source: James H. Pedrick, "Modeling Deal Effects Using Scanner Pannel Data," Working paper, Graduate School of Business, University of Chicago (January 1987).

SUMMARY

We have traced the evolution of choice models used to analyze promotions. We have noted a distinct similarity between the more recent models and the earlier ones. For example, the loyalty variable of Guadagni and Little corresponds to the linear learning model, and Fader and McAlister's γ corresponds to Lilien's C. However, there is a clear progression of sophistication and insight that undoubtedly has not yet plateaued.

The most controversial difference among the models involves their assessment of the long-term, or at least post–immediate purchase occasion, effect of promotions. The linear learning model is associated with a positive effect, the bargain value is associated with a negative effect, the logit models are associated with a negative effect that may net out to be positive when compared to the buildup in habit, and the choice restriction model is associated with no effect! Given the tantamount importance of this issue, there is clearly more research to be done.

Recently, more attention has been placed on combining purchase incidence, quantity, and brand choice models. It is necessary to estimate not only brand choice effects but also purchase timing changes and stockpiling. This research direction is important if these models are going to be applied in real applications.

9

Time Series Analysis Applied to Sales Promotion

OVERVIEW

Time series analysis consists of a wide range of techniques designed to examine data that evolve over time. We will consider a logical progression of three time series techniques: univariate time series analysis, transfer function analysis, and intervention analysis. Univariate time series analysis attempts to predict the value of a dependent variable, in our case sales, as a function of previous sales and random "error" terms. The key difference between univariate time series analysis and multivariate regression as discussed in Chapter 7 is that the former technique does not include independent variables such as the level of sales promotion.

Transfer function analysis starts with a univariate time series analysis model and then adds independent variables such as promotion. The interesting philosophical difference between transfer function analysis and regression stems from the fact that transfer function analysis allows promotion to explain only that part of variation in sales that is not correlated with the systematic, periodic variation in promotion. The reasoning behind this is if sales and promotion share the same systematic, periodic fluctuation, it could be due to a third causal factor. The philosophy behind regression is to include as many theoretically sound variables in the model as possible, and let them compete as potential explainers of sales. If the regression cannot choose among the competing explanations, this will show up as high multicollinearity.

Intervention analysis is similar to transfer function analysis but is particularly suited to the analysis of promotions. This is because intervention analysis is especially useful for analyzing the effects of short-term pulses on the dependent variable sales. Many sales promotions, including special sales, displays, feature advertising, and special events, can be viewed as short-term pulses "intervening" with the normal progression of the sales time series.

Having pointed out the distinction among univariate time series, transfer function, and intervention analysis, it is important to note their close relationship. Both transfer function and intervention analysis use Box-Jenkins ARIMA (autoregressive integrated moving average) univariate time series analysis as the underlying model to which they add independent variables. Transfer function analysis is appropriate for continuous independent variables such as advertising, while intervention analysis is appropriate for the standard one- or two-week promotions. However, we may want to include advertising and promotion effects in the same model, and therefore it is possible to use a combination of transfer function and intervention analysis.

Because univariate time series analysis does not explicitly consider any independent variables such as promotion, one might wonder how it could possibly be of use in analyzing promotions. The answer is that univariate time series analysis can be used to extrapolate into the promotion period the "baseline" level of sales that would have occurred had there not been a promotion. The effect of the promotion is then "read off" as the difference between actual sales in the promotion period and the time series analysis forecast of baseline sales. This use is illustrated in Figure 9.1. Techniques that involve measuring the deviation of actual sales from a forecasted baseline are generally called "bump analyses" (Kuehn and Rohloff, 1967, pp. 86–91; Appelbaum, 1985).

Managerially, univariate time series analysis is oriented toward helping the manager to evaluate previous promotions and therefore learn what to anticipate for future promotions. Transfer function and intervention analysis can be used to evaluate previous promotions but also provide an explicit prediction of future sales in various promotion environments. These techniques thus would appear to be most useful. However, they are much more difficult to apply than univariate

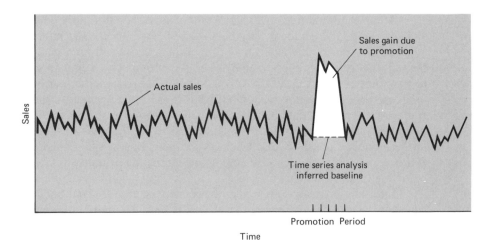

FIGURE 9.1 Univariate Time Series Analysis Used to Perform a "Bump Analysis" Evaluation of a Promotion

time series analysis. They require more data, more sophisticated computer software, and more conceptual thought. The problem with univariate time series analysis is that, under certain circumstances, it can give simply derived but incorrect estimates of the effects of sales promotions. We will discuss these circumstances in the section on "Cautions."

UNIVARIATE TIME SERIES ANALYSIS

Univariate time series analysis is actually a collection of statistical techniques, all with the common orientation of analyzing the current values of a time series such as sales in terms of previous sales and error terms. We will not attempt to describe in detail all these methods here. The reader is referred to several excellent books on time series analysis, including Makridakis et al. (1983), Makridakis and Wheelwright (1982), Nelson (1973), and Brown (1963). Introductory business statistics texts such as Lapin (1987), Wonnacott and Wonnacott (1984), Iman and Conover (1983), and Hanke and Reitsch (1989) also include good discussions of basic time series analysis techniques.

In the next section, we introduce the basic time series decomposition model. Following that, we discuss ARIMA models, which build upon the basic decomposition model. Then we discuss the circumstances under which these models are appropriate. Finally, we close with an analysis of real data utilizing the ARIMA method and techniques for estimating the basic time series decomposition model.

The Basic Time Series Decomposition Model

The basic time series decomposition model provides a framework that is embedded in all time series analysis techniques. In this section, we present the model and describe two methods for estimating it.

The Model.   The basic time series decomposition model posits that the time series progression of the dependent variable sales can be explained by trend (T), seasonality (S), cycle (C), and irregularity (I). That is,

$$\text{SALES} = f(T, S, C, I) \tag{9.1}$$

Trend represents the long-term systematic change in sales. For example, sales might be increasing steadily at a rate of 2,000 units per month. Seasonality is systematic, periodic variation in sales within a given year. For example, December may consistently be a high sales month, and the summer months may characteristically have low sales. Cycle is essentially a long-term seasonality. It occurs over several years rather than within each year. Cycle is often related explicitly to the state of the economy and is especially relevant to the sales of durable goods. The irregular component of the time series is assumed to be random noise unrelated to trend, seasonality, or cycle.

Equation (9.1) can be operationalized in several ways. There are multiplicative models, additive models, and mixed models (see Makridakis et al., 1983, Ch. 3). A multiplicative model would be

$$\text{SALES} = T \times S \times C \times I \tag{9.2}$$

The trend component would be scaled in terms of sales units. The seasonality and cycle components would be scaled as indices that indicate how sales deviate from the long-term trend in the data. Various estimation techniques (we will describe the ratio–to–moving average and regression methods shortly) are used to estimate the trend, seasonality, and cycle components so that they can be used to forecast future sales or project a sales baseline from which the effects of a promotion can be assessed. The irregularity component would also be scaled as an index, indicating how the data depart from the trend, seasonality, and cyclic components present at a particular point in time. However, the irregularity indices would only be estimated for currently existing data. Irregularities cannot be predicted for future periods.

Ratio–to–Moving Average Method. The ratio–to–moving average method uses "moving averages" of the data to decompose the data into its trend, seasonality, and cyclic components. Once these components are isolated, the trend level, along with seasonal and cyclic indices, can be estimated using curve fitting techniques such as regression or simple averages of the data. We will demonstrate the method with an example later in this chapter, and the reader is referred to Makridakis et al. (1983, Ch. 4), for complete details. At this time, we illustrate the basic principle of the ratio–to–moving average method, which is based on taking judicious moving averages of the data. For example, assume we have the following sales time series on a quarterly basis:

Quarter	1	2	3	4	1	2	3	4	1	2	3	4
Sales	100	120	230	150	170	190	320	225	260	300	450	375

We can clearly see the trend and seasonal components to these data—the trend is upward, and the third quarter of every year is noticeably strong. If we take four-quarter moving averages of these data, the results are as follows:

Quarter	1	2	3	4	1	2	3	4	1	2	3	4
Avg. Sales			150	168	185	208	226	249	276	309	346	

These numbers were calculated by averaging the first four original sales numbers, then averaging the next four, and so on. For example, $150 = (100 + 120 + 230 + 150)/4$, $168 = (120 + 230 + 150 + 170)/4$, and so on. The first important observation concerning the averaged data is that they reflect trend but do not include seasonality. By having all four seasons present in each average, the new numbers differ because of the long-term trend in the data, but not because of seasonality. Another important property of the moving average data is that a good deal of the irregularity present in the original data will be averaged or "smoothed" out. For example, since we assume that irregularities are random noise, the first quarter might contain an abnormally large irregularity, the second might contain a small irregularity, and so on, so taking moving averages allows the irregularities to balance out. The foregoing calculation therefore illustrates how judicious calculation of moving averages can smooth out periodic seasonalities and random irregularities from the data. As will be illustrated later, the ratio–to–moving average method utilizes this principle to help isolate components of a time series and then estimate trend level as well as seasonal and cyclic indices.[1]

Regression Method. Another method for estimating the basic decomposition model is to formulate the model in terms of a regression equation. This is often done by using a time index and seasonal dummy variables as independent variables to capture trend and seasonality. For example, assume we have quarterly sales data. Let

$$\text{Sales}_t = \text{sales in quarter } t$$

$$\text{First}_t = \begin{cases} 1 \text{ if quarter } t \text{ is the first quarter of the year;} \\ 0 \text{ otherwise} \end{cases}$$

$$\text{Second}_t = \begin{cases} 1 \text{ if quarter } t \text{ is the second quarter of the year;} \\ 0 \text{ otherwise} \end{cases}$$

$$\text{Third}_t = \begin{cases} 1 \text{ if quarter } t \text{ is the third quarter of the year;} \\ 0 \text{ otherwise} \end{cases}$$

$$t = \text{time index, going from 1 to } T \text{ (the number of time periods)}$$

We could estimate the following regression model:

$$\text{Sales}_t = \beta_0 + \beta_1 t + \beta_2 \text{First}_t + \beta_3 \text{Second}_t + \beta_4 \text{Third}_t \tag{9.3}$$

The term β_1 captures linear trend. (Other forms of trend can be modeled as well by appropriate quantification of the time index. For example, quadratic trend could be modeled by adding a t^2 term to equation 9.3.) The β_2, β_3, and β_4 terms measure seasonality. Note that we do not need a separate variable for the fourth quarter—the seasonalities for the first, second, and third quarters are estimated relative to the fourth quarter. Equation (9.3) is an additive model. Multiplicative models such as (9.2) can be estimated by appropriate use of logarithms. For example, we could formulate the multiplicative model

$$\text{Sales}_t = \beta_0 t^{\beta_1} e^{\beta_2 \text{First}_t} e^{\beta_3 \text{Second}_t} e^{\beta_4 \text{Third}_t} \tag{9.4}$$

Taking logs of both sides of equation (9.4), we obtain

$$\ln(\text{Sales}_t) = \beta_0 + \beta_1 \ln(t) + \beta_2 \text{First}_t + \beta_3 \text{Second}_t + \beta_4 \text{Third}_t \tag{9.5}$$

---

[1] The reader will also notice that each moving average has been "centered" between the middle two quarters making up that average. This is because the sales rate represented by that average corresponds to the middle of the data making up that average. The ratio–to–moving average method sometimes takes moving averages of moving averages to re-center the results directly at particular time periods (see Makridakis et al., 1983, Ch. 4).

Equation (9.5) can be estimated using a commonly available linear regression computer package.

Once equation (9.3) or (9.5) is estimated, we can use it to project a baseline sales forecast into a promotion period. The incremental sales generated by the promotion can then be estimated by subtracting baseline sales from actual sales during the promotion period. We will illustrate this in the "Example" section.

Comparing the regression method for estimating the basic time series decomposition model to the ratio–to–moving average method, the former has the advantage of a well-developing statistical theory. This can be used to test hypotheses concerning trend or seasonality and to form confidence intervals for forecasts. One problem, however, is that by using dummy variables to handle seasonality, we can quickly use up degrees of freedom for estimation. For example, if our data were monthly, we would use 11 monthly dummies to capture the monthly seasonalities. If we only had two years of data, the resulting seasonality estimates would most likely be unstable, that is, have large standard errors. One way around this problem is to use a more parsimonious representation of seasonality. This can be done using sine and cosine variables, and this is the goal of Fourier analysis (see Makridakis et al., 1983, Appendix 8-B). Fourier analysis can also be used to model cycle.

The ratio–to–moving average method does not circumvent the problem of too many parameters to estimate with too few data points. It has the same number of parameters to estimate as does the regression model and the same data with which to work. In this respect, the regression model may be preferred, because it has a well-developed statistical theory to measure the stability of its estimated parameters. The regression method is also more flexible, since unimportant seasonality parameters can be pruned from the model, and sophisticated methods such as Fourier analysis can add even more flexibility.

In conclusion, we generally recommend the regression method for estimating the time series decomposition model. The ratio–to–moving average method, however, does have its adherents. For example, it forms the basis for the Census II forecasting package used by the U.S. government to predict economic variables (see Makridakis et al., 1983, Ch. 4). Its use of moving averages also forms the conceptual basis for the PROMOTER method, which we review in "The PRO-MOTER Methodology" section. Finally, there is no systematic research that has compared regression to the ratio–to–moving average method in terms of the quality of projected sales baselines to evaluate promotions.

ARIMA Models

Autoregressive integrated moving average (ARIMA) modeling is a very general univariate time series analysis technique. It is capable of uncovering complex seasonality, cyclic, and lag structures that may be present in the data. To the extent that these complexities are important in explaining variation in sales over time, ARIMA potentially can produce more accurate forecasts, and hence a more accurate baseline projection on which to evaluate a promotion. In addition, ARIMA modeling is fundamental to transfer function and intervention analysis. We therefore briefly describe and illustrate use of the procedure here. For a detailed discussion, the reader is referred to the Box-Jenkins description (Box and Jenkins, 1976) and to the excellent discussions in Makridakis and Wheelwright (1982, pp. 129–152) and Makridakis et al. (1983, Ch. 9).

The basic components of an ARIMA model are the autoregressive (AR) and moving average (MA) parts. The autoregressive component shows how current values of the dependent variable (sales) can be predicted from previous values, while the moving average component shows how current values of the dependent variable can be predicted from previous irregularities or "error" terms. If the original data exhibit trend, it is necessary to use differences between successive values rather than their absolute values, since ARIMA assumes the mean of the data is constant over time. For example, assume the following sales data:

$$10 \quad 22 \quad 28 \quad 40 \quad 52 \quad 60 \quad 71 \quad 80 \quad 89 \quad 100$$

These data obviously exhibit positive trend. By taking successive differences, we eliminate the trend, obtaining

$$12 \quad 6 \quad 12 \quad 12 \quad 8 \quad 11 \quad 9 \quad 9 \quad 11$$

where $12 = 22 - 10$, $6 = 28 - 22$, and so on. Note that if we are given the differenced data and the first-undifferenced sales figure, we can derive the rest of the original sales data by adding successive differences. For example, $10 + 12 = 22$, $22 + 6 = 28$, $28 + 12 = 40$, and so on. We are summing, or "integrating," the difference data to obtain the original data—hence the "I" for "integrated" in the name ARIMA.

Notationally, it is common to use the backward shift operator "B" in describing ARIMA models. This operator is defined as follows:

$$BS_t = S_{t-1}$$
$$B^2 S_t = S_{t-2}, \text{ and so on} \tag{9.6}$$

so that $(1 - B)S_t = S_t - BS_t = S_t - S_{t-1}$ is the first difference between successive sales values. A second difference, $(S_t - S_{t-1}) - (S_{t-1} - S_{t-2})$, can be written as $(1 - B)S_t - (1 - B)S_{t-1} = (1 - B)(S_t - S_{t-1}) = (1 - B)(1 - B)S_t = (1 - B)^2 S_t$. The ARIMA (p, d, q) model (without seasonality) is defined as follows:

$$(1 - \phi_1 B - \phi_2 B^2 \cdots \phi_p B^p)(1 - B)^d S_t = \mu + (1 - \theta_1 B - \theta_2 B^2 \cdots \theta_q B^q)e_t \tag{9.7}$$

where p is the order of the autoregressive component, d is the order of differencing, q is the order of the moving average component, e_t is the error term, and μ is the mean assumed to be constant over time.

Since ARIMA models of even low order are very flexible, in the interest of parsimony, p and q are usually set less than or equal to 2. An ARIMA (2, 1, 1) model would be

$$(1 - \phi_1 B - \phi_2 B^2)(1 - B)S_t = \mu + (1 - \theta_1 B)e_t$$

$$\Rightarrow (1 - \phi_1 B - \phi_2 B^2)(S_t - S_{t-1}) = \mu + e_t - \theta_1 e_{t-1}$$

$$\Rightarrow S_t - \phi_1 S_{t-1} - \phi_2 S_{t-2} - S_{t-1} + \phi_1 S_{t-2} + \phi_2 S_{t-3} = \mu + e_t - \theta_1 e_{t-1} \quad \text{(9.8)}$$

$$\Rightarrow S_t = \mu + (\phi_1 + 1)S_{t-1} + (\phi_2 - \phi_1)S_{t-2} - \phi_2 S_{t-3} + e_t - \theta_1 e_{t-1}$$

Equation (9.8) is a linear representation of sales as a function of previous sales values and error terms.

A fully specified ARIMA model often has a seasonal component, and the seasonal component may in fact evolve over time. This is much more flexible than the ratio–to–moving average and regression methods we examined for analyzing the basic decomposition model. With those methods, the same seasonal index was assumed to apply for a given season in each year of the data. Notationally, the full ARIMA model is specified as ARIMA$(p, d, q)(P, D, Q)^s$ using the notation of Makridakis et al. (1983). The $(P, D, Q)^s$ term signifies that the seasonal component of the model is of periodicity s (e.g., $s = 12$ months or 4 quarters) and the seasonality itself follows a (P, D, Q) ARIMA process. Since a seasonality of period s can be removed from the data by taking the difference between $S_t - S_{t-s}$, a seasonal model will include terms like $(1 - B^s)$. As an example, an ARIMA$(2, 1, 1)(0, 1, 2)^{12}$ model would be as follows:

$$(1 - \phi_1 B - \phi_2 B^2)(1 - B^{12})(1 - B)S_t = \mu + (1 - \theta_1 B)(1 - \omega_1 B^{12} - \omega_2 B^{24})e_t$$

$$\begin{array}{cccccc}
\uparrow & \uparrow & \uparrow & \uparrow & \uparrow & \\
p = 2 & s = 12 & d = 1 & q = 1 & s = 12 & \text{(9.9)} \\
 & D = 1 & & & Q = 2 &
\end{array}$$

where the $p = 2$ term represents the underlying autoregressive component of the data, the $s = 12$ term represents the 12-period seasonal component, the $d = 1$ term represents first differencing of the data to remove trend, the $q = 1$ term represents the underlying moving average component of the data, and the $Q = 2$ term represents a moving average seasonal component.

Once a particular ARIMA model is specified, it can be estimated using an iterative least squares algorithm. The algorithm searches for the parameters that allow the given model to recover the data best. While the algorithm is not guaranteed to converge or reach a global optimum, it generally works well in practical applications. The biggest hurdle in ARIMA analysis is identifying the appropriate model.

There are occasions when theory dictates the values for p, q, and so on, especially at least for the periodicity of seasonality. Usually, however, the analyst has very little a priori reason to specify the p's and q's. Endemic to the use of ARIMA, then, is allowing the data to reveal the appropriate model specification. The analyst looks at the graph of the data and at several orders of auto and partial correlations (e.g., the fifth-order autocorrelation is the correlation between every fifth value in the time series).

It is beyond the scope of our discussion here to address the various ways of inferring ARIMA specifications. Makridakis et al. (1983, Ch. 9) provide an excellent introduction on how to interpret autocorrelation and partial correlation coefficients. Suffice it to say that specifying an ARIMA model is often more art and data manipulation than science. Typically, several models will be tried before settling on the best one. There would appear to be a potential problem with overfitting a given set of data by capturing that particular data set but no general properties of the data, and indeed, Box and Jenkins urge the analyst to search for parsimonious models (hence the reliance on p and q less than or equal to 2). However, with proper validation, overfitting can be avoided, and as Makridakis, Wheelwright, and McGee suggest, the differences between alternative models after eliminating the obviously bad ones are often small. As a result, the decision to go with a $(2, 2, 1)(1, 1, 1,)^{12}$ or a $(2, 2, 1)(2, 1, 1)^{12}$ model may not be so critical.

Cautions in Applying Univariate Time Series Analysis

As discussed earlier, univariate time series analysis can be used to extrapolate a baseline estimate onto the period in which a promotion is to be evaluated. The baseline estimate is derived from data observed prior to the promotion to be evaluated. The viability of using univariate time series analysis for this purpose depends on the nature of the data in the "preperiod." In Chapter 7, we used a simulated data illustration to investigate the potential biases in omitting relevant explanatory variables in analyzing sales data. Since univariate time series analysis does not include explanatory variables, the lessons learned from that illustration are relevant. In particular, from the illustration in Chapter 7, we can infer that it is dangerous to use univariate time series analysis to derive a baseline under two circumstances:

- Promotions are used frequently during the periods prior to the promotion being evaluated.
- Promotions in this preperiod are highly correlated with seasons.

In the first circumstance, the presence of promotions in the preperiod inflates the baseline because the promotions make average sales during the preperiod higher than the no-promotion sales level the estimated baseline is supposed to represent. In the second circumstance, the seasonality estimates for the seasons correlated with promotion become inflated, because the positive effect of promotions is embedded in those seasons. This results in underestimating the effect of a subsequent promotion that takes place during one of these seasons.

The recommendation then is to use univariate time series analysis only when the preperiod data are "clean," that is, relatively free of the brand's promotions, and, if the analysis is to be used to evaluate promotions that occur in a particular season, these seasons in the preperiod should not be highly correlated with use of promotion. Unfortunately, we cannot provide quantitative guidelines that specify what is meant by "relatively free" and "not highly correlated." Judgment is often needed to decide whether these conditions hold. It is, however, possible to provide at least some quantitative guidance to this judgment. This is one of the concepts underlying the PROMOTER methodology (Abraham and Lodish, 1987; see also the "PROMOTER" section in this chapter).

An Example of Using Univariate Time Series Analysis to Evaluate a Promotion

In this section, we use univariate time series analysis to evaluate a promotion. Specifically, we use the baseline bump analysis approach illustrated in Figure 9.1. The data are based on a real packaged goods promotion. The promotion was a special consumer premium offer accompanied by a trade deal, in-store point-of-sale material, and television advertising. It was offered during the last two months of the year. Warehouse withdrawal sales data were available for two years prior to the promotion, during which there was little promotion activity for the brand. The warehouse data divide the year into 13 four-week periods. A total of 29 periods of data were available, consisting of 25 periods prior to the promotion, 2 periods during the promotion, and 2 periods after the promotion. The data are displayed in Figure 9.2.

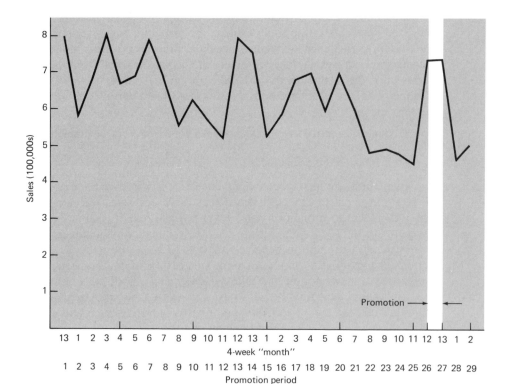

FIGURE 9.2 Sales Data for Time Series Analysis Example

Data courtesy of General Foods, Inc., White Plains, NY.

We see in Figure 9.2 that the promotion is associated with a large increase in sales, but we notice that the periods during which the promotion was offered (periods 12 and 13) are traditionally high sales months. There is obvious seasonality in the data that must be taken into account in evaluating the promotion. We will assume that the cycle exerts little influence on brand sales, since (1) the brand is a small-ticket item probably impervious to swings in the economy and (2) the cycle would ordinarily not vary too much over two years, unless, for example, a sudden recession occurred in the middle of the data. This was not the case with this example.

We will evaluate this promotion by using univariate time series analysis to project a baseline onto the promotion period. Specifically, we will use three methods: ratio–to–moving average, regression, and ARIMA.

Table 9.1 presents the analysis of the data using the ratio–to–moving average method. Column 1 presents the original data. Columns 2 and 3 show the calculation of seasonality. The data in column 2 were obtained by computing 13-period (one-year) moving averages. For example, 676,805 is the average of the first 13 numbers in column 1, 673,227 is the average of the second 13 numbers, and so on. Since seasonality occurs within a one-year or 13-period interval, and because taking a 13-period average should smooth out most irregularities, we assume that the data in column 2 should differ mainly because of trend (signified by the "T" heading for column 2). Since column 1 consists of trend, seasonality, and irregularities, and column 2 consists of trend, dividing column 1 by column 2 yield seasonality and irregularities. The results of doing these divisions (these are the "ratios" in the "ratio"–to–moving average name) are displayed in column 3. We note in column 3 that the results for periods 12 and 13 suggest high seasonality in those periods.

The results in column 3 contain seasonality and irregularity. If we had had enough data, column 3 would have contained more numbers, and we would have been able to calculate at least two seasonality/irregularity indices for each seasonal period. We could then average these indices to smooth out irregularities and produce an estimate of seasonality largely free of irregularities. However, in this case, with only 25 periods before the promotion period, we can only calculate one seasonality/irregularity index for each period, and we take those quantities as our estimates of seasonality. Since we assume that on average irregularities cancel out, these estimates should on average equal the true seasonality index.

In column 4 of Table 9.1, the seasonal indices have been divided into the first 25 periods of original data to produce deseasonalized sales. These data consist of trend and still some irregularities, but seasonality has been removed.[2] A simple regression trend line, $S = a + bt$, was then fit to these data, with the estimate of a being 719,987 and that of b being $-6,127$. That is, sales of this product are falling at a rate of 6,127 units per four-week period. In column 5, this trend line

---

[2] Note that there are still some irregularities in column 4 because the data in column 2 are not completely free of irregularities. Dividing column 2 into column 1 to produce column 3 thus yields a different set of irregularities than was present in column 1. As a result, irregularities do not completely cancel out when we divide column 3 into column 1 to yield column 4.

TABLE 9.1 The Ratio–To–Moving Average Method Applied to the Data in Figure 9.2

Period	Year	13-Period "Month"	Original Sales Data (T × S × I)	13-Period Moving Avg. (T)	Seasonality Estimates (Column 1 ÷ 2) × 100	Deseasonalized Data Column 1 ÷ 3	Estimated Trend Line	Seasonally Adjusted Sales Predictions	Incremental Sales Columns 1–6
1	1	13	805,584			678,672	713,860	847,352	
2	2	1	582,344			705,359	707,733	584,304	
3	2	2	682,118			731,572	701,606	654,177	
4	2	3	806,201			732,843	695,479	765,096	
5	2	4	675,605			586,717	689,352	793,789	
6	2	5	693,976			700,703	683,225	676,666	
7	2	6	793,750	676,805	117.28	676,805	677,098	794,094	
8	2	7	685,728	673,227	101.86	673,227	670,971	683,430	
9	2	8	554,807	668,673	82.97	668,673	664,844	551,630	
10	2	9	621,902	661,253	94.05	661,253	658,717	619,516	
11	2	10	569,136	651,571	87.35	651,571	652,590	570,026	
12	2	11	523,616	653,774	80.09	653,774	646,463	517,761	
13	2	12	803,692	646,572	124.30	646,572	640,336	795,940	
14	2	13	759,071	639,500	118.70	639,500	634,209	752,790	
15	3	1	523,142	633,625	82.56	633,625	628,082	518,566	
16	3	2	585,669	628,123	93.24	628,123	621,955	579,918	
17	3	3	680,331	618,418	110.01	618,418	615,828	677,481	
18	3	4	704,237	611,595	115.15	611,595	609,701	702,056	
19	3	5	600,357	606,146	99.04	606,146	603,574	597,809	
20	3	6	701,816			598,411	597,447	700,686	
21	3	7	609,346			598,219	591,320	602,319	
22	3	8	483,281			582,477	585,193	485,535	
23	3	9	495,743			527,106	579,066	544,612	
24	3	10	480,436			550,013	572,939	500,462	
25	3	11	452,780			565,339	566,812	453,960	
26	3	12	736,047[a]				560,685	696,931	32,116
27	3	13	737,002[a]				554,558	658,260	78,742
28	4	1	462,856[a]				548,431	452,785	10,071
29	4	2	506,183[a]				542,304	505,644	539
									128,468

[a] Periods 26 and 27 are the promotion periods. Periods 26–29 are not included in the computation of seasonality and trend in columns 2–5.

246

is computed for all periods. The computations for periods 26–29 represent the projected baseline level of sales for those periods, taking into account trend but not seasonality. Column 6 then displays the results of multiplying the seasonal indices in column 3 by the appropriate trend levels in column 5, to produce a baseline that takes into account seasonality as well as trend. Thus, sales of 696,931 units is what we would have expected in period 26 if just trend and seasonality were at work.

Since the promotion was offered in period 12 of year 3 and sales were 736,047 units, we estimate that $736,047 - 696,931 = 39,116$ incremental units were generated in that period by the promotion. Likewise, we calculate 78,742 incremental units in period 13 of year 3. We also carry the incremental sales calculation two additional periods, since the promotion might have borrowed sales from those periods. The calculations suggest that this did not occur. If anything, the immediate postpromotion effect was positive. The total incremental sales generated by the promotion is estimated as 128,468 units. The cost of the promotion must now be balanced against the contribution margin per unit, but the difficult part— the calculation of incremental sales—has been achieved.

We next analyze the data in Figure 9.2 using regression. A model similar to equation (9.3) was formulated, except that this time there were 12 seasonal dummies. The R^2 for this model was .9686, the F-statistic was significant at $p < .001$. The estimated model was

$$\text{Sales}_t = 602,793 + 87,038\text{MON2} + 202,299\text{MON3} + 154,843\text{MON4}$$

$$+ 117,976\text{MON5} + 224,481\text{MON6} + 130,123\text{MON7} \qquad (9.10)$$
$$+ 7,518\text{MON8} + 53,185\text{MON9} + 25,037\text{MON10} - 5,663\text{MON11}$$

$$+ 277,446\text{MON12} + 223,696\text{MON13} - 5,888t$$

where MON2, MON3, and so on are the dummy variables for the 4-week "month" seasonalities and t signifies time. Notice that there is no first month dummy, so the estimated seasonalities are relative to the first month. We see that months 12 and 13 have very high seasonalities, similar to the results of the ratio–to–moving average method. The trend estimate of $-5,888$ is also similar to the $-6,127$ estimate found using the ratio–to–moving average method. To produce a baseline estimate for year 3, month 12, we simply substitute into equation (9.10) the appropriate values. This yields

$$602,793 + 277,446 \text{ (the estimated seasonality for period 12)}$$

$$- 5,888 \times 26 \ (t = 26 \text{ for year 3, month 12}) = 727,151 \quad (9.11)$$

Table 9.2 displays the incremental sales results for the regression method, along with the ratio–to–moving average method and ARIMA model to be described next. The regression estimate is 88,438 incremental sales.

The ARIMA technique was next used to analyze the data in Figure 9.2. The model was fit on the first 25 periods and used to forecast a baseline for the next four periods. After noting the downward linear trend and apparent 13 period

TABLE 9.2 Incremental Sales Results for Data in Figure 9.2

Period			Ratio-to–Moving Average Method		Regression with Period Dummy Variables		ARIMA	
Year	Period	Actual	Predicted Sales	Incremental Sales	Predicted Sales	Incremental Sales	Predicted Sales	Incremental Sales
3	12	736,047	696,931	39,116	727,145[a]	6,902	687,460	48,587
3	13	737,002	658,260	78,742	667,508	69,494	661,256	75,746
4	1	462,856	452,785	10,071	437,923	24,933	427,481	35,375
4	2	506,183	505,644	539	519,074	−12,891	468,673	37,510
		2,442,088	2,313,620	128,468	2,353,650	88,438	2,244,870	197,218

[a] This number differs from that in equation (9.11) due to rounding error. The number in this table is exact.

seasonality, $d = 1$ and $S = 13$ were specified. Examining auto- and partial correlations yielded the specification $(2, 1, 0)(0, 1, 0)^{13}$. The estimated model was

$$(1 + .829B + .579B^2)(1 - B)(1 - B^{13})S_t = -3686 + e_t \qquad (9.12)$$

or

$$S_t = .171S_{t-1} + .250S_{t-2} + .579S_{t-3} + S_{t-13} - .171S_{t-14}$$

$$- .250S_{t-15} - .579S_{t-16} - 3686 + e_t \quad (9.13)$$

This model was used to forecast a baseline onto the last four periods of the data. The results are displayed in Table 9.2. The ARIMA estimate of incremental sales is 197,218.

The estimates of incremental sales for the three methods range from 88,438 to 197,218. The highest number is more than double the lowest. However, as a percentage of total sales (approximately 2,000,000), the range of incremental sales estimates is only approximately 5 percent. We therefore conclude that the methods generate similar estimates of incremental sales. It might be possible, depending on the actual margins and costs involved, that these differences could make a difference in whether or not the promotion is calculated to be profitable. However, we should recognize that there is plenty of uncertainty in the forecasted baseline. For example, the 95 percent confidence interval for the 727,145 sales forecasted for the regression model in period 12, year 3, ranges from 633,775 to 820,516, while the 95 percent confidence interval for the ARIMA forecast of 687,460 for that period ranges from 581,083 to 793,837. Certainly the differences in incremental sales estimates is within the range of uncertainty the models assign to their estimates.

In summary, the example in this section illustrates the use of three univariate time series methods to evaluate a sales promotion by projecting a baseline estimate into the promotion period. The methods yielded similar estimates of incremental sales, so no one can be concluded as superior. The strong statistical theory underlying regression and its relative ease of implementation would suggest it as the preferred technique. However, if more data were available and if more complex seasonalities or lags were present in the data, ARIMA would provide a powerful tool for estimating the promotion effect.

The two key features that allowed us to use univariate time series analysis in this example were (1) although the promotion was implemented in the high sales season, previous years' sales results for that season, when (we assume) no promotion was used, allowed an uncontaminated estimation of seasonality, and (2) the prepromotion period was not plagued by other major promotions, so that the univariate models did not leave out important variables. We therefore assume that the cautions raised earlier did not pertain to this example. If they had, we would have implemented one of the methods that are described in the remaining sections of this chapter and in Chapter 7.

A final interesting and important point concerns the evaluation of the post-promotion effects of the promotion. The issue here is for how long the baseline should be extended after the promotion to capture the promotion's full effect. In theory, we could extend the baseline for several post-promotion periods and eventually sales should return to the baseline level. In practice, however, one may run into the next promotion using this approach. The PROMOTER methodology (described next) utilizes the analyst's judgement to address this question. Transfer function and intervention analysis specify a model that directly estimates the duration and magnitude of any long-term effect.

THE PROMOTER METHODOLOGY

We now turn our attention to a time series methodology developed by Abraham and Lodish (1987) to circumvent some of the pitfalls of univariate time series analysis discussed earlier. Their method, incorporated in a decision support system called "PROMOTER," particularly addresses the problem of an elevated baseline caused by too many promotions during the analysis period. It also takes into account some of the blatant aberrations that often accompany sales data, such as a consistent end of the quarter surge in sales as the sales force endeavors to meet its quotas.

An outline of the PROMOTER methodology is depicted in Figure 9.3. It is an iterative procedure, whose goal is to calculate baseline sales, the sales that would have occurred had there not been a promotion. The PROMOTER model is

$$S(t) = T(t) \times SI(t) \times X(t) \times [b(t) + p(t) + e(t)] \tag{9.14}$$

where

$S(t)$ = sales level, time t

$T(t)$ = impact on sales of trend in time t

$SI(t)$ = impact on sales of seasonality in time t

$X(t)$ = impact on sales of exceptional events in time t

$b(t)$ = base sales, sales that would occur in time t after adjusting for trend, season and exceptional events, and assuming no promotions were influencing sales

$p(t)$ = effect of promotion on sales in time t

$e(t)$ = random noise or irregularities, averaging zero

The analysis strategy is to first detrend, deseasonalize, and de-"exceptionalize" the data, leaving $b(t) + p(t) + e(t)$. Next, periods are identified when $p(t) = 0$. In those periods, since according to the model the data equal $b(t) + e(t)$, one can get a direct estimate of $b(t)$ by taking moving averages of the data. The moving averages smooth out the irregularities. This baseline is then extrapolated onto the periods when $p(t) > 0$.

Seasonality is first estimated using either the ratio–to–moving average or

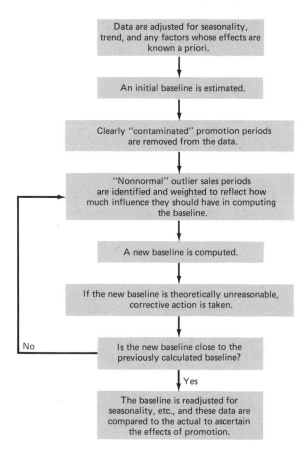

dummy variable techniques demonstrated earlier. Exceptional event effects are next estimated using methods depending on the event under consideration. For example, if distribution were known to increase by 20 percent, an index of 1.20 could be used. The purpose here is to try to purify the data using independent information before using the data themselves. Exceptional events not considered at this step will be picked up as outliers later in the analysis. Trend is then estimated by adjusting the data for seasonality and exceptions, and then fitting a curve to a smoothed version of the adjusted data. The original data are then adjusted for seasonality, exceptions, and trend, so we are left with a series representing $b(t) + p(t) + e(t)$.

Baseline estimates are calculated by taking moving averages of the data. This will average out the $e(t)$ term to zero, but including the periods where $p(t) > 0$ would bias the estimated baseline, as we discussed earlier. PROMOTER therefore incorporates a series of judgment-based rules for diagnosing when $p(t) > 0$ and omits those data points from the moving average calculation of $b(t)$. Data points from a more extended period of time are then used in the moving average calculation. For example, say that the $b(t) + p(t) + e(t)$ data are as follows:

t	1	2	3	4	5	6	7	8	9	10	11	12	13	14	15	16
	20	22	18	19	23	20	21	19	41	10	19	20	22	21	23	18

and a promotion occurred in period 9. We might assume that periods 9 and 10 are contaminated by promotion, and thus omit that data. We then calculate $b(t)$ as three-period moving averages of the remaining data:

t	1	2	3	4	5	6	7	8	9	10	11	12	13	14	15	16
$b(t) + e(t)$	20	22	18	19	23	22	21	19	—	—	19	20	22	21	23	18
$b(t)$		20	19.7	20	21.3	22	20.7	20.2	19.7	19.3	19.8	20.3	21	22	20.7	

$b(t)$ is calculated in this case by taking a moving average of three successive periods (the length of the moving average is a user-specified parameter). For example, in period 2, the estimated baseline is $(20 + 22 + 18)/3 = 20$. When we get to period 8, we want to average periods 7, 8, and 9, but period 9 has been omitted, so we use period 11. The resulting average, $(21 + 19 + 19)/3 = 19.7$, is centered at period 9. We can then infer a baseline for period 8 of $(20.7 + 19.7)/2 = 20.2$.

In this example, the evaluation of the promotion is therefore $41 - 19.7 \cong 20.3$ incremental units in period 9, followed by a postpromotion dip of $10 - 19.3 \cong -9.3$ units. The net result of the promotion is therefore $20.3 - 9.3 = 11$ incremental sales.

While the foregoing calculation shows the essence of how PROMOTER works, the method also contains a detailed assessment of outliers. Depending on how much of an outlier a particular point is, it is either omitted completely from the calculation (implicitly assigned a weight of zero as are promotion contaminated periods) or assigned some intermediate weight between 0 and 1. This allows the analyst to use as much data as possible. Finally, the process beginning with the detection of outliers is iterated until the successive baselines are close to each other (see Figure 12.3).

Figure 9.4 shows a PROMOTER-calculated baseline and a validation period. The promotion periods are obvious in these data. Beginning in August 1983, the brand ceased promotions, and the sales follow the baseline calculated prior to that time. PROMOTER seems to have identified the correct baseline.

PROMOTER represents an important and very innovative application of time series analysis to evaluating promotions. It directly confronts the problem

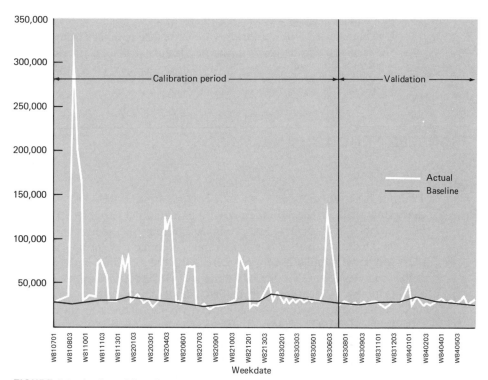

FIGURE 9.4 An Actual Baseline and Validation Test for PROMOTER

Source: Magid M. Abraham and Leonard M. Lodish, "PROMOTER: An Automated Promotion Evaluation System," *Marketing Science*, Vol. 6, no. 2 (Spring 1987), p. 113.

that promotion activity contaminates a time series calculated baseline. However, the method does have some limitations:

- It does not address the seasonality-promotion correlation problem. Seasonality is assumed to be known a priori.

- A PROMOTER analysis using factory shipments data can be biased *downward* in the presence of frequent promotions (Abraham and Lodish, 1987, pp. 108–110). Since frequent promotions encourage deal to deal buying, and PROMOTER eliminates promotion periods, the sales level left will be unrealistically low. Abraham and Lodish recommend using data closer to the consumer (e.g., warehouse withdrawals rather than factory shipments) under the premise that such data will be less prone toward such problems.

- PROMOTER does not generally include competition. Competition is part of the marketing environment, and its effect of driving down the baseline is endemic to that environment. However, if competitive activity is correlated with the brand's own promotions, the extrapolation of the baseline to promotion periods will be inaccurate. PROMOTER includes a regression-based option for including factors such as competition, but this feature is not commonly used (Abraham and Lodish, 1987, p. 118).

- The method is conceptually straightforward but is not simple. There is a need to compare PROMOTER's accuracy with simple time series and regression techniques.
- The method relies on judgment for key factors such as the period of time during which promotions affect sales, how long the various moving averages should be, and the quantification of outliers. The statistical properties of the baseline estimates are not known.

TRANSFER FUNCTION ANALYSIS

The Method

Transfer function analysis, also called multivariate ARIMA or MARIMA, combines univariate ARIMA modeling with explanatory variables. That is, independent variables such as price and promotion are now included in the analysis. While transfer function analysis is not extremely common in the marketing literature, there are some notable exceptions, including the excellent papers by Helmer and Johansson (1977) and Doyle and Saunders (1985). Helmer and Johansson studied sales response to advertising using the Lydia Pinkham data and found that transfer models had greater forecast accuracy than certain conventional regression models. Doyle and Saunders studied the *pre*promotion dip in sales. We will review this paper since it is directly relevant to promotion. First, it is necessary, however, to provide an overview of the transfer function technique.

The goal of transfer function series analysis is to first model the progression of the independent variables as an ARIMA process and then determine whether there is any relationship between the independent variables and the dependent, other than what would be explained by the ARIMA process. The techniques used to identify this relationship are "prewhitening" and "cross-correlation functions." If it is determined that the independent and dependent variables are related to each other, the function describing this relationship is called the transfer function.

The general form of the transfer function model (with error a_t and one independent variable x) is

$$s_t = \frac{\omega(B)}{\delta(B)} x_{t-b} + \frac{\theta(B)}{\phi(B)} a_t \tag{9.15}$$

where

$$\phi(B) = 1 - \phi_1 B - \phi_2 B^{2-} \cdots - \phi_p B^p$$

$$\theta(B) = 1 - \theta_1 B - \theta_2 B^{2-} \cdots - \theta_q B^q$$

$$\omega(B) = 1 - \omega_1 B - \omega_2 B^{2-} \cdots - \omega_s B^s$$

$$\delta(B) = 1 - \delta_1 B - \delta_2 B^{2-} \cdots - \delta_r B^r$$

$\theta(B)$ and $\phi(B)$ are the moving average and autoregression terms familiar to us from our discussion of ARIMA models. For example, if x was not included in the model, we would be left with a pure ARIMA model for equation (9.15). The ratio $\omega(B)/\delta(B)$ of backward shift operator functions is the transfer function. A ratio is used because even if $\omega(B)$ and $\delta(B)$ are low order, for example, $s = r = 1$, their ratio can be very complex. Using a ratio expression for the transfer function allows us to express fairly complicated lag structures with few parameters. Note that we express sales and the independent variable in lowercase letters.[3] This is because we assume that the data have been adjusted for trend and seasonality. That is, $s_t = (1 - B)(1 - B^{12})S_t$ if sales are monthly data with a linear trend. We briefly summarize the steps in identifying and estimating a transfer function model (see Makridakis et al., 1983, Ch. 10 for more details).

1. Adjust S_t and X_t for seasonality and trend, yielding s_t and x_t.
2. Identify an ARIMA model to describe x_t. That is, identify a model so that $\phi_x(B)x_t = \theta_x(B)\alpha_t$, where α_t is the error term for the x_t ARIMA model.
3. Use the x_t ARIMA model to infer α_t. This is called prewhitening x_t: $\alpha_t = [\phi_x(B)/\theta_x(B)]x_t$.
4. Use the same x_t ARIMA model to prewhiten s_t. That is, let $U_t = [\phi_x(B)/\theta_x(B)]s_t$.
5. Correlate α_{t-k} with U_t, for positive and negative values of k. These are called cross-correlations.
6. Specify r, s, and b by examing the cross-correlations.
7. Obtain estimates of the noise series $[\theta(B)/\phi(B)]a_t$, and identify the order of θ and ϕ using standard univariate ARIMA techniques.
8. Estimate all parameters.
9. Validate and check the model for reasonableness.

Note, the basic mechanism is to first explain x_t in terms of a univariate ARIMA model (step 2), and then, in steps 3–5, see whether there is any relationship between the residuals of applying that model to both the x_t and s_t series. The philosophical difference between this approach and regression modeling is profound. Regression tries to maximize the causal explanation of sales by factors such as promotion. Transfer function analysis only allows promotion to explain variation in sales that cannot be explained by moving average and autoregression factors common to promotion and sales. For example, assume a brand was promoted on a periodic basis, not correlated with season, and was perfectly correlated with sales. The ARIMA model $\phi_x(B)$ and $\theta_x(B)$ would provide a good fit to the x_t (promotion) time series and implicitly to the s_t series. The correlations between the prewhitened sales and promotion series (α_{t-k} and U_t) would be zero, because the prewhitening removes the part of correlation between sales and promotion explainable in terms of common periodic movement. We would then conclude that promotion does not influence sales and be left with a pure ARIMA model. In summary, since promotion can be modeled in terms of previous levels of promotion, and promotion is perfectly related to sales, transfer function analysis will infer no causal effect of promotion on sales. Sales will be modeled as a function

---

[3] The reader should not confuse s with s_t. We follow the notation of Makridakis et al. in using s to signify the order of the $\omega(B)$ function. The term s_t represents sales in period t.

of previous sales and random noise values. In the same case, a regression analysis would ascribe causality to promotion, and noise would have little role in the determination of sales.

The question of whether the transfer function or regression approach is appropriate is a philosophical one. From the transfer function point of view, a perfect correlation between sales and promotion may be spurious if promotion can be explained in terms of previous promotion levels. Perhaps sales causes promotion, rather than the reverse. Or, perhaps a third variable, for example, seasonality, causes both promotion and sales. The econometric approach makes an assumption, namely, that if anything, promotion causes sales rather than the reverse. A regression model would also include as many factors as possible, for example, seasonality, and allow the estimation process to disentangle promotion from seasonal effects. If multicollinearity prevents this, it will show up as large standard errors for both promotion and seasonality effects. In summary, transfer function analysis looks for alternative explanations (for example, seasonality in both promotion and sales) before ascribing causality to promotion. A regression assumes that the model has been correctly specified. If there is reverse causality, the model should be simultaneous.[4] If there are other important factors, they should be included in the model.

Examples of Transfer Function Models

We now review a few transfer function models. Doyle and Saunders (1985) examined department store sales as a function of six marketing instruments: leaflets, display, press, TV advertising, price promotion, and commission structure for sales personnel. The hypothesis of interest was that a temporary increase in commission rate accompanying a promotion would be *preceded* by a dip in sales, as salespeople attempt to get customers to purchase during the time their commission rates were higher.

Table 9.3 displays the results of steps 2 and 5 in the Doyle and Saunders study. We see that the ARIMA models for the independent variables were not very complicated. All variables were first-differenced to remove trend and 52-period differenced since the data were weekly. All the ARIMA models were moving average models with order not greater than one. For example, commission rate followed a moving average process in which both the raw data and the seasonal effect evolved over time. The cross-correlations in Table 9.3 indicate clearly a lead effect of commission. Higher commissions in period t are associated with lower sales in the two preceding periods.

---

[4] Transfer function analysis as discussed in this section is not appropriate for studying simultaneous relationships. The technique can be modified, however, to investigate such situations. See Aaker et al. (1982) for an application of this modified technique to studying the advertising-sales relationship.

TABLE 9.3   ARIMA Models and Cross-correlations for the Doyle-Saunders Study on Lead Effects

ARIMA models for the independent variables (step 2)

Variable	ARIMA Model
Leaflets	$l_t = (1 - .78B^{52})a_t$
Display	$d_t = (1 - .55B)(1 - .71B^{52})a_t$
Press	$p_t = (1 - .54B)(1 - .67B^{52})a_t$
TV	$t_t = (1 - .68B^{52})a_t$
Price promotion	$r_t = (1 - .53B)(1 - .82B^{52})a_t$
Commission	$c_t = (1 - .25B)(1 - .80B^{52})a_t$

$l_t = (1 - B)(1 - B^{52})L_t$ where L_t is the original leaflet variable, et cetera, a_t is random noise.

Cross-correlation coefficients (step 5, correlations with prewhitened sales)

	Lead					Lag			
	4	3	2	1	0	−1	−2	−3	−4
Leaflets	.00	.04	.01	−.01	−.02	.09	.02	.03	.01
Display	−.11	−.07	−.06	−.06	.04	.23[a]	.20[a]	.19[a]	.16
Press	.09	.12	.11	.08	.08	.16	.00	−.08	−.13
TV	.02	.04	.01	.03	.08	.20[a]	−.06	−.07	−.06
Price promotion	.02	.01	.04	.03	.44[a]	.01	.01	.01	.00
Commission	.05	.04	−.13	−.29[a]	.54[a]	−.09	−.03	.01	−.01

[a] Significant, $p < .05$.

Source: Peter Doyle and John Saunders, "The Lead Effect of Marketing Decisions," *Journal of Marketing Research*, Vol. 22, no. 1 (February 1985), pp. 58–59. Adapted from the *Journal of Marketing Research*, published by the American Marketing Association.

Using the information in Table 9.3, Doyle and Saunders specified their transfer functions. For example, the three significant lagged correlations for display suggest a transfer function consisting of three lag terms beginning at time $t − 1$. Doyle and Saunders estimate the following model for the effect of display on sales:

$$(.255B + .043B^2 + .032B^3)D_t,$$

where D_t is the amount of display advertising in period t (note the B^2 and B^3 terms were not statistically significant). The effect of commission rates on sales was estimated as:

$$(2006B^{+2} + 4676B^{+1} − 8355)C_t,$$

where B^{+2} and B^{+1} can be viewed as "forward shift" operators, that is, $B^{+2}C_t = C_{t+2}$. C_t was operationalized as a fraction of the regular price, so that smaller C_t signifies larger commissions. This explains the positive signs for the B^{+2} and B^{+1} coefficients, and the negative sign for the current period effect. Specifically, larger commissions imply smaller C_t, and then the positive signs for lead effects imply smaller sales in the periods before the commission rate actually is increased. Using this function, Doyle and Saunders calculated that about 7 percent of total sales during an 8-week promotion period consisted of sales that would have taken place prior to the promotion period had commission rates not been increased during that period.

We note that Doyle and Saunders estimate their model using an autoregressive regression procedure instead of a transfer function algorithm. However, the important point is that they use the transfer function approach to specify their model. We note also that although the transfer function approach is capable of very complicated lag structures, the ones estimated by Doyle and Saunders were relatively straightforward. They were not ratios of B or B^+ functions, but simple linear functions of B or B^+.

Other researchers have usually used simple transfer functions in marketing applications. For example, Helmer and Johansson (1977) estimated the following two functions to model the Lydia Pinkham data:

$$S_t = \frac{.5206}{(1 - .3599B)} A_t + \frac{a_t}{(1 - .2557B)}$$

$$S_t = .4827A_t + .881A_{t-1} + \frac{a_t}{(1 - .2755B)}$$

where S_t is first-differenced sales, A_t is first-differenced advertising, and a_t is error. Jenkins (1979) estimated the following model:

$$S_t = 7.9A_t - 40.5P_t + (1 - .45B)a_t$$

where P_t is first-differenced price. Montgomery and Weatherby (1980) estimated the following model:

$$S_t = \frac{(.550 + .482B)}{(1 - .847B + .286B^2)} A_{t-2} + \frac{a_t}{(1 - 1.022B + .267B^2)}$$

As the Doyle and Saunders example indicates, transfer function analysis has strong potential in marketing, and we expect that it will be used more to study promotion. The problems with transfer function analysis are similar to those with ARIMA modeling. For example, specification is more an art than a science. There is also what may be a problem for some analysts in the method's philosophy of trying to explain as much as possible using extrapolative moving average and autoregression components, and leaving the leftover variance for promotion. In discussing this issue earlier, we suggested that this is a philosophical rather than an analytical issue. A final problem with transfer function modeling is its reliance on ARIMA models for the independent variables. Often, sales promotions are one-week zero-one pulses, not amenable to the correlational analysis setting embedded in the transfer function approach. A method perhaps more fitting in these cases is intervention analysis, which is a derivative of transfer function analysis. We now study this method.

INTERVENTION ANALYSIS

The Method

The intervention model is a transfer function model with the independent variable(s) being a temporary pulse or a permanent step change. Also, the methodology for estimating intervention models does not use prewhitening or cross-correlation functions. The model is, therefore,

$$S_t = \frac{\omega(B)}{\delta(B)} X_t + \frac{\theta(B)}{\phi(B)} a_t \tag{9.16}$$

where X_t is the intervention, for example, a dummy variable signifying the presence or absence of promotion in week t[5] and $\omega(B)/\delta(B)$ is a transfer function.

The methodology for specifying the transfer function relies much more on the analyst's a priori hypotheses than on letting the data dictate the transfer function. Importantly in this regard, there are a few basic transfer functions that have particularly useful implications for the effect of X_t on S_t. These, shown in Figure 9.5, are by no means exhaustive, but have particular application to sales promotion.

In Figure 9.5 function 6 would be particularly relevant to studying promotion: ω_0 measures the immediate promotion impact, $\omega_1 + \omega_2$ measures the postpromotion dip, and ω_2 represents the long-run effect of the promotion. Function 6 captures a very rich set of phenomena with only four parameters.

The intervention analysis methodology can therefore be summarized as follows (see Box and Tiao, 1975; Montgomery and Weatherby, 1980):

1. Hypothesize a transfer function for X_t.

2. If the promotion event takes place subsequent to a long string of promotion free data, estimate the noise model $\theta(B)/\phi(B)$ using standard ARIMA analysis on the data prior to the intervention.

3. If the promotion takes place in the middle of the data, or at multiple occasions, so that there is no long promotion-free period, estimate the parameters for $\omega(B)/\delta(B)$ first, and then use ARIMA procedures on the residuals to identify the $\theta(B)/\phi(B)$ model (Montgomery and Weatherby, 1980, p. 304).

In the case of promotion, we would expect step 3 to be commonly followed. Notice the shift in emphasis now: The intervention transfer function is prespecified rather than dictated by the data. Intervention analysis is indeed closer in philosophy to regression modeling.

---

[5] Note we use uppercase letters for S_t and X_t, meaning these variables are not differenced. This makes the exposition easier. In the course of estimating intervention analysis models, it sometimes is necessary to difference the data to eliminate trend or seasonality.

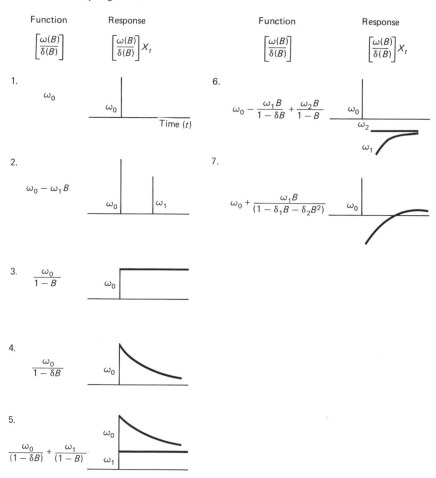

FIGURE 9.5 Alternative Transfer Functions for Intervention Analysis Assuming X_t Is a One-Period Pulse

Sources: Douglas C. Montgomery and Ginner Weatherby, "Modeling and Forecasting Time Series Using Transfer Functions and Intervention Analysis," *AIIE Transactions*, 12, 4 (December 1980), pp. 292, 303; G. E. P. Box and G. C. Tiao, "Intervention Analysis with Application to Economic and Environmental Problems," *Journal of the American Statistical Association*, 70, 349 (March 1975), p. 72.

Examples of Intervention Analysis

One of the earliest studies to use intervention analysis in a marketing context is Wichern and Jones's (1977) investigation of the effect of the American Dental Association endorsement on sales of Crest toothpaste. This marketing event was a step rather than a pulse input, and in that sense it was not a promotion. An intervention model for analyzing sales promotions is provided by Jenkins (1979, pp. 70–75). The example involved estimating the effects of trade and consumer promotions on sales of a consumer product. Three years of data were available,

One estimated model was

$$s_t = 2778t_t - 572c_t + (1 - .56B - .35B^2)(1 + .61B^{13})a_t \tag{9.17}$$

where

s_t = first-differenced sales

t_t = first-differenced zero-one presence of trade promotion

c_t = first-differenced zero-one presence of consumer promotion

Equation (9.17) indicates that trade promotions have a dramatic effect on sales, while consumer promotions have a slight negative impact. Actually, the consumer promotion was not statistically different than zero, but inspection of the data showed that consumer promotions occurred only in the presence of trade deals, and never alone. This means the correct interpretation of equation (9.17) is that when trade promotions are run, sales increase in that period by an average of 2,778 units. When consumer promotions are run in addition to the trade promotion, the effect is no different from when trade promotions are run alone. The results indicate that a consumer promotion overlay does not improve the effectiveness of a trade promotion. This begs the question of whether a consumer promotion alone would be equally or even more effective at lower cost.

Interestingly, the Jenkins model is again a very simple one. Aside from the more complex structure on the error term, the model is basically a dummy variable regression. Jenkins reports trying $(\omega_0 - \omega_1 B)$ for the intervention transfer function but that the ω_1 term did not increase the precision of the model.

Leone (1987) recently reports an application of intervention analysis to evaluating a promotion for wet cat food. The data are displayed in Figure 9.6. The promotion was a "5 for $1.00" sale in period 10, much more extreme than the "3 for $1.00" sales that were offered roughly on a monthly basis. The data revealed the quintessential bump-trough effect for promotions (see Chapter 5). Leone employed transfer function 6 in Figure 9.5 to describe the effect of the promotion on sales. The final estimated model was

$$\text{Sales}_t = \left(492.24 - \frac{355.7B}{1 - .57B} + \frac{60.9B}{1 - B}\right) X_t + \frac{1 - .76B}{1 - .97B^3} a_t \tag{9.18}$$

where X_t is a zero-one dummy depicting presence of the "5 for $1.00" promotion and a_t is error. The results imply that the initial effect of the promotion was to increase sales by 492.24 units. In the next period, sales decrease by 294.8 units $(-355.7 + 60.9)$ below normal sales. These are sales presumedly accelerated forward to the week of the promotion. Finally, the model estimates a positive long-term effect of 60.9 units per week, approximately a 10 percent increase. The long-term effect seems to hold throughout the postpromotion period.

In summary, intervention analysis holds much promise for the study of sales promotion because promotions often take the form of single-period pulses. The rich array of potential responses to promotion are displayed in Figure 9.5, but

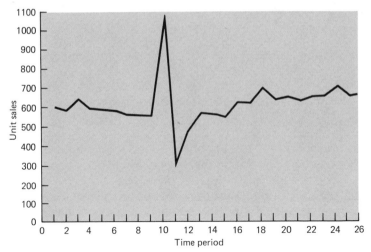

FIGURE 9.6 Weekly Sales Data for Wet Cat Food from the Leone Intervention Analysis Study

Source: Robert P. Leone, "Forecasting the Effect of an Environmental Change on Market Performance: An Intervention Time-Series Approach," *International Journal of Forecasting*, Vol. 3 (1987), p. 476, published by Elsevier Science Publishers, Physical Sciences and Engineering Division.

these have not been fully exploited in the sales promotion literature. Further research is needed to investigate the potentially important contributions to be yielded by intervention analysis.

SUMMARY

We have reviewed the methods, existing literature, and potential contribution of time series analysis to the study of sales promotion. We have traced through univariate time series models including ARIMA useful for bump analysis, the PROMOTER methodology, transfer function analysis, and intervention analysis. Each technique has built upon the previous ones.

If we compare the attention to time series methods to that given to regression models, experiments, and choice models, we see that time series analysis has not yet enjoyed its "day in the sun." This might be due to a number of reasons, including

- The univariate time series models are not useful in a heavy promotion environment, and the other models are a quantum leap more complicated.
- Computer software for ARIMA models and transfer function and intervention analysis is not as readily available as it is for regression analysis or analysis of variance.
- The philosophical emphasis of these techniques, with the important exceptions of intervention analysis and PROMOTER, is less on phenomenological model building than on data fitting.

All three of these reasons should not dissuade the researcher or practitioner from pursuing time series analysis. First, univariate time series methods work quite well under certain circumstances. Also, when the environment is more complex, it makes sense that we would need the complexity afforded by the ARIMA models. Second, good computer software is available for ARIMA, transfer function, and intervention analysis (e.g., the SAS ETS routines) (SAS Institute, 1984). Third, the philosophical orientation does give us pause to reflect on possible reverse or spurious causality, and intervention analysis strikes a balance between data fitting and hypothesis testing. Our conclusion is that time series models of sales promotion should and, it is hoped, will receive more attention in the future.

10

Coupons

INTRODUCTION

Distribution Trends

C. W. Post, the producer of ready-to-eat cereals, is commonly recognized as the first manufacturer to distribute coupons. The first coupon was a 1 cent savings certificate that could be used toward the purchase of a new cereal called Grape Nuts. The date was 1895. Since then, the distribution and processing of coupons has grown into a major industry, and coupons have become a significant marketing tool. Traditionally the domain of packaged goods manufacturers, coupons now are being used for restaurants, champagne, mass transit, and even automobiles.

Figure 10.1 displays the trend in number of coupons distributed. These data are collected by the Manufacturers Coupon Control Center (MC3). The data represent coupons distributed by packaged goods manufacturers, so do not include the use of coupons in other industries or those distributed by retailers. Even so, MC3 reports that manufacturers distributed 221.7 billion coupons in 1988 (Manufacturers Coupon Control Center, 1989a), or approximately 2,460 for each of the 90 million American households. As Figure 10.1 illustrates, much of the growth that led to this astronomical level occurred after the recession of 1975.

As reported by MC3 (1988a, 1989a), the total number of coupons redeemed in 1988 was 7.05 billion, for an average redemption rate of 3.2%. Consumers saved $2.93 billion using coupons, an average of approximately $32.56 per household. Adding to these savings is evidence that face values (the amount of discount offered per coupon) have more than kept pace with inflation in recent years. For example, the average coupon face values for grocery products in 1987 was 33.9 cents, approximately double the level in 1979, representing a higher growth rate than inflation. In addition, retailers received $572 million from manufacturers to

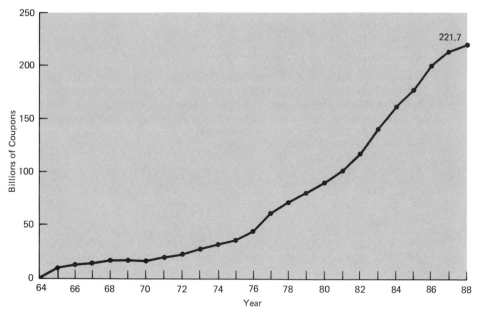

FIGURE 10.1 Trend in Coupon Distribution

Sources: 1988: Manufacturers Coupon Control Center, *Coupon Distribution and Redemption Patterns,* 1989a, p. 1; 1984–1987: Manufacturers Coupon Control Center, *Coupon Distribution and Redemption Patterns,* 1988a, p. 2; 1979–1983: Nielsen Clearing House, *Coupon Distribution and Redemption Patterns,* 1984, p. 3; 1965–1978: Nielsen Clearing House, *A Product Manager's Guide to Effective Couponing,* 1982, p. 6.

compensate them for handling coupons. Clearly, coupons have an important economic impact on both consumers and retailers.

From the point of view of an individual brand manager, couponing can be a significant investment. For example, the cost of a free-standing insert coupon drop—currently the most common form of coupon—can easily be $1,000,000 (see Table 10.7). It is not uncommon for brands that employ couponing to have four or five coupon drops a year (see Neslin, 1989, and the promotion plan discussed in Chapter 13). Vilcassim and Wittink (1987) calculated that 21 percent of purchase transactions for instant coffee and 9 percent of purchase transactions for regular coffee involved a manufacturer coupon. Clearly, couponing can have a significant financial impact not only on consumers and retailers, but on individual brands as well.

Types of Coupon Distribution Vehicles

There are four main "vehicles" for distributing coupons: media-distributed, direct-mail, package, and retailer-distributed coupons. Table 10.1 lists and describes these vehicles. Currently, the most popular distribution method is a media-distributed vehicle known as the "free-standing insert," a leaflet of coupons inserted usually in a Sunday newspaper (see Chapter 1, Figure 1.2F, for an illustration).

TABLE 10.1 Coupon Distribution Vehicles

Media Distributed

Free-standing insert. A leaflet of coupons for various products that can be inserted into a (usually Sunday) newspaper.

ROP (run-of-press) newspaper. Coupons that appear on the actual pages of newspapers, rather than being inserted as a separate page or section. Often these coupons appear in an advertisement for a brand (these are called "in-ad" coupons).

Sunday supplements. Coupons that appear on the pages of a newspaper "Sunday supplement" magazine such as *Parade* and *Family Weekly*.

Magazine. Coupons that appear in magazines other than Sunday supplements, such as *Better Housekeeping*. The coupons can be actually on a page, or attached using special "tip-in" or "pop-up" cards.

Direct Mail

Coupons are mailed directly to consumers using the U.S. Postal Service. One mailing usually includes several coupons from various manufacturers, although much more expensive solo mailings are possible.

Package

On-package. The coupon appears on the outside of the package and can be used for a subsequent purchase.

Instantly redeemable. The coupon is on the outside of the package but can be easily removed and used on the current purchase.

In-package. The coupon is inside the package and can be used for a subsequent purchase.

Cross-ruff. The coupon is for another brand, manufactured either by the same or a different firm. The coupon itself can be either in or on package.

Retailer Distributed

Retailer coupons. Coupons distributed by the retailer rather than the manufacturer. The coupons can be distributed by ROP newspaper, included in "Best Food Day" circulars, or handed out in the store.

Coupon-dispensing machines. Manufacturer coupons are distributed by a machine located in the store. The machine displays which coupons are available and the shopper specifies which coupons he or she wants.

Direct-mail and newspaper coupons for a particular brand can be distributed either alone ("solo") or with those of other brands ("co-op"). Solo coupons generally cost much more than co-op coupons. Package coupons appear on or in the actual product package, good for either the current or next purchase. Sometimes a coupon contained in a particular brand's package is for another brand. This is called a "cross-ruff" coupon. It might be used by a manufacturer to stimulate trial of a new product. Retailer coupons are distributed by the retailer, often but not necessarily in response to a trade deal offered by a manufacturer. For example, the retailer may distribute a coupon for one of its own "store brands."

One characteristic of coupons not captured in Table 10.1 is the coupon's

TABLE 10.2 Manufacturers' Use of Coupon Vehicles, 1979–1988

	1979	1980	1981	1982	1983	1984	1985	1986	1987	1988
Free-standing inserts										
Sunday newspaper	14.9%	18.4%	26.2%	33.3%	36.6%	42.7%	50.4%	68%[a]	72.7%[a]	77.3%[a]
Daily newspaper	<1%	<1%	<1%	<1%	6.4%	8.8%	9.5%	—	—	—
ROP newspaper										
Solo	36.2%	31.1%	27.3%	23.1%	20.0%	17.3%	12.2%	7.4%	5.9%	5.4%
Co-op	16.1%	17.1%	17.7%	15.2%	12.2%	10.0%	8.0%	7.1%	4.6%	2.4%
Direct mail	3.2%	3.4%	3.3%	3.8%	4.3%	4.4%	4.4%	4.0%	5.3%	5.0%
Sunday supplements	9.5%	9.0%	7.3%	6.3%	4.9%	3.3%	2.1%	1.2%	[b]	[b]
Package coupons	7.9%	7.7%	6.4%	6.9%	5.6%	5.0%	4.8%	5.8%	5.3%	5.2%
Magazine	12.2%	13.3%	11.8%	11.4%	10.0%	8.5%	8.6%	6.5%	3.7%	2.4%

[a] Combined Sunday and daily.

[b] In 1987, 2.5% of coupons were distributed through Sunday supplements and other vehicles. In 1988, this number was 2.3%.

Sources: Manufacturers Coupon Control Center, "Coupon Distribution and Redemption Patterns," 1989a, p. 6; Manufacturers Coupon Control Center, "Coupon Distribution and Redemption Patterns," 1988a, p. 5; Manufacturers Coupon Control Center, "Coupon Distribution and Redemption Patterns," 1986, p. 5; Nielsen Clearing House, "Coupon Distribution and Redemption Patterns," 1984; Nielsen Clearing House, "A Product Manager's Guide to Effective Couponing," 1982.

expiration date. The expiration date stipulates a date by which the coupon can be redeemed. Attempts to redeem the coupon after this date should not be allowed by the retailer. If often proves difficult for the manufacturer to police expiration dates. However, retailers often stipulate one-week expiration dates for their coupons and enforce these regulations.

Table 10.2 displays the relative popularity of the various coupon alternatives used by manufacturers. The most dramatic trend in these data is the increased usage of free-standing inserts (FSI's) and the corresponding decline in ROP newspaper coupons. FSI's have the advantage of clear, full-color graphics and ready accessibility for the consumer. Sunday free-standing inserts are becoming as much a part of the Sunday paper as the comics. In fact, one newspaper study found that a free-standing insert received recall scores between 75 and 85 percent (Starch, 1985). The front news section received the highest score, 88 percent, while comics received a score of 64 percent. Direct-mail, package, and Sunday supplement coupons have traditionally been less commonly used. Sunday supplements have especially been declining in usage, probably as a result of the popularity of FSI's.

Table 10.3 shows that the popularity of alternative couponing vehicles varies considerably across general product categories. While all product categories include heavy users of FSI's, beverages and food products rely relatively more on ROP newspaper. One possible reason for this is that ROP newspaper coupons often appear in the food section of the newspaper, where there can be considerable synergies. The shopper may peruse the food section to obtain ideas for meals, and therefore food coupons are a natural companion.

TABLE 10.3   Usage of Coupon Vehicles, by Type of Product, 1985

	Household Products	Health and Beauty Aids	Beverages	Frozen Foods	Refrigerated Products	Other Packaged Foods
Free-standing inserts						
Sunday paper	53%[a]	63%	33%	46%	37%	50%
Daily newspaper	11%	4%	10%	12%	14%	9%
ROP Newspaper						
Solo	9%	3%	28%	22%	20%	13%
Co-op	9%	3%	8%	8%	10%	10%
Direct mail	6%	7%	3%	3%	2%	3%
Sunday supplements	4%	4%	2%	1%	2%	2%
Package coupons	4%	5%	3%	3%	5%	6%
Magazine	4%	11%	13%	5%	10%	7%

[a] To be read: 53% of coupons for household products were distributed in Sunday free-standing inserts.

Source: Manufacturers Coupon Control Center, *The Scanner,* Volume 2, Issue 1, 1987, Chart 1.

OBJECTIVES SERVED BY COUPONING

In this section, we review the managerial objectives served by couponing and discuss the evidence in support of each objective. Table 10.4 displays these objectives, organized under four main headings: Direct Sales Impact, Retail Trade Related, Integrate with Advertising and Other Promotions, and Use as a Strategic Tool.

Direct Sales Impact

Attract New Triers.   A new trier may be defined as a consumer trying a new product for the first time, or a consumer who has not tried an existing brand for several purchase occasions but now purchases the brand. In both cases, it is reasonable to expect that the availability of a coupon would enhance the consumer's probability of making an initial purchase.

The concept of perceived risk is especially relevant to the objective of attracting new triers (see Chapter 2, "Perceived Risk"). Despite an effective advertising communication of clear product benefits, consumers face uncertainty with respect to whether the product will actually achieve these benefits, compared to the certainty with which they know the benefits of their current brand. A coupon essentially compensates the consumer for the risk of trying a potentially faulty brand.

Couponing competes with sampling as a trial vehicle, although many companies use both vehicles in an all-out effort to gain trial. Both vehicles have their separate merits. By requiring the consumer to make some effort and actually spend money to try the product, couponing can avoid some of the negative attributions

TABLE 10.4 Couponing Objectives

Direct Sales Impact	Retail Trade Related	Integrate with Advertising and Other Promotions	Use as a Strategic Tool
Attract new triers	Gain in-store promotional support	Reinforce or enhance print media advertising	Preempt the competition
Attract brand switchers	Increase distribution	"Synergize" with other marketing instruments	Price discriminate
Increase category consumption	Motivate the sales force		Cushion a price increase
Maintain or enhance repeat purchase rates	More directly control retail price		Reach the appropriate target group
Defend market share			Gain trial for another product

consumers might make if they try a product for free (e.g., "The only reason I tried this product was because I got it for free, so I must not really like it"; see Chapter 2, "Attribution Theory"). Couponing also allows formation of a clear reference "regular" price in the consumer's mind (see Chapter 2, "Theories of Price Perception"), whereas sampling does not communicate price. Sampling, however, may be required if the perceived risk is high or if the target group is not prone to use coupons.

There is fairly good empirical support for couponing as a trial vehicle. In an econometric analysis, Nakanishi (1973) found that provision of a direct-mail coupon was more highly associated with product trial than either network or spot television. As part of a coupon proneness study, Teel et al. (1980) found that 18 percent of consumers felt that coupons usually influence their decision to try a new product, 52 percent said they occasionally do, and 30 percent said they never do. Rosen (1985), drawing on a national sample of consumers, found that heavy coupon users are more likely to agree that they "like to buy new and different things." Neslin and Clarke (1987) found in questioning consumers about the brands for which they had used a coupon that 14 percent of uses were for a first trial and 34.1 percent of coupon uses were for a brand bought rarely or occasionally. In summary, coupons appear to be an effective vehicle for stimulating consumer trial.

Attract Brand Switchers. There are many reasons to suspect that coupons are powerful switching devices. From an attitude model or utility theoretic viewpoint, they offer a powerful economic incentive that overcomes attitudinal or budget barriers to purchase (see Chapter 2, "Attitude Models"). In addition, coupons provide important psychological mechanisms for inducing a switch. First is the "smart-shopper" phenomenon: The coupon redeemer has a feeling of exclusivity and control that provides psychological as well as economic benefit to using a coupon for a brand that would otherwise not be bought (see Chapter 2, "Application 2," in "Attitude Models," and "The Redemption Decision" of this chapter). Second, the coupon provides a clear, undebatable communication of price reduction: The consumer can see that he or she is getting 50 cents off the regular price clearly marked on the package. This is much more believable than a "price marked is 50 cents off regular price" price-pack message or the "special sale price" communication that accompanies in-store price discounts.

There is ample empirical support for the hypothesis that coupons induce brand switching. Much of this research will be reviewed in "The Effect of Coupons upon Brand Sales." It includes econometric analyses (Neslin, 1989), time series analyses (Hee, 1981), field experiments (Bawa and Shoemaker, 1987b; Klein, 1985), redeemer profiles (Neslin and Clarke, 1987), laboratory experiments (Schindler, 1984a, b), and simple brand-switching statistics (Johnson, 1984).

For example, in Chapter 5, we provided panel data statistics for the regular caffeinated coffee category that showed that 56.1 percent of purchases involving a coupon were of a different brand from that bought last time. This compared to a 32.1 percent chance of buying a different brand if no promotion was used. The respective statistics for the instant caffeinated category were 47.1 percent and 32.2 percent. Johnson (1984) compiled similar statistics for 14 packaged goods brands. He reported that in 7 cases, purchases with a coupon were more likely to be associated with purchasing a different brand from the purchases involving a consumer-reported "store special." In 5 cases, there was no difference in association with purchasing a different brand, and in 2 cases, the association was stronger for store specials.

Increase Category Consumption. For certain discretionary purchase categories, coupons could increase actual usage by attracting new category users or encouraging current category users to consume more. A coupon might stimulate problem recognition, or simply might increase consumers' top-of-mind awareness of the category (see Chapter 2, "The Consumer Decision Process"). However, it is difficult to see how coupons could be a more effective category usage device than other promotions. In fact, the consumer's need to plan use of coupons (clip, save, and bring to the store) may impede impulse buying that can be more readily stimulated by an in-store display or special sale.

Some empirical support for coupons as a stimulant to category usage comes from Ward and Davis (1978a). In an econometric analysis of orange juice sales, they found a strong association between coupon redemptions and total category sales of orange juice. There was some evidence that the coupon worked by stimulating top-of-mind awareness of the category.

Maintain or Enhance Repeat Purchase Rates. A longer-term objective of couponing is to maintain repeat purchase rates of frequent brand users or enhance those for new triers or infrequent users. One tactic for enhancing repeat purchase rates would be to use an FSI coupon to attract new customers and then an on-package coupon to help establish the new habit of buying the brand. A second strategy is based on the supposition that the simple act of buying the brand once encourages consumers to repurchase, because the consumer learns about the brand or begins to form a habit. Therefore, employing a coupon to induce a switch will by itself result in more subsequent purchases. This is the "purchase effect" described in Chapter 5. A third motivation for using coupons to maintain or enhance repeat purchase rates is that coupons serve as rewards, and rewarded behavior will be sustained in the long term. This is the "promotion usage effect" described in Chapter 5.

There are several theories that support the use of couponing to maintain or enhance repeat rates. One theory that supports a positive role for coupons in establishing repeat rates is the operant conditioning framework, which emphasizes coupons as reinforcement. Coupons can also potentially serve as rewards for shaping and reinforcing the formation of a new purchase habit. Theories that emphasize the importance of habit, such as the Hullian model and low-involvement decision making, also support a positive role for coupons in the establishment of increased repeat purchase rates. The potential peril in using coupons stems from the attribution literature, which suggests the possibility that consumers will attribute their purchase to the availability of the coupon rather than to the intrinsic merits of the brand. (See Chapter 2 for more detailed discussions of these theories.)

The empirical evidence on couponing's effect on repeat purchase rates is not definitive. In Chapter 2 and Chapter 5, we reviewed laboratory experiments and panel data analyses supporting all three possibilities: negative effect, positive effect, and no effect. As discussed in Chapter 2, one key issue is whether the type of coupon used, the context of the purchase occasion, and the consumer's a priori knowledge of the brand will be conducive to the consumer attributing the cause of the coupon purchase exclusively to the coupon or to internally motivated causes. To the extent that the coupon purchase is attributed to internal motivations, the coupon can serve as a reward and enhance attitudes toward the brand. For example, the work of Tybout and Scott (1983) suggests that if a consumer has well-defined knowledge of the brand before using the coupon, the coupon is likely to serve as a reward. This suggests that coupons can maintain or enhance the loyalty of frequent users or consumers who through word-of-mouth or advertising are well informed about the brand. However, it may be dangerous to use coupons for example in the early periods of a new product introduction.

Defend Market Share.   For existing brands, the concern is often with maintaining a given market share. At the consumer level, coupons can help achieve this goal in three ways: first, by serving as a reward to loyal consumers; second, by preempting a competitive promotion from luring away a loyal user; and third, by assuring that the brand will attract its share of brandswitchers. From an economic point of view, using coupons to defend market share can be represented by the prisoner's dilemma (see Chapters 4 and 15). The strategic problem faced by the manufacturer is that its market share is vulnerable to the couponing activities of its competition. However, this view is shared by both manufacturers, so both end up using coupons and succeed in protecting their market share, but have eroded their profits by incurring the costs of couponing.

Neslin (1989) examined the competitive effects of couponing, and his empirical results support the notion that competitive coupons steal market share unless matched by the brand's own coupon (see more discussion of this analysis in this chapter, "Econometric Studies"). However, his results suggest that the situation is less accurately described by the prisoner's dilemma. He finds that there are winners and losers in the promotions wars. Winners are defined as brands whose market share in a coupon-competitive environment is larger than their estimated "baseline" market share that would be achieved if no manufacturers used coupons. Note, however, that from the standpoint of profitability, all brands may be losers.

Retail Trade Related

Gain In-Store Promotional Support. One potential strategy for inducing a retailer to promote a brand is to provide evidence that the brand will shortly be promoted directly to the consumer via a coupon. This "news," it is hoped, has the effect of showing the retailer how serious the manufacturer is about wanting to sell the brand, and suggests that by promoting the brand in-store, a mutually beneficial synergy can occur between the coupon and the in-store promotions, resulting in a quick turnover of retailer inventory.

Curhan and Kopp (1986) recently conducted a thorough study of factors that influence retailer support of trade deals. They identified eight fundamental factors, one of which was called "accompanying manufacturer support." This factor included not only couponing, but advertising and sampling as well. In comparison with other factors, accompanying manufacturing support was only weakly associated with the overall attractiveness of a trade deal to a retail buyer and actually had a directionally negative influence on trade performance (the degree to which the retailer actually promoted the brand).

While Curhan and Kopp offer methodological caveats for their results (Curhan and Kopp, 1986, p. 22), there are compelling reasons to believe them. As noted by Quelch (1982), retailers are becoming more and more sophisticated in planning their merchandising. Using scanner data, they can calculate the benefits of their own promotions more readily than those of a manufacturer coupon, where the impact may be less immediate. The retailer may also believe that couponing by itself will generate sales, so their simultaneous promoting of the brand would be unnecessary and in fact inefficient.

Another pragmatic reason why couponing might be unpopular among retailers is that many retailers offer double or even triple coupon savings to consumers redeeming at their store. For example, a consumer redeeming a 35 cent coupon would receive a 70 cent discount on the item. In fact, retailers may be in their own prisoner's dilemma with respect to this strategy, as all stores in the service area undertake this policy (Bhasin and Dickinson, 1987, p. 295). In this retailing environment, the last thing retailers want is a splashy new coupon distributed in their area. Some retailers have limited the maximum amount by which they will increase the value of a coupon. For example, they will double the face value of a coupon, up to $1.00.

Increase Distribution.   Another retail-related objective for using coupons is to gain distribution or shelf-facings for the brand. The strategy would pertain particularly to new products, but would be viable for existing products as well. The managerial argument here is that by distributing a coupon, the manufacturer will generate unusually high demand for the brand. In this case, an out-of-stock is just as detrimental to the retailer as it is to the manufacturer.

The argument becomes more compelling if the manufacturer can establish that a disgruntled customer will go to another store. In fact, a survey (Nielsen Clearing House, 1985) revealed that 25 percent of consumers stated that they would try to find the couponed brand at another store if the couponed brand were out of stock. The retailer would lose that sale plus an additional amount of sales that the consumer would undoubtedly make when going to the other store.

Motivate the Sales Force.   Couponing is sometimes used as a "news item" for motivating the sales force. A coupon signals the sales force that management really wants to sell the brand and gives the sales representative something to talk about during a sales call. There is little published evidence to substantiate the role of couponing in helping to motivate the sales force, although brand managers often mention it as an important factor. Especially if the decision is to decrease couponing efforts, the signal of less support for the brand may cause a sales representative to shift efforts toward other brands.

If Curhan and Kopp's findings are correct, coupons should become less of a motivator to the sales force. Reflecting the retailer's considerations, sales representatives should become excited only about steep price discounts on major items.

More Directly Control Retail Price.   Direct manufacturer control of absolute price in a retail establishment is forbidden under the Sherman Act, and manufacturers are constantly frustrated in their efforts to push through the type of price discounts they feel will increase sales. Manufacturers may stipulate trade performance requirements involving a price reduction from a "regular" price, but this is difficult to monitor. Without the requirements, retailers will do anything ranging from no passed-along price decrease to a full passed-along decrease. Price-packs are another alternative for controlling a price discount, but these have added administrative cost, and some retail outlets will not accept price packs. Coupons provide manufacturers with a means to bypass the retailer and deliver the price decrease they desire.

Integrate with Advertising and Other Promotions

Reinforce or Enhance Print Media Advertising. A potentially important role for couponing is in enhancing the value of a particular advertising message. This can occur either by bringing attention to the advertisement or by making the advertising message more believable.

As noted in the earlier-cited Starch study, coupons are readily noticed. It therefore is logical that the accompanying advertisement may also be more likely to be noticed. In fact, further evidence cited by Bowman (1980) indicates that print advertisements containing coupons are more likely to be noticed and recalled than are the same ads not containing coupons.

One obvious concern, however, is that a coupon lowers the overall image of the product (see discussion of object-perception theory in Chapter 2). The notion of "distraction," however, provides an explanation of how a coupon might increase the persuasiveness of an advertisement. Under this theory (Festinger and Maccoby, 1964) a normal human response is to argue against the message advanced in any persuasive communication. This counterarguing "cognitive response" lessens the persuasiveness of the communication (Wright, 1973). The distraction hypothesis is that some part of the communication not directly related to its message, for example, a coupon, may distract the consumer from undertaking these counterarguments and therefore results in a more persuasive advertisement. Consider Figure 10.2, an example of a simple advertising message used to introduce a new coffee brand. The communication makes a claim that the new coffee is superior tasting. If the distraction effect is at work, rather than counterarguing, "But it's still an instant coffee, it probably tastes lousy," the consumer is quickly enticed by the $1.00 coupon to at least try the brand. Since the taste claim was not counterargued, it perhaps has a better chance of being accepted.

Petty et al. (1976) found in a laboratory experiment that distraction could either enhance or detract from the persuasiveness of a communication, depending on the nature of the message. If the message was implausible and readily counterarguable, then distraction enhanced persuasiveness. If the message was plausible and difficult to counterargue, distraction *decreased* persuasiveness. Applying these findings to couponing, coupons may have a place in distracting counterarguments to common claims such as "new improved," although would be less effective in the situation that there was powerful news to communicate.

Other empirical evidence is somewhat equivocal with respect to the role of coupons in enhancing advertising effectiveness. Hopkins and Parsons (1984) found that a direct-mail advertisement accompanied by a coupon favorably changed consumer attitudes toward the test brand. However, the coupon-plus-advertisement treatment was not compared to an advertising-alone treatment. Perhaps the advertisement was effective despite the deleterious effects of the coupon. Bearden, et al. (1984) conducted an experiment in which they examined the effect of coupons on price perceptions, overall purchase attitude, and behavioral intention. Drawing on attribution theory, the authors hypothesized that couponing would

FIGURE 10.2 Possible Synergy Between an Advertisement and a Coupon

Courtesy of Taster's Choice, Nestle Foods, Inc., Purchase, NY.

have a deleterious effect on those variables. In the authors' words, "No definitive support was found for the coupon hypothesis" (p. 31).

"Synergize" with Other Marketing Instruments. One motivation for this coupon objective is the phenomenon of clutter. The consumer is bombarded daily by thousands of advertising messages, premiums, sweepstakes, and coupons. One philosophy is that the only way to break through this clutter is to do everything at once. That is, the consumer has to see the brand advertised on television, see the brand coupon as he or she is reading the newspaper, and then go to the store and be reminded by a huge display. Couponing then becomes part of a big marketing event.

A theoretical justification for this strategy lies in the "just-noticeable-difference" phenomenon embodied in Weber's law. In this instance, a significantly large marketing effort is needed to be noticeable above the ambient marketing "noise." However, no theory encompasses by itself how consumers will react to several simultaneously appearing yet different motivators to buy the brand. In fact, one danger of the increased level of marketing activity is that in defense, consumers will resort to low-involvement decision making or judgment heuristics.

While the "big-bang" theory is popular with many managers, the published empirical evidence is less persuasive. Eskin and Baron (1977) found that when a market received heavy coverage of a free sample accompanied by a coupon, advertising was less effective than it would have been otherwise. Neslin (1989) found that feature advertising did not increase coupon redemptions, yet had a minor cannibalization effect in diluting the incremental sales impact of a coupon.

Use as a Strategic Tool

Preempt the Competition. Competitors often launch new products by employing a huge advertising and promotion blitz. One way an incumbent brand can insulate its own loyal customers from this massive effort is to "load up" the consumer on the brand, thus taking the consumer out of the market during the competitor's new product launch. Coupons can be used in this role. For such a strategy to work, one or more of a number of conditions should exist: Interpurchase time should be long, the product should be inventoryable, the brand's loyal customers should be prone toward using coupons, and the exact timing of the competitive activity should be known. A good example might be in the colds medicine market. The interpurchase time is certainly fairly long, and the product is small and hence inventoryable. Aside from using competitive intelligence, a manufacturer can safely conjecture that the new cold medicine would be launched during the peak colds months and could time its coupon drop to precede this time.

There is ample theoretical justification for the use of promotions as "loading up" devices. Most of this comes from the economics literature (Blattberg et al., 1981) and is based on the economic trade-offs to the consumer between price reduction and household inventory carrying cost. Empirical evidence suggests that coupons are much more effective at increasing purchase quantity than changing purchase timing (Neslin et al., 1985; Grover and Rao 1985). If in a particular instance, purchase timing does not need to be altered and the potential increase in quantity will result in a long enough delay until repurchase, then using coupons to preempt a competitive action is supported by this research.

Price Discriminate. Price discrimination is a pricing structure where different segments of consumers are charged different prices for the same item. As discussed in Chapter 4, if distinct segments exist with different price elasticities, price discrimination may be more profitable than charging one price. The problem in implementing price discrimination is that it is normally not possible to charge different consumers different prices within the same market area.

Coupons potentially provide a mechanism for selectively delivering a price discount. Under this mechanism, the coupon redeemer self-selects to use the coupon, so that the manufacturer does not have to literally decide which consumers can receive a discount. Narasimhan (1984a) showed that consumers who have lower opportunity costs of time will be more price sensitive and will be more likely to redeem coupons. He also showed some empirical evidence that coupon users were more price sensitive than noncoupon users. (See Chapter 4, "Price Discrimination," for more detailed discussion; see Houston and Howe (1985) for a theoretical analysis of couponing as a price discrimination device under monopolistic competition.)

Cushion a Price Increase. The distribution of coupons provides a plausible strategy for softening the negative effect of a price increase. If carefully implemented, there is ample theoretical justification for this strategy. The new price may be much higher than the current reference price the consumer uses to judge an available price (see Chapter 2, "Theories of Price Perception"). By providing a coupon that places the brand's net price between the current reference price and the new price, the consumer begins to adapt to a new, higher reference price. Once the coupon is no longer available, the new price does not seem so high relative to the newly formed reference price. For example, assume a brand costs $1.50 and its price is raised to $2.00. A 25 cent coupon makes the effective price $1.75. After the coupon is no longer available, $2.00 does not seem to be as severe a price increase as it once was.

As Sawyer and Dickson (1984) point out, however, many things can go wrong with this strategy. For example, if the price is raised from $1.50 to $1.60, and a 25 cent coupon is provided, consumers may adapt to a new price level of $1.35, making the new price even more unacceptable. The timing of the coupon also must be exactly right. One lost purchase occasion, in which the heretofore loyal consumer switches to another brand because of the new price, may result in the long-term loss of that consumer. Instantly redeemable on-package coupons might be the answer, although even they must be timed effectively and may provide a price discount to too broad an audience.

There are a series of papers, positioned in the coupons and price discrimination literature, that empirically investigate the relationship between prices and use of coupons. Levedahl (1984, 1986) found that when no coupon was used, shelf price was lower than when a coupon was used. Vilcassim and Wittink (1987) examined several brand sizes of coffee and found a positive relationship between shelf price and percentage of sales made with a coupon, even after controlling for package size, use of other promotions, and store versus national label brands.

These studies provide intriguing evidence on the relationship between retail prices and couponing. There are some methodological issues, however, which should be noted. In the Levedahl studies, consumers might not seek out low prices when using a coupon. This could happen, for example, if consumers have a finite amount of time they are willing to allocate to shopping. Coupon redeemers might find that they can get bigger discounts by using coupons, and after investing their time in searching for coupons, they do not wish to devote additional time to searching for still further price reductions. In the Vilcassim and Wittink study, differences in product quality or advertising could be a factor. Higher quality or more heavily advertised brands would tend to have larger market shares, and market share is positively correlated with redemption rates. Meanwhile, higher quality or more highly advertised brands might command higher prices, so there would be a positive correlation between price and number of coupons redeemed. Having noted these caveats, however, the Levedahl and Vilcassim and Wittink studies provide important evidence on the use of coupons to cushion price increases.

Reach the Appropriate Target Group. Coupons can be used to deliver a price decrease to a selected target group. For example, manufacturers can insert coupons in magazines more likely to be read by a competitor's loyal users. Direct-mail coupons can be directed at special geographic targets, or with the aid of a screening questionnaire such as that employed by Donnelly, mailed directly to a competitor's loyal users (Alsop, 1985; Stern, 1985). With the increasing sophistication of the direct marketing industry, selective targeting of coupons is likely to become a more viable objective for couponing.

The potential efficiency of using coupons to deliver a price decrease to the appropriate target group is compelling. However, there is little empirical evidence as to whether the high cost of delivering this selected price decrease is outweighed by the benefit. Note, for example, that in the case of delivering the coupon to the competition's loyal users, the coupon might achieve a lower redemption rate, but the incremental sales per redemption would be higher. The net result on profit could be calculated using the methods illustrated in the upcoming "Coupon Profitability" section.

Gain Trial for Another Product. Managers often utilize the strategy of "cross-ruffing." For example, packages for a flagship brand might contain coupons for a new or less popular brand. There are several reasons to justify this practice: First, it is an inexpensive method for distributing coupons. Second, by identifying the new brand with the flagship brand, a favorable transfer of attitude may result. Third, if the new brand is related to the flagship brand, or the target group for

TABLE 10.5 Quality of Evidence in Support of Various Coupon Objectives

Managerial Objective	Conceptual/Theoretical Support	Empirical Support
Direct sales impact		
Attract new triers	Strong	Strong
Attract brand switchers	Strong	Strong
Increase category consumption	Strong	Moderate
Maintain or enhance repeat purchase rates.	Mixed	Mixed
Defend market share	Strong	Moderate
Retail trade impact		
Gain in-store promotional support	Strong	Weak
Increase distribution	Strong	Little research
Motivate the sales force	Strong	Little research
More directly control price	Strong	Strong
Integrate with advertising and other promotions		
Reinforce or enhance print media advertising	Mixed	Weak
Synergize with other marketing instruments	Moderate	Weak
Use as a strategic tool		
Preempt the competition	Strong	Moderate
Price discriminate	Strong	Moderate
Cushion a price increase	Mixed	Moderate
Reach the appropriate target group	Strong	Little research
Gain trial for another product	Strong	Little research

the new brand is similar to that for the flagship brand, then the coupon is being effectively targeted. Cross-ruff couponing is inexpensive and has little downside risk, but it is not clear that the benefits are large. Redemption rates for cross-ruff coupons are usually very low, and package space might be more effectively used for other purposes. Again, very little has been studied about the benefits of cross-ruff couponing.

Summary

Table 10.5 provides a summary of the quality of conceptual and empirical evidence in support of various couponing objectives. The table suggests that the conceptual side is more developed than the empirical side. For certain objectives, however, the conceptual support is "mixed," meaning there are arguments for and against the objective. A primary example of this is the objective of maintaining or enhancing repeat purchase rates.

Considering both conceptual and empirical support, the best established roles for couponing are for attracting new triers and brand switchers. There is a particular need to sort out the effects of coupons on repeat purchase rates. The various objectives relating to retail trade impact, integration with advertising and other promotions, and use of coupons as a strategic tool also need empirical investigation.

COUPON PROFITABILITY

Calculating Profit

Table 10.6 presents an example of calculating profit for a particular coupon drop. The calculation measures whether the incremental profits contributed by the coupon outweigh its incremental cost. In the example in Table 10.6, the costs outweight the benefits, and the coupon results in a loss of $344,520. There are two major components of cost: distribution and redemption. Distribution costs entail the costs of making the coupon available to consumers. For example, free-standing inserts are assembled and distributed by private companies that charge manufacturers a fee for including a coupon for their brand. Similarly, newspaper and magazine coupons entail the cost of buying space in the appropriate publications. Distribution costs are usually stated on a "per 1,000" basis. Redemption costs largely consist of the amount of money, represented by the face value of the coupon, that the manufacturer must return to each consumer who redeems the coupon. The actual reimbursement is usually done by the retailer at the point of purchase (e.g., a consumer purchasing a $1.00 item with a 25 cent coupon only pays the retailer 75 cents). The manufacturer then pays the retailer a "handling fee," for example, 7 cents per redeemed coupon, for this service. Sometimes a third-party "clearinghouse" collects redeemed coupons from retailers, counts them, and bills the manufacturer. When a clearinghouse is used, sometimes an additional 2–3 cents cost per coupon is incurred as payment to the clearinghouse.

In the example in Table 10.6, the coupon drop entails the distribution of 30 million 40 cent coupons. The cost to distribute these coupons is $10 per thousand, or $300,000. Assuming a 7 percent redemption rate, redemption costs total $897,000, representing 80 percent of total costs. Note that for each redemption, the manufacturer is liable for the 40 cent face value plus 10 cents processing fee for the retailer and clearinghouse.

The incremental profit side of the ledger depends directly on the incremental sales generated by coupon redemptions. Note, first, that we include a factor re-

TABLE 10.6 Calculating Coupon Profitability

Incremental costs	
Distribution: 30,000,000 × $10 per thousand	$ 300,000
Redemption: 30,000,000 × 7% redemption	
× (40 cents face value + 10 cents processing)	1,050,000
	$1,350,000
Incremental profit contribution:	
2,100,000 redemptions (×.95 legitimate)	
× .6 incremental sales per legitimate redemption	
× $2.80 wholesale price × 30% margin	1,005,480
Net incremental profit	$(344,520)

flecting the possibility that not all redeemed coupons correspond to actual sales of the product. This is the problem of misredemption. Coupons might be inadvertently redeemed for a wrong brand, or deliberately submitted by a fraudulent retailer to receive the face value and processing fee. We will discuss this issue in the upcoming section "The Problem of Misrepresentation." On the cost side, the manufacturer must pay for all redemptions, but on the incremental profits side, only legitimate redemptions can be a source of incremental sales.

Another important quantity here is "incremental sales per legitimate redemption," which in Table 10.6 is assumed to be .6. In general, this quantity can be anything greater than zero. Values greater than one are certainly possible. This could occur for example if redeeming the coupon had an effect on repeat purchase probabilities. It could also occur if the coupon enhanced the effectiveness of advertising. If we think of the effects of couponing, however, to be largely constrained to the immediate purchase, incremental sales per legitimate redemption will range between 0 and 1. Unfortunately, of all the quantities required to calculate coupon profitability, incremental sales per redemption is the least well studied.

In the example shown in Table 10.6, the 30 percent profit margin means that each incremental sale contributes 84 cents to profit (.30 times \$2.80 wholesale price). This profit margin is net of costs of goods sold, but also may be net of some allocation of overhead or other marketing costs, depending on the accounting practice of the company.

We can gain more insight into the profit calculation shown in Table 10.6 by formally expressing the calculation. First, let

C = distribution cost per coupon

D = number of coupons distributed

F = face value of coupon

P = processing cost per redeemed coupon

R = redemption rate (fraction of distributed coupons redeemed)

L = fraction of redemptions that are legitimate, that is, not misredemptions

M = profit contribution per unit sold (wholesale price times fraction contribution margin)

I = fraction of redemption sales that are incremental

Then, by definition, we have

total incremental costs = distribution costs + redemption costs

$$= (C \cdot D) + (D \cdot R \cdot (F + P))$$

total incremental profit = number of incremental sales × profit margin

$$= D \cdot R \cdot L \cdot I \cdot M$$

net incremental profit $= (D \cdot R \cdot L \cdot I \cdot M) - (C \cdot D) - (D \cdot R \cdot (F + P))$ **(10.1)**

Equation (10.1) represents the net incremental profit contributed to the manufacturer, after accounting for the incremental costs involved with running the coupon program. From equation (10.1), we can solve for I^*, the incremental sales per coupon necessary for the promotion to break even, by setting the equation equal to zero. This yields

$$\text{required incremental sales to break even} = \frac{C}{R \cdot L \cdot M} + \frac{F + P}{L \cdot M} = I^* \qquad \textbf{(10.2)}$$

The first term in equation (10.2) reflects the need to make up coupon distribution costs, while the second represents the need to make up redemption costs. The required I^* increases as these costs increase and decreases as margin, redemption rate, and the legitimate redemption percentage increase. In the example shown in Table 10.6, we would have

$$I^* = \frac{.01}{.07 \cdot .95 \cdot .84} + \frac{.40 + .10}{.95 \cdot .84} = .179 + .627 = .806$$

In this case, we see that the second term, representing redemptions costs, drives up our required incremental sales per redemption. One way to control that cost would be to decrease face value, but if we did this, we would get a lower redemption rate and the first term in the I^* equation would become dominant. For example, if face value were lowered to 30 cents, the redemption cost term would only equal .501, but if this reduced redemption rate to 4 percent, the distribution cost term would equal .313, and I^* would equal .815. We see that lowering face value decreases redemption costs, but makes it less likely that we will cover the distribution costs.

While this example illustrates some of the trade-offs entailed with changing coupon face value, it also suggests that it might be possible to find an optimal face value. This would require explicit functional relationships for redemption rate (R) and incremental sales per redemption (I) as a function of face value. That redemption rate is a function of face value is pretty well established in the literature, although the particular function varies across brands and product categories (see the "Coupon Redemption" section). Less research has been conducted on the relationship between incremental sales and face value, although there is some work on this issue (Irons et al., 1983; Shoemaker and Tibrewala, 1985; Bawa and Shoemaker, 1987b). Once the relationships between R and F and between I and F were specified, they could be substituted into equation (10.1) and the optimal face value calculated. The resulting profit equation could also be used in a decision calculus investigation of coupon design decisions (e.g., Neslin and Shoemaker, 1983a).

There are two other potential extensions of the foregoing analysis. One would be to adjust profit margins upward if coupon distribution were accompanied by a price increase (Vilcassim and Wittink, 1987). Another would be to incorporate explicitly a separate parameter for incremental sales beyond the redemption purchase occasion, as opposed to subsuming both current and repeat purchase sales within the parameter I (see Levedahl, 1986).

Managing the Costs of Couponing

Due to the difficulty in measuring incremental sales, managers often find themselves concentrating on managing costs. Criteria such as cost per redemption replace profit as a means for evaluating a coupon promotion. Table 10.7 illustrates the calculation of this criterion, based on a 35 cent coupon distributed through a number of alternative vehicles. The table reveals that cost per redemption can range from 66 cents to $1.36. Face value is therefore usually no more than 50 percent of the cost per redeemed coupon. The distribution costs of the entire coupon drop must be allocated to a relatively small number of redeemed coupons and, as a result, face value is a major but not dominant cost. While the arithmetic of this is straightforward, the managerial psychology may not be. Managers must realize that in distributing a 35 cent coupon, they are really investing at least double that for each coupon redeemer. One needs a large number of incremental redemptions to recover that investment.

Since the arithmetic of Table 10.7 is so straightforward, the results so concrete, and the data so available, managers may find it tempting to ignore the revenue side of coupon profitability. Indeed, if all coupon vehicles yielded the same incremental sales per redemption, then the issue of cost efficiency would be paramount. However, there are reasons to believe that different vehicles will yield different incremental sales.

First, the various vehicles reach different target groups, and different target groups will yield different incremental sales (see Neslin and Clarke, 1987, for evidence). Second, some vehicles are easier to target than others. For example, magazine on-page coupons may be most expensive on a cost per redemption basis, but using readership data cross-tabulated by product usage (available, for example, from M. R. Simmons, Inc., see Lehmann, 1985, pp. 263–265), the coupon can be targeted directly toward nonusers of the brand. This differs from the undifferentiated reach of many free-standing inserts.

Third, there are reasons to believe that even if two coupon vehicles are targeted toward the same population, they will yield different incremental sales (Matosian, 1982; also see "Experiments Involving Coupons" in this chapter). For example, one might hypothesize that free-standing inserts would yield lower incremental sales than direct mail (see Neslin and Shoemaker, 1983a). The logic here is that FSI coupons require more consumer effort, and only a brand's loyal customers will be willing to make that effort.

In summary, coupons are often managed from the cost side rather than the revenue side. Cost data are more available and easier to understand. However, different incremental sales per redemption ratios can offset an apparent cost-efficiency advantage of one coupon vehicle over another.

The Problem of Misredemption

Our discussion has shown how misredemption can decrease the profitability of a coupon promotion. When a "redeemed" coupon does not correspond to an actual sale, the manufacturer loses the face value of the coupon plus the processing

TABLE 10.7 Calculating Costs per Redemption: Illustrations for Various Coupon Vehicles

Vehicle	(A) Number Distributed	(B) Cost per Thousand	(C) Face Value	(D) Processing Fee	(E) Redemption Rate	(F) Total Redemptions[a]	(G) Total Cost[b]	(H) Cost per Redemption[c]
Free-standing insert	50,324,000	$7.06	$.35	$.11	3.6%	1,811,664	$1,188,653	$.656
Newspaper ROP, Solo	35,018,000	12.92	.35	.11	2.1	735,378	790,706	1.08
Sunday supplement	20,586,000	10.80	.35	.11	1.2	247,032	335,964	1.36
Magazine on-page	38,013,000	13.96	.35	.11	1.8	684,234	845,409	1.24
Direct mail	45,000,000	16.47	.35	.11	5.8	2,610,000	1,941,750	.744

[a] F = A × E
[b] G = (C + D) × F + (A/1000) × B
[c] H = G/F

Note: Calculations do not include misredemption. See Table 10.6 for including misredemption in a profit calculation.

Source: Adapted from D'Arcy Masius Benton and Bowles, "Couponing as a Marketing Tool: A Special Report," December, 1988 Edition.

fee, so the costs of misredemption can be quite high. Much of the published evidence regarding misredemption is in the form of anecdotes rather than formal research studies. However, there is enough evidence for us to define clearly the nature of the problem, estimate its extent, and discuss ways of minimizing the problem.

The form of misredemption commonly alleged to account for the most misredemptions is referred to as "gang clipping." Gang clipping involves an organized effort to clip hundreds of coupons and then submit them for reimbursement to either a clearing house or the manufacturer. The "gang" may be the retailer, literally, the store manager or owner, or might be a criminal who works with an accomplice who has access to the lines of coupon communication between a store's central chain office and a coupon clearinghouse. Gang clipping often involves the use of a paper cutter to cut out hundreds of coupons from stacks of newspapers or magazines. When this is done, the redeemed coupons are often in suspiciously mint condition, but fraudulent redeemers have been known to deliberately crinkle or wash their gang-cut coupons before submitting them.

A dramatic example of misredemption occurred in 1977, when manufacturers, the New York district attorney, and the U.S. Post Office collaborated to distribute a newspaper ROP coupon for a nonexistent BREEN detergent. Although coupons were distributed only in local newspapers, (mis)redemptions were received from more than 2,300 retailers from almost all states (Bowman, 1980). There have been other examples of similar stakeouts: The results clearly indicate that the problem is real.

While organized, deliberate criminal efforts are behind a great deal of misredemption, misredemption can also have more humble origins. The consumer may mistakenly redeem a coupon for the wrong size, or even for the wrong brand. The cashier may honestly forget to check that the coupons the consumer submits correspond to actual products purchased. In order to speed up the checkout process, the cashier often asks customers to submit coupons after all the groceries have been tabulated. This makes it very difficult for the cashier to perform a detailed accounting of the correspondence between coupons used and items bought. It is also possible that consumers and cashiers participate in the deliberate misredemption of coupons. This problem is quite similar to shoplifting and pilferage. It undoubtedly occurs, but no one has quantified its prevalence.

Some of the discussion of misredemption can at times seem melodramatic, or even like an excuse managers make to alibi for the inefficient performance of marketing funds. However, the costs of misredemption can be significant. Returning to the example in Table 10.6, if 5 percent of redemptions are misredemptions, then the manufacturer is spending 2,100,000 redemptions × 5 percent × 50 cents equals $52,500 that is completely wasted. The wastage is equal to about 2.6 cents per legitimate coupon redemption, meaning that if misredemption could be eliminated, almost 3 cents could be added to coupon face value. Also, considering that many brands have four or five coupon drops per year, the lost money due to misredemptions can easily amount to hundreds of thousands of dollars.

Estimates of misredemption rate are not well documented and range anywhere from 1 to 25 percent (Bowman, 1980; Neslin and Shoemaker, 1983a; D'Arcy MacManus Masius, 1984). Clearly there is a need for more precise estimates of misredemption. Perhaps scanner-based panels provide a means for being of help. As part of compiling these databases, all the coupons redeemed by a given consumer are collected and later matched with electronic records of actual purchases. This could at least yield an estimate of the misredemption taking place at the point of purchase.

Unfortunately, many of the proposed solutions to the misredemption problem can be self-defeating. These include relax purchase quantity or size requirements, decrease face value, use long expiration dates, avoid high misredemption vehicles, and issue stern warnings to both retailers and consumers. All these steps can be counterproductive. Stern warnings can turn off retailers and consumers, ROP newspaper and free-standing inserts may have higher misredemption but generate a more immediate sales response than other vehicles, lower face values will reduce legitimate redemptions. Perhaps the best steps to take are selective prosecution of gang clippers and other law breakers (*Marketing News*, 1985), positively framed information campaigns for retailers and consumers emphasizing the benefits of couponing (Bowman, 1980), and retailer involvement with the training and management of cashiers. Until the problem is eliminated, the most practical solution is to allow for an anticipated misredemption level when planning coupon promotions (see Bowman, 1980, p. 92; Neslin and Shoemaker, 1983a).

COUPON REDEMPTION

The Redemption Decision

A number of theories have been advanced to explain how consumers reach a decision to use a coupon. These include attitude models (Shimp and Kavas, 1984), scripts (Gardener and Strang, 1984), the collection-intention-redemption process (Henderson, 1985), price benefit versus time cost trade-off (Narasimhan, 1984a), the "smart-shopper" phenomenon (Schindler, 1984a, b), and price benefit versus preferred brand substitution and effort cost trade-off (Bawa and Shoemaker, 1987a). The importance of these theories is that they have implications for the design of couponing programs. In this section we will review these theories and their implications.

The attitude model proposed by Shimp and Kavas follows the traditional belief-attitude-intention model advanced by Fishbein et al. (see Chapter 2, "Application 2" in "Attitude Models"). Shimp and Kavas found that both the consumer's own beliefs about using coupons as well as the consumer's beliefs regarding peer and spouse attitudes influenced the decision to use coupons. For example, beliefs that substantial financial savings could be gained by using coupons were highly associated with positive attitudes toward redeeming coupons.

In addition, so was the belief that one's spouse would approve of redeeming coupons. One important implication of these findings is that manufacturers wishing to increase redemption rates should emphasize the family approval in their coupon design. For example, a heading over the coupons in a free-standing insert might say, "Use these coupons for savings your family will appreciate."

A script simply is a time-saving routinized action scheme that enables a consumer to translate coupon availability into behavior (Gardner and Strang, 1984). One script, the "null," is simply to ignore all coupons. Another is to use coupons to formulate the shopping list. Another one would be to scan coupon FSI's and direct mailings, and then clip and use coupons for brands currently in household inventory. There is a mindless element to the use of scripts, and thus managers might initially think the phenomenon would be difficult to harness. However, depending on whether the predominant scripts used by the population are advantageous to the brand in question, the manager may be able to reinforce their usage. For example, Gardner and Strang suggest that "normal" format coupons might foster script usage, while innovative coupon schemes might thwart usage. The concept of scripts is potentially very useful. However, procedures for measuring and quantifying scripts are needed to make the concept more actionable.

Henderson (1985) proposed a pragmatic model of the coupon redemption decision, consisting of three steps: collection, intention to use, and actual usage. Collection involves clipping and saving the coupon. Intention is the consumer's deliberate intent to use a particular coupon. Actual usage takes place when the consumer brings the coupon to the store and redeems it. Henderson proposes that all three stages of the decision process can be influenced by the design of the coupon. For example, perforated coupons are easier to detach from a free-standing insert and hence are more collectable. A high face value makes it more likely the consumer will intend to use the coupon. A "coupon wallet," available in supermarkets or through mail-in offers in free-standing inserts, makes it more convenient actually to use coupons.

Schindler (1984a) proposed a coupon redemption model that showed the interplay between coupon usage and brand choice. He viewed the normal (coupon not available) choice process as one of processing price and processing the brand and its benefits, and then reconciling the two to make a choice. Coupons are hypothesized to influence the price-processing side, through three potential mechanisms: increasing the salience and hence awareness of the actual price being paid, providing reassurance of a price reduction, and providing the consumer with the internally rewarding feeling that he or she is in control of determining the final cost of the brand. This last mechanism, the "smart-shopper phenomenon," reflects a sense of pride on the part of the consumer at having "won" something. Schindler (1984a, b); Shimp and Kavas (1984); Chapter 2, "Application 2," and Babakus et al. (1988) find evidence to support the smart-shopper phenomenon.

Bawa and Shoemaker (1987a) provide a conceptual framework for computing the net benefits of using a coupon. The model can be applied to the general behavior of using coupons, or to the specific choice of using a coupon to buy a particular brand. We will first present the model as it applies to the more general use of coupons. The model is as follows:

net benefits = economic and psychic benefits − (substitution costs + effort costs)

Economic and psychic benefits refer to face value savings and to nonfinancial benefits such as the smart-shopper phenomenon. Substitution costs are the disutility the consumer incurs by possibly purchasing brands he or she would not otherwise have bought. The substitution cost would be zero for the most preferred brand. Effort costs are due to the consumer searching for coupons and handling them. In thinking about a particular household's total use of coupons, Bawa and Shoemaker assume that both benefits and costs will be monotonically increasing functions of the extent of coupon usage. Figure 10.3 illustrates this using particular relationships.

Figure 10.3 reveals an "optimal" level of coupon usage, determined by the specific shapes of the costs and benefits curves. Bawa and Shoemaker do not explicitly measure these curves, but the figure suggests that as a result of balancing benefits versus costs of using coupons, many consumers within a given category will not use coupons on either 0 percent or 100 percent of purchases, but rather at some level between those extremes (see Bawa and Shoemaker, 1987a, pp. 105–106).

The Bawa-Shoemaker model can also be applied to using a particular coupon

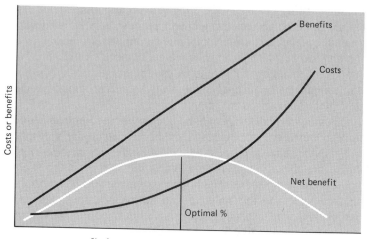

FIGURE 10.3 Consumer Costs and Benefits of Using Coupons for Category Purchases

Source: Kapil Bawa and Robert W. Shoemaker, "The Coupon-Prone Consumer: Some Findings Based on Purchase Behavior Across Product Classes," *Journal of Marketing*, 51 (October, 1987), p. 102. Adapted from the *Journal of Marketing*, published by the American Marketing Association.

to purchase a specific brand. One might be interested in relating consumer preference for this brand to likelihood of using the coupon. Financial benefits, psychological benefits, and effort costs will probably be independent of brand preference. A 30 cent face value is worth the same in economic terms no matter how much preference one has for the brand. The smart-shopper phenomenon refers to the general use of coupons, so feelings of pride in using a coupon to control price paid should be independent of brand preference. If the coupon is distributed in an untargeted manner, randomly with respect to brand preference (e.g., via an FSI), effort costs should also be independent of brand preference. Substitution costs, however, will be a decreasing function of preference for the brand. Balancing the costs and benefits as they relate to brand preference, we would predict that net benefits for using a coupon to buy a specific brand would increase as a function of brand preference. As a result, current users should be more likely to redeem a brand's coupon than nonusers. This conjecture is verified by Shoemaker and Tibrewala (1985) and Bawa and Shoemaker (1987b).

The Bawa and Shoemaker model suggests strategies to overcome the tendency for coupons to be redeemed by consumers already loyal to the brand. One idea would be to make effort costs higher for consumers with high preference for the brand. This could be done by targeting the coupon toward current nonusers. For example, the coupon could be distributed in a magazine that was known to have among its readers relatively few current users of the brand. The relatively recent appearance of services for targeting direct-mail coupons toward nonusers fits well with this strategy (see the earlier discussion in this chapter).

Narasimhan (1984a) proposes an economic model of coupon usage that is not as complete as Bawa and Shoemaker's, but relates coupon usage to price sensitivity so as to justify the use of coupons as a price discrimination device. Narasimhan views the decision to redeem a coupon as a trade-off between a potential price savings and the effort required to redeem a coupon. Narasimhan shows that under a certain set of assumptions (see Chapter 4), consumers with lower opportunity costs of time will be more price sensitive and will be more apt to redeem coupons. Narasimhan finds some empirical evidence to support his model. The important implication for management is that coupons provide a method for increasing profits through price discrimination (see "Price Discriminate" earlier in this chapter and Chapter 4).

In summary, a variety of theories have been offered to explain the coupon redemption process, and they all have implications for the design of couponing programs. Most of the theories need more empirical support to substantiate these implications.

Who Redeems Coupons?

Estimates are that between 71 and 88 percent of American households redeem coupons (Bowman, 1980, pp. 16–18; Nielsen Clearing House, 1985; Food Marketing Institute, 1987; Manufacturers Coupon Control Center, 1989b). In its nationwide survey of 1,007 shoppers, the Food Marketing Institute (1987) found that

37 percent of respondents said they used coupons "pretty much every time," 22 percent said "fairly often," 30 percent said "only occasionally," and only 12 percent said "never."

Coupon usage has an ambiguous association with income (see Chapter 3, Table 3.1). Some researchers find no relationship, some find a positive relationship, and some find that coupon usage peaks at middle income. In terms of other demographic variables, coupon proneness has a generally positive relationship with education and household size, a less consistent relationship with age, female employment outside the home, and presence of young children. Demographic groups' usage of couponing undoubtedly reflects coupon distribution patterns. The majority of coupons are distributed through magazines and newspapers, and circulation of these media is lower among lower-income groups as well as less educated groups. Given the more recent emphasis on free-standing inserts, Sunday newspaper subscription is undoubtedly an important variable influencing use of coupons (e.g., see Moody, 1987a). Other factors related to particular demographic group usage of coupons include brand preference (Levedahl, 1988) and institutional barriers such as store acceptance of coupons (Hernandez, 1988).

Researchers have been more successful in developing a psychographic portrait of the coupon-prone consumer. Summarizing from Table 3.1 of Chapter 3, the coupon-prone consumer consistently emerges as price conscious, venturesome (eager to try new products, opinion leaders), and highly involved with shopping (plans trips, enjoys shopping, etc.), and often is found not to be brand loyal. These findings are consistent with price discrimination theory, the smart-shopper phenomenon, and Bawa and Shoemaker's notion of lower substitution costs for consumers who are not brand loyal.

A final important consideration regarding who uses coupons is whether coupon usage is a general household trait or product class specific. The empirical evidence, gleaned primarily from Bawa and Shoemaker's work but also from Narasimhan's (1984b) analysis, is that household coupon usage across categories is certainly more consistent than random usage. However, the consistency is not perfect. Therefore, while there are some common demographic and psychographic traits among coupon users, manufacturers should conduct category-specific coupon proneness studies before they finalize their coupon targeting strategies.

Average Redemption Levels

Table 10.8 breaks down average redemption rates by vehicle and product class. The table shows that there is considerable variation both across vehicles and across product classes. In- and on-pack coupons for the brand in the package redeem highest, undoubtedly because the target group for such coupons is the brand's loyal users, and they have zero substitution costs. In-pack redeems higher than on-pack, because of lower effort costs. In fact, direct mail is the third highest redeemer, undoubtedly because of low effort required of the consumer. FSI's generally redeem higher than newspaper ROP, also because they are easier to find and also possibly because they more easily attract attention.

TABLE 10.8 Average Coupon Redemption Rates by Vehicle and Category, 1983 and 1985[a]

Vehicle	Grocery Products	Refrigerated Products	Other Packaged Foods	Frozen Foods	Beverages	Household Products	Health and Beauty Aids
Newspapers							
ROP solo	2.3/2.8	2.1/2.7	2.3/2.9	1.7/2.5	3.2/4.2	2.1/2.6	1.3/1.8
ROP co-op	2.4/3.0	2.2/2.8	2.5/3.1	1.9/3.0	3.0/3.4	2.2/2.7	1.7/2.1
FSI (daily)	4.0/3.9	4.1/3.7	4.1/4.0	3.0/3.2	4.5/5.0	3.6/3.7	2.2/2.6
FSI (Sunday)	4.2/4.3	4.0/4.8	4.3/4.4	3.3/3.6	4.7/5.4	3.9/4.0	2.6/2.8
Sunday supplement	2.0/2.4	2.0/2.5	2.0/2.5	1.9/1.9	1.8/2.2	2.1/1.9	1.0/1.1
Magazine							
On-page	2.0/2.4	1.8/2.4	2.0/2.4	1.4/1.8	2.3/2.6	1.5/1.9	.8/1.0
Pop-up	4.3/5.1	4.3/5.3	4.2/5.1	3.4/4.0	4.7/5.6	4.0/4.9	2.7/3.8
Direct mail	7.0/8.9	6.8/8.5	7.2/9.1	6.2/7.5	7.7/9.5	6.5/9.0	6.4/7.5
Package[b]							
In-pack	18.3	18.6	18.2	16.0	20.2	17.8	10.5
On-pack	12.2	12.7	12.3	11.0	14.9	11.3	12.3
Cross-ruff in	6.4	6.4	6.1	6.6	6.9	6.2	3.1
Cross-ruff on	4.1	4.3	3.9	4.8	4.5	3.7	3.0

[a] Left number is 1985, right number is 1983.

[b] Only 1983 data.

Source: Manufacturers Coupon Control Center, *The Scanner,* Volume 2, Issue 1, 1987, Chart 2; Nielsen Clearing House Reporter, "Coupon Distribution and Redemption Patterns by Product Group," No. 2 (Chicago: A.C. Nielsen Company, 1984), pp. 8–9.

Among categories, beverages redeem the highest and health and beauty aids the lowest. This may reflect brand loyalty. For example, coffee products use many coupons and may have lower brand loyalty than health and beauty aids such as shampoo. This would explain why health and beauty aid on-pack coupons redeem quite well, but would not explain why in-pack is so low. In any case, it is clear that while redemption rates are typically in the single digits (excluding regular package coupons), the numbers can vary widely.

Average coupon redemption rates (the percentage of distributed coupons that are ultimately redeemed) have generally declined across all product categories and distribution vehicles. These rates are as follows (compiled from Nielsen Clearing House Reporter, 1984; Manufacturers Coupon Control Center, 1989a):

1979	4.2%
1980	4.2%
1981	4.0%
1982	3.7%
1983	3.9%
1984	3.8%
1985	3.6%
1986	3.5%
1987	3.3%
1988	3.2%

A number of trends influence the foregoing statistics. As Table 10.2 indicates, distribution has moved away from run-of-press newspaper and Sunday supplement coupons and toward free-standing inserts and direct mail. This trend would tend to increase redemption rates. Table 10.8, however, shows that within a given distribution vehicle, redemption rates have decreased in recent years. For example, Sunday FSI's for beverages achieved 5.4 percent redemption in 1983, but 4.7 percent redemption in 1985. Three explanations for the downward trend in redemption rates within distribution vehicle are as follows: (1) As the absolute numbers have increased, coupons become less well targeted, and hence redemption rate is a negative function of amount of the level of distribution (Ward and Davis, 1978b, obtain this finding). (2) Couponing has spread to weaker brands which command lower redemption rates. (3) During the recent upturn in economic prosperity, consumers have become less price conscious.

Forecasting Coupon Redemption Rates

The Problem. As our discussion of coupon profitability showed, swings of one or two percentage points in redemption rate can have a significant impact, because the redemption percentage is multiplied by several million distributed coupons. In addition, the cost side of coupon management is very real. It represents hard cash that the manufacturer must pay to the retailer. As a result, a critical part of planning coupon programs is the accurate forecasting of redemption rates.

To explore how accurate a forecast is needed, consider the example of a 40,000,000 coupon drop in a Sunday FSI. The drop cost would be approximately $9 per thousand, and assume a 30 cent face value and 10 cent processing cost. Let r equal actual redemption rate. Total coupon costs will be (see equation 10.1)

$$\$360,000 + (.40 \cdot 40,000,000 \cdot r) = \$360,000 + (\$16,000,000 \cdot r)$$

If our forecast is off by a fraction Δ, then our error in budgeting will be $\$16,000,000 \cdot \Delta$, or $160,000 if we are off by one percentage point. As a percentage of actual total costs, this would be

$$\frac{16,000,000 \cdot \Delta}{360,000 + (16,000,000 \cdot r)}$$

If $\Delta = .01$ and $r = .032$, this works out to 18.3 percent of total costs. A forecast error of half a percentage point would work out to 9.2 percent of total costs. If the redemption rate turned out to be 7 percent, then a forecast error of one percentage point would be 10.8 percent of total costs, and half a percentage point would be 5.4 percent of total costs. While standards for required budget accuracy differ from company to company, these calculations suggest that we would like to be able to forecast coupon redemption rates for a specific coupon drop to at least within one percentage point of the actual.

The general approach to forecasting coupon redemption rates is to formulate and estimate a model, and then use that model, along with managerial judgment, to produce a forecast. Specific steps are as follows:

1. Identify factors determining redemption rate.
2. Specify a model.
3. Collect data.
4. Estimate the model.
5. Validate the model.
6. Use the model.

Identify Factors Determining Redemption Rate.   Reibstein and Traver (1982) compiled an extensive list of factors that determine redemption rates. Table 10.9 lists these factors. Most of the factors listed in Table 10.9 make good intuitive sense, but we elaborate on two of them.

Size of the coupon drop warrants particular attention. The logic here is that size might be substituting for how well the coupon is targeted. Note that "target match" is really the factor of interest. A small drop is most likely targeted toward the right audience. In contrast, a very large drop may mean that the coupon has not been targeted toward particular regions or particular newspapers known to be read by coupon-prone consumers.[1] As a result, size of distribution drop is generally thought to be negatively correlated with redemption rate (e.g., Ward and Davis, 1978b).

Brand loyalty to the couponed brand is considered a positive factor affecting redemption. This is because brand loyals have low substitution costs and are therefore inclined to redeem a coupon for the brand to which they are loyal (see discussion of the Bawa-Shoemaker model discussed earlier in this chapter). Note the apparent contradiction of this hypothesis with our early findings that brand loyalty is negatively correlated with coupon proneness. This contradiction is reconciled by the proposition that loyal consumers will be very apt to redeem a coupon for the brand to which they are loyal, but they find it difficult to find such coupons, and therefore have lower overall coupon usage than nonloyal consumers. A brand with a loyal franchise picks up its share of nonloyals plus a larger number of loyals and, hence, commands a higher redemption rate than does a brand with a smaller number of loyal users.

Specify the Model.   The general approach to forecasting redemption rates will be to specify and estimate a regression model. Many of the same issues discussed in Chapter 7 therefore become relevant. One of the key issues is the level of aggregation with respect to brands. That is, should we have one model for each brand, or one model for all brands? If we have a separate model for each brand, we only use the data for a given brand's coupon drops in estimating its model. If we have one model for all brands, we can pool the data and have many more observations for estimating the model.

The penalty for pooling the data when separate models should be estimated

---

[1] Note that repetition is not the problem for large coupon drops. For example, distributing more FSI coupons means that more consumers receive the coupon, not that particular consumers are exposed several times to the same coupon.

TABLE 10.9 Factors Affecting Coupon Redemption Rates

Factor	Hypothesized Relationship to Redemption Rate
Distribution vehicle	
Face value	
Absolute	+
Percentage discount	+
Design of coupon	
Area of country	
Competitive activity	−
Size of coupon drop	−
Purchase requirements	−
Advertising and promotion support	+
Seasonality	
Product class penetration	+
Brand market share	+
Brand loyalty to couponed brand	+
Brand distribution	+
Stage in product life cycle	−
Brand image	+

Source: David J. Reibstein and Phillis A. Traver, "Factors Affecting Coupon Redemption Rates," *Journal of Marketing,* Vol. 46 (Fall 1982), p. 104. Adapted from *Journal of Marketing,* published by the American Marketing Association.

is that the coefficient estimates will be biased. The penalty for estimating separate models when the data really can be pooled is the low sample size for each model, which results in wide variances around the coefficient estimates. Either error can result in inaccurate forecasts. The best approach to deciding whether or not to pool the data is to conduct specific tests for equality of coefficients across brands (Bass and Wittink, 1975) and to test the accuracy of alternative models (see Chapter 7).

Another issue in specifying the redemption forecasting model is the functional form of the model, which could be linear, log-linear (Ward and Davis, 1978b), or logit (Reibstein and Traver, 1982). Linear and log-linear models are easy to estimate, while logit has the advantage of naturally constraining the forecasts to lie where they must, between zero and one. Again, the best approach to selecting a functional form is to test several.

Collect Data. Collecting data is not always an easy task. Some companies have detailed coupon information, including face value, vehicle, number of coupons distributed, and geographic region available for previous coupon drops. Competitive activity data are more difficult to collect. It is especially difficult to anticipate competitive activity when deriving a forecast. When pooling data across brands, brand-specific characteristics such as penetration, market share, distribution, and life cycle are typically easy to obtain, while brand loyalty and image data are less available.

Data on the dependent variable, redemption rate, become available from the company's own clearinghouse or an independent clearinghouse. In either case, one must recognize that hundreds of thousands of coupons must be counted, and redemption rate is therefore probably measured with some error. This error will decrease the ability of any regression model to forecast redemption rates.

Estimate the Model.   Ordinary least squares regression usually is the appropriate technique for estimating the model. However, seemingly unrelated regression may be appropriate if models are estimated for separate brands and error terms are correlated between equations, nonlinear regression may be needed if the model specified is nonlinear and cannot be converted to a linear model, and logistic regression would be appropriate if the logistic functional form were used (see Reibstein and Traver, 1982). If the observations used to estimate the model vary in terms of the number of coupons distributed, heteroscedasticity can be present— one would expect larger variance for observations with larger numbers of coupons distributed. In this case, weighted least squares would be the appropriate estimation technique (see Pindyck and Rubinfeld, 1981, Ch. 6).

Table 10.10 summarizes the estimation results of three published and two unpublished redemption forecasting models. The first unpublished study was made available to the authors after it was completed. The second unpublished study was conducted by the authors using data generously donated by a packaged goods firm. Distribution vehicle and face value are the two most commonly used independent variables. Vehicle is uniformly highly significant. Face value occasionally is not statistically significant. In the two cases where this occurred, both studies alluded to a lack of variation in face value that probably accounted for a lack of statistical significance.

When distribution size is considered, it generally relates negatively to redemption rates. Unpublished study 1 finds that the relationship is at first positive, but then negative after the size of the coupon drop reaches a certain point. Market share also has the hypothesized positive impact on redemption rate. Reibstein and Traver estimated their model for one brand, but market share varied from area to area and was positively related to redemption rate. Note that in their model, area of the country itself was not related to redemption rate. Neslin and Clarke estimated their model across brands and geographic areas, and both market share and geographic area were significant predictors.

Most of the models displayed in Table 10.10 are estimated for single brands. Reibstein and Traver had 140 observations available for a single brand. This is a relatively large number of observations. It is doubtful that one brand would have 140 coupon drops over any reasonable amount of time. However, observations were available for various geographic areas, and hence several observations were available from essentially one coupon drop. In the unpublished studies, we see relatively small sample sizes when estimating for single brands.

TABLE 10.10 Coupon Redemption Forecasting Models: Summary of Estimation Results

	Reibstein and Traver	Ward and Davis	Neslin and Clarke	Unpublished Study 1
Dependent variable	Redemption rate	Number of redemptions	Redemption rate	Redemption rate
Explanatory variables included				
Vehicle	Significant	Significant	Significant	Significant
Coupon value (absolute)	+	+	Not significant	Not significant
Coupon % reduction	+			
Distribution size	−	+[a]		Concave parabola
Market share	+		+	
Category penetration			+	
Area of country	Not significant		Significant	
Seasonality	Not significant			Not significant
R^2	0.92	0.82	0.51	Not available
Sample size	140	90	400	17
Level of aggregation	One brand	One category (coupons were not brand specific)	Across brands for different categories using two distribution vehicles	Single brand

	Unpublished Study 2			
	Model I (Brand A)	Model II (Brand B)	Model III[b] (Brands A and B)	Model IV[b]
Dependent variable	Redemption rate	Redemption rate	Redemption rate	Redemption rate
Explanatory variables included				
Vehicle	Significant	Significant	Significant	Significant
Coupon value	+	+	+	+
Coupon % reduction				
Distribution size				
Market share				
Category penetration				
Area of country				
Seasonality				
R^2	.891	.844	.876	.933
Sample size	26	16	42	59
Level of aggregation	One brand	One brand	Across two brands in a narrowly defined category	Across five brands in a narrowly defined category

[a] The relationship with number of coupons redeemed was positive. The relationship with redemption rate was negative.

[b] Brand-specific dummy variables were included in these models. These variables were statistically significant.

See further notes on p. 297.

Validate the Model.   Table 10.10 and the foregoing discussion reveals that fore-casting models can be estimated that fit the data rather well and yield coefficients that are consistent directionally with hypotheses. The acid test of these models, however, is the accuracy of their forecasts for future coupon drops. Reibstein and Traver state that (1) fit held up well in moving from estimation to validation samples but (2) median discrepancy between actual and predicted relative to actual redemption rates was as high as 23.5 percent (pp. 111–112). Reibstein and Traver suggest that including more variables in the model (e.g., coupon design) would improve prediction if the data could be obtained. They state that median forecast error was reduced from 30.8 percent to 23.5 percent by including more variables than the distribution vehicle factor. Reibstein and Traver do not state absolute forecast errors, but the lowest predicted redemption rate for a particular vehicle with an average face value, drop size, and so on was 5.039 percent. This would translate to an average absolute prediction error of approximately one percentage point (.235 times .05039). Since most distribution vehicles had higher redemption rates, this suggests that average prediction accuracy was usually worse than one percentage point.

Unpublished study 2 also sheds some light on forecast accuracy. The study investigated the redemption rate forecast accuracy for two specific brands, using either a brand-specific model or a model estimated across the two brands. Two approaches were used for updating the model while forecasting redemption rates over time. The first approach used no updating. A model was estimated using the first two sevenths of the data and used to predict on four successive sevenths of the data covering about two years. (A one-seventh length period separated esti-mation from the forecasts because data would not become instantly available in an actual application.) A second approach was to estimate models on successive two-sevenths of the data. Using this approach, a model was estimated for periods 1 and 2 and used to forecast for period 4; then one was estimated for periods 2 and 3 and forecast for period 5, and so on. We call this the periodic updating approach. A typical model was based then on a few month's data. For brand A, the sample size for a typical model was 25, for brand B, it was 15. Therefore, the models aggregated across the two brands typically had about 40 observations. Table 10.10 displays the initial two-sevenths models, based on 26, 16, and 42 observations.

Further Notes for Table 10.10

Sources: David J. Reibstein and Phillis A. Traver, "Factors Affecting Coupon Redemption Rates," *Journal of Marketing,* 46 (Fall, 1982), pp. 106–108, adapted from *Journal of Marketing,* published by the American Marketing Association; Ronald W. Ward and James E. Davis, "Coupon Redemption," *Journal of Advertising Research,* 18, 4 (August 1978b), p. 33, adapted from the *Journal of Advertising Research,* © Copyright 1978 by the Advertising Research Foundation; Scott A. Neslin and Darral G. Clarke, "Relating the Brand Use Profile of Coupon Redeemers to Brand and Coupon Characteristics," *Journal of Advertising Research,* 27, 1 (February/March, 1987), p. 30, adapted from the *Journal of Advertising Research,* © Copyright 1987 by the Advertising Research Foundation.

Note: A blank space indicates that the variable was not considered.
A "+" means a significant positive relationship was uncovered.
A "−" means a significant negative relationship was uncovered.

TABLE 10.11 Accuracy of Redemption Rate Forecasting (Unpublished Study 2)

Brand A	Model Aggregated Across Brands A and B		Brand-Specific Model	
	Periodic Updating	No Updating	Periodic Updating	No Updating
Mean absolute error	1.224	1.051	1.328	1.187
Standard deviation	1.409	1.2	1.358	0.98
% ≤.5 percentage points				
error	47%	52%	18%	25%
≤1	60%	55%	62%	55%
≤2	80%	88%	83%	88%
≤3	92%	92%	90%	95%
Minimum error	0.01	0.01	0.02	0.19
Maximum error	7.44	5.1	7.63	4.56
Number of predictions	60	60	60	60

Brand B	Model Aggregated Across Brands A and B		Brand-Specific Model	
	Periodic Updating	No Updating	Periodic Updating	No Updating
Mean absolute error	1.214	2.453	1.858	2.523
Standard deviation	0.918	1.115	1.089	1.273
% ≤.5 percentage points				
error	24%	0%	24%	0%
≤1	53%	3%	35%	29%
≤2	88%	50%	38%	32%
≤3	97%	53%	91%	56%
Minimum error	0.03	0.75	0.14	0.98
Maximum error	3.40	4.55	3.80	4.78
Number of predictions	34	34	34	34

The results of these studies are shown in Table 10.11 and can be summarized as follows:

- Mean absolute error ranges from 1.051 to 2.523 across brands and methods. The best methods for each brand produce MAE's of 1.051 and 1.214. It therefore appears possible to develop models with *average* absolute errors in the vicinity of one percentage point.
- There is ample variation in forecast accuracy across specific predictions. Sometimes a model is able to predict redemption rate for a specific coupon drop to within .01 percentage points. Other times the prediction is off by as much as 7.63 percentage points.
- No one method emerges as clearly the best. For brand A, mean accuracy is statistically equal across methods, with an initial model estimated across two brands edging out the others. For brand B, a periodically updated two-brand model is clearly best.

Implementation. Once a model is estimated, it is relatively easy to use. For example, the brand-specific model estimated for brand B in unpublished study 2 and summarized in Table 10.10 was as follows:

redemption rate (in hundredths) = 2.485 + .093 × face value − 1.12

$$× (1 \text{ if ROP newspaper, 0 otherwise})$$

$$+ 2.677 × (1 \text{ if FSI, 0 otherwise}) − .193$$

$$× (1 \text{ if Sunday supplement, 0 otherwise})$$

Therefore, our forecasted redemption rate for a 40 cent FSI coupon would be 2.485 + .093 × 40 + 2.677 = 8.88%. FSI is a very strong vehicle for this brand. The equivalent coupon inserted in ROP newspaper would yield 2.485 + .093 × 40 − 1.12 = 5.09%.

The forecasts of the model could be used as part of a cost-oriented planning calculation such as shown in Table 10.7, a profit-oriented planning calculation as shown in Table 10.6, or in a full-scale planning model (Neslin and Shoemaker, 1983a).

Summary. To summarize this section on forecasting redemption rates, it appears that forecast accuracy at least to within one percentage point is desirable. Evidence from the Reibstein and Traver study and from unpublished study 2 suggest that such accuracy cannot be guaranteed. Unpublished study 2 found that average accuracies of one percentage point could be achieved after testing various levels of aggregation and updating schemes, but even then, there was large variation in forecast accuracy from coupon drop to coupon drop. These results, however, must be considered exploratory. More detailed and systematic research is needed in this area.

Possibilities for improving coupon redemption rate forecasting accuracy not considered here include use of managerial judgment in conjunction with the quantitative models (e.g., Lawrence et al., 1986; Gupta and Wilton, 1987) and using more variables. Coupon designs can be pretested for attractiveness to the consumer and these results included in a redemption rate model. Advertising and promotion also can be included, and perhaps competitive activity should be considered.

The Timing of Coupon Redemptions

Part of the budgeting and planning process is to forecast not only how many coupons will be redeemed, but when they will be redeemed. There are really two important questions here: First, when will the coupons be redeemed at retail, and second, when will the manufacturer become liable for the cost of the coupon redemption. The first question becomes more relevant when one is planning for how coupons will affect retail sales. For example, perhaps management wants to know when advertising and promotion support should take place. The second question is more relevant when cost control is important, that is, when a budget needs to be implemented and controlled.

Figure 10.4 shows that the timing of free-standing insert coupon redemptions at retail, when viewed on a monthly basis, generally follow an exponential distribution, where close to half of total redemptions (44.5%) take place in the first month. A monotonically decreasing distribution of redemptions over time is intuitively appealing. Drawing on the collection-intention-redemption decision model advanced by Henderson ("The Redemption Decision"), one would conjecture that the translation of intention to redemption would dwindle over time, as collected coupons became used, lost, or forgotten.

Free-standing insert and newspaper ROP coupons generally redeem the fastest, while direct-mail and magazine coupons redeem less quickly, and package coupons are slow to redeem. In fact, the redemption pattern for package coupons looks more like a gamma than an exponential distribution (see Bowman, 1980, pp. 56–60). This is because redemptions of package coupons come at least one purchase cycle after the initial purchase. An important factor influencing the timing of redemptions is the presence of an expiration date. An expiration date will obviously push forward the timing of redemptions. (An interesting issue in need of research is how over-all redemption rate is affected.) Pushing forward the timing of redemptions has two potential benefits. First is the better control and limited financial liability that comes with expenditures taking place within a compact period of time. Second is the possibility that redemptions that take place earlier after coupon distribution might be more likely to represent incremental sales (see the forthcoming section on Experiments Involving Coupons). In any case, it is noteworthy that the use of short expiration date coupons has doubled between 1986 and 1988 (Manufacturers Coupon Control Center, 1989a).

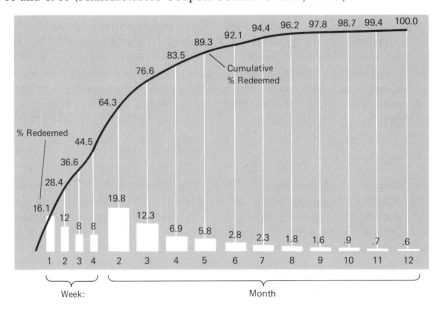

FIGURE 10.4 Timing of Coupon Redemption at Retail, Monthly Data, Free-Standing Insert

Source: Manufacturers Coupon Control Center, "Speed of Redemption at Retail Level," 1988b, Copyright © 1988 by A. C. Nielsen Company.

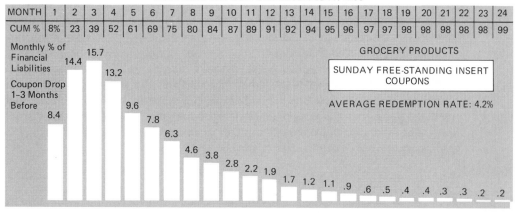

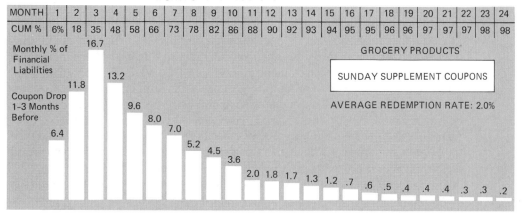

FIGURE 10.5 Time of Manufacturer Financial Liability for Coupon Redemption

Source: Manufacturers Coupon Control Center, "Coupon Distribution and Redemption Patterns," 1986, p. 16, Copyright © 1986 by A. C. Nielsen Company.

The degree to which manufacturer liability for coupon redemptions lags retail redemption depends on the practices of the clearinghouse used. Figure 10.5 reveals, for example, that the time distribution of manufacturer liability generally follows a gamma distribution, beginning one to three months after the coupon drop. Charts such as those shown in Figure 10.5 can be compiled and used for budgeting purposes.

THE EFFECT OF COUPONS UPON BRAND SALES

Perhaps the most important issue concerning coupons is their effect upon brand sales. However, managers do not typically have firm estimates of the number of incremental sales generated by a coupon. This is in stark contrast to the issue of coupon redemption rate. As we saw in Section 10.4, average redemption rates are published by commercial sources, and previous researchers have investigated databases that included brand-specific, coupon drop–specific redemption rates. The basic problem is that coupon redemptions simply have to be counted and that count is undertaken because it feeds into a direct cost of the coupon program, whereas the effect on sales must be inferred from the retail sales time series. There are a few studies, however, that are beginning to shed light on the incremental sales benefit of coupons. The methodologies employed in these studies vary. They include controlled experiments, profiles of coupon redeemers, baseline extrapolation, and econometric analysis.

Experiments Involving Coupons

We will discuss three experiments that have measured the incremental sales effect of couponing. The first is the series of "Couponlab" experiments (Klein, 1985, and Irons et al., 1983; see Chapter 6, "Two-Group Pre-Post Experiments"). Couponlab was a commercially available service for testing coupon promotions. The service employed a consumer panel in a large Midwestern city, whose purchases could be monitored using supermarket scanner equipment. The panel could be divided into control and treatment groups, and then various direct-mail coupons were distributed to the appropriate groups. With judicious design of treatment groups, so that competitive coupons were not distributed to different cells, several experiments could be run at once. However, the essence of the experimental design was quite simple: One group of consumers in a given location would receive a coupon for the test brand (the test group), while another group, in the same location, would not receive the coupon (the control group).

Figure 10.6 shows an example of the results of such an experiment (Klein, 1985). Actually plotted are test minus control sales over time. The results clearly show a common finding in Couponlab experiments: The coupon drop causes a definite increase in market share. In this case, the cumulative effect was equivalent to 8.2 share points over a 12-week period. The test brand had a base share of 12 percent.

On the basis of more than 50 such experiments, Klein (1985), made some important conclusions. These include

- Incremental sales are easier to get for small brands and harder to get for bigger brands.
- Higher face values yield more incremental sales.
- High redemption rates are not necessarily associated with more incremental sales.
- The earlier redemptions are more likely to be incremental sales.

The first two conclusions were explicitly tested by Irons et al. (1983) using data from several Couponlab experiments. Using 46 observations across categories of coupon-generated incremental sales per thousand households, they estimated a regression model to explain differences in this number as a function of several independent variables. Face value and brand market share were among

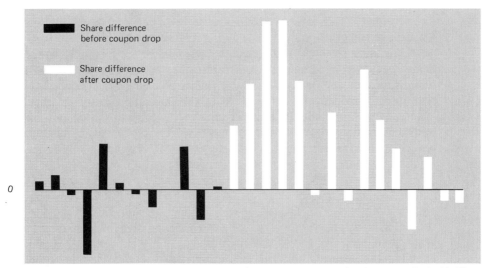

Weeks after coupon drop   1 2 3 4 5 6 7 8 9 10 11 12 13 14 15
Sales increase quickly when a $0.35 coupon is offered.

FIGURE 10.6 Incremental Sales Generated by a Couponlab Experiment

Source: Robert L. Klein, "How to Use Research to Make Better Sales Promotion Marketing Decisions." In *Handbook of Sales Promotion*, ed. Stanley Ulanoff (New York: McGraw-Hill, 1985), p. 461.

those variables. The results were that face value had a highly significant effect, whereas market share was not statistically significant.

The finding that the earlier redemptions are incremental sheds light on the possible nature of the redemption decision. Klein conjectures that those who do not redeem coupons immediately are probably saving for the brand they would have bought anyway. The consumer who redeems more quickly has possibly used the coupon to help structure his or her shopping list in the week the coupon is distributed. This finding, if it generalizes, is important because it supports the use of expiration dates for coupons (see Neslin, 1989, for confirmatory evidence, and Neslin and Clarke, 1987, and Moody, 1987b, for contrary evidence).

There are no published estimates of incremental sales per coupon redemption for the Couponlab experiments. However, evidence displayed in Irons et al. shows that incremental sales per 1,000 households varied from virtually zero to 1,300! Most of the variation, however, was between 0 and 100.

Two other experiments have been published regarding coupon effectiveness in two entirely different applications: bus ridership and pizza restaurant sales. The bus ridership experiment (Matosian, 1982), tested the effect of a free-ride coupon on long-term bus-ridership. Three distribution vehicles were tested: direct mail, free-standing insert, and direct hanging of the coupon on the doors of residences. The experimental design was identical to the Couponlab work, except ridership was observed three months after the coupon drops. Results were that passenger counts were up significantly, approximately 192 on a base of 825 for direct mail, 162 on a base of 848 for the door hanger, and 89 on a base of 317 for the free-standing inserts.

The pizza restaurant experiment (Chapman, 1986) was more complicated in design because of the need to control for different service areas and the nature of housing in those areas. The experiment tested a direct-mail coupon, either with a menu or combined with a menu and an information brochure. Results indicated at least an approximate doubling in sales for three weeks after the coupon drop and 50 percent increases lasting another three weeks. The exact magnitude of the percentage increase depended primarily upon the distance of the couponed area from the restaurant.

The experiments reported here are all field studies, and hence have good external validity. We should, however, point out two issues regarding the Couponlab experiments. First, direct-mail couponing represents only 5 percent of coupon distribution, yet the Couponlab experience is exclusively direct mail. The Matosian experiment shows that there is reason to believe that incremental sales effectiveness depends on distribution vehicle. Second, the Couponlab experiments may not have captured the typical environment in which a direct-mail coupon is distributed. Manufacturers will often step up advertising or try to coordinate in-store promotion activities to coincide with a coupon drop. Those activities may either help or hurt the effectiveness of the coupon, depending on whether they create additional excitement for consumers or cannibalize the coupon's effect. Despite these limitations, Couponlab as well as the other two experiments reported here clearly support the potential benefits of couponing.

Profiles of Coupon Redeemers

Another method of gauging the sales effects of coupons is to profile the redeemers of coupons in terms of whether they are already loyal users of the product, brand switchers, new triers, and so on. A profile that is skewed toward brand switchers and new triers is more desirable in the sense that coupon purchases are more likely to represent incremental sales. The two quantities that must be measured when developing a redeemer profile are the consumer's purchase rate of the brand and her or his use of coupons for that brand. These data can be collected using self-report surveys or panel data. In this section, we review three studies that profiled coupon redeemers.

Shoemaker and Tibrewala (1985) measured consumers' self-reported likelihood of using either a 15 cent or 50 cent coupon for four brands. They then cross-tabulated this likelihood by previous purchase history. Aggregated across brands and face values, their results were as follows:

Number of Prior Brand Purchases over Five Purchase Occasions		Fraction Who Said They Would Redeem a Coupon (sample size in parentheses)	Fraction of All Redemptions
"Occasional" buyers	0	.074 (609)	.169
	1–2	.349 (274)	.361
"Regular" buyers	3–4	.564 (101)	.214
	5	.613 (111)	.256

Although regular buyers of the brand were more likely to redeem a coupon for that brand, their smaller absolute numbers resulted in a redeemer brand use profile much more evenly spread out among regular buyers and occasional buyers. Shoemaker and Tibrewala also found that higher face values shifted the brand use profile more toward occasional users. This is consistent with the Couponlab experiments relating face values to incremental sales.

Neslin and Clarke (1987) studied not only the consumer profile of the average coupon redeemer, but how that profile changed as a function of market share position of the brand, distribution vehicle, face value, geographic location, timing of redemption, and redemption rate. Specifically, a "coupon book" containing 59 coupons for various brands was distributed in Memphis and Milwaukee. The book was distributed either using direct mail (unsolicited) or as a result of a consumer request in response to a newspaper advertisement. Consumers were contacted at two weeks and four weeks after they were mailed the coupon book. Consumers were asked which coupons they had redeemed, and if so, how they would characterize their prior behavior with respect to that brand: Was this a brand they bought "almost always," "occasionally," "rarely," or was this the first time they had bought the brand? Across all coupon redemptions, the average redeemer profile was

> Fifty-two percent almost always bought the brand.
> Thirty-four percent rarely or occasionally bought the brand.
> Fourteen percent were buying the brand for the first time.

Therefore, for example, 52 percent of all coupon redemptions were by consumers who almost always bought the couponed brand anyway. First, it is noteworthy that these results correspond well with Shoemaker and Tibrewala's. The 14 percent new triers corresponds to their 16.9 percent who had not purchased in the previous five occasions, the 34 percent rarely or occasional corresponds to their 36.1 percent one to two previous purchase consumers, and the 52 percent almost always bought corresponds to their 47 percent "regular buyers." Making a value judgment of whether this is a favorable or unfavorable profile depends on a half-empty or half-full viewpoint. On the negative side, about 52 percent of redemptions are probably having no effect on sales, at least for the coupon purchase occasion. On the positive side, 48 percent of redemptions are by those who otherwise would be highly unlikely to buy the brand.

Neslin and Clarke demonstrated that the profile varied significantly as a function of brand and coupon characteristics. Their conclusions were as follows:

- Market share is a significant determinant of redeemer profiles. Generally, lower share brands have better profiles. High share brands, especially in concentrated markets, have much poorer profiles.
- The consumer-request distribution method yielded a much more favorable profile.
- Profiles differed by city.
- Higher redemption rates were associated with worse redeemer profiles, while face value did not affect profiles.
- Redemptions recorded four weeks after distribution were associated with better profiles than were those recorded after two weeks.

This study supports the conclusion that the average redeemer profile, and hence the number of incremental sales, can change dramatically depending on brand or coupon characteristics. The market share results provide empirical support for Klein's statement, which was not verified by Irons et al., that low-market-share brands find it easier to generate incremental sales. The distribution vehicle result reinforces Matosian's findings that different vehicles achieve different amounts of incremental sales. The better profiles found in the later measurement period would seem to contradict the Couponlab finding that the earliest redemptions are incremental, as does the finding that face value did not influence the redeemer profile. In the former case, however, Neslin and Clarke's late redemptions were still within one month of distribution, and in the latter case, the authors note that there was little variation in face value.

The conclusion that higher redemptions are associated with a less favorable redeemer profile and hence fewer incremental sales (per redemption) is consistent with Klein's conclusions, but nevertheless is still intriguing. Neslin and Clarke's results control for face value and brand market share, so these variables do not explain the result.

The result implies that after controlling for face value and brand share effects, larger redemption rates bring along more loyal users. There does not appear to be any immediate explanation for this, but two independent studies found similar results, so the finding is probably not serendipitous.

Bawa and Shoemaker (1987b) computed a couponed brand's share of purchases for each consumer in a scanner purchase panel, for the 24-week period prior to a coupon drop. They then cross-tabulated these results by actual propensity to redeem the coupon and found the following:

Prior Share of Purchases		% of Consumers	Redemption Rate	% of Total Redemptions
0	(nonusers)	66.2%	4.2%	28.5%
.01–.20	(infrequent users)	27.3%	17.8%	50.4%
.20–1.0	(frequent users)	6.5%	31.3%	21.1%

Similar to the Shoemaker and Tibrewala study, this table suggests that frequent users of the brand are much more likely to use the coupon than nonusers, but there are so many nonusers that more redemptions come from nonusers than frequent users: 78.9 percent of the coupon redemptions are from consumers who had purchased the brand less than 20 percent of the time over the previous six months. As a result, it appears that many of the redemptions represent incremental sales. The preceding table was calculated for the case of a ''medium'' size face value (Bawa and Shoemaker, 1987b, p. 373). As we move from ''low'' to ''medium'' to ''high'' face values, the Bawa and Shoemaker data show that frequent users become less represented in the redeeming population, but the representation of nonusers and infrequent users does not move in a consistent direction.

Baseline Extrapolation Studies

Hee (1981) developed a market share logit model similar to Guadagni and Little (1983) and used it to extrapolate a baseline estimate of sales into the time periods when a Couponlab coupon distribution had taken place. The model applied to individual consumers and took into account the promotional environment apart from couponing, as well as the consumer's inferred loyalty to various brands (based on consumer's purchase history prior to the current purchase occasion). (See Chapter 8 for a more detailed discussion of logit models.)

The model was aggregated across consumers to derive a prediction of market share in any given period, conditional on each consumer's previous purchase history and knowledge of the promotions (besides coupons) available in that period. Hee tested the model for holdout data periods and found good predictive validity. She then extrapolated these predictions to the coupon drop period. One set of results is reprinted in Figure 10.7. Figure 10.7 depicts an estimated gain of 35 share points for brand B, accumulated over a 24-week period, on a base of a 20 percent market share (Hee, 1981, p. 49). As shown in Figure 10.7, a good portion of the market share gain came at the expense of brand C.

Econometric Studies

Neslin (1989) formulated a multi-equation econometric time series model to directly infer incremental sales per coupon redemption. The model traced the relationship between coupon distribution and coupon redemption, and then modeled how redemptions translate into increased market share. The key idea behind modeling this translation is that if coupons are redeemed exclusively by those who would have bought the brand anyway, then in periods when there are many coupon redemptions, the market share among those *not* redeeming the coupon will be low. This is because the coupon takes out of the nonredeeming population a disproportionate number of loyal users. Conversely, if coupons are used exclusively by those who ordinarily would not buy the brand, then market share among nonredeemers will increase in periods where there are many redemptions, because coupons disproportionately draw nonusers from the population.

Neslin modeled coupon redemptions as a function of coupon distribution, previous period redemptions, competitive coupons, and the brand's retailer promotions. However, he also included market share as an explanatory variable for redemptions. This introduces simultaneity due to the tendency of higher market share by itself to bring about more redemptions.

When the complete model is used to calculate incremental sales, it does not count as incremental sales that would have been gained by the brand's in-store activities. However, the stores covered in Neslin's data had implemented "every-day-low-price" strategies (see Chapter 14), where in-store price cuts were less important merchandising tools. This environment would tend to yield strong incremental effects for coupons for the particular data base Neslin used to test his model.

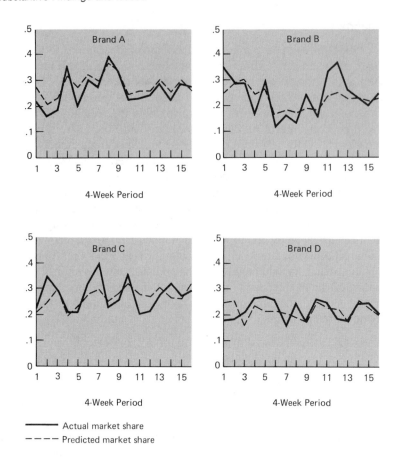

FIGURE 10.7 Incremental Sales Generated by a Coupon, Relative to a Logit-Derived Baseline

Source: Judith Ann Hee, "Determining Manufacturers' Couponing Strategies," unpublished masters thesis, Sloan School of Management, MIT, Cambridge, MA (June 1981), p. 48.

The major results of Neslin's model are summarized in Table 10.12. The results show that incremental sales per coupon redemption ranged from 0.21 to .53. The median across the seven brands is that 39.8 percent of coupon redemptions represent incremental sales.

Table 10.12 shows that the three brands whose average actual market share is greater than their estimated baseline have the highest incremental sales per redemption. This supports the importance of considering incremental sales for redemption in coupon planning.

Table 10.12 also shows that there is a strong relationship between a brand's

TABLE 10.12 Results from an Econometric Model of Coupons' Effect on Sales

Brand	Estimated Incremental Sales per Redeemed Coupon	Average Market Share	Estimated Baseline Share
A	.398	.176	.180
B	.483	.084	.063
C	.437	.085	.062
D	.361	.136	.149
E	.208	.207	.264
F	.341	.031	.073
G	.534	.280	.209

Source: Scott A. Neslin, "A Market Response Model for Coupon Promotions," Working Paper, Amos Tuck School of Business Administration, Dartmouth College (May, 1989).

estimated baseline (market share that would be obtained in an environment without couponing) and the actual market share it achieves in the marketplace. However, neither of these are related to incremental sales per redemption. The reason for this is that while Neslin's model implies that baseline market share should be negatively related to incremental sales, there are other factors as well that influence incremental sales, including competitive draw and the brand's own other promotions. These effects offset the built-in negative relationship between brand market share and incremental sales per redemption.

Summary and Discussion

The results of experimental research, consumer profiles, baseline extrapolation, and econometric studies sheds important light on the incremental sales impact of couponing. Some of these conclusions are as follows:

- Coupons can have a pronounced and measurable effect upon short-term brand sales.
- The number of incremental sales per redemption can vary significantly by brand and by coupon characteristics.
- Most studies have not directly measured incremental sales per redemption. One study did explicitly do so and found that across seven brands, the average incremental sales per redemption was approximately .40, but this study was in an every-day-low-pricing retail environment where we would expect higher than usual sales effects from coupons.

The good news for managers is that indeed coupons can generate incremental sales. Unfortunately, however, there is not enough uniformity in the research findings so that managers can easily anticipate the incremental sales impact of coupons for their specific brands. The recommendation to managers is therefore to commission either experiments, profile research, baseline analyses, or econometric analyses for their specific brands. For researchers, the need is clear to study generalizations in incremental sales results, following up most specifically on the work of Irons et al. (See Moody, 1988, for recent work in developing a general model for forecasting incremental sales due to couponing.)

In closing this section, we should note that we have concentrated on short-term sales gains, not on the potential long-term effects on brand loyalty and repeat rates. Future analyses should begin to include long-term as well as short-term effects (see "Maintain and Enhance Repeat Purchase Rates" in this chapter).

WHY ARE THERE COUPONS? THE CONSUMER VIEWPOINT

When one casually asks consumers whether they like coupons, opinions range from "I hate coupons" to "What do you mean by coupons" to "I love coupons." The conversation then usually progresses to the consumer asking, "Why are there coupons?" The textbook answer is that coupons serve the managerial objectives discussed earlier in this chapter. The consumer's retort is, "Well, what's in it for me?"

There are two potential benefits of couponing: First, coupons might result in lower price (both with and without the coupon), and second, they might allow consumers to consume more of the products they prefer. Economists have examined both these potential benefits from a theoretical perspective (LaCroix, 1983; Sweeney, 1984; Levedahl, 1984; Houston and Howe, 1985, 1986; Rieber, 1986). This research has found that whether these benefits are realized depends on issues such as whether the marginal cost of production is an increasing or decreasing function of quantity, whether total consumption is constant or could increase, and whether there are positive carryover effects of brand purchasing. Lower prices and higher consumption are more likely when marginal costs decline, primary demand is elastic with respect to price, and there are carryover effects. However, if these conditions are not met, regular prices may be higher and quantity consumed may be lower. The social benefit of couponing thus becomes an empirical issue.

Earlier in this chapter, we reviewed empirical evidence that coupons are associated with increased list prices. This evidence was not completely conclusive, but does shift the debate toward those who might suggest that coupons result in lower prices. As one would expect, the casual empiricism of the consumer is split on this issue, depending on whether the consumer uses or does not use coupons. A recent survey found that only 17 percent of coupon users think prices would decrease if coupons were discontinued, while 30 percent of nonusers think prices would decrease (Nielsen Clearing House, 1985).

Another way to look at the price issue is from a macroeconomic perspective. A 1978 study (Strang, 1981) concluded that the costs of manufacturer couponing constitute one quarter of 1 percent of total retail sales of products in couponed categories. However, things have changed drastically since that time. In the absence of a replication of Strang's rigorous analysis, we must make a few assumptions to update the one quarter of 1 percent figure. In our numerator is coupon costs while in our denominator is retail sales in couponed categories. We would first note that prices have approximately doubled since 1978, so our denominator has doubled. However, there is reason to believe our numerator has more than doubled. The number of coupons distributed has more than doubled. Costs per thousand have increased due to inflation *and* use of more expensive free-standing inserts. In addition, face values have about doubled. If we assume then that total coupon costs have increased by a factor of 2 (double distribution) × 3 (triple cost per thousand) × 2 (double face value), we would conclude that our numerator has increased 12-fold. Our ratio of coupon costs to retail sales has therefore increased 6-fold (12/2). Our updated estimate then is that coupons now constitute 1.5 percent of retail sales in coupon categories.

If that 1.5 percent could be directly passed on to consumers, the household spending $80 per week would save $1.20 per week in grocery costs. However, if this household were a heavy user of coupons, then savings might be 10 coupons per week × 33.9 cents average face value (Manufacturers Coupon Control Center, 1988a), or $3.39. This suggests that couponing distributes a uniform level of savings for all consumers toward those willing to collect and redeem coupons. The question of whether this is fair from the consumer's viewpoint depends on a number of issues. Since coupon users are more price sensitive, the coupon is distributing savings among those who care about getting those savings. However, not every consumer has equal access to coupons. Lower-income households that do not buy newspapers or rural households that are not on the FSI circulation route have little chance to accumulate these savings. One might argue that these households are the ones that need the savings the most.

The major supposition in the preceding paragraph was that the cost of couponing could be passed along to consumers if coupons were eliminated. There is no guarantee that this is possible. Couponing might be a more efficient way for firms to compete than, for example, advertising or trade dealing, so that eliminating coupons would result in higher marketing expenditures (Antil, 1985, pp. 319–322, argues this both conceptually and empirically). Coupons might also serve the role of keeping prices low for lower-quality brands. By allowing an upper price tier (and presumedly higher-quality) brand to compete with lower-price tiers, the coupon forces the lower-quality brands to price themselves lower than the higher-quality brands minus the coupon discount, since otherwise, their price-conscious consumers will switch to the higher-quality brands.

Another argument for coupons as a stimulus to price competition is that coupons provide manufacturers with an important means of combatting the growing power of retailers. Coupons allow the manufacturer to reach consumers directly with a price decrease, whereas retailers are loath to pass along trade discounts to consumers (Chevalier and Curhan, 1976; Curhan and Kapp, 1986). It may therefore be wishful thinking to assume that the full 1.5 percent potential reduction in price would be forwarded to consumers if coupons were eliminated.

In summary, then, the social value of couponing is open to debate (see, for example, Antil, 1985, and Uhl, 1982). To put the debate in perspective, the same debate could be waged about any marketing expenditure. There is conceptual as well as empirical evidence for and against the social value of couponing. Theoretical research is needed that takes into account the role of the retailer as well as alternative marketing vehicles. Empirical research is needed to measure the economic impact of coupons as well as to build upon the work relating couponing to shelf price. Until this research is completed, the debate on couponing will reflect the rich emotional and psychological processes that coupons tend to invoke.

11

Trade Dealing

INTRODUCTION

One of the primary mechanisms used by manufacturers to promote products are trade deals. The "trade" is simply the members of the channel of distribution. Trade deals have many objectives as will be discussed later in the chapter, but it is important to recognize that it is "push money" intended to push the product through the channels of distribution to the end user.

In spite of its importance in the promotional mix of the manufacturer and the total dollars in expenditures devoted to it, almost none of the standard marketing texbooks discuss trade dealing, and there are very few academic articles written on the topic. Only in the last few years have articles begun to appear about trade dealing (Brown, 1973; Blattberg and Levin, 1987; Abraham and Lodish, 1987; Chevalier and Curhan, 1976). However, it is expected that in the next few years more articles will appear and the topic will generate more research.

It is useful to begin by defining a trade deal. A trade deal is simply a promotion directed to the members of the channels of distribution. The results of trade deals are readily apparent to most consumers. On "Best Food Day" in the newspaper (often Thursday) one sees all the advertisments run for grocery and other packaged good products by food retailers. The items in the advertisement are stimulated by trade deals. When an appliance dealer runs a General Electric or Whirlpool advertisement, it has usually been generated through a trade promotion. While trade promotions are directed to the trade, the goal is to receive promotions, advertising, and displays from the trade directed to the consumer.

The remainder of this chapter will explore trade dealing: describing the objectives of trade dealing, giving the types of trade deals used for durables and nondurables, discussing the measurement of the effects of trade deals, giving empirical results from measuring trade deals, and finally, describing when trade deals are likely to be most effective.

OBJECTIVES OF TRADE DEALS

Trade dealing is used for many purposes. In fact one of the problems with analyzing trade deals is that managers and researchers often state multiple objectives for trade deals making it more difficult to isolate the sales and profit effect.

Before proceeding, it is important to recognize one of the reasons trade deals are used. The manufacturer does not control the retail price in most situations. The price the manufacturer controls is only to the next level in the channel. In some industries this is very far from the end user. In industries where the manufacturer has control over the channel, trade deals are not used. Trade dealing is a mechanism for the manufacturer to try to induce actions for its direct customer just as the retailer tries to influence the consumer.

The following are a list of objectives for trade promotions. Each will be discussed in more detail.

- Induce retailers to offer a price discount.
- Induce retailers to display the brand.
- Induce retailers to advertise the brand.
- Offer incentives for the retailer's/dealer's sales force to push the brand to the customer.
- Gain or maintain distribution for a model or item within the product line.
- Gain or maintain distribution for the brand.
- Load the retailer, dealer, or distributor with inventory to avoid out-of-stocks.
- Shift inventory from the manufacturer to the channels of distribution and the consumer.
- Avoid price reductions.
- Defend the brand against competitors.
- Induce price fluctuations into the market.
- Finance retailer inventories.

This is a long list and does not cover all the explanations given. However, it highlights the primary reasons often given for running a trade deal.

To shorten the discussion of objectives, some will be grouped because their purpose is similar.

Inducing Retailer Merchandising Activities

The first, and probably primary, objective of trade promotions is to induce the retailer to advertise, price discount, and display the item. By having the retailer run promotions, the manufacturer will experience large sales increases. (Chapter 12 shows how retailer promotions can increase sales for grocery products.)

In looking at desired retailer actions, the manufacturer would like to have its items discounted. The exact amount cannot be specified (legally), but the manufacturer would like the retailer to discount the product as much or more to the consumer than the discount offered to the retailer. In other words, the retailer would pass through 100 percent (or more) of the trade deal. Once a price discount is offered, the manufacturer would like the retailer to advertise the brand in the weekly or periodic advertisement run by the retailer to inform consumers of the price promotion. Finally, a display is desired because when a consumer comes into the store and sees the brand displayed, it results in a greater chance of a purchase. Displays can induce sales even if the consumer did not see the advertisement or when there is no price discount (see Chapter 12).

Retail Sales Force Incentives

In certain product categories where the retailer's salesperson has a strong effect on the customer, it is important to try to induce him or her to push the manufacturer's product. For example, many customers come into the store uncommitted about which appliance brand to buy. A recommendation by the salesperson can strongly influence the customer's choice. Having that salesperson push a specific brand is very advantageous for that manufacturer. A SPIFF (defined in "Description of Trade Deals for Consumer Durable Goods") is needed to induce this behavior on the part of the salesperson.

Loading the Retailer

The manufacturers of many products would like to load the retailer or channel for several reasons. First, it decreases the chances of an out-of-stock. Second, larger inventories may cause the channel members to push the product to the end user. Third, the manufacturer may have seasonal products which must be loaded into the retailer at the beginning of the season. Fourth, it may be cheaper for the manufacturer to make long production runs and then pass the inventory carrying costs on to the retailer or other channel members.

Gaining or Maintaining Distribution

A commonly held belief by manufacturers is that trade deals can induce the retailer to maintain distribution on weaker products. The gross margin increases when the item is promoted, and therefore, the profitability of the channel member increases. For weaker brands, which receive little retailer push, this is the reason commonly given for running trade promotions. It should be noted that the alternative of reducing price does not work as well because retailers and dealers believe that price reductions will ultimately be passed through which does not increase retailers' margins whereas trade promotions do increase their margins. Whether this is true requires empirical research.

Avoiding Price Reductions

In the early 1970s when the Nixon administration, much to the surprise of the business community, instituted wage-price controls, the manufacturers were unable to increase price. Reducing price was legal. Therefore, in a situation where price increases are not allowed but price decreases are, the manufacturer wants to set its price as high as possible and then offer *temporary* price reductions. Since the price can go back up once these temporary reductions expire, the manufacturer has an incentive to use trade deals.

While this explanation is still given by United States manufacturers, it is not a very plausible reason for running trade deals. Trade deals existed long before wage-price controls. If the United States ever does go back to price controls, trade dealing would be very advantageous as a mechanism for managing price. However, in the current environment, it is unlikely to be an important reason to run a trade promotion. In other countries with high inflation rates, such as Brazil, Israel, and Argentina, trade dealing could be a very important mechanism for controlling price.

Competitive Tool

Several articles have been written recently which argue that if the brand has low market share and if there is a segment of switchers who choose the lowest-priced brand, then the firm should randomize its price. (For example, see Lal, 1988; Narasimhan, 1988; Raju, et al., 1988; Lattin, 1988.) Trade dealing is viewed as a means to randomize price though some of these articles do not explicitly incorporate the retailer-manufacturer link. (See Chapter 4 for a further discussion of this issue.) Therefore, weaker brands would want to trade deal heavily to increase the frequency of deals in the category and "break" the loyalty patterns of some of the consumers.

Along those lines, then, higher-share firms offer trade deals as a defensive mechanism to avoid erosion in market share. While the higher-share firms would be better off not promoting, it is necessary for competitive reasons. The retailer will only promote those brands offering trade deals, and if weaker share brands begin offering promotions, then so will the stronger share brands. (See Chapter 4 for more details.)

In summary there are many reasons for a manufacturer to offer a trade deal. There are also many types of trade deals designed to meet these objectives. These are discussed in the next section.

TYPES OF TRADE DEALS

To understand the types of trade deals offered to the channels of distribution, it is useful to divide them into trade deals offered for nondurable and durable goods. Durable goods' trade deals often are designed to build and finance the dealers' inventory as well as gain passthrough, whereas for nondurables, they are more focused on gaining advertising, display, and price discounts. After the trade deals are described, a table is created which relates the objectives given in ''Objectives of Trade Deals'' of the chapter to the types of trade deals manufacturers can offer.

Description of Trade Deals for Consumer Durable Goods

Many consumer durable goods manufacturers are frequent users of trade deals. The following are the types commonly used.

1. *Off invoice*. The purpose of an off-invoice promotion is to discount the product to the dealer for a fixed period of time. It is a price cut but is temporary, and when the time period elapses, the price goes back to its normal level. The specific terms of the discount usually require performance, and the discount lasts for a specified period (e.g., one month). Sometimes the trade can buy multiple times and sometimes only once.

2. *Cumulative volume rebates*. The total purchasing by the dealer over a fixed period of time (e.g., quarter, year) is cumulated and then a discount is offered depending on the total volume. (See Dolan, 1987, for a discussion of quantity discounts.)

3. *Floor planning or inventory financing*. Financing of the dealers' inventories is called floor planning. The dealer is given financial terms to acquire items. Payment is required 90 days or some fixed period after delivery. This allows the dealer to try to sell the items before they need to pay for them.

4. *Free goods*. Occasionally a manufacturer will offer free merchandise along with the purchase of an item. This allows the dealer to sell the merchandise or to offer it to the customer as an incentive. For example, microwave cookware may be offered with the purchase of microwave ovens.

5. *Cooperative advertising*. Paying for part of the dealers' advertising is called cooperative advertising which is often abbreviated as co-op advertising. The manufacturer either offers the dealer a fixed dollar amount per unit sold or offers to pay a percentage of the advertising costs. The percentage varies depending upon the type of advertising run. If the dealer is prominent in the advertisement, then the manufacturer often pays less, but if the manufacturer is prominent, then he pays more.

6. *SPIFFS*. SPIFFS are incentives offered to the dealer's sales force to push a manufacturer's product. Rather than being given to the dealer, the incentive is given directly to the salesperson. For example, Whirlpool will offer a $25 SPIFF on a 21-cubic-foot refrigerator. If the salesperson sells a unit, then he or she receives $25. The amount of the SPIFF varies, and the willingness of dealers to allow their sales personnel to receive SPIFFS also varies.

7. *Contests*. Hawaii is filled with dealers who have won free trips from manufacturers. Contests are frequently used to try to increase volume above last year's level. The specific contest varies from free goods to trips to almost anything promotion agencies can generate.

8. *Quota incentives*. Quota incentives are similar to volume rebates except they are tied to quotas. The quotas are often a percentage increase over last year's volume. For example, Ford Truck division might offer a $300 incentive if a dealer sells 110 percent of last year's units in the same time period this year. Or $500 may be offered for every unit above 130 percent. Thus, the incentives may be increasing as a function of the volume increase the dealer has to generate.

The list just given is not exhaustive. However, it does indicate the wide variety of incentives offered and shows that they can induce different behavior from the dealers.

Description of Trade Deals for Consumer Nondurable Goods

As will become apparent, the types of trade deals offered for consumer nondurables are similar. However, the emphasis is toward price incentives. The following is a partial list of the types of trade deals offered.

1. *Off invoice*. The same as for durable goods. It gives the retailer a discount for every item purchased during a fixed period of time.

2. *Bill-back*. Bill-backs are similar to off-invoice except that the retailer computes the discount per unit for all units bought during the promotional period and then bills the manufacturer for the units sold and any other promotional allowances that are owed after the promotional period is complete. The advantage from the manufacturer's position is the control it gives and guarantees that the retailer performs as the contract indicates before payment is issued. Generally, retailers do not like bill-backs because of the time and effort required.

3. *Free goods*. Usually free goods takes the form of extra cases at the same price. For example, buy 3 get 1 free is a free goods offer. For nondurables because the cost is less, free goods usually takes the form of extra cases rather than ancillary products as it is for durable goods.

4. *Cooperative advertising allowances*. The same as for durable goods though the manufacturer rarely pays for the whole advertisement. The main issue is the prorata charges for a given page. Theoretically, to receive an allowance, the retailer must demonstrate that the advertisement ran.

5. *Display allowances*. A display allowance is similar to cooperative advertising allowances. The manufacturer wants the retailer to display a given item when a price promotion is being run. To induce the retailer to do this and to help defray the costs, a display allowance is offered. Display allowances are usually a fixed amount per case, such as 50 cents per case.

6. *Sales drives*. For manufacturers selling through brokers or wholesalers, it is also necessary to offer incentives. Sales drives are intended to offer the brokers and wholesalers incentives to push the trade deal to the retailer. For every unit sold during the promotional period, the broker and wholesaler receive a percentage or fixed payment per case sold to the retailer. It works as an additional commission for an independent sales organization or additional margin for a wholesaler.

7. *Terms or inventory financing*. Just as durable goods manufacturers receive financing, so do retailers and wholesalers. The manufacturer may not require payment for 90 days, thus increasing the profitability to the retailer who does not need to borrow to finance inventories.

8. *Count-recount*. Rather than paying retailers on the number of units ordered, the manufacturer does it on the number of units sold. This is accomplished by determining the number of units on hand at the beginning of the promotional period (count) and then determining the number of units on hand at the end of the period (recount). Then, by tracking orders, the manufacturers know the quantity sold during the promotional period. (This differs from a bill-back because the manufacturer verifies the actual sales in count-recount.)

9. *Slotting allowances*. Recently, manufacturers have been paying retailers funds known as slotting allowances to receive space for new products. When a new product is introduced the manufacturer pays the retailer X dollars for a "slot" for the new

product. Slotting allowances are a fixed payment to the retailer for accepting and testing a new product.

10. *Street money.* Manufacturers have begun to pay retailers lump sums to run promotions. The lump sum, not per case sold, is based on the amount of support (feature advertising, price reduction, and display space) offered by the retailer. The name comes from the manufacturer's need to offer independent retailers a fixed fund to promote the product because the trade deal goes to the wholesaler.

The foregoing description of trade deals is intended to give the reader some understanding of how the system works. (Also see Chapter 13 for additional examples.) To make it more concrete, a specific trade deal from a manufacturer is given in Figure 11.1.

 **COLGATE-PALMOLIVE** *COMPANY*

A Delaware Corporation

300 Park Avenue
New York, NY 10022-7499
Telephone 212-310-2000
Cable Address PALMOLIVE

November 5, 1988

To Our Valued Customers:

We are pleased to offer an allowance of $5.60 off invoice on Ajax Laundry Detergent Giant size for the six week shipping period beginning Monday, February 6, 1989 and ending Friday March 17th. Invoice protection will be provided for the two weeks prior this Ajax Giant off invoice promotion, and your final order date is Friday, March 10th.

Product Information

Item	UPC	Case Packout	Case Weight	Case Cube	Pallet Pattern
Ajax Giant	05281	14/36oz.	37.5 lbs.	1.85	9x5=45

On a truckload basis, this brings your cost per case from $19.90 down to $14.30, or $1.021 per unit, making this package a very attractive feature and display item. Together with Ajax Liquid Detergent King and Ajax Family Size Cleaner, an advertising and display event may qualify for support from the Ajax Line Special Event Merchandising Contract.

Sincerely

Vice President - Sales

FIGURE 11.1

Source: Colgate-Palmolive Company, N.Y., N.Y.

C-P COLGATE-PALMOLIVE COMPANY

Ajax Line Special Event
Merchandising Contract
Household Products Division

☐ DIRECT   ☐ INDIRECT   ☐ COOPERATIVE JOBBER

AGREEMENT made as of this ____ day of _____ , 19 __ , between COLGATE-PALMOLIVE COMPANY (COLGATE) and the undersigned DEALER.

COLGATE agrees to pay DEALER for "SPECIAL EVENT" promotional services on selected Ajax brands during each of the two performance periods of this agreement (January 1 to June 30, 1989, and July 1 to December 31, 1989) on the following terms and conditions:

TERMS AND CONDITIONS:

1. A fund for each performance period will be accrued equal to 50¢ per case on all sizes (*selected case pack changes are accrued at the equivalized base case rate as set forth in the attached addendum to this agreement) of AJAX LINE items, shipped to the DEALER during each base period which will be the same six month periods noted above, prior year.

2. Monies under this fund may be earned only when DEALER renders "SPECIAL EVENT" type of promotions (for example, Rotogravure, Television, Radio, or Other), and when such performance is in support of and in addition to performance rendered under an applicable COLGATE sponsored short term Promotion. The DEALER will qualify for maximum payment by selecting three different Ajax brands per performance period (approved by the COLGATE SALES REPRESENTATIVE), and featuring them together in the primary "SPECIAL EVENT" type of promotion used by DEALER.

   NOTE: *If Print Media is used advertising space must be a minimum of 4 column inches.*

3. COLGATE agrees to pay the DEALER for each performance period 1.15 per case on all cases (*selected case pack changes are paid at the equivalized base case rate as set forth in the attached addendum to this agreement) purchased and shipped to DEALER'S stores in support of the "SPECIAL EVENT" and the COLGATE applicable sponsored short term promotion (s), providing that total payment for each period does not exceed the available fund for that period. Monies available for any one promotional period must be earned by the DEALER during that period.

4. The "SPECIAL EVENT" Advertising must include the unit retail price of the item(s); must not be included or combined with any competing brands; nor can it be combined with more than three other items within a 30-second radio/television commercial.

5. Payment will be made to the DEALER upon receipt of the Certificate of Performance which must indicate in the "Remarks" section the Jobber's invoice number(s) if invoiced by Jobber; a copy of the applicable short term agreement which indicates the number of cases shipped in support of the COLGATE sponsored short term promotion(s); and documentary proof (script/storyboard, tear sheet of rotogravure, and any other appropriate proof of performance as may be required) satisfactory to COLGATE that the "SPECIAL EVENT" performance was rendered as required under the Terms and Conditions of this agreement. Such payments may not be used to reduce, or as set off against, the sale price of any COLGATE product, nor is any amount claimed to be due hereunder to be deducted by the DEALER from any invoice or bill for COLGATE products. In no event shall COLGATE have any liability to make payment unless proof of performance is submitted within 30 days after the termination of the performance period.

6. If DEALER arranges or sponsors advertising on behalf of two or more retail stores, DEALER represents that he has received written authorization to perform the services for which allowances are available hereunder.

7. DEALER operating stores under more than one trade name will accrue a fund based only on purchases for stores operating under the name or names which advertising is run.

8. COLGATE may initiate separate "SPECIAL EVENT" agreements with individual members of voluntary chains or associations and make payment on such agreements direct to individual stores. The amount of money paid will be deducted from the gross amount earned by the voluntary chain or association under the agreement.

9. All "SPECIAL EVENT" promotions must be for the benefit of all stores operated or regularly serviced by the DEALER.

0. This agreement terminates on December 31, 1989, unless it is sooner terminated by either party upon not less than five (5) days written notice to the other party, in which event DEALER shall be paid upon the basis of his performance up to the date of termination. This agreement is available to all competing customers of COLGATE.

11. For those DEALERS who do not advertise on television/radio or in rotogravure, off-shelf display will be acceptable providing the item(s) covered by this agreement are floor displayed in each of the DEALER'S stores for a period of at least three (3) consecutive weeks and the item(s) are supported by a price reduction that is to be in excess of any other price reduction which may be in effect on the short term promotion(s) applicable to this agreement.

Dealer's Name (Print)	Account Number	Advertising As (Trade Name, If Any)
Street Address City State Zip		Authorized Representative (Signature)
Colgate Representative (Signature)		District

010

FIGURE 11.1 (cont.)

In looking at Figure 11.1, one sees that the trade deal is offering a $5.60 off invoice for a period from January 23 (two weeks prior to shipping) to March 10. The ship dates are from February 6 to March 17. Notice that the regular price is $19.90 making the discount approximately 23%.

The second page of Figure 11.1 shows a special event merchandising contract listing the performance required of the retailer. Term 1 gives an accrual fund which is used for "special events" such as television or radio advertising. Term 2 states the terms under which this fund can be used and indicates using 3 Ajax brands increases the payments under the contract. Term 3 gives $1.15 for special events such as newspaper advertising. Term 10 terminates the agreement. Term 11 allows the "dealer" to substitute displays. Note that a 3-week display is required which explains why displays often continue after the price discount is discontinued by the retailer.

To understand how the different types of trade promotion fit the objectives given earlier, Table 11.1 has been generated. The rows of the table show the trade promotion type and the columns different promotional objectives. Some promotions have more than one objective.

The most frequently used promotions are designed to load the dealer, to serve as a competitive tool, to reduce the retail price temporarily, or to advertise the item through the retailer. These promotions correspond with inventory financing, off invoice, and cooperative advertising.

TABLE 11.1 Objectives of Trade Promotional Tactics

	Objectives[a]						
Tactics	1	2	3	4	5	6	7
Off invoice	x		x	x	x	x	
Bill-back	x		x	x	x	x	
Volume rebate					x		x
Free goods	x			x			
Floor planning			x			x	
Cooperative advertising	x					x	x
Display allowances	x					x	
SPIFFS		x					
Contests							x
Quota incentives	x		x		x		
Sales drives	x		x				
Slotting allowances			x	x			
Street money	x					x	

[a] Objectives:
1. Retailer merchandising activities
2. Retailer sales force incentives
3. Loading the retailer
4. Gaining or maintaining distribution
5. Obtain price reduction
6. Competitive tool
7. Retailer "goodwill"

In summary, the manufacturer has many trade promotional vehicles available. By setting objectives it becomes easier to decide which promotions to run. The ability to measure the execution of these objectives is very important, but most manufacturers do not have systems in place to determine how best to assess the impact of trade deals. The next section discusses several approaches that are used for measurement of trade deal effects.

MEASUREMENT OF TRADE DEAL EFFECTIVENESS

One of the important issues confronting brand managers is the measurement of the effectiveness and profitability of trade promotions. Three approaches will be discussed: (1) before-after analysis, (2) statistical models, and (3) frequency of retailer promotions based on trade deals.

Before-After Analysis

Many manufacturers use a system that will be called before-after analysis to assess the profitability and sales effect of a promotion. In this analysis manufacturers view their sales promotions as if they are time series quasi-experiments. (See Chapter 6 for a discussion of the problems in using this type of experimental design and analysis procedure.) The system looks at sales before, during, and after promotions. The before sales serve as a "baseline" which indicates what sales would have been if no promotion was run. The during indicates the sales increase due to the promotion, and the after indicates the sales dip after the promotion is completed. The dip occurs because retailers load their inventories when a trade deal is offered. After it is over, they sell off their excess inventory.

To understand how before-after analysis works, consider this example: Suppose for two months a firm offers a $2.00 off-invoice trade deal with a 50 cent advertising allowance. The regular price of a case of 24 units is $20.00. Assuming the retailer runs an ad (to receive the case allowance), the trade deal cost per case is $2.50. The incremental gross margin for the product is 50 percent or $10.00 per case.

Sales in the two months prior to the trade deal averaged 10,000 cases per month. "Average sales" is used as the baseline. During the two months of the trade deal, sales averaged 30,000 cases per month. For the two months after the trade deal sales dropped to 2,000 cases per month. Using this information it is possible to determine: (1) incremental sales and (2) incremental profits.

1. *Incremental sales.* For the four months during and after the trade promotions, case sales would have been 10,000 cases a month assuming the same sales rate that occurred before the trade deal was offered. Thus, 40,000 cases would have been sold. The actual sales were 30,000 × 2 plus 2,000 × 2 = 64,000 cases. Incremental case sales were 24,000 cases.

2. *Incremental profits.* Normal sales would have been 40,000 cases during the promotion at $20 per case or $800,000. Profits would have been $10 per case times 40,000 cases or $400,000 if no trade promotion had been run.

When the promotion was run, 60,000 cases were sold at a net price of $17.50 or $1,050,000 in sales. After the promotion ended, the sales were 4,000 cases at $20.00 per case or $80,000. The net sales during and after the promotion was $1,130,000.

The profit during the promotional period was 60,000 cases times $7.50 or $450,000. For the period after the promotion, the profits were 4,000 cases times $10.00 per case or $40,000. The profit for the during and after period is $490,000.

The incremental profit is simply $490,000 (the profit during and after the promotional) minus $400,000, the profit if no trade deal had been run, or $90,000.

The before-after analysis has several limitations. First, the "baseline" sales estimate is often very inaccurate. (See Chapters 7 and 9.) When a manufacturer promotes frequently, it is difficult to generate a baseline because sales are always influenced by promotions whether it is before, during, or after a particular deal. As a result, it is difficult to estimate baseline sales which assumes there are no promotions.

Another important limitation is due to the possibility that the promotion is offered at the same time as some other significant event occurs. The promotional estimate includes the effect of this unusual event. For example, the manufacturer offers a trade deal during the Christmas season. Did the trade deal or the seasonal effect cause the sales increase? This cannot be determined using a "before-after" analysis.

To overcome this problem more complex analysis of shipment data are needed. The next section describes how statistical models can be used to estimate promotional effectiveness.

Statistical Models

An alternative to before-after analysis is a statistical model. The model generates better estimates of the baseline. Two statistical models to measure trade dealing effectiveness will be discussed: Blattberg-Levin (1987) and PROMOTER (Abraham-Lodish, 1987). Both models use manufacturer shipments data and develop procedures to predict what sales would be in the absence of a trade promotion. Earlier work by Brown (1973) is not discussed but was the first attempt at building a trade promotion model and is the basis of a service called SPAR which analyzes trade promotions. The statistical methods are discussed in more detail in Chapters 7 and 9.

Blattberg-Levin Model.   The purpose of the Blattberg-Levin model is to measure the effectiveness and profitability of trade deals. The model is based on the structure given in Figure 11.2. It shows that the trade promotion affects the willingness of the retailer to offer a retail promotion. If the retailer runs a promotion, the brand's volume increases because the consumer switches to the promoted brand and, in some cases, increases consumption. However, the retailer also buys the trade dealt item for inventory (forward buying), and this increases shipments during the trade dealing period but decreases shipments after the trade deal is over.

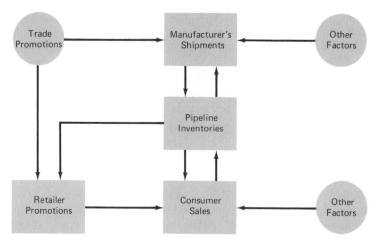

FIGURE 11.2 How a Trade Promotion Influences Sales

Source: Robert C. Blattberg and Alan Levin, "Modelling the Effectiveness and Profitability of Trade Promotions," *Marketing Science*, Vol. 6, no. 2 (Spring 1987), p. 127.

To summarize the effects from a trade deal,

1. The retailer runs a promotion in which a percentage of the units bought on trade deal are sold to the consumer at a discounted price (passthrough percentage).
2. Consumers increase their purchase of the brand when the retailer runs a promotion.
3. The retailer usually buys inventory at the end of the trade dealing period.
4. The retailer decreases its buying after the trade deal ends and relies on inventory bought during the trade dealing period.

Figure 11.3 shows the variablity in bimonthly consumer sales and monthly shipments. It indicates that monthly shipments are far more variable than bimonthly consumer sales. The implication from this plot is that when a trade promotion is run, the retailer forward buys for inventory and then decreases purchases immediately afterward.

To capture these effects Blattberg and Levin developed a four-equation model. One of the equations was subsequently dropped because data were not available. However, with scanner data it is now possible to estimate all four equations.

The model contains the following equations:

Shipments:

$$\text{shipments}_t = f_1(\text{inventory}_{t-1}, \text{trade promotions}_t, \text{other factors}_t) \qquad \textbf{(11.1a)}$$

Retail promotions:

$$\text{retail promotions}_t = f_2(\text{trade promotions}_t, \text{trade promotions}_{t-1},$$
$$\text{inventories }_{t-1}) \qquad \textbf{(11.1b)}$$

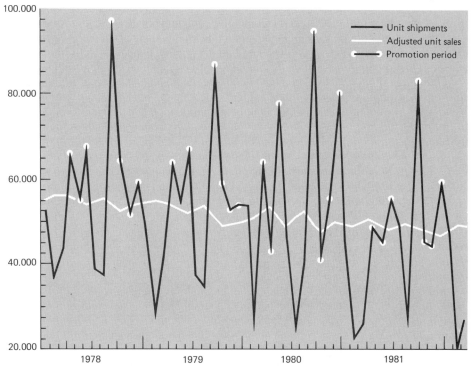

FIGURE 11.3 Nielsen Adjusted Sales versus Factory Shipments: Product X, Market 1

Source: Robert C. Blattberg and Alan Levin, "Modelling the Effectiveness and Profitability of Trade Promotions," *Marketing Science*, Vol. 6, no. 2 (Spring 1987), p. 128.

Consumer sales:

consumer sales$_t$ = f_3(retailer promotions$_t$, other factors$_t$) **(11.1c)**

Inventory:

inventories$_t$ = f_4(inventories$_{t-1}$, shipments$_t$, consumer sales$_{t-1}$) **(11.1d)**

where t = the time period and $f(\ \ )$ is a function.

The retailer promotion equation was omitted from the statistical estimation because no data existed to measure the frequency of retail promotions. Majers data exists, but the company did not purchase it.[1]

Using Nielsen bimonthly data, company shipments, trade deals, plus some other data (advertising, trend, and seasonality), Blattberg and Levin estimated the parameters in the shipments and consumer sales equation. Because Nielsen bimonthly data were used and these are not very sensitive to retail promotions, some adjustments were needed. As scanner data become available to measure

---

[1] Majers data will be discussed in the "Analysis of the Frequency of Retail Promotions" section. It is a service that identifies the type of feature advertising a manufacturer receives.

the effects of retail promotions, the precision of the estimates of consumer response of deals will be far more accurate.

Table 11.2 reproduces the model coefficients estimated by Blattberg and Levin. They show that trade promotions have a significant effect on shipments. They also show that inventory level works in the opposite direction of the promotional effects. If the retailer's inventory level is high, then shipments will be lower.

Blattberg and Levin's empirical results can be summarized as follows:

1. Trade deals increase shipments to the retailer.
2. Retailers forward buy, which decreases shipments after a promotion has ended (trough after trade deal.)
3. Consumer sales increase but not as much, as retailers forward buy as demonstrated by troughs in shipments after the deal.

To understand how these two conflicting effects work (forward buying versus consumers increasing purchasing of the trade dealt brand), Figure 11.4 has been reproduced from the Blattberg and Levin article.

Based on the model, Figure 11.4 shows how a trade deal affects shipments. It then overlays consumer sales and shows the long-run effect of a trade promotion. During the trade dealing period, the shipments increase and peak the last

TABLE 11.2 Coefficient Estimates for Two Markets and Sizes

| | Market 1/Size 2 | | Market 2/Size 2 | |
Variable	Coefficient	T-Ratio	Coefficient	T-Ratio
Shipments equation				
Lagged inventory	-3.29×10^{-5}	-2.94	-4.26×10^{-5}	-3.15
Trend	-5.964×10^{-3}	-0.72	-7.24×10^{-3}	0.88
Off invoice	36.9071	6.51	25.6119	4.93
End of deal	3.4142	0.75	4.2845	0.99
Sales drive	21.4402	3.27	3.4890	0.55
Price change	13.5317	2.31	4.6786	0.89
Fall premium	0.2029	1.34	0.2290	1.61
Constant	8.8366	45.32	8.7882	45.54
	$R^2 = .845$		$R^2 = .611$	
	No. of obs. = 35		No. of obs. = 35	
Consumer sales equation				
Lagged inventory	3.295×10^{-6}	2.10	4.880×10^{-7}	0.17
Seasonality	0.0127	2.69	0.0270	4.60
Trend	-0.0005	-2.01	1.737×10^{-3}	0.92
Lagged advertising	0.0005	0.33	1.990×10^{-3}	1.08
Constant	7.89	16.45	6.2365	10.65
	$R^2 = .446$		$R^2 = .511$	
	No. of obs. = 35		No. of obs. = 35	

Source: Robert C. Blattberg and Alan Levin, "Modelling the Effectiveness and Profitability of Trade Promotions," *Marketing Science*, Vol. 6, no. 2 (Spring 1987), p. 134.

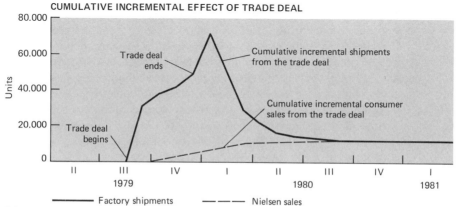

FIGURE 11.4 September–December 1979 8.3 Percent Off-Invoice Deal: Product X, Market 1

Source: Robert C. Blattberg and Alan Levin, "Modelling the Effectiveness and Profitability of Trade Promotions," Marketing Science, Vol. 6, no. 2 (Spring 1987), pp. 137–138.

week of the promotion when most retailers forward buy. Then, shipments fall off radically because the retailer uses warehouse inventory to replenish the stores. Once inventories are reduced to normal levels, the retailer will begin buying at "normal" levels. By aggregating across retailers, shipments will rise gradually because not all retailers forward buy the same number of weeks supply for inventory.

Consumer sales, on the other hand, increase during and immediately after the promotion (depending on when the retailer promotes) and cumulatively equal the long-run increase in shipments (due to the promotion). By definition, in the long-run consumer sales increase equals the shipments increase.[2] If, during the promotion, shipments increase above the long-run consumer sales increase, they must be reduced at another point in time. The result is that shipments during the

---

[2] The quantity consumers buy determines the incremental shipments since the retailer is simply "storing" the goods.

trade deal period are partially stolen from future period sales. Because sales during the trade deal are at a discount, these "lost" sales decrease the profitability of the trade deal.

Given these models Blattberg and Levin were able to determine deal profitability. To understand the procedure, suppose that incremental consumer sales were 15,000 cases. Long-run incremental shipments also has to be 15,000 cases. Regular sales (baseline) were approximately 20,000 cases per month. A promotion was run for four months. During the four months of the promotion, 135,000 cases were sold. Regular shipments (80,000) plus incremental shipments (15,000) were 95,000 cases. The retailer, therefore, forward bought 135,000 − 95,000 = 40,000 cases.

The promotion being analyzed was an $8\frac{1}{3}$ percent off-invoice promotion. Regular price was $12.00 per case, and so the discount was $1.00. Total shipments sold on promotion were equal to 80 percent[3] of product shipments during the promotion period. If the off-invoice allowance is $1.00 per case, the total cost of the promotion is $1.00 × [(.8 × 135,000)] = $108,000.

The gross margin percentage for this product was 50 percent, or $6.00 per case. The long-run incremental increase in case shipments was 15,000 cases resulting in an incremental profit for the additional units sold of $90,000.

Combining the two calculations of deal costs and incremental profits shows that the deal lost $18,000 ($90,000 − $108,000). While shipments had increased approximately 15,000 units, the cost of discounting shipments normally sold was greater than the profit gained from the promotion.

PROMOTER. Abraham and Lodish (1987) developed a modeling procedure that they called PROMOTER. The concept of PROMOTER is to develop a statistical procedure to offer a better estimate of the baseline sales than a simple "before-after" analysis does. The following is the basic model that they use. (See Chapter 9 for a more detailed description.)

$$S(t) = T(t) \times SI(t) \times X(t) \times [b(t) + p(t) + e(t)] \qquad (11.2)$$

where

$S(t)$ = sales at time t

$P(t)$ = promotion at time t

$T(t)$ = trend of sales not due to promotions

$SI(t)$ = seasonal index

$X(t)$ = exception index representing special factors

$B(t)$ = baseline sales at time t

$E(t)$ = noise at time t

$p(t)$ = promotion after removing seasonality and trend

$e(t)$ = noise after removing seasonality and trend

---

[3] Some retailers did not buy on promotion so 80 percent, not 100 percent, was sold.

$b(t)$ = baseline after removing seasonality and trend

$AS(t)$ = adjusted sales at time t

The following relationships are used by Abraham and Lodish:

$$p(t) = \frac{P(t)}{T(t) \times SI(t) \times X(t)} \tag{11.3a}$$

$$e(t) = \frac{E(t)}{T(t) \times SI(t) \times X(t)} \tag{11.3b}$$

$$b(t) = \frac{B(t)}{T(t) \times SI(t) \times X(t)} \tag{11.3c}$$

$$AS(t) = b(t) + p(t) + e(t) \tag{11.3d}$$

Using various estimation techniques, they estimate $b(t)$, which is the baseline sales adjusted for seasonality and trend when *no promotions* are run. Then, using the data when promotions are run it is possible to estimate $p(t)$.

Baseline Methods versus Consumer/Shipment Models.   The difference between the Blattberg-Levin model and PROMOTER is related to the need to model the consumer sales equation versus simply using a baseline for *shipments*. One of the controversies that will loom in the future will be whether shipment models can be used to evaluate trade deals.

To make the problem more concrete Table 11.3A gives an example of shipment data for a brand. The data show sales of 75 units during "normal periods," 0 units after a trade deal, and varying peaks during the trade deal "week." The baseline is clearly 75.

TABLE 11.3A   Shipment and Trade Deal (Example)

Week	Shipments	Trade Deal
1	75	
2	75	
3	75	
4	300	$2.00 off invoice
5	0	
6	0	
7	0	
8	225	$2.00 off invoice
9	0	
10	0	
11	75	
12	75	
13	225	$1.50 off invoice
14	0	
15	0	

Consumer sales data are given in Table 11.3B along with the shipment data. Normal sales are 50 units, and sales during retail promotions are 175. The total is the same as shipments. However, the true baseline is 50, not 75, which can be determined from consumer sales not shipments. The reason a shipment model is required is to estimate the quantity the retailer forward buys.

A model of shipments is necessary because one needs to assess the response to specific types of trade deals *holding fixed other variables.* For example, if inventories are high, then sales will be lower when a given trade deal is run. Using before-after measures does not adjust for these other variables.

By looking at both shipments and consumer sales, passthrough becomes clear. Figures 11.5A and 11.5B show two different situations. In Figure 11.5A, shipments are being passed on to the consumer. In Figure 11.5B, shipments are not being passed on even though the retailer is forward buying, particularly in later time periods. A baseline model looking only at shipments would not be able to show the lack of passthrough during the latter periods. Figure 11.5C shows a case where baseline analysis will work because there is a preperiod to develop a baseline.

In summary, more research is needed to learn the "best" modeling procedure for trade dealing. Both modeling approaches need refinement, and no doubt there will be other researchers working in this area who will provide different and superior models.

Analysis of the Frequency of Retail Promotions

The two models just described are designed to measure the profitability of a trade promotion given certain tactics. The users of the models and "before-after" anal-

TABLE 11.3B Shipment, Consumer Sales, Trade Deal, Consumer Promotion (Example)

Week	Shipments	Trade Deal	Consumer Sales	Consumer Promotion
1	75		50	
2	75		50	
3	75		50	
4	300	$2.00 off invoice	175	20¢ discount
5	0		50	
6	0		50	
7	0		50	
8	225	$2.00 off invoice	175	20¢ discount
9	0		50	
10	0		50	
11	75		50	
12	75		50	
13	225	$1.50 off invoice	175	20¢ discount
14	0		50	
15	0		50	

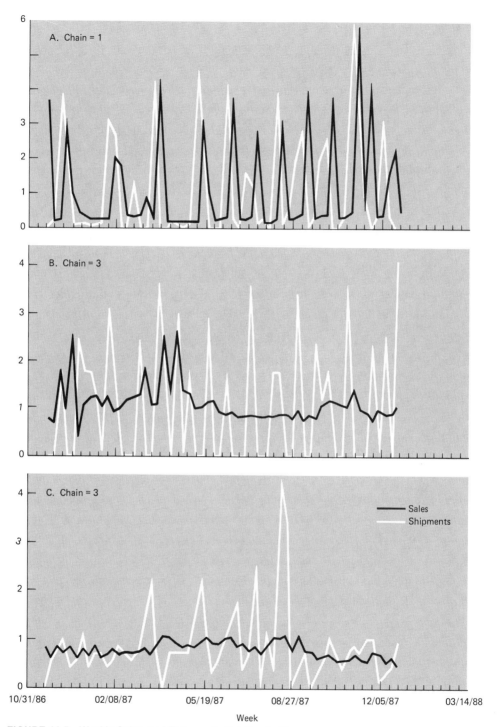

FIGURE 11.5   Weekly Sales and Shipments Relative to Mean

Source: A. C. Nielsen.

ysis are the brand management group. However, there is another equally important group, the sales force, who needs to understand the effectiveness of trade promotions.

The sales force is evaluated on how well they execute the marketing plan. In the case of trade deals, this means how often a retail promotion runs when a trade deal is offered. If the sales force is not receiving retail promotions, it means that the trade promotion is simply allowing the retailer to buy at a lower price without any increase in consumer sales. Majers (now part of A. C. Nielsen) has developed a service called Majers Feature Service that allows the manufacturer to track retail feature activity. Many of the leading package goods companies use this service.

Majers Feature Service records all retail promotions in a market for a given product category. Majers receives the newspapers, flyers, circulars, Roto sections and other media in the market which indicate which items have received retailer promotions. Then, reports are generated indicating the manufacturer's share of promotion by retailer and for the total market. If the retailer is not running ads and competitors are heavily featuring the item, the sales force will try to use this information to convince the retail buyer to run a promotion on a given item. The manufacturer can use the information to evaluate the performance of the sales force. When Majers Feature Service is combined with scanner data, management can also begin to learn which types of retail promotions generate the most profitable sales increases. This can be used by the brand manager to set promotional goals for the sales force.

To make this discussion concrete an example will be given. Suppose the sales force is looking at the promotional activity for smoked sausage in Atlanta in March 1987. Figure 11.6A shows all the retail feature activity for the top three chains in the market, Kroger, Food Giant, and Winn Dixie. The share of market is listed on the report which shows that Kroger has 29 percent and Food Giant and Winn Dixie each have 14 percent. One sees all the advertisements listed by day of the week. The report also lists the product size, the featured price and quantity, and the type of advertisement. The type of feature is divided into A, B, and C. Also listed are the ad lines.

Brand and sales management can look at the report and compare it to the activity (trade dealing) going on during the month to see how effective it has been. However, there is a summary report generated for the same data which is given in Figure 11.6B. The report shows a summary of the feature activity during a bimonthly period (February–March 1987).

In looking at the report one sees that Kroger does not run A ads for this category. The preponderance of the ads run by Kroger for the category are C ads with an occasional B ad. Winn-Dixie, on the other hand, runs A ads for the category and is the heaviest advertiser. Food Giant and Big Star, the other two large chains, are more heavily B and C advertisers. For the sales force this helps direct their activity. Can the sales force convince Kroger to run A ads for their brand? If the answer is no, then their effort should be devoted to the other three chains plus A&P who has 9 percent of the market.

Advertising Detail Report / Smoked Sausage, Seven-Day Retail Grocery Ad Activity. Current Period Is: March 1987, 26 Markets.

Market: Atlanta
% National Acv: .99%
% of Mkt Audited: 94%
# of Accts Audited: 10

Nspr & Vehic	Week of Ad	Day Adv	Brand	Style	Type	Product Size	Featured Qty/Price	Ad Rate/ Lines	Fam/ Shr	Promo & Ils Value	Wtd Value
Kroger	Shr of Mkt: 29%										
CN N	03/01	TU*	Eckrich	Choice of style	Unspecified	16 oz	1/1.99	A/150	F	X	1.72
MR	03/01	MO	Hillshire Farm	Choice of style	Unspecified	16 oz	1/1.99	B/ 20			.86
MR	03/08	MO	Old Village	Choice of style	Unspecified	16 oz	1/1.99	C/ 20			.29
CN N	03/08	TU*	Sunnyland	Beef	Unspecified	16 oz	1/1.99	A/ 80	F	X	1.72
CN N	03/15	TU*	Eckrich	Choice of style	Unspecified	16 oz	1/1.99	A/165	F	X	1.72
MR	03/15	MO	Old Village	Choice of style	Unspecified	16 oz	1/1.99	C/ 18			.29
MR	03/22	MO	Old Village	Choice of style	Unspecified	16 oz	1/1.99	C/ 16			.29
Food Giant	Shr of Mkt: 14%										
CN SR	03/01	MO	Hillshire Farm	Choice of style	Unspecified	16 oz	1/2.19	A/ 60	F		.83
CN SR	03/08	MO	Bryan	Choice of style	Unspecified	16 oz	1/2.19	B/ 25			.42
CN N	03/08	TU*	Bryan	Choice of style	Unspecified	16 oz	1/2.19	A/ 50	F	X	.83
CN N	03/08	TU*	Bryan	Beef	Unspecified	16 oz	1/2.59	A/ 16	F	X	.83
CN N	03/08	TU*	Mr Turkey	Unspecified	Unspecified	16 oz	1/1.89	A/ 15	F	X	.83
CN N	03/08	TU*	Smokey Hollow	Hot	Unspecified	16 oz	1/2.19	A/ 50	F	X	.83
CN N	03/08	TU*	Smokey Hollow	Smokies, choice	Cocktail	16 oz	1/2.59	A/ 50	F	X	.83
CN N	03/15	TH*	Hillshire Farm	Choice of style	Unspecified	16 oz	1/1.99	C/ 14			.14
CN N	03/15	TH*	Hillshire Farm	Hot	Links	16 oz	1/2.49	C/ 9	F		.14
CN N	03/15	TH*	Hillshire Farm	Beef	Links	16 oz	1/2.19	C/ 7			.14
CN N	03/15	TH*,	Hillshire Farm	Beef	Unspecified	16 oz	1/1.99	C/ 14	F		.14
CN SR	03/15	MO	Hillshire Farm	Choice of style	Unspecified	16 oz	1/1.99	A/ 70	F		.83
CN SR	03/22	TU*	Bar S	Unspecified	Unspecified	48 oz	1/4.59	A/ 60	F	X	.83
CN SR	03/22	MO	Mr Turkey	Turkey	Unspecified	16 oz	1/1.98	B/ 25	F		.42
Winn Dixie	Shr of Mkt: 14%										
CN SR	03/01	TH	Bryan	Choice of style	Unspecified	16 oz	1/2.29	A/ 14	F	X	.83
CN SR	03/01	TH	McEvers	Unspecified	Links	24 oz	1/2.49	A/ 50	F	X	.83
CN N	03/08	TH	Unspecified	Unspecified	Unspecified	48 oz	1/4.99	C/ 16			.14
CN N	03/15	TH	Bryan	Choice of style	Unspecified	16 oz	1/2.29	A/127	F	X	.83
CN N	03/15	FR*	Eckrich	Choice of style	Unspecified	16 oz	1/1.99	A/530		X	.83

* = Non-Best Food Day.

Source: A. C. Nielsen.

FIGURE 11.6A Advertising Detail Report/Smoked Sausage, Seven-Day Retail Grocery Ad Activity. Current Period Is: March 1987, 26 Markets.

Source: A. C. Nielsen.

Key Account Report/Smoked Sausage, Best Food Day Retail Grocery Ad Activity Only. Current Period Is: Feb. 1987–Mar. 1987.

Total Number of Ads and Ads by Type

Account	Acv %	Total Category				Total Eckrich Lean Supreme				Total Eckrich				Total Lean Supreme				Total Hillshire/ Kahn				Tot Hillshire/ Kahn Rope				Bryan/Smky Bryan Lean			
		A	B	C	Tot	A	B	C	Tot	A	B	C	Tot	A	B	C	Tot	A	B	C	Tot	A	B	C	Tot	A	B	C	Tot
Kroger	29																												
Bi-month T.Y.		1	6		7																			1	1			1	1
Bi-month L.Y.			6		6																		3		3	3			3
Current 12 Mo.		12	30		42	2	2		4	2	2		4						3		3					1	1		2
Food Giant	14																												
Bi-month T.Y.		3	5		8	1			1	1			1					2	2		4	2	2		4	1			1
Bi-month L.Y.		4	1	4	9		2		3		2		3						1		1		1		1				
Current 12 Mo.		14	31	31	76	5	6	7	18	4	6	7	17					5	8	8	21	5	6	4	15	2	4	3	9
Winn Dixie	14																												
Bi-month T.Y.		11	4		15	2			2	2			2					2	1		3	1	1		2	3			3
Bi-month L.Y.		11	11		22	2	5	7	14	2	5	7	14					1			1	1			1	11			11
Current 12 Mo.		53	20	29	102														1		1		1		1				
Big Star	13																												
Bi-month T.Y.		1	4	2	7	1			1	1			1										3	1	4				
Bi-month L.Y.		2	5		7	1			1	1			1						3	1	4		5		5	1	4	1	6
Current 12 Mo.		5	29	8	42	3	11		14	3	11		14					1	7	4	12	1	7	4	12	1			1
A & P	9																												
Bi-month T.Y.		1	4		5	2			3	2			3													1	1		2
Bi-month L.Y.		4	9		13	2	5		7	3	1		5	7					3		3		3		3	2	1		3
Current 12 Mo.		8	7	38	53	3	1	15	19	5			15	19						6	7	1	6		7	3	6	13	22
Big Apple Food W	4																												
Bi-month T.Y.		3	5		8	1			1	1			1					2	2		4	2	2		4	1			1
Bi-month L.Y.		4			4	1			1	1			1					3			3		1		1				
Current 12 Mo.		15	30	14	59	5	4	5	14	4	5	5	14	1				5	8	5	18	5	6	1	12	2	4	2	8
Thriftown/Big Bu	4																												
Bi-month T.Y.		2	4		6																								
Bi-month L.Y.		1	2	3	6																								
Current 12 Mo.		1	16	18	35																								
Cub Foods	3																												
Bi-month T.Y.		1			1																								
Bi-month L.Y.						Added—6/23/85				2			2	2			2	2											
Current 12 Mo.		5			5																								

A = Best—Most Dominant Pkg Product Feature / B = Good—Medium Dominance / C = Mention—Least Dominant.

Source: A. C. Nielsen.

FIGURE 11.6B Key Account Report/Smoked Sausage, Best Food Day Retail Grocery Ad Activity Only. Current Period Is: Feb. 1987–Mar. 1987.

Source: A. C. Nielsen.

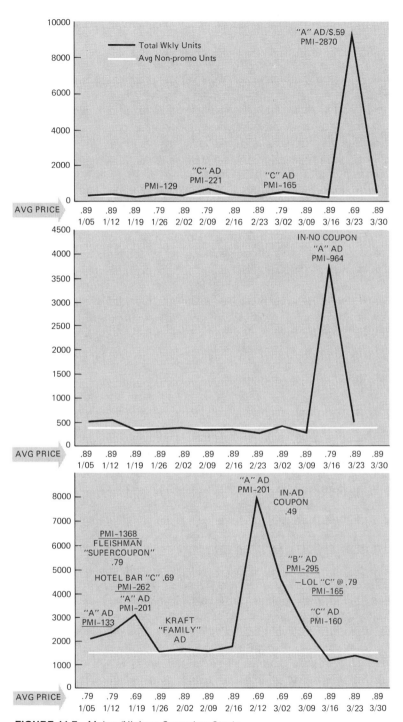

FIGURE 11.7 Majers/Nielsen Scanning Study

Source: A. C. Nielsen.

The data generated from these reports serves to direct the sales force and to evaluate the effectiveness of various trade promotions. The major problem is that it would be helpful to be able to relate the cost and return from running an A, B, and C ad to actual sales.

Nielsen Marketing Research has begun to use scanner data to evaluate promotional effectiveness of various newspaper feature advertising. The following is an example they have generated. Using a Majers/Nielsen Scanning Study of scanner data from a large retail chain in New York, they were able to study the effectiveness of A, B, and C ads. Beginning with Land O'Lakes stick margarine, Figure 11.7A shows that when an A ad is run with a $.59 price, sales go up 28.7 times the normal level whereas running a C ad with a price of $.79 generates only a 2.21 increase in sales. In both cases the regular price is $.89. Figure 11.7B shows that when Imperial margarine had a price decrease to $.79 from $.89 it received a 9.64 increase in sales.[4]

Figure 11.7C shows that Parkay received far more support since it was the brand leader. It received three promotions during the period and received three A ads, one B, and one C. Sales for Parkay increased less dramatically as a percentage, but the overall volume increase was much larger. When Parkay ran an A ad with a $.69 price and a $.20 in ad coupon, sales went up 4.14 times by about 6,000 units on a base of 1,500. When Parkay ran other A ads, they were less effective because competition was also running ads.

The analysis presented is simply to show how advertising evaluation can be enhanced with an accurate description of the advertising combined with scanner data. (Chapter 12 discusses the measurement of retail promotions in more detail.)

In summary, several approaches have been described which analyze trade promotional effectiveness. These range from the simple before-after analysis to more complex statistical models of Blattberg-Levin and PROMOTER. For the sales force Majers Feature Service offers information about the degree of retail feature advertising a brand received.

FINDINGS REGARDING PASSTHROUGH

While little has been written about trade dealing, it is possible to indicate several key findings regarding passthrough of trade promotions. In discussing these results it is important to understand the key trade-off which influences the profitability of a trade promotion: increase consumer sales versus the retailer forward buying at the lower prices. In other words, does the manufacturer receive enough passthrough to justify the cost of trade dealing? This section begins with a brief discussion of forward buying and continues with a discussion of the research results of Bucklin (1987), Curhan and Kopp (1986), and Blattberg and Levin (1987).

---

[4] Note that these data are analyzed using time series quasi-experimental models described in Chapter 6.

Forward Buying

The retailer, being a rational economic agent, has learned that when a trade promotion is offered, it is possible not only to buy the quantity needed during the promotional period but also to buy an increased quantity just as the promotional period ends to reduce the future cost of goods paid by the retailer or wholesaler. This is called forward buying.

Most large retail chains use some form of an EOQ (economic order quantity) model which trades off the storage cost, financial holding cost, and labor costs with the reduced discount available from the manufacturer. Many retailers have reduced the computation to a simple chart which shows the buyer how much should be ordered. (See Chapter 14.)

A buying chart has the following variables listed on it: price per case, number of units per case, number of cases per pallet, and interest rate. A pallet is simply the device used to store the good and represents a fixed quantity of space. The chart then indicates for a given discount how many weeks of supply the buyer should purchase. Weeks supply will vary by item, and the buyer needs to have an estimate of normal volume of the item. For many items it is possible that the retailer will not need to buy all the weeks supply implied by the model because the manufacturer will offer another trade deal before the period has ended.

Which items will be forward bought? Those items with high absolute dollar discounts and low storage costs (many cases per pallet) are forward bought extensively. Those items with high storage costs and low dollar value are forward bought significantly less. The manufacturer knowing this behavior of the retailer should then design mechanisms to limit the quantity bought by the retailer for items that have low storage costs and high dollar discounts. These procedures are discussed in "Strategies for Trade Dealing."

Passthrough

As was stated, the critical issue that the manufacturer faces is: Will my trade promotion be passed through to the consumer? It is therefore important to understand what causes the passthrough of a trade deal.

Bucklin (1987) developed a simple model to see what factors influence retailers' passthrough of a trade deal. He defined passthrough as the percentage of the trade deal that is given to the consumer. Another definition is the percentage of the promotion passed through to the consumer given that the retailer accepts it[5] as well as the percentage of the dollar amount passed through.

Bucklin's model implies that leading brands will receive greater passthrough than weaker brands and that weaker retailers will run more promotions than strong retailers. Then using a coffee database from SAMI/Burke and trade dealing data from a private source, he analyzed the degree of passthrough. He finds that the

---

[5] Accepting a promotion means the retailer offers the consumer some type of price cut and/or merchandising (feature and/or display) for the item.

hypotheses generated are confirmed in the data. Thus, being a strong brand increases trade dealing effectiveness through greater passthrough.

Curhan and Kopp (1986) use a database in which they analyze the promotional decisions of five retail chains. They divided trade support (passthrough) into four groups: none, nominal, moderate, and strong. The empirical results were

1. None—53.8%
2. Nominal—28.7%
3. Moderate—8.7%
4. Strong—8.6%

This clearly indicates that a high percentage of promotions do not receive any retailer support.

What factors influence the level of support that the retailers receive? The following were found by Curhan and Kopp:

1. Item profitability
2. Manufacturer reputation
3. Item importance
4. Promotional elasticity
5. Manufacturer brand support
6. Incentive amount

One can redefine these into the following four variables:

1. Economic structure of the trade deal
   a. Deal discount, allowances, and terms
   b. Performance requirements and restrictions
   c. Length of the deal
2. Item importance
   a. Volume
   b. Category
   c. Competitive retailer promotional activity
3. Manufacturer's reputation
4. Promotional elasticity
   a. Own promotional elasticity
   b. Cannibalization

Based on this study it is easy to understand why trade deals are unprofitable. A high percentage of items are not passed through. It is also clear that the brand's position is critical to the effectiveness of a trade promotion. Leading brands are more likely to receive passthrough than a weak brand. Before a brand's trade promotions are effective it is necessary to create a strong "consumer" pull for the product. Thus, other marketing variables such as advertising and other pull strategies interact with trade deals.

Profitability of Trade Deals

Blattberg and Levin (1987) analyze passthrough and trade dealing costs to determine brand profitability. (See "Blattberg-Levin Model" for the methodology.) Figure 11.8 shows the results. Trade dealing is almost always unprofitable for the

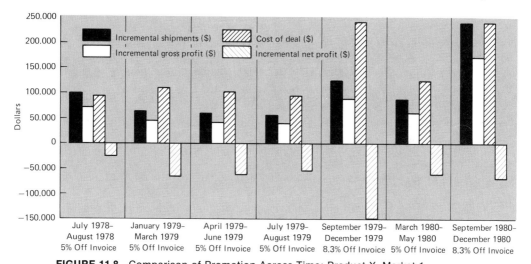

FIGURE 11.8 Comparison of Promotion Across Time: Product X, Market 1

Source: Robert C. Blattberg and Alan Levin, "Modelling the Effectiveness and Profitability of Trade Promotions," *Marketing Science,* Vol. 6, no. 2 (Spring 1987), p. 140.

brand under study. In fact, as the company increased the level of trade promotions (frequency and off-invoice discount), its profitability declined even further. This result appears to be consistent with those found by other manufacturers. (IRI reports only 15 percent of trade deals pay out.) It is very difficult to show that trade deals are profitable.

Chevalier and Curhan (1976) give some indication about why this happens. First, not all trade deals are "passed through" to the consumer. Many retailers "pocket" the trade deal dollars and do not offer a retail promotion or offer only a C ad with almost no price discount. In either case, the consumer sales increase from the trade deal is minimal, but the retailer forward buys extensively.

Second, even if there is consumer passthrough of the trade deal, is it enough to overcome the forward buying? In the Blattberg and Levin analysis, the brand under study sold almost 70 percent of its annual volume on trade deal and yet received very little consumer passthrough. Even if a product triples its sales for one week during the trade promotion period, it may not be enough to compensate for the high volume sold to the retailer during the trade dealing period. Some brands would be better off decreasing their market share but selling less on trade promotion. However, brand managers are reluctant to follow this strategy.

Third, the brand's position in the market is important in explaining the degree to which passthrough occurs. If the brand has high market share, the retailer is much more likely to pass it through. Further, the retailer's deal profitability is significantly higher to the retailer if a leading brand is offered because all its sales will not come from other brands in a category. Sales come from store switchers or infrequent category buyers. Blattberg and Wisniewski (1987) give an example of deal profitability to the retailer and show that the weaker brands, particularly those that are not differentiated, gain their sales from other brands in the category. (See Chapters 12 and 14 for further discussion of this issue.)

In summary, the profitability of trade promotions is generally negative. Since this is commonly found, then what justification can be given for continuing to run trade promotions? The answer usually given is competition (prisoner's dilemma), though Chapter 4 offers other explanations.

Conclusions Regarding Passthrough

The following are the conclusions from the limited number of studies of trade promotions:

1. Retailers forward buy when trade deals are offered.
2. Leading brands receive more promotions than weaker brands.
3. Factors influencing passthrough are
   a. Promotional elasticities
   b. Item importance
   c. Manufacturer incentives

Given these conclusions, the key issues facing the manufacturer are: How can more effective trade deals be run? What marketing mix tools can be used as a substitute for trade dealing? Very few firms have been able to answer either question.

STRATEGIES FOR TRADE DEALING

The purpose of this section is to discuss the strategies and tactics that a firm can use in trying to improve its trade dealing activities. The section begins by describing when it is advantageous for the manufacturer to trade deal. Then, some alternative tactics are described which can improve the effectiveness of trade deals. (Also see Chapter 15 for a discussion of this issue.)

When Manufacturers Should Trade Deal

Most firms feel that trade dealing is the necessary cost of doing business. Unfortunately, the high cost of trade dealing means managers will no longer be able to rely on this argument. It is, therefore, useful to understand the conditions when trade deals are advantageous to the firm.

Table 11.4 shows a simple matrix which has two axes: retail deal elasticity and holding costs by the retailer. For simplicity the matrix is divided into four cells, categories with high and low holding costs, and brands with high and low deal elasticities. The matrix indicates whether the brand should trade deal. If the category has high carrying costs and high promotional elasticities, then it should be trade dealt. The reason is that the retailer will not forward buy significantly and has an incentive to promote the brand (high promotional elasticity). At the other extreme is a product with low promotional elasticity and low holding cost.

TABLE 11.4 When a Brand Should Trade Promote

		Holding Costs	
		High	Low
Promotional Elasticity	High	Promote Paper Products	? Tuna Fish
	Low	Do Not Promote Specialty Cheeses	Do Not Promote Laxatives

The retailer will forward buy this item and not pass it through because there is very little reason to promote it to the consumer.

One cell of the matrix contains a case in which neither the retailer nor the manufacturer wants to promote the item: high holding costs and low deal elasticity.[6] The most difficult cell is low holding cost but high deal elasticity. The retailer definitely wants the product trade dealt because it will promote it and forward buy it. However, for the manufacturer it is a more difficult decision because the trade deal will result in significant forward buying. However, competitors will force trade promotions to be run unless their is some form of collusion.

Table 11.4 also lists some product categories that fit into each cell. Paper products are ideal products to trade deal because it is difficult for the retailer to stock months of supplies. Tuna is an example of a category with high promotional elasticities and low holding costs. Laxatives are an example of low holding cost but low promotional elasticity. Specialty cheeses are an example of high holding costs (refrigeration is required) and low promotional elasticities (directed to small market segments).

The brand manager can determine where his or her products fit into this matrix and then decide if trade promotions should be a significant part of the marketing mix.

Tactics for Improving Trade Promotion Results

Given all the problems with trade dealing discussed throughout this chapter, what are possible alternative tactics which can improve the effectiveness of trade promotions? The ones listed are not new to brand managers and are often viewed negatively by the retailer. However, if the firm is relying heavily on trade dealing to improve market share and sales, then these remedies discussed should be tried.

The first is *count-recount* which is used only by a few manufacturers. Count-

---

[6] The manufacturer may want to promote the item to pass on holding costs, but the retailer may be less efficient than the manufacturer at storing the items.

recount simply pays the retailer on the number of units moved from the warehouse to the store, which serves as a surrogate for consumer sales. Thus, for every unit sold to the consumer the retailer will be paid a certain dollar amount. The advantage of count-recount is that the manufacturer only pays for the units passed through and not for the units forward bought. Some forward buying can take place but it is usually limited. The disadvantages of count-recount are the monitoring cost and the retailer's dissatisfaction with it and unwillingness to accept the promotion because it limits the forward buying for the brand.

For a manufacturer with strong brands count-recount may be very effective because no retailer is going to want a key competitor promoting the item without the opportunity to promote the brand. They will therefore accept the trade deal. For a manufacturer with weak brands just the opposite will be true. The retailer will simply not accept the promotion. Thus, weak brands are at a distinct disadvantage when count-recount is used effectively by leading brands.

The second tool, also disliked by the retailer, is *bill-backs*. A bill-back is similar to an off invoice promotion, but the retailer must bill back the manufacturer for the promotional allowances achieved during the trade promotion. These include price discount, display, and ad allowance. The advantage is compliance. If the manufacturer requires an A ad for the retailer to receive the promotional allowances, then the retailer will not be paid unless the appropriate actions were taken. Bill-back gives the manufacturer the chance not to pay the retailer, whereas off invoice makes it very difficult to enforce the promotional contracts.

The third technique is *allocations*. The manufacturer determines the normal volume a retailer sells in a fixed time period. When a trade deal is run, then the retailer is allowed to buy only a certain number of additional weeks supply. Thus, the forward buy quantity is limited, and the profitability of the trade deal increases.

The final issue addresses problems that weak brands face. Most trade dealing is unprofitable for a weaker brand because the retailer passthrough is less. What actions should a weak brand take? Contrary to practice, a weak brand should increase its expenditures on pull, not push. Pull strategies can strengthen the brands position in the market and then allow it to receive more trade support. Without a strong consumer position, it is difficult to receive trade support. Therefore, investing in advertising, couponing, product reformulation, and other actions directed to increase the brand's underlying preference to the consumer is money well spent. Trade promotions are likely to be simply used to "maintain" distribution but result in very limited passthrough.

All these actions are easy to describe theoretically, but most manufacturers are reluctant to enforce them for fear of alienating the retailer. However, unless some action is taken, the firm's trade deals are highly unprofitable. Therefore, it may be worth taking some risk by enforcing the contracts and seeing what will happen.

SUMMARY

This chapter has described how trade dealing works. While it represents a significant part of the marketing manager's budget for most consumer product companies and products sold through dealers and distributors such as tractors, there are very few academic articles or books written about it. However, with the increased interest in promotions as a marketing mix tool, far more will be written about trade deals resulting in a greater understanding about when to use a trade promotion and how to best design a trade promotion.

The chapter gave many of the objectives of trade promotions and then a description of the types of trade deals used by durable and nondurable consumer product companies. It is clear from this discussion that the objectives of trade promotions are complex and it makes measurement of the effectiveness of trade promotions more difficult.

Several methods of measuring trade promotion effectiveness were given, ranging from the simple before-after analysis used by many packaged goods companies, to statistical models such as Blattberg-Levin or PROMOTER, to MASTER TRACK, which shows how effective a trade promotion is in receiving retailer support. While these procedures exist, the state of measurement of trade dealing is very crude, and far more work is needed in this area.

The chapter ended with a discussion of the empirical findings and actions that a firm can take to improve their trade dealing effectiveness. The empirical findings highlighted the low consumer passthrough percentage of most trade deals. The recommendations ranged from instituting a count-recount system to decrease retailer forward buying to shifting trade promotion expenditures to consumer pull strategies. Again far more research is needed into how and when a trade promotion is effective.

12

Retail Promotions

Promotions are a way of life for retailers. Every week when the consumer goes to the grocery store, there are as many as 100 items on sale that have been advertised in the newspaper and 15 to 20 items on display. Department stores run periodic sale events, automobile dealers offer clearance sales, heavy equipment companies give free demonstrations. Promotions, which include price discounts, feature advertising, displays, special events, are one of the primary marketing mechanisms retailers use.

To understand the impact of promotions better, Figure 12.1 shows data for sales and promotion frequency for Northern Bathroom Tissue within one chain in a Northeastern market. Every three to four weeks Northern is promoted. The promotional discount is usually in the range of 10 percent, and the sales increase is two to three times normal sales. Approximately 50 percent of the brand's volume is sold on a retail promotion. Figure 12.2 shows the promotional frequency for the same product across the major chains in the market. It shows at least one chain is promoting Northern almost every week.

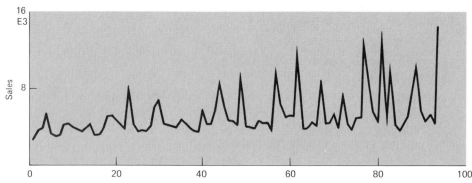

FIGURE 12.1 Discounts versus Sales—Northern

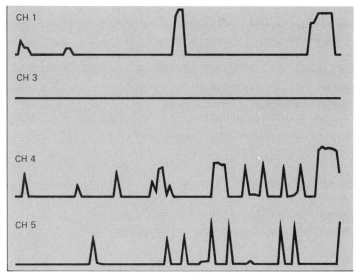

FIGURE 12.2   Promotional Frequency Across the Major Chains in the
Market—Northern

Source: A. C. Nielsen.

While bathroom tissue is a heavily promoted product, it does show how important retail promotions are to a brand. Table 12.1 shows the percentage of the sales sold on deal for four categories. Clearly for most of the brands analyzed a high percentage (50 percent) of total sales are from retail promotions. It is therefore very important for manufacturers and retailers to understand how these promotions influence sales.

The remainder of this chapter will explore retail promotions, namely, types of retail promotions, empirical findings about how retail promotions work, measurement of retail promotions, measuring the profitability of retail promotions, and future research issues.

TYPES OF PROMOTIONS OFFERED BY RETAILERS

Before discussing the measurement of promotions, it is useful to understand the different types of retail promotions. The list given in this section is not necessarily inclusive but will highlight some of the more common promotions used by retailers.

Price Discounts

Probably the most prevalent promotional tool is a price discount. A special price is offered with discounts ranging from 2–10 percent on items such as automobiles

TABLE 12.1 Effect of Retailers' Promotions on Individual Brand Sales

Brand	Market Share	Percentage of Units Sold on a Retail Promotion
Flour		
Pillsbury	19.7%	67.3%
Gold Medal	11.9	55.8
Ceresota	10.5	36.0
Jewel Maid	9.2	49.9
Margarine		
Imperial	14.3	65.5
Land O' Lakes	11.1	71.1
Parkay	7.2	75.4
Chiffon	5.9	40.6
Blue Bonnet	3.0	81.3
Blue Brook	39.7	34.9
Sunnyland	7.1	32.3
Generic	11.7	0
Bathroom tissue		
Charmin	15.0	42.7
Scott Tissue	14.6	51.6
Northern	7.2	61.3
White Cloud	6.3	43.1
Soft 'N Pretty	3.9	54.8
Jewel	1.8	52.6
Coronet	2.8	34.9
Generic	48.4	0
Tuna fish		
Chicken of the Sea	16.9	60.7
Bumble Bee	8.4	83.7
Starkist	6.8	64.2
Blue Brook	13.3	37.9
Generic	54.6	0

Source: Robert C. Blattberg and Kenneth J. Wisniewski, "How Retail Price Promotions Work: Empirical Results," working paper 42, University of Chicago, December, 1987.

to as much as 70 percent on obsolete inventories, floor samples, and out-of-season items.

While price discounts are straightforward, retailers are cognizant of using psychological mechanisms to enhance price image. Retailers will indicate the level of the price cut to the consumer in the form of "regularly *x* and now *y*" (e.g., regularly $1.89, now $1.69). This might encourage the consumer to anchor on the regular price discount, enhancing the perceived value of the price discount. (See Chapter 2.)

It is common for food retailers to offer a "2 for" or "3 for" price to the consumer. An item might be priced at 3 for $1 rather than 34 cents. The consumer behaves differently depending upon which of the two discounts is offered. The suggestion that the consumer should buy three items to get the discount often motivates the customer to buy more units. A retailer may actually sell more units at 3 for $1 than at 31 cents because the consumer reacts to the suggestion of buying three. Empirical evidence will be given later showing that "N for" are powerful promotions.

Displays

One of the most important forms of retail promotions is a display. Displays greatly increase sales, but the space available is limited and expensive. In a grocery store there may be only 10–15 items that receive major display space at a given time, and they are usually reserved for high-volume items.

The types of displays differ by type of store. By way of example, in a grocery store there are four major types of displays. The first is an end-of-aisle in which the item is displayed at the end of a major aisle in the store. It attracts high store traffic and is usually a large display. It is strategically placed so that the customers must pass it numerous times in going through the store.

The second is a "front-of-the-store" display which is similar to an end-of-aisle display except that it is located at the front of the store so that it is seen when the customer enters the store. It has high traffic volume, and the customer does not have his or her shopping cart filled yet. This is viewed as the "premier" display type.

The third type is an in-aisle display. It is located in the aisle in which the item is sold. It usually highlights some form of special promotion. The advantage of an in-aisle display is that if focuses the consumer on the promoted item relative to the non-promoted items in the category. If the item is more profitable to the retailer, then shifting the consumer's purchases to the promoted item will result in greater profitability.

The final type of display is a "shelf-talker." It is a tag or some type of sign that is displayed on the shelf above or below the item being displayed. The shelf-talker signifies to the consumer the item is being promoted. For items in the dairy case or other items that are difficult to display, shelf-talkers are frequently used.

Displays, along with retail feature advertising, may interact with price discounts. If the consumer is not informed that a price discount is offered, the price elasticity is likely to be small. Chapter 7 identifies statistical procedures which take into account the joint effect of price discounts, displays, and feature advertising.

There are other forms of point-of-purchase (POP) displays used in the store. Sweepstakes and contests are usually announced with some form of POP. Retailers view these types of displays as "background" information for the consumer regarding some type of event a manufacturer is offering.

Retail Newspaper Advertising

The other heavily used promotional tool is feature advertising. A feature advertisement is run in the daily or weekly local newspapers or a special circular distributed around the store. For grocery products feature advertising is run on Wednesday or Thursday which is known as "Best food day." The items advertised usually appear with special prices. Most general merchandisers (e.g., Sears, K Mart) use Sunday for newspaper inserts.

Feature advertising on best food day usually contains several pages of items. The size of the advertising for an item is divided into three major categories. Major ads (A ads) are large and feature the highest volume items with the largest price reductions. The next are medium-sized ads (B ads), which contain items which are either lower in volume or have a smaller deal discount than the items in the A ads. Finally, there are line ads (C ads) containing items that may not have a price discount but are advertised to receive the advertising allowance from the manufacturer.

Manufacturers use co-op or advertising allowances to induce the retailer to feature their items in the ad. For a department store, many of the items that are run in their ads are partially paid for by co-op advertising. For appliance dealers, between 50 and 75 percent of the advertising cost is covered by the co-op advertising allowance depending upon whether the dealer uses the manufacturer's ad or their own. Food retailers pay for almost 100 percent of their ad by using advertising allowances supplied by the manufacturers. Therefore, the promotional dollars offered by the manufacturers play an important part in determining the items that are featured in a given week's advertisement.

Other Promotions

There are many other types of price promotions offered by retailers. For example, a bank in Tennessee offered its customers two options for the purchase of a certificate of deposit (CD). The customer could buy a CD worth $50,000 at an interest rate of 8.5 percent for a five-year period, or he or she could have a lower interest rate of 7.5 percent but receive an Apple computer. Many of the customers chose the Apple computer even though its actual value was less than 1 percent of $50,000 for a five-year period. The reason is that the retailer (bank) is able to find situations in which customers have a difficult time comparing offers and often choose the one that appears to offer a higher value.[1] The form of the discount has as much influence on the promotion's effectiveness as the amount of the price reduction.

Occasionally retailers will use other forms of promotions. Rather than use a price discount, an "in-ad" coupon is used which is available to anyone shopping in the store. This limits the quantity that can be bought on a promotion. Durable

---

[1] Chapter 2 discusses "mental accounting" and its implications for promotions.

goods retailers will offer special financing charges rather than a lower price. This often discriminates against cash buyers but avoids actually cutting price. Premiums have long been offered to consumers who purchased gasoline in the 1970s prior to OPEC (Organization of Petroleum Exporting Countries). Banks and savings and loans offer special premiums if consumers make a certain size of deposit or open new accounts.

Free trial for a service is also offered to induce initial trial. Some brokerage houses offer free "first trades." Banks will offer free checking accounts as a mechanism to obtain other accounts from the consumer.

There are many other forms of retailer promotions that are used, but the primary types have just been described. No doubt over the next several years there will be additional forms of retailer promotions. As long as there is an opportunity to attract customers or to sell additional items through some form of promotion, retailers will focus on the best way to do this.

EMPIRICAL EVIDENCE ABOUT RETAIL PROMOTIONAL EFFECTS

This section will describe the empirical results from research on retail promotions to provide empirical evidence about how promotional effects work. The individual effects drawn from this section are combined into the measurement model in the next section. The empirical findings are divided into the following areas: (1) psychological pricing, (2) shape of deal effect, (3) own and cross-deal elasticities, (4) price versus promotional elasticities, (5) feature advertising and display, (6) promotional elasticities across markets, (7) stockpiling, (8) deal decay, (9) deal carryover effects, and (10) price tiers.

Psychological Pricing

Retailers frequently price using the last digit ending in "9" and "2 for 99 cents" pricing. The question is: Do these techniques work? Blattberg and Wisniewski (1987) studied this question using the University of Chicago Retail Scanner Database. The model used to produce these results is given in the next section.

Table 12.2 shows the results of an analysis of prices ending in "9" and those not ending in "9." If a promotion ends in "9," there is a positive increase in sales. As hypothesized, 16 out of 20 cases had the correct positive sign. The average effect is in the range of 10 percent sales increase except for tuna. (An outlier caused tuna to have a larger effect.) Thus, if a promotion were priced at 71 cents, a decrease to 69 cents would increase sales 10 percent *above* the effect simply due to the price decrease.

Why does ending in "9" work? There have been several studies trying to evaluate the reasons (see Shindler, 1987). A possible explanation is related to how individuals approximate price in their mind. Whatever the answer, it has important implications, since a retailer should never price at 78 cents rather than 79 cents

TABLE 12.2 Ending in "9" Effect

Flour	End 9	Bath Tissue	End 9
Pillsbury	1.244[a]	Charmin	1.077[b]
Gold Medal	.660[b]	Scott Tissue	1.100[b]
Ceresota	.859[b]	Northern	1.009[b]
Jewel Maid	1.347	White Cloud	1.115
Average	1.028	Soft 'N Pretty	.768
		Jewel	1.275[b]
Margarine		Coronet	1.510
Imperial	1.409	Average	1.122
Land O' Lakes	1.320		
Parkay	1.343	Tuna Fish	
Chiffon	1.575	Chicken of the Sea	1.289
Blue Bonnet	1.950	Bumble Bee	1.728
Blue Brook	1.156[b]	Starkist	4.442
Average	1.459	Blue Brook	1.765
		Average	1.594[c]

[a] 1.244 is a sales multiplier implying sales increase by 1.244 when Pillsbury flour has an "ending in 9" price.

[b] Insignificant at the .10 level.

[c] Excludes Starkist.

Source: Robert C. Blattberg and Kenneth J. Wisniewski, "How Retail Price Promotions Work: Empirical Results," working paper 42, University of Chicago, December, 1987.

because sales will be the same at 78 cents as 79 cents.[2] A retailer may be able to increase profits by reducing price from 71 cents to 69 cents because the increased sales is greater than the 2 cent price decrease effect.

Another phenomenon analyzed is "*N* for *X*," which means the price is expressed in multiple units. The theory behind this type of pricing is that the consumer buys the quantity suggested by the multiple units. Again, one would expect an increase in sales *above* the hypothesized price cut. Table 12.3 gives estimates of the "*N* for" effect. Out of 6 cases, there were 5 with the correct sign. In margarine it was 3 out of 4. For bathroom tissue, the effect was positive and highly significant (Scott ran a 7 for $3.00 sale), and for tuna fish, the effect had the correct positive sign but was small. The results indicate that "*N* for *X*" increases sales significantly. This conclusion is based on small samples and requires additional testing to evaluate the magnitude of the effect.

Shape of Deal Response

An important managerial question is the shape of the deal response. Figure 12.3 gives examples of three alternative deal response curves. If the deal response has "increasing returns to scale," then increasing the deal discount can be very advantageous. If the shape follows an "S," then small discounts and large dis-

---

[2] Some retailers use endings in "8" rather than "9" to differentiate their pricing. If the consumer perceives 78 cents the same as 79 cents, then the retailer is losing 1 cent on every item sold.

TABLE 12.3 "N for" Effect

Margarine	N for	Bath Tissue	N for
Imperial		Charmin	
Land O' Lakes	1.365[a]	Scott Tissue	1.113
Parkay	1.094[b]	Northern	
Chiffon	1.214	White Cloud	
Blue Bonnet	1.523	Soft 'N Pretty	
Blue Brook	.984[b]	Jewel	
Average	1.236	Coronet	
		Average	1.113
Tuna Fish			
Chicken of the Sea			
Bumble Bee	.995[b]		
Starkist			
Blue Brook			
Average	.995[c]		

[a] 1.365 is a sales multiplier implying that sales of Land O'Lakes increase by 1.365 when it is run as a "N for" promotion.

[b] Insignificant at the .10 level.

[c] Excludes Starkist.

Source: Robert C. Blattberg and Kenneth J. Wisniewski, "How Retail Price Promotions Work: Empirical Results," working paper 42, University of Chicago, December, 1987.

counts are not profitable. Therefore, the shape of the deal response influences the tactics the retailer will use.

To date there is very little evidence about the general shape of the deal response. Wisniewski and Blattberg (1983) did some preliminary analysis of deal responses and found that the deal shape fit an S-shaped function. However, this study was flawed because it included promotions from multiple categories; therefore, the S-shape was related to different deal elasticities across categories as well as the deal response curve.

More recently, Blattberg and Wisniewski (1987) developed several alternative models of deal discounts and evaluated the shapes. It showed that over the relevant range deals follow an increasing returns curve (not an S-shape). The study analyzed a limited range of deal discounts. If a retailer never tests extremely large discounts, it will not be possible to see the upper part of the S-curve. Their conclusion was that retail promotions appear to have an increasing returns to scale over the specific deal range studied.

Deal Elasticities and Cross-Elasticities

Deal discounts strongly influence a brand's sales. In many cases the sales increase is in the range of three to seven times the normal level for deal discount feature advertising and display in the range of 15 to 20 percent. Table 12.4 was constructed to show the sales response to retailer promotions. It gives the deal coefficient for all brands in four product categories: tuna fish, flour, margarine, and bathroom

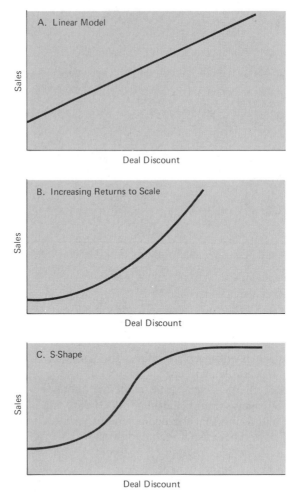

FIGURE 12.3   Three Alternative Response Curves.

tissue. These categories are not intended to be representative of deal responsiveness but rather to show the actual level of sales increases that result from
deals (which includes price decrease, feature advertising, and display).

The results show several interesting effects. First, the category with the
highest responsiveness is flour which is a commodity. Second, the deal responsiveness across categories and brands are surprisingly close to each other. In
building models this indicates that it may be possible to constrain deal elasticity
parameters to be close to one another. Further research is needed to see how
elasticities vary across categories.

Cross-elasticities have also been analyzed for the different brands in the
same categories. Table 12.5 shows the magnitude of the cross-elasticities for dif-

TABLE 12.4 Deal Elasticities

Flour		Tuna Fish	
Ceresota	5.34	Bumble Bee	10.28
Gold Medal	10.08	Chicken of the Sea	8.04
Pillsbury	5.79	Starkist	8.50
Jewel	14.34	Blue Brook	8.10
Generic	—		
Bathroom Tissue		Margarine	
Northern	9.03	Blue Bonnet	6.57
Soft 'N Pretty	11.63	Chiffon	6.42
White Cloud	10.35	Imperial	5.05
Charmin	10.32	Land O' Lakes	4.84
Scott Tissue	7.72	Parkay	8.65
Coronet	4.66	Blue Brook	.49
Jewel	11.26	Sunnyland	9.56
Generic	—	Generic	—

Source: Robert C. Blattberg and Kenneth J. Wisniewski, "How Retail Price Promotions Work: Empirical Results," working paper 42, University of Chicago, December, 1987.

ferent brands in the four product categories being studied. One can see that the cross sales effect varies significantly by brand. The reason is due, in part, to statistical variation and, in part, to differences by brand.

An issue that can be answered using cross-elasticities is the question of the net sales increase a brand generates. If the deal discount causes an increase in sales of 300 percent, how much of that comes from other brands (cross-elasticities) and how much is incremental volume? Incremental brand volume comes from four sources: (1) other retailers, (2) competitive brands, (3) purchase and quantity acceleration, and (4) increased consumption. To date, little research has been conducted analyzing these alternative sources of volume. Figure 12.4 shows the percentage increase in sales for a given brand due to increased category volume versus cannibalization. For example, for Land O'Lakes margarine the sales increase is due to category volume increase with only a small percentage coming from competitive brands, but for Bluebonnet most of the volume increase comes from cannibalization.

The implication for the retailer is that brands that cannibalize other brands in the category are not good targets for retail promotions *unless it has a higher gross margin* than the other brands in the category. The "Profitability" section discusses this issue in more detail.

In summary, deal elasticities are quite large, as seen in Table 12.4. Deal elasticities within a category appear to be much closer in magnitude than they are across categories. Cross-elasticities are more difficult to measure but are very important to the retailer in determining which items to promote. If an item cannibalizes other brands, there are serious problems in promoting it if there is not an increase in category profitability.

TABLE 12.5 Cross-Elasticities[a]

	Flour				
	CER	GDM	PIL	JWL	GRC[a]
Ceresota (CER)	—	−.46	1.47[b]	.42	—
Gold Medal (GDM)	−.42	—	1.10	1.23	—
Pillsbury (PIL)	−.13	.74	—	−.66	—
Jewel Maid (JWL)	.30	.83	1.86	—	—
Generic (GRC)	.02	−.30	.98	.45	—

	Margarine							
	BBT	CHF	IMP	LOL	PKY	BBK	SNY	GRC[a]
Blue Bonnet (BBT)	—	−.38	.55	.28	.14	−.21	.34	—
Chiffon (CHF)	.36	—	.16	.71	.19	−.12	−.07	—
Imperial (IMP)	.15	.37	—	.19	−.01	−.05	−.07	—
Land O' Lakes (LOL)	.33	.34	.19	—	.33	.07	−.13	—
Parkay (PKY)	.14	.18	.26	.08	—	−.08	−.02	—
Blue Bonnet (BBK)	.27	.49	.17	.20	.17	—	.28	—
Sunnyland (SNY)	.29	.83	.07	.30	.17	.07	—	—
Generic (GRC)	.06	.21	.10	−.06	−.02	.00	.15	—

	Tissue							
	NTH	SFT	WTC	CHM	SCT	JWL	CNT	GRC[a]
Northern (NTH)	—	0.37	0.55	0.67	0.22	−0.33	−1.02	—
Soft 'N Pretty (SFT)	1.40	—	2.65	1.73	0.28	1.16	0.33	—
White Cloud (WTC)	1.38	0.80	—	1.78	−0.18	0.44	1.38	—
Charmin (CHM)	1.15	0.85	0.80	—	0.38	0.53	−0.72	—
Scott Tissue (SCT)	−0.22	0.21	0.27	0.26	—	0.18	−1.99	—
Jewel (JWL)	−0.92	−0.28	−0.61	1.04	0.82	—	−1.53	—
Coronet (CNT)	−0.22	0.43	4.74	1.26	−0.13	2.66	—	—
Generic (GRC)	0.42	0.03	0.52	0.23	0.19	0.18	0.96	—

	Tuna				
	BBB	CKN	STK	BBK	GRC[a]
Bumble Bee (BBB)	—	.59	.44	1.30	—
Chicken of the Sea (CKN)	.43	—	.34	.52	—
Starkist (STK)	.37	.42	—	1.09	—
Blue Brook (BBK)	1.22	.48	.97	—	—
Generic (GRC)	.05	.09	.00	.19	—

[a] For generic means it did not promote.

[b] Numbers in the table are the percentage decrease/increase in the row brand's unit sales as the column brand decreases/increases its price 1 percent; e.g., for each 1 percent decrease in Pillsbury's price, Ceresota sales drop 1.47 percent.

Source: Robert C. Blattberg and Kenneth J. Wisniewski, "How Retail Price Promotions Work: Empirical Results," working paper 42, University of Chicago, December, 1987.

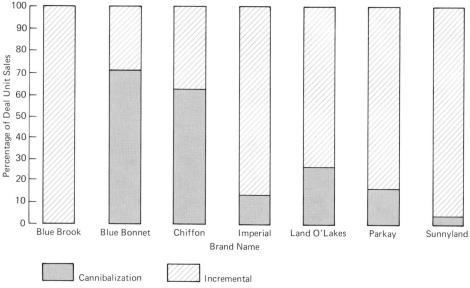

FIGURE 12.4 Source of Promotional Sales: Margarine at 20% Deal Discount

Source: Center for Research in Marketing, University of Chicago.

Price Versus Promotional Elasticities

Retailers have long known that price elasticities are significantly lower than promotional elasticities (deal discount elasticity).[3] There have been several research studies showing this effect (e.g., Blattberg and Wisniewski, 1987). The two critical issues are (1) How different are the magnitudes of the elasticities? and (2) Why are they different?

To see the magnitude of the difference in the two elasticities, Table 12.6 shows the average price elasticities and promotional for four product categories. The price elasticities are in the range of 2.5 and the promotional elasticities are 8 to 11. Therefore, consumers are far more responsive to promotions than permanent price changes.

The reasons, in one sense, are obvious. Because price deals are temporary, the consumer buys more on deal than the normal quantity and stockpiles additional units. Also because promotions are temporary, deal-oriented customers search for reduced price and respond during the promotion, again changing their purchase timing, whereas if a price reduction occurs, the consumer can delay the purchase until they are out-of-stock. Thus, one explanation hinges on purchase timing.[4]

---

[3] It should be noted that promotional elasticities may interact with display and feature advertising increasing the observed promotional elasticity. These results also contradict Guadagni and Little (1983, p. 22), who found price and promotional elasticities are equal.

[4] This explanation raises an issue about measuring promotional elasticities. The appropriate measurement period may be longer than the week in which the promotion occurred. If this longer period is used, the promotional elasticity will be lower because of the decreased buying in the weeks following the deal.

TABLE 12.6 Deal vs. Price Elasticity

	Deal Elasticity	Price Elasticity[a]
Flour		
Ceresota	5.34	1.85
Gold Medal	10.08	2.59
Pillsbury	5.79	1.32
Jewel	14.34	2.47
Generic	—	[b]

	Deal Elasticity	Price Elasticity[a]
Tuna Fish		
Bumble Bee	10.28	−4.99
Chicken of the Sea	8.04	−.72
Starkist	8.50	−3.08
Blue Brook	8.10	−2.59
Generic	—	[b]

	Deal Elasticity	Price Elasticity[a]
Bathroom Tissue		
Northern	9.03	3.17
Soft 'N Pretty	11.63	6.53
White Cloud	10.35	1.69
Charmin	10.32	1.21
Scott Tissue	7.72	[b]
Coronet	4.66	2.02
Jewel	11.26	[b]
Generic	[b]	3.59

	Deal Elasticity	Price Elasticity[a]
Margarine		
Blue Bonnet	6.57	[b]
Chiffon	6.42	2.86
Imperial	5.05	[b]
Land O' Lakes	4.84	2.34
Parkay	8.65	3.88
Blue Brook	.49	2.23
Sunnyland	9.56	—
Generic	—	[b]

[a] Absolute values are shown. All elasticities are negative.

[b] No regular price variation in the data series used to estimate the model.

Source: Robert C. Blattberg and Kenneth J. Wisniewski, "How Retail Price Promotions Work: Empirical Results," working paper 42, University of Chicago, December, 1987.

Another explanation is based on price discrimination. Consumers who buy on deal have different cost parameters (see Jeuland and Narasimhan, 1985). Those with lower cost parameters buy and consume more when a deal is run. Therefore, when a promotion is run, more consumers enter the market and buy on deal. The result is a larger spike for a deal than for a price reduction.

Finally, promotions are "announced" through feature advertising and display whereas price reductions are not announced. Therefore, price elasticities are lower.

In summary, promotional elasticities are significantly higher than price elasticities. This means that retailers have an incentive to keep the price high and then reduce it through promotions rather than keep the price at a lower everyday level.

Feature Advertising and Display Elasticities

Feature advertising and displays are key components of most promotional activity. It is difficult to measure their elasticities because they are usually combined with significant price decreases. However, in a recent article Wittink et al. (1987) estimate feature advertising and display elasticities. Their results show that a feature ad and a display increases sales approximately 100 percent. These appear low compared to deal discount elasticities covered earlier.

While these estimates are valuable to retailers, they need to be refined. Retailers would like to know how the size of an ad and different display locations affect elasticities. Clearly, more work is going to be needed to document the magnitude of these effects.

Promotional Elasticities Across Markets

Very few studies have documented differences in elasticities across markets. However, Wittink et al. have studied how deal elasticities vary across markets. Their results are shown in Table 12.7. They show that Seattle has significantly

TABLE 12.7   Parameter Estimates for Starkist 6.5-oz Chunk Light Tuna in Ten Major Markets

Market	Price Elasticity	Feature Multiplier	Display Multiplier	Display and Feature Multiplier	Product of Feature and Display Multiplier
Boston	−2.53	1.77	1.96	4.75	3.47
Chicago	−3.30	1.98	2.13	3.95	4.22
Houston	−1.51	1.93	1.60	2.94	3.09
Indianapolis	−1.42	1.84	1.84	2.71	3.39
Jacksonville/ Orlando	−1.30	1.19	2.39	2.39	2.84
Kansas City	−1.93	2.02	2.00	3.69	4.04
Los Angeles	−3.19	1.52	1.71	2.20	2.60
New York	−2.67	1.86	2.05	5.88	3.81
Seattle	−2.52	4.03	1.90	6.77	7.62
San Francisco	−1.90	2.29	1.98	4.11	4.53

Source: Dick R. Wittink, Michael J. Addona, Willima J. Hawkes, and John C. Porter, "SCAN-PRO®: A Model to Measure Short-Term Effects of Promotional Activities on Brand Sales, Based on Store-Level Scanner Data," Working paper, Johnson Graduate School of Management, Cornell University, Ithaca, NY (May 1987), p. 36.

lower deal elasticities than Jacksonville. The question is: Are these differences simply statistical variation or true differences?

Possible explanations about why deals vary across markets are (1) different frequency in trade deals, (2) different levels of retail competition, (3) differences in consumer responsiveness to deals, and (4) different market structures.

The implication to the manufacturer is that the type of trade deals should vary by market depending on deal responsiveness. However, this is difficult to execute because of diverting.

Stockpiling

A phenomenon discussed frequently in the literature is consumer stockpiling when a deal is offered. Blattberg et al. (1981) show significant stockpiling in several categories using Chicago *Tribune* data from the 1960s. (See Chapter 5 for a more detailed discussion of the theory and empirical evidence.) Several recent articles (e.g., McAlister, 1985) argue that consumers do not stockpile or that the effect is small.[5] However, most studies have found some form of stockpiling by the consumer.

The importance of stockpiling to the retailer is that if the consumer does increase purchasing but does not increase consumption, then the deal is less profitable because in the next period the consumer does not buy his or her normal quantity at regular price. Using retail scanner data, if there is stockpiling then one would expect a "trough" after a promotion. This results from the consumer not buying the dealt brand after the promotion ends because of the additional unconsumed units bought during the deal period. Very few researchers have been able to find a trough after a deal, even though when scanner panel data are analyzed, there appears to be stockpiling.

If consumers stockpile, then why are these troughs not observed? Chapter 7 discusses this issue. The explanation offered is based on the fact that timing and quantity acceleration balance out. Several additional reasons can be hypothesized. First, most retail stores continue to display an item several weeks after a deal has ended. While the price goes back to the normal level and no retail feature advertising is being used, the store manager does not want to have to tear down the display because there is nowhere to put the excess stock. Therefore, they continue with the display. If the display has a significant effect on sales, then no trough would occur.

The second explanation is that there is a segment of consumers that shop from deal to deal. These deal-oriented customers cause a major sales spike, and therefore, one would not observe a trough. However, there is not strong evidence to show this explanation is correct.

Figure 12.5 shows the spikes for a brand of margarine in which the individual consumers are divided into different promotional groups. The groups are those

---

[5] McAlister actually computed the number of multiple units purchased and concluded consumers were not stockpiling. However, purchase timing could have changed.

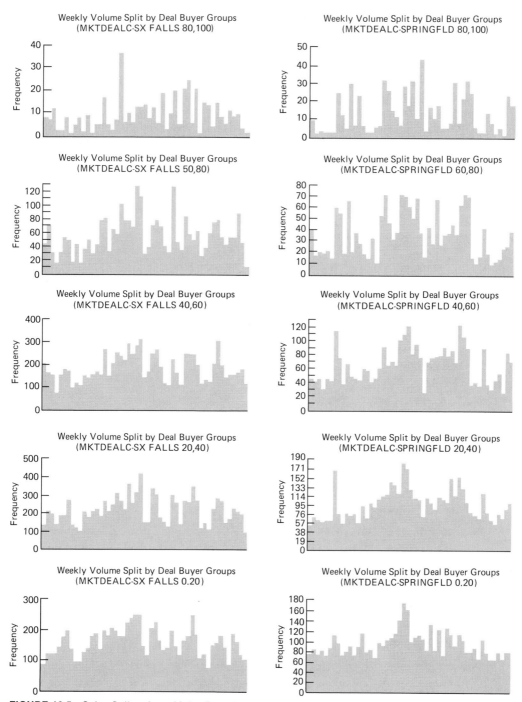

FIGURE 12.5 Sales Spikes for a Major Brand of Margarine.

Source: Center for Research in Marketing, University of Chicago.

consumers who buy 0–20, 20–40, 40–60, 60–80, and 80–100 percent of their purchases on deal. While the consumers who are more deal oriented do cause the spike to increase, so do light and medium deal buyers. Thus, when a deal is offered, the spike cannot be explained simply by deal buyers.

The third explanation is that there is no stockpiling. As was stated earlier, McAlister found that in Kansas City in the coffee category, there was no evidence of stockpiling by purchasing multiple units. However, in another study, Pedrick (1987), using margarine data supplied by ERIM, showed that consumers definitely increase purchasing rates. The increase was approximately 25 percent. If the consumers increase their usage rate by 25 percent, there would be no stockpiling. However, Pedrick also showed that there was an increase in the interpurchase time after a deal which would imply that the consumption rate did not increase enough to overcome the increased purchase rate. (This is similar to Neslin et al., 1985.)

Thus, it appears that consumers stockpile. However, it is still difficult to detect troughs after promotions in retail scanner panel data. The preceding discussion may explain the phenomenon, but to date there has been very little theoretical work trying to describe how and when a trough after a deal should be evident.

Deal Decay

For a retail promotion, sales decay the longer the deal lasts. Figure 12.6 is an example for a flour promotion. As can be seen, the deal effectiveness is decaying the longer the promotion lasts. Only when retail advertisements were run did the sales curve shift.

Figure 12.7 gives a general picture of how deal effectiveness decays the longer the retailer runs the promotion. One sees that the promotional decay fits an exponential decay. Thus, the first weeks of the promotion are far more effective than later weeks.

Rao and Thomas (1973) and Blattberg and Wisniewski (1987) reported this result, though retailers have understood the phenomenon for many years. The cause of this effect is unknown though the answer is related to why promotional elasticities are higher than price elasticities. However, it appears that after a promotion is run for several weeks, the consumers' expectation is that they can buy the item at the special price for many more weeks. Thus, it is viewed as a regular price change which has much lower responsiveness than a deal.

Deal Carry-over Effect

A critical issue for manufacturers is the deal carry-over effect. If the consumer buys an item on deal in one period, is there a higher or lower probability of buying on deal the next period? The profitability of a deal is higher or lower depending on the deal carry-over effect.

Several studies have been conducted which have analyzed deal carry-over

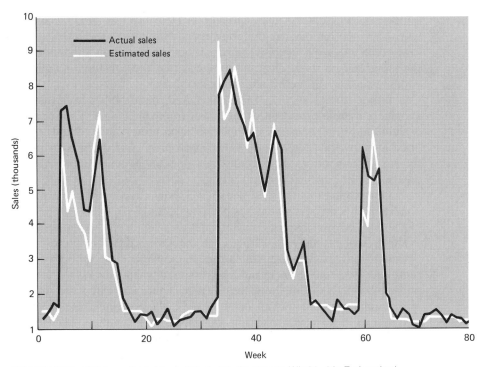

FIGURE 12.6   Pillsbury 5-Lb Flour (Wk 1–30: Backcast; Wk 31–80: Estimation)

Source: Robert C. Blattberg and Kenneth J. Wisniewski, "How Retail Price Promotions Work: Empirical Results," working paper 42, University of Chicago, December, 1987.

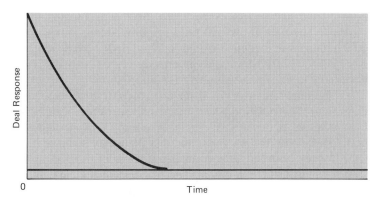

FIGURE 12.7   How Deal Effectiveness Decays the Longer the Retailer Runs the Promotion.

effects. As was discussed in Chapter 2, Dodson et al. (1978) have shown that when a promotion occurs, the consumers who bought the brand on deal have a lower than average probability of repeat buying that brand than those who bought the brand not on deal. Their reasoning is that the consumer's image of a brand is diminished when the brand is bought on deal.

Other studies such as Shoemaker and Shoaf (1977) have also shown that average purchase probabilities are lower following a deal. Their rationale is that promotions attract consumers who have lower utility for the brand. The promotion price is below the consumer's reservation price, but the regular price is above the reservation price. Thus, consumers do not repeat buy when the price increases.

One reason that these studies have shown declining repeat purchase probabilities is that no adjustment has been made for the nondeal purchase probability of the deal buyers. Neslin and Shoemaker (1988) have argued and shown some evidence that promotions attract customers with different preferences than the "regular" buyers. When a deal is run, the lower preference buyers have greater representation among the brand's buyers than when a deal is not run. These low-preference buyers bring down the average repurchase rate when one looks at the next purchase occasion. This occurs *even* if the next purchase occasion is a deal purchase. The next purchase does not include a promotion, and so the low-preference deal buyers do not repeat purchase. By looking only at the aggregate results and not separating consumers by preference, the repeat purchase probability appears to decline.

To demonstrate this result, Table 12.8 gives the repeat buying rates for consumers buying margarine. The table is divided into three cells: total sample, switchers, and brand-loyal consumers. The table entries show that the repeat purchase probability depends on whether the consumer did or did not buy on deal for the i and $i + 1$st purchase.

The results indicate that if one does not adjust for the aggregation bias, it appears that promotions decrease the purchase probability between i and $i + 1$. However, if one separates switchers from brand loyals, the results are far less obvious. The data show that only for Bluebonnet is there a negative carry-over effect. Thus, the evidence would indicate that there is no carry-over effect which was also found by Bawa and Shoemaker (1987). However, additional studies are necessary to draw "conclusive" results.

The empirical work just described contradicts Dodson et al. However, in defense of their position, short-term analysis of promotions is likely to show very little positive or negative carry-over effect. Why should a consumer who regularly shifts brands view the brand less favorably because it was promoted? However, for the brand-loyal consumers, a series of promotions may change the consumer's image of the product. The real test of the carry-over effect would be to find cases in which products were not promoted for a long period of time and then are promoted. One could see then if a set of loyal consumers switch to less frequently dealt brands.

TABLE 12.8 Model Predictions for Repeat Purchase Probabilities[a] (Evaluated for the Average Household)

Brand	Imperial	House	Blue Bonnet	Parkay
Occasion: All Households				
No deal to no deal	.144	.647	.648	.385
Deal to no deal	.016	.565	.328	.223
No deal to deal	.146	.712	.792	.674
Deal to deal	.090	.637	.502	.487
Occasion: Brand-Switching Households				
No deal to no deal	.028	.666	.509	.309
Deal to no deal	.022	.643	.301	.282
No deal to deal	.122	.807	.760	.648
Deal to deal	.110	.792	.569	.617
Occasion: Brand-Loyal Households				
No deal to no deal	.926	.973	.949	.990
Deal to no deal	.917	.943	.979	.986
No deal to deal	.943	.981	.961	.974
Deal to deal	.936	.951	.984	.988

[a] These are the estimated conditional probabilities of repurchasing brand i at time $t + 1$, after purchasing i at time t. The estimates are obtained from the brand choice model using the coefficients reported in Table 12.2. Household-specific variables are evaluated for the average household.

Source: James H. Pedrick, "Modelling Deal Effects Using Scanner Panel Data," Working paper, Graduate School of Business, University of Chicago, (April 1987).

Price Tiers

Retailers have used the concept of price tiers to price and promote items. Department stores classify items according to good, better, best.[6] Each level represents a price point. Retailers then promote items as a function of price points. They assume if the higher price point is promoted, customers trade up.

Blattberg and Wisniewski (1987) and Kumar and Leone (1988) have shown that consumer nondurables also behave according to price tiers. The implication for modeling is that certain cross-elasticities will be zero or small. If a lower-tier brand promotes, it does not attract customers from a higher-tier brand. Therefore, the cross-elasticity coefficient for "good" (low tiers) is small in a model analyzing "best" sales.

Summary

The empirical results have shown that there are many different factors influencing promotional effectiveness. The key findings in this section are

1. Promotional responsiveness is much greater than price responsiveness.
2. There are certain effects that cannot be explained by standard economic models. These include "ending in 9" effects and "N for X" prices.

---

[6] Other designations are often used but the concept is still a rank ordering in price.

3. Panel data show that consumers appear to stockpile goods when promotions are offered, but it is very difficult to measure "troughs" after deals using retail scanner data.

4. Some items within a product category derive their sales increase by cannibalizing the sales of other items in the category. These items may not always be profitable for the retailer to promote.

5. The magnitude of the deal response across brands and product categories are approximately the same. While there is substantial variation, it may be possible to use the mean elasticity level and shrink all the coefficients to this grand mean.

6. Deal effectiveness decays exponentially the longer the deal is run. The reason given is that consumers begin to treat the price decrease as though it was permanent. However, the exact cause is not well understood.

7. Display and feature advertising increases sales in the range of 75 to 100 percent. They may interact with price promotional discounts.

The next section uses these findings in the development of models to measure retail promotions.

MEASURING THE EFFECTS OF RETAILER PROMOTIONS

Retailers have used very simple methods to measure the effectiveness of retail promotions. This section begins with the standard procedure used by retailers, before-after analysis, and then describes several alternative approaches, which include models of retail scanner data and models of scanner panel data.

Data to Measure the Effectiveness of Retail Promotions

Before beginning to describe measurement procedures, it is important to understand the data available for measuring retail promotions. The data can be divided into two types: (1) store level point-of-sale (POS) data and (2) individual purchase histories (panel data). Each type is important. Currently, store-level POS data is more readily available to retailers. However, POS data cannot answer questions about brand switching and store loyalty, whereas individual purchase histories can. While individual purchase history data would be extremely valuable to a retailer, they are not easy to collect, and therefore, most retailers focus on using POS data to analyze retail promotions. (See Chapter 7.)

The data required to measure retail promotions include

- Accurate history of the types of promotions run
  - Price reductions
  - Display activities
  - Detailed description of retail advertising
  - Description of other promotional activities
- Daily or weekly sales data (from POS system)
  - Prior to the promotion
  - During the promotional period
  - After the promotion

— Total retail sales for the category or department
— Customer counts (optional)
- Cost and margin information
  — Cost of the promotions including the retail advertising and display costs
  — Marginal cost of the item promoted
  — Trade discounts, cooperative advertising, and display allowance

These data are then used in various types of analyses to determine the effectiveness of retail promotions.

Before-After Measurement of Retail Promotions

A commonly used method for measuring the effects of a retail promotion is to analyze the sales before, during, and after the promotion has ended. The approach is simple to use but may not give an accurate estimate of the effectiveness of a specific promotional type (versus promotional event). This will be shown after the "before-after" analysis is described. (Also see Chapter 6.)

Example of the Methodology

Suppose the retailer runs a promotion on April 9 (Thursday) and it lasts one week (ends Wednesday). The retailer's regular price is reduced from $1.09 to $.89. A major ad (A ad) and an end-of-aisle display are run. The sales results were

- Sales for the four weeks prior to the promotion averaged 960 units at $1.09.
- Sales during the week of the promotion were 2,640 units at $.89.
- Sales the week following the promotion were 720 units at $1.09.
- Advertising space costs for the feature ad were estimated to be $300, and the cost to set up the display was $18. No cost of the space was given by the retailer.
- The regular case cost of the item was $21.50.
- A trade deal was offered by the manufacturer. The discount per case was $2, the advertising allowance was $1 per case along with a display allowance of $.50 per case. The case contained 24 units.
- The retailer did not forward buy (to make the analysis simpler) the item when it was offered on trade deal.

The following calculations were made to estimate the profitability of the deal.

1. The revenue expected during the promotion if no deal is offered was 960 units times $1.09 equals $1,046.40. The 960 is the average volume before the promotion.
2. If no deal were run, profits would have been one week's revenue, $1,046.60, minus the cost of goods which was 40 cases (960 divided by 24) times $21.50, which equals $860.00. The profit was then $186.40
3. The actual revenue during the deal was 2,640 units (110 cases) times $.89, $2,349.60. The cost per case was $21.50 minus the trade allowance and advertising and display allowance, which was $2.00 + $1.00 + $.50 or $3.50 resulting in a cost per case of $18.00 ($21.50 − $3.50). The total cost during the promotion was 110 × $18.00 = $1,980.00. The profit was the revenue minus the cost per case. This is $369.60
4. There is one other cost. The sales after the promotion were less than expected. This also has to be taken into account. The normal sales level would have been 960 units,

but it fell to 720 units. The retailer's sales decreased by 240 units. The lost profit was 240 units times $1.09 minus $21.50 times 10 (240 divided by 24 units per case), which equals $46.60.

5. Combining all the calculations one sees that the profit from the promotion is $369.60 − $186.40 − $46.60 = $136.60 in profits *before* advertising and display costs. These costs were $300.00 + $18.00 = $318.00 The net *loss* after advertising and display costs is $181.60

For the retailer the promotional loss signals that the price discount ($1.09 to $.89) is too large. The next time the same trade deal is offered, a lower discount can be given.

Advantages and Limitations of the "Before-After" Promotional Analysis

As was stated earlier, the advantage of "before-after" analysis is simplicity and ease of use. Whether explicitly or implicitly most retailers use some type of before-after analysis to evaluate promotions. The method is simple, requires short promotional histories, can be done using a calculator, and does not require user sophistication.

The major problems with "before-after" analysis are (1) The results do not generalize,[7] (2) it does not take into account the cannibalization of other items in the product category, (3) it does not adjust for other variables that influence sales during the promotion, and (4) it has wide variation.

Table 12.9 shows sales for the same promotion offered four times by a retailer. The retailer estimated normal weekly sales to be 1,450 cases. Looking at the first or third promotion gives very different results than the second or fourth. Which is correct? Obviously none of them. Some type of average response is required, not individual promotional response.

The second problem is the failure to analyze the cannibalization in the category and how it affects the promotion's profitability. By studying "before-after"

---

[7] The results are unbiased but have large variation.

TABLE 12.9 Sales Response to Specific Promotion

Promotion:	Price reduction from $1.29 to $.99 Display in the front of the store A ad	
Normal Weekly Movement:	1,450 cases	
	Date	*Unit Sales (cases)*
Week	88-03	11,361
	88-11	8,804
	88-17	3,247
	88-25	8,671

category profitability rather than brand profitability, it is possible to overcome this problem. While in theory one can apply before-after analysis to the category, it is difficult to isolate the individual effects without some type of statistical model.

The final problem with "before-after" analysis is that it does not adjust for other variables that could explain sales changes. If an item is promoted when another promotion is run in the category, "before-after" analysis cannot identify the effect of the other promotion. "Before-after" analysis also cannot separate the price effect from the merchandising and feature advertising effect. Most retailers would like to understand the effects for the separate components of a promotion.

Thus, while "before-after" analysis is simple to use, it is very limited in being able to explain promotional effects.

Statistical Modeling of Store-Level Scanner Data

An alternative approach to "before-after" measurements is statistical modeling. A model adjusts for variations from promotion to promotion, and the parameter estimates give "average" measurements of promotional effects. This section will describe two models, developed by Blattberg and Wisniewski (1987) and Wittink et al. (1987), that are currently being used by retailers and manufacturers. At the end of the section, modeling problems will be discussed.

Blattberg and Wisniewski Model. Blattberg and Wisniewski (1987) developed a statistical model to be used by retailers. As such, it incorporates many of the effects described in the preceding discussion explaining "how deals work." The variables used in the model are described and then the functional form is given. Estimation results are not given, though they can be found in Blattberg and Wisniewski (1987, 1988).

VARIABLES USED IN THE MODEL: PRICE. Regular price and promotions are entered separately into the model because promotional elasticities are substantially higher than price elasticities.

DEAL. Deals are modeled so that the function can either represent increasing returns to scale or an S-shape. The specific variable used is $1/1 + D$, where D is deal discount which allows the deal discount to have an S-shaped effect. Other functions of D could be used, though some require nonlinear estimation.

COMPETITIVE PRICES. Competitive prices should also be split between deal and regular price. The problem is that the number of variables entered into the model becomes excessive. To solve the problem competitive prices were entered using $1/P$, where P is the price of the competitive item. The form is similar to the dealing variable except that 1 has not been added. The 1 is unnecessary because the price is never 0 whereas deal discount can be 0.

ADVERTISING AND DISPLAY. The ads were entered as three dummy variables to represent the size (A, B, and C) of the ads. Display captured the number of stores actually displaying the brand. It ranges from 0 to 7 because seven stores were audited to see if a display was present. Display ultimately needs to be divided into type of display to see the sales impact of different locations in the store.

DECAY.   As was discussed, deal effectiveness decays over time. The variable was included as λ^t (actually it is $e^{-\lambda t}$). This is simply a Koyck lag, which indicates that the effectiveness decays geometrically.

ENDING IN 9 AND N FOR.   To model "ending in 9" and "N for," it is necessary to use dummy variables. When a deal ended in 9, a dummy was inserted. A similar procedure was used for "N for" deals; a dummy was inserted when it occurred.

SCANNER WEEK ADJUSTMENT.   Because the scanner week begins on Sunday and ends on Saturday but deals are offered on Thursdays, an adjustment is needed. A variable was introduced so that in the first week of the deal, it was equal to .65 and in the last week of the deal it was .35. The .65 and .35 were used because Thursday, Friday, and Saturday's sales are 65 percent of a weeks sales and Sunday through Wednesday represent 35 percent. Thus, if the deal runs only for 65 percent of the week (based on volume), then its impact needs to be adjusted downward. The specific variable used is ln .65 in the first week and ln .35 in the last week.

OTHER VARIABLES.   Other variables such as seasonality and trend need to be added to the model. These adjustments are commonly used in models and standard procedures were used.

THE MODEL.   The model is a semilog functional form:

$$S_{it} = \exp[\alpha + \beta_1 R_{it} + \beta_2/(1 + D_{it}) + \sum_{k \neq i} \delta_k/P_{k,t} + \gamma_1 A_{i,1,t} + \gamma_2 A_{i,2,t}$$

$$+ \gamma_3 A_{i,3,t} + \phi_1 X_{i,t} + \phi_2 E9_{i,t} + \phi_3 NF_{i,t} + \lambda T_{i,t} + \phi_5 C_{i,t} + \epsilon_{i,t}] \quad \text{(12.1)}$$

where

S_{it} = unit sales of brand i in period t

R_{it} = regular price of brand i in period t

P_{it} = actual price of brand i in period t

D_{it} = deal discount, defined as $(R_{it} - P_{it})/R_{it}$

$A_{i,1,t}$ = dummy variable for an A ad

$A_{i,2,t}$ = dummy variable for a B ad

$A_{i,3,t}$ = dummy variable for a C ad

$X_{i,t}$ = display activity (ranges from 0 to 7 depending on the number of stores displaying the item)

$E9_{i,t}$ = dummy variable for a promotion ending in 9

$NF_{i,t}$ = dummy variable for an "N for" promotion

$T_{i,t}$ = time the promotion began with 0 being the first week

$C_{i,t}$ = scan/deal week correction

$\begin{cases} \text{ln .65 in the first week} \\ \text{ln .35 in the last week} \end{cases}$

$\epsilon_{i,t}$ = random error time

α, β, γ, δ, and λ are parameters

In summary, the model captures the following effects:

1. The deal variable (1/1 + D) allows for an S-shape or increasing returns to scale.
2. A scanner week correction is used to adjust for the first and last week of the deal.
3. A deal decay is built into the model.
4. "Ending 9" and "*N* for" are modeled using dummy variables.
5. Retail advertising, display, and advertising are estimated separately.

The model has then been applied to retail scanner data. Blattberg and Wisniewski (1987, 1988) describe the fits and estimation results. Figure 12.8 shows the fits of the model. For a more detailed discussion see Blattberg and Wisniewski (1987, 1988). The model will serve as the basis for the "Profitability Model for Retailers" section.

SCAN*PRO

Another model, using retail scanning sales and promotional data has been developed by Wittink et al. (1987). The basic model was developed at the store level

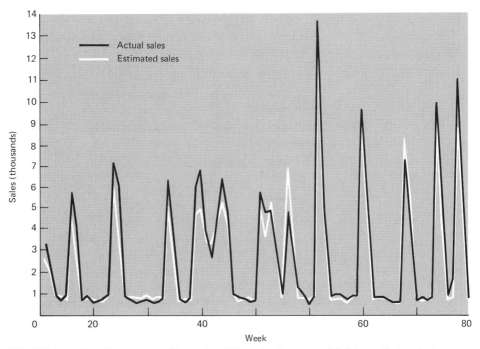

FIGURE 12.8 Blue Bonnet 1-Lb Margarine (Wk 1–30: Backcast; Wk 31–80: Estimation)

Source: Robert C. Blattberg and Kenneth J. Wisniewski, "How Retail Price Promotions Work: Empirical Results," working paper 42, University of Chicago, December, 1987.

and then aggregated across stores and chains to develop market-level estimates of the promotional effects.

In contrasting the Wittink et al. model to the Blattberg-Wisniewski (B-W) model, the primary difference is in the level of aggregation. The B-W model is aggregated at the price zone level for a chain, whereas Wittink et al. is developed at the store level. B-W are assuming that the promotional effects are identical (or almost identical) across stores within a price zone. Wittink et al. add many more parameters but can model individual store differences. (See Chapter 7 for a discussion of aggregation issues.)

A second difference is that B-W include many more promotional effects than do Wittink et al. because the model is designed to be used by the retailer. SCAN*PRO is designed to be used by the manufacturer to understand how the retailer makes decisions.

The model estimated is

$$S(i, 1, t) = \alpha_{i1} \prod_{j=i}^{j} P(i, j, t)^{\beta(ij)} \gamma_{1,i,j}^{D(1,i,j,t)} \gamma_{2,i,j}^{D(2,i,j,t)} \gamma_{3,i,j}^{D(3,i,j,t)} e^{u(i,1,t)}$$

where

$S(i, 1, t)$ = unit sales (e.g., number of pounds) for brand 1 in store i, week t

$P(i, j, t)$ = unit price for brand j in store i, week t

$D(1, i, j, t)$ = an indicator variable for feature

$= \begin{cases} 1 \text{ if brand } j \text{ is featured (but not displayed) by store } i, \text{ in week } t \\ 0 \text{ otherwise} \end{cases}$

$D(2, i, j, t)$ = an indicator for display

$= \begin{cases} 1 \text{ if brand } j \text{ is displayed (but no feature) for brand } j \text{ in store } i \text{ in week } t \\ 0 \text{ otherwise} \end{cases}$

$D(3, i, j, t)$ = an indicator variable for the simultaneous occurrence of feature and display

$= \begin{cases} 1 \text{ if both display and feature occur} \\ 0 \text{ otherwise} \end{cases}$

$u(i, 1, t)$ = an error term

J = the number of brands

N = the number of stores

T = the number of weeks

An interesting part of Wittink et al.'s paper is the tables showing elasticities across markets and the effects of displays and feature advertising. The feature multiplier is in the range of 2, indicating that sales double when a feature advertisement is run. Display activity is also in the same range. When both are run simultaneously, the combined effect is slightly less than the two effects multiplied together. This would indicate a slight negative interaction between the two effects. (Chapter 7 discusses incorporating interaction effects into the model.)

Modeling Issues. In trying to model retail scanner data two critical statistical issues arise: (1) multicollinearity and (2) wrong signs. These will be discussed briefly because they were covered in Chapter 7.

MULTICOLLINEARITY. A common problem is the interrelationship between deal discounts, feature price, and display activity. The retailer frequently runs all three in combination, particularly when a large deal discount is offered. The result is multicollinearity.

Measures of multicollinearity exist such as looking at the eigenvalues of the design matrix $(X'X)$ to see if the range between the largest and smallest is too great. The result is very large standard errors for the coefficients.

If multicollinearity exists, there are several possible solutions (see Chapter 7). However, they are generally not satisfactory. One is to create a "combination" variable which incorporates large deal discounts, feature advertising and display activity. The advantage is that multicollinearity is reduced but the disadvantage is that the separate effects cannot be identified.

In summary, researchers must be aware of multicollinearity. Unfortunately, no adequate solution exists for solving the problem.

WRONG SIGNS. It is common for cross-elasticities to be measured with the wrong signs. The reason is that there are a large number of coefficients to be estimated in a model such as the one given in the section on the B-W model. If wrong signs are present, then retailers, when trying to optimize the model to determine the best deal discount, see a deal on one item increasing sales on another item.[8] Also the optimal deal discount is affected such that it is overstated. Therefore, it is critical to produce models with the correct signs.

The solution again is not simple. Allenby (1988) generated a procedure in which cross-elasticities are constrained based on the assumption that the consumer follows a Luce model. If one accepts this assumption, Allenby then shows that the cross-elasticity matrix can be constrained. The constraints arise because lost sales due to a competitive promotion are proportional to the market share of the two brands. (This is the same assumption used in logit models.) The result is that far fewer cross-elasticities need to be estimated thus increasing the chances that the estimates have the correct sign.

Allenby and Blattberg (1988) investigate this assumption and show that the constrained model outperforms unconstrained models in both predictive accuracy on a hold-out sample and in the number of correct signs. The model developed uses market share as the dependent variable. The cross-elasticity coefficients are constrained based on the brand's market share. The ratio of the cross-elasticities for two brands is proportional to the market shares for the two brands, assuming they are in the same market segment.[9] More research needs to be conducted on methods to constrain coefficients, but it is important to use estimation procedures which will generate correct signs.

---

[8] It is possible that a deal on one item can increase the sales of other items in a category. However, in categories such as tuna, margarine, flour, and bathroom tissue it is unlikely.

[9] Brands with the same form and price point are in a market segment.

Models Fit to Scanner Panel Data

Retailer scanner data offers one type of database to analyze promotions, but most of the recent research conducted on the effects of retailer promotions has utilized scanner panel data. Scanner panel data provides purchase information at the individual level and, therefore, is an excellent source of analyzing promotional effects.

Currently, the main problem with scanner panel data is that the data are available only from small cities such as Marion, Indiana, which are not necessarily representative of major markets such as Chicago. The data providers (e.g., Nielsen, IRI, and SAMI-Burke) are beginning to offer diary panel data from larger markets. It is therefore important to understand the types of models that can be applied to these data.

The best known study of promotions using scanner panel data is by Guadagni and Little (1983) in which they fit a logit model to scanner panel data. This model has been discussed in Chapter 8, and so only the results will be provided.

The empirical results of the Guadagni and Little model indicated that both deals and price elasticities are surprisingly high. Since their paper, other researchers (e.g., Blattberg and Wisniewski, 1987) have observed that deal elasticities are high but not price elasticities.

While Guadagni and Little's article is pioneering, there are some dealing effects not considered. First, competitive effects are not directly modeled but are proportional to market share. This may be a good way to model competition, but no test of this form of competition was undertaken.

Second, stockpiling was not considered. While stockpiling seems to be difficult to show in some categories, it is generally believed that the consumer stockpiles when a promotion is offered. However, Guadagni and Little focused on the probability of buying the brand size and not on the quantity bought.

Finally, the concept of independence of irrelevant alternative[10] is not considered. For promotional modeling this may not be critical because the set of brands under investigation can be fixed. Only when a new brand is introduced will this become a problem.

After Guadagni and Little several other papers appeared using variants of their model to evaluate promotions. Fader and McAlister (1985) argued that consumers sometimes restrict their choice to acceptable brands on promotion. Again, their model is given in Chapter 8, and only the implications of the model will be discussed.

In looking at their model, there are two key components. If no acceptable brand is promoted, the purchase probability simply becomes the same as a stan-

---

[10] Independence of irrelevant alternatives means that adding another brand to the category automatically reduces sales of all brands in the category proportionally, but this may only fit sub-categories.

dard logit model. If an acceptable brand is promoted, then a coefficient, γ, determines how much the promotion influences the purchase decision. The larger γ, the more the promotion influences the probability of buying the promoted brand.

The model offers an interesting way to include promotions into the individual purchase choice decision. It also allows for differences across households because γ varies by consumer. Thus, one can see how many promotion responsive consumers buy in a category. For a retailer, this indicates the percentage of consumers who are likely to switch stores to buy an item at a better price.

Lattin (1985) also uses a logit model to add competitive effects. His model includes several additional variables that Guadagni and Little did not consider: "a contextual attraction" to the brand, perceived value of the brand, and competitive infringement on the brand. As price decreases or the deal discount increases, the perceived value of the brand is increased. Competitive infringement focuses on which brands compete. For example, private label volume is influenced by national brand volume, but national brands are not influenced by private label brands. Hence, he models competitive infringement specifically to account for asymmetric cross-elasticities. Clearly, Lattin has identified a critical issue. His approach is difficult to make operational but is interesting conceptually because it focuses on competitive effects.

The final article is by Pedrick (1987) (also see Kristnamurthi and Raj, 1988) who also uses a logit model to model promotional effects. The interesting difference between Pedrick's model and the ones just described is that Pedrick adds another model which tries to incorporate quantity into the analysis. Quantity is modeled using a tobit model. A tobit model allows for the fact that the customer buys 0 units when not buying but X units when buying. It is not constrained to be a (0, 1) decision variable the way a logit model is. The other key feature of the tobit model is that it incorporates the interrelationship between the two decisions. Thus, if the consumer buys more of brand A when a promotion is run than when brand B is promoted, the tobit model can incorporate differences in the quantity bought into the estimation procedure.

Pedrick finds two interesting effects. First, consumers stockpile (from the tobit model), and stockpiling depends upon demographic factors. Second, future brand purchase probabilities are not influenced by the consumer buying on deal. As was discussed earlier, this is counter to Dodson et al.'s (1978) finding.

In summary, several approaches have been used to model the effects of retail promotions. These range from using data from a single retailer (Blattberg and Wisniewski) to many retailers (Wittink et al.). Some researchers have used scanner panel data starting with Guadagni and Little. In general all have found large promotional elasticities. The key issue that still needs to be addressed is the analysis of cross-elasticities to understand competitive effects of deals.

PROFITABILITY MODEL FOR RETAIL PROMOTIONS

For manufacturers and retailers, it is essential that they understand the profitability of retail promotions. Several factors are important in computing the profitability of promotions such as the type of trade deal received, brand cannibalization, and gross margins for the items in the category including the dealt brand.

Using the statistical model given earlier and some of the empirical results given in the section on empirical evidence, a profitability model was developed. The model allows the retailer to "optimize" the deal discount for a specific item when a trade deal is offered. The following paragraphs describe how the model works, give sample output from the models, and conclude with a discussion of the implications for the retailer and the manufacturer.

Sales and Promotion Models

The model estimates given earlier can be used to assist retailers in determining the effects of offering different deal discounts and different levels of feature advertising and displays. To make this more concrete, the stick margarine category will be analyzed using the Blattberg-Wisniewski model.

Before using the model a key restriction must be tested: the unit sales increase for a specific item due to a deal discount *must* be greater than the unit sales loss for the other items in the category. In addition, all deal cross-elasticities must have the correct sign. If they do not, then a deal on one item will increase the sales on another item, which is theoretically and intuitively incorrect.

In looking at the coefficients in Table 12.5 one notes that most of the signs are correct. The major exception is BBK, a Jewel private label brand. The second step is to check the other restriction to see if it holds for all the items in the table. However, it is common to violate these restrictions. Then, the models need to be adjusted so that these constraints hold. This can be through the user modifying the coefficients or using some type of constrained estimation to require the restrictions to hold.

To see how the unit sales are affected when an item is promoted, Blue Bonnet 1-lb stick margarine was used. The model estimates given in Table 12.10 are used. A deal discount is set, and the decision to advertise the item is made. Then, these values are entered into the equations and a unit sales estimate is made for each item in the category. For the other items in the category, it is assumed that no promotion is being run simultaneously.

Table 12.10 shows the sales increase in Blue Bonnet and the lost unit sales of the other brands in the category. Blue Bonnet sales increase was 176 percent at a 10 percent discount and 340 percent at a 20 percent discount. However, the net category increase in unit sales for a 10 percent price discount was 2.4 percent and for a 20 percent discount it was 4.4 percent. Thus, unit sales for the brand grew far more than the category. Over half of the Blue Bonnet sales came from other brands within the category. The unit sales increase is then entered into the financial model described in the next section.

TABLE 12.10 Blue Bonnet Deal Discount Profit Computation (profits in dollars)

	Brand: Blue Bonnet		Regular price: 85 cents		
			Regular cost: 71 cents		
			Discount cost: 59 cents		

| | | | Discount | | |
Brand	0%	10%	20%	30%	9.41% Optimal
Blue Bonnet	238	442	362	31	427
Chiffon	190	182	173	162	183
Imperial	693	681	668	649	682
Land O' Lakes	444	427	409	384	429
Parkay	317	312	307	299	313
Blue Brook	1,280	1,241	1,198	1,139	1,245
Sunnyland	266	257	247	234	258
Generic	147	145	144	143	146
Total	3,545	3,687	3,509	3,040	3,683

Source: Center for Research in Marketing, University of Chicago.

Financial Model

Even though a deal discount of 20 percent for Blue Bonnet increased sales by 340 percent, it came at the cost of lost sales to other brands in the category. If the profitability of Blue Bonnet is less than the other brands, the category profit could decrease. A financial model is required to compare the profitability of different promotional alternatives for Blue Bonnet.

The model begins with the deal discount, the advertising levels, display activity, and the unit sales increase or decrease by item in the subcategory. Then, the item's gross margin is entered. For example, the gross margin for the private label brands are approximately 35 percent, for the generic brand it is 45 percent, and for national brands it varies. The gross margin in cents for each brand is given in Table 12.11. Next, the deal discount for the brand is entered. For Blue Bonnet margarine a trade deal discount of 12 cents was offered to the retailer.

Using these financial data one can then calculate the profitability of different deal discounts. For each deal discount offered, one calculates the lost profits from the other items in the category. Table 12.10 shows this calculation. One then calculates the increase in profit (or loss) for the item being dealt. Table 12.10 shows the profit calculation for Blue Bonnet at four different discount levels: 0 percent, 10 percent, 20 percent, and 30 percent.

Once the two separate profit calculations are completed (for the loss in profits from the other items and the gain/loss for the dealt item), they are combined to indicate the profitability of the promotion. Table 12.10 shows the net profit (loss) for the four deal discounts offered. Table 12.10 also shows that the optimal deal discount is in the range of 10 percent. The retailer can then determine the level within this range that is optimal and decide whether to offer the promotion at this discount or use a larger discount because of the store traffic generation. However, if the retailer uses a larger discount, the lost profit from the optimal

TABLE 12.11 Prices, Costs, and Margins of Brands of Margarine

Brand	Price	Cost	Margin (in cents)
Blue Bonnet	$.85	$.71	$.14
Chiffon	.59	.49	.10
Imperial	.89	.73	.16
Land O' Lakes	.75	.61	.14
Parkay	.83	.68	.15
Blue Brook	.49	.39	.10
Sunnyland	.53	.43	.10
Generic	.25	.21	.04

level can be determined. Then, a more "rational" decision regarding the question of offering a larger discount for the item can be made by deciding whether the additional store traffic is likely to offer enough additional profit to justify the lost profit.

The profit model does not take into account the retailer's forward buying decision. For this discussion, it is assumed to be a separate decision from the size of the deal discount. The quantity bought after the deal is completed does not depend on the quantity sold during the deal (assuming there is no trough after a deal). However, models can be constructed which jointly optimize promotions *and* inventory.

The most difficult part of setting deal discounts is estimating the store traffic that results from a promotion. As was stated, the model helps the retailer concentrate on the loss sustained by offering a large discount, but it cannot estimate the gain in profits from attracting additional customers.[11]

Another related issue is the price image of the retailer. If price promotions influence the retailer's price image, then deep deal discounts on high-volume categories are important. The model cannot answer this question.

Implications of Profitability Model for the Retailer and Manufacturer

The model just described has significant implications for the manufacturer and retailer. The manufacturer needs to understand how the retailer's promotional strategy will affect retail passthrough of the trade deals offered. If the brand is strong and likely to attract customers into the retail chain, then the passthrough and deal discount is likely to be large. However, if the brand simply cannibalizes the category, then it is clear the retailer should not pass on 100 percent of the trade deal received. Thus, weaker brands or product categories which do not increase the store traffic for the retailer are vulnerable to lower passthrough levels.

---

[11] A model in which store traffic $ST = f$ (brand i's promotion at time t) can be built. However, the effect on total traffic is likely to be very small because there are 50–200 items on sale in any given week.

The optimal strategy for the retailer, when receiving a trade promotion on a weaker brand (Blue Bonnet in the previous section) is to offer a discount on the dealt brand which increases the gross margin in cents above the other brands in the category and then use merchandising to try to switch the customers to the dealt brand. If, instead, the retailer tried to discount the item so that the gross margin was less than the competitive items, then when the consumer switched, the retailer would lose profits. Thus, the position of the brand has a significant effect on the retailer's strategy.

To demonstrate this point, a second brand was analyzed to determine the optimal deal discount. Table 12.12 shows that Land O' Lakes sells for less than Blue Bonnet, 75 cents versus 85 cents. However, to make the example comparable, it was assumed that they both had the same initial gross margin cents, and therefore, the cost of Land O' Lakes was 61 cents compared to 71 cents for Blue Bonnet. Both received a 12 cent trade deal. The question is: What is the optimal deal discount? For Blue Bonnet it was 9.4 cents and for Land O' Lakes it was 13.3 cents. Thus, the retailer pocketed 2.6 cents in the case of Blue Bonnet, but actually added 1.3 cents to the Land O' Lakes trade deal. The reason was the increase in overall volume. Land 'O Lakes has more than three times the volume than Blue Bonnet, which means that more customers are likely to switch to it from other stores.

One can summarize the strategy of the retailer. If a brand has a "strong franchise" and is likely to attract customers, then pass on more than the trade deal allowance but if the brand is weak or the category is not likely to attract new customers, do not pass through 100 percent of the trade promotion. The result is that weaker brands or brands in weaker categories are not likely to receive the passthrough that a strong brand in a strong category does. The retailer should

TABLE 12.12 Land O' Lakes Deal Discount Profit Computation

	Brand: Land O' Lakes		Regular price:	75 cents	
			Regular cost:	61 cents	
			Discount cost:	49 cents	

| | | | Discount | | |
Brand	0%	10%	20%	30%	13.3% Optimal
Blue Bonnet	128	124	119	113	123
Chiffon	190	174	159	138	170
Imperial	693	678	661	638	673
Land O' Lakes	825	1,387	1,159	512	1,330
Parkay	317	314	311	306	313
Blue Brook	1,280	1,250	1,218	1,171	1,241
Sunnyland	266	257	247	233	254
Generic[a]	147	148	149	151	148
Total	3,846	4,331	4,022	3,263	4,252

[a] Land O' Lakes has the wrong cross price sign in the generic model.

Source: Center for Research in Marketing, University of Chicago.

promote the weaker brands but use it more to cannibalize the other brands in the category because the profit margin (in cents) is higher for the weaker brand during a promotion. The brand manager should be aware of this strategy of the retailers and design promotions accordingly.

FUTURE RESEARCH TOPICS

Promotions have become the subject of much academic research over the last five years. The availability of scanner data has been a major impetus for this research. It is interesting to note that most of the research has focused on the "own" effects of promotions from the brand managers' point of view. There are many other issues that need to be addressed in research on retailer promotions.

1. Do retailer promotions increase store traffic? Which products affect store traffic?
2. How does retailer profitability influence the passthrough and discounts offered?
3. What percentage of a retail promotion is incremental profit to the retailer and what percentage is cannibalization of other brands? What are the implications of these percentages to the manufacturer?
4. How do promotional elasticities vary across product categories and brand's market share position? Why?
5. Why do researchers have trouble finding troughs after retail promotions when consumers seem to stockpile?
6. Does a change in the level of promotions in a product category influence the number of brand-loyal consumers in the category?
7. Why do promotional elasticities for the same product category vary across markets?

No doubt there are many more research topics which can be analyzed. However, it is interesting to note that many of the topics listed focus on "why" certain phenomenon exist rather than showing they exist. Academic research needs to concentrate on explaining why certain responses are observed not merely documenting that they do exist.

SUMMARY

The following conclusions can be drawn from the research described.

1. Retail promotional elasticities are quite high and explain a significant percentage of the variation in a brand's sales.
2. Competitive effects (cross-elasticities) have not been the primary focus of most researchers though Blattberg and Wisniewski (1986), Allenby (1988), and SCAN*PRO developed by Wittink et al. (1987) have begun to analyze the competitive effects of promotions.
3. Display and feature advertising effects, both very important components of retail promotions, have not been analyzed to any major extent. The analysis conducted to date is very limited and looks at these promotional tools in a very crude way. Yet most retailers rely heavily on them.

4. Very few articles have analyzed the profitability of promotions to retailers and its implication for the manufacturer, though this is a critical element in the design of trade promotions.
5. Scanner panel data have been used in several studies, though the underlying theory of dealing behavior needs to be expanded.

In summary, the analysis of retail promotions is a new area for both academics and business researchers. Given the expenditure devoted to retail promotions, it is surprising that so little research has been conducted. However, this is likely to change over the next few years, and many more articles will be produced developing new theories and concepts.

13

The Manufacturer Promotion Planning Process

THE MANUFACTURER'S PLANNING PROCESS

Overview

Figure 13.1 depicts the framework for the manufacturer promotion planning process that will be examined in this chapter. The framework is normative—it prescribes how promotions *should* be planned—but to some extent does reflect the reality at several firms. The framework was derived based on personal interviews with managers, corporate documents, and several excellent references, including Strang (1980), Farris and Quelch (1983), Lodish (1986), Schultz and Robinson (1982), and Ulanoff (1985).

The core of the planning framework is the development of marketing objectives and strategies and then promotion objectives and strategies. The budgeting process, consisting of three distinct steps, is seen as coincident to and obviously intertwined with this core. "Background" factors determined by corporate policy and the marketing environment play a critical role in framing the entire promotion planning process. The process is often interactive, especially with regard to budgeting and involves feedback through the review of past promotion performance.

The parallel processes of advertising and other marketing mix planning are included in our framework because while these processes are parallel, they are not independent. Promotion and advertising planning must be coordinated at the levels of objective setting, strategy formulation, tactic design, implementation, and evaluation. For large organizations, this task can be especially formidable, since different departments can be involved and large events encompassing the entire country may be in the works.

The planning process shown in Figure 13.1 is for one brand or perhaps one closely-knit product line. The figure therefore omits the importance of coordi-

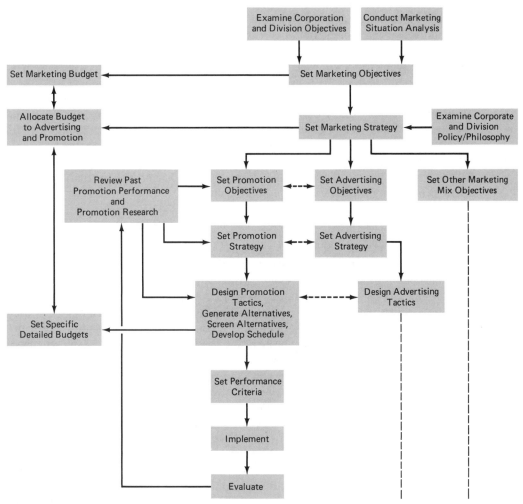

FIGURE 13.1 The Manufacturer Promotion Planning Process

nating efforts across products. In packaged goods companies, it is quite common for several brands to join together in sponsoring a special event or contest. Cross-ruff couponing is another example of promotion involving more than one brand. The issue, however, is particularly relevant for durable goods manufacturers (Quelch et al., 1987). For example, branding is an important assurance of quality in the household appliance market. A promotion for one appliance in the firm's product line is therefore likely to enhance the sales for other items carrying the same brand name. That is, a promotion for a Black and Decker variable speed drill enhances sales for Black and Decker painting equipment. Likewise, a promotion that degrades the image of one product in the Black and Decker line degrades the image of all Black and Decker equipment and can decrease the morale of the sales force. In conclusion, then, the issue of coordinating planning efforts across brands represents an opportunity for efficiency and cost sharing among a given firm's packaged goods brands, but may represent a requirement for a firm's durable goods brands.

A final point regarding Figure 13.1 is the timing of the planning process. A promotion plan is usually part of a one-year marketing plan, so the objectives and strategies pertain to a one-year time horizon. Typically, several promotions will be designed to implement the promotion strategy. One should recognize, however, the need to be flexible as the year progresses. Unexpected developments in competitive activity or in the performance of the brand may require that promotion tactics or even strategy and objectives be changed.

Corporate and Division Objectives

Corporate and division objectives serve as the starting point for planning all marketing activities. These objectives are often stated in very specific numerical terms, involving sales, market share, profit, or ROI (return-on-investment) goals. In addition, they are often stated on a quarterly basis. In large corporations, quarterly profit performance is often critical in maintaining the company's stock price, and as a result, quarterly quantitative goals permeate the planning process. At some level between the corporation and the brand, however, these goals must be divided up among the firm's several brands. For large corporations, the goals are first parceled out to divisions and then brand groups.

Corporations and divisions also often set general strategies for achieving the sales and profit objectives. These include strategies such as ''more efficient use of marketing expenditures'' (e.g., Webster, 1981) which have a definite impact on the promotion planning process, and also explicit guidelines for sales promotion expenditures to sales ratios (Strang, 1980, p. 10).

Strang concludes (1980, pp. 50–61, 99) that corporate and division-level senior management are taking on more important roles in the promotion planning process, involving the setting of objectives and strategy guidelines, as well as the approval of promotion plans. This is undoubtedly both a blessing and a problem. It does attest to the increased importance of sales promotion and bodes well for additional financial resources being devoted to managing sales promotion. However, this could increase the emphasis on sales promotion as a short-term tool if senior management pays more attention to quarterly profit goals than long-term brand viability.

Situation Analysis

Situation analyses are a prerequisite to any planning process. Various checklist approaches are available for covering the appropriate bases relevant for sales promotion planning (e.g., Robinson, 1985, pp. 390–393). Topics to be reviewed include brand performance, competitive performance, and consumer behavior.

Particularly relevant areas for sales promotion planning are consumer response to promotions and competitive promotion activities.

Examining historical competitive activity can give important clues as to the competition's future plans as well as how competitors would react to changes in the brand's own activities. Perhaps a leading competitor has cut trade promotion in a selected geographic area, providing a signal that he or she wishes to extricate the category from a ruinous prisoner's dilemma trade promotion war. Alternatively, perhaps the category has been spiralling into a promotion war over the past several years, and it is time for the brand in question to send a signal to the competition.

Corporate and Division Policy/Philosophy

Many times corporations have a policy or philosophy with regard to sales promotion that sets the tone for sales promotion planning. This policy may be stated in corporatewide memos. Other times, it is part of an implicit attitude rooted in senior management and transferred over time to junior managers through the process of approving (and disapproving) promotional plans. One such philosophy, elements of which the authors have seen in a few companies, is stated by Maier (1985, p. 43) as follows:

1. "Sales promotion is an integral part of the marketing mix."
2. "Sales promotion should be used as an offensive weapon in the brand's marketing arsenal, not merely as a defensive reaction when a problem arises."
3. "Sales promotion should extend and reinforce the brand's advertising and positioning, whenever possible."
4. "Sales promotions should be developed as campaigns, not as single, unrelated events."
5. "Good sales promotions are built upon sound strategic planning."

As single sentence summaries, these statements seem innocuous enough, but they are not universally shared. Other corporate philosophies with respect to sales promotion include a necessary evil, a cost of doing business that should be decreased if possible, or a tool to be used as a defensive measure for attracting one's share of brand switchers. In a qualitative sense, promotion still does not enjoy the status of advertising, which is often viewed by managers as "nicer" or "better for the company image" (Strang, 1980, p. 60). Perhaps the most widespread philosophical view of promotion is that it cannot build a long-term consumer franchise (e.g., Schultz and Robinson, 1982, pp. 68–70). Others might state this view more emphatically: Sales promotion is for short-term sales movement, while advertising builds the long-term viability of the brand.

One can certainly quarrel with any of these philosophies. They get at the basic roots of questions such as the profitability of promotions and their reinforcement properties, and these questions are not yet resolved (see Chapters 2, 5, and 10–12). In studying the promotion planning process, we note, however, that the corporate philosophy toward promotions sets the stage for the objectives that will be defined for promotion, as well as the evaluation criteria. If the corporate line is that promotions are a necessary cost of doing business that can be used to move inventory short term, then promotions will indeed be used sporadically and will be designed to achieve noticeable sales bumps. The reality thus becomes a self-fulfilling prophecy of the philosophy.

Corporate philosophies undoubtedly form gradually, based on real and imagined experiences, but this issue is particularly salient for the durables and service industries, which are only now beginning to use sales promotion, especially consumer promotions, in greater amounts. These companies therefore do not have a well-established corporate philosophy on sales promotion. In this case, senior management should recognize that whatever philosophical tone they set will have important ramifications for how promotion is used in their companies.

Marketing Objectives and Strategy, Sales Promotion Objectives and Strategy

The distinctions among these four components of the promotion planning process are theoretically clear but often confused in practice. In general, objectives are goals, often stated in numerical terms. Schultz and Robinson (1982, p. 149) stipulate that objectives should be specific, measurable, clear and concise, practical and realistic, affordable, and attainable. Strategies are general approaches to achieving those goals. Marketing objectives and strategies pertain to the marketing mix as a whole, while promotion objectives and strategies pertain just to that aspect of the marketing mix.

Table 13.1 gives examples of coordinated sequences of marketing and pro-

TABLE 13.1 Three Examples of Marketing and Promotion Objectives and Strategies

	I	*II*	*III*
Marketing objective	Increase market share from 5% to 7%.	Increase sales by 20%.	Increase profit by 20%.
Marketing strategy	Promotion will "push" the product while advertising will "pull" it.	Increase purchase rate of product.	Decrease marketing expenditures while holding sales as high as possible.
Promotion objectives	Gain 90% distribution for the product.	Decrease interpurchase time from 10 to 8 weeks.	Maintain distribution at 90%.
Promotion strategy	Use trade deals, especially in low-distribution areas.	Use trade dealing to encourage frequent price cuts. Use consumer promotions to encourage faster use-up rate.	Cut consumer promotions that do not pay out. Use trade deals only to extent necessary to maintain distribution.

motion objectives and strategies. Note that the role for promotion depends directly on the marketing strategy, and not the marketing objectives. For example, consider scenario I. Starting with the marketing objective of increasing market share, a number of promotion objectives and strategies could be developed. However, once the marketing strategy assigns promotion the role of pushing the product through the trade, the promotion objectives become trade oriented and the promotion strategies involve trade deals.

Note that the specific strategies and objectives displayed in Table 13.1 are influenced greatly by corporate objectives and policies, situation analysis, and review of previous promotion effectiveness. For example, in scenario II, consumer research might have indicated that product usage is a variable—that is, its consumption rate is established by getting the product in the home and then getting the consumer to use it. In addition, the trial rate might have been high, and loyalty levels might generally be high in this category. As a result, increasing loyalty or attracting brand switchers would not have been good strategies. Once the strategy of increasing consumption rate had been established, the ample usage of promotion could not have been a viable strategy unless corporate guidelines allowed for heavy promotion expenditure and the corporate philosophy allowed for promotion having long-term effects. Finally, the strategy would not have been viable if previous research had shown that in-store promotions do not accelerate purchase timing.

As discussed earlier, most promotion plans have a one-year time horizon. This does not have to be the case however. In fact, one might argue that three-year promotion plans would help to extricate promotion from its role as a short-term sales generator. Table 13.2 shows an example of a three-year plan in which promotion's role is to attract and retain new triers. The theoretical basis for the plan is of the operant conditioning framework discussed in Chapter 2.

TABLE 13.2 Marketing and Promotion Objectives and Strategies: A Long-Term Planning Example

Marketing objective	Increase market share by 50% over three years.	
Marketing strategy	Initiate and establish habit using promotion; reinforce using advertising.	
Promotion objectives	Year 1:	Increase percentage ever tried from 50% to 75%.
	Year 2:	Induce 50% repeat rate among new triers.
	Year 3:	Maintain 40% repeat rate among new triers.
Promotion strategy	Years 1 and 2:	Use direct-mail couponing and sampling to attract new triers. Use in-pack coupons to stimulate repeat purchase.
	Year 3:	Gradually phase out in-pack coupons and use limited FSI coupon distribution.

Promotion Tactics

Promotion tactics are the specific tools for executing a particular strategy. The output of the tactics plan is a promotion calendar showing when each promotion event will occur, and separate detailed descriptions for each event. The best way to specify promotion tactics is through a process of generating and screening alternatives.

Generating Alternatives. The easiest and most common way to generate alternatives is by consulting a list. Sometimes a company will cross-reference such a list with various promotion objectives. An example of this is provided by Strang (1976) and displayed in Table 13.3. Lists such as this can be made much more specific, for example, distinguishing between the various types of coupons. Lists can also be cross-referenced by product type, to reflect past research or corporate philosophy on which promotions work best for which products. Table 13.4, from Quelch et al. (1987) displays such a list for durables.

The use of lists often gets the planner in the ballpark of what type of promotion to use, but there are still many details to be worked out. For example, if we decide we want to use a coupon, we must then decide on vehicle, face value, circulation and expiration dates, and overlay or accompanying advertising. Thus, a simple coupon promotion can explode into several alternatives. Trade deals are similar in this respect.

TABLE 13.3   Generating Promotion Alternatives for Packaged Goods: A List Cross-referenced by Promotional Objectives

| | Primary Impact | | |
Technique	Brand Awareness	Attract New Customers	Increase Sales to Present Customers
Bonus packs			●
Cash refunds			
Single purchase		●	
Multiple purchase			●
Contest/sweepstakes	●		
Couponing			
Media/mail		●	
In/on pack			●
Multiple			●
Premiums			
Single purchase		●	
Multiple purchase			●
Price-off			●
Sampling		●	

Source: Reprinted by permission of *Harvard Business Review.* An exhibit from "Sales Promotion: Fast Growth, Faulty Management," by Roger A. Strang (July/August, 1976). Copyright © 1976 by the President and Fellows of Harvard College; all rights reserved.

TABLE 13.4 Generating Promotion Alternatives for Durable Goods: A List Cross-referenced by Product Type

Price	Lower Ticket (Disposables)				Higher Ticket (Serviceables)			
Product Type	Item		System		Item		System	
Cascaded Demand	No	Yes	No	Yes	No	Yes	No	Yes
Example	Iron	Insta-matic Camera	Tires	Skis	Refrig-erator	Auto-mobile	Home Security System	Personal Computer
Rebates	★	★	★	★	★	★	★	★
Price/quantity promotions		★	★					
Coupons		★						
Sweepstakes	★	★						
Accessories/premiums		★		★				★
Testers/loaners/samples						★		★
Tie-in promotions		★		★				★
Trade-in allowances			★	★	★	★		★
Financing incentives					★	★		★
Service contracts					★	★		★
Finders fees							★	

Source: Reprinted from "Opportunities and Risks of Durable Goods Promotion," by John A. Quelch, Scott A. Neslin, and Lois Olson, *Sloan Management Review*, Vol. 28, No. 2 (Winter, 1987), p. 33, by permission of the publisher. Copyright © (1987) by the *Sloan Management Review* Association. All rights reserved.

Other ways to generate promotion alternatives include the standard idea-generation methods used in new product development (Urban and Hauser, 1980, Ch. 6). These methods include suggestions from employees, competitive searches, focus groups, and creative brainstorming sessions. In the case of promotions, the sales force is often a good source of promotion ideas. The sales force is in contact with retailers and is quick to learn about an innovative competitive promotion. Sales promotion agencies also bring a broad and fresh perspective to the task of generating promotion alternatives. Formal marketing research in the form of focus groups or in-depth interviews with retailers or consumers can be fruitful, but such alternatives might be more successful at evaluating ideas than generating them.

Creative brainstorming has a tremendous amount of potential, especially in designing contests, sweepstakes, overlays, or premiums. Typically, a creativity consultant will run a day-long meeting, using various levels of managers from several departments (see Urban and Hauser, 1980, Ch. 4). Many packaged goods firms have experience with using such consultants for designing advertising or new products, and may even employ a creativity consultant in-house. Durable goods companies with little experience in using promotions would have very challenging problems, for example, "competition-proofing" a promotion (Quelch et al., 1987), to address using creativity.

In conclusion, the number of promotion tactic executions available for implementing a particular strategy will be very large. In light of this, Strang's finding that packaged goods companies consider only a limited number of alternatives (1980, pp. 26–28, 60–61) is somewhat surprising. There are several reasons, however, why managers might only consider a limited number of alternatives:

- An exhaustive generation of all alternatives takes time and can be frustratingly inefficient.
- There is a general tendency to use last year's plan as a benchmark.
- Corporate policy/philosophy toward promotion may discourage creativity.
- Many alternatives are in fact considered, but only implicitly, since planners develop a talent for immediately focusing on the best alternatives.

Screening Alternatives. Screening promotion alternatives involves evaluting them on the criteria of consistency with strategy and achievement of objectives. Evaluating consistency with strategy can often be made on a judgmental basis. For example, if the strategy is to use trade deals to gain distribution although not to gain in-store promotions, heavy performance allowances will obviously be off-strategy. Determining whether a given alternative will achieve quantifiable objectives is a more difficult task. There are four methods for making this determination.

1. *Judgment based on experience.* The feedback provided from previous promotion evaluation becomes important here. If no feedback is available, the judgment becomes "seat of the pants."
2. *Pretesting.* A narrowed-down list of alternatives can be evaluated by either retailers or consumers (Block et al., 1985; Schultz and Robinson, 1982, pp. 418–420).

3. *Market tests.* Executions are tested via experimentation in the actual marketplace.
4. *Decision models.* Statistical models based only on hard data, or "decision calculus" models that incorporate management judgment, can be used to calculate the effectiveness of alternative promotions.

It is difficult to gauge the relative use of these four screening methods. Certainly, the formal use of research is less common in promotion planning than in advertising planning (Schultz and Robinson, 1982, p. 416; Strang, 1980, pp. 67, 69). However, there are several examples in the literature where pretesting methods (Levy et al., 1983; Block et al., 1985), experiments (Chapter 6), decision calculus models (Little, 1975; Neslin and Shoemaker, 1983a), and statistical analyses (Abraham and Lodish, 1987; Lodish, 1986, pp. 56–59) have been used in situations with real managers. We will review some of these techniques later in the chapter.

The Promotion Calendar. Once the tactics planning is complete, the results can be summarized in a promotion calendar. The promotion calendar is a schedule that lists each promotion event. Often the calendar includes budget information. It also serves as a way to coordinate promotions across brands and for a given brand over time. It is thus an important component of the planning process, in addition to being an implementation document. We will examine an actual promotion calendar in this chapter.

Performance Criteria

The "bottom line" performance criteria for a promotion should relate directly to the objectives of the promotion. However, intermediate measures are also useful. For example, the objective of a trade promotion may be to achieve 90 percent distribution, and this is the key performance criterion. However, intermediate measures such as percentage of retailers participating in the trade promotion are also important. Other intermediate measures include percentage display and featuring achieved at retail, and coupon redemption rates. Intermediate measures are valuable for diagnosing the reasons for promotion performance. However, caution must be taken to guard against using intermediate measures as primary performance criteria.

Implementation

Implementing promotions can be a very painstaking task, especially when several different components need to be coordinated. Implementation often has been the role of a merchandising department or an advertising or promotion agency. However, firms are beginning to use their own managers for this purpose. For example, an associate brand manager may be developed as a liaison between the brand group and the sales force, or simply as a troubleshooter helping to coordinate a firm's sponsorship of an athletic event. In summary, most managers can recall a horror story involving display material that never arrived or advertising that broke two weeks after a major in-store promotion. More and more attention is being paid to these details.

Another aspect of implementation deals with the brand management process itself, in particular, the execution of a budget. A significant problem can arise when promotions are managed by intermediate rather than bottom-line criteria. For example, a brand manager may panic when a coupon redemption rate comes in higher than expected—this means that costs will soar over budget. However, perhaps this means the coupon generated even more incremental sales than expected, and a future coupon drop can be curtailed to remain within budget. Likewise, perhaps a redemption rate on target might not correspond to a sales increase on target, and a future coupon promotion needs to be altered in terms of face value or distribution vehicle. In summary, promotion objectives are always stated in terms of benefits, and they should finally be evaluated in terms of benefits. Unfortunately, promotions are often managed in real time using performance data readily available: cost and intermediate measures (Strang, 1980, p. 31; Lodish, 1986, p. 10). Most textbook discussions on budget control (Schultz and Robinson, 1982, p. 412; Zoul, 1985, p. 419) emphasize its role in tracking expenditures *and performance* against the promotion plan. However, the latter function is less concrete and less easily quantified on an ongoing basis.

Once the promotion plan is being implemented, various deviations may become necessary. Strang (1980, p. 32) reports fairly high flexibility in changing promotion plans during the year, although promotion plans appear to be more fixed than advertising plans. Interestingly, senior management often takes the lead in initiating these changes.

Evaluation

Promotion evaluation is a critical aspect of the entire planning process; however, the evidence is weak as to the extensiveness and quality of promotion evaluation. Strang (1980, pp. 102–103) reaches a rather dim view of the practice of promotion evaluation and its use in future planning. He notes, for example, that "it is reasonable to say that more than 90 percent of the allocation decisions made by executives in the study were made without the benefit of formal research guidance" and that "much sales promotion evaluation appeared to consist of a simple count of the number of cases of the brand that were sold during the promotional period without consideration of the effect on contribution or to the slump in sales that usually followed." Lodish (1986) reaches a similar conclusion: "Most firms evaluate the cost of promotion, but few firms even attempt to measure the profitability of a long- or short-term promotion compared to not doing it at all" (p. 10). (See also Lemont, 1981.)

This evidence should be contrasted with other findings that formal evaluation does take place. Strang himself found that 86 percent of managers stated they undertook some formal evaluation of sales promotions. Farris and Quelch (1983, pp. 194–197) note increased manufacturer interest in "investing in decision support systems to evaluate past promotions and to facilitate promotion planning.'' They document use of one time series methodology and mention another system in use by Chesebrough-Ponds, which can ''retrospectively compute the profit impact of individual promotions, in total or by account, or project the profit impact of planned promotion programs.''

To synthesize these findings, there appears to be three fundamental issues regarding the evaluation of promotions:

1. Are formal evaluations undertaken?
2. Are the evaluations high quality?
3. Are the results used for future planning?

Summarizing the evidence, it does appear that formal evaluations are undertaken, but the quality and actual usage of these reviews may be suspect.

Budgeting

Figure 13.1 suggests that the promotion planning process consists of three levels of budgeting decisions: the total marketing budget, the allocation of that budget to promotion versus advertising and other marketing mix elements, and the preparation of individual promotion budgets. As the figure shows, there should be give-and-take among these budgeting decisions and the process should not necessarily be ''top-down.'' For example, a well-conceived promotion event may require a large budget, which tilts the allocation more toward promotion and possibly enlarges the total marketing budget.

The Marketing Expenditure Decision.   The marketing expenditure decision is often made using strict guidelines if not actual participation by senior management (Strang, 1980, pp. 40, 53). Often, the establishment of a total marketing budget involves negotiation between a brand manager and senior management. The brand manager will argue invariably that more can be accomplished with a higher budget. The final control of total marketing expenditures, however, is usually considered the domain of senior management. A full discussion of the determination of the marketing budget is beyond the scope of this book. The reader is urged to read the discussions in Kotler (1988), Lilien and Kotler (1983), as well as Larreche and Srinivasan (1982) for more detailed information.

The Allocation to Promotion Versus Other Marketing Elements.   Synthesizing from Strang (1980), Farris and Quelch (1983), and Schultz and Robinson (1982), there are five principal ways of allocating funds to promotion.

1. *Predetermined ratios.* These involve rules of thumb based on company policy or historical precedent, possibly modified by the strategic position of the brand.
2. *Objective and task method.* Objectives for both advertising and promotion are stated and plans are developed to accomplish those objectives at minimum cost.
3. *The build-up approach.* The budget begins with the ''necessary'' promotion expenditures and successively adds the less necessary programs. At some point, using

either objectives, predetermined ratios, or a total budget constraint as a cut-off criterion, the least necessary expenses are deleted.

4. *Competitive parity*. The budget mirrors that of a close competitor, scaled up or down accordingly.

5. *Theoretically optimal expenditures*. A sales response model is used to find the budget that will maximize profits. The model is either solved analytically or by using a simulation approach. The "optimal" budget may be not taken literally, but stated as a guideline or starting point to other budgets.

Strang reports that, while senior managers often specified ratio guidelines, historical precedent—namely, last year's allocation—was the most commonly used method of allocation. This is rather discouraging since the objective and task and theoretically optimal methods have much more intuitive appeal. However, both these techniques rely on an explicit representation of the sales response function. Given the mixed status of promotion evaluation noted earlier, this is a rather ambitious requirement. Lodish, however, argues that this is where the use of experimentation can become important (1986, pp. 82–89). Others argue that reasonable knowledge of the sales response function often does exist, either in the form of documented empirical evidence or managerial experience, and therefore decision calculus models can be used as part of the optimal expenditures approach.

Budgets for Individual Events. Preparing detailed event budgets is usually a straightforward task, once the details of the promotion have been specified. However, given the complexity of some of these events, costs can escalate rapidly unless care is paid to the details of purchasing items such as point-of-purchase material and premiums (Schultz and Robinson, 1982, pp. 409–413).

An additional problem in budgeting promotions arises when the market response to the promotion determines the cost of the program. This occurs with couponing, where redemption rate and timing is a key uncertainty. As discussed in Chapter 10, forecasting of redemption rates to within one percentage point is feasible but not always obtainable, and a one-percentage-point change in redemption rate can easily represent 10 percent of a coupon promotion's cost. Similar problems occur with rebates, premiums, and trade deals, where retailer participation rate as well as amount purchased on deal can easily vary from a budgeted target. As discussed in "Implementation," the key to managing sales promotions is to have a view of the sales implications of a cost overrun. In this way, management can diagnose the true significance of the cost discrepancy.

EXAMPLES OF PROMOTION PLANNING

In this section, we provide two examples of actual promotion plans. The first summarizes the derivation of a promotion calendar and shows an example of the calendar. The calendar is disguised but is based on an existing product's actual calendar. The second example illustrates the materials needed to implement a specific promotion event for a national brand of peanut butter.

Devising a Promotion Calendar

The manufacturer in this instance was very oriented toward current profits and was concerned about the efficient use of marketing funds. The concern was that marketing funds were not currently being deployed in a way that maximized the return per dollar spent. This corporate goal exerted pressure throughout the organization to produce profits by using current marketing resources more efficiently.

The particular brand in question was a medium market share brand in a stagnant market. It was a mature brand with an established brand franchise. Between 1980 and 1987, the brand had moved from 18 percent of its volume sold on promotion to 51 percent. This increased emphasis on promotion was not of concern. What was of concern was the balance between trade promotion and consumer promotion. The company believed that trade promotions were more likely to pay out than consumer promotions and that trade promotions ensured distribution and trade support, critical factors in the company's view for maintaining and enhancing purchase frequency among current users. Consumer promotions were believed to be good trial inducers, but for a mature brand with a loyal following, this was not seen as important.

The marketing objective for this brand therefore was to increase profits while maintaining market share or growing it slightly. The strategy was to emphasize continuity of purchase, that is, continued purchase by the brand's loyal segment. Although total marketing funds would increase due to inflation and competitive pressures, those funds were to be used in the most efficient manner possible. The role for promotion in this strategy was to contribute to enhanced continuity, and the promotion strategy was to shift funds toward trade promotion, away from consumer promotion. This shift in funds was seen as being consistent with the corporate concern about efficiency, and with the general organization belief that trade funds were more appropriate for enhancing continuity as opposed to trial.

Table 13.5 displays the promotion calendar for both the current year (1986–1987) and the new year (1987–1988). The calendar illustrates the detail that is needed to plan a year of promotion activity. While most of the calendar is self-explanatory, a few points of clarification are appropriate. The presell date, which appears without parentheses, is the date at which the sales force will inform the trade of the trade promotions listed until the next presell date. The dates in parentheses pertain to the dates during which factory shipments would be accompanied by the adjacent trade discount(s). For example, on May 26, 1987, the sales force would inform retailers in regions 4, 5, and 6 that a $2.40-per-case allowance would be available on all 8-oz packages shipped during the period July 1–August 14, 1987. In regions 2, 3, 9, and 10, the discount would not be quite as steep—

TABLE 13.5 A Promotion Calendar: Brand X National Promotion Plans

1986–1987

Presell (Shipment)	Event (Regions)	Cases[a] (000)	$'s (000)
5/26 (7/14–8/15)	Free-standing insert	(195)	1,100
	$2.13-per-case 8-oz allowance (nat'l)	700	1,495
	In-store sampling (R1)	—	50
		895	2,645
8/11 (9/22–10/24)	8-oz 30 cent price pack	383	1,263
	$2.59-per-case 8-oz preprice (R1, 2, 3)	255	1,550
	$2.59-per-case 8-oz incremental allotments	43	250
	Magazine subscription offer (R6)	(22)	115
	$1.09 2-oz preprice (R2)	5	40
	$2.13-per-case 8-oz allowance (R4, 5)	50	107
	Challenge refund (R7)	—	40
	4-oz 40 cent price pack (R2, 3)	12	46
	Hispanic coupon (R5, 8)	—	55
		770	3,466
8/11 (12/8–1/16)	$.10 mailed coupon	(368)	1,355
	$1.86-per-case 8-oz allowance (R3, 4, 7, 8, 9)	415	780
	"Free 2-oz" (R10)	—	115
	$2.40-per-case 2-oz allowance (R6)	8	20
	$2.67-per-case 1-oz allowance (R2)	200	535
		983	2,670
8/11 (2/2–3/6)	8-oz "Buy 2 Get 1 Free" (R3)	(1)	21
	2-oz bonus pack (nat'l ex. R4, 6, 8)	455	2,850
	$1.11-per-case 2-oz allowance (R3, 4, 7, 8, 9)	66	75
	$2.13-per-case 8-oz allowance (R2, 3, 8)	175	375
	$1.86-per-case 8-oz allowance (R5)	25	50

1987–1988

Presell (Shipment)	Event (Regions)	Cases (000)	$'s (000)
5/26 (7/1–8/14)	Free-standing insert (nat'l)	(100)	1,225
	$2.40-per-case 8-oz allowance (R4, 5, 6)	920	2,235
	$2.08-per-case 8-oz allowance (R2, 3, 9, 10)	69	160
	$1.00 off two defense coupon (R2, 4)	(25)	485
	Local radio promotions (R3, 5)	—	30
	$2.27-per-case 4-oz allowance (R6)	10	25
9/7–10/9	$2.27-per-case 4-oz allowance (R1, 8)	14	35
	$2.90-per-case 4-oz allowance (R11)	16	50
	Magazine promotion	—	500
		1,154	4,745
8/17 (10/5–11/6)	5 cent 8-oz price-pack (nat'l)	495	1,880
	$2.69-per-case 8-oz preprice (R3, 6, 9, 11)	122	1,095
11/2–11/27	$2.08-per-case 8-oz allowance (R, 2, 4, 10)	26	60
	$2.27-per-case 4-oz allowance (R12)	6	15
	Near pack test (R5)	—	205
	Hispanic sampling, NHSF (LA)	—	100
	R2 sampling	—	5
		649	3,360
8/17 (12/7–1/8)	$.10 mailed coupon (nat'l)	(105)	900
	$2.08-per-case 8-oz allowance (R2, 4, 6, 9, 12)	325	679
	$2.20-per-case 8-oz allowance (R3, 5, 7)	210	465
	$2.40-per-case 8-oz allowance (R1, 8, 10, 11)	181	440
		821	2,484
11/23	Free-standing insert (R1, 2, 3, 4)	(35)	665

Date	Item	Cases	Dollars
	8-oz "Buy 2 Get 1 Free" (R2)	—	11
	4-oz 40 cent price pack (R3)	60	210
	Challenge refund (R5)	(7)	110
		797	3,837
2/16	Free-standing insert (nat'l)	—	300
(3/30–5/1)	$2.17-per-case 8-oz allowance (R4)	350	775
	$2.40-per-case 8-oz allowance (R2)	240	580
	Little League promotion (1.8MM circ.)	—	17
	Walking/ret. fitness effort (R7)	—	67
	$2.34-per-case 4-oz allowance (R3, 6, 9)	215	510
	$2.40-per-case 8-oz allowance (R2, 4, 7, 10)	360	875
	Defense coupon (R5)	—	85
		1,165	3,209
	Total working cases and dollars	4,610	15,827
	Nonworking (military, misc.)	—	904
	Total promotion	4,610	16,731

Date	Item	Cases	Dollars
(2/8–3/11)	$2.20-per-case 8-oz allowance (R5)	497	1,095
(1/25–3/11)	$2.16-per-case 8-oz allowance (R6)	130	285
(3/7–4/8)	$1.89 8-oz preprice (R7)	106	590
	$2.40-per-case 8-oz allowance (R8)	45	110
	$2.08-per-case 8-oz allowance (R9)	181	377
	$3.18-per-case 4-oz allowance (R10)	69	220
	$2.27-per-case 4-oz allowance (R11)	6	15
	Trade incentive program (nat'l)	—	1,339
	Radio promotions (R5)	—	90
	Hispanic sampling (R3)	—	50
		1,069	4,836
2/5	Free-standing insert (R1, 2, 3)	(50)	1,275
(4/4–5/6)	$2.27-per-case 4-oz allowance (R4)	135	306
	$2.08-per-case 8-oz allowance (R5, 6)	156	330
	$2.20-per-case 8-oz allowance (R8)	122	295
(4/4–5/13)	$2.13-per-case 8-oz allowance (R9)	208	451[b]
(5/30–6/30)	$2.20-per-case 8-oz allowance (R11)	262	577
	$2.20-per-case 4-oz allowance (R13)	24	53
	Jackets (300) (R10)	—	12
	$2.27-per-case 4-oz allowance (R12)	91	210
(5/23–6/30)	$2.08-per-case 8-oz allowance (R14)	132	285
	Consumer service coupon	—	10
	$2.27-per-case 4-oz allowance (R3, 9, 12)	30	75
	Trade slicks (R1, 2, 8, 11)	—	60
	Special event	—	300
		1,210	4,239
	Total working cases and dollars	4,903	19,664
	Nonworking (military, misc.)	—	1,250
	Total promotion	4,903	20,914

TABLE 13.5 (*continued*)

Year	Volume	% Vol Promoted	Promotion Expenditures[c] % Trade	Promotion Expenditures[c] % Consumer
1980–81	8,200	18	38	62
1981–82	8,834	33	37	63
1982–83	9,384	34	39	61
1983–84	8,880	38	33	67
1984–85	8,881	41	29	71
1985–86	9,391	46	21	79
1986–87	9,027	51	38	62
Proposed 1987–88	9,200	53	50	50

[a] Numbers in parentheses indicate cases over and above those sold on trade promotion.
[b] Includes $5.67-per-case 8-oz allowance (R15).
[c] Trade promotion includes allowances, incremental allotments, trade incentive program, jackets, and special event.

$2.08 rather than $2.40. Also beginning May 26, 1987, the sales force would inform the trade of various consumer promotions, for example, a nationally distributed free-standing insert coupon. These consumer promotions might impress retailers with the need to buy additional quantities of the brand (see Chapter 14).

The promotion calendar also includes a budget. For example, the free-standing insert coupon mentioned was expected to cost $1,225,000. It was expected that 920,000 cases would be shipped under the $2.40-per-case allowance. Note that $2.40 times 920,000 multiplies to $2,208,000 whereas $2,235,000 is listed as the cost of this promotion. The company believed in allowing some leeway in the budget and wanted to guard against budget overruns.

Visual inspection of Table 13.5 reveals more trade promotion in more regions during 1987–1988 than during the previous year. This is reflected in the statistics that 50 percent of promotion sales this year would be allocated to trade promotions, in contrast to 38 percent in the previous year. The promotion calendar appears to be consistent with the promotion strategy outlined.

Implementing a Particular Promotion Event

In this section we discuss the materials needed to implement a particular promotion event for Jif peanut butter. This event was designed to help launch a new plastic jar for Jif. The appendix to this chapter has several of these materials: (1) a one-page summary of the marketing plan sent to the sales force, (2) materials prepared for the sales force to present the full marketing campaign to the trade, (3) a "shelf card" to be placed on the store shelf to highlight the new package, (4) a free-standing insert coupon announcing the plastic jar and presenting a refund offer, and (5) a storyboard for the television advertising that supported the event. Additional materials not shown in the appendix included a "tear pad" consumer promotion, located on the supermarket shelf, where the consumer would tear off a mail-in refund offer; "ad slicks" depicting the new plastic jar, which the trade uses to prepare feature promotions; and a large shelf card for use in a special display.

These materials illustrate the care and detail that must go into implementing a particular promotion event. The sales force material for informing the trade is much more than a simple listing of events. The material carefully builds a case for the retailer to buy more Jif peanut butter and suggests appropriate merchandising strategies for the retailer. The material is clearly a marketing communications piece directed at the trade. It communicates the benefits of the plastic jar for the retailer, as well as for the consumer. Recommendations for merchandising strategies are supported by test market results. The ability of this material to convince the retailer of the worthwhileness of the promotion will be critical to the overall success of the introduction of the plastic jar.

In addition to the detail displayed in the materials in the appendix, the coordination of messages among the various materials is clear. The plastic jar benefit is communicated in all promotion materials, whether they be for the trade, the consumer, or the sales force. This is the coordination needed to implement a unified marketing campaign. One aspect that cannot be displayed is the need for coordinated timing. For example, if the advertising appears in a two-week flight that begins two months before the appearance of the plastic jars, the effect will be diluted as consumers fail to find the plastic jar on the shelf.

PLANNING MODELS

While virtually all the research discussed in this book potentially has a role in planning promotions, a few models have been developed specifically as planning tools. We will review five of these methods in this section. Two of these methods are decision calculus models (Little, 1975, and Neslin and Shoemaker, 1983a), two are models based on survey data (Block et al., 1985, and Levy et al., 1983), and one is an optimization model (Rao and Thomas, 1973). Two noteworthy planning models not reviewed here are a time series–analysis-based decision support system developed by Abraham and Lodish (1987) and a regression-based model developed by Blattberg and Levin (1987). These are discussed in Chapter 11. The five models reviewed here complete the spectrum of methodological approaches to promotion planning.

BRANDAID

BRANDAID (Little, 1975) is a marketing mix model representing a classic example of Little's decision calculus approach (Little, 1970). The model is very comprehensive, covering advertising, pricing, distribution, and the sales force, as well as promotion. It is especially useful for deriving marketing strategies and allocating the marketing expenditure budget. Figure 13.2 shows the array of factors considered by the model. We will briefly review the promotion submodel. The reader is referred to Little's original articles plus the lucid discussion in Lilien and Kotler (1983) for more detail.

Model Formulation. BRANDAID models a brand's sales rate, $s(t)$, as a function of baseline reference sales, s_0, multiplied by a set of "effect indices," where there is an effect index for each influence on brand sales. Little defines $e(i, t)$ as the effect of influence i on brand sales in time t. The overall sales model is, therefore,

$$s(t) = s_0 \times e(1, t) \times e(2, t) \, x \cdots x \, e(I, t) \tag{13.1}$$

where there are "I" influences of sales (promotion, advertising, etc.). The effect indices are calibrated so that a value of 1 refers to a reference level of that influence, where the reference level could be the promotion plan used in the previous year. If actions were taken this year to increase promotion's effectiveness by 20 percent in time t, we would have $e(1, t) = 1.2$ (where $i = 1$ refers to promotion).

The numerical value of $e(1, t)$ can be specified directly by the manager or can be modeled as a function of controllable actions. The actions included in the

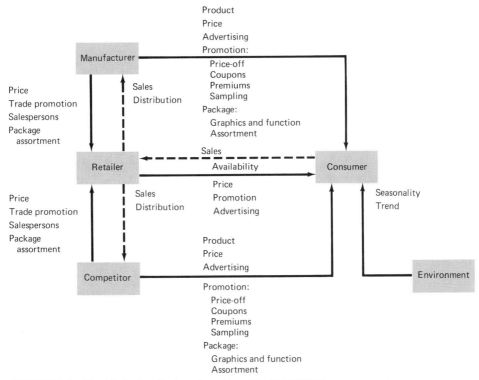

FIGURE 13.2   The Marketing System Considered by BRANDAID

Source: John D. C. Little, "BRANDAID: A Marketing-Mix Model. Part I: Structure; Part II: Implementation," *Operations Research,* Vol. 23, no. 4 (July–August 1975), p. 632.

promotion model are expenditures in time t, $x(t)$, the fraction of consumers (or geographic territories) covered by the promotion in time t, $h(t)$, and the relative effectiveness of the particular promotion used in time t, $k(t)$. Note that the values $x(t)$, $h(t)$, and $k(t)$ refer to the promotion under consideration in time t. The corresponding values for the "reference promotion" in time t are x_0, h_0, and k_0. Little then defines promotional intensity in time t as

$$a(t) = \frac{h(t)k(t)x(t)}{h_0 k_0 x_0} \tag{13.2}$$

As the intensity of promotion is increased, by spending more money, covering more consumers, or using a more effective promotion vehicle, the effect index will also increase, but not in direct proportion. Little assumes an s-shaped response curve relating promotion intensity to promotion's effect on sales. To capture the dynamics of the promotion effect and the net impact on sales, BRAND-AID incorporates the classic "bump-dip" dynamic effect of promotions (see Chapter 5) and cannibalization by the brand's promotions of other brands in the product line. In addition, note that BRANDAID can evaluate not just one promotion, but several taking place over the year.

Application. The BRANDAID model was applied to a packaged good fictitiously called "GROOVY" (Little, 1975). The model helped to derive a new promotion plan as part of the annual marketing plan process, and also was used during the year to help track the brand's progress and recommend remedial action as necessary. In fact, the implementation process for the model was gradual: First, it was used for the annual promotion plan; then it was used for tracking and "firefighting."

The fundamental issue facing brand management for GROOVY was the allocation of a budget to advertising and promotion. A regression model was formulated for sales as a function of advertising and promotion expenditures, and this provided the basic means to relate promotional intensity, $a(t)$, to promotion impact, $e(1, t)$. Figure 13.3 shows the effectiveness indices for seasonality, price,

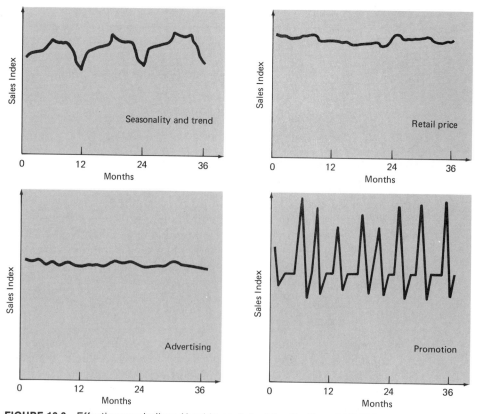

FIGURE 13.3 Effectiveness Indices Used in an Actual Application of BRANDAID

Source: John D. C. Little, "BRANDAID: A Marketing-Mix Model. Part I: Structure; Part II: Implementation," *Operations Ressearch*, Vol. 23, no. 4 (July–August 1975), p. 666.

advertising and promotion used in one of several plans evaluated by the model. The promotion effects manifest the classic bump-dip promotion pattern, although the height and depth of the bumps and dips differ across promotions, due to differences in expenditure level. The four indices in Figure 13.3 multiply together (see equation 13.1) to produce the sales forecast for the brand. Little (1975, pp. 667–669), shows that the model fit historical data well and also had good predictive validity.

The model was used to evaluate several different marketing plans. A marketing plan consisting of an additional promotion and a 50 percent increase and new media allocation for advertising was predicted by the model to be most profitable. Interestingly, management turned out to feel less certain about the advertising effect indices and so decided to fund the additional promotion but not the additional advertising. Little also describes the tracking and firefighting uses of BRANDAID. In particular, the model helped to diagnose a potential softness in forthcoming sales, and an additional promotion was implemented as a result of the analysis. Clearly, BRANDAID represents an important application of models to the planning process, especially on the question of budgeting.

A Model for Planning Coupon Promotions

Neslin and Shoemaker (1983a) devised a decision calculus model for planning coupon promotions. Compared to BRANDAID, this model concentrates on one element of the marketing mix—promotion—and adds particular detail on couponing. While Neslin and Shoemaker position their model clearly as a coupon-planning tool, it does include enough detail on trade deals to be useful for this type of promotion as well.

Model Formulation. The Neslin-Shoemaker model takes into account the actions of the manufacturer, retailers, and consumers as they affect the ultimate profitability of a coupon promotion (see Figure 13.4). The manufacturer sets the process in motion by specifying a coupon program aimed at consumers, and a trade deal aimed at retailers. Retailers respond by stocking up on the brand and running retailer promotions. Consumers then respond to both the retailer promotions and the coupon promotion, which depending on actual implementation, often hit the consumer at about the same time. The resultant increase in consumer sales then takes away the additional inventory built up by retailers. Of course, depending on the exact effectiveness of the coupon, the degree of stocking up among retailers, and the extent of retailer promotions, the net result may or may not leave the trade with excess inventory. The Neslin-Shoemaker model calculates profit based on the net impact of the entire promotion. The model is modular in that it can certainly handle situations when just a coupon is distributed, with no accompanying trade deal. However, coupons in fact are often implemented as part of a larger promotional campaign, and the model therefore captures this practice.

The Neslin-Shoemaker model consists of three submodels representing retailer response to the trade deal, consumer response to the coupon promotion,

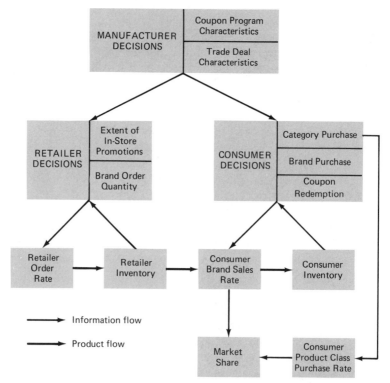

FIGURE 13.4 The Marketing System Considered by the Neslin-Shoemaker Coupon Model

Source: Scott A. Neslin and Robert W. Shoemaker, "A Model for Evaluating the Profitability of Coupon Promotions," *Marketing Science,* Vol. 2, no. 4 (Fall 1983), p. 364.

and consumer response to in-store promotions. Consumer sales in period t, $s(t)$, is modeled as equal to baseline sales, s_0, plus changes induced by couponing activity, $c(t)$, and retailer promotions, $r(t)$:

$$s(t) = s_0 + c(t) + r(t) \qquad (13.3)$$

The terms $c(t)$ and $r(t)$ are modeled as a function of coupon distribution and extent of retailer promotions. For both models, the net effect of any promotion depends on the degree of brand switching and accelerated purchasing induced by the promotion, as well as repeat purchase effects. In Chapter 5 we reviewed the details of how these effects are modeled (see discussion of ΔSALES$_t$ in Chapter 5). This submodel translates the number of coupon redemptions in time t into incremental sales in time t, using the assumed degree of switching, acceleration, and repeat purchase effects to be present for couponing. The complete Neslin and Shoemaker model consists of nine major equations representing the system depicted in Figure 13.4.

Application.   The coupon model was applied to the selection of a couponing plan for a packaged good. The brand manager was faced with deciding between a free-standing insert and a direct-mail coupon for a particular promotion campaign. In either case, the coupon would be coordinated with a trade deal consisting of a 15 percent price discount plus an additional 8 percent advertising allowance for participating retailers. Table 13.6 presents all the parameters necessary for running the model.

TABLE 13.6   Parameter Estimates Used to Run the Neslin-Shoemaker Coupon Model

		Type of Coupon	
		Direct Mail	Free-Standing Insert
A.	*Program Specifications*		
	Number of coupons (millions)	20	20
	Drop cost/1,000 coupons	$15	$5
	Face value	15¢	15¢
	Discount to all retailer participants	15%	15%
	Ad allowance	8%	8%
	Process cost/coupon	5¢	5¢
	Week of coupon drop	20	20
	Sell-in period (week numbers)	10–13	10–13
	Retail promotion schedule (% of promoting	18: 10%	5%
	retailers beginning promotion in given week	19: 22%	20%
	number)	20: 36%	50%
		21: 22%	20%
		22: 10%	5%
B.	*Coupon Program Performance Assumptions*		
	Redemption rate (%RED)	5%	2.5%
	Percent legal redemptions (LEGAL)	90%	75%
	Average time until redemption, $\psi(x)$ (weeks)	8	7
	% coupon sales that are accelerated purchases (ACC)	0%	0%
	Predeal average purchase probability among accelerators (MSA)	0%	0%
	Predeal average purchase probability among nonaccelerators (MSU)	50%	60%
	% coupon sales resulting in new repurchases (TEMP)	9%	7.2%
	% coupon sales resulting in permanent gain (PERM)	0%	0%
	# purchase occasions to reach PERM (DECAY)	3	3
C.	*Retail Promotion Performance Assumptions*		
	Participation rate (MAXPAR)	70%	80%
	Increase in promotion sales (Δ)	3.00	3.00
	Average length of retailer promotion (Γ) (weeks)	2	2
	Increase in retailer order during promotion (ANTICINC)	125%	125%

TABLE 13.6 *(continued)*

	Type of Coupon	
	Direct Mail	Free-Standing Insert
% promotion sales that are accelerated purchases (RACC)	50%	50%
Predeal average purchase probability among accelerators (RMSA)	100%	100%
Predeal average purchase probability among nonaccelerators (RMSU)	67%	67%
% promotion sales resulting in new repurchases (RTEMP)	2%	2%
% promotion sales resulting in permanent gain (RPERM)	0%	0%
# purchase occasions to reach RPERM (RDECAY)	3	3
D. *General Baseline Constants*		
Baseline market share (MS_0)	10%	10%
Baseline category sales/week ($PURCH_0$) (units)	3,000,000	3,000,000
Average purchase cycle (C) (weeks)	8	8
% retailers visited/week (η)	25%	25%
Average retail inventory on hand (weeks) (WEEKSINV)	4.5	4.5
Delivery schedule on retail orders $\gamma(x)$	within 1 week—20% 2 weeks—80% 3 weeks—100%	within 1 week—20% 2 weeks—80% 3 weeks—100%

Source: Scott A. Neslin and Robert W. Shoemaker, "A Model for Evaluating the Profitability of Coupon Promotions," *Marketing Science*, Vol. 2, no. 4 (Fall 1983), p. 372.

Part A of the table shows that both coupons would use a 15 cent face value, and 20,000,00 of them would be distributed in week 20. The major difference between the coupons was that the direct-mail coupon would cost three times as much to distribute.

Part B of the table shows the manager's assumptions on how the consumers would respond to the coupons. The direct-mail coupon would achieve double the redemption rate, fewer of these would be misredemptions, and redemptions would be spread over a longer period of time (average redemption time of 8 versus 7 weeks). The direct-mail coupon was expected to attract more brand switchers (MSU = .50 versus .60), and because many of those switchers were expected to be new triers (the brand was relatively new), the direct-mail program would produce more repeat sales (TEMP = 9 percent versus 7.2 percent). (See Chapter 5 for the exact formulas into which these assumptions are inserted.)

Part C of Table 13.6 shows that retailers would more than double their orders in response to the trade deal (ANTICINC = 125%) and that, when in-store promotions were implemented by retailers, consumer sales would increase by an average of 300% (Δ = 3) in the stores running such promotions. However, under the direct-mail coupon, fewer retailers would promote (MAXPAR = 70% rather than 80%). This might turn out actually to be a mixed blessing, since the brand manager assumed that 50 percent of the sales generated by retailer promotions represented sales accelerated from future periods (RACC = 50%) and that virtually all accelerators were already loyal users of the brand (RMSA = 100%).

The performance assumptions in parts B and C are rather detailed and one might ask the basis on which the manager made these assumptions. Many of the assumptions were very solid. For example, the manager had ample experience with redemption rates and was quite confident in the redemption rate assumptions. The brand-switching assumptions were based on panel data analyses plus the manager's own views. For example, the manager believed that the effort involved in redeeming a free-standing insert, relative to a direct-mail coupon, would mean that fewer brand switchers would be attracted by a free-standing insert. In summary then, the assumptions were based on support ranging from ample experience to panel data analyses to personal judgment. One might quarrel with the assumptions. Indeed it turned out that one of them was obviously wrong. However, the decision on whether to use a free-standing insert or direct mail would hinge on these assumptions, whether they be made implicitly or explicitly. The model required that the assumptions be made explicit so they could be rigorously evaluated. The model also allowed for a variety of "what if" analyses to determine the impact of changing the assumptions.

Figure 13.5 shows the results of simulating the model using the assumptions in Table 13.6. In Figure 13.5A, we see that both programs (recall that at the consumer level, each program included a coupon and accompanying retailer promotions) would produce a notable effect on market share, in fact, the quintessential bump-dip effect. Notice that the effect is accentuated for the free-standing insert. This is because that promotion would result in more retailer participation and hence more in-store promotions, and according to the manager's assumptions, it was in-store promotions and their accelerated sales that generated the bump-dip effect. This can be seen in Figure 13.5B. The coupon's effect on sales is more dispersed since there is no acceleration and coupons are redeemed over several weeks.

Calculating the net relative profit impact of the two revealed that the direct-mail program was more profitable by $55,474. This result held up under extensive sensitivity analysis (Neslin and Shoemaker, 1983a, p. 377). However, the manager decided to go with the free-standing insert. If the model had shown a much greater sacrifice in profit, the manager would have been inclined to go with the direct-mail coupon. However, the FSI would be more popular with the sales force, and the trade-off of $55,000 in profit on one promotion versus the long-term benefits of a happy sales force was deemed worth it. Neslin and Shoemaker were able to track the performance of the promotion in one market. The results were that the model forecasts made a systematic error due to the manager's assumption that retailer promotions largely just accelerate sales that would have occurred anyway. Actual sales data showed no evidence of acceleration. After the model was ad-

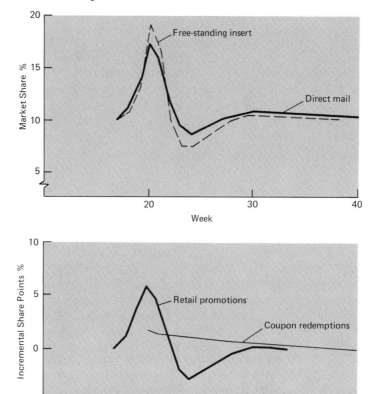

FIGURE 13.5 13.5A. The Simulated Effect of Two Coupon
Promotions on Market Share (Each coupon program is
accompanied by retailer promotions)
13.5B. The Separate Impacts of Retailer Promotions
and Couponing on Market Share, $c(t)$ and $r(t)$

Source: Scott A. Neslin and Robert W. Shoemaker, "A Model for Evaluating the Profitability of Coupon Promotions," *Marketing Science*, Vol. 2, no. 4 (Fall, 1983), p. 375.

justed for this finding, it fit the actual data well, and the revised profit calculation
put the direct-mail coupon as $45,000, not $55,000, more profitable. In view of
the manager's emphasis on sales force contentment, a correct decision had apparently been made.

An Optimization Model

The problem of planning sales promotions would apparently lend itself to optimization procedures. The decision alternatives are numerous but well defined, and
the objective function, while not usually known with certainty, is also clearly
defined. Rao and Thomas (1973) developed a set of optimization models for plan-

ning price promotions. The decision variables considered included the size of the price cut, its duration, and in the most ambitious case, the placement of several promotions throughout the year. Rao and Thomas used simple calculus and dynamic programming to solve their models.

Planning a Single Promotion. Rao and Thomas assumed as a general response to promotion, a "dip-bump-dip" pattern. That is, sales would decrease just before the promotion, then increase dramatically during the promotion (although the increase would dwindle if the promotion was extended in time), and finally, sales would decrease right after the promotion was withdrawn. The "prepromotion dip" is not particularly common in real-world situations, but has been documented clearly by Doyle and Saunders (1985). The mechanism for this phenomenon is that customers learn about the promotion beforehand, either because of a set of patterns of previous promotions, or through the sales force. Figure 13.6 shows the basic pattern of sales response Rao and Thomas used.

To review the Rao and Thomas model, it is necessary to define the following terms:

R_1 = average percentage reduction in sales rate during prepromotion period
R_2 = average percentage increase in sales rate during promotion period
R_3 = average percentage reduction in sales rate during postpromotion period
p = percentage price discount, as a fraction of profit margin
w_1 = length of prepromotion period
w_3 = length of postpromotion period
w = length of promotion period

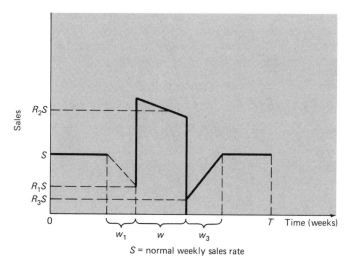

S = normal weekly sales rate

FIGURE 13.6 Pattern of Sales Response to Promotion Assumed
by Rao and Thomas

Source: Reprinted with permission from *Operational Research Quarterly*, Vol. 24, no. 2, Vithala R. Rao and L. Joseph Thomas, "Dynamic Models of Sales Promotion Policies," p. 405, Copyright 1973. Pergamon Press plc.

Rao and Thomas modeled sales response to promotion as follows:

$$R_1 = 1 - apw \qquad a > 0 \qquad\qquad (13.4)$$

$$R_3 = 1 - cpw \qquad c > 0 \qquad\qquad (13.5)$$

$$R_2 = 1 + b_1 p + b_2 pw \qquad b_1 > 0, \quad b_2 < 0 \qquad (13.6)$$

Equations (13.4) and (13.5) say that the dip periods will be steeper for promotions that have steeper price reductions and last longer. Equation (13.6) says that the average percentage sales rate increase during the promotion bump will be greater if the price discount is large, but smaller if the promotion period is longer. Rao and Thomas used the foregoing definitions to derive a profit equation and then derived the following expressions for the optimal price discount p^* and its length w^*:

$$p^* = \tfrac{3}{4} - \tfrac{1}{4}\sqrt{(1 + 8d/b_1)} \qquad\qquad (13.7)$$

$$w^* = \frac{-b_1 p^*}{b_2} \qquad\qquad (13.8)$$

where

$$d = \frac{aw_1 + cw_3 + 2}{2}$$

Equation (13.7) provides the intuitive results that the optimal price discount should be smaller if the pre- and postpromotion dips are steeper, as measured by $d = (aw_1 + cw_3 + 2)/2$, and larger if promotion period response is greater (b_1 large). The optimal length of the promotion will be greater if the promotion period response is greater, if the price discount is greater, and if the effect of promotion length an average promotion period sales is smaller (b_2 closer to zero). As an example, consider the following parameter values:

$w_1 = 1$ (the prepromotion dip lasts 1 week)

$w_3 = 2$ (the postpromotion dip lasts 2 weeks)

$\left.\begin{array}{l} a = 1 \\ c = 3 \end{array}\right\}$ (the postpromotion dip is steeper than the prepromotion dip)

$\left.\begin{array}{l} b_1 = 10 \\ b_2 = -1 \end{array}\right\}$ (a one-week 10 percent promotion will result in a 90 percent increase in sales during that week, and each additional week the promotion is run reduces the average weekly increase by 10 percentage points)

Then, we would calculate

$$d = \frac{1(1) + 3(2) + 2}{2} = 4.5$$

$$p^* = \tfrac{3}{4} - \tfrac{1}{4}\sqrt{(1 + 8(4.5)/10)} = .2138$$

$$w^* = \frac{-10(.2138)}{(-1)} = 2.138 \text{ weeks}$$

Thus, the optimal price promotion is a 21 percent reduction run for a little more than two weeks.

This simple model is easy to "run." One could change the parameter values to examine the sensitivity of p^* and w^*. Note also that the model does not always recommend holding a promotion. If $d > b_1$, that is, if the pre- and postpromotion dips are large relative to the gain in sales during the promotion period, p^* will be negative in equation (13.7), an infeasible value.

Planning Multiple Promotions. The problem of planning multiple promotions over a given time horizon is much more complicated. First, equations (13.7) and (13.8) cannot be used repeatedly, because once a time constraint is added, it may be better to run several one-week promotions rather than a lesser number of two-week promotions, each of which were optimal if we were planning for only one promotion. This could happen, for example, if the two-week promotion were less than two times more profitable than the best one-week promotion. Second, response to subsequent promotions is undoubtedly not independent of the number and proximity of previous promotions. To address the first problem, Rao and Thomas used dynamic programming to place the several promotions optimally over the time horizon. To address the second issue, they explictly modeled sales during the promotion period as a function of the number and proximity of previous promotions. In particular, let

P_t = percentage discount employed in period t

N_t = number of promotions run previously to period t

D_t = number of periods between period t and the last discount

L_t = length of the promotion period up to period t

One model proposed by Rao and Thomas (p. 414) for sales during a promotion period ($s(P_t, N_t, D_t, L_t)$) was as follows:

$$s(P_t, N_t, D_t, L_t) = \text{normal sales} \times (1 + aP_t - cN_t + dD_t)e^{-b(L_t - 1)} \tag{13.9}$$

Therefore, sales during the promotion period would be initially smaller if the discount were smaller, if a large number of promotions had been run previously, and if another promotion had recently been run. Irrespective of initial promotion response, sales during the promotion period would decrease exponentially with the length of the period.

Rao and Thomas included equation (13.9) in a dynamic program, in which P_t was the decision variable and L_t, N_t, and D_t were state variables. They did not provide an example of running the model, but it has strong potential. Today's advent of powerful personal computers would make even a complicated dynamic program a practical tool. The required parameters for running the model are difficult to estimate empirically, but no more difficult than the parameters required for a full-fledged run of BRANDAID or the Neslin-Shoemaker model. The Rao-Thomas model itself is quite intuitive and simple.

Survey Methods for Planning Promotions

Most promotion planning models are based on describing the relationship between a planning action (budget allocation, coupon face value, etc.) and sales or profit. However, certain potential planning actions are not easily related to sales. These include various overlay designs for coupons, different types of premiums, and levels of trade deal offers that go beyond the realm of previous experience. In these cases, a potentially rewarding planning tool is to survey the target group and determine their preferences for the various alternatives under consideration. We will examine two such planning techniques here, one utilizing mulitdimensional scaling (Block et al., 1985) and one using conjoint analysis (Levy et al., 1983).

Multidimensional Scaling. Multidimensional scaling has enjoyed popularity for developing product positioning strategies. The technique can produce a perceptual map on which products are located to capture their perceived similarity to each other. An ideal point can also be located on the map, and this provides guidance concerning which products are closest to the one consumers would prefer.

In the promotion planning context, instead of products, we have alternative promotion executions. These could be, for example, seven different premiums, or could be five different types of consumer promotions.

One might ask why there should be any differences in preference among promotion alternatives, aside from that due to their objective or economic value. First, there is the amount of effort required by the promotion, which translates into perceived economic value. Second, there are noneconomic attributes of promotions that relate to their use, for example, the smart-shopper phenomenon (Chapter 10, "The Redemption Decision"). Third, mental accounting theory posits that different packaging of the same economic incentive can yield different consumer utility (Chapter 2, "Prospect Theory and Mental Accounting").

In an exploratory study, Block et al. (1985) developed multidimensional scaling maps for three different product categories. These maps are reproduced in Figure 13.7.

The cereal map shows that sweepstakes and in-pack premiums are closest to the ideal point, although not perfectly on top of it. To improve consumer response to these promotions, the manufacturer needs to make them more like a coupon and refund offer, because then perceptions of B and C on the map will move toward E. Perhaps this means that sweepstakes and premiums should have some immediate economic value. Stated differently, perhaps a coupon combined with a sweepstakes would be a popular alternative.

The diaper map shows a coupon to be closest to the ideal point, although a coupon with some of the elements of a contest or sweepstakes would probably move even closer. Perhaps a coupon with contest or sweepstakes overlay might be in order, or a mail-in offer in which the consumer would receive several coupons might be popular.

The tissue map shows coupons to be the overwhelming favorite among con-

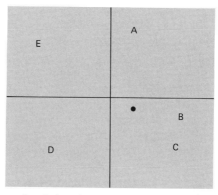

Cereal plot using INDSCAL and Ideal Point
A — Coupons
B — Sweepstakes
C — In-pack premium
D — Self-liquidating premium
E — Coupon and refund offer
● — Ideal point

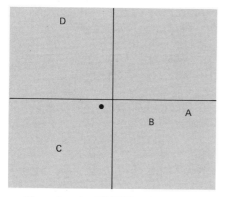

Diaper plot using INDSCAL and Ideal Point
A — Self-liquidating premium
B — Coupon plus refund for free product
C — Contest
D — Swepstakes
● — Ideal point

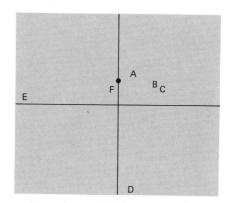

Tissue plot using INDSCAL and Ideal Point
A — Coupon for free product
B — Coupon and refund offer
C — Coupon and refund offer
D — Sweepstakes
E — On-pack price off
F — Coupon plus refund for free product
● — Ideal point

FIGURE 13.7 Multidimensional Scaling Maps of Promotion Alternatives

Source: Martin Block, Tamara S. Brezen, and Don. E. Schultz, "An Exploratory Study of Pretesting Sales Promotion Executions Using Individual Differences Scaling and Preference Mapping," Working paper, Department of Advertising, Michigan State University, East Lansing (1985), pp. 11–13.

sumers. Price packs and sweepstakes definitely have little appeal. Interestingly, Block et al. note that the brand manager involved in this situation admitted after seeing the results that price-packs had been overused in the category, and this had probably diluted their perceived value.

As the foregoing examples indicate, the diagnostics generated by this process are qualitative. They are useful for screening alternatives and serving as a stimulus for creating new alternatives. As Block et al. note, the departure from relating the alternatives to sales may be a bit discomforting. They propose a field test validation study and that would be an important undertaking. However, it is important to point out that advertising copy is routinely evaluated using purchase intent and recall scores, which are valid, but certainly imperfect correlates with sales.

The more sinister potential problem with using this technique is the danger of maximizing usage of the promotion but not incremental sales. For example, Neslin and Clarke (1987) find that higher coupon redemption rates by themselves may indicate fewer incremental sales per redemption. The solution to this problem requires more work but is conceptually simple. Namely, maps should be examined for different consumer segments: loyal users, switchers, and so on.

Conjoint Analysis. Conjoint analysis, like multidimensional scaling, has a rich history of helping in the product design process (Cattin and Wittink, 1982). We will review a recent application of the procedure to planning trade promotion activities, by Levy et al. (1983). The key benefit of conjoint analysis, especially in a trade promotion context, is that it provides an explicit measure of how much of one trade support variable retailers are willing to trade-off to get a certain amount of another variable.

A survey instrument was devised and administered to 68 retail buyers. Levy et al. considered four decision variables: level of cooperative advertising, level of couponing in local newspapers, financial terms of sales, and service level. These variables were not part of a specific trade deal, but represented a year-long representation of the manufacturer's overall trade promotion strategy. Each respondent evaluated nine trade promotion profiles, each consisting of different combinations of the decision variables. Respondents were prescreened as to their normal sales level and then asked to indicate by how much they would change their sales order if the displayed activities were implemented. This represented an attempt by Levy et al. to link decision variables directly with actual sales. The researchers showed that the data they collected were reliable and predicted well on hold-out samples of respondents. They did not, however, validate the results in an actual field setting.

The respondent's self-reported change in sales order level for each profile served as the dependent variable in a dummy variable regression. The levels of each decision variable served as the dummy variables. The aggregate results are shown in Table 13.7. As the table shows, cooperative advertising was a very

TABLE 13.7 Numerical Results of the Levy, Webster, and Kerin Conjoint Study

Marketing Mix Variable (Level)	Estimated Impact on Sales	Relative Importance
Cooperative Advertising		
(0) 3 times at 15¢/lb	$2,477	
(1) 4 times at 10¢/lb	873	
(2) 6 times at 7¢/lb	0	41%
Coupons in Local Newspapers		
(0) 2 times at 25¢/lb	0	
(1) 4 times at 10¢/lb	481	15
(2) 3 times at 15¢/lb	913	
Financial Terms of Sale		
(0) 2%/10 days/net 30	0	
(1) 2%/30 days	1,366	23
"Service Level" Percentage of Items Shipped That Were Ordered:		
(0) 96%	0	
(1) 98%	1,283	
(2) 99.5%	1,173	21

Source: Michael Levy, John Webster, and John Kerin, "Formulating Push Marketing Strategies: A Method and Application," *Journal of Marketing*, Vol. 47 (Winter 1983), p. 27. Reprinted from the *Journal of Marketing*, published by the American Marketing Association.

important variable to the retailers. If the sales order scaling can be taken literally, as much as $2,477 in additional sales per retailer could be gained by using fewer cooperative advertising offers but with higher reimbursements per offer. Retailers would sacrifice their most preferred couponing level and their most preferred financial terms to obtain this most preferred cooperative advertising level.

The Levy et al. research demonstrates the practicality and richness of conjoint analysis in a promotion context. While these researchers made an effort to relate their results to actual sales, the predictive validity of self-reported statements of how much retailers would change orders in response to different trade terms has not been established in terms of actual behavior. For example, although annual manufacturer-retailer agreements are sometimes negotiated, it is more common for retailers to make decisions on individual, specific trade deals. The particular measurement task used by Levy et al. might therefore have been atypical. In conclusion then, the dollar amounts shown in Table 13.7 should probably not be taken literally. However, the potential usefulness of the technique is still apparent: Conjoint analysis can yield important guidance for designing trade promotion programs.

Summary

Table 13.8 provides a comparative summary of the planning models reviewed in this chapter. These models provide tools for making a number of decisions, especially regarding promotion tactics. All the methods are complementary and in fact can be ordered in a somewhat hierarchical manner: BRANDAID is the broadest of the models and could be used to set an initial budget, develop a marketing strategy, and recommend the timing of promotions. The coupon model could be used to evaluate specific alternative executions of trade deals and coupons. The optimization model could be used to generate alternative price promotions that could be evaluated within the BRANDAID context of an entire marketing strategy. The multidimensional scaling technique could be used to generate couponing alternatives which could be costed out with the coupon model or more generally defined consumer promotions that could be evaluated using BRANDAID. Conjoint analysis could be used in the same way, except would probably be more appropriate for trade dealing.

This scenario, while certainly plausible, is very ambitious given the current state of managers' use of quantitative tools (see "Evaluation" earlier in this chapter). Undoubtedly, the diffusion process for these tools will be enhanced by the availability of computer power, but organizational commitment, led by senior management, is probably the key ingredient. It is beyond the scope of our dis-

TABLE 13.8 Summary of Promotion Planning Models

Model	Decisions	Phases of Planning Process
BRANDAID (Little)	Multiple promotions (and other marketing mix variables)—dollar expenditures, scheduling, coverage, vehicle	Budgeting, marketing strategy, tactics
Coupon model (Neslin-Shoemaker)	Single coupon promotion—timing, face value, vehicle; single trade deal—timing, off-invoice, and ad allowance amounts	Tactics
Optimization model (Rao-Thomas)	Single and multiple price promotions—timing, duration, discount amount	Budgeting, tactics
Multidimensional scaling (Block, Brezen, and Schultz)	Select most preferred promotion from point of view of customer—guidance on creating new promotions	Tactics
Conjoint analysis (Levy, Webster, and Kerin)	Best promotion design from point of view of customer—considers concrete design alternatives	Tactics

cussion to address this process in detail, however, the reader should see Lodish (1986) for a specific discussion of adopting models for promotion planning and Little (1979) for a more general discussion.

FURTHER RESEARCH DIRECTIONS

In this chapter, we have presented a framework for planning promotion, reviewed what is known about that process, and discussed planning models designed to facilitate that process. There are several questions which remain unanswered or unaddressed by the literature, and it is worthwhile to list them here. First, with regard to the planning process itself,

1. What are the key ingredients of successful planning? There are two elements to this issue: First, how do we measure the success of any planning operation? Second, which elements of the planning process (strategy setting, objective setting, tactics, budgeting, etc.) are most critical to a successful planning process?

2. What is the proper role of senior management? How much should they control? How much should they participate?

3. How can the planning process be altered to guard against myopic or short-term promotion strategies?

4. What are the aspects of promotion planning that companies generally do worst? Is it objective setting, strategy setting, tactics, coordination, and so on? Once identified, how can these aspects be improved?

5. Which budgeting methods work best? How does this differ, if at all, for various types of firms or products?

With respect to planning models, there are also a number of issues:

1. Exactly what is the current state and nature of managers' use of planning models? We have some information on this but need to examine what types of managers use models, what types of model are used, and so on.

2. Does use of models improve the planning process?

3. What is the proper relationship between optimization and decision calculus models in the planning process?

4. Specific planning models in the following areas would be useful:
   a. Integrating a knowledge base generated by an evaluation tool such as PROMOTER with a decision calculus model such as BRANDAID or the Neslin-Shoemaker model.
   b. Helping to generate objectives, for promotion as a whole and for individual promotions in particular.
   c. Planning trade deal tactics by including both the trade and consumer response to in-store promotions. The Neslin-Shoemaker model includes this but not in enough detail (see also Blattberg and Levin, 1987).
   d. Deriving a promotion calendar. This might extend the Rao-Thomas methodology to handle multiple promotion types as well as multiple periods. If an optimization model, the technique could start with a sales or profit objective and allocate promotions to achieve this objective for least cost, or it could start with the budget and maximize some objective, or be unconstrained.
   e. Planning premiums, sweepstakes, and contests. The multidimensional scaling and conjoint analyses provide help here, but a more profit-oriented tool is needed.

A final general area of potential research is on the use of expert systems for promotion planning (McCann, 1986). Expert systems are computer programs that codify expert knowledge on how to tackle a particular problem. The large volume of potential promotion alternatives, coupled with a complex array of situation variables, might make expert systems an attractive planning tool. Some research is already underway in this area (Bayer et al., 1986; Keon and Bayer, 1986) and further work could yield important promotion planning tools.

Appendix 13.A

A COMPENDIUM OF MATERIALS NEEDED TO IMPLEMENT A PROMOTION CAMPAIGN

A. MEMO TO THE SALES FORCE
B. SALES FORCE PRESENTATION MATERIALS
C. SHELF CARD
D. FREE STANDING INSERT COUPON
E. STORYBOARD FOR TELEVISION ADVERTISING

Source: Courtesy of The Procter & Gamble Company, Cincinnati, Ohio.

JIF PLASTIC INTRODUCTION

SOUTHERN DIVISION:	Presell:	11/23/87
	Shipments:	1/11/88
SOUTHWESTERN/EASTERN	Shipments:	2/1/88
WESTERN	Shipments:	2/29/88
CENTRAL	Shipments:	3/7/88 (preliminary; to be confirmed 2/11/88)

The Jif Plastic introductory plan has it all. From preferred product, preferred packaging, DPC category leadership and new TV advertising, the Jif Plastic introduction gives Jif a competitive edge as outlined below.

Packaging
Jif Plastic jar is the category leader with the lowest DPC (see DPC info this tab). Jif Plastic will be shipped in new red (creamy) and blue (crunchy) displayable trays. This tray will have a lower front lip for increased product visibility without having to case cut (labor savings).

Promotion Plan
Jif's initial consumer trial event will be a Sunday supplement coupon reaching 55% of U.S. households. This FSCI is scheduled for April 17 in Eastern and Southwestern Divisions, May 1 for the Western Division and June 14 for the Central Division. This coupon, with a 15¢ value, will be accompanied by a full-page color advertisement. This Plastic challenge offer will "bet consumers $1.00 that they will love Jif's new shatterproof jar." Consumers may receive two 50¢ coupons by mail or a 75¢ refund by participating in the challenge offer. During the following months, Jif will be fielding a variety of high impact promotions designed to further stimulate new trial and distribution.

Mobile Merchandiser
A mobile display unit will be provided for in-store display. A mobile merchandiser is a wooden cart with locking wheels that provide a space efficient method to display Jif. This display piece, combined with displayable shipping containers, provide further incentive to display Jif.

Distribution/Shelf Management
Coinciding with the Jif Plastic introduction will be a category shelf management drive. The focus will be on 50/50 (50% peanut butter/50% all other spreads) shelf set with Jif receiving space according to movement within the peanut butter section. Regional Nielsen data will be provided for the entire spread category (peanut butter, jam, jelly, honey, marmalade, fruit butter) with by-market rankings.

Advertising
Jif will begin airing special "Oops" advertising concurrent with the Plastic package national expansion. Jif "Oops" copy is a special introductory commercial which visually demonstrates the shatterproof benefit of Jif's Plastic jar.

dz
005
10/19/87

A. Memo to the Sales Force

Source: Courtesy of Procter & Gamble Company, Cincinnati, Ohio.

THE BRAND
TO BUILD WITH:

- Leader IN Peanut Butter Category Sales Nationally
- Leader IN TASTE and QUALITY according to consumers
  Preferred 62 to 33 in overall preference*
- Leader IN INNOVATION
  Freshness Seal, Straightwall Jar, Displayable Cases, Plastic Cap.

**JIF CHANGED
WITH THE TIMES...
AND SAVED
YOU MONEY!**

COST SAVINGS + .21¢ CASE.
YOUR SAVINGS ANNUALLY + _____.

*Company Research MRD

B. Sales Force Presentation Materials

Source: Courtesy of Procter & Gamble Company, Cincinnati, Ohio.

ANNOUNCING: A PROFIT AND VOLUME BUILDER

PLASTIC JAR
CONSUMERS LOVE IT!

12 OZ. 18 OZ. 28 OZ. 40 OZ.

FEATURE	PREFERENCE
Unbreakable	44 to 0
Lightweight	28 to 0
National	25 to 0
Handling/Opening	16 to 2
Overall Pkg.	77 to 23*

AND YOU WILL TOO!

— 33% reduction in breakage**
— Takes less space (7% reduction in case cube)
— Lighter weight for easier handling (27% average reduction in case weight)
— First Peanut Butter with Freshness Seal
— Clear, Heavy Duty Plastic (same as 2 liter soft drink bottle)
— Reduced case pack on 12 oz. & 28 oz.

CLEVELAND TEST MARKET RESULTS:
JIF SHARE: +6%
CATEGORY CONSUMPTION: +5%

*MRD   **Company Research

B. Sales Force Presentation Materials (cont.)

Source: Courtesy of Procter & Gamble Company, Cincinnati, Ohio.

HOW TEST MARKET RESULTS HAPPENED:

HOW YOU CAN MAKE IT HAPPEN

DISTRIBUTION: Test • 100% distribution Jif Peanut Butter all accounts
Idea • Stock full distribution Jif Peanut Butter

FEATURING: Test • Feature levels +20%
Idea • Feature Jif in support of Plastic Plan

DISPLAY: Test • Display levels +72%
Idea • Display Jif in support of Plastic Plan

PRICE: Test • Resales equal to or below competitor
Idea • Price Jif competitively

SHELF: Test • 50/50 Shelf Sets* (50% Peanut Butter/50% all other spreads) with Jif spaced according to movement
Idea • Set spread category according to movement

*55% Cleveland ACV

B. Sales Force Presentation Materials (cont.)

Source: Courtesy of Procter & Gamble Company, Cincinnati, Ohio.

THE JIF
PLASTIC PLAN:

- **NEW DISPLAYABLE CASE**

The New Jif Tray Pack..

- **350 GRPS T.V. ADVERTISING**
  (Double Advertising Weight)

- **SPECIAL "OOPS" SHATTERPROOF T.V. ADVERTISING COPY**

- **SHELF EXPERTS TO ASSIST IN DEVELOPING AND EXECUTING SPREAD CATEGORY SHELF MANAGEMENT PROGRAM.**

- **PROMOTIONAL EVENTS**

- **NEW PLASTIC IN-STORE P.O.P. MATERIAL PLUS JIF PLASTIC CHALLENGE REFUND**

  Includes...
  - **High Value Coupon** _____.
  - **Mail-In refund up to $2.00 Value**
  - **FSCI Drops** _____.

B. Sales Force Presentation Materials (cont.)

Source: Courtesy of Procter & Gamble Company, Cincinnati, Ohio.

JIF PLASTIC:

BENEFITS

- Cost Savings + .21¢ case means savings of $ _____ to you annually.
- 33% reduction in breakage
- Takes less space (7% reduction in cube)
- Lighter weight for easier handling (27% average reduction in case weight).
- Proven in test — builds JIF business and total category consumption + 5 over balance U.S.*
- Test increase in consumption would mean _____ to you!
- Peanut Butter stimulates spread category.

BUILD PEANUT BUTTER and SPREAD CATEGORY WITH JIF PLASTIC PLAN.

*Company Research

B. Sales Force Presentation Materials (cont.)

Source: Courtesy of Procter & Gamble Company, Cincinnati, Ohio

NEXT STEPS:

1. Carry Full Distribution JIF Peanut Butter Plastic Jar.

2. Price JIF Competitively — Recommended Resales:

12 OZ. — _____
18 OZ. — _____
28 OZ. — _____
40 OZ. — _____

3. Use 50/50 Shelf Plan to Maximize Peanut Butter Sales.

4. Feature and Display JIF _____ oz. on _____.
Recommended Feature Resales:

B. Sales Force Presentation Materials (cont.)

Source: Courtesy of Procter & Gamble Company, Cincinnati, Ohio

B. Sales Force Presentation Materials (cont.)

Source: Courtesy of Procter & Gamble Company, Cincinnati, Ohio

JIF/CRISCO MOBILE MERCHANDISER DISPLAY

FORM #102-6608

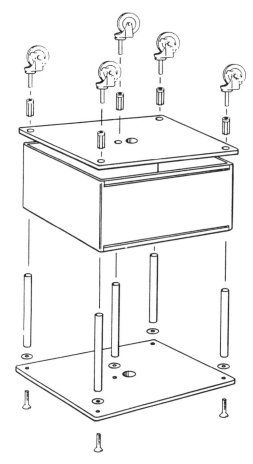

1. Remove all parts from carton. Install a flathead screw in a small counter-sunk (recessed) hole in top wood panel from label side. Place washer over screw, hold screw head with finger and screw on threaded end of one steel tube. Tighten firmly. Repeat with four other screws, washers and steel tubes. Tighten firmly. This assembly should now be on floor with tubes pointing up.

2. Open corrugated sleeve to a rectangle and install upside down around tubes. Press down to top wood panel.

3. Place bottom wood panel on steel tube ends so that all vie tubes fit into five holes in wood panel. Note: Locate two butes from one side into holes in wood panel, hold in position, and adjust others into other holes. Press down and make sure wood panel is touching corrugated sleeve under it.

4. Install a plastic insert on each wheel. Note: Make sure insert is fully seated onto wheel stem down to bearing. Install wheel without lock on side into center steel tube. Install wheels with locks into corner steel tubes. Press all wheels down firmly so that bearings touch wood panel. Turn cart over onto wheels.

5. Slide signs into sign tracks on corrugated sleeve. Use proper side of signs to match product.

6. Roll cart to display location and lock wheels by pushing wheel lock counter clockwise. Note: Refer to top wood panel label for product layout.

> CAUTION: DO NOT ROLL OVER LARGE CRACKS OR BUMPS WHEN LOADED WITH PRODUCT.

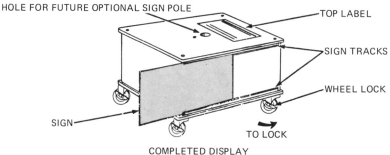

HOLE FOR FUTURE OPTIONAL SIGN POLE — TOP LABEL — SIGN TRACKS — WHEEL LOCK — SIGN — TO LOCK

COMPLETED DISPLAY

B. Sales Force Presentation Materials (cont.)

Source: Courtesy of Procter & Gamble Company, Cincinnati, Ohio

C. Shelf Card

Source: Courtesy of Procter & Gamble Company, Cincinnati, Ohio

D. Free-Standing Insert Coupon

Source: Courtesy of Procter & Gamble Company, Cincinnati, Ohio

GREY ADVERTISING INC.

CLIENT: PROCTER & GAMBLE
PRODUCT: JIF
TITLE: "OOPS"   LENGTH: 30 SECONDS

DATE: 8/11/87
CODE NO.: PGJF 5873

1. (MUSIC UP)

2. (MUSIC UNDER) ANNCR: (VO) Moms of America, Jif Peanut Butter is proud to announce

3. the end of...

4. 1ST BOY: Oops.

5. 2ND BOY: Uh, oh.

6. (MUSIC)

7. 1ST GIRL: I'm sorry.

8. (MUSIC)

9. 3RD BOY: Oh, boy!

10. ANNCR: (VO) Introducing the shatter proof, smatter proof,

11. even all spatter proof

12. all plastic

13. jar of Jif.

14. So now, Jif,

15. the only peanut butter with a peanutty Jifference, is the only big brand

16. with a plastic jar

17. that puts an end to...

18. 1ST BOY: Oops.

19. 2ND GIRL: It's okay.

20. It's okay. (MUSIC OUT)

E. Storyboard for Television Advertising

Source: Courtesy of Procter & Gamble Company, Cincinnati, Ohio

14

The Retailer Promotion Planning Process

Retailers, like manufacturers, must plan promotions. While the process is similar to many other organizations designing a plan, it is important to understand the specific issues and approaches retailers use to make promotional decisions. The purpose of this chapter is to describe "state-of-the art" techniques used to plan retail promotions.

The chapter covers (1) the retailer's planning process, (2) an example of the retail planning process, (3) promotional tactics, and (4) research issues.

THE RETAILER'S PLANNING PROCESS

The planning process for manufacturers presented in Figure 13.1 applies to the retailer. As with manufacturing, the core of the retailer's planning process is the progression from corporate objectives to marketing strategy to promotion objectives to promotion strategy to promotion tactics. Table 14.1 gives an example of how these objectives and strategies might be spelled out for a particular supermarket retailer. The supermarket has decided on an everyday-low-pricing (EDLP) strategy, and that dictates the objectives, strategies, and tactics for sales promotion. In particular, the role of promotions is to generate traffic and help communicate the EDLP strategy. Promotion sales should be kept at a low percentage of total sales, and the markup, even on promoted items, should be positive.

In the rest of this section we elaborate on the strategies and objectives available to retailers.

Marketing Strategy

A retailer must make several critical strategic decisions which relate to its positioning in the market place. The major dimensions of this decision are

- Pricing (high or low)

TABLE 14.1 Objectives and Strategies for a Hypothetical Supermarket

Corporate objectives	Capture 20% of the local market
Marketing strategies	Everyday low pricing Parity with competition on variety, convenience, service Less emphasis on price-oriented sales promotions More emphasis on advertising to build image
Promotion objectives	Generate traffic Help communicate image
Promotion strategy	Maintain promotion sales as a percentage of total sales at 10% Maintain margin of 5% on promoted merchandise Promote items with broad appeal
Promotion tactics	Feature items in circular and in-store Use displays to reinforce feature advertising

- Promotional strategy (high/low or everyday low pricer)
- Service level (high or low)
- Variety (high or low)
- Focus (specialty or department store)
- Convenience (multiple locations, few locations)

In general, the decisions listed are not dichotomous, but they highlight the possible strategies a retailer can use. These choices have a strong influence on promotional planning objectives.

In looking at the options listed, it is clear that there are several alternative strategies a retailer can follow. It can become a specialty store or it can carry many lines of merchandise. Generally, it is felt that specialty stores are higher priced, but recently they are becoming far more competitive, particularly in areas such as appliances and electronics, home improvement products, auto accessories and repair, and clothing. By specializing, they are able to obtain better promotions from the manufacturers because of their high volumes in one specific category.

Service level affects the cost structure of the retailer. The higher the service level, the higher the cost. A retailer that offers higher service levels is less likely to present a low price image through promotions. Instead, promotions are used to reinforce the store's image. For example, a high-service-level retailer promotes a new line of Calvin Klein clothing to reinforce its "designer" shops. The promotion is *not* a series of price discounts but rather a "fall preview" for selected customers. This promotion is intended to (1) affect the image of the store, (2) presell the merchandising line, and (3) offer selected customers a feeling of "exclusivity."

A difficult but important decision is determining whether the retailer should be an everyday low pricer or have higher prices and higher promotional discounts. Some food retailers offer lower everyday prices and consequently do not discount heavily. Others offer higher everyday prices but have frequent price discounts. In many markets it appears that the majority of customers prefer periodic deep price discounts based on the higher share these stores represent. On the other hand, EDLP is growing in share. Clearly, the promotional strategies of these two types of retailers will be very different.

The final issue is variety. There is a trend toward larger stores resulting in greater category variety. Large stores frequently offer a wide variety of brands and sizes within a given category. This means that promotions are available within a specific category almost every week. The retailer may in fact want to use a promotion to interest the customer in the category with the hope he or she will "trade up" to a better, more profitable model or item. This type of promotional activity is common in appliance, electronic, and clothing retailers.

In summary, the retailer's strategy will influence the promotional objectives set. It is important to understand how different retailer strategies affect the type of promotional strategies that will be run. The next section gives examples of different promotional objectives.

Sales Promotion Objectives

Four promotion objectives particularly important to retailers are (1) generating store traffic, (2) moving excess inventory, (3) enhancing the store's image, and (4) creating a price image. Each of these will be discussed in the paragraphs that follow.

Traffic building can occur through "event" promotions. For example, an automobile dealership will feature a sports figure on the premises so as to attract customers. A more common approach is to induce consumers to purchase a particular item plus a host of other items through a price promotion. In the case of supermarkets, the chain might promote a "loss leader," that is, an item priced below cost, in the hopes that the loss leader will attract customers to the store and those customers will buy other items at regular price (see Walters and Rinne, 1986). In the case of appliance or automobile dealers, sales of the promoted item may lead to a lucrative service contract from the customer. The traffic building objective, then, opens a broader set of roles for promotions beyond the "sell that item now" that often permeates manufacturers' promotional goals. This makes retail promotional planning more complex.

Retailers often find that they must use promotions to reduce or eliminate excess inventory. While the retailer is similar to the manufacturer in this regard, reducing inventories is more salient to retailers (Bolen, 1978, pp. 128–129; Wingate and Sampson, 1975, pp. 313–316). Inventory reduction often results in unplanned promotions. The retailer knows that a certain percentage of stock must be sold at markdown because of excess inventory, but occasionally it is necessary to have an additional promotion to reduce inventories further.

The third objective is store image. Retailers may use feature advertising and displays to emphasize specific merchandise being carried. Because the retailer carries this type of merchandise, it influences the customer's perception of the store's image. For example, while a retailer carries designer clothing such as

Giorgio Armani, the retailer may sell very little of this clothing, but will advertise that the store carries this type of merchandise to "position" the store in the customer's mind. The customer may buy lower-priced clothing at that store but enjoys shopping at an upscale store. One frequently sees department stores using this type of advertising to create an upscale image for their stores.

The fourth objective is to use promotions to influence the price image of the store. It is assumed the consumer uses the items advertised in the retailer's weekly flier to determine whether the store is low priced. By having the "lowest price in town" on key items, the consumer gains the impression the store is low priced. If the customer then walks in and finds only the promoted items are low priced, the customer is disappointed and unwilling to return. Thus, a delicate balance exists between promoting a price image and the pricing of nonpromoted items. Retailers try to institute a promotional policy consistent with their pricing strategy.

Promotion Tactics

Once the promotional objectives are set, it is necessary to decide on the promotional tactics. The following is a very brief review of promotion tactics. These are discussed in more detail in "Promotional Tactics" in this chapter.

Event Planning   Most retailers begin their tactical promotion planning by deciding on a series of events for the next year. For a food retailer these events can be "Back to School," "Lenten Meals," "Christmas Baking Special." For a department store, the events are tied to seasons or holidays such as Columbus Day or Easter. For appliance and electronic retailers, they may devise special events. These events offers a theme to the promotion, making it easier to advertise to the consumer.

Items to Promote.   The typical retailer carries thousands of items, not all of which can or necessarily should be promoted at the same time. This contrasts to the manufacturer's planning problem in which each brand or product line has its own promotional plan. The retailer needs selection criteria. One commonly used is store traffic generation, another is the profitability of the item, and a third is the image it creates. These will be discussed in more detail later in this chapter.

Discount Level.   Once items are selected, it is necessary to determine the level of discount offered. The decision depends on the manufacturer's discount (if any), the deal responsiveness of the consumer, competitive deals, and the price image the store is trying to portray. Specific models will be discussed later regarding how to set the deal discount.

Merchandising and Feature Advertising.   In combination with the price discount decision, it is necessary to determine whether to feature the item in the weekly store advertising and what type of display, if any, to use. These decisions are driven in part by the co-op money offered by the manufacturer.

Forward Buying.   When manufacturers offer retailers special promotions, the opportunity arises to build inventories. The retailer buys future weeks supplies of the item at the discounted cost and then warehouses them until it can be sold. This practice is called forward buying. In food retailing, forward buying is a major source of profits and researchers have estimated that food retailers would become unprofitable if forward buying were stopped. (This of course assumes that retailers would not raise price or seek other sources of revenue.)

Understanding how retailers forward buy is critical because it influences the profitability of a manufacturer's trade deal. Later, in this chapter, an example will be given of the inventory model food retailers use to forward buy.

Executing Promotional Tactics

After retailers design promotional tactics they must be executed. Surprisingly execution often leaves something to be desired. The following are some of the problems the retailer faces.

Coordinating the Selling Effort. Since many retailers rely on their sales staff to push their products, sales incentives must be considered part of the design of the retailer's promotions. For example, an automobile retailer cutting the price on the bottom of the line model may want to cut sales commissions for that model. This will encourage the salesperson to trade the customer up to a more profitable model. Coordinating the selling effort is often very difficult in large multilocation retailers. Videotapes are used so that the "headquarters" can effectively communicate the promotional program to the "field."

Availability of Merchandise. A problem that plagues retailers is lack of merchandise when a promotion is run. It is caused by the retailer's inability to forecast an item's sales. The same item at the same price may sell twice as much on one promotion as another. Forecasting sales with this type of variability is extremely difficult. (See Chapter 7.)

A second cause of the problem is the lack of available merchandise in the store. The store managers occasionally fail to order or receive the promoted item. This is common in department stores and other types of retailers where the items stocked change regularly. The ad manager, who spent thousands for an ad only to see no merchandise available, wants ways to reduce the chances of these errors occurring. The solution is careful communication to the local outlets and possible bonuses for adequately stocking the items. However, with hundreds of items promoted per week mistakes can easily occur.

Poor Pricing. Occasionally a retailer will price the larger size of an item well above the smaller size. For example, the 1-lb size might be $1.09 on sale and the 2-lb size will be $2.59. The retailer must decide whether they want this type of pricing. The customer may perceive that the retailer is trying to "trick" them. The solution is to ask the manufacturer for special product line pricing rather than item pricing.

In summary, the execution of promotional tactics requires great attention to detail. It is easy to alienate customers because of the types of tactics the firm has used. Many retailers do a poor job of executing their promotions, and the customer becomes disenchanted with the retailer.

EXAMPLE OF THE RETAIL PLANNING PROCESS

To help make the planning process more concrete, an example will be used which shows how a retailer actually plans promotions. The example is based on interviews with several retailers and is an amalgam of their planning processes.

Description of the Retailer

The retailer in this example is a department store which offers a broad range of merchandise. It is located in three major Midwestern cities, and each city has its own marketing manager who takes the plan designed by headquarters and adapts it to his or her individual market.

Management has adopted the promotion strategy of being a high-low pricer. Every month a newspaper insert and direct mail are used to advertise the promoted items. The initial promotional plan is developed at headquarters and then modified by the three major regional offices of the chain to meet local competition and to target the buying habits in local markets.

Design of the August Promotion

In September of the prior year, management met to decide on the annual promotion calendar. For next August it was decided to run a promotion centered around the theme of "Back to School." This event was chosen because most parents begin to buy children's clothing and other merchandise early in August to prepare their children to return to school. Over the last several years the chain found that this promotional event was very successful, as evidenced by their monthly sales levels, customer counts, and improved profitability.

The actual planning process begins in March. The advertising manager must decide (1) items to include in the promotion, (2) margins, (3) advertising and merchandising, (4) order quantities, and (5) executional issues.

As to the items selected for the promotion, the merchandising and advertising team were each asked to list items to be considered for inclusion in the promotional event. Not all departments will be included because they may not fit into the promotional theme or because they may be of limited appeal to the customer segment being targeted.

The following categories were selected:

- Children's apparel
- Computers
- Bicycles
- Sporting goods

- Home fashions (directed to college students)
- Hardware (directed to college students)
- Stationary and "school supplies"

Once the general categories had been selected, it was then necessary to begin working with manufacturers and distributors to see what types of promotional discounts they would be willing to offer. For example, one large computer manufacturer indicated a willingness to offer a broad promotional discount if the retailer would run a full-page feature advertisement and provide a special display in the computer area, including all the peripheral equipment offered by the manufacturer. Another computer manufacturer was willing to provide a rebate on the product plus include software valued at $250 free with a purchase if the retailer would run a half-page feature advertisement.

The marketing manager responsible for the promotion must then decide which of these promotions will have the greatest appeal to the store's customers. The retailer cannot run both promotions because the computer manufacturers indicated they would recind their promotional offer if they did not receive an exclusive advertisement.

Once they are received, a committee meets and studies all the available promotional offers. They decide which items to include, what discounts to offer, and the size of the advertising to use for each item. Once these decisions are made, the buyers are then responsible for obtaining the promotional discounts from the manufacturers and ordering the merchandise. The ordering decision is made by looking at past sales during similar promotions, trend data, and other information available from publications which indicate general market conditions.

The advertising is then designed and a preliminary mockup is available for viewing. This is sent to the three divisional offices and they make changes to meet their local market needs. These are then reviewed with headquarters to make sure that the changes do not violate any of the agreements reached by the buyers.

Execution of the August Promotion

After the chain has designed the promotion, merchandising needs to distribute the plan to each of the divisions. These divisions then ask their merchandising managers to evaluate the plan and decide if any changes are needed. Each division removes some items felt to be of limited importance in their market and adds special merchandise for their local market. By adding four pages to the middle of the insert, they are each able to tailor the August promotion to meet their specific market demand.

It is then necessary to order the merchandise. For the August promotion, this occurs in April. The regional buyers estimate the quantities to be sold during the promotion and then make the appropriate buying decisions. The quantity decision is extremely difficult, and the buyers always order more than they think they can sell because they are afraid of alienating customers if they are out-of-stock on items in the advertisement. This poses problems after the promotion ends because there are always excess inventories that must be liquidated through other outlets or by extending the sale period. Developing a more sophisticated procedure for determining the optimal inventory level is of prime importance to this retailer.

Once the promotion has been planned, the individual stores within the region are informed of the dates and the quantities they should stock. Then, each store manager is responsible for displaying the appropriate merchandise. This is a critical executional issue. The local merchandising staff periodically checks each store to ensure that the items have been ordered, displays put up, and the correct prices entered into the cash register. Even with this periodic checking mistakes sometimes occur and customers become upset. The chain wants to pursue a procedure to automate the process of price marking.

Postpromotion Evaluation

Once the promotion ended, the buyers and merchandisers evaluated the success of the promotion. They found that store sales increased by 7.8 percent compared to the same period last year. Sales in certain categories exceed expectations, others below expectations. These are noted for next year's back-to-school promotion.

The difficult question that management could not answer was the traffic generated by the promotion. They could compare sales with the last several years, but if no promotion was run, they did not know what would have happened. The result was uncertainty about the effectiveness of these event promotions.

The final issue was the profitability of the promotion. Overall store margin was below expectation partly because sales were concentrated more heavily in the promoted items than was planned. This concerned management because they were afraid that their customers were beginning to buy only promoted items. It was agreed margins should be tracked over time to see if this problem persisted.

In summary promotional planning is based on managerial intuition. The analysis of the effectiveness of the promotion is simplistic. The difficult question is: Can marketing models and analysis improve the retailer's profitability? This will be discussed in "Promotional Tactics."

PROMOTIONAL TACTICS

This section will describe how retailers set promotional tactics. This section begins with event planning, covers margin planning and item planning, and then focuses on discount levels and merchandising to support this promotion. It ends with a discussion of forward buying.

Since statistical models delivered through decision support systems will be available to retailers in the future, this section also includes how the models developed in Chapter 12 (Retail Promotions) can be used to help plan promotional tactics.

Event Planning

Retailers usually begin the planning process by determining the events that will be run throughout the year. As was stated before, an event is usually related to some period of the year such as Easter, Christmas, Thanksgiving, back-to-school, and summer holidays. The retailer then decides the appropriate type of items to promote for these events.

For example, department stores use Columbus Day to offer a fall promotion and promote certain types of items such as linens. The timing of this event is the middle of the fall fashion season, and it is designed to generate traffic between the beginning of the Christmas season and after the initial fall buying season. January, on the other hand, is used to offer large markdowns for Christmas merchandise.

Food retailers also use holidays and seasonal periods to create events. Items are chosen to be consistent with the event. In summer, vegetables are frequently featured; in fall, soup is promoted.

By planning the events long before they occur, retailers can negotiate with the suppliers. The negotiations take the form of asking for co-op advertising, special price allowances, and occasionally special merchandise. The suppliers are willing to cooperate because they can receive large incremental sales from the promotional event.

Obviously, the planning process may need to be changed if economic conditions change. Retailers might offer a pre-Christmas sale because their inventory is too high and cannot be liquidated during the January sale. Events are often modified as economic or market conditions change.

In summary, the retail promotion process begins with event planning. Once the events are determined, then margins are set.

Margin Planning

A critical issue to retailers is their margins. After determining the events to run, the retailer tries to estimate seasonal or annual margins for the store or chain. Two approaches are discussed in the paragraphs that follow. The first defines markup and markdown and shows how the retailer can use some simple equations to plan margins. The second, recommended by Lodish (1982), uses a decision calculus approach.

Markup and Markdown Planning. When planning a promotional strategy, two critical issues are the percentage of total sales sold on promotion and the average markup of these promoted sales. A simple equation can be derived involving three quantities and used for planning purposes. Define

S = total retail sales over the planning horizon ($)

N = total retail sales for product sold at regular price ($)

D = total retail sales for product sold at reduced price ($)

X = total markup for product sold at regular price ($)

Y = total markup for product sold at reduced price ($)

Given these definitions, $S = N + D$, and $X + Y$ = gross profit.
We can then define

$P = D/S$ = fraction of total sales made at reduced price

$1 - P = 1 - D/S = N/S$ = fraction of total sales at regular price

$M_r = X/N$ = average fraction markup on product sold at regular price

$M_p = Y/D$ = average fraction markup on product sold at reduced price

$M_t = (X + Y)/S$ = average fraction total markup

The following identity can then be easily derived:

$$M_t = \frac{(X + Y)}{S} = \left(\frac{N}{S}\right)\left(\frac{X}{N}\right) + \frac{(D/S)}{(Y/D)}$$
$$= (1 - P)M_r + PM_p$$

(14.1)

In other words, the total average markup for a retailer is a weighted average of markups achieved for regular price sales and reduced price sales, the weights being the relative proportion of regular versus reduced price sales.

Equation (14.1) can be very useful at the strategic planning level. For example, Table 14.2 compares pricing and promotion strategies for two supermarkets. For the "high-low" retailer, reduced price merchandise accounts for 20 percent of sales, and it is sold at a loss. The everyday-low-price retailer, in comparison, sells regular priced merchandise at a slightly lower markup (hence, slightly lower regular prices) and sells fewer products at a reduced price with the price reductions not as steep as the "high-low" retailer. The net result is that both retailers achieve a total 18 percent markup, with the everyday-low-price retailer doing this through lower regular price and higher reduced prices.

As illustrated in Table 14.2, equation (14.1) provides a good overview of the retailer's pricing and promotion strategies. In this case, we have considered only one type of promotion, price reduction. However, the equation is easily expanded to include "seasonal sales," "inventory clearance sales," and "weekly features." In addition, the equation can be used to run through various scenarios. For ex-

TABLE 14.2 Pricing and Promotion Strategies for Two Hypothetical Supermarkets

	Standard Retailer	Everyday-Low-Price Retailer
Percentage of sales sold at reduced price (P)	20%	10%
Average regular price markup (M_r)	25	20
Average reduced price markup (M_p)	-10	0
Total average markup ($M_t = (1 - P)M_r + PM_p$)	18	18

ample, what average reduced price markup is required to achieve a 20 percent total markup if 80 percent of our product is sold at 25 percent markup? (The answer is 0 percent.)

While the equation does provide insight, its simplicity can be misleading. The problem is that P, the fraction of sales sold at reduced price, and total sales, S, are functions of regular markup and reduced price markup, as well as the frequency at which reduced prices are offered, F, and the percentage of merchandise that are placed at reduced price, E. In fact, the retailer's problem is

$$\text{max profit} = SM_t = NM_r + DM_p \qquad (14.2)$$

where

$$N = f(M_r, M_p, F, E) \qquad (14.3)$$

$$D = f(M_r, M_p, F, E) \qquad (14.4)$$

For example, assume that for a *given* frequency and price reduction (fixing F and E), we have the following relationships:

$$N = B_0 - \beta_1 M_r + \beta_2 M_p \qquad (14.5)$$

$$D = \gamma_0 + \gamma_1 M_r - \gamma_2 M_p \qquad (14.6)$$

with $\beta_0 > 0, \beta_1 > 0, \beta_2 > 0, \gamma_0 > 0, \gamma_1 > 0, \gamma_2 > 0$. Then, using calculus, we can derive the optimal values for M_p and M_r:

$$M_p^* = \frac{2\gamma_0\beta_1 + \beta_0(\beta_2 + \gamma_1)}{4\beta_1\gamma_2 - (\beta_2 + \gamma_1)^2} \qquad (14.7)$$

$$M_r = \frac{2\beta_0\gamma_2 + \gamma_0(\beta_2 + \gamma_1)}{4\beta_1\gamma 2 - (\beta_2 + \gamma_1)^2} \qquad (14.8)$$

Equations (14.7) and (14.8) show the complicated way in which the relationships depicted in equations (14.5) and (14.6) filter through to determine the optimal pricing and promotion policy.

As a numerical example, let $\beta_0 = 5,000$, $\beta_1 = 200$, and $\beta_2 = 100$, and $\gamma_0 = 500$, $\gamma_1 = 200$, and $\gamma_2 = 300$. Then,

$$N = 5,000 - 200M_r + 100M_p$$

$$D = 500 + 200M_r - 300M_p$$

Using equations (14.7) and (14.8) we obtain

$$M_p = 11\tfrac{1}{3}\%$$

$$M_r = 21\%$$

Using these values, we obtain

$$N^* = 10,333$$

$$D^* = 1,300$$

so approximately 9 percent of sales are from price-reduced merchandise selling at a ll⅓ percent markup, while 91 percent are from sales at regular prices sold at 21 percent markup.

This example illustrates the richness of going beyond the "first-order" analysis displayed in Table 14.2. The point is that margin decisions for both regular and promoted merchandise change the overall level of demand, and it is therefore necessary to take these effects into account in order to produce an optimal pricing and promotion plan.

Clearly, the analysis illustrated by equations (14.2) to (14.8) is seldom used in practice, although the first-order analysis illustrated in Table 14.2 is commonly used. The main obstacle precluding use of the more sophisticated analysis is operationalizing equations (14.3) and (14.4). This requires a functional form and estimation of the parameters. In practice, this could be quite complicated, and very little research has attempted to estimate the effect of pricing and promotion strategy on *overall* sales (Walters and Rinne, 1986). One exception is the work of Walters and MacKenzie (1988). These researchers estimated the relationship between various store promotions and store sales, profit, and store traffic. Their analysis was at a somewhat more tactical level than the demand equations required for equations (14.2)–(14.4). However, their work is an encouraging first step toward that end.

Decision Calculus Model.   Lodish (1982) devised a decision calculus model to investigate the type of complexities demonstrated in the analysis based on the retailer's optimization problem. Lodish's purpose was to provide directional guidance to issues such as average markup rather than derive an optimal level. This pragmatic approach is consistent with the decision calculus paradigm as well as the reality that exact demand equations are not generally available.

Table 14.3 outlines the demand equations that form the heart of Lodish's model. These equations are analogous to equations (14.3) and (14.4) proposed earlier. Lodish partitions total sales into regular sales (sales at regular prices), price event sales (sales from planned price promotions, e.g., Washington's Birthday), and markdown sales (sales for merchandise marked down because of excess

TABLE 14.3   Outline of the Demand Equations for a Retailer Strategy Model

total sales	= regular sales + price event sales + markdown sales
regular sales	= f (national advertising, inventory, retail space, regular markup, local advertising, merchandise, competitive activity, market growth)
price event sales	= f (national advertising, inventory, retail space, regular markup, price-off, number of events, merchandise, price event advertising, market growth, competition)
markdown sales	= f (markup, merchandise, inventory, competition, price event sales, regular sales)

Source: Leonard Lodish, "A Marketing Decision Support System for Retailers," *Marketing Science*, vol. 1, no. 1 (Winter 1982), pp. 31–56.

inventory). As explanatory variables, Lodish includes several strategic decision variables, including national advertising expenditures, retail space, regular markup, and character of merchandise, as well as exogenous variables such as competitive activity and market growth.

The model could be estimated at the department level for a single store or for an aggregate of several stores in a particular region. Table 14.4 illustrates the questions posed to managers to elicit their judgments of the model parameters. Examination of this chart suggests that the questions are often difficult to answer. Lodish reports that a planning team rather than one individual was required to answer the questions. As with any decision support system, Lodish reports the implementation of experiment and campaign evaluation assisted in developing a knowledge base necessary for calibrating the model.

Table 14.5 displays the output for a full-scale application of the model. The particular scenario played out in this example is not particularly bright. The current state of the retailer is shaky, and becomes more so as inventory growth outpaces sales.

In conclusion, Lodish's model represents an ambitious planning tool for retailer promotions. The model obviously demands management commitment to be implemented successfully, plus allocation of resources to analyze historical data and experiments. However, Lodish reports that the model "has actually been productively used to support decisions for a large, national retailer."

Selecting Items to Promote

One of the difficult issues that retailers face is what items to select for a promotion. Part of the decision is made when the event is selected. However, there are usually many candidates to include in the promotion. The retailer must decide which of the candidate items to select.

Curhan and Kopp (1986) analyzed how food retailers make item selection decisions. Through surveying retailers they obtained information on a series of variables which were thought to influence promotions. They then put these variables into a factor analysis and obtained factors which influence retail item selection. Table 14.6 shows the results. The factors Curhan and Kopp found to be important are

- Item importance
- Promotion elasticity
- Manufacturer's brand support
- Promotion wear-out
- Sales velocity
- Item profitability
- Incentive amount

Nowhere on this list are issues about category cannibalization (does the item increase category sales) and the complementarity of the promoted item with other items in the store. For example, if turkeys are sold at Thanksgiving, then cranberry

TABLE 14.4 Questions Posed to Managers for Calibrating the Retailer Strategy Model

Question 1 (for E_{PB} (POFF))
   What would the percentage change be in price break sales, if price reductions were other than the average percent off?
   10% off _____   15% off _____   (20% is current average) _____
   25% off _____   30% off _____

Question 2 (for E_{PB} (PBLADV))
   What would the percentage change be in price break sales if local price break advertising expenditures were doubled, provided the number of price break events remained the same? _____

Question 3 (for E_{PB} (PBEVENTS))
   What would the percentage change be in price break sales if the number of price break events were doubled, provided local price break advertising dollars remained the same? _____

Question 4A (for E_{TS} (N.ADV))
   For those entities with no present national advertising, what would the percentage increase be in total sales if national advertising were to be at
   $2 million _____ $4 million _____

Question 4B (for E_{TS} (N.ADV))
   For those entities with national advertising what would be the percentage of increase or decrease in total sales if there was

	Half	Twice	Four times
No adv. _____	the adv. _____	the adv. _____	the adv. _____

Question 5A (for E_{PB} (MCHAR), and E_{RS} (MCHAR))
   If the character of merchandise were improved increasing the average unit price 5% over normal inflation and markup percentage remained constant, what would the percentage change in total sales be? _____

Question 5B (for E_{MD} (MCHAR))
   What percentage increase or decrease in store markdown sales would there be if this character change were implemented? _____

Question 6 (for E_{MD} (MARKUP))
   What percentage increase or decrease in store markdown sales would there be if markups were increased by three percentage points? _____

Question 7 (for E_{RS} (MARKUP), and E_{PB} (MARKUP))
   What would the percentage change be in total sales if markup increased by three percentage points? _____

Question 8 (for E_{TS} (SPACE))
   What would the percentage change be in total sales if selling square feet were to increase or decrease?
   -50% _____ -25% _____ $+25\%$ _____ $+50\%$ _____

Question 9 (for E_{TS} (INV))
   What would the percentage change be in total sales, if the average inventory were increased or decreased from the inventory level necessary to sustain normal sales growth?
   -20% _____ -10% _____ $+10\%$ _____ $+20\%$ _____

Question 10 (for E_{RS} (LADV))
   What would the percentage change be in regular sales, if total local advertising were increased by 10 percent and 50 percent for regular item advertising?
   $+10\%$ _____ $+50\%$ _____

Source: Leonard Lodish, "A Marketing Decision Support System for Retailers," *Marketing Science*, Vol. 1, no. 1 (Winter 1982), pp. 31–56.

TABLE 14.5 Output Generated by the Retailer Strategy Model (000 omitted)

	1977 Ref	1977 Plan	1978 Plan	1979 Plan	1980 Plan	1984 Plan
Merchandise sales	157	157	184.909	186.674	187.182	200.559
Service sales	0	0	0	0	0	0
Store markdowns	10.1988	10.1988	12.3224	11.389	11.4196	12.3172
Price breaks	7.67415	7.67415	9.59793	10.2721	1.88884	0
Price reductions	1.68352	1.68352	1.8435	1.9725	2.13029	2.30072
Associate discount	1.73511	1.73511	2.04355	2.06305	2.06867	2.21651
Shrinkage	4.71	4.71	5.54726	5.60021	5.61546	5.01677
Beginning inventory	65	65	106.241	136.692	155.036	154.044
Purchases at retail	198.241	198.241	215.36	205.018	186.19	199.573
Ending inventory	106.241	106.241	136.692	155.036	154.044	153.058
Gross margin	47.455	47.455	57.8707	55.1039	59.0344	63.3294
Service expense	0	0	0	0	0	0
Merchandise charge	1.98241	1.98241	2.1536	2.05018	1.8619	1.99573
Freight	7.15575	7.15575	8.42777	8.50822	8.53139	9.14108

Salaries						
Management	6.84635	6.84635	8.06337	8.14034	8.16251	8.74584
Selling and service	13.6141	13.6141	16.0342	16.1872	16.2313	17.3913
Other	9.30651	9.30651	10.9609	11.0655	11.0956	11.8886
Total salaries	29.767	29.7669	35.0584	35.393	35.4894	38.0257
Payroll tax	2.3059	2.3059	2.7158	2.74173	2.74919	2.94566
General expense	10.5754	10.5754	12.4553	12.5742	12.6084	13.5095
Interest	5.08614	5.08614	7.0193	8.66482	8.93055	9.12144
P.B. local advertising	4.6508	4.6508	5.34824	5.57119	5.99953	6.4181
Other local advertising	2.4192	2.4192	2.84999	1.37842	2.92211	3.13752
National advertising	0	0	0	0	0	0
Display	*1.57505	1.57505	1.85503	1.87274	1.87784	2.01204
Total advertising and display	8.64505	8.64505	10.0534	8.82235	10.7995	11.5677
Operating expense	56.3794	56.3794	67.3022	68.1961	70.5771	75.1699
Operating profit/loss	-18.063	-18.063	-20.013	-23.651	-21.936	-22.977
Rent	12.6105	12.6105	14.8522	14.9939	15.0348	16.1092
Plant and equipment	3.88267	3.88627	4.57286	4.61651	4.62908	4.9599
Taxes	1.6186	1.6186	1.90633	1.92452	1.92976	2.06767
Distributing and reg	7.76943	7.76943	9.15054	9.23789	9.26304	9.92502
Corporate service	1.11077	21.11077	1.30822	1.32071	1.32431	1.41895
Store profit/loss	-45.055	-45.055	-51.803	-55.744	-54.117	-47.458

Source: Leonard Lodish, "A Marketing Decision Support System for Retailers," Marketing Service, Vol. 1, no. 1 (Winter 1982), pp. 31–46.

TABLE 14.6 Criteria Examined by Curhan and Kopp for Selecting Items to Promote Factors Influencing Trade Promotional Support

Factor	Factor Name (% var. explained)	Loading	Variables Included in the Factor
F1	Item importance (16.3%)	.77	Item is significant enough to warrant promotion
		.75	Category responds well to promotion
		.66	Closest trade competitor is likely to promote item
		.64	Importance of promoted product category
		.59	Item regular (nondeal) sales volume
		.57	Deal meshes with trade promotional requirements
			Buyer's estimate of sales increase on the basis of
F2	Promotion elasticity (9.3%)	.86	Price reduction and display
		.82	Display only
		.80	Price reduction only
		.70	Price reduction, display, and advertising
			Manufacturer's brand support in the form of
F3	Manufacturer brand support (8.2%)	.85	Coupons
		.81	Radio and television advertising
		.80	Newspaper advertising
		.75	Point-of-purchase promotion (e.g., display)
F4	Manufacturer reputation (7.3%)	.72	Manufacturer's overall reputation
		.72	Manufacturer cooperates in meeting trade promotional needs
		.64	Manufacturer cooperates on emergency orders, backhaul, etc.
		.55	Quality of sales presentation
		.51	Manufacturer's overall product quality
F5	Promotion wear-out (6.4%)	.93	Product category is overpromoted
		.93	Item is overpromoted
F6	Sales velocity (5.4%)	−.81	Brand market share rank (SAMI)[a]
		.69	Item regular sales volume (SAMI)[a]
		.46	Item regular sales volume
F7	Item profitability (4.5%)	.79	Item regular gross margin
		.72	Item regular gross margin[a]
		.49	Reasonableness of deal performance requirements
F8	Incentive amount (4.2%)	.83	Absolute amount of deal allowances
		.81	Deal allowances as percent of regular trade cost[a]
		.49	Absolute amount of deal allowances[a]

[a] Denotes objective (archival) measure.

Source: Ronald C. Curhan and Robert J. Kopp, "Factors Influencing Grocery Retailers' Support of Trade Promotions," Report No. 86-104 (Cambridge, MA: Marketing Science Institute, July 1986).

sauce, sweet potatoes, dressing, and so on are also sold. The retailer is willing to lose money on the first item to generate sales of the other items.

Translating the factors given by Curhan and Kopp plus the other factors just described results in the following set of questions which help determine item selection.

1. Does the item generate store traffic?
2. Does the item increase sales of other items in the store?
3. What type of trade allowances are being offered on the item?
4. Which items in a category or department offered the best trade allowances?
5. When was the item or product category last promoted?
6. At what price has competition promoted the item and can the retailer match the price?

No doubt there are many other questions that need to be answered, but these offer a sample of the issues the merchandisers must address when selecting items to promote.

Most retailers use some type of planning heuristic such as identifying "H, M, L" items. H's are high-volume items, M moderate-volume items, and L low-volume items. Then, categories are selected to be promoted a given number of times a year. Items in H categories are rotated so that they are not used too frequently. M items are run when they have good promotional allowances or they relate to the promotional event in some special way. L items are used as fillers, and it is hoped that they will be purchased in combination with H or M items.

In one sense, the actual selection of items to be promoted should be very amenable to computerized procedures. There are many alternative portfolios of items to promote, and usually there is only one or two grand objectives underlying the promotion, for example, generate store traffic, increase profits, or clear inventories. However, even if we could tie the promotion to just one objective, the response function relating that objective to possible portfolios would be very complicated, undoubtedly containing many interaction terms. In addition, we have seen that in practice there are several criteria retailers use to select promoted items. These can be viewed as tactical objectives, all of which should be consistent with the global objective.

It is not surprising then that the state of current practice is not to use computer models to select promoted items. In the authors' experience, the process in supermarkets seems to be one of quantifying some economic aspect of the promotion, be it absolute movement, promoted margin, even return on investment, and then making a final selection by reconciling these economic factors with the qualitative considerations.

The best way to visualize how this process works is to review how the supermarket chain might select its items pictured in Table 14.7. For this chain, the overall objectives of promotion are to generate store traffic and communicate an everyday-low-pricing image. The promotion strategy is, first, to maintain promotion sales at 10 percent of total sales and maintain a margin of 5 percent on promoted items. This ensures that price reductions are not too steep, and thus

TABLE 14.7 Typical Deals Available to Supermarket Retailer Planning Promotions

Item	Normal Unit Movement	B Ad Unit Movement	Unit Cost Regular	Unit Cost Deal	Other Deal Notes	Current Price	Promotion Recommendation[a]
Cranberry sauce	200	1,200	$ .64	$ .58	[b]	$ .70	
Cocoa mix	50	300	1.52	1.22	[c]	1.85	C, $1.36
Spaghetti	200	1,400	.37	.33		.45	A, 3/$1.00
Coffee	350	2,000	3.37	2.44		3.75	
Diapers A	50	400	2.62	2.51	[d]	3.22	B, $2.69
Diapers B	25	175	1.84	1.20		2.21	
Brownie cake mix	150	750	.83	.66		1.09	A, $.69
Dish detergent	30	180	1.06	.91	[d]	1.25	
Cereal A	100	700	1.23	1.19	[d]	1.54	
Cereal B	22	130	1.21	1.11	[b]	1.47	
Cereal C	28	140	1.28	1.11		1.69	
Candy	40	200	1.71	1.55		2.55	

[a] Predicted by buyer based on past experience.

[b] A sum of $2,000 is offered for ad performance.

[c] Buyer made previous commitment to feature item at some point.

[d] FSI coupon to be distributed soon, plus increased advertising.

price does not vary too much from week to week, and that promotions are not playing too large a role. Second, to generate traffic, the items promoted should have general appeal. The main advertising used by this retailer are a weekly news circular, containing featured items, and in-store support for these featured items. Additional items are featured in the store using shelf-talkers.

The particular chain might have several stores within a geographic area, and promotion decisions are made by a merchandising director in chain headquarters. Reporting to this director are several buyers, who inform the director, a month in advance of the week being planned, the items that are or will soon be on deal. There might be 200 deals available and the director must select 40 items to promote in the circular. The rough layout of a circular page is depicted in Figure 14.1.

Figure 14.1 shows that there are three sizes of advertisements on the page, and the standard plan is to feature items at cost in the A ads, at 5 percent markup in the B ads, and 10 percent markup in the C ads. Given the general percentage incremental sales generated by these ads, the overall margin on promoted merchandise should be close to 5 percent.

The economic aspects of each deal are then quantified and also are displayed in Table 14.7. For the A ads, the director is looking for traffic builders to be sold at cost. Spaghetti is attractive here. It is a big mover, has broad appeal, and could be featured at 3 for a dollar, which sounds inexpensive. Coffee is also a big mover with broad appeal, and the deal discount is very steep. However, the unit price would still be large in absolute terms, and the cost price reduction would be too steep—the everday-low-price image would be hurt. Cranberry sauce looks attractive, but does not have as wide appeal and is a seasonal item. Brownie cake mix has broader appeal and can be featured at under a dollar. This is selected for

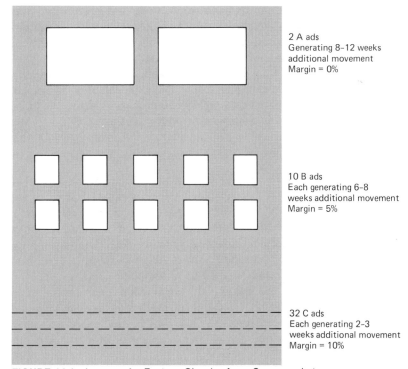

2 A ads
Generating 8–12 weeks
additional movement
Margin = 0%

10 B ads
Each generating 6–8
weeks additional movement
Margin = 5%

32 C ads
Each generating 2–3
weeks additional movement
Margin = 10%

FIGURE 14.1 Layout of a Feature Circular for a Supermarket

the second A ad. Diapers make for a good B ad. Their appeal is limited, but they are very promotion responsive. Two brands are on deal. Brand A is a bigger mover and normally is quite expensive. It is being supported by a manufacturer coupon. Brand B, the smaller brand, is offering a very steep discount, but we do not want to reduce price too much. Brand A is the selection for a B ad.

Cocoa mix was selected for a C ad. The buyer had made a previous commitment, and although cocoa mix is not a big seller, winter is coming soon and the deal is steep enough so that 10 percent margin can be obtained.

The process would go on as described. In this case, item movement, breadth of appeal, absolute price, and other manufacturer supporting activities played an important role. The prominence of these tactical objectives derives from the everyday-low-pricing strategy of the chain and the promotion objectives involving store traffic and price image. Undoubtedly the results would be different for other types of chains. Another chain might carry the economic calculations farther, as follows (using B ad figures for incremental sales):

	Normal Cost	Normal Revenue	Promoted Cost	Promoted Revenue	Incremental Cost	Incremental Profit	ROI
Diapers A	$131.00	$161.00	$1,004.00	$1,116.00	$817.69	$82.00	10%
Cake mix	124.50	163.50	495.00	517.00	370.50	− 16.50	−4
Cocoa mix	76.00	92.50	366.00	447.00	290.00	64.50	22

Referring to the previous example, we see that promotions were selected with widely different returns on investment (ROI's). This is sensible—ROI on the individual item promotion was not a criterion. Other supermarkets might look closer at this figure.

In summary, item selection is an art form. It is based on the merchandiser's intuition. A planning model, using decision calculus combined with statistical models, can be created to simplify the process. Currently, though, very few retailers use a scientific approach to item selection.

A Decision Calculus Model for Planning Individual Retailer Promotions

Once a particular item or set of items has been selected for promotion, the task still remains to plan the details of the promotion. In the supermarket example reviewed previously, most of the details were ironed out as part of the selection process. However, this is often not the case. For example, an automobile dealer may select a particular model to promote, but details have to be worked out regarding the specific pricing, advertising expenditures, and sales compensation plan. In durables retailers such as automobile dealers, a host of issues arise in trying to evaluate any particular plan, including repeat sales, trade-ins, service contracts, and competitive response. Dhebar et al. (1987) devised a decision calculus model for addressing these issues. The model is particularly appropriate for relatively small durable goods stores and was developed for an automobile retailer.

Figure 14.2 gives a description of the Dhebar et al. model. The model recognizes a basic dichotomy to be short- and long-term impact of the promotion. The short-term impact is embodied in immediate sales of additional cars and accompanying options. The design of the promotion directly influences store traffic, closing rate (percentage of customers who agree to buy a car), delivery acceptance rate (the percentage of customers ordering a car who accept the car once it is delivered), the purchase rate of options, and the particular models sold. For example, a sports figure promotion might build traffic, but most customers would just be looking for a free autograph, and the closing rate might be small. By reducing the price of a stripped-down model *and* lowering sales commissions on that model, customers might be induced to trade up to the more "loaded" models. The long-term portion of the model focuses on used car sales, service revenues, and long-term, new car sales. These three factors depend on the immediate short-term sales generated by the promotion and contribute to long-term profit.

The authors formulate their model in nine equations, most of which are simple multiplications and summations of the factors feeding into a dependent variable. For example,

immediate sales (cars/day) = traffic (customers/day)

$\times$ closing rate (percentage)

$\times$ acceptance rate (percentage) **(14.9)**

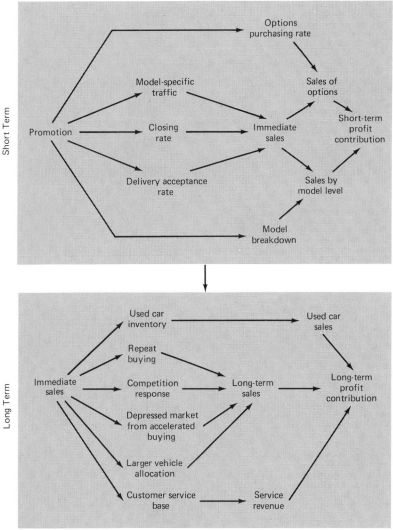

FIGURE 14.2 Schematic Outline of a Decision Calculus Model for Planning Individual Automobile Dealer Promotions

Source: Anirudh Dhebar, Scott A. Neslin, and John A. Quelch, "Developing Models for Planning Retailer Sales Promotions: An Application to Automobile Dealerships," *Journal of Retailing*, Vol. 63, no. 4 (Winter 1987).

They then present an application of their model in which estimates of model parameters were provided by the dealer and reconciled versus a regression analysis of sales as a function of previous promotions.

Table 14.8 displays the output from running the model on a Lotus spreadsheet. The figure compares two scenarios: promotion versus no promotion. The Basic, Medium, and High columns refer to the level of optional equipment au-

TABLE 14.8 Output from the Dhebar, Neslin, Quelch Model for Planning Individual Retailer Promotions

	No Promotion				Promotion			
		Basic	Medium	High		Basic	Medium	High
Sales								
Sales mix		20%	60%	20%		20%	60%	20%
Inquiries/day	18				40			
% inquiries—promoted model	5%				50%			
% closings	23%				29%			
% closings delivered	80%				80%			
Sales/day—promoted model	0.17	0.03	0.11	0.03	4.64	0.93	2.78	0.93
Contribution								
Unit contribution		$1,000	$1,200	$1,500		$0	$1,200	$1,500
Alarms								
Penetration	35%				35%			
Profit/unit	$75				$75			
Unit contribution		26	26	26		26	26	26
Rustproofing								
Penetration	50%				50%			
Profit/unit	$50				$50			
Unit contribution		25	25	25		25	25	25
Scotchguard protection								
Penetration	30%				30%			
Profit/unit	$75				$75			
Unit contribution		23	23	23		23	23	23
Radio upgrade								
Penetration	75%				75%			
Profit/unit	$100				$100			
Unit contribution		75				75		
Financing & insurance								
% financed	60%				60%			
Insurance penetration	80%				80%			
Financing profit/unit	$300				$300			
Insurance profit/unit	$150				$150			
Unit contribution		252	252	252		252	252	252

Service	
Year 1 contribution	$150 ... $150
Year 2 contribution	$425 ... $425
Year 3 contribution	$300 ... $300
Year 4 contribution	$425 ... $425
Discount rate	15% ... 15%
Unit contribution	892 ... 892 ... 892 ... 892 ... 892 ... 892
Trade-ins	
% trading in	60% ... 60%
Profitable trade-ins	10% ... 10%
Unit profit	$1,500 ... $1,500
At-loss trade-ins	90% ... 90%
Unit loss	($80) ... ($80)
Net unit contribution	47 ... 47 ... 47 ... 47 ... 47
Sales commission	(180) ... (180) ... (180) ... (50) ... (180)
Total contribution/unit	$2,160 ... $2,285 ... $2,585 ... $1,290 ... $2,285 ... $2,585
Sales/day—promoted model	0.17 ... 0.03 ... 0.11 ... 0.03 ... 4.64 ... 0.93 ... 2.78 ... 0.93
Total contribution/day (first-time sales)	$408 ... $72 ... $251 ... $86 ... $9,956 ... $1,197 ... $6,360 ... $2,399
Repeat sales (4 years after initial sale, no promotion, medium model)	30% ... 30% ... 30%
Additional contribution from repeat sales	$65 ... $1,818
Effective total contribution/day	$473 ... $11,774
Increase in contribution resulting from promotion	
Contribution/day	$11,301
Promotion period	4 days
Total for promotion period (gross)	$45,202
Promotion expenses	$10,000
Total for promotion period (net)	$35,202

Source: Anirudh Dhebar, Scott A. Neslin, and John A. Quelch, "Developing Models for Planning Retailer Sales Promotions: An Application to Automobile Dealerships," *Journal of Retailing,* Vol. 63, no. 4 (Winter 1987), pp. 352–355.
160

tomatically included in the car. Looking at the unit contribution, we see that under the promotion, unit profit contribution of the basic model is reduced from $1,000 to zero. This is because the promotion design is to reduce the basic model's price by that amount. Farther down, we see that none of the options, contributions change, since the promotion is on the basic model and not on any particular options. Still farther down, we see that sales commissions are reduced from $180 to $50 under the promotion, for the basic model only. This sets up the sales force incentive to trade up customers away from the promoted model. As a result, we see at the very top now that the mix of models sold is assumed to be the same in the nonpromotion and promotion scenarios. Traffic is expected to increase from 18 to 40 inquiries per day, and the closing rate is also expected to increase, from 23 percent to 29 percent. In addition, the percentage of traffic who will be interested in the promoted model will increase from 5 percent to 50 percent. Combined with an acceptance rate of 80 percent, we calculate 4.64 immediate sales per day during the four-day promotion, in contrast to an average of only .17 sales of this model per day without the promotion. This is a very large increase, but the manager is assuming that this could only be sustained for four days. Following toward the bottom of Table 14.8, we see that service, trade-in, and repeat sales are factored in and that the promotion is expected to increase profit by $35,202.

Dhebar et al. illustrated the flexibility of their model by applying it to evaluate a new manufacturer financing plan. They also conducted extensive sensitivity analysis, revealing, for example, that traffic, closing rate, and acceptance rate were not only the diagrammatic foundation of the model, but the numerical foundation as well. The model's results were most sensitive to deviations in assumptions regarding these factors.

The Dhebar et al. model gives encouraging support to the use of decision calculus models in designing retailer promotion events. As with all decision calculus applications, however, this approach requires ample cooperation and involvement on the part of management.

Statistical Models to Plan Promotional Discounts

As was stated earlier, retailers use certain rules in trying to set promotional discounts. As with item selection, the retailer divides items into H's, M's, and L's. The H items are promoted at a price which will bring in customers (traffic builders). The goal is to be the lowest priced retailer in the market, and so it is necessary to anticipate competitors' pricing. The trade deal offers the retailers savings but the promotion will pass on more than the amount of the trade dealing.

For moderately responsive items, M items, many retailers pass on the exact amount of the trade deal savings. Thus, the promotional discount to the consumer is significantly less than for H items. For low-volume, low-response items, L items, retailers will not necessarily discount them. The retailer will pocket the trade deal savings for L items depending upon whether there are enough B items to fill up the ad.

Obviously, the system is very simplistic. However, it does demonstrate the types of heuristics that retailers use. Implicitly they are estimating elasticities by categorizing items into H's, M's, and L's.

As an alternative an item planning model can be developed to assist the retailer in determining the optimal discount. To demonstrate how the model works, a specific example will be used. The cost of the item is $24.00 per case. The retail price is $30.00 per case. The retailer received a co-op advertising allowance of 50 percent of the cost of the advertisement and $.50 per case display case allowance.

The following demand model is used (based on Blattberg and Wisniewski, 1988):

$$q = k \exp(\beta_0 - \alpha P + \beta_1 D + \gamma_1 FA + \gamma_2 DIS) \tag{14.10}$$

where

q = quantity sold

D = deal discount (in dollars)

$FA = \begin{cases} 0 \text{ no feature advertising} \\ 1 \text{ feature advertising} \end{cases}$

P = regular retail price

$DIS = \begin{cases} 0 \text{ no display} \\ 1 \text{ display is present} \end{cases}$

k = constant

$\alpha, \beta_0, \beta_1, \gamma_1,$ and γ_2 are parameters.

To apply the model, $k, \alpha_1, \beta_0, \beta_1, \gamma_1,$ and γ_2 need to be estimated. In empirical research with grocery products, the deal elasticities (Blattberg and Wisniewski, 1988) have been estimated in the range of 5 to 6, display elasticities doubles volume, and feature advertising elasticities increase volume by 75 percent. Using these assumptions, the retailer can then determine the item's discount and whether to use a feature ad and display (discussed in the next section).

The profit function is

$$\pi = (p - c + DISA + TD) \times q - (D \times q) - DISC + FAA - FAC \tag{14.11}$$

where

p = retail price per unit

c = cost per unit

q = quantity in units

$DISA$ = display allowance per unit

D = deal discount (in dollars)

$DISC$ = cost of a display

FAA = feature advertising allowance

FAC = feature advertising cost

TD = trade deal in dollars

Define $m = P - C + DISA + TD$ = product's margin. Using standard calculus, the optimal deal discount is

$$D = \frac{m\beta_1 - 1}{\beta_1} \qquad\qquad (14.12)$$

Using the assumption that $m = (30 - 24 + .50) = 6.50$, β_1 can be derived by noting that elasticities at 20 percent discounts are in the range of 5. The discount in dollars is 6. Then $\exp(6\beta_1) = 5$, or $\beta_1 = .27$.
Thus,

$$D = \frac{(6.50)(.27) - 1}{.27} = \$2.80$$

or a 9.3 percent markdown from the retail price. Notice that no trade deal was necessary for the retailer to promote this item. The reason is that consumers respond differently to promotions than to price decreases. (See Chapter 12 for a discussion of this issue.)

Suppose a $2.50 trade deal was offered which is an 8.3 percent discount. Then, the retailer will increase the promotion offered to the consumer. How much? m becomes $9.00 ($6.50 + $2.50), and

$$D = \frac{(9.00)(.27) - 1}{.27} = 5.30$$

or 17.6 percent markdown from retail price.

Comparing the optimal discount to the heuristics given, one sees that passing on the trade deal discount "penny for penny" is not optimal. Rather, for an item that has a high elasticity, it is better to pass on a larger discount than the trade deal.

To see the optimal passthrough for an item that has a lower elasticity, suppose β_1 is decreased to .12 (a doubling of sales at a 20 percent discount). Then

$$D = \frac{(9.00)(.12) - 1}{.12} = .44$$

or a discount of 1.4 percent. Thus, for low elasticity-products, the optimal policy is not to pass through the discount.

The foregoing model focuses on one of the critical issues, setting promotional discounts. Clearly, the more sales responsive the category is to a price discount, the larger should be the discount. Further, the example shows that "penny-for-penny" passthrough is not an optimal policy for the retailer. The passthrough should depend on the price responsiveness of the item.

There are many limitations to the model. In particular it did not include category cannibalization (discussed shortly). It also did not consider the degree to which the item generated additional traffic or sales of complementary goods.

Currently, no models exist that analyze the increase in store traffic for a given item being promoted.

The model did not include the effects of the deal discount on other competitive items. However, this can be analyzed using a slightly different model. Suppose the category has three items and the model for the sales of the three items is

$$q_i = k \exp (\beta_{i1} D_1 + \beta_{i2} D_2 + \beta_{i3} D_3) \tag{14.13}$$

where

q_i = quantity sold of item i

D_i = the deal discount for the ith item

β_{ij} = the cross-deal elasticity

β_{ii} = own deal elasticity

k = a constant which represents normal sales when no deals are occuring

For simplicity, feature advertising and display activity have not been included in the model.

The retailer's problem is to maximize profits for the category, which is simply

$$\pi = \sum_{i=1}^{I} m_i q_i - \sum_{i=1}^{I} d_i q_i \tag{14.14}$$

where m = gross margin for item i including the trade deal.

Optimizing equation (14.14) does not result in a closed form solution. However, one can obtain the optimal discount through a simple search procedure.

To analyze how competitive effects influence the optimal discount, the following example was constructed. Suppose the own deal coefficient $\beta_{11} = .27$. The competitive coefficients are $\beta_{12} = \beta_{13} = -.05$. They represent a 25 percent loss in volume at a 20 percent price reduction for the dealt item. Margins are assumed equal and are $6.50 and a trade deal of $2.50 is offered. The market share of all three brands is assumed to be equal when no deal is offered. Table 14.9 shows the optimal deal discount compared to the model which includes competitive category effects. The discount drops from $5.30 per case to $4.80 per case.

Now suppose the competitive coefficients are higher, implying greater intracategory cannibalization. Let $\beta_{12} = \beta_{13} = .1$. Then, as is shown in Table 14.9, the optimal deal discount drops to $4.30. Now suppose the margins for the two competitive items are higher ($10 versus $6.50) and the initial volume is the same. Then, the optimal policy is *not* to deal.

Clearly, what we see from the example is that cannibalization and category margins influence the optimal deal discount. Does a retailer's merchandiser understand this intuitively? The answer is probably not. The analysis given shows

TABLE 14.9 Optimal Deal Discount

Model Assumptions	Optimal Discount by Retailer (per case)
No competition	$5.30
Competition (low cannibalization)	4.80
Competition (high cannibalization)	4.30
Competition (high cannibalization and higher margins for nondealt items)	0.00

that the calculations are difficult to make and the optimal discount depends on the deal elasticity and cannibalization in the category. For this reason models are going to become far more important to the retailer in determining optimal deal discounts.

Feature Advertising and Display Activity

To determine whether to run a feature advertisement, the calculations are somewhat different. For the example, suppose the size of the advertisement is a "major" ad, and it results in a 75 percent sales increase. If normal sales for the item is 200 cases per week, then the increased sales from the feature advertisement is 150 cases with a margin of $6.00 per case, or $900. The cost is $500, and the manufacturer will pay half. Thus, running the major advertisement generates $900 − $250 or $650 in incremental profit.

While the calculation is simple, the problem is that the true cost of the advertisement is the opportunity cost of the space. This may be significant since other major advertisements can be run. Thus, when considering all advertisements that can be run, the retailer needs to use some type of linear or integer programming model. The objective function is the response to different types of advertisements. The constraints are page space and category frequency. The model then selects the set of items to advertise.

Display activity is similar to feature advertising except that the payment is per case. For the example, it will be assumed that the payment only relates to cases sold during the retail promotion, but in reality it includes additional cases the retailer buys during the deal. It is assumed that displays double sales. If normal volume is 200 cases, then by running a display, sales increase by 200 cases at a profit margin of $6.00 per case. The cost of the display is $750 and the allowance is $.50 per case, or $100. Thus, the profit is $550 ($1,200 − $750 + $100). Again, the problem is that a display pays out but there is a high opportunity cost of the space, and therefore some type of optimization model is needed to select the items to display.

One last point is worth mentioning. In Chapter 12 it was shown that the length of the deal frequency influences the response. The longer the deal, the lower the sales in latter periods. This explains in part why a retailer cannot deal the same item every week. Not shown is the fact that the frequency of dealing an item influences the responsiveness to a deal. The more frequently a deal is offered, the lower is the elasticity. This also needs to be incorporated into a planning model. (See Rao and Thomas, 1973, for further discussion of this issue.)

Forward Buying

Certain types of retailers forward buy merchandise when trade promotions are offered. The reason is obvious. The storage cost plus reduced price is less than the future purchase price. Forward buying is an important part of promotional planning because the retailer often makes significant profits from managing the forward buying process.

Forward buying in its simplest form is based on inventory management models. It is useful to understand the basic model that some retailers use so that the implications of offering trade deals which induce forward buying can be better understood.

Forward Buying Models

The model to be discussed was developed for a food retailer, but the basic principles apply to any other type of retailing. The forward buying process is a trade-off between the deal discount and specific costs of carrying and handling the merchandise. These include carrying cost, which is the investment required to buy the inventory; storage costs, which is based on a per pallet cost; and handling costs, which is the incremental cost of bringing the goods to the warehouse, putting them into storage, and then removing them. (A pallet is simply a portable platform for storing materials.) The savings result from buying the product at a reduced cost. The following is an example of the type of economic order quantity (EOQ) model used by retailers.

The variables to be used in the model are

W = weeks to purchase

G = gross profit dollar per case (difference between regular cost and deal cost)

PC = purchase cost (deal cost)

P = number of cases per pallet

HC = handling cost per pallet (includes in and out charges and transportation)

SC = storage cost per pallet per month

CC = cost of capital

X = number of cases to be purchased

F = weekly forecast of cases shipped to the stores

To determine the amount to forward buy, X, the net profit from forward buying is differentiated with respect to X resulting in the incremental profit by investing in one more case. When this is equal to zero, the retailer does not benefit from buying an additional case.

Net profit (NP) is defined as

Gross profit less carrying costs less storage costs less handling costs.

gross profit $= G * X$

carrying costs $= PC * X/2 * CC/52 * X/F$

where

$$PC * X/2 = \text{average investment}$$

$$CC/52 = \text{weekly carrying cost}$$

$$X/F = \text{weeks of investment}$$

storage cost $= (X/2) * (1/P) * (SC/4) * (X/F)$

where

$$X/2 * 1/P = \text{average pallets}$$

$$SC/4 = \text{weekly storage charge per pallet}$$

$$X/F = \text{weeks of investment}$$

handling cost $= X * 1/P * HC$

where

$$X * 1/P = \text{number of pallets}$$
$$HC = \text{handling cost per pallet}$$

Combining terms weekly net profit is

$$NP = G * X - (PC) * (X/2) * (CC/52) * (X/F) \\ - (X/2) * (1/P) * (SC/4) * (X/F) - (X) * (1/P) * HC \quad \textbf{(14.15)}$$

Differentiating with respect to X gives

$$dNP/dX = G - PC * CC/52 * X/F - 1/P * SC/4 * X/F - HC/P \quad \textbf{(14.16)}$$

Setting the derivative to 0 and solving for X gives

$$X = \frac{52 * F * (G * P - HC)}{(PC * P * CC + 13 * SC)} \quad \textbf{(14.17)}$$

Dividing by the weekly forecast, which is assumed constant, gives the number of weeks supply to buy as[1]

$$W^* = \frac{52 * (G * P - HC)}{(PC * P * CC + 13 * SC)} \quad \textbf{(14.18)}$$

---

[1] If the weekly forecast is not constant, which occurs for highly seasonal products and holidays, the retailer needs to adjust the formula. However, over most of the year demand is stable in food and drug categories.

TABLE 14.10 Effects of Warehousing Costs on Forward Buying Volume

Cases per Pallet	Handling Cost	Storage Cost	Quantity to Order	Weeks' Supply
20	$14	$ 4	3,133	15.7
30	14	4	4,139	20.7
20	20	4	2,611	13.1
20	14	10	1,896	9.5

The equations given show that several variables influence the degree to which the retailer should forward buy. The first is the storage costs which are related to the number of cases that can be put on a pallet. Bulkier items result in fewer cases per pallet which means that fewer units will be purchased. Second, the higher the investment holding all other factors fixed, the less that will be purchased. Third, because the handling cost is a fixed amount, if the savings is not large enough to overcome the handling costs, then the retailer will not necessarily forward buy. Thus, for items with low volumes, the handling cost may be sufficiently high so that the item will not be forward bought.

To understand the inventory model just given, it is useful to substitute some numbers and see how the formula works. Suppose the storage cost per month per pallet is $4.00 and the handling cost is $14.00 per pallet. The retailer's cost of capital is 15 percent. The weekly forecast is 200 cases of the item and 20 cases fit on a pallet. The case selling price is $25.00. A 10 percent trade deal is offered. How much should the retailer forward buy? Using equation (14.17), the quantity to purchase is 3,133 units which is 15.7 weeks supply (dividing by 200 units forecasted per week).

Table 14.10 shows the effect of varying certain parameters and their effect on the quantity to buy. It shows ceteris paribus, as holding cost and storage cost increase and the number per pallet decreases, the quantity forward bought decreases. Any type of retailer can use the model, though a key assumption is that demand is constant over time. As demand varies over time, the formulas need to be modified.

RESEARCH ISSUES

In evaluating the relevant research questions for retail planning, the following topics have received little or no attention in the marketing literature.

- How can the traffic effect of promotions be measured?
- How is a store's price image created?
- How should retailers select items for advertising and display?

Each topic is discussed briefly in the paragraphs that follow.

Store Traffic

The primary issue associated with retail planning is estimating the "traffic" effect of promotions which is obviously the most difficult question to answer. Very little empirical research has been conducted trying to answer this question. The problem is that retailers always advertise. There are no nonadvertised periods. Hence, the only way to measure traffic effects is to build some type of econometric model.

Walters and MacKenzie (1988) and Walters and Rinne (1986) have used econometric procedures to try to estimate the effect of promotions on store traffic. This research offers an interesting starting point, but further research is needed. Examples of research questions that need to be addressed include

1. What percentage of consumers shop stores offering special promotions and why?
2. How much is a consumer's choice of store influenced by promotions offered?
3. How do consumers make the decision between "high-low" retailers and everyday-low-price retailers?
4. How can reliable econometric models be built which use store traffic as the dependent variable and item prices as the independent variables?

Price Image

A critical issue facing retailers is how consumers develop a price image for a chain. Specific questions are

- How does this image determine store choice?
- Does a consumer select items which are used to establish a price image?
- Does the consumer use only high volume items to determine a store's price image?

Once it is determined how to estimate a chain's price image how do promotions influence price image? Do promotions drive traffic but not price image?

A final issue is the relationship between price image and store choice. Which comes first? Do consumers indicate their store has lower prices than consumers who do *not* shop that store? This relates to the key issue: How does price image *cause* shopping behavior?

Selecting Items to Merchandise

Retailers are constrained in the number of items that should be merchandised (advertised, displayed, and promoted). No formal model exists that determines the optional items to select.

The problem can be constructed as a linear programming model in which the constraints are the number of items, frequency of promotions in a category, and time between promotions for an item. The objective function is total store profitability. Using this type of model, the retailer can select those items which have the highest margins and lowest cross-elasticities and generate the most traffic. An additional component of this model could be an inventory management model, so that the forward buy decision could be combined with the item selection decision.

15

Strategic Issues in the Design of Promotional Strategies

INTRODUCTION

The purpose of this chapter is to discuss strategic issues in the design and use of promotions. Promotions are classified as tactics used by the firm as part of the marketing mix. There are, however, broader promotional issues that become strategic. These include

- How do firms use promotions to meet marketing objectives?
- Push or pull?
- How do promotions influence a brand's franchise?
- How do firms avoid the "prisoner's dilemma"?
- How do firms avoid "hostaging" their brands?

The remainder of this chapter covers these issues.

HOW DO FIRMS USE PROMOTIONS TO MEET MARKETING OBJECTIVES?

Promotions are increasingly being called upon to meet an ever-expanding set of marketing objectives. It is therefore important to understand how and when promotions can be used as part of the overall marketing strategy.

First a set of marketing objectives is listed and then the type of promotion that can be used to meet these objectives is described. While promotions can be used to meet certain objectives, they can have an adverse effect on a product's marketing strategy as will be discussed in the section on consumer franchise building. Therefore, at the end of the section some of the negative consequences of promotions are listed.

Meeting Marketing Objectives

The following list of specific objectives is given along with the types of promotions that can be used. Only a partial list is given, but it shows how promotions are used to meet these objectives.

Objective	*Promotional Type*
Increase repeat buying	In-pack coupons, continuity programs (e.g., frequent flyer), "*N* for" retail promotions
Increase market share among brand switchers	FSI coupons, targeted coupons to other brand users, retail promotions
Increase retailer's promotion frequency	Trade deals, combination of consumer promotions and trade deals (big-bang theory)
Influence the product's image	Co-op image advertising with image-oriented retailers
Increase category switching	Retail promotions, FSI coupons, large rebates
Target deal–sensitive consumers	Coupons, "*N* for" retail promotions
Increase category consumption	Retailer promotions, promotions tied to events (e.g., back to school)
Increase trial among nonusers	Cross-couponing, free samples, trial packs, direct-mail coupons
Liquidate short-term inventories	Trade deals, rebates, inventory financing
Increase distribution	FSI coupons (increase demand), trade deals (increase DPP)

Limitations of Promotions

While promotions can be used to affect many of the product manager's objectives there are clearly risks and limitations to promotions. The following is a list of some of the problems. (Quelch, 1987, offers an excellent discussion of these issues.)

Decreasing Brand Loyalty. The use of promotions by one brand may lead to increased promotional activity for all brands which in turn increases brand switching within the category. Thus, while the brand may benefit in the short run from initial promotional activity, the long-term consequence is decreased brand loyalty.

Increasing Price Sensitivity. Some product categories have low price sensitivity because of low historical promotional activity. By using promotions, category price sensitivity increases because consumers become conditioned to promotions. The result is lower long-term profits (unless category demand increases enough to cover the lower average price).

Forward Buying and Diversion. As is discussed in Chapter 11, one of the problems with trade deals is that retailers and wholesalers forward buy. Because of forward buying, some retailers and wholesalers are buying almost 100 percent of their merchandise on deal. Manufacturers must run their plants at full capacity to generate inventories to sell during trade deals and then "stop" production after the trade promotion. This is very inefficient because all the retailers and wholesalers do is hold excess production in inventory in warehouses. The retailer, wholesaler, and manufacturer would be better off if no forward buying occurs. (It should be noted for some products it is efficient to produce periodically and then transfer inventories. In this case using trade dealing to load the retailer or wholesaler makes sense. Also if it is more economical for the consumer to hold inventories than the manufacturer, then trade promotions will be used.)

Diversion is another problem created by trade deals and quantity discounting. Because manufacturers offer different trade deals by region of the United States (and in some cases countries), it is efficient for wholesalers and retailers to buy from diverters who buy excess merchandise and ship it to other regions of the United States. The manufacturer would be better off shipping directly to the retailer and making the differential that shipping costs represent. Diverting forces the manufacturer to charge the same prices (adjusting for transaction costs) by region.

An excellent example of diverting is the "gray" market. For products such as computers, discounters buy merchandise from dealers and wholesalers who buy on deal or receive quantity discounts. Using this low purchase price, discounters then sell at costs below the authorized dealers causing the manufacturer to lose dealers. Identical pricing across markets eliminates the problem, but then the manufacturer cannot use promotions to adjust to local competitive conditions, which is the impetus for regional trade deals in the first place.

As one can see from the foregoing discussion, arbitragers in the market decrease the ability of manufacturers to use promotions and quantity discounts to price discriminate.

Detracting from Quality Image. Later, the effect of promotions on a brand's consumer franchise is discussed in detail. Clearly this is a potential consequence of the use of promotions. As will be stated, it is not clear that promotions do detract from a brand's consumer franchise. However, it is important to recognize the possibility exists when advocating promotions.

Short-Term Orientation. Promotions are generally thought to represent a short-term "fix." They generate revenue and profits but they may be mortgaging the future. Upper management should attempt to control short-term spending simply to drive sales to meet annual objectives because it may have some of the negative consequences given.

In summary, there are definite risks and problems in using promotions. The advantage of promotions is that sales results are measurable. It is important to recognize, however, that promotions rarely are used to create a brand franchise or to position a product. However, they can induce consumers to try the product, repeat buy it, and possibly become loyal to it. Thus, promotions strongly influence

consumers' actions but they do not necessarily create "positive" consumer attitudes.[1] This is left for advertising, positioning, and public relations.

PUSH OR PULL?

A critical question facing a brand or product manager is: should marketing expenditures be directed to the end-user (pull) or to the intermediaries in the channel
(push)?

Figure 15.1 shows a simple schematic explaining these two alternative strategies. Spending money on the "end-user" stimulates consumer demand and hence
brand or product sales. Spending money with the "trade" (intermediaries in the
channel) causes them to reduce price, offer special displays, or provide other
forms of merchandising which increases consumer demand and brand or product
sales. The problem is most managers want to know whether push or pull is more
efficient. Unfortunately, they are interrelated, not mutually exclusive.

Push Versus Pull Promotional Strategies

Table 15.1 gives examples of push and pull promotional strategies. Pull promotions
go *directly* from the manufacturer to the consumer and are frequently called consumer promotions. Push promotions go *through* the retailer or intermediary to
the end-user.

The advantage of direct promotions to the consumer (pull) is that intermediary compliance is not required. Unfortunately, they are generally less responsive and generate fewer short-term sales than a retail price reduction.

To see this, suppose a market has 1 million households. The product being

---

[1] The marketing literature (e.g., attribution theory) discusses how promotions create negative
attitudes toward products. See Chapter 2.

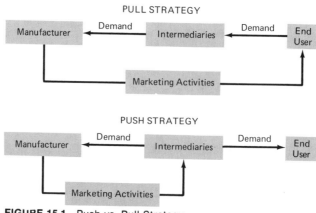

FIGURE 15.1 Push vs. Pull Strategy

TABLE 15.1 Push and Pull Promotional Vehicles

Push Promotions	Pull Promotions
• Off-invoice	• Couponing
• Spiffing	• Rebates
• Floor planning	• Continuity programs
• Co-op advertising	(e.g., frequent flyer)
• Display allowances	• Contests, sweepstakes
• Free goods	

studied comes from a category with 80 percent penetration and the product has a 20 percent market share. Assume it is purchased once a month. An FSI (free-standing insert) has a redemption rate of 4 percent. (See Chapter 10.) FSI's reach approximately 45 percent of U.S. households. Using these assumptions, 18,000 coupons will be redeemed.

In contrast, a retail promotion frequently increases the item's sales three times its normal level. (See Chapters 12 and 14.) Category sales are 800,000 units per month and hence brand sales are 160,000 units per month or 40,000 per week (four weeks to a month for simplicity). Suppose a retail promotion lasts one week. If sales increase three times the normal level, then 120,000 units are sold during the promotional week or an additional 80,000 units. The FSI generates 18,000 units or 22.5% of the volume.[2]

Thus, *if* the retailer or channel intermediary passes through the savings from the promotion to the consumer, then push strategies are highly effective. If a significant percentage of promotions are not passed through, then pull promotions become more advantageous.

Push and pull can be used together. Most successful push promotions are for products with strong end-user pull. In other words, those products which have strong demand receive a disproportional amount of "trade push." A marketing manager should use pull to develop strong customer demand and then use push to receive promotions from the trade.

Exclusive investment in push or pull can result in a less effective unbalanced marketing strategy because (1) intermediaries may not be willing to push the product when the firm is emphasizing customer pull or (2) intermediaries might be willing to push the product but there is no end-user demand. The marketing manager must balance push and pull expenditures to create demand for the product through consumer acceptance so that when distribution is generated, the product is being purchased. This "balancing act" continues throughout the product life cycle with more or less emphasis on push and pull depending on the maturity

---

[2] If the retail sales increase is less (e.g., 1.5 times normal) or the retailer does *not* offer a promotion, trade deals will be less effective than coupons.

of the category and the ability to differentiate the product. (See "Push Versus Pull Promotions over the Product Life Cycle" for a more detailed discussion.)

In summary, the marketing manager can use both push and pull in combination depending upon the specific objectives desired. There may be certain circumstances where only pull or push should be used. In general, most firms use both push and pull. The next section shows how push can be used with pull to benefit the intermediaries and manufacturers.

Partnership Push

In some industries the manufacturer and channel members have learned that it is advantageous to cooperate rather than be adversaries. In its extreme form there are exclusive dealers or franchisees who are supported by manufacturer programs. Department stores, for example, try to differentiate themselves by carrying items that create an image to the consumer. By having exclusive arrangements with certain designers, the department store *and* the designer (manufacturer) are able to convey a joint image to the consumer. In Chicago, when Marshall Fields has an exclusive arrangement to carry a certain line, it advertises the line to its customers to "position" its stores. Simultaneously, the designer is also being positioned within the market as "upscale" because Marshall Fields carries the line. If, instead of Marshall Fields, Montgomery Ward carries the line, a different image would be created. Thus, the retailer and the manufacturer create a general image in which they are tied together in the consumer's mind.

The advantage of partnership push is that both the retailer and the manufacturer jointly benefit rather than having an adversarial relationship. The concept is based on offering certain key retailers (or other channel members when appropriate) an exclusive franchise for the product or service. Without an exclusive franchise, no advantage accrues to the retailer for pushing the product. If competitors can buy the same product or brand, then the retailer has nothing unique to advertise. The partnership is not intact.

Shugan (1986) offers an example of partnership push. The retailer is given a unique model or product line to sell which only a few retailers in the trading area can sell. For instance, in cameras the model may be differentiated by a specific lens which only a small set of retailers can carry. These retailers will promote the item since the model is carried only by a few retailers. Thus, there is a form of cooperation between the retailer and the manufacturer to reduce price competition and to allow the retailer to push a given item because it is unique to that retailer.

The disadvantage of offering retailers exclusive products is that it limits availability. The manufacturer has to make the trade-off between greater retailer push (exclusive franchise) and greater market coverage. By offering branded variants (Shugan, 1986) the manufacturer can gain market coverage and retailer push (exclusive franchise for a given model number).

The types of products likely to be used for partnership push are ones that help to create an "image" for the store. This means items that are differentiated. For department stores, designer clothing offers the ability to create an "image" for the store. For grocery stores, standard products such as coffee, margarine, and paper products cannot easily be used. However, specialty items can be. Thus, an exclusive line of ice cream can be used to position the quality image of the store. Exclusive brands of coffee can also be used.

In summary, partnership push is being used by manufacturers and retailers to overcome problems of lack of exclusivity in items being stocked by the retailer (or other channel members). Promotions can be used to enhance this concept by emphasizing the unique product lines a retailer is stocking. The retailer should be willing to invest more push money into those items that are exclusively theirs. The manufacturer's challenge is to create a partnership without reducing volume to the point where it is not economical to limit the number of retailers' selling the product.

Push Versus Pull Promotions over the Product Life Cycle

In developing a promotional strategy (push versus pull), it is important to consider where the brand is in the product life cycle. A new product introduction requires different types of promotional tactics than does a mature or declining product. For each of the four stages of the product life cycle, a set of recommended promotional tactics is given. The recommendations are summarized in Table 15.2.

TABLE 15.2 Push and Pull over the Product Life Cycle

Introductory stage	
Push: Gain distribution	Pull: Gain trial
Vehicles: Trade deals, free goods	Vehicles: Sampling
	FSI's
	Trial sizes
	In-store demonstrations
Growth stage	
Push: Gain additional distribution	Pull: New triers
	Repeat buying
Vehicles: Off-invoice	Vehicles: Trial sizes
free goods	Coupons (FSI's, in-pack, on-pack)
	Special premium packs
Maturity stage	
Push: Gain switchers	Pull: Gain switchers and maintain loyalty
Vehicles: Off-invoice	Vehicles: Direct-mail coupons
Co-op advertising	On-pack and in-pack coupons
Spiffing	
Display allowances	
Declining stage	
Push: Maintain brand profitability	Pull: Generate volume
Vehicles: Off-invoice	Vehicles: FSI's
	Value packs

Introductory Stage.   During the introductory stage the key objectives are to generate initial trial and distribution. To generate trial the promotional tools that can be used effectively are (1) sampling, (2) trial sizes, (3) FSI coupons (broad reach), and (4) in-store demonstrations. These are all pull promotions.

To gain distribution, it is essential to use some type of trade deal to increase gross margin and hence the economic return for stocking the product. Slotting allowances have also become a popular promotional tool.[3] Special allowances can be used for displays, though many retailers will not display a new product. These are clearly push strategies. However, without pull, most new products will be unsuccessful. In the introductory stage, pull dominates push.

Growth Stage.   The objectives in the growth stage are to generate additional new triers and repeat buying among triers. Therefore, the goals of the promotions are (1) to increase the trial base, (2) to reinforce repeat buying, and (3) to expand (or maintain) distribution.

The same pull tools given in the introductory stage can be used to increase trial, though sampling becomes less cost effective as trial rates go up. To generate repeat buying, in-pack and on-pack coupons can be used. This allows customers to become regular users of the product. Special premium packs that offer additional quantities at the same price offer triers an incentive to repeat purchase. However, retailers do not like to stock these special packs because they require additional UPC's and special slots in the warehouse.

Push again is used to expand distribution through stocking of additional sizes and new retailers carrying the product. The type of trade promotions used focuses on free goods, off-invoice, and other discounts aimed at making the product profitable to stock.

Maturity Stage.   During the maturity stage, the product category becomes price sensitive because many similar brands are available to the consumer. During this period push promotions are increased relative to pull promotions. The promotional goals are to reinforce loyalty and to capture a significant share of switchers. The focus shifts to more retailer promotions and couponing. Feature advertising, displays, and price discounts become important even though consumer promotions are still heavily used in the promotional mix. Couponing is used to entice brand switchers.

To generate feature advertising, displays, and price reductions, the product's position (market share) influences the degree to which the retailer will promote the item. The product's position has been determined, in part, from the promotional strategies used during the introductory and growth stages. Ironically, underspending early in the product life cycle may decrease the opportunity to generate effective promotions during the mature stage.

Pull promotions are used to reach new users, though this becomes less crit-

---

[3] A slotting allowance is used to gain a "slot" in the retailer's warehouse. A fixed payment is usually made by the manufacturer to the retailer.

ical because the brand's sales are primarily from consumers who have already tried the product. Targeted couponing to users of competitive brands can be very advantageous because loyal customers are not promoted.

To reinforce loyalty, on-packs and in-packs are used. These reduce the risk of losing a loyal customer to another brand because of a coupon received. They also reinforce the customer's habitual behavior.

Declining Stage. During the declining stage the goal is to maintain distribution and try to be a surviving brand. If this can be accomplished, the brand can be very profitable. The retailer looks at volume to determine which brands to delete from the category. Any promotion that generates volume becomes important.

The major problem facing the brand is that the retailer may not want to promote brands in a declining category as often as brands in a growth or large mature category because the customer base is declining. Therefore, it is important to rely heavily on pull promotions.

Pull promotions should take the form of FSI's because they reach a broad audience. In addition, special value packs offering more volume at the same price or cents-off packs will reduce the price to the consumer without trade cooperation.

Finally, push promotions in the form of trade deals need to be used to try to guarantee margins to the retailer. Most likely, competitors are also offering extensive trade deals, and the strategy has to be to match competition while trying to gain a dominant position in terms of share.

Once competitors have been driven out of the market, the firm should reduce the level of promotions. The consumer buys declining product categories for specific uses, not because it is promoted.

Summary. In summary there are different strategies depending upon the product's stage in the product life cycle. Table 15.2 summarized the promotional strategies just described. It is essential to plan for the promotional strategies required at each stage so that the firm is well positioned all through the product life cycle. The general theme is: Balance push and pull, though push increases in importance as the product matures.

CONSUMER FRANCHISE BUILDING

One of the most common arguments against the use of promotions is that it diminishes a brand's consumer franchise. The definition of a brand's consumer franchise is vague, and so this section will begin by trying to define the term. Then, a discussion of some of the empirical evidence will be given. Finally, tentative (only because of the lack of strong evidence) conclusions will be given.

Consumer Franchise

Diehard battery has it, Kitchen Aid has it, Mercedes and BMW have it. Shell batteries don't. General Electric doesn't, Chevy doesn't. IBM, Apple, and Compaq have it, but Zenith, Radio Shack, and AT&T don't. What is "it"? A consumer franchise.

What, then, is a consumer franchise? The Marketing Science Institute (MSI) ran a conference (Leuthesser, 1988) to define and study "brand equity" which is similar to a consumer franchise. The following were some of the definitions of brand equity (consumer franchise).

1. Utility not measured by attributes
2. Loyalty
3. Differentiated clear image that goes beyond product preference
4. Brand commitment
5. Low cross-elasticities with respect to advertising
6. Retailer's willingness to carry a brand at lower margins than competition.

An interesting and simple way to look at all these definitions is to divide the concept between the trade and the consumer. To the trade, it refers to "the market share leader." To the consumer, brand equity refers to "the preferred brand." These definitions fit nondurables but may not perfectly fit higher-priced durable goods which have a low market share but are strongly preferred such as Mercedes-Benz. To the trade, Mercedes-Benz also has a strong pull.

Translating these definitions into English, a product has a consumer franchise if it has developed a loyal following and its customers walk into a store and demand the product from the retailer; they are not willing to take a substitute. Thus, someone desiring a Mercedes will not be satisfied buying a Cadillac even if the Cadillac is priced significantly lower. In the extreme this argument will not hold, but the consumer is not swayed to switch from their desired brand by small price differences. In the consumer's mind the utility for the product with a consumer franchise exceeds similar products.

In the 1970s a major appliance manufacturer conducted an unpublished study in which it evaluated the consumer franchise for a number of appliance manufacturers. The study found that Kitchen Aid and Maytag had a strong consumer franchise, but General Electric and Whirlpool did not.

To evaluate the meaning of this strong consumer franchise, the company sent "blind" shoppers (scripted shoppers) into retail stores to see how the salesperson reacted to different scenarios. If someone walked in committed to a brand name (e.g., General Electric), then the salesperson discussed only models within that brand's line and did not try to shift the customer to another brand. However, if the customer walked in uncommitted, the salesperson tried to shift him or her to the brand with the highest margin to the retailer. The higher margins were generated from promotions. Being committed (a strong franchise) helps insulate the brand from the sales force pushing higher-margin brands.

The moral of the story is that brands with strong consumer franchises are less vulnerable to competitors' promotional strategies.

Do Promotions Destroy a Brand's Consumer Franchise?

For years advertising executives have been warning marketing executives that promotions will destroy their brand's image. If a premium product promotes, the consumer then wonders why this has occurred, attributes lower quality as the reason, and the brand loses its consumer franchise. Promotions destroy all the positive imagery advertising agencies work so hard to create. Is this true? Is Madison Avenue right?

Strang (1975) in his Ph.D. thesis argued that the Madison Avenue was right. He cited several examples in which brands that were heavily promoted began to lose market share. The cause was assumed to be attributable to a loss in the brand's consumer franchise. Other empirical evidence in his thesis showed that brands that increased their advertising budgets increased their market share.

Shortly after Strang's work, Dodson et al. (1978) gave a theoretical reason why promotions cause brands to lose market share. (This article has been covered extensively in Chapter 2, so only the conclusions are given.) They argued the reason for the loss in a brand's sales is attribution theory. The brand's quality image is diminished because the consumer attributes reasons why a promotion is run. For example, since high-quality products rarely promote but low-quality products frequently promote, the brand must be low quality if it promotes.

The empirical evidence given by Dodson et al. shows that consumers are less likely to buy the promoted brand on subsequent purchases. Several other studies (Shoemaker and Shoaf, 1977; Neslin and Shoemaker, 1989; Scott, 1977) have evaluated repeat buying effects. These studies generally agreed with the Dodson et al. results, though Scott gives examples in which repeat buying rates are increased after a promotion. While there is evidence on both sides, the issue has not been resolved (Chapter 5). Both sides can cite examples, but it is difficult to find strong evidence that promotions hurt a brand's franchise.

The primary problem is causation. When a brand has weakening sales, it frequently increases promotions. Sales are declining but not necessarily because of the brand's promotional activity. Strong brands frequently do not promote because they want to maximize profits, and if promotions do not payout, then why promote? Strang (1980) cites evidence that managers increase promotions when sales are down, but increase advertising when sales are high.

In most packaged goods categories, the brand leader receives more retailer promotions than weaker brands. One would expect that the higher level of retail promotions would decrease the consumer franchise for these brands and their market share would decrease. However, there is no evidence this is occurring.

Johnson (1984) studied brand loyalty over a long time frame. Surprisingly (or maybe not so surprisingly), the leading brands in most categories are still the leading brands. This finding implies that the increasing promotion seen in the late 1970s and early 1980s has not eroded the market position of the brand leader. While some research has shown a negative effect of the promotion on the brand's franchise, Johnson's study brings into question whether leading brands have had their market position eroded through increasing promotions.

How to Interpret the Data and Some Tentative Conclusions

The empirical analysis and theories appear to be too simplistic. The answer may depend upon the type of product being analyzed. Figure 15.2 gives a grid Foote, Cone, and Beldling uses to characterize products. One axis of the grid divides products into high and low involvement; the other axis divides them into think and feel products. Examples are given of products in each quadrant.

In evaluating the types of products whose franchise is less vulnerable to promotional activities, it would appear to be think products. The consumer tries to develop an objective evaluation of these products. Feel products, particularly in the high-involvement quadrant, are much more suspectible to promotions eroding their image. If a customer buys a product for prestige and then finds out that it is heavily discounted, it changes the image of the product. Of course, heavy discounting at the end of the fashion season is expected and so the customer is less likely to "attribute" lower quality to the product.

Another problem with promoting prestige products is that they become too accessible. Consumers buy certain products because of their exclusivity. If everyone can own a "prestige" product, then its "utility" diminishes. Promotions increase the number owning the product thus diminishing the "franchise" of the

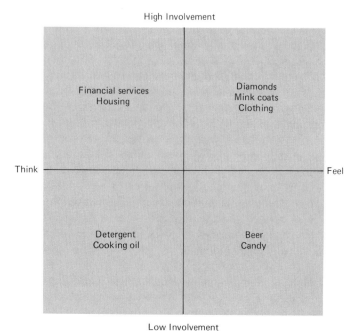

FIGURE 15.2 Foote, Cone, and Belding Grid

product. Prestigious products which are conspicuously consumed may be poor candidates for promotions.

Based on this discussion, the following conclusions can be drawn:

1. Mixed results have been found that a brand or product's consumer franchise erodes when promotions are used.
2. Brand loyalty studies show very little change in brand shares in established categories. During the same period there has been a dramatic increase in the amount of promotional activity. (See Johnson, 1984.) Thus, increased promotions do not appear to have eroded the consumer franchise for these brands.
3. The effect of promotions on a brand's consumer franchise may depend upon the type of product it is. The consumer franchise for "feel," high-involvement products may be vulnerable to the use of promotions because consumers are buying the exclusivity of the product. "Think" products may not have their consumer franchise eroded by promotions because the consumer is making a "rational" decision.

PRISONER'S DILEMMA

One reason frequently stated for running promotions is the prisoner's dilemma. In Chapter 4 a brief explanation was given. The prisoner's dilemma implies that promotions are used because of competitive pressure. Before discussing what actions a firm can follow to reduce unprofitable promotions resulting from being in the prisoner's dilemma, it is useful to review the theory.

Theory and Solutions to the Prisoner's Dilemma

Rather than using prisoners as the players in the prisoner's dilemma, two firms, both making the decision to promote or not, will be used. Firm 1 has two decisions: run trade deals or do not run trade deals. Firm 2 has exactly the same decisions. Both have a profit function which depends upon their action and their competitor's action. The following payoff matrix shows the results of the different actions of firm 1 and firm 2.

		Firm 2	
		No trade deal	Trade deal
Firm 1	No trade deal	(a_{11}, b_{11})	(a_{12}, b_{12})
	Trade deal	(a_{21}, b_{21})	(a_{22}, b_{22})

where $a_{11} > a_{22}$, $a_{21} \gg a_{11}$, $a_{22} \gg a_{12}$, $b_{12} \gg b_{11}$, $b_{11} > b_{22}$, and $b_{22} \gg b_{21}$.

The two firms face a prisoner's dilemma because firm 1 and firm 2 are better off if neither promotes, but the "best" action based on the payoff matrix is to promote because each firm loses large profits if the competitor promotes and it does not. The issues are: How should one play? Can both firms avoid cutting each other's throat?

For the example just given, the prisoner's dilemma is not totally realistic. In most markets there are multiple players, and the "game" is played over multiple time periods. (In the jargon of game theory this is an *N*-person, noncooperative, supergame.)

Many authors have tried to look at how firms should play repeated games in a noncooperative environment. No definitive answers have resulted. There are, however, several strategies worth noting. The first is a Nash equilibrium. A Nash equilibrium assumes that the firm's competitors will defect, meaning run a promotion. If a firm knows its competitors will promote, then its best move is to promote. The result is that all firms move to the least profitable strategy (cell 2, 2 in the matrix).

Griffith and Rust simulated an *N*-person multiplay prisoner's dilemma. They show that if there are a large number of players, then it pays to play a Nash strategy in which they defect and offer a promotion.

They also show that if there are few players, then a tit-for-tat can work. Tit-for-tat means that the firm always matches the competitor's move. Thus, if its competitor raises price, the firm matches. If its competitor does promote, the firm promotes. However, this strategy works only when there are very few competitors. Thus, it appears that the number of competitors influences the optimal strategy.

Fader and Hauser (1987) using a tournament show the winning strategy is a variant of tit-for-tat. Firms offer "moderate" promotions. However, in their tournament there were only three firms. The optimal strategy may not be tit-for-tat if there are more firms involved as Griffith and Rust show.

Application of Prisoner's Dilemma to Promotions

As soon as marketing managers learn about the prisoner's dilemma, they immediately recognize that it fits their dilemma in managing promotions. They ask if the "solution" can be applied to the real world. Can they play tit-for-tat. Should they continue running promotions? The answer depends upon two factors: (1) Can a firm communicate its strategy to competitors? and (2) Is the firm really facing the prisoner's dilema?

If competitors know a firm's promotional actions immediately after they are taken, it is easier to escape from the prisoner's dilemma because each firm can signal its action to the others. Looking at it from another perspective, immediate knowledge of a competitor's activity decreases the chances of facing the prisoner's dilemma. For example, three gasoline stations on a corner can all learn when one competitor raises price as a signal to the other two to also raise price without too much of a loss. If the others do not match, then the firm immediately lowers its price back to the level of the other two. Thus, each firm can signal the others in the market. Airlines, for example, notify the customer publicly (and hence the competitors) of a price increase. This serves as a signal. Burke (1988a) studied various forms of signaling in a prisoner's dilemma.

For some industries, it is far more difficult to learn about competitive promotional activities. Take a firm selling consumer products to food retailers. A trade deal is offered. The field sales force may learn about it within a week, but no standard tracking mechanism exists to maintain information about competitors' promotions. By not maintaining the information in a systematic way, it is difficult for competitors to see signals. Thus, how easy is it to signal? Even if a competitor was trying to signal reduced trade promotions, the other competitors may not be able to "read" the information. The signal did not work and the signaler simply lost money. Thus, noise is added to the process which decreases the advantage of signaling. See Burke (1988b) for a discussion of signaling and screening of information.

A similar problem exists with mass distribution of coupons. Can competitors "read" a signal that one competitor has significantly reduced its volume of coupons distributed? It is unlikely. Therefore, the signal may not effectively communicate the relevant information to a competitor.

The conclusion is that many of the strategies used to "escape" the prisoner's dilemma assume the competitors can observe the signal. Unfortunately, this is difficult for certain types of promotions. Therefore, tit-for-tat and other strategies may not work, even for markets where there are a small number of players.

The other issue is: Do all promotions result in a prisoner's dilemma? The answer is no. The frequency of promotions and the own and cross-elasticities have a significant effect on the answer.

To understand the issue better, an example has been constructed. Suppose that when a retail promotion is offered, sales double. The retailer promotes the item four times per year. However, the retailer purchases 80 percent of its volume at the manufacturer's trade deal price. If no trade deal is offered, 100 percent of its volume is sold at regular price. The trade deal price is 10 percent below regular price.

Assume there are two identical firms in this market. When the retailer promotes the competitor's item, its volume decreases by 50 percent. (The additional volume comes from price-sensitive customers who switch brands.) The normal volume per week for each firm is 200 units. The price per case is $10.00 and the trade deal price is $9.00. The manufacturer's marginal cost of goods is $5.00 per case. Assume the dealing period is 13 weeks and only one retail promotion is offered during the 13 weeks.

Using these assumptions one can construct the payoff matrix for each manufacturer. The firm must decide: Should it offer a series of trade promotions next year? Table 15.3 gives the payoffs for the two options each firm has (promote or do not promote).

It shows that if firm 1 does not offer a trade deal, it is better off even if firm 2 offers a trade deal. Assuming firm 2 does not offer a trade deal, what action should firm 1 take? Profits are $12,500 if firm 1 does not offer a trade deal and $11,220 if firm 1 offers a trade deal. Suppose, now that firm 2 does not offer a trade deal. Firm 1's profits are $13,000 if no trade deal is offered and $11,720 if

TABLE 15.3 Promotional Payoff Matrix

		Firm 2	
		No trade deal	Trade deal
Firm 1	No trade deal	13,000, 13,000	12,500, 11,720
	Trade deal	11,720, 12,500	11,220, 11,220

a trade deal is offered. The result is: firm 1 should *not* offer a trade deal. The same is true for firm 2. Yet, if firm 2 promotes, firm 1's profits are less. However, the payoff matrix is just the opposite of the prisoner's dilemma; firm 1 (or firm 2) should never run a trade promotion. The reason is that the passthrough is low relative to the volume sold on the trade deal, and therefore, it does not pay to promote. While the firm loses market share, it is not enough to justify the continual cost of a trade promotion.

What happens if five firms are in the market rather than one? Assume that each promotes, and firm 1 loses the same volume, 100 units. However, there are 20 (not 5) promotional weeks run by the retailer for four competitive items. Should firm 1 promote? The answer depends upon the retail deal elasticity and the amount the retailer buys on trade promotion. Unless the firm can gain enough volume when a promotion is run to cover the cost, it does not pay to run trade promotions. (In this example, issues about distribution and shelf space are not included. By increasing volume, it may help keep the firm's products in distribution.) The firm may be better off investing in advertising or other types of actions which will increase "normal" sales.

The same type of example can be constructed for coupons. It would show that while the brand loses share from not couponing, its profitability will increase *even if* competitors continue to promote. The competitor's profit will increase when the firm stops promoting, but it is still less profitable than if promotions were run.

To summarize, there may be many situations where a firm would be better off not promoting. Because market response (deal elasticities) is low, it may be advantageous to stop promoting even if market share drops. This is a difficult decision for the firm to make, but it may be optimal. Analysis of retail deal elasticities and incremental coupon volume are critical in making this decision.

HOSTAGING

The last section discussed the strategic dilemma associated with noncooperation between firms in an industry. A similar problem exists between retailers and manufacturers. Promotions are forcing manufacturers to lose their power in the channel. The concept to be covered in this section is called "hostaging." It refers to the ability of the retailer (or trade channel) to exert significant pressure on manufacturers to force them to continually offer trade promotions.[4]

Concept of Hostaging

"Hostaging" is defined as the condition in which a brand permits the trade to control over 50 percent of its direct marketing budget. Over time the process advances to the point where consumer promotions work to support trade events, and advertising becomes too expensive, or at best a minor budget item. The brand ultimately becomes completely dependent on the trade for volume and promotional support. It can exceed 90 percent of the brand's marketing activity.

What is the result of a brand being "held hostage"? The answer is the brand loses its identity and functions almost like a private-label brand. Its share is driven by a lower retail price (a lower price tier than national brands) and promotions to attract the price-sensitive consumer. Its volume does not depend on preference and loyalty, but on price. When new products enter the market, these brands frequently lose distribution because the retailer substitutes the new brand for those brands with the least consumer demand. (See Blattberg, Buesing, and Sen, 1980, for an example in which brands lose volume when a new brand enters the market.)

Hostage Index

The hostage index is derived from four factors:

1. Percentage of volume sold on deal
2. Weighted depth of deal
3. Percentage of the marketing budget represented by trade spending
4. Private label share of category volume

The higher the hostage index, the lower the manufacturer's control of the brand.

The matrix in Figure 15.3 shows the hostage index versus a brand's market share. It also gives a description of the brand's position in each of the four quadrants of the matrix. Brands in quadrant I have high trade control, low share and are called hostage brand. Brands in quadrant II have high share and high trade control and are hostage-vulnerable brands. Brands in quadrant III have high share and low trade control and are leveraged brands. Finally, brands in quadrant IV have low trade control and low share and are secure brands.

A firm can then place each of its brands in the matrix and then use this information to develop a trade strategy for each brand.

Strategies

Jones recommends the following strategies to overcome hostaging. First, sacrifice volume and share in order to reduce promotional spending. While the brand will lose some distribution, the money can be reinvested into consumer spending and

---

[4] This concept was developed by Keith Jones of Summa.

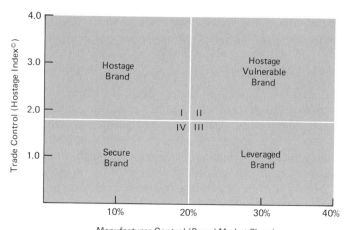

FIGURE 15.3 Hostage Control Grid

repositioning to try to increase the "consumer franchise" of the brand. The reinvestment is critical because, otherwise, the brand will simply become a cash generator and will ultimately die.

Second, reduce costs and try to position the brand in a "moderate" price tier below the national brands. For categories in which there are moderate-quality buyers, this strategy may work. Shedd margarine is lower cost than the national brands and, in some markets, has captured significant share. It has lower costs because it is a blend and contains lower-cost ingredients. This strategy works only if the consumer wants a product whose primary premise is "value," that is, national brand attributes and lower prices. When it is difficult for the consumer to evaluate the quality of these brands, the strategy may not work.

Third, acquire several hostage brands and try to gain enough volume so that promotional activity can be reduced. This means that the retailer will not be able to remove all brands from the store if they are not promoted. However, this is a risky strategy. The best current example is Dr Pepper and 7-Up. Through economies of scale in distribution and production, they were able to drive down their costs. They can also negotiate with the trade and threaten to pull all their brands if one loses distribution.

While these strategies are designed to overcome hostaging, an equally important issue is avoiding hostaging. The recommended steps are (1) reduce trade deal frequency, (2) convert trade spending into consumer promotions and advertising, and (3) focus on product modification to differentiate the brand and make it less reliant on price.

All the recommended steps are reasonable actions, but they offer no guarantee of success. It is extremely difficult to turn a brand around once it is "held hostage." It is not easy to avoid hostaging when the competition is offering large trade deals. However, a strong focus on benefits and value to the customer can increase a brand's market share. The problem is that it takes time. Pepsi took decades to overcome Coke. No one has been able to reduce Budweiser's share in the beer market. Recommending strategies is easier than implementing them. However, it is important to remember, promotions are a short-run "fix," and brand enhancement can lead to long-run success.

References

AAKER, DAVID A., "Toward a Normative Model of Promotional Decision Making," *Management Science*, Vol. 19, no. 6 (February 1973), pp. 593–603.

AAKER, DAVID A., "The New-Trier Stochastic Model of Brand Choice," *Management Science*, Vol. 17, no. 5 (April 1971), pp. 435–450.

AAKER, DAVID A., JAMES M. CARMAN, and ROBERT JACOBSON, "Modeling Advertising-Sales Relationships Involving Feedback: A Time Series Analysis of Six Cereal Brands," *Journal of Marketing Research*, Vol. 19, no. 1 (February 1982), pp. 116–125.

ABRAHAM, MAGID M., and LEONARD M. LODISH, "PROMOTER: An Automated Promotion Evaluation System," *Marketing Science*, Vol. 6, no. 2 (Spring 1987), pp. 101–123.

ADDLEMAN, SIDNEY, "Orthogonal Main-Effect Plans for Asymmetrical Factorial Experiments," *Technometrics*, Vol. 4 (February 1962), pp. 21–46.

AHMED, SADRUDIN A., and GARY M. GULAS, "Consumers' Perception of Manufacturers' Suggested List Price," *Psychological Reports*, Vol. 50 (April 1982), pp. 507–518.

AILLONI-CHARAS, DAN, *Promotion: A Guide to Effective Promotional Planning, Strategies, and Executions*. New York: John Wiley, 1984.

ALLENBY, GREG M., "A Unified Approach to Identifying, Estimating and Testing Demand Structures with Aggregate Data," Working paper, Ohio State University, Columbus (January 1988).

ALLENBY, GREG M., and ROBERT C. BLATTBERG, "How Do Brands Compete," Working paper, Graduate School of Business, University of Chicago (November 1988).

ALSOP, RONALD, "Companies Seek Ways to Put Coupons Where They'll Count," *The Wall Street Journal*, August 8, 1985, p. 25.

AMEMIYA, TAKESHI, *Advanced Econometrics*. Cambridge, MA: Harvard University Press, 1985.

ANDERSON, EVAN E., "The Effectiveness of Retail Price Reductions: A Comparison of Alternative Expressions of Price," *Journal of Marketing Research*, Vol. 11, no. 3 (August 1974), pp. 327–330.

ANTIL, JOHN H., "Couponing as a Promotional Tool: Consumers Do Benefit," *Journal of Consumer Affairs*, Vol. 19, no. 2 (Winter 1985), pp. 316–327.

APPELBAUM, MEL, "Test Prices, Evaluate Promotions Using Models, Supermarket Scanner Data, and 'Bump Analysis,'" *Marketing News* (March 1, 1985), pp. 16, 20.

ASSAEL, HENRY, *Consumer Behavior and Marketing Action*, 3rd ed. Boston: Kent, 1987.

AXELROD, ROBERT, "Effective Choice in the Prisoner's Dilemma," *Journal of Conflict Resolution*, Vol. 24, (March 1980a), pp. 3–25.

AXELROD, ROBERT, "More Effective Choice in the Prisoner's Dilemma," *Journal of Conflict Resolution* (September 1980b), pp. 379–403.

BABAKUS, EMIN, PETER TAT, and WILLIAM CUNNINGHAM, "Coupon Redemption: A Motivational Perspective," *Journal of Consumer Marketing*, Vol. 5, no. 2, (Spring 1988), pp. 37–43.

BAGOZZI, RICHARD P., "A Field Investigation of Causal Relations Among Cognitions, Affect, Intentions, and Behavior," *Journal of Marketing Research*, Vol. 19, no. 4 (November 1982), pp. 562–584.

BASS, FRANK M., and ROBERT P. LEONE, "Temporal Aggregation, The Data Interval Bias, and Empirical Estimation of Bimonthly Relations from Annual Data," *Management Science*, Vol. 29, no. 1 (January 1983), pp. 1–11.

BASS, FRANK M., and DICK R. WITTINK, "Pooling Issues and Methods in Regression Analysis: Some Further Reflections," *Journal of Marketing Research*, Vol. 15, no. 2 (May 1978), pp. 277–279.

BASS, FRANK M., and DICK R. WITTINK, "Pooling Issues and Methods in Regression Analysis with Examples in Marketing Research," *Journal of Marketing Research*, Vol. 12, no. 4 (November 1975), pp. 414–425.

BASS, FRANK M., M. GIVON, M. KALWANI, D. REIBSTEIN, and G. P. WRIGHT, "An Investigation into the Order of the Brand Choice Process," *Marketing Science*, Vol. 3, no. 4 (Fall 1984), pp. 267–287.

BASS, FRANK M., ABEL JEULAND, and GORDON P. WRIGHT, "Equilibrium Stochastic Choice and Market Penetration Theories: Derivations and Comparisons," *Management Science*, Vol. 22, (June 1976), pp. 1051–1063.

BAUER, RAYMOND A., "Consumer Behavior as Risk Taking." In *Proceedings of the 43rd National Conference of the American Marketing Association*, ed. Robert S. Hancock, pp. 389–398. Chicago: American Marketing Association, 1960.

BAWA, KAPIL, and ROBERT W. SHOEMAKER, "The Coupon-Prone Consumer: Some Findings Based on Purchase Behavior Across Product Classes," *Journal of Marketing*, Vol. 51, no. 4 (October 1987a), pp. 99–110.

BAWA, KAPIL, and ROBERT W. SHOEMAKER, "The Effects of a Direct Mail Coupon on Brand Choice Behavior," *Journal of Marketing Research*, Vol. 24, no. 4 (November 1987b), pp. 370–376.

BAYER, JUDY, STEPHEN LAWRENCE, and JOHN W. KEON, "PEP: An Expert System for Promotion Marketing," Working paper 4-87-88, Graduate School of Industrial Administration, Carnegie-Mellon, Pittsburgh (October 1986).

BAYUS, BARRY L., "Accelerating the Durable Replacement-Cycle with Marketing Mix Variables," *Journal of Product Innovation Management* (September 1988), 216–226.

BEARDEN, WILLIAM O., DONALD LICHTENSTEIN and JESSE E. TEEL, "Comparison Price, Coupon, and Brand Effects on Consumer Reactions to Retail Newspaper Advertisements," *Journal of Retailing,* Vol. 60, no. 2 (Summer 1984), pp. 11–34.

BEEM, EUGENE R., and H. JAY SHAFFER, "Triggers to Customer Action—Some Elements in a Theory of Promotional Inducement," Report No. 81-106 Marketing Science Institute, Cambridge, MA (rev. December 1981).

BELSLEY, DAVID A., EDWIN KUH, and ROY E. WELSCH, *Regression Diagnostics: Identifying Influential Data and Sources of Collinearity*. New York: John Wiley, 1980.

BEM, D. J., "Self-perception Theory." In *Advances in Experimental Social Psychology*, Vol. 6, ed. L. Berkowitz, pp. 1–62. New York: Academic Press, 1972.

BEN-AKIVA, M., "Program for Maximum Likelihood Estimation of the Multinominal Logit Model," Transportation Systems Division of Civil Engineering, MIT, Cambridge, MA. (January 1973).

BHASIN, AJAY, and ROGER DICKINSON, "Extra Value Couponing—Strategic Implications for Supermarkets," *Agribusiness*, Vol. 3, no. 3 (1987), pp. 293–306.

BLAIR, EDWARD A., and E. LAIRD LANDON, JR., "The Effects of Reference Prices in Retail Advertisements," *Journal of Marketing*, Vol. 45, no. 2 (Spring 1981), pp. 61–69.

BLATTBERG, ROBERT C., and KENNETH J. WISNIEWSKI, "Modelling Store-Level Scanner Data," Marketing working paper no. 43, University of Chicago (January 1988).

BLATTBERG, ROBERT C., and ALAN LEVIN, "Modelling the Effectiveness and Profitability of Trade Promotions," *Marketing Science*, Vol. 6, no. 2 (Spring 1987), pp. 124–146.

BLATTBERG, ROBERT C., and KENNETH J. WISNIEWSKI, "How Retail Price Promotions Work: Empirical Results," Marketing working paper no. 42, University of Chicago (December 1987).

BLATTBERG, ROBERT C., and KENNETH J. WISNIEWSKI, "Price-Induced Patterns of Competition," Working paper, Graduate School of Business, University of Chicago (December 1986).

BLATTBERG, ROBERT C., and ABEL P. JEULAND, "A Micromodeling Approach to Investigate the Advertising-Sales Relationship," *Management Science*, Vol. 27, no. 9 (September 1981), pp. 988–1004.

BLATTBERG, ROBERT C., THOMAS BUESING, and SUBRATA K. SEN, "Marketing Strategies for New Brands," *Journal of Marketing*, Vol. 44, no. 4 (Fall 1980), pp. 59–67.

BLATTBERG, ROBERT C., and SUBRATA K. SEN, "Market Segments and Stochastic Brand Choice Models," *Journal of Marketing Research*, Vol. 13, no. 1 (February 1976), pp. 34–45.

BLATTBERG, ROBERT C., and SUBRATA K. SEN, "A Bayesian Technique to Discriminate Between Stochastic Models of Brand Choice," *Management Science*, Vol. 21, no. 6 (February 1975), pp. 682–696.

BLATTBERG, ROBERT C., and SUBRATA K. SEN, "Market Segmentation Using Models of Multidimensional Purchasing Behavior," *Journal of Marketing*, Vol. 38, no. 4 (October 1974), pp. 17–28.

BLATTBERG, ROBERT C., GARY D. EPPEN, and JOSHUA LIEBERMAN, "A Theoretical and Empirical Evaluation of Price Deals for Consumer Nondurables," *Journal of Marketing*, Vol. 45, no. 1 (Winter 1981), pp. 116–129.

BLATTBERG, ROBERT C., THOMAS BUESING, PETER PEACOCK, and SUBRATA K. SEN, "Identifying the Deal Prone Segment," *Journal of Marketing Research*, Vol. 15, no. 3 (August 1978), pp. 369–377.

BLATTBERG, ROBERT C., PETER PEACOCK, and SUBRATA K. SEN, "Purchasing Strategies Across Product Categories," *The Journal of Consumer Research*, Vol. 3, no. 3 (December 1976), pp. 143–154.

BLOCK, MARTIN, TAMARA S. BREZEN, and DON E. SCHULTZ, "An Exploratory Study of Pretesting Sales Promotion Executions Using Individual Differences Scaling and Preference Mapping," Working paper, Department of Advertising, Michigan State University, East Lansing (1985).

BOLEN, WILLIAM H., *Contemporary Retailing*, Englewood Cliffs, NJ: Prentice Hall, 1978.

BOWMAN, RUSSELL, "Sales Promotion: The 1985 Annual Report," *Marketing and Media Decisions* (July 1986), pp. 170–174.

BOWMAN, RUSSELL, *Couponing and Rebates: Profit on the Dotted Line*. New York: Chain Store Publishing, 1980.

BOX, GEORGE E. P., and GWILYM M. JENKINS, *Time Series: Analysis Forecasting and Control* (San Francisco: Holden-Day, 1976).

BOX, G. E. P., and G. C. TIAO, "Intervention Analysis with Applications to Economic and Environmental Problems," *Journal of the American Statistical Association*, Vol. 70, no. 349 (March 1975), pp. 70–79.

BRODIE, RODERICK, and CORNELIS A. DE KLUYVER, "Attraction Versus Linear and Multiplicative Market Share Models: An Empirical Evaluation," *Journal of Marketing Research*, Vol. 21, no. 2 (May 1984), pp. 194–201.

BROWN, ROBERT G., "Sales Response to Promotions and Advertising," *Journal of Advertising Research*, Vol. 14, no. 4 (August 1974), pp. 33–39.

BROWN, ROBERT G., "A Model for Measuring the Influence of Promotion on Inventory and Consumer Demand," *Journal of Marketing Research*, Vol. 10, no. 4 (November 1973), pp. 380–389.

BROWN, R. G., *Smoothing, Forecasting and Prediction*. Englewood Cliffs, NJ: Prentice Hall, 1963.

BUCKLIN, RANDOLPH E., "Pass-through of Manufacturer Trade Promotions by Grocery Retailers," Working paper, Stanford University, Stanford, CA (October 1987).

BURKE, MARIAN C., "The Dynamic Effects of Competitor Signals on Managers' Choice in an Iterated Prisoner's Dilemma," Working paper FSB 8801, Duke University, Durham, NC (January 1988a).

BURKE, MARIAN C., "Signaling and Screening: Tactics in Negotiations Across Organizations," Working paper FSB 8803, Duke University, Durham, NC (January 1988b).

BUSH, ROBERT R., and FREDRICK MOSTELLER, *Stochastic Models in Learning*. New York: John Wiley, 1955.

BÜYÜKKURT B. KEMAL, "Integration of Serially Sampled Price Information: Modeling and Some Findings," *Journal of Consumer Research,* Vol. 13, no. 3 (December 1986), pp. 357–373.

CAMPBELL, DONALD T., and JULIAN C. STANLEY, *Experimental and Quasi-Experimental Designs for Research*. Chicago: Rand McNally, 1963.

CATTIN, PHILIPPE, and DICK R. WITTINK, "Commercial Use of Conjoint Analysis: A Survey," *Journal of Marketing*, Vol. 46, no. 3 (Summer 1982), pp. 44–53.

CHAPMAN, RANDALL G., "Assessing the Profitability of Retailer Couponing with a Low-Cost Field Experiment," *Journal of Retailing*, Vol. 62, no. 1 (Spring 1986), pp. 19–40.

CHEVALIER, MICHEL, and RONALD C. CURHAN, "Retail Promotions as a Function of Trade Promotions: A Descriptive Analysis," *Sloan Management Review* (Fall 1976), pp. 19–32.

CHEVALIER, MICHEL, "Increase in Sales Due to In-Store Display," *Journal of Marketing Research*, Vol. 12, no. 4 (November 1975), pp. 426–431.

CHURCHILL, GILBERT A., JR., *Marketing Research: Methodological Foundations*, 4th ed. Chicago: Dryden, 1987.

CLARKE, DARRAL G., "Econometric Measurement of the Duration of Advertising Effects on Sales," *Journal of Marketing Research*, Vol. 13, no. 4 (November 1976), pp. 345–357.

COCHRAN, W. G., and G. M. COX, *Experimental Designs*, 2nd ed. New York: John Wiley, 1957.

COHEN, JOEL B., "Involvement and You: 1000 Great Ideas." In *Advances in Consumer Research*, Vol. 10, eds. Richard Bagozzi and Alice Tybout, pp. 325–328. Ann Arbor, MI: Association for Consumer Research, 1983.

COLE, CATHERINE, and GOUTAM CHAKRABORTY, "Laboratory Studies of Coupon Redemption Rates and Repeat Purchase Rates," in *AMA Educators' Proceedings*, eds. Susan P. Douglas, Vijay Mahajan, William M. Pride, Gary T. Ford, Peter Doyle, Michael R. Solomon, Mark I. Alpert, Gary L. Frazier, and James C. Anderson, pp. 51–54, Chicago: American Marketing Association, 1987.

COTTON, B. C., and EMERSON M. BABB, "Consumer Response to Promotional Deals," *Journal of Marketing*, Vol. 42, no. 3 (July 1978), pp. 109–113.

CUNNINGHAM, SCOTT M., "Perceived Risk as a Factor in Diffusion of New Product Information." In *Science, Technology and Marketing, Fall Conference Proceedings of the American Marketing Association*, ed. Raymond M. Haas, pp. 698–721. Chicago: American Marketing Association, 1966.

CURHAN, RONALD C., and ROBERT J. KOPP, "Factors Influencing Grocery Retailers' Support of Trade Promotions," Report No. 86-104. Cambridge, MA: Marketing Science Institute, July 1986.

CURRIM, IMRAN S., and LINDA G. SCHNEIDER, "A Taxonomy of Consumer Purchase Strategies in a Promotion Intensive Environment," Working paper, Amos Tuck School of Business Administration, Dartmouth College, Hanover, NH (August 1988).

CURRIM, IMRAN S., ROBERT J. MEYER, and NHAN T. LE, "Disaggregate Tree-Structured Modeling of Consumer Choice Data," *Journal of Marketing Research*, Vol. 25, no. 3 (August 1988), pp. 253–265.

D'ARCY MACMANUS MASIUS, "Couponing as a Marketing Tool: A Report on the Industry," St. Louis, MO: D'Arcy MacManus Masius, April 1984.

D'ARCY MASIUS BENTON and BOWLES, "Couponing as a Marketing Tool," St. Louis, MO: D'Arcy Masius Benton and Bowles, December 1988.

DAVIS, KENNETH R., *Marketing Management*, 4th ed. New York: John Wiley, 1981.

DEIGHTON, JOHN, "The Interaction of Advertising and Evidence," *The Journal of Consumer Research*, Vol. 11, no. 3 (December 1984), pp. 763–770.

DELLA BITTA, ALBERT J., and KENT B. MONROE, "The Influence of Adaptation Level on Selective Price Perceptions." In *Advances in Consumer Research*, Vol. I, eds. Scott Ward and Peter Wright, pp. 359–369. Association for Consumer Research, 1974.

DESHPANDE, ROHIT, WAYNE D. HOYER, and SCOTT JEFFRIES, "Low Involvement Decision Processes: The Importance of Choice Tactics." In *Marketing Theory: Philosophy of Science Perspectives*, eds. Ronald F. Bush and Shelby D. Hunt, pp. 155–158. Chicago: American Marketing Association, 1982.

DESLAURIERS, BRIAN C., and PETER B. EVERETT, "Effects of Intermittent and Continuous Token Reinforcement on Bus Ridership," *Journal of Applied Psychology,* Vol. 62, no. 4 (August 1977), pp. 369–375.

DHEBAR, ANIRUDH, SCOTT A. NESLIN, and JOHN A. QUELCH, "Developing Models for Planning Retailer Sales Promotions: An Application to Automobile Dealerships," *Journal of Retailing*, Vol. 63, no. 4 (Winter 1987), pp. 333–364.

DICKSON, PETER R., and ALAN G. SAWYER, "Point-of-Purchase Behavior and Price Perceptions of Supermarket Shoppers," Report No. 86-102. Cambridge, MA: Marketing Science Institute, June 1986.

DODSON, JOE A., ALICE M. TYBOUT, and BRIAN STERNTHAL, "Impact of Deals and Deal Retraction on Brand Switching," *Journal of Marketing Research*, Vol. 15, no. 1 (February 1978), pp. 72–81.

DOLAN, ROBERT J., "Quantity Discounts: Managerial Issues and Research Opportunities," *Marketing Science*, Vol. 6, no. 1 (Winter 1987), pp. 1–22.

DONNELLEY MARKETING, "10th Annual Survey of Promotional Practices." Stamford, CT: Donnelley Marketing, 1988.

DOOB, ANTHONY N., J. MERRILL CARLSMITH, JONATHAN L. FREEDMAN, THOMAS K. LANDAUER, and TOM SOLENG, JR., "Effect of Initial Selling Price on Subsequent Sales," *Journal of Personality and Social Psychology*, Vol. 11, no. 4 (1969), pp. 345–350.

DOYLE, PETER, and JOHN SAUNDERS, "The Lead Effect of Marketing Decisions,: *Journal of Marketing Research*, Vol. 22, no. 1 (February 1985), pp. 54–65.

DOYLE, PETER, and B. ZEKI GIDENGIL, "A Review of In-Store Experiments," *Journal of Retailing*, Vol. 53, no. 2 (Summer 1977), pp. 47–62.

EHRENBERG, A. S. C. *Repeat Buying*. Amsterdam: North-Holland, 1972.

EINHORN, HILLEL J., "The Use of Nonlinear, Noncompensatory Models in Decision Making," *Psychological Bulletin*, Vol. 73 (1970), pp. 211–230.

ENGEL, JAMES F., and ROGER D. BLACKWELL, *Consumer Behavior*, 4th ed. Chicago: Dryden, 1982.

ESKIN, GERALD J., and PENNY H. BARON, "Effects of Price and Advertising in Test-Market Experiments," *Journal of Marketing Research*, Vol. 14, no. 4 (November 1977), pp. 499–508.

ESTES, W. K., "Toward a Statistical Theory of Learning," *Psychological Review*, Vol. 57 (1950), pp. 94–107.

ETGAR, MICHAEL, and NARESH K. MALHOTRA, "Determinants of Price Dependency: Personal and Perceptual Factors," *Journal of Consumer Research*, Vol. 8, no. 2 (September 1981), pp. 217–222.

FADER, PETER S., and JOHN R. HAUSER, "Implicit Coalitions in a Generalized Prisoner's Dilemma," Working paper 88-017, Harvard Business School, Cambridge, MA (October 1987).

FADER, PETER S., and LEIGH MCALISTER, "A Promotion-Induced Choice Restriction Model of Consumer Choice," Wharton (University of Pennsylvania) Marketing Department Working paper 88-014 (rev. February 1989).

FADER, PETER S., and LEIGH MCALISTER, "A Note on the Relationship Between Promotion Sensitivity and Consumer-Specific Variables," Working paper 1663-85, Sloan School of Management, MIT, Cambridge, MA (June 1985).

FARLEY, JOHN U., and L. WINSTON RING, "An Empirical Test of the Howard-Sheth Model of Buyer Behavior," *Journal of Marketing Research*, Vol. 7, no. 4 (November 1970), pp. 427–438.

FARRIS, PAUL W., and JOHN A. QUELCH, *Advertising and Promotion Management: A Manager's Guide to Theory and Practice*. Radner, PA: Chilton, 1983.

FESTINGER, LEON, and N. MACCOBY, "On Resistance to Persuasive Communications," *Journal of Abnormal and Social Psychology*, Vol. 68 (1964), pp. 359–366.

FESTINGER, LEON, *A Theory of Cognitive Dissonance*. New York: Harper & Row, 1957.

FISHBEIN, MARTIN, and ICEK AJZEN, *Belief, Attitude, Intention, and Behavior: An Introduction to Theory and Research*. Reading, MA: Addison-Wesley, 1975.

FOMBY, THOMAS B., R. CARTER HILL, and STANLEY R. JOHNSON, *Advanced Econometric Methods*. New York: Springer-Verlag, 1984.

FOOD MARKETING INSTITUTE, "Trends: 1987 Consumer Attitudes and the Supermarket." Washington, DC: Food Marketing Institute, 1987.

FRANK, RONALD E., "Brand Choice as a Probabilistic Process," *Journal of Business*, Vol. 35, (1962), pp. 43–56.

FRASER, CYNTHIA, "Customer Responses to Promotions by Established Brands: Theories, Methodology, and Managerial Implications," paper presented at Marketing Science Institute Conference, Measuring and Evaluating Sales Promotion to the Trade and to Consumers, October 3–4, 1985, Cambridge, MA.

GABOR, ANDRE, and CLIVE GRANGER, "On the Price Consciousness of Consumers," *Applied Statistics*, Vol. 10 (November 1961), pp. 170–188.

GALLANT, A. R., and J. J. GOEBEL, "Nonlinear Regression with Autoregressive Errors," *Journal of the American Statistical Association*, Vol. 71 (1976), pp. 961–967.

GARDNER, MERYL, P., and ROGER A. STRANG, "Consumer Response to Promotions: Some New Perspectives." In *Advances in Consumer Research*, Vol. 11, ed. Thomas Kinnear, pp. 420–425. Provo, UT: Association for Consumer Research, 1984.

GATIGNON, HUBERT, "Competition as a Moderator of the Effect of Advertising on Sales," *Journal of Marketing Research*, Vol. 21, no. 4 (November 1984), pp. 387–398.

GHOSH, AVIJIT, SCOTT A. NESLIN, and ROBERT W. SHOEMAKER, "A Comparison of Market Share Models and Estimation Procedures," *Journal of Marketing Research*, Vol. 21, no. 2 (May 1984), pp. 202–210.

GLOEDE, WILLIAM F., "Postal Probe Clips $1M-a-Week Coupon Scam," *Advertising Age*, March 31, 1986, p. 10.

GORN, JERALD J., "The Effects of Music in Advertising on Choice Behavior: A Classical Conditioning Approach," *Journal of Consumer Research*, Vol. 9, no. 3 (Winter 1982), pp. 94–101.

GREEN, PAUL E., FRANK J. CARMONE, and DAVID P. WACHSPRESS, "On the Analysis of Qualitative Data in Marketing Research," *Journal of Marketing Research*, Vol. 14, no. 1 (February 1977), pp. 52–59.

GREEN, PAUL E., "On the Design of Choice Experiments Involving Multifactor Alternatives," *Journal of Consumer Research*, Vol. 1, no. 2 (September 1974), pp. 61–68.

GRIFFITH, DAVID E., and ROLAND T. RUST, "Effective Pricing Strategies Under Varying Expectations of Competitor Behavior," Working paper, Department of Marketing, University of Texas at Austin (n.d.).

GROVER, RAJIV, and VITHALA R. RAO, "Inferring Competitive Market Structure Based on a Model of Interpurchase Intervals," Working paper, Cornell University, Ithaca, NY (June 1985).

GUADAGNI, PETER M., and JOHN D. C. LITTLE, "A Logit Model of Brand Choice Calibrated on Scanner Data," *Marketing Science*, Vol. 2, no. 3 (Summer 1983), pp. 203–238.

GUPTA, SUNIL, "Impact of Sales Promotions on When, What, and How Much to Buy," *Journal of Marketing Research,* Vol. 25, no. 4 (November, 1988) pp. 342–355.

GUPTA, SUNIL, and PETER C. WILTON, "Combination of Forecasts: An Extension," *Management Science*, Vol. 33, no. 3 (March 1987), pp. 356–372.

HANKE, JOHN E., and ARTHUR G. REITSCH, *Business Forecasting*, 3rd ed. Boston, Allyn and Bacon, 1989.

HASTORF, ALBERT H., DAVID J. SCHNEIDER, and JUDITH POLEFKA, *Person Perception*, Reading, MA: Addison-Wesley Publishing Company, 1970.

HAUSER, JOHN R., and STEVEN M. SHUGAN, "Defensive Marketing Strategies," *Marketing Science*, Vol. 2, no. 4 (Fall 1983), pp. 319–360.

HAUSER, JOHN R., and GLEN L. URBAN, "Assessment of Attribute Importances and Consumer Utility Functions: Von Neumann-Morgenstern Theory Applied to Consumer Behavior," *Journal of Consumer Research*, Vol. 5, no. 4 (March 1979), pp. 251–262.

HECKMAN, J. J., "The Common Structure of Statistical Models of Truncation," *Annals of Economic and Social Measurement*, Vol. 5 (1976), pp. 475–492.

HEE, JUDITH ANN, "Determining Manufacturers' Couponing Strategies," unpublished masters thesis, Sloan School of Management, MIT, Cambridge, MA (June 1981).

HELMER, RICHARD M., and JOHNY K. JOHANSSON, "An Exposition of the Box-Jenkins Transfer Function Analysis with an Application to the Advertising-Sales Relationship," *Journal of Marketing Research*, Vol. 14, no. 2 (May 1977), pp. 227–239.

HELSON, HARRY, *Adaptation-Level Theory*. New York: Harper & Row, 1964.

HENDERSON, CAROLINE M., "Modeling the Coupon Redemption Decision." In *Advances in Consumer Research*, Vol. XII, eds. Elizabeth C. Hirschman and Morris B. Holbrook, pp. 138–143. Provo, UT: Association for Consumer Research, 1985.

HENDERSON, CAROLINE M., "Sales Promotion Segmentation: Refining the Deal-Proneness Construct," Working paper, The Amos Tuck School of Business Administration, Dartmouth College, Hanover, NH (September 1984).

HERNANDEZ, SIGFREDO A., "An Exploratory Study of Coupon Use in Puerto Rico: Cultural vs. Institutional Barriers to Coupon Use," *Journal of Advertising Research*, Vol. 28, no. 5 (October/November 1988), pp. 40–46.

HILGARD, ERNEST R., and GORDON H. BOWER, *Theories of Learning*, 4th ed. Englewood Cliffs, NJ: Prentice Hall, 1975.

HOLBROOK, MORRIS B., "Integrating Compositional and Decompositional Analyses to Represent the Intervening Role of Perceptions in Evaluative Judgments," *Journal of Marketing Research*, Vol. 18, no. 1 (February 1981), pp. 13–28.

HOPKINS, PATRICIA M., and LEONARD J. PARSONS, "The Impact of a Cents-Off Direct Mail Coupon in Repositioning a Product," Working paper, Georgia Institute of Technology, College of Management, Atlanta, GA (rev. December 1984).

HOUSTON, DOUGLAS A., and JOHN S. HOWE, "Reply to 'An Economic Rationale for Couponing: A Comment,'" *Quarterly Journal of Business and Economics*, Vol. 25 (Fall 1986), pp. 75–76.

HOUSTON, DOUGLAS A., and JOHN S. HOWE, "An Economic Rationale for Couponing," *Quarterly Journal of Business and Economics*, Vol. 24 (Spring 1985), pp. 37–50.

HOWARD, JOHN A., "Learning and Consumer Behavior." In *Perspectives in Consumer Behavior*, 3rd ed., eds., Harold H. Kassarjian and Thomas S. Robertson, pp. 96–104. Glenview, IL: Scott, Foresman, 1981.

HOWARD, JOHN A., and JAGDISH N. SHETH, *The Theory of Buyer Behavior*. New York: John Wiley, 1969.

HULL, CLARK L., *Principles of Behavior*. New York: Appleton-Century-Crofts, 1943.

IMAN, RONALD L., and W. J. CONOVER, *Modern Business Statistics*. New York: John Wiley, 1983.

IRONS, KARL W., JOHN D. C. LITTLE, and ROBERT L. KLEIN, "Determinants of Coupon Effectiveness." In *Proceedings of the 1983 ORSA/TIMS Marketing Science Conference*, ed. Fred Zufruden, pp. 157–164, University of Southern California, Los Angeles, CA (1983).

JACOBY, JACOB, and ROBERT W. CHESTNUT, *Brand Loyalty, Measurement Management*. New York: John Wiley, 1978.

JENKINS, GWILYM M., *Practical Experiences with Modelling and Forecasting Time Series*. Jersey, Channel Islands, U.K.: Jenkins and Partners, 1979.

JENNRICH, ROBERT I., and SAMUEL D. OMAN, "How Much Does Stein Estimation Help in Multiple Linear Regression," *Technometrics*, Vol. 28, no. 2 (May 1986), pp. 113–121.

JEULAND, ABEL P., and CHARKRAVARTHI NARASIMHAN, "Dealing-Temporary Price Cuts-by Seller as a Buyer Discrimination Mechanism," *Journal of Business*, Vol. 58, no. 3 (1985), pp. 295–308.

JEULAND, ABEL P., FRANK M. BASS, and GORDON P. WRIGHT, "A Multibrand Stochastic Model Compounding Heterogeneous Erlang Timing and Multinomial Choice Process," *Operations Research*, no. 28 (March–April 1980), pp. 225–277.

JOHNSON, TOD, "The Myth of Declining Brand Loyalty," *Journal of Advertising Research*, Vol. 24, no. 1 (February–March 1984), pp. 9–17.

JOHNSTON, J., *Econometric Methods*, 2nd ed. New York: McGraw-Hill, 1972.

JOLSON, MARVIN A., JOSHUA L. WIENER, and RICHARD B. ROSECKY, "Correlates of Rebate Proneness," *Journal of Advertising Research*, Vol. 27, no. 1 (February–March 1987), pp. 33–44.

JONES, EDWARD E., and KEITH E. DAVIS, "From Acts to Dispositions: The Attribution Process in Person Perception." In *Advances in Experimental Social Psychology*, Vol. 2, ed. L. Berkowitz. New York: Academic Press, 1965.

JONES, J. MORGAN, and JANE T. LANDWEHR, "Removing Heterogeneity Bias from Logit Model Estimation," *Marketing Science*, Vol. 7, no. 1 (Winter 1988), pp. 41–59.

JONES, J. MORGAN, and FRED S. ZUFRYDEN, "An Approach for Assessing Demographic and Price Influences on Brand Purchase Behavior," *Journal of Marketing*, Vol. 46, no. 1 (Winter 1982), pp. 36–46.

JONES, J. MORGAN, and FRED S. ZUFRYDEN, "Adding Explanatory Variables to a Consumer Purchase Behavior Model: An Exploratory Study," *Journal of Marketing Research*, Vol. 17, no. 3 (August 1980), pp. 323–334.

JONES, J. MORGAN, and FRED S. ZUFRYDEN, "Relating Deal Purchases and Consumer Characteristics to Repeat Purchase Probability," *Journal of the Market Research Society*, Vol. 23, no. 2 (1981), pp. 84–99.

KAHN, BARBARA E., and THERESE A. LOUIE, "The Effects of Price Promotions on Brand Choice Behavior," Working paper, Anderson Graduate School of Management, U.C.L.A., Los Angeles, CA (August 1988).

KAHNEMAN, DANIEL, and AMOS TVERSKY, "Prospect Theory: An Analysis of Decision Under Risk," *Econometrica*, Vol. 47 (March 1979), pp. 263–291.

KALWANI, MANOHAR U., HEIKKI J. RINNE, YOSHI SUGITA, and CHI-KIN YIM, "A Reference Price Based Model of Consumer Brand Choice," Working paper 935, Krannert Graduate School of Management, Purdue University, West Lafayette, IN (April 1988).

KALWANI, MANOHAR U., and ALVIN J. SILK, "On the Reliability and Predictive Validity of Purchase Intention Measures," *Marketing Science,* Vol 1, No. 3 (Summer 1982), pp. 243–286.

KAMEN, JOSEPH, and ROBERT TOMAN, "Psychophysics of Prices," *Journal of Marketing Research*, Vol. 8, no. 1 (February 1970), pp. 252–257.

KASSARJIAN, HAROLD H., "Presidential Address." In *Advances in Consumer Research*, Vol. 5, ed. H. Keith Hunt, pp. xiii–xiv. Ann Arbor, MI: Association for Consumer Research, 1978.

KELLER, F. S., and W. N. SCHOENFELD, *Principles of Psychology*. New York: Appleton-Century-Crofts, 1950.

KELLEY, HAROLD, "Attribution Theory in Social Psychology," In *Nebraska Symposium on Motivation*, ed. David Levine. Lincoln: University of Nebraska Press, 1967.

KEON, JOHN, "The Bargain Value Model and a Comparison of Managerial Implications with the Linear Learning Model," *Management Science*, Vol. 26, no. 11 (November 1980), pp. 1117–1130.

KEON, JOHN W., and JUDY BAYER, "An Expert Approach to Promotion Management," *Journal of Advertising Research*, Vol. 26 (June–July 1986), pp. 19–26.

KLEIN, ROBERT L., "How to Use Research to Make Better Sales Promotion Marketing Decisions." In *Handbook of Sales Promotion*, ed. Stanley Ulanoff, pp. 457–466. New York: McGraw-Hill, 1985.

KLEIN, ROBERT L., "Using Supermarket Scanner Panels to Measure the Effectiveness of Coupon Promotions." In *Marketing: Measurement and Analysis, 1981, Proceedings of the Third ORSA/TIMS Special Interest Conference on Market Measurement and Analysis*, ed. John W. Keon, pp. 118–124. Providence, RI: The Institute of Management Sciences, 1981.

KOTLER PHILIP, *Marketing Management: Analysis, Planning, Implementation, and Control*, 6th ed. Englewood Cliffs, NJ: Prentice Hall, 1988.

KRISHNAMURTHI, LAKSHMAN, and ARVIND RANGASWAMY, "The Equity Estimator for Marketing Research," *Marketing Science*, Vol. 6, no. 4 (Fall 1987), pp. 336–357.

KRISHNAMURTHI, LAKSHMAN, and S. P. RAJ, "A Model of Brand Choice and Purchase Quantity Price Sensitivities," *Marketing Science*, Vol. 7, no. 1 (Winter 1988), pp. 1–20.

KUEHN, A. A. "Consumer Brand Choice—A Learning Process?" *Journal of Advertising Research*, Vol. 2 (1962), pp. 10–17.

KUEHN, ALFRED A., and ALBERT C. ROHLOFF, "Consumer Response to Promotions." In *Promotional Decisions Using Mathematical Models*, ed. Patrick J. Robinson, pp. 45–148. Boston: Allyn & Bacon, 1967.

KUMAR, V., and ROBERT P. LEONE, "Measuring the Effect of Retail Store Promotions on Brand and Store Substitution," *Journal of Marketing Research*, Vol. 25, no. 2 (May 1988), pp. 178–185.

LACROIX, SUMNER J., "Marketing, Price Discrimination, and Welfare: Reply," *Southern Economic Journal*, Vol. 49, no. 3 (January 1983).

LAL, RAJIV, "A Theory of Manufacturer Trade Deals and Retail Price Promotions," Working paper, Stanford University, Stanford, CA (May 1988).

LANCASTER, KELVIN, *Consumer Demand*. New York: Columbia University Press, 1971.

LAPIN, LAWRENCE L., *Statistics for Modern Business Decisions*, 4th ed. New York: Harcourt Brace Jovanovich, 1987.

LARRECHE, JEAN-CLAUDE, and V. SRINIVASAN, "STRATPORT: A Model for the Evaluation and Formulation of Business Portfolio Strategies," *Management Science*, Vol. 28, no. 9 (September 1982), pp. 979–1001.

LATTIN, JAMES M., "The Impact of Store Brands on the Nature of Manufacturer's Trade Deals and Retail Price Promotion," Working paper, Stanford University, Stanford, CA (January 1988).

LATTIN, JAMES M., "A Model of Balanced Choice," *Marketing Science*, Vol. 6, no. 1 (Winter 1987), pp. 48–65.

LATTIN, JAMES M., "Modeling Competitive Infringement on Brand Share," Working paper 855, Graduate School of Business, Stanford University, Stanford, CA (rev. November 1985).

LAWRENCE, M. J., R. H. EDMUNDSON, and M. J. O'CONNOR, "The Accuracy of Combining Judgmental and Statistical Forecasts," *Management Science*, Vol. 32, no. 12 (December 1986), pp. 1521–1532.

LAZEAR, EDWARD P., "Retail Pricing and Clearance Sales," *The American Economic Review*, Vol. 76, no. 1 (March 1986), pp. 14–32.

LEEFLANG, PETER S. H., and JAN C. REUYL, "On the Predictive Power of Market Share Attraction Models," *Journal of Marketing Research*, Vol. 21, no. 2 (May 1984), pp. 211–215.

LEHMANN, DONALD R., *Market Research and Analysis*, 2nd ed. Homewood, IL: Richard D. Irwin, 1985.

LEMONT, FRED L., "Room at the Top in Promotion," *Advertising Age*, March 23, 1981, p. 61.

LEONE, ROBERT P., "Forecasting The Effect of an Environmental Change on Market Performance: An Intervention Time-Series Approach," *International Journal of Forecasting*, Vol. 3 (1987), pp. 463–478.

LEUTHESSER, LANCE, "Defining, Measuring, and Managing Brand Equity," Marketing Science Institute, Report No. 88-104, May, 1988.

LEVEDAHL, WILLIAM J., "Coupon Redeemers: Are They Better Shoppers?" *Journal of Consumer Affairs*, Vol. 22, no. 2 (1988), pp. 264–283.

LEVEDAHL, WILLIAM J., "Profit Maximizing Pricing of Cents Off Coupons: Promotion or Price Discrimination?" *Quarterly Journal of Business and Economics* (Fall 1986), pp. 56–70.

LEVEDAHL, WILLIAM J., "Marketing, Price Discrimination, and Welfare: Comment," *Southern Economic Journal* (January 1984), pp. 886–891.

LEVEDAHL, W. J., "The Pricing of Cents-Off Coupons: Multipart Pricing or Price Discrimination?" Faculty working papers 37, Departments of Economics and Business, North Carolina State University, Raleigh (1983).

LEVY, MICHAEL, JOHN WEBSTER, and ROGER A. KERIN, "Formulating Push Marketing Strategies: A Method and Application," *Journal of Marketing*, Vol. 47, no. 1 (Winter 1983), pp. 25–34.

LIEFELD, JOHN, and LOUISE A. HESLOP, "Reference Prices and Deception in Newspaper Advertising," *Journal of Consumer Research*, Vol. 11, no. 4 (March 1985), pp. 868–876.

LILIEN, GARY L., "A Modified Linear Learning Model of Buyer Behavior," *Management Science*, Vol. 20, no. 3 (March 1974a), pp. 279–285.

LILIEN GARY L., "An Application of a Modified Linear Learning Model of Buyer Behavior," *Journal of Marketing Research*, Vol. 11, no. 3 (August 1974b), pp. 279–285.

LILIEN, GARY L., and PHILIP KOTLER, *Marketing Decision Making: A Model-Building Approach*. New York: Harper & Row, 1983.

LITTLE, JOHN D. C., "Decision Support Systems for Marketing Managers," *Journal of Marketing*, Vol. 43, no. 3 (Summer 1979), pp. 9–26.

LITTLE, JOHN D. C., "BRANDAID: A Marketing-Mix Model. Part 1: Structure; Part II: Implementation," *Operations Research*, Vol. 23, no. 4 (July–August 1975), pp. 628–673.

LITTLE, JOHN D. C., "Models and Managers: The Concept of a Decision Calculus," *Management Science*, Vol. 16, no. 8 (April 1970), pp. B466–B485.

LITVACK, DAVID S., ROGER J. CALANTONE, and PAUL R. WARSHAW, "An Examination of Short-Term Retail Grocery Price Effects," *Journal of Retailing*, Vol. 61, no. 3 (Fall 1985), pp. 9–26.

LODISH, LEONARD M., *The Advertising and Promotion Challenge: Vaguely Right or Precisely Wrong?* New York: Oxford University Press, 1986.

LODISH, LEONARD, "A Marketing Decision Support System for Retailers," *Marketing Science*, Vol. 1, no. 1 (Winter 1982), pp. 31–56.

LODISH, LEONARD M., and DAVID J. REIBSTEIN, "Keeping Informed," *Harvard Business Review* (January–February 1986), pp. 168–182.

LOVELOCK, CHRISTOPHER H., and JOHN A. QUELCH, "Consumer Promotions in Service Marketing," *Business Horizons* (May –June 1983), pp. 66–75.

LUCE, R. D., *Individual Choice Behavior: A Theoretical Analysis*. New York: John Wiley, 1959.

MADDALA, G. S., *Limited-Dependent and Qualitative Variables in Econometrics*. New York: Cambridge University Press, 1983.

MAIER, JOSEPH S., "The Big Event and the Sales Promotion Campaign." In *Handbook of Sales Promotion*, ed. Stanley M. Ulanoff, pp. 429–442. New York: McGraw-Hill, 1985.

MAKRIDAKIS, SPYROS, STEVEN C. WHEELWRIGHT, and VICTOR E. McGEE, *Forecasting: Methods and Applications*, 2nd ed. New York: John Wiley, 1983.

MAKRIDAKIS, SPYROS, and STEVEN C. WHEELWRIGHT, *The Handbook of Forecasting: A Manager's Guide*. New York: John Wiley, 1982.

MANSFIELD, EDWIN, *Statistics for Business and Economics: Methods and Applications*, 2nd ed. New York: W. W. Norton, 1983.

MANUFACTURERS COUPON CONTROL CENTER, "Coupon Distribution and Redemption Patterns," Wilton, CT: Manufacturers Coupon Control Center, 1989a.

MANUFACTURERS COUPON CONTROL CENTER, "Special Release: Household Size and Coupon Use," Wilton, CT: Manufacturers Coupon Control Center, 1989b.

MANUFACTURERS COUPON CONTROL CENTER, *Coupon Distribution and Redemption Patterns*. Wilton, CT: Manufacturers Coupon Control Center, 1988a.

MANUFACTURERS COUPON CONTROL CENTER, "Speed of Redemption at Retail Level," Wilton, CT: Manufacturers Coupon Control Center, 1988b.

MANUFACTURERS COUPON CONTROL CENTER, "The Scanner," Vol. 2, Issue 1, Wilton, CT: Manufacturers Coupon Control Center, 1987.

MANUFACTURERS COUPON CONTROL CENTER, *Coupon Distribution and Redemption Patterns*. Wilton, CT: Manufacturers Coupon Control Center, 1986.

Marketing News, "Retail Coupon Cheats Are Tracked Down with Assistance from Computer Records," May 24, 1985, p. 2.

MASSY, WILLIAM F., and RONALD E. FRANK, "Short Term Price and Dealing Effects in Selected Market Segments," *Journal of Marketing Research*, Vol. 2, no. 2 (May 1965), pp. 171–185.

MASSY, WILLIAM F., DAVID B. MONTGOMERY, and DONALD G. MORRISON, *Stochastic Models of Buying Behavior*. Cambridge, MA: MIT Press, 1970.

MATOSIAN, JACKLINE, "Effectiveness of Different Coupon Delivery Methods in Building Mass Transit Ridership," *Journal of Advertising Research*, Vol. 22, no. 3 (June–July 1982), pp. 54–59.

MAZURSKY, DAVID, PRISCILLA LABARBERA, and AL AIELLO, "Why Satisfied Consumers Switch Brands: The Effects of Experience and Intrinsic and Extrinsic Incentives on Brand Switching Disposition," Working paper, School of Business, New York University (1984).

MCALISTER, LEIGH, "The Impact of Price Promotions on a Brand's Market Share, Sales Pattern, and Profitability," Report No. 86-110, Cambridge, MA: Marketing Science Institute, December 1986.

MCALISTER, LEIGH, "A Theory of Consumer Promotions: The Model," Working paper 1457-83, Sloan School of Business, MIT, Cambridge, MA (July 1983).

MCCANN, JOHN M., "Market Segment Response to the Marketing Decision Variables," *Journal of Marketing Research*, Vol. 11, no. 4 (November 1974), pp. 399–412.

MCCANN, JOHN M., *The Marketing Workbench: Using Computers for Better Performance.* Homewood, IL: Dow Jones-Irwin, 1986.

MCFADDEN, D., "Econometric Models of Probabilistic Choice." In *Structural Analysis of Discrete Data: With Econometric Applications*, eds. C. Manski and D. McFadden. Cambridge, MA: MIT Press, 1981.

MCFADDEN, D., "Modelling the Choice of Residential Location." In *Spacial Interaction Theory and Residential Location*, eds. A. Karlquist et al., pp. 75–96. Amsterdam: North Holland, 1978.

MCFADDEN, D., "Conditional Logit Analysis of Qualitative Choice Behavior." In P. Zarembka (ed.), *Frontiers in Econometrics*. New York: Academic Press, 1973.

MCKINNON, GARY F., J. PATRICK KELLY, and E. DOYLE ROBISON, "Sales Effects of Point-of-Purchase In-Store Signing," *Journal of Retailing*, Vol. 57, no. 2 (Summer 1981), pp. 49–63.

MIZERSKI, RICHARD W., LINDA L. GOLDEN, and JEROME B. KERNAN, "The Attribution Process in Consumer Decision Making," *Journal of Consumer Research*, Vol. 6, no. 2 (September 1979), pp. 123–140.

MONROE, KENT B., "Buyers' Subjective Perceptions of Price," *Journal of Marketing Research*, Vol. 10, no. 1 (February 1973), pp. 70–80.

MONROE, KENT B., ALBERT J. DELLA BITTA, and SUSAN DOWNEY, "Contextual Influences on Subjective Price Perceptions," *Journal of Business Research*, Vol. 5 (December 1977), pp. 277–291.

MONTGOMERY, DOUGLAS C., and GINNER WEATHERBY, "Modeling and Forecasting Time Series Using Transfer Function and Intervention Methods," *AIIE Transactions* (December 1980), pp. 289–308.

MONTGOMERY, DAVID B., and ALVIN J. SILK, "Estimating Dynamic Effects of Market Communications Expenditures," *Management Science*, Vol. 18, no. 10 (June 1972), pp. 485–501.

MONTGOMERY, DAVID B., "Consumer Characteristics Associated with Dealing: An Empirical Example," *Journal of Marketing Research*, Vol. 8, no. 1 (February 1971), pp. 118–120.

MOODY, MARK J., "The Impact of Manufacturer Coupons on Consumer Buying and Manufacturer Profits," Working paper, Cincinnati, Ohio: SAMI/Burke, Inc., September, 1988.

MOODY, MARK J., "Demographic Analysis of Coupon Usage Tendencies," Technical report 87-5-1-MJM, Burke Marketing Services, Cincinnati, OH (1987a).

MOODY, MARK J., "Are 'Early' Coupon Redeemers Better than 'Late' Coupon Redeemers? or When Does the Incremental Volume of a Coupon Occur?" Technical report 87-5-2-MJM, Burke Marketing Services, Cincinnati, OH (1987b).

MOORE, WILLIAM L., and RUSSEL S. WINER, "An Experiment to Determine the Effects of Package Size on Consumption," Working paper, Graduate School of Business, Columbia University, New York (1978).

MORIARTY, MARK, "Retail Promotional Effects on Intra- and Interbrand Sales Performance," *Journal of Retailing*, Vol. 61, no. 3 (Fall 1985), pp. 27–48.

MORIARTY, MARK, "Feature Advertising-Price Interaction Effects in the Retail Environment," *Journal of Retailing*, Vol. 59, no. 2 (Summer 1983), pp. 80–98.

MORRISON, DONALD G., "Purchase Intentions and Purchase Behavior," *Journal of Marketing*, Vol. 42, no. 2 (Spring 1979), pp. 65–74.

NAERT, PHILIPPE A., and MARCEL WEVERBERGH, "Market Share Specification, Estimation, and Validation: Toward Reconciling Seemingly Divergent Views," *Journal of Marketing Research*, Vol. 22, no. 4 (November 1985), pp. 453–461.

NAERT, PHILIPPE A., and MARCEL WEVERBERGH, "On the Prediction Power of Market Share Attraction Models," *Journal of Marketing Research*, Vol. 18, no. 2 (May 1981), pp. 146–153.

NAGLE, THOMAS T., *The Strategy and Tactics of Pricing.* Englewood Cliffs, NJ: Prentice Hall, 1987.

NAKANISHI, MASAO, "Advertising and Promotion Effects on Consumer Response to New Products," *Journal of Marketing Research*, Vol. 10, no. 3 (August 1973), pp. 242–249.

NAKANISHI, MASAO, and LEE G. COOPER, "Parameter Estimation for a Multiplicative Competitve Interaction Model: Least Squares Approach," *Journal of Marketing Research*, Vol. 11, no. 3 (August 1974), pp. 301–311.

NAKANISHI, MASAO, and LEE G. COOPER, "Simplified Estimation Procedures for MCI Models," *Marketing Science*, Vol. 1, no. 3 (Summer 1982), pp. 314–322.

NARASIMHAN, CHAKRAVARTHI, "Competitive Promotional Strategies," *Journal of Business*, Vol. 61, no. 4 (October 1988), pp. 427–449.

NARASIMHAN, CHAKRAVARTHI, "A Price Discrimination Theory of Coupons," *Marketing Science*, Vol. 3, no. 2 (Spring 1984a), pp. 128–146.

NARASIMHAN, CHAKRAVARTHI, "Tobit Analysis of Coupon Usage," Proceedings of the American Statistical Association, Economic Statistics Section, 1984b, pp. 227–242.

NARASIMHAN, CHAKRAVARTHI, and RAM C. RAO, "Models of Price Promotion Under Endogenous Search," Working paper, Graduate School of Business, University of Chicago (April 1984).

NATIONAL RETAIL MERCHANTS ASSOCIATION, "Financial and Operating Results of Department and Specialty Stores in 1986." New York: National Retail Merchants Association, 1987.

NATIONAL RETAIL MERCHANTS ASSOCIATION, "Financial and Operating Results of Department and Specialty Stores of 1971." New York: National Retail Merchants Association, 1972.

NELSON, CHARLES R., *Applied Time Series Analysis for Managerial Forecasting.* San Francisco, CA: Holden-Day, 1973.

NESLIN, SCOTT A., "A Market Response Model for Coupon Promotions," Working paper, Amos Tuck School of Business Administration, Dartmouth College, Hanover, NH (May 1989).

NESLIN, SCOTT A., "Anticipating the Profitability of Coupon Promotions Using a Logit Choice Model," Working paper, Sloan School of Management, MIT, Cambridge, MA (January 1984).

NESLIN, SCOTT A., "Designing New Outpatient Health Services: Linking Service Features to Subjective Consumer Perceptions," *Journal of Health Care Marketing*, Vol. 3, no. 3 (Summer 1983), pp. 8–21.

NESLIN, SCOTT A., "Linking Product Features to Perceptions: Self-Stated Versus Statistically Revealed Importance Weights," *Journal of Marketing Research*, Vol. 18, no. 1 (February 1981), pp. 80–86.

NESLIN, SCOTT A., and ROBERT W. SHOEMAKER, "An Alternative Explanation for Lower Repeat Rates After Promotion Purchases," *Journal of Marketing Research*, Vol. 26, no. 2 (May 1989), pp. 205–213.

NESLIN, SCOTT A., and DARRAL G. CLARKE, "Relating the Brand Use Profile of Coupon Redeemers to Brand and Coupon Characteristics," *Journal of Advertising Research*, Vol. 27, no. 1 (February–March 1987), pp. 23–32.

NESLIN, SCOTT A., CAROLINE HENDERSON, and JOHN QUELCH, "Consumer Promotions and the Acceleration of Product Purchases," *Marketing Science*, Vol. 4, no. 2 (Spring 1985), pp. 147–165.

NESLIN, SCOTT A., and ROBERT W. SHOEMAKER, "A Model for Evaluating the Profitability of Coupon Promotions," *Marketing Science*, Vol. 2, no. 4 (Fall 1983a), pp. 361–388.

NESLIN, SCOTT A., and ROBERT W. SHOEMAKER, "Using a Natural Experiment to Estimate Price Elasticity: The 1974 Sugar Shortage and the Ready-to-Eat Cereal Market," *Journal of Marketing*, Vol. 47, no. 1 (Winter 1983b), pp. 44–57.

NICOSIA, FRANCESCO M., *Consumer Decision Processes: Marketing and Advertising Implications*. Englewood Cliffs, NJ: Prentice Hall, 1966.

NIELSEN CLEARING HOUSE REPORTER, "Coupon Distribution and Redemption Patterns by Product Group," No. 2, pp. 2–9. Chicago: A. C. Nielsen Company, 1984.

NIELSEN CLEARING HOUSE, "What Consumers Think of Coupons: A Study of Consumer Actions and Reactions." Chicago: A. C. Nielsen Company, 1985.

NIELSEN CLEARING HOUSE, "Coupon Distribution and Redemption Patterns." Chicago: A. C. Nielsen Company, 1984.

NIELSEN CLEARING HOUSE, "A Product Manager's Guide to Effective Couponing." Chicago: A. C. Nielsen Company, 1982.

Nielsen Researcher, "Analyzing Promotions: The Free-Standing Insert Coupon," no. 4, pp. 16–20. Chicago: A. C. Nielsen Company, 1982.

NORD, WALTER R., and J. PAUL PETER, "A Behavior Modification Perspective on Marketing," *Journal of Marketing*, Vol. 44, no. 2 (Spring 1980), pp. 36–47.

NYSTROM, HARRY, HANS TAMSONS, and TOBER THAMS, "An Experiment in Price Generalization and Discrimination," *Journal of Marketing Research*, Vol. 12, no. 2 (May 1975), pp. 177–181.

OLSON, CHARLES L., and MARIO J. PICCONI, *Statistics for Business Decision Making*. Glenview, IL: Scott, Foresman, 1983.

OMAN, SAMUEL D., "Shrinking Towards Subspaces in Multiple Linear Regression," *Technometrics*, Vol. 24, no. 4 (November 1982), pp. 307–311.

ORTMEYER, GWENDOLYN, JAMES LATTIN, and DAVID MONTGOMERY, "Routinized Choice Behavior, Brand Commitment, and Consumer Response to Promotions," Stanford Business School Research Paper Series, 935 (March 1987).

PARSONS, LEONARD J., and RANDALL L. SCHULTZ, *Marketing Models and Econometric Research*. New York: American Elsevier, 1976.

PASHIGIAN, B. PETER, "Demand Uncertainty and Sales: A Study of Fashion and Markdown Pricing," Working paper, University of Chicago (January 1987).

PEDRICK, JAMES H., "Modeling Deal Effects Using Scanner Panel Data," Working paper, Graduate School of Business, University of Chicago (April 1987).

PETER, J. PAUL, and WALTER R. NORD, "A Clarification and Extension of Operant Conditioning Principles in Marketing," *Journal of Marketing*, Vol. 46, no. 3 (Summer 1982), pp. 102–107.

PETTY, RICHARD E., GARY L. WELLS, and TIMOTHY C. BROCK, "Distraction Can Enhance or Reduce Yielding to Propaganda: Thought Disruption Versus Effort Justification," *Journal of Personality and Social Psychology*, Vol. 34, no. 5 (1976), pp. 874–884.

PINDYCK, ROBERT S., and DANIEL L. RUBINFELD, *Econometric Models and Economic Forecasts*, 2nd ed. New York: McGraw-Hill, 1981.

PLANE, DONALD R., and EDWARD B. OPPERMANN, *Business and Economic Statistics*. Plano, TX: Business Publications, 1981.

PORTER, MICHAEL E. *Competitive Strategy*. New York: The Free Press, 1980.

QUELCH, JOHN A., "Influences on Promotion Design," Working paper, Harvard Business School, Cambridge, MA (March 1987).

QUELCH, JOHN A., "Trade Promotion by Grocery Products Manufacturing: A Managerial Perspective," Report No. 82-106 Marketing Science Institute, Cambridge, MA, August 1982.

QUELCH JOHN A., SCOTT A. NESLIN, and LOIS B. OLSON, "Opportunities and Risks of Durable Goods Promotion," *Sloan Management Review*, Vol. 28, no. 2 (Winter 1987), pp. 27–38.

QUELCH, JOHN A., CHERI T. MARSHALL, and DAE R. CHANG, "Structural Determinants of Ratios of Promotion and Advertising to Sales." In *Research on Sales Promotion: Selected Papers*, ed. Katherine E. Jocz, Report 84-104, pp. 83–105. Cambridge, MA: Marketing Science Institute, July 1984.

RAJU, JAGMOHAN S., V. SRINIVASAN, and RAJIV LAL, "The Effects of Brand Loyalty on Competitive Price Promotional Strategies," Working paper, Graduate School of Business, Stanford University, Stanford, CA (May 1988).

RAO, RAM C., "Pricing and Promotions in Aysmmetric Duopolies," Working paper, University of Texas at Dallas (November 1987).

RAO, VITHALA R., and L. JOSEPH THOMAS, "Dynamic Models for Sales Promotion Policies," *Operational Research Quarterly*, Vol. 24, no. 3 (1973), pp. 403–417.

RATCHFORD, BRIAN T., "Operationalizing Economic Models of Demand for Product Characteristics," *Journal of Consumer Research*, Vol. 6, no. 1 (June 1979), pp. 76–87.

RAY, MICHAEL L., "Psychological Theories and Interpretations of Learning." In Scott Ward and Thomas S. Robertson, eds., *Consumer Behavior: Theoretical Sourcebook*. Englewood Cliffs, NJ: Prentice Hall, 1973.

REIBSTEIN, DAVID J., and PHILLIS A. TRAVER, "Factors Affecting Coupon Redemption Rates," *Journal of Marketing*, Vol. 46, no. 4 (Fall 1982), pp. 102–113.

REICHARDT, CHARLES S., "The Statistical Analysis of Data from Nonequivalent Group Designs." In *Quasi-Experimentation: Design and Analysis Issues for Field Settings*, eds. Thomas D. Cook and Donald T. Campbell, pp. 147–202. Chicago: Rand McNally, 1979.

RIEBER, WILLIAM J., "An Economic Rationale for Couponing: A Comment," *Quarterly Journal of Business and Economics* (Fall 1986), pp. 71–74.

ROBINSON, WILLIAM A., "Planning a Sales Promotion." In *Handbook of Sales Promotion*, ed. Stanley M. Ulanoff, pp. 389–412. New York: McGraw-Hill, 1985.

ROSELIUS, TED, "Consumer Rankings of Risk Reduction Methods," *Journal of Marketing*, Vol. 35, no. 1 (January 1971), pp. 56–61.

Rosen, Cheryl Ann, "The Cents-Off Lure: Identifying the Coupon-Susceptible Consumer," Unpublished M.B.A. thesis, Graduate School of Business, The University of Texas at Austin (May 1985).

Rothschild, Michael L., "A Behavioral View of Promotions Effects on Brand Loyalty." In *Advances in Consumer Research*. Vol. XIV, eds. Melanie Wallendorf and Paul Anderson, pp. 119–120. Provo, UT: Association for Consumer Research, 1987.

Rothschild, Michael L., and William C. Gaidis, "Behavioral Learning Theory: Its Relevance to Marketing and Promotions," *Journal of Marketing*, Vol. 45, no. 2 (Spring 1981), pp. 70–78.

Ryan, Michael J., and E. H. Bonfield, "The Fishbein Extended Model and Consumer Behavior," *Journal of Consumer Research*, Vol. 2, no. 2 (September 1975), pp. 118–136.

Sahakian, William S., *Learning: Systems, Models, and Theories*, 2nd ed. Chicago: Rand McNally, 1976.

Salop, Steven, and Joseph Stiglitz, "The Theory of Sales; A Simple Model of Equilibrium Price Dispersion with Identical Agents," *The American Economic Review*, Vol. 72, no. 3 (December 1982), pp. 1121–1130.

Salop, Steven, and Joseph Stiglitz, "Bargain and Ripoffs: A Model of Monopolistic Competitive Price Dispersion, *Review of Economic Studies*, Vol. 4 (1977), pp. 493–510.

SAS Institute, *SAS User's Guide: Statistics, Version 5 Edition*. Cary, NC: SAS Institute, 1985.

SAS Institute, *SAS/ETS User's Guide, Version 5 Edition*. Cary, NC: SAS Institute, 1984.

Sawyer, Alan G., and Peter R. Dickson, "Psychological Perspectives on Consumer Response to Sales Promotion." In *Research on Sales Promotion: Collected Papers*, Report No. 84-104, ed. Katherine E. Jocz, pp. 1–21. Cambridge, MA: Marketing Science Institute, July 1984.

Schindler, Robert M., "Image Effects of Odd Pricing," University of Chicago, Marketing working paper (July 1987).

Schindler, Robert M., "How Cents-Off Coupons Motivate the Consumer." In *Research on Sales Promotion: Collected Papers*, Report 84-104, ed. Katherine E. Jocz, pp. 47–62. Cambridge, MA: Marketing Science Institute, 1984a.

Schindler, Robert M., "How Sales Promotions Stimulate Consumer Response: Implications for Designing More Effective Programs," Working paper, University of Chicago (September 1984b).

Schneider, Linda G., and Imran S. Currim, "Consumer Purchase Behaviors Associated with Active and Passive Deal Proneness," Working paper, Amos Tuck School of Business Administration, Dartmouth College, Hanover, NH (March 1989).

Schultz, Don E., and William A. Robinson, *Sales Promotion Management*. Chicago: Crain Books, 1982.

Scott, Carol A., "Forming Beliefs from Experience: Evidence from Self-perception Theory." In *Perspectives in Consumer Behavior*, 3rd ed., eds. Harold H. Kassarjian and Thomas S. Robertson, pp. 296–305. Glenview, IL: Scott, Foresman, 1981.

Scott, Carol A., "Modifying Socially-Conscious Behavior: The Foot-in-the Door Technique," *Journal of Consumer Research*, Vol. 4, no. 3 (December 1977), pp. 156–164.

Scott, Carol A., "The Effects of Trial and Incentives on Repeat Purchase Behavior," *Journal of Marketing Research*, Vol. 13, no. 3 (August 1976), pp. 263–269.

Scott, Carol A., and Richard F. Yalch, "Consumer Response to Initial Product Trial:

A Bayesian Analysis," *Journal of Consumer Research*, Vol. 7, no. 1 (June 1980), pp. 32–41.

SCOTT, CAROL A., and ALICE M. TYBOUT, "Extending the Self-perception Explanation: The Effect of Cue Salience on Behavior." In *Advances in Consumer Research*, Vol. VI, ed. William L. Wilkie, pp. 50–54. Ann Arbor, MI: Association for Consumer Research, 1979.

SHERIF, CAROLYN, "Social Categorization as a Function of Latitude of Acceptance and Series Range," *Journal of Abnormal and Social Psychology*, Vol. 67 (August 1963), pp. 148–156.

SHERIF, MUZAFER, and CARL HOVLAND, "Judgmental Phenomena and Scales of Attitude Measurement: Placement of Items with Individual Choice of Number of Categories," *Journal of Abnormal and Social Psychology*, Vol. 48 (January 1953), pp. 135–141.

SHIMP, TERENCE A., and ALICAN KAVAS, "The Theory of Reasoned Action Applied to Coupon Usage," *Journal of Consumer Research*, Vol. 11, no. 3 (December 1984), pp. 795–809.

SHIMP, TERENCE A., ROBERT F. DYER, and SALVATORE F. DIVITA, "An Experimental Test of the Harmful Effects of Premium-Oriented Commercials on Children," *Journal of Consumer Research*, Vol. 3, no. 1 (June 1976), pp. 1–11.

SHOCKER, ALAN D., and V. SRINIVASAN, "Multiattribute Approaches for Product Concept Evaluation and Generation: A Critical Review," *Journal of Marketing Research*, Vol. 16, no. 2 (May 1979), pp. 159–180.

SHOEMAKER, ROBERT W., "An Analysis of Consumer Reactions to Product Promotions." In *Educators' Conference Proceedings,* eds. Neil Beckwith, Michael Houston, Robert Mittelstaedt, Kent B. Monroe, and Scott Ward, pp. 244–248. Chicago: American Marketing Association, 1979.

SHOEMAKER, ROBERT W., and VIKAS TIBREWALA, "Relating Coupon Redemption Rates to Past Purchasing of the Brand," *Journal of Advertising Research*, Vol. 25, no. 5 (October–November 1985), pp. 40–47.

SHOEMAKER, ROBERT W., and F. ROBERT SHOAF, "Repeat Rates of Deal Purchases," *Journal of Advertising Research*, Vol. 17, no. 2 (April 1977), pp. 47–53.

SHOEMAKER, ROBERT W., and F. ROBERT SHOAF, "Behavioral Changes in the Trial of New Products," *Journal of Consumer Research*, Vol. 2, no. 2 (September 1975), pp. 104–109.

SHUGAN, STEVEN, "Branded Variants," University of Chicago, Center for Research in Marketing, October 1986.

SKINNER, B. F., *The Behavior of Organisms: An Experimental Analysis.* New York: Appleton-Century-Crofts, 1938.

STARCH INRA HOOPER, *Study of Readers of the January 6, 1985 Issue of the Atlanta Journal-Constitution Regarding Product Movers Insert*, prepared for Marketing Showcase, New York.

STERN, AIMÉE, "New Marketing Game: Stealing Customers," *Dun's Business Month*, Vol. 125, no. 2 (February 1985), pp. 48–50.

STERNTHAL, BRIAN, and C. SAMUEL CRAIG, *Consumer Behavior: An Information Processing Perspective.* Englewood Cliffs, NJ: Prentice Hall, 1982.

STRANG, ROGER A., "The Economic Impact of Cents-Off Coupons," *Marketing Communications* (March 1981), pp. 35–44.

STRANG, ROGER A., *The Promotional Planning Process.* New York: Praeger, 1980.

STRANG, ROGER A., "Sales Promotion: Fast Growth, Faulty Management," *Harvard Business Review* (July–August 1976), pp. 115–124.

STRANG, ROGER A., *The Relationship Between Advertising and Promotion in Brand Strategy.* Cambridge, MA: Marketing Science Institute, 1975.

STRAZEWSKI, LEN, "Sales Promotion: Jostling for Consumers', Marketers' Attention," *Advertising Age*, February 6, 1986, pp. 13–14.

STUART, ELNORA W., TERENCE A. SHIMP, and RANDALL W. ENGLE, "Classical Conditioning of Consumer Attitudes: Four Experiments in an Advertising Context," *Journal of Consumer Research*, Vol. 14, no. 3 (December 1987), pp. 334–349.

SWEENEY, GEORGE, and J. WILLIAM LEVEDAHL, "Marketing, Price Discrimination, and Welfare: Comment," *Southern Economic Journal* (January 1984), pp. 892–899.

TEEL, JESSE E., ROBERT H. WILLIAMS, and WILLIAM O. BEARDEN, "Correlates of Consumer Susceptibility to Coupons in New Grocer Product Introductions," *Journal of Advertising*, Vol. 9, no. 3 (1980), pp. 31–46.

TELSER, LESTER, "Least Square Estimates of Transition Probabilities." In *Measurement in Economics*, Christ et al., (Stanford, California: Stanford University Press, 1963), pp. 270–292.

THALER, RICHARD, "Mental Accounting and Consumer Choice," *Marketing Science*, Vol. 4, no. 3 (Summer 1985), pp. 199–214.

THEIL, H., "A Multinomial Extension of the Linear Logit Model," *International Economic Review,* Vol. 10 (October 1969), pp. 251–269.

THEIL, HENRI, *Principles of Econometrics.* New York: John Wiley, 1971.

THOMPSON, PATRICK, and THOMAS NOORDEWIER, "Effects of Consumer-Oriented Sales Promotion on Durable Goods: The Case of Domestic Automobile Sales," Working paper, College of Business, The Ohio State University, Columbus, Ohio, 1988.

TOTTEN, JOHN C., and MARTIN P. BLOCK, *Analyzing Sales Promotion: Text and Cases* (Chicago, Commerce Communications, Inc., 1987).

TYBOUT, ALICE M., and CAROL A. SCOTT, "Availability of Well-Defined Internal Knowledge and the Attitude Formation Process: Information Aggregation Versus Self-perception," *Journal of Personality and Social Psychology*, Vol. 44, no. 3 (1983), pp. 474–479.

UHL, J. N., "Cents-Off Coupons: Boon or Boondoggle for Consumers?" *Journal of Consumer Affairs*, Vol. 16, no. 1 (Summer 1982), pp. 161–165.

ULANOFF, STANLEY M., ed., *Handbook of Sales Promotion.* New York: McGraw-Hill, 1985.

URBAN, GLEN L., and JOHN R. HAUSER, *Design and Marketing of New Products.* Englewood Cliffs, NJ: Prentice Hall, 1980.

VANDAELE, WALTER, *Applied Time Series and Box-Jenkins Models.* New York: Harcourt Brace Jovanovich, 1983, pp. 334–347.

VANHONACKER, WILFRIED R., "Carryover Effects and Temporal Aggregation in a Partial Adjustment Model Framework," *Marketing Science*, Vol. 2, no. 3 (Summer 1983), pp. 297–315.

VARADARAJAN, P. RAJAN, "Horizontal Cooperative Sales Promotion: A Framework for Classification and Additional Perspectives," *Journal of Marketing*, Vol. 50, no. 2 (April 1986), pp. 61–71.

VARIAN, HAL R., "A Model of Sales," *The American Economic Review*, Vol. 70, no. 4 (September 1980), pp. 651–659.

VILCASSIM, NAUFEL J., and DICK R. WITTINK, "Supporting a Higher Shelf Price Through Coupon Distributions," *Journal of Consumer Marketing*, Vol. 4, no. 2 (Spring 1987), pp. 29–39.

WALLACE, T. D., "Weaker Criteria and Tests for Linear Restrictions in Regression," *Econometrica*, Vol. 40, no. 4 (July 1972), pp. 689–698.

WALTERS, ROCKNEY G., and SCOTT B. MACKENZIE, "A Structural Equations Analysis of the Impact of Price Promotions on Store Performance," *Journal of Marketing Research*, Vol. 25, no. 1 (February 1988), pp. 51–63.

WALTERS, ROCKNEY G., and HEIKKI J. RINNE, "An Empirical Investigation into the Impact of Price Promotions on Retail Store Performance," *Journal of Retailing*, Vol. 62, no. 3 (Fall 1986), pp. 237–266.

WARD, RONALD W., and JAMES E. DAVIS, "A Pooled Cross-Section Time Series Model of Coupon Promotions," *American Journal of Agricultural Economics* (November 1978a), pp. 393–401.

WARD, RONALD W., and JAMES E. DAVIS, "Coupon Redemption," *Journal of Advertising Research*, Vol. 18, no. 4 (August 1978b), pp. 51–55.

WARSHAW, PAUL R., "Predicting Purchase and Other Behaviors from Contextually Specific Intentions," *Journal of Marketing Research*, Vol. 17, no. 1 (February 1980), pp. 26–33.

WEBSTER, FREDERICK E., JR., "Top Management's Concerns About Marketing Issues for the 1980s," *Journal of Marketing*, Vol. 45, no. 3 (Summer 1981), pp. 9–16.

WEBSTER, FREDERICK E., JR., *Marketing Communication.* New York: Ronald Press, 1971.

WEBSTER, FREDERICK E., JR., "The 'Deal-Prone' Consumer," *Journal of Marketing Research*, Vol. 2, no. 2 (May 1965), pp. 186–189.

WHITE, B. A. "Comparison Shopping and the Economics of Manufacturers' Coupons," Discussion paper 517, Department of Economics, State University of New York, Buffalo (1983).

WICHERN, DEAN W., and RICHARD H. JONES, "Assessing the Impact of Market Disturbances Using Intervention Analysis," *Management Science*, Vol. 24, no. 3 (November 1977), pp. 329–337.

WILKIE, WILLIAM L., and EDGAR A. PESSEMIER, "Issues in Marketing's Use of Multiattribute Attitude Models," *Journal of Marketing Research*, Vol. 10, no. 4 (November 1973), pp. 428–441.

WILKIE, WILLIAM L., and PETER R. DICKSON, "Shopping for Appliances: Consumers' Strategies and Patterns of Information Search." Cambridge, MA: Marketing Science Institute, November 1985.

WILKINSON, J. B., J. BARRY MASON, and CHRISTIE H. PAKSOY, "Assessing the Impact of Short-Term Supermarket Strategy Variables," *Journal of Marketing Research*, Vol. 19, no. 1 (February 1982), pp. 72–86.

WILSON, R. DALE, LARRY M. NEWMAN, and MANOJ HASTAK, "On the Validity of Research Methods in Consumer Dealing Activity: An Analysis of Timing Issues." In *Educators' Conference Proceedings*, eds. Neil Beckwith, Michael Houston, Robert Mittelstaedt, Kent B. Monroe, and Scott Ward, pp. 41–46. Chicago: American Marketing Association, 1979.

WINER, B. J., *Statistical Principles in Experimental Design*, 2nd ed. New York: McGraw-Hill, 1971.

WINER, RUSSELL S., "A Reference Price Model of Brand Choice for Frequently Purchased Products," *Journal of Consumer Research*, Vol. 13 (September 1986), pp. 250–256.

WINGATE, JOHN W., and HARLAND E. SAMPSON, *Retail Merchandising.* Cincinnati, OH: South-Western, 1975.

WISNIEWSKI, KENNETH J., and ROBERT C. BLATTBERG, "Response Function Estimation Using UPC Scanner Data." In *Advances and Practices of Marketing Science*, ed.

Fred S. Zufryden, Proceedings of ORSA/TIMS Marketing Science Conference, March 1983.

WITTINK, DICK R., MICHAEL J. ADDONA, WILLIAM J. HAWKES, and JOHN C. PORTER, "SCAN-PRO®: A Model to Measure Short-Term Effects of Promotional Activities on Brand Sales, Based on Store-Level Scanner Data," Working paper, Johnson Graduate School of Management, Cornell University, Ithaca, NY (May 1987).

WONNACOTT, RONALD J., and THOMAS H. WONNACOTT, *Econometrics*, 2nd ed. New York: John Wiley, 1979.

WONNACOTT, THOMAS H., and RONALD J. WONNACOTT, *Introductory Statistics for Business and Economics*, 3rd ed. New York: John Wiley, 1984.

WOODSIDE, ARCH G., and GERALD L. WADDLE, "Sales Effects of In-Store Advertising," *Journal of Advertising Research*, Vol. 15, no. 3 (June 1975), pp. 29–34.

WRIGHT, PETER, "The Cognitive Processes Mediating Acceptance of Advertising," *Journal of Marketing Research*, Vol. 10, no. 1 (February 1973), pp. 53–62.

ZAICHKOWSKY, JUDITH LYNNE, "Measuring the Involvement Construct," *Journal of Consumer Research*, Vol. 12, no. 3 (December 1985), pp. 341–352.

ZALTMAN, GERALD, and MELANIE WALLENDORF, *Consumer Behavior: Basic Findings and Management Implications*, 2nd ed. New York: John Wiley, 1983.

ZOUL, ROBERT N., "Promotions Cost Money: Don't Overlook the Budget." In *Handbook of Sales Promotion*, ed. Stanley M. Ulanoff, pp. 413–428. New York: McGraw-Hill, 1985.

ZUFRYDEN, FRED S., "Multibrand Transition Probabilities as a Function of Explanatory Variables: Estimation by a Least-Squares-Based Approach," *Journal of Marketing Research*, Vol. 22, no. 2 (May 1986), pp. 177–183.

Author Index

Subject Index